OWEN LATTIMORE
AND THE ''LOSS'' OF CHINA

A

Philip E. Lilienthal

Book

The Philip E. Lilienthal imprint
honors special books
in commemoration of a man whose work
at the University of California Press from 1954 to 1979
was marked by dedication to young authors
and to high standards in the field of Asian Studies.
Friends, family, authors, and foundations have together
endowed the Lilienthal Fund, which enables the Press
to publish under this imprint selected books
in a way that reflects the taste and judgment
of a great and beloved editor.

OWEN LATTIMORE

AND THE "LOSS" OF

CHINA

ROBERT P. NEWMAN

UNIVERSITY OF CALIFORNIA PRESS
BERKELEY   LOS ANGELES   OXFORD

University of California Press
Berkeley and Los Angeles, California

University of California Press, Ltd.
Oxford, England

© 1992 by
The Regents of the University of California

Library of Congress Cataloging-in-Publication Data

Newman, Robert P.
Owen Lattimore and the "Loss" of China / Robert P. Newman.
p.   cm.
"Philip E. Lilienthal book."
Includes bibliographical references and index.
ISBN 0-520-07388-6
1. Lattimore, Owen, 1900–   .   2. China—Foreign relations—United
States.   3. United States—Foreign relations—China.   4. Governmental
investigations—United States—History—20th century.   5.
McCarthy, Joseph, 1908–1957.   I. Title.
E748.L34N48   1992
327.51073—dc20   91-21888
                                                            CIP

Printed in the United States of America
9 8 7 6 5 4 3 2 1

The paper used in this publication meets the minimum requirements of
American National Standard for Information Sciences—Permanence of Paper
for Printed Library Materials, ANSI Z39.48-1984. ♾

For THURMAN ARNOLD

ABE FORTAS

JOSEPH O'MAHONEY

WILLIAM D. ROGERS

LUTHER YOUNGDAHL

CONTENTS

PREFACE

One of the bitterest debates in American history took place at midcentury, when the Republic of China, our friend and ally in World War II and the object of our most vigorous Protestant missionary enterprise, went over to "the enemy": atheistic communism. Americans could not believe that China had made this choice freely. Its adherence to the "World Communist Conspiracy," many thought, must have been coerced both by Soviet manipulation and by the treasonous actions of American diplomats and politicians. We had "lost" China because some Communist mastermind in the American government had deliberately sabotaged the efforts of Chiang Kai-shek (a Methodist) to defeat Mao Tse-tung in the Chinese civil war. After Mao won the war in 1949, the same Communist mastermind tried to influence the U.S. Department of State to recognize Mao's People's Republic and sell the remnant Nationalists on Taiwan down the river.

The "Who Lost China?" debate intensified in 1950, when Kim Il-sung attacked the South Korean government under Syngman Rhee. South Korea was an American protectorate in the same sense that China had been. MacArthur's successful early prosecution of the Korean War lessened the scapegoating over China, but when the Chinese armies joined the North Koreans and smashed the U.S. Eighth Army in December 1950, American fear and outrage became uncontrollable. The search for a scapegoat expanded: whoever had lost China had also lost Korea.

Harry Truman caught much of the blame, and the damage to his popularity because of these disasters in Asia seared the consciousness of American politicians for a generation. He was not the only person to suffer from the loss of China. Secretary of State Dean Acheson, General George Marshall, Ambassador Philip Jessup, and a handful of China specialists in the foreign service also came under attack. But a prominent China scholar who had never been in the State Department at all caught most of the blame when the American inquisition escalated in 1950: Owen

Lattimore. Lattimore was dead center in the gunsights of the politicians, journalists, Chinese Nationalist operatives, American Legionnaires, professional anti-Communists, internal security alarmists, and religious leaders who made up the China lobby. Lattimore was alleged to be the shadowy Communist mastermind behind American policy in Asia.

Two decades after the attack on Truman, Acheson, and Lattimore, a Republican who had been part of the attack, Richard Nixon, reversed course and began negotiations with the People's Republic of China. Nixon could do so because he could not be outflanked on the right.

Four decades after the midcentury attack on Democratic treason, another Republican president, George Bush, came full circle, defending continued friendship with a repressive Maoist government in Peking against almost universal outrage over the slaughter in Tiananmen Square. Lattimore did not live quite long enough to savor the irony. He died in May 1989.

Lattimore, a Johns Hopkins University professor specializing in China and Asia, became a headline figure when Senator Joseph R. McCarthy charged him with being the "top Soviet spy, the boss of the whole ring of which Hiss was a part" in the United States. Lattimore at that time was persona non grata in the Soviet Union, and this canard would not fly, even in the cold war atmosphere of the times. McCarthy downgraded Lattimore to merely "the architect of our Far Eastern policy," which still made him responsible for the loss of China. Lattimore was not only the alleged mastermind of U.S. Asian policy but also a heretic for advocating diplomatic recognition of the People's Republic of China. For those who did not buy the conspiracy charge, the heresy was sufficient damnation. The charges against him have never died; they are enshrined in our tribal memory.

Now that records of behind-the-scenes maneuvering during the midcentury Red Scare are becoming available, it is time that the full story be brought out. Our tribal memory needs correction. Nowhere in print are the corruption and viciousness of the forces behind Lattimore's persecution exposed. Even reputable scholars accept the conclusion that where there was so much smoke, there must have been some fire. According to this reasoning, since Hiss and the Rosenbergs were found guilty by juries of their peers, Lattimore was probably guilty also, even though never convicted.

To understand the United States since the 1950s, one must understand the pathology of that decade. A major symptom of that pathology was the U.S. pretense that the rump Chinese Nationalist government on Taiwan was the legitimate government of China and that we should therefore refuse to recognize the People's Republic. It was the furious argument over the recognition of Peking that drew me into the China policy arena. In 1954 I was directing the intercollegiate debate program at the University of Pittsburgh. College and university debate coaches that year selected as the national debate topic "Resolved: That the United States Government should extend diplomatic recognition to the Communist Government of China." College debating is not usually a high-profile activity, but in 1954 the choice of the recognition topic attracted the wrath of a vast constituency. Hearst, Scripps Howard, and McCormick Patterson newspapers began a crusade to shut down this subversive activity. The Chiang Kai-shek bloc in Congress joined in. The conservatives partially succeeded: West Point, Annapolis, teachers' colleges in Nebraska, Catholic colleges in Ohio, and other skittish institutions canceled debates on this topic.

On Pearl Harbor Day, 1954, the *Pittsburgh Sun-Telegraph*, a Hearst paper, published a column by E. F. Tompkins under the headline "Coddling Communism: Campus Propaganda." Tompkins attacked the University of Pittsburgh for holding a tournament on the recognition topic. In each of these terrible debates one team would have to "advocate the Communist cause." Pitt trustees read the *Sun-Telegraph*, and some of them phoned Pitt's acting chancellor, Charles Nutting, inquiring, "Who's the subversive professor indoctrinating Pitt debaters?"

A strong believer in First Amendment freedoms, Nutting fended off the nervous trustees, and so far as I know, my career was not damaged by the Hearst attack. But the view that debating a topic such as recognition was a subversive activity stimulated anguished reflection, leading me to a six-year investigation of U.S. China policy and the publication in 1961 of *Recognition of Communist China? A Study in Argument*. I concluded that the arguments in favor of recognition were strong.

Not until 1977, however, did my path cross that of the preeminent advocate of recognition: Lattimore. As we talked, it became clear that this man not only had been a fearless opponent of the American inquisition but also had led a fascinating life. He began to tell me about it. When his Freedom of Information documents began to come from the FBI in 1978, he was living in France, and he commissioned me to read and evaluate them. This work led to a decade of correspondence, hundreds of hours of interviews, and access to Lattimore's private papers.

This book is the result. Lattimore had begun his memoirs but never finished them. I have had access to his manuscript and have borrowed parts of it, but the basic story and the judgments of his career and opinions are my own.

This book is not just a biography; it is a study in American political demonology.

ACKNOWLEDGMENTS

The truth about Lattimore's career, and the charges against him, could not have been fully established without the 1974 amendments to the Freedom of Information Act, whose prime mover was Congressman William S. Moorhead, ably assisted by Norman G. Cornish. I carefully followed the hearings that led to these amendments. In the 1970s Congress was on the side of the public's right to know what its servants in the executive branch were doing.

Nor could this book have been written without a good-faith effort by the FBI to honor the Freedom of Information Act and the companion Privacy Act. One can quarrel with specific decisions of FBI clerks who sanitized the Lattimore and Budenz files for release, particularly their frequent denials on grounds of national security for items that could not conceivably affect the national security. Nonetheless, FBI releases give a candid and remarkably complete picture of events in the U.S. Senate and the Department of Justice from 1950 to 1955. The same cannot be said about the CIA. That agency's nine-year stall before releasing a trivial fraction of its Lattimore holdings was plain malfeasance. The CIA has much to hide about its activities during its first decade, and no mere Congress is going to force it to come clean. One has to agree with Taylor Branch in his preface to *Parting the Waters:* in many areas, "the logic of secrecy has been allowed to reach levels of royalist absurdity."

Many generous people have taken the time to comment on early drafts of this book, and without them it would have been much the poorer: William Acheson, Betty Barnes, Dauna Bartley, Lewis Bateman of the University of North Carolina Press, Susan Biesecker, Douglas Bishop, Marie Buscatto, Samuel C. Chu of Ohio State University, Jerome Edwards of the University of Nevada at Reno, Robert Frank of Berry College, Richard B. Gregg of the Pennsylvania State University, William Hall, Waldo Heinrichs of Temple University, Steve Jenkins of Sacramento State University, Thomas Kane of the University of Pittsburgh, Thomas Kerr of Carnegie Mellon University, Kathy Klenner, Stanley I. Kutler of the University of Wisconsin at Madison, Gerald Mast, Evelyn Stefansson Nef, Morris Ogul of the University of Pittsburgh, Gerard and Eleanor Piel, William D. and Suki Rogers, John Stewart Service, Roger Stemen of Gettysburg College, Jean Ann Streiff, and Shawnalee Whitney. Parts of the manuscript were read by Lloyd Eastman of the University of Illinois, Caroline Humphrey of Cambridge University, Dale Newman, Fujiko Isono, David Lattimore, Maria Lattimore, and Michael Lattimore.

I am also indebted to many people who have furnished documents or information otherwise unavailable: Charles Palm and Ernie Tompkins of the Hoover Institution; Donald Brown and David Hoffman of the Pennsylvania State Library; Clem Vitek, formerly librarian of the Sun Papers, Baltimore; Julia B. Morgan and James Stimpert of Johns Hopkins University; Harold L. Miller and Lloyd F. Vilicer of the State Historical Society of Wisconsin; Thomas C. Reeves of the University of Wisconsin, Parkside; Donald Ritchie, Office of the Historian, U.S. Senate; Marius Jansen, Princeton University; F. Alan Coombs, University of Utah; Gene M. Gressley, University of Wyoming; David Kepley and Robert W. Coren, National Archives; Stanley I. Kutler, E. Gordon Fox Professor at the University of Wisconsin, Madison; Evelyn Stefansson Nef; Patti Goldman of the Public Citizen Litigation Group; Robert Kully, California State University, Los Angeles; Alec Stewart, Dean, University of Pittsburgh Honors College; David Harvey, Mackinder Professor of Geography, Oxford; Harold Isaacson, University of North Carolina, Charlotte; William D. and Suki Rogers, Arnold and Porter; Von V. Pittman, Jr., University of Iowa; Jerome Edwards, University of Nevada, Reno; Lionel S. Lewis, State University of New York, Buffalo; Darwin H. Stapleton, Rockefeller Archive Center; Betty Barnes; Gerard and Eleanor Piel; Charlotte Riznik; Senator Claiborne Pell; James Cotton, Australian National University; Steve MacKinnon, Arizona State University; Neil Smith, Rutgers University; George McT. Kahin, Cornell University; Howard Schonberger, University of Maine; and Urgunge Onon, Cambridge University. The staff of Hillman Library of the University of Pittsburgh was, as always, magnificent. For the University of California Press, Peter Shwartz, Dan Gunter, and Marilyn Schwartz offered a great deal of invaluable advice.

September 18, 1969, in the meeting room of the Academy of Sciences of the Mongolian People's Republic, Ulan Bator: Bagaryn Shirendyb, president of the Academy, calls the ten members and twenty or so associate members to order. The Academy, founded in 1961 on Russian lines to recognize scholarly achievement and to supervise the state library, the sixteen research institutes, the academic publishing house, the astronomical observatory, the seismic station, and similar enterprises, is about to invest its first foreign member.

The new member, surprisingly, is neither Russian nor Chinese. Until at least 1960 the Mongols had considered him an apologist for Western imperialism, a capitalist oppressor, and an enemy of all patriotic Mongols. But he read and spoke Mongol fluently, and beginning in the 1920s he had followed the ancient caravan routes across the Inner Mongolian Gobi to Turfan and Urumchi and Tahcheng. He had made himself an authority on the history and culture of the Mongol peoples. He was now the foremost proponent of Mongol nationalism and culture in the Western world. He was Owen Lattimore.

The ceremony was simple, as befitted such an establishment in a nation not yet numbering two million people. There were three speeches. Shirendyb began by announcing the occasion and calling on two assistants to robe Lattimore in a colorful gown, a traditional *khadaq* scarf, and a cap with a button on top. Academician Lobsanvandan then gave a five-minute biography, emphasizing that the honoree was not just a scholar but also a true friend of the Mongols. Then Lattimore spoke.

No text of his speech survives, but Lattimore says the first part was a challenge to the Mongols to intensify their fledgling studies of folklore, songs, and legends; to join these with rigorous study of the documentary remains of their once-powerful civilization; and to continue the scientific studies that had enabled them to move so swiftly from feudalism to a highly literate polity. He closed with an invocation to world peace, performed in the traditional alliterative rhapsodic style—a five-line stanza, the only part of his speech he had memorized. The speech was acclaimed as a great success.

A success it should have been. Lattimore, ambivalent toward the Russians, grudgingly respectful of the Chinese, held an unbounded affection for the Mongols. These descendants of the great khans had fascinated and captivated him since he first met a Mongol camel puller on the Desert Road to Turkestan. Now, his tribulations over, he could savor the respect and attention the Mongols offered him in return.

PART ONE

The Heresy

CHAPTER ONE

A Fascination with Central Asia

On July 18, 1951, when the Senate Internal Security Subcommittee under Patrick McCarran of Nevada was well into its investigation of Owen Lattimore, Robert Morris, special counsel to the subcommittee, went to the FBI with a hot tip. Lattimore, said Morris, "was a Russian orphan who was born in Russia and was adopted by his parents, although Lattimore claimed to have been born in Washington, D.C., in 1900."

Clyde Tolson, J. Edgar Hoover's alter ego at the FBI, appreciating the implications of this startling item, sent an agent to check birth records. At the Bureau of Vital Statistics the agent obtained a copy of certificate number 105986, showing that one Owen Lattimore had been born in Sibley Hospital on July 29, 1900, to David and Margaret Lattimore, both native Americans.[1]

Lattimore's father taught high school in the District of Columbia. Owen was the second child, and the family expected to have more. Teaching salaries then were not adequate even for a family of four. David Lattimore was open to a job with a better salary.

Such an offer came from the shaky Manchu Empire, suffering in 1900 from the aftermath of the Boxer Rebellion. Western armies had thoroughly defeated Chinese troops; it was clear to the Manchus that China had to bring its science and technology up to Western standards. This meant Western education: training young Chinese in Western languages, then sending them to foreign colleges. David Lattimore was a language teacher, skilled in English, French, Greek, and Latin. He took a job teaching English and French in Shanghai and moved the family there in 1901. He taught in China for twenty years, moving from Shanghai to Paotingfu to Tientsin. Three more children were born in China.

In China, businessmen, diplomats, and secular teachers lived in compounds where the only Chinese were servants. The playmates of the Lattimore children were other foreigners. David did not encourage his offspring to learn Chinese from the servants, fearing that they would acquire a servant mentality. Owen and his brother Richmond were to be grounded in Western culture and languages; they could learn proper Chinese, as their father had done, when they were older.

Perhaps most dramatic of Lattimore's memories of these early years were those from 1911, when Sun Yat-sen started his revolution. The Lattimores were in Paoting-fu. Fearing another Boxer-type uprising, the American embassy ordered American citizens in outlying areas to come to Peking for safety. For several months the Lattimores lived as refugees in a small temple near the southern wall. No serious disturbances developed, however, and though the Nationalist general in charge of Peking ruled with a heavy hand, people were allowed to move about. Lattimore recalled, "When we went along the big streets we would see human heads nailed on telephone poles to intimidate the people of Peking. Seeing these heads did not bother us. It simply strengthened the idea that we were living in one world and the Chinese were living in another, and that this was the kind of thing that Chinese did to each other. It had nothing to do with us."[2]

The Lattimore children were taught at home until 1912. Then, wanting them to be cosmopolitan, David Lattimore sent them to Switzerland with their mother. Owen was enrolled at the Collège Classique Cantonal near Lausanne, the beginning of a six-year separation from his family that forced him to develop an independence that stayed with him all his life. Had he finished his autobiography, it would have borne the title *Happiness Is among Strangers*. Living alone, in countries where the native language was not English, forced him to relate to strange people and to absorb unfamiliar cultures. Lattimore felt that under these conditions "you have to gain access; you have to work at it: and to work at a problem, get the feel of it and succeed—that is happiness."

Lattimore adjusted well to his Swiss school, despite initial concern that his French was not up to that of his fellows. He was the only English speaker in the school. Later he recalled surprisingly little about the school, but his adventures during vacations stuck in his memory. His Uncle Alec, his father's younger brother, was in Europe and took him on a tour of Italy in 1913. They went to Verona, where *Aida* was performed in the Roman amphitheater with elephants, camels, and horses "trampling across, while all around the amphitheater people lit matches, their flames trembling in the still air.''

When war broke out in 1914, Owen was sent to England with his Uncle Alec, while his mother and the other children returned to China. Owen and Uncle Alec stayed for a time in Oxford, where Owen temporarily attended school. He spent many nights pub-crawling with Alec, from which excursions he acquired a technique that was to serve him well. It was not wise, he learned, for an ''ignorant youngster'' to interrupt conversations among adults. But he could ''put in a remark or even a question that helped to move the talk along in a direction in which I was interested. Developed into a technique, this became useful in later years, in Chinese inns or a peasant hut far up in the mountains, or around a campfire in Mongolia. The way to learn is to nudge people to talk about what they know (or, sometimes, what they think they know). Avoid the kind of question that gets the quick, simple answer. There is a difference between people supplementing each other's knowledge or opinions and when they are just fobbing off the outsider who 'wouldn't understand, anyway.' '' Lattimore's ability to extract information from strangers later became legendary.

Uncle Alec left England before the end of 1914, and Owen was enrolled at St. Bees School in Cumberland. There, despite the troubled stirring of adolescence, he spent five happy years. St. Bees was a minor but sound public school, preparing its best literary students for Oxford and its prospective scientists for Cambridge. Lattimore was the literary type, fond of poetry; his favorite book was A. E. Housman's *Shropshire Lad*. In his fourth year at St. Bees he and several friends started a literary magazine, with Lattimore contributing much of the poetry. He liked G. K. Chesterton and Hilaire Belloc, who romanticized the Middle Ages, and had desultory contact with social studies, reading Gibbon, John Stuart Mill, and Herbert Spencer. He also did scattered reading in anthropology, especially on primitive and ancient religions, later remembering Sir James Frazer's *Golden Bough* and Thomas Huxley's *Science and Christian Tradition*. Karl Marx did not penetrate the walls of St. Bees.

Lattimore's account of his years at St. Bees suggests that stories of youthful shenanigans at British public schools are not exaggerated. One of Lattimore's more revealing stories about St. Bees concerned his flirtation with the Catholic church. Uncle Alec, a Catholic, had sometimes taken him to hear mass. Owen's father was agnostic and strongly anti-Catholic, and part of Owen's religious adventure was simple rebellion. During his first year at St. Bees, Owen started going to an Irish priest in a nearby village for religious instruction; he then "went the whole way and had myself baptized. My father was coldly angry. He stopped writing to me, so that for a couple of years I communicated only with my mother." At St. Bees, however, this deviance gave Lattimore a certain prestige, enabling him "to mark out an individual position. I enjoyed asking for permission to cycle from school to Whitehaven to attend Mass, and I enjoyed letting it be known, in a carefully unostentatious way, that I had a Latin Missal."

But the conversion did not take. In Owen's very first confession the priest "was only interested in whether I masturbated or was already going to bed with girls. . . . I cycled back bewildered, but by the time I got home the shock was wearing off. There had been no revelation, no glimpse of the divine, just the gross attempt to ferret out the sex life of a boy of fifteen. There followed very quickly, but probably not as quickly as I now think I remember, a counter-revelation: I was liberated. So that was all there was to it: not God, but a man telling me about God and commanding me to believe him." Lattimore later pursued religious matters with a local Scottish Presbyterian minister, whose humaneness and sympathetic understanding, along with his advice to read Ernest Renan, established a tolerant acceptance of religion, though not an active belief in a specific creed, for the rest of Lattimore's life. After several years Lattimore wrote his father about his new attitude toward religion; David responded immediately and warmly, and the religious crisis was over.

Lattimore flourished and grew at St. Bees. During his last year (1918–19) his major concern was getting into Oxford. His father could not afford to send him there without a scholarship, so Owen worked hard in preparation for the scholarship exams. He did well, but the superior background of his British competitors in classical languages was too great to overcome. He did not win. Bitterly disappointed, he returned to China at age nineteen to seek employment.

Years later he was glad that he had not attended Oxford. "It was the generation of Evelyn Waugh, Aldous Huxley, and all those people. I would have come out an insufferable esthete, or perhaps have been influenced by one of the extremist ideologies of the day, fascism or Marxism."

Lattimore's father was then in Tientsin, the port serving Peking. The British firm Arnhold and Company had a branch office in Tientsin, and Owen secured a job there. Arnhold "imported into China everything that the West had to sell, and exported everything that the West would buy."

He worked first in the department that imported cotton textiles. This was a dying trade, and Lattimore found it boring. Several months after he began work, the chief of Arnhold's insurance department in Shanghai visited Tientsin, decided Lattimore was a promising young employee, and asked if he would like to transfer to Shanghai to work on insurance. Lattimore readily agreed.

Shanghai and the insurance business suited Lattimore better than his previous position. Because assessing insurance risks involved travel in the interior, where interpreters were scarce, he began serious study of Chinese. In 1921, after Owen had been in Shanghai a year, his father accepted an invitation to teach at Dartmouth College. Lattimore went to Tientsin to say good-bye to his family.

While in Tientsin on this visit, he met H. G. W. Woodhead, an Englishman who was editor of the *Peking and Tientsin Times*, the most influential English-language paper north of Shanghai. Woodhead offered him a job at the paper, and Lattimore accepted, thinking it would give him an opportunity to develop his literary interests. But the job was a disappointment. He had few opportunities to investigate and write stories of his own, spending most of his time proofreading.

After Lattimore had worked a year at the newspaper, Arnhold and Company lured him back with an offer to take charge of the insurance business at the Tientsin branch, with better pay and a chance for more travel. The travel especially attracted him. As a frustrated intellectual, he hated the Chinese port cities. The foreigners were hopeless philistines, with no interest in poetry, literature, or history. Peitaiho, the nearby summer resort, was no better: "There Ministers of Legation from Peking hoist their flags for the summer, and the Diplomatic body *in partibus infidelium* resting from the strict routine of dancing, scandal, and gambling, refreshed itself with swimming, gambling, and scandal."[3]

The insurance business did not take all of Lattimore's time; he worked hard at learning Chinese and read widely in the one cultural resource available, the library of the Tientsin Club. Arnhold gradually delegated to him much of the traveling required in matters other than insurance, occasionally sending him to negotiate with corrupt officials demanding outrageous bribes to allow passage of a shipment of wool, peanuts, or some commodity already purchased by Arnhold but held up in the interior.

Lattimore was not, however, the typical foreign business traveler. Most foreigners entered the countryside armed with extensive supplies and staff. Not Lattimore:

I took a small suitcase with a few clothes in it, and carried it myself.
No interpreter, no food, no cook, no servant. I fended for myself on the
journey. When I got where I was going, I would find an old-fashioned
Chinese firm of the kind where the clerks and apprentices lived on the
premises and all ate together, the food being supplied by the firm. There
would be consternation when I arrived. "Where are your servants and
your baggage?" I would explain that I hadn't any, but if they would
make room for me on one of the big brick sleeping platforms (heated
by flues in winter), and lend me a quilt, I would roll up in it to sleep.
After the first astonishment, this would lead to great cordiality and
hospitality.[4]

Four years of navigating the countryside for Arnhold and Company
taught Lattimore much about politics, economics, banditry, landlordism,
and peasant unrest. At the time he viewed his early years in Tientsin as a
kind of purgatory. Later he realized that his travels gave him the equivalent of a Ph.D. in economics. The bottom line was always profit or loss;
for the rest of his life he measured economic theories against what he
knew of business as Arnhold and Company practiced it. When orthodox
Communists, the American New Left, or other ideologues presented what
he called "the oversimplified picture of Wall Street's insatiable ambitions,
I always say to them, 'Look, don't talk to me about American and Western imperialism in China. I was part of it. And I know what's propaganda
and what's real.' " Lattimore believed the cliché had some validity: the
trouble with the New Left was that "they haven't met a payroll."

There was more to his travels for Arnhold than just business. The mystery and excitement of the vast Chinese inland territory began to claim
his spirit. One journey in particular he called a "turning point" in his life.
Early in 1925 he was sent to the railhead at Kweihwa (now Hohhot) on
the border of Inner Mongolia to negotiate the passage of a trainload of
wool owned by Arnhold that had been stalled because of a fight between
two warlords.

Kweihwa, a trading town founded by the Mongol Altan Khan in the
sixteenth century, was the eastern terminus of camel caravans from Sinkiang (then called Chinese Turkestan) and the western terminus of the
railroad from Peking. Lattimore was fascinated by the business of the
railyard:

Here at the end of the last stage of journeys of 1200 or 1500 miles,
sometimes more, the caravans filed into the dusty railway yard. In long
lines the camels halted and one after another sagged to their knees and
squatted, their lower lips drooping sarcastically and their heads turning

contemptuously on their swan-curved necks while the bales of wool or other goods were slipped from their backs and thudded to the ground. There lay the loads, between the lines of camels and the line of railway wagons: a distance of two paces, perhaps four paces, bridging a gap of two thousand years, between the age when the caravans had padded back and forth into the obscure distances dividing the Han Empire from the Roman Empire, and the age of steam, destroying the past and opening the future.[5]

After seeing the caravans, Lattimore was determined to follow them out through the Mongolian plains and the Gobi to their point of origin. He returned to Tientsin and tried to persuade Arnhold and Company to stake him to such an exploration; surely it would yield information useful for future commerce. Lattimore's employers were skeptical of the commercial utility of such a venture, and they feared that he would be captured by bandits and held for ransom; nevertheless, they were sympathetic to his wanderlust. They suggested that he work another year for them, this time in their Peking office, dealing with government officials and transportation agents. This work would provide him both with additional savings so he could travel on his own and with contacts that might ease his entry into the turbulent western provinces. Moreover, Peking was appealingly cosmopolitan, with a vigorous intellectual and cultural life. He accepted.

During his year (1925) in Peking, Lattimore met Eleanor Holgate, daughter of a Northwestern University professor who had brought her to China on a year's sabbatical. Enamored of Peking, Eleanor later deserted Evanston and returned with another adventurous girl to work in the Institute of Art History. She was thirty (five years older than Lattimore), attractive, and vivacious. Both Lattimore and Eleanor Holgate participated in the social life of the young foreign community. They met on a camping trip to the Western Hills and after a brief courtship married on March 4, 1926.

They began to think of a honeymoon journey through the enticing lands of Central Asia. Lattimore was already committed to following the caravan route through Inner (Chinese) Mongolia to Sinkiang, but he could not take Eleanor on this trip. There was much antiforeign sentiment in the area, and most American missionaries had withdrawn from the interior to the safety of the Treaty Ports. Furthermore, the rigid customs of the caravan men would not allow a woman on the journey, and marauding soldiery made her presence exceedingly dangerous. But Eleanor could travel to Sinkiang by a relatively safe railroad journey, north from Peking through Manchuria, and then west on the Trans-Siberian to the edge of Sinkiang. Owen would meet her at the terminus of the Russian railroad, and they could then travel together through the more stable areas of Sinkiang, through the Heavenly Mountains (Tien Shan), around the vast Taklamakan Desert, across the Karakorum Pass, and south into India. It would be a honeymoon for the ages.

So the plans were made. They would both go by train to Kweihwa, where he would arrange his caravan. When he left, she would return to Peking to await word that he had arrived in Sinkiang. They would then meet in Semipalatinsk, four hundred miles across the Soviet border from Sinkiang.

The Chinese civil wars of the mid-1920s, however, frustrated their plans. Lattimore was set to go, camels and camel puller ready, in March 1926, but his camels were commandeered by a warlord's army and he was left stranded in Kweihwa. Eleanor was still with him, and together they explored the area around Kweihwa, talking to caravan people and learning the ways of avoiding military conscription of one's camels. The trick was to assemble a caravan in one of the secluded valleys away from town, where provisions could be carried by modest cart trips that attracted no attention. By August 1926 Lattimore had digested caravan lore so thoroughly and honed his evasive skills so successfully that he was able to get a caravan of nine camels together and begin his westward journey on the twentieth. Eleanor entrained for Peking to await word of his progress.

As a lone Caucasian among the brawling, polyglot camel men of Central Asia, Lattimore could not afford to make a single false move. His ability to go native, acquired during his travels for Arnhold, his facility in Chinese, and the company of a devoted retainer inherited from his father enabled him to survive.

The trip, despite its rigors, was all he expected of it. Buried in the spare prose of *Desert Road to Turkestan* are lyrical phrases capturing the aesthetic heights of this adventure: "The camels and the long road, with glimpses, before the sun set, of rolling country and a world without end, were the fulfillment of an old ambition, but they became suddenly tinged with the emotion of a new dream." When he came to the Inner Mongolian uplands, he was "childishly thrilled to . . . be travelling with a caravan into that great plateau of depth and color, with mountains in sight; mountains on whose far side lay strange country, where I might travel but the one time in my life, living for a few score days the life of men in other ages." When he reached the Heavenly Mountains, "the sudden sight of them was like a prophecy fulfilled."[6]

If traveling for Arnhold had provided an education in economics, the caravan trip to Sinkiang provided an education in sociology and grassroots geopolitics. Unlike earlier institutionally sponsored and elaborate expeditions by professional explorers through Central Asia, Lattimore's small group met and attached itself to regular caravans. From camel pullers, cooks, traders, and provisioners met en route Lattimore absorbed the mystique of the Inner Mongolian desert. He liked most of the caravan men and became especially fond of a camel puller with the large caravan of the House of Chou:

> When he was not in my tent, I was usually in his, and both his men and those of the House of Liang were cheery fellows. They had at first a forced and wary politeness not natural to their own habits, but before long this wore off and they began to accept me without reserve as an understandable person of their own kind. This was in part because I had smoothed out my own awkwardnesses. I had fallen into the way of gossiping with them instead of asking questions point-blank about things I did not understand. There is nothing that shuts off the speech of simple men like the suspicion that they are being pumped for information; while if they get over the feeling of strangeness they will yarn as they do among themselves Then in their talk there comes out the rich rough ore of what they themselves accept as the truth about their lives and beliefs, not spoiled in trying to refine it unskillfully by suiting the words to the listener.[7]

Though he did not then speak Mongol, the occasional Mongols he met knew some Chinese, and he began to develop the empathy with that long-suffering people that dominated the rest of his life. *Desert Road* contains several outraged passages about the exploitation of Mongols by Han Chinese. One Mongol trader came from a well-watered district ten miles from the caravan route that had been taken over by the Chinese, who were to move in the next year. Lattimore grieved with him: "So the Mongols were to withdraw from the menace of fields and houses and a life they did not understand; the game would be scared from the pretty hills, and instead of ponies and sheep and white yurts there would be only a few squalid villages. To my way of thinking it was tragic."[8]

Worse, Chinese expropriation of Mongol grazing lands was no solution to China's immemorial famines.

> The prostration of the Chinese people is due to the almost superstitious veneration of the family, from the ancestral tomb to the newborn son, which is carried out in practice by reckless marrying and begetting. The

fine philosophy of the classic Chinese civilization, when interpreted in
its lowest terms by the most ignorant and numerous part of the nation,
is a fatal thing. In his haste to found a family, attached forever to family land, the Chinese peasant simply cannot comprehend the idea of a
fertile leisure, cautious marriage, and the fostering of his sons by en-
larging the measure of their opportunities. This vice in Chinese political economy might be corrected by saner marriage customs; certainly
never by merely expanding the area of their breeding grounds and marriage grounds. . . . In the meantime, the Chinese are evicting the Mongols, as near as I can compute, at about the rate of ten miles a year, all
along the edge [of the caravan route].[9]

Toward the end of the caravan journey, Lattimore met a different group
of Mongols, "driven out of their own country [the Mongolian People's
Republic, or as it was earlier known, Outer Mongolia] by the crushing
taxation under the new Russian- and Buriat-directed regime. As things
go in that part of the world a man makes himself an outlaw by moving away from his tribal region—a grave crime in the eyes of the rulers
who tax him."[10] Ultimately Lattimore came to believe that the Soviet-
sponsored Mongolian People's Republic, despite taxation and sometimes
repression, offered the Mongols a far better life than either Chinese or
Japanese hegemony.

The journey to Urumchi, Sinkiang's capital, was not all aesthetic de-
lights and fascinating campfire talk. There were anxious moments. Reports of marauding soldiers were frequent, and several times the caravan's
leaders prepared elaborate tales about their various sponsors and missions
hoping to ward off severe robbery; other times they made detours around
areas where soldiers were reported to be active. They came through un-
challenged. Lattimore arrived in Urumchi in January 1927.

Urumchi had a primitive wireless station, and Lattimore ordered many
messages sent to Eleanor in Peking. Some of them she received, and in
early February she was off via the Trans-Siberian railway to Semipalatinsk. She had no trouble getting a Soviet transit visa. Lattimore, preparing to cross the border to meet her at railhead, had a quite different experience.

The Soviet Consul General at Urumchi was cordial and helpful, cabling
Moscow to request permission for Lattimore to travel to Semipalatinsk.
Lattimore noted in *High Tartary* that it was "easier" for bureaucrats to
grant a woman permission to travel through "political" territory to join
her husband than it was to grant the husband permission to cross cherished boundaries to fetch his wife. And he knew, "both from reading and

from my slight acquaintance with Russians of the old regime: in the Russia of the Tsars, if the reports on a traveler in Central Asia read innocently, the conclusion drawn was that either the officials on the spot were stupid or they had been bribed."[11] Thus when Moscow denied his request, "It was the official attitude toward Central Asia that was at fault, not the personal attitude toward me of the Russian consular representatives in Chinese territory." He was stuck in the Chinese border town Chuguchak (now Tahcheng), hoping that Eleanor would know he was there and be able somehow to make the long sled journey by herself.

In the dead of the Siberian winter, speaking no Russian, Eleanor managed to obtain passage on a sled carrying matches from Novosibirsk to China. The journey, as she described it in *Turkestan Reunion*, was as frigid and uncomfortable as one could imagine. But she survived. She found Lattimore in Chuguchak late in March, and after a month for Eleanor's recuperation they began their six-month honeymoon through Central Asia. It was an idyllic journey. Travel now was by horse cart; there were no camel caravans. They went first to Urumchi, then on a side trip to the great Turfan Depression. Lattimore had met a Turki merchant in Urumchi who entertained them in his native Turfan; an all-day picnic he gave for them in a nearby vineyard, under a 150-year-old grapevine, took three pages for Lattimore to describe.

After Turfan the Lattimores traveled along the rim of the desert to Aksu, Kashgar (now Kashi), Yarkand, and finally over the Karakorum Pass to Srinigar in India. The intense heat of the summer months led them to travel mostly at night. By the end of the journey, in September, they were crossing 17,000-foot mountain passes covered by glaciers.

Lattimore recorded fewer geopolitical observations in his account of this journey than in the caravan saga. His travelogue dealt mostly with horses, mountains, nomadic customs, cities and ruins of cities, Kazakhs, Uighurs, and fascinating people. There was danger and hardship, but he and Eleanor arrived in Srinigar triumphant and healthy.

From India they went to Rome, reputed to be the least expensive European city at that time. They spent the winter of 1927–28 writing their respective books with the help of the Royal Italian Geographical Society. For a pittance they occupied the third floor of the house near the foot of the Spanish Steps where, a century before, John Keats had spent his last months.

From Woodhead and other acquaintances in China, Lattimore had learned that the prospect for publishing his book in England was very good. When he finished the manuscript of *Desert Road*, he and Eleanor went to England,

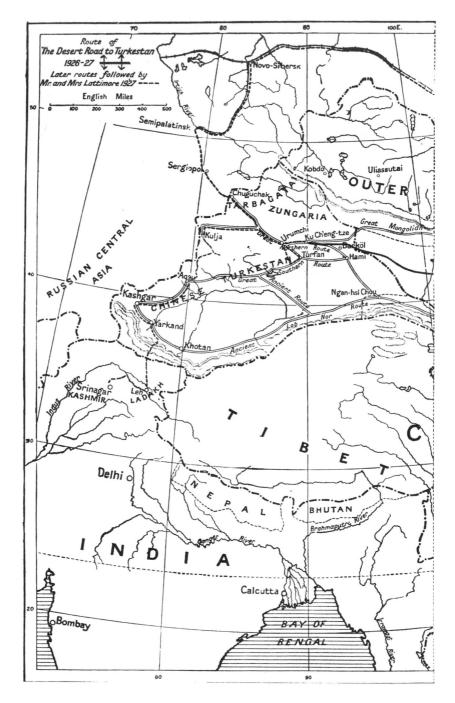

Route of Lattimore's Central Asian journey, 1927. From Owen Lattimore, *Desert*

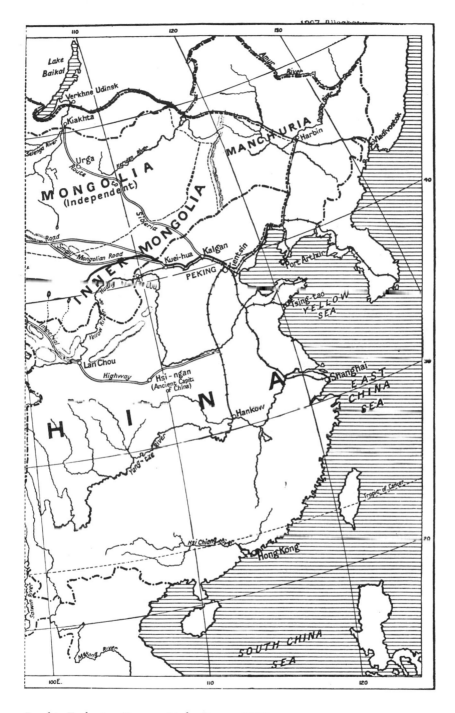

Road to Turkestan (Boston: Little, Brown, 1929).

where he found a publisher who issued the book within the year. Lattimore also contacted Douglas Carruthers, a famous English naturalist whose *Unknown Mongolia* Lattimore had carried with him on his travels. Carruthers received him warmly, advised him about publishing, and introduced him to many of London's orientalists. While in London, at the age of twenty-eight, Lattimore was invited to lecture to the British Royal Geographical Society and the Royal Central Asian Society. He and Eleanor left for the United States in midsummer.

In the summer of 1928, for the first time since Lattimore had been taken to China in 1901, he was back on American soil—broke, married, with no job in sight. He wanted to continue to travel and study in the frontier regions of China. Quite by accident, he was put in touch with the Social Science Research Council (SSRC), a dispenser of funds to promising scholars. Lattimore hardly fit the usual criteria. He had no Ph.D., no graduate study, no college work at all. But he had remarkable experience and the manuscript of *Desert Road* to prove it. Isaiah Bowman, head of the American Geographical Society and influential in the SSRC, liked Lattimore's proposals for the study of Inner Asia and pushed for approval of an unusual grant: a year of informal study at Harvard to gain some acquaintance with the methods and standards of social scientists, and then a year of subsidy to work in China.

One of the anthropologists Lattimore worked with at Harvard was Roland B. Dixon, who had traveled extensively in Central Asia. Dixon insisted that the Lattimores should meet Robert LeMoyne Barrett, also an Asian explorer, who was in Boston on a brief visit. The heir of a wealthy Chicago businessman, Barrett had rejected the business world to travel. Lattimore called Barrett "one of the last of the great eccentrics." Barrett and his wife found the Lattimores to be kindred spirits and began to subsidize Lattimore's travels, providing extras not covered by the SSRC grant when he got back to China. It was a relationship that lasted, with one interruption, until Barrett's death in 1969.

The eight months Lattimore spent at Harvard (1928–29) were rewarding, but Asia beckoned, and much was happening in China; the revolution begun by Sun Yat-sen was accelerating under Chiang Kai-shek. Lattimore returned to China, free to travel and study full-time.

During 1929–30 Owen and Eleanor traveled throughout Manchuria, seeking "surviving communities of the fast-vanishing Manchus who were once the principal inhabitants of Manchuria and the conquerors of China."[12] The Manchus were but one of many non-Chinese races scattered around the central core of Han Chinese. Lattimore was interested in all the minority races, but he was most drawn to the Mongol communities. He knew that the Chinese were steadily displacing Mongol herders with Han farmers, and on a trip to a Chinese colonization project in western Liaoning Province he saw in detail the practices that had been described to him during his caravan trip:

> This colonisation was brutally carried out: the Mongols were evicted at the point of the bayonet and Chinese colonists planted on their land. If any Mongols resisted, they were dealt with as "bandits.". . . Clearly, the military colonisation which my wife and I had seen was not strengthening the Chinese position but preparing the Mongols to accept (and in some cases to welcome) any Japanese aggression against the Chinese that would put an end to the Chinese aggression against the Mongols. Shocked by what we had seen, I tried to learn more about the policies of the various provincial governments dealing with different sectors of Inner Mongolia. I soon found that a great deal of money was being made. The families of generals accompanying the troops acquired expropriated Mongol land at nominal prices and colonised it with refugees from famine areas, imposing on them "sharecropping" rents that kept them poor and powerless.[13]

To Western minds, "Mongol" was synonymous with the "barbarian hordes" of Genghis Khan. Lattimore, though, saw the Mongols as a fascinating, persecuted, intelligent people who suffered the fate of all minorities dominated by neighboring goliaths: in the Mongol case, Russia, China, and Japan. As Han Chinese steadily encroached on Inner Mongolian territory, many Mongols lost their native language and spoke only Chinese. This loss did not, Lattimore observed, eradicate Mongol nationalism: "This phenomenon of the national minority whose loss of the national language has only intensified its nationalism is easily overlooked. It is found among some Welshmen who speak only English, some Bretons who speak only French, and I daresay among some Basques who speak only Spanish or French."[14]

Beyond his growing sympathy for Mongol nationalism, Lattimore began to appreciate the geopolitical significance of the Sino-Soviet border areas. In *High Tartary* (1930) he speculates on the turmoil that yet lay ahead before these much-fought-over territories were finally stabilized. It would, he predicts, be bitter: "The mountains and deserts of Inner Asia have now lain for several centuries like a buffer between Russia and China— one of the greatest nations of the West, and the greatest nation of the East. From both sides a flow has begun into these thinly-held lands. Russian and Chinese must in time come face to face. There is no meeting in history to compare with it. . . . Already a thrust and counter-thrust is bearing on them (as in Manchuria and Mongolia). It is a play of primal forces, far more significant than superficial considerations of politics, which are only symptomatic, and will vary and be transformed, in the confounding way that symptoms have."[15]

His prophecy was strikingly fulfilled in the 1960s, refuting the ignorant American belief of 1950 that Russia had made a satellite of China or, as the supporters of Chiang Kai-shek put it, had created a "Slavic Manchukuo."[16] To many Americans, Marxism was *the* compelling force of the century in determining national policies. To Lattimore, geopolitics was more vital. His "primal forces," the expansionism of China and Russia, proved to be determining, and ideology to be merely incidental.

Also very early in his career Lattimore discerned that Russian policies toward the minorities of Central Asia were more enlightened than those of China. The Russian, he wrote, "has shown less race animosity than any other white race would ever have shown." And "the measure of autonomy granted to the native republics under Russian 'advisory' government appears like comparative freedom, especially the privileges of carrying arms and policing themselves." Thus "the advantages of Russian allegiance being vehemently borne in upon the tribes on the hither side of the border, who chafed under the Chinese restrictions on the bearing of arms," these peoples began to see that Russian hegemony was preferable to the only alternative, Chinese hegemony.[17] Lattimore did not say, then or later, that the Soviet Union provided anything approximating Western-style democracy, which no one in that turbulent corner of the globe knew anything about. But his observation about the Soviet "power of attraction" was correct.

By the summer of 1930, when his SSRC fellowship expired, Lattimore had published not only *Desert Road* and *High Tartary* but also three articles in *Asia* magazine and two in *Atlantic Monthly*. These publications were sufficient to induce the Harvard-Yenching Institute to award him a fellowship for 1930–31. He moved to Peking and began systematic study of written Chinese and the Mongol language.[18] During this period he wrote *Manchuria: Cradle of Conflict* and *The Mongols of Manchuria*, in which he espouses the cause of Mongol nationalism.

When these books were published in 1932 and 1934, they aroused immediate controversy. Since Lattimore condemned Chinese frontier policy, the Japanese praised his books, believing that they served Japanese purposes in Manchuria. Since the Japanese praised them, the Russians accused Lattimore of being an "imperial apologist." And, of course, nationalistic Chinese were offended. Lattimore was always to be controversial because of his outspoken views on the rights of the Mongols and other Inner Asian peoples; neither Japanese nor Chinese found his sympathy for the subject races tolerable.

Even though Peking was his headquarters from 1930 until the summer of 1933, Lattimore continued traveling in native fashion: "Going up to the Inner Mongolian frontier I bought some camels, a Mongol tent, and local provisions, and found as a guide and companion a Mongol who did not know any Chinese. By the end of my first journey of this kind, I had made a good start in the Mongol language. I had also become the first and only American with a combined experience of many months of travel in all three of the great northern frontier areas of China—Manchuria, Mongolia, and Sinkiang—and the ability to travel in those areas, and in North China, without an interpreter." [19]

When the Harvard-Yenching fellowship expired, the Guggenheim Foundation awarded Lattimore grants for 1931 through 1933; he thus had foundation support for five full years of study and travel. During this period the Japanese seized Manchuria, then Jehol, and began to spread out in Inner Mongolia and North China. Lattimore did not approve of this development; he began the opposition to Japanese aggression that dominated his beliefs for a decade.

Also during his fellowship years he met the Dilowa Hutukhtu, one of the "living Buddhas" of the Lama Buddhist church, roughly equivalent to a cardinal in the Catholic church. The Dilowa's former monastery at Narobanchin in the Mongolian People's Republic had both civil and religious jurisdiction over a territory of approximately 1,250 square miles. In 1931 the Dilowa was arrested by the Communist government of the Mongolian People's Republic; he was convicted of antigovernment activities, given a suspended sentence of five years, and told to remain at the monastery. Knowing the Buddhist church had little future under the Communists, he fled to Chinese jurisdiction in Inner Mongolia, and then to Peking.

Lattimore found the Dilowa fascinating; he "was a man of the old order, deeply imbued with the ethos of Tibetan-Mongolian Buddhism, a system of ideas and beliefs that had not changed since the Middle Ages." [20] The Japanese courted the Dilowa, trying to get him to sign on as one of their collaborators, proclaiming their intention of liberating the Mongolian People's Republic from Soviet domination. The Dilowa would have none of this collaboration. He told Lattimore that the Japanese would, "whatever they might say about 'alliance' with the Mongols, make Mongolia into a kind of colony. He did cling, as long as he could, to the hope that American policy might do something to restrain Japan's continuing expansion."[21] Lattimore clung, also vainly, to the same hope.

In addition to the Dilowa and other refugees from the Mongolian People's Republic, Lattimore met and learned about Mongol life from the major Inner Mongolian leaders. One of these leaders was Merse, who headed a school that trained Mongol interpreters for service in the administration of Chang Hsueh-liang, the Nationalist warlord controlling the eastern part of Inner Mongolia. Chang ordered Merse killed in September 1931. Another, Te Wang, was the principal leader of the Inner Mongolian autonomy movement. Unable to secure backing for Mongol autonomy, Prince Te was wooed by the Japanese and eventually threw in his lot with them. Lattimore remarked of him, "As for Te Wang, he has not 'gone over' to Japan; he has been tied hand and foot and thrown to the Japanese."[22]

Lattimore not only absorbed the lore of Mongol culture during his trips into isolated Mongol communities but also read everything available in Peking about the great empires of the khans and their interaction with China. He was absorbed by a tantalizing question: How had such a noble people come to their twentieth-century subjection by the Han? This was the most salient inquiry in his lifelong pursuit of the mysteries of Central Asia. James Cotton summarizes the development of his scholarship:

> He wished to determine how a nomadic society with many egalitarian characteristics had come to be dominated by an entrenched nobility and clergy; he also sought to understand why this entrenched elite had so signally failed to provide that leadership which the Mongols required in the crisis of the past two decades, an enquiry which led to speculation on what future course of action would preserve them as a people. And since the fate of the Mongols was related at every turn with developments in China, Lattimore was also led to contemplate the past and the present of the relationship between these two civilizations, and what failing in Chinese society had prevented that alliance which would have been so advantageous to both peoples.[23]

No ideological system determined his search for answers, though he acknowledged the influence of Oswald Spengler. He took the first volume of *The Decline of the West* with him on his travels in 1929 and 1930.

The years traveling through North China also brought Lattimore into close contact with warfare, not just with the skirmishes between rival generals but with the tactics being developed by the Japanese army. To a great extent these tactics involved systematic "brutality and arrogance" on the part of Japanese soldiers, equaling those of the Germans less than a decade later. Lattimore later found that isolationist sentiment in the United States was so strong that few wanted to hear about Japanese brutality in China. That was not our business.

Nor were Americans interested in field tactics, though they should have been. One of Lattimore's journeys provided him with insight that might have been salutary for many Western commanders a decade later:

> In 1933 I went up to the province of Jehol as guide, interpreter, and ghostwriter to an Englishman who was reporting for an American news syndicate, and together with an American reporter and a couple of American military observers watched the Japanese overrun 100,000 square miles of territory in ten days. They did it by the use of motorized transport and by cutting through the Chinese forces and driving deep, paying no attention to their exposed flanks. This Japanese campaign in 1933 and not the German campaign in Poland in 1939, was the first tryout of the modern blitzkrieg. Only the Germans and the Russians seemed to have paid much attention. Other people thought it was just a lot of Japanese overrunning a lot of Chinese, and not worth study by professional soldiers.[24]

There was an addition to the Lattimore family during these fellowship years in North China. Eleanor became pregnant in the summer of 1930 and on March 24, 1931, entered the hospital in Peking for what turned out to be a very difficult delivery. The son born to her on March 25 was named David, after his grandfather. The Dilowa Hutukhtu became David's godfather.

By the end of his second Guggenheim year, in the summer of 1933, Lattimore and his family were ready to return to the United States. Fellowship money had run out; it was time to look for a job. And there were more books and articles to be written from the experiences of his four years as a student in China.

CHAPTER TWO

The IPR Years

One organization likely to have a job for someone with Lattimore's background was the Institute of Pacific Relations (IPR), headquartered in New York. The IPR was a prestigious study and discussion group founded in Hawaii in 1925 by prominent Americans affiliated with the YMCA. The founders' motivating idea was that YMCA-tested procedures for bringing members of different races together, encouraging frank discussion to meliorate conflicts, should be applied to all the peoples of the Pacific basin.

The IPR was therefore organized to "study the conditions of the Pacific peoples with a view to the improvement of their mutual relations." The idea caught on, various national councils were created, and a Pacific IPR secretariat (the Pacific Council) was established to coordinate conferences and publications. By the summer of 1933 the American Council of the IPR was a well-funded operation, the Pacific Council was publishing a prestigious journal, and the fifth conference of the organization was about to be held at Banff. Lattimore applied to attend the Banff conference and was accepted.

The major IPR journal, *Pacific Affairs*, happened to need an editor that summer. H. G. W. Woodhead, under whom Lattimore had worked a decade earlier on the *Peking and Tientsin Times*, was at the Banff conference and recommended Lattimore for the job. The IPR approved, and Lattimore accepted. The position fit his ambitions perfectly. He could do his editing from whatever base he chose and have time to carry out his own travel, research, and writing.

Lattimore spent the remaining months of 1933 and the first part of 1934 in New York, talking to IPR personnel and learning about editing. He had met many of the IPR staff at Banff; in New York he got to know them better. Most prominent was Edward C. Carter, secretary general of the Pacific Council, hence Lattimore's boss. Carter was innovative, brash, dynamic, and fully supportive of the fledging editor. Carter's main assistant, Frederick V. Field, had been editor of the *Harvard Crimson* and had studied imperialism at the London School of Economics. When he went to work for the IPR, he was a Socialist; shortly after Lattimore met him, though, Field moved further left, supporting the Communist party, but he kept his politics out of IPR activities. Lattimore was friendly with Field and respected him.

One IPR staff member who became Lattimore's lifelong friend was Joseph Barnes. Barnes was with the IPR from 1931 to 1934, after which he joined the *New York Herald-Tribune*, serving as Moscow correspondent, then in Berlin, and from 1939 to 1948, as foreign editor.[1] During World War II Barnes and Lattimore both worked for the Office of War Information. Until his death in 1970 Barnes was foremost among those whose opinion on world events Lattimore valued.

After his apprenticeship with IPR headquarters Lattimore and his wife went back to Peking via Hawaii, where he lectured to the IPR chapter. From Honolulu to Yokohama he and Eleanor shared passage on the SS *President Coolidge* with Agnes Smedley, perhaps the most volatile and adventurous radical American woman of the times. (The Chinese Communist party rejected her application for membership because of this volatility.) Lattimore, who had never met anyone like Smedley, was fascinated. Five pages of the eight-page letter he wrote to Barnes while aboard the *President Coolidge* were devoted to Smedley:

> She's very intense, and extraordinarily naive, and owing I suppose to her life in India and Shanghai has a spy-phobia, detecting detectives behind every pillar and peepers at every porthole. She sees the world in what I can only describe as folklore terms—capitalist consuls, police and other officials are all agents of the Devil; Soviet generals, instead of being militarists, are servants of the Kingdom of God. Her face glowed rapturously as she told of travelling across Siberia, too sick to get out of her berth, in a compartment she shared with a Red Army general. You could tell by the insignia on his collar that he was a general, she said, her eyes widening, and shining with remembered bliss. This angelic being, when he found that she was too sick to share his black bread and herrings, bought her milk at the stations.[2]

From this sarcasm it is clear that Lattimore had no maudlin sentiments about the Russians.

When the Lattimores arrived back in Peking, China was still in turmoil, but the unrest did not stop his forays into the countryside to study trade patterns, agriculture, peasant life, and the effects of Japanese encroachment on the Mongols. In 1935 the Dilowa, who was then a high-ranking official with the national minorities office of the Chiang Kai-shek government, arranged with Inner Mongolian authorities for Lattimore to visit the annual ritual honoring the relics of Genghis Khan at Ejen Horo, deep in the Ordos Desert. This pilgrimage, similar to that of devout Muslims to Mecca, was restricted by the Mongols to those deeply sympathetic to Mongol nationalism and required a hair-raising trip of four weeks. Lattimore later wrote an account of part of the trip for *Atlantic Monthly*.[3] He was impressed and affected by the ceremony but did not credit most of the relics in the shrine as genuine.

The years from 1934 to 1938 were the most productive of Lattimore's life. The combination of field trips and study in Peking was everything he anticipated. The foreign community with which he interacted constituted a stellar group; it included, among others, Joseph Stilwell, I. A. Richards, John Stewart Service, John King Fairbank, Edgar Snow, Anna Louise Strong, H. G. Creel, O. Edmund Clubb, Nelson T. Johnson, and Harold Isaacs. These were both social and intellectual friends.

The scholar from whom Lattimore learned the most was the archaeologist Carl Whiting Bishop, later one of the curators of the Smithsonian Institution. Lattimore's affinity with Bishop was based not only on the latter's mastery of Chinese language and history but also on his scholarly methods. Bishop was a field archaeologist rather than a theoretician working from other people's findings. Lattimore remarked, "He worked in the way in which I myself was trying to work: observe the facts, and see if from these facts you can derive a generalization. I showed Bishop the typescript of my first draft of *Inner Asian Frontiers of China*, and where I would enter into speculation, trying to identify this or that primitive tribe in the earliest Chinese references, Bishop would send my draft back, saying: 'This is complete nonsense, and must be thoroughly rewritten.' "

Karl Wittfogel, also then in Peking, was another to whom Lattimore showed his first drafts. A refugee from Hitler's Germany, Wittfogel was trying to establish himself as a scholar among American and British sinologues. At Wittfogel's request Lattimore added footnotes to *Inner Asian Frontiers* citing Wittfogel's work. Lattimore said later, "It was over Wittfogel that I had my only real quarrel with my wife. Eleanor was always a much better judge of people than I was. She said, 'Be careful. This man is flattering you in order to get started in the United States. He is the kind who is always either licking your boots or jumping on you with his own boots. He could turn against you at any time.' But I refused to listen to her.''

In addition to intellectuals and diplomats Lattimore had contact with two future politicians of great influence. In the summer of 1934 the Lattimores vacationed at a mountain resort in Shansi Province, where their son David came down with tonsillitis. In the nearest medical facility, a remote mud-brick hospital, Dr. Walter Judd took out David's tonsils. John Foster Dulles, touring Asia on behalf of American Protestant missions, visited Peking during the early 1930s. Lattimore met him at lunch in the U.S. embassy: "He was quite firm in his opinion that it was ridiculous for the Chinese to resist Japanese invasion until they had settled the Communist question in China. Only then could they turn to other business.'' Lattimore did not agree but held his peace.

There was one big difference between Lattimore's 1934–38 tour of duty in Peking and his earlier stays: as editor of *Pacific Affairs* he was sitting atop an active volcano. The YMCA idea of decreasing intergroup hostilities by getting people together in the same room may have worked reasonably well, but publishing a journal that had to carry highly partisan authors with irreconcilable national animosities did not produce harmony.

By the time of Lattimore's editorship, active national IPR councils included the British, Australians, Canadians, New Zealanders, French, Dutch, Chinese, and Japanese. Each national council was autonomous, and Lattimore, as editor, worked for them all. Several times he requested the IPR Pacific Council for guidance on what topics *Pacific Affairs* was to cover, and how. But such guidance was not forthcoming, and Lattimore found that any editorial decision would offend someone. "As the editor of the magazine that served as the international forum of the Institute, I was right in the middle, and no matter who was throwing a brickbat at whom I was likely to get clipped."[4] Colonialism and imperialism were the topics that occasioned the most anguish. Should discussions about Asian independence movements be included in *Pacific Affairs*? Surely this was a topic important to the "conditions of the Pacific peoples," but when Lattimore published scholarly analyses predicting the end of colonialism in Asia, the British, Dutch, and French all raised hell.

Lattimore was immediately caught up in the bitter Sino-Japanese quarrel. *Pacific Affairs* carried articles exposing, and damning, the most glaring imperial operation of the day—that of the Japanese in China. Muted though they were, these articles not only put him in the middle of Sino-Japanese rivalry but also caught him between pro- and anti-Japanese officials of the U.S. State Department. Press correspondents covering Asia, American businessmen, and even university people were similarly divided.

Few Americans remember that before Pearl Harbor a substantial group of Japanophiles in this country thought that the Japanese program for developing Asian resources—the Greater East Asia Co-Prosperity Sphere—was reasonable and should be encouraged. Many of them also believed that the stories about Japanese atrocities in China were false or exaggerated and that the Chinese, disorderly and politically incompetent, would benefit by Japanese discipline. The pro-Japanese group had much in common with the pro-Hitler people. Both factions were attracted to the order and efficiency of the Fascist countries, which they regarded as the last bulwark against the horrifying spread of bolshevism, and both thought Fascist leaders could be reasoned with, appeased, and kept under control.

Lattimore rejected the Japanophile position entirely. He had seen the atrocities, did not think the Chinese politically incompetent, and did not trust the Japanese militarists in Manchuria.[5] As to obstructing bolshevism, he did not believe fascism was an effective defense against whatever designs the Russians might have, and he insisted that the main task of students of Asia was to alert the world to the dangers of Japanese imperialism. He later acknowledged that he "failed to perceive that Communism was opening a new chapter in the history of Chinese politics."[6] But geopolitics was still for him primary, and ideology secondary.

The only Pacific power that refused to participate in IPR activities was the Soviet Union. In 1927 IPR Secretary General Merle Davis went to Moscow to encourage Soviet participation, but was unsuccessful. John N. Thomas, author of a perceptive study of the IPR, notes that "in retrospect it seems likely that the Soviets were somewhat suspicious about the benefits of joining a 'bourgeois' institution funded by 'monopoly capitalists' such as the Rockefeller Foundation."[7] The American Communist party had a similar attitude. Bella Dodd, a prominent former Communist, told the FBI in 1952 that "people in the Communist Party did not think too highly of the Institute of Pacific Relations." She quoted Alexander Trachtenberg, head of International Publishers and chief Party theoretician, as saying that the IPR was "an instrument designed to further the commercial interests of the member countries."[8]

Like his predecessor, Edward C. Carter found Soviet noncooperation in the IPR galling. As Lattimore put it, "Carter set out to infiltrate the Soviet Union." Carter's crusade to get the Russians involved in the IPR was one of the major themes at the Banff conference; the proceedings of that conference lament the Russian absence, attributing it largely to U.S. refusal to recognize the Soviet Union diplomatically. American recognition in 1933 improved the situation, and Carter went to Moscow in 1934 to see if the Russians would now join. Minutes of a meeting Carter held with A. Arosev, president of the Soviet society for foreign cultural relations, show Carter trying to convince Arosev that the IPR did not intend to "use the Soviet Union for political purposes." The IPR simply recognized the importance of Soviet studies of the Pacific area. Arosev, unconvinced, responded, "It would be hard to convince anyone in the Soviet Union that the Institute was not political. Any organization in which England, Japan, China and the United States are working, because of the delicate relations between these countries, is of necessity political."[9]

However reluctantly, the Soviets did then designate their Pacific Ocean Institute, a branch of the Soviet Academy of Sciences, as the Russian unit affiliated with the IPR. This was a government bureau, not an independent private organization as were the other IPR national councils, but for Carter it was welcome progress anyway.

In 1935, for the first and only time, a Soviet author submitted an article to *Pacific Affairs*. In one sense Lattimore was delighted to receive it. Under the czars, Russian scholarship on the Mongols and other Central Asian peoples had been extensive; the Soviets appeared to be equally interested in their frontier areas, and Lattimore hoped for many high-quality contributions by Soviet authors. Unfortunately, the 1935 contribution killed that expectation. It concerned the sale by Russia of its share in the Chinese Eastern Railway, and it contained some rough language. Lattimore considered it "rank propaganda" and "an uncomfortable wallop in the midriff" to his hopes for serious Soviet contributions.[10] But despite his misgivings he felt obliged to print it, including its derogatory references to "Chinese reactionaries" and "Japanese adventurers." The Japanese IPR protested bitterly; by contrast, the Chinese, noted Lattimore, "took the attitude that the Soviet Council was a member, that the origin of the article was quite clear, and that the Soviet Council was entitled to have its say."[11]

The quality of possible Soviet contributions to IPR journals was less important to Secretary General Carter than was the gain in prestige if the Soviets became active in IPR affairs. In early 1936, as the IPR conference to be held that summer at Yosemite approached, Carter decided to make a maximum push to obtain Soviet participation. He went to Moscow to confer with Soviet Pacific Ocean Institute officials, taking with him Harriet Moore, a scholar specializing in Russian affairs at IPR headquarters in New York. Carter also wrote to Lattimore in Peking, instructing him to travel to the Yosemite Conference via Moscow and meet Carter and Moore there.

Lattimore was ambivalent about this mission. The Soviets had been rough on him in their own publications, saying that "his scholasticism is similar to Hamlet's madness," vilifying him for publishing an article by then-Trotskyite Harold Isaacs, and accusing him (contrary to facts they should have known) of justifying the Japanese invasion of Manchuria. Lattimore told the FBI in 1950 that "the Russians seemed to reserve their roughest and most uncomplimentary remarks for me."[12] The Carter summons to Moscow also involved some personal inconvenience for the Lattimores. Two weeks on the Trans-Siberian railroad with a five-year-old was a journey decidedly inferior to simply boarding a Pacific liner at Shanghai. But Carter's wishes, plus the fact that Lattimore had never been in the Soviet Union, governed his decision. This time the Soviets gave him a visa.

The Lattimores arrived in Moscow toward the end of March 1936, staying for several days at the home of U.S. Consul Angus Ward. Eleanor and David then went on to England while Owen stayed for two weeks with Demaree Bess, then *Christian Science Monitor* correspondent in Moscow.

Much of Lattimore's time was spent in meetings with Soviet officials, including V. E. Motylev, who complained about Lattimore's editing of *Pacific Affairs*. Lattimore did not back down, especially on Motylev's charge that Lattimore was pandering to Japanese aggression. Motylev demanded that the IPR and its journal support the line that Japanese aggression should be dealt with through collective security arrangements involving all the great powers. Lattimore responded that *Pacific Affairs* served all the national councils, even the Japanese, and had to avoid outright partisanship.[13]

Lattimore hoped that he would be able to make contacts in Moscow that would allow him to visit the Mongolian People's Republic, access to which was controlled by the Russians. Motylev would have none of it. Japan was threatening in the area, he said, and "Mongolia now is constantly ready for war and conditions are very unstable." Lattimore did not believe these excuses, suspecting instead that the Russians simply did not trust him.[14]

All things considered, Carter achieved little on his mission to Moscow. The Soviets did send two representatives to Yosemite, but they never again attended an IPR conference, never submitted another article to *Pa-*

cific Affairs, continued carping about Lattimore's editing, and reneged on most of the literature exchanges and other commitments they made in the Moscow meetings. As World War II drew closer, the Soviets did not even answer mail from IPR headquarters. But Carter got some publicity from the Soviet promise to attend Yosemite.

Despite rebuffs, Lattimore did benefit from the Moscow trip. He talked at length with Academician B. Pankratov, a Mongolist whom he had met in Peking, and with other Asian specialists to whom he was introduced by Demaree Bess. Lattimore was also invited to address the Soviet Academy of Sciences about his views on Asia, but he was not then fluent in Russian and did not know how well his lecture was translated.[15] He noticed, however, that a man in the back of the room got up and moved several rows forward during his speech, repeating this maneuver until he was right in front of the podium. At the end of the lecture the man disappeared in the crowd. Lattimore turned to his hosts and asked who the person so intent on hearing every word was. His hosts were amazed: "Why that was Borodin. Didn't you recognize him?" Lattimore knew well that Mikhail Borodin was the famous Soviet agent who had advised Sun Yat-sen and Chiang Kai-shek from 1923 to 1927, enabling them to establish the Kuomintang as a powerful force. But Lattimore had been in North China while Borodin was in Canton, and they had never met.[16]

Carter thought that Lattimore, while in Moscow, should see U.S. Ambassador William Bullitt to give him the latest information about developments in China. Impressed with Lattimore's critique of events in Inner Mongolia, Bullitt took Lattimore to see a Soviet vice-commissar of foreign affairs. The vice-commissar listened impassively; Lattimore felt it was a waste of time.[17]

Perhaps the most significant event of Lattimore's stay in Moscow was his exposure to Freda Utley, who was at a discussion of Chinese problems held by a Soviet research institute.[18] Utley, a British Communist, had married a Russian working in London and then moved to Moscow with her husband. While there she worked for the Soviets in various capacities, bore a son, and saw her husband disappear in Stalin's purges. She thought her husband had been sent to a labor camp. In later years her path crossed Lattimore's in ways that neither could have foreseen.

After Moscow Lattimore went to Holland, then joined his family in England, where he lectured to IPR groups before going on to Yosemite. The Yosemite Conference of August 16–19, 1936, was the largest and most publicized IPR gathering to date.[19] There were 113 accredited delegates representing eleven national councils, with press and other observ-

ers in addition. The preface to the printed conference proceedings contains
a paean to Soviet attendance, and the presence of Motylev, delegation
head, and Vladimir Romm, *Izvestia* correspondent, no doubt contributed
something to discussions. Other notables were also present, among them
Newton D. Baker, U.S. Secretary of War during World War I, and Hu
Shih, the eminent Chinese philosopher. Lattimore kept a low profile, though
he did deliver himself of his pro-Mongol sentiments, which, as usual,
irritated Russians, Chinese, and Japanese alike.

Motylev predictably pushed the major Soviet foreign policy "line":
peace was indivisible, collective security was the only way to avoid another war, and the League of Nations had to be rejuvenated. But it was
the Japanese "line" that got the most attention. The edited conference
proceedings reveal the naïveté of the editors, who, a mere five years before Pearl Harbor and with eyewitness accounts of Japanese atrocities in
Manchuria circulating widely among the delegates, incorporated in the
document Japanese propaganda so childish as to defy common sense. Japanese naval expansion, claimed one Japanese delegate, was "largely to
replace obsolete ships. We are not interested in entering a naval race."[20]
A "formal evening address by a Japanese member" declared "we may not
all own Ford cars, but we still are happy with raising morning glories in
our less expensive flower pots."[21] War, said all the Japanese, was un-
thinkable.

Not all the utopian rhetoric about Japan's intentions came from the
Japanese. Elizabeth Boody, an American economist and journalist who
later married the Harvard economist Joseph Schumpeter, contributed her
share to the glorification of Japan's forward-looking policies. But while
IPR editors and conference leaders downplayed their opposition to Japanese aggression in China, Lattimore and most of the conferees regarded
that as the most important issue.

Yosemite was the high-water mark of Soviet activity in the IPR. Soviet
officials continued to complain about Lattimore and *Pacific Affairs*; none
of the efforts of Carter or Lattimore to mollify their sensitivities brought
them back into the fold.

After Yosemite, Lattimore spent twelve weeks in London studying
Russian with a tutor. Dealing with the prickly Soviets through an interpreter annoyed him, and he had little faith in available translations of the
extensive czarist sources of Inner Asia. Freda Utley was also then in London, having left Moscow in despair of ever seeing her husband again.
Relations between Utley and Lattimore were cordial; she had admired his
talking back to Motylev and his crew in Moscow. Carter, she thought,

had been much too sycophantic. Lattimore hoped to improve his newly acquired Russian language capability by spending some time in Moscow before returning to China, but he was again denied a visa. In spring 1937 he and his family went back to China via the Suez Canal.

During Lattimore's absence from China the famous Sian kidnapping of Chiang Kai-shek occurred. Chang Hsueh-liang, former warlord of Manchuria, was stationed in Sian as commander of Nationalist troops arrayed against the Communists; Chang felt that Chiang Kai-shek was wasting resources fighting the Chinese Communists, whom he wanted to see included in a United Front opposed to the Japanese. In December 1936 Generalissimo Chiang was on a visit to Sian; Chang Hsueh-liang's forces arrested him and threatened his life if he did not make peace with the Communists and promise vigorous action against Japan. Chou En-lai was instrumental in getting Chiang released and in working out terms of the United Front.[22]

When Lattimore arrived in China soon after the Sian Incident, he was impressed by the outpouring of popular support for Chiang as a result of the United Front agreement. Later Lattimore came to believe that he had been misled by this surge of popularity into an exaggerated belief in Chiang's leadership skills.

The Chinese Communists were then quartered in Shensi Province, first at Paoan, then Yenan, establishing a separate jurisdiction in northwest China and developing their own armies, mostly guerrillas, to harass the Japanese. These Communist activities were unknown to the outside world until 1936, when journalist Edgar Snow visited Shensi and wrote glowing reports of Communist efficiency, morale, and popular support. After Snow's revelations in newspaper articles and his book *Red Star over China*, a trip to Yenan became the top priority of every Western journalist covering China.

Getting to Yenan was not easy. The Nationalist government was outraged at Snow's favorable accounts of Mao and followers. From early 1937 on, the Nationalists tried to block attempts by Westerners to reach Yenan. The Communists, on the other hand, broadcast invitations to any and all to come inspect their operations. Sian was the gateway to Yenan; many Western journalists tried to get there, but most were apprehended and turned back by Nationalist authorities.

One of the would-be travelers to Yenan was Thomas A. Bisson, a sinologue and fellow of the Foreign Policy Association who was studying Chinese politics from Peking. Bisson knew Lattimore and was aware of Lattimore's celebrated ability to get to remote places (except in the Soviet

Union). Shortly after Lattimore got back to Peking from London, Bisson approached him about visiting Yenan. Lattimore had never been there and had in fact no contacts with Chinese Communists, but he was intrigued by Edgar Snow's accounts and immediately agreed. As Lattimore described events in an article he wrote for the London *Times*, "Not knowing of any underground tunnels that would lead me to north Shensi, I set about planning the journey in trustful innocence. I sent a letter to the Red capital, by ordinary mail, with my address candidly printed on the back of the envelope—and got in answer a cordial invitation."[23]

By the time Lattimore got his invitation from Yenan, Philip Jaffe and his wife had asked to join the party. Lattimore had not previously met Jaffe but knew he was launching a new magazine about the Far East to be called *Amerasia;* Lattimore had agreed to serve on its editorial board.

If any Caucasian could bring off a trip through the turbulent Chinese countryside, Lattimore was that person. And in Sian he met a kindred soul who was not only wise in the ways of the countryside but also ran a motor repair shop: Effie Hill. Lattimore described Effie in his foreword to Bisson's *Yenan in June 1937:*

> Effie was a prime example of that picaresque genus, "the parson's profligate son," of whom there were quite a lot in old China. His parents were Swedish Lutheran missionaries. He had grown up on a sector of the Inner Mongolian frontier long ago settled by Chinese colonists where the local Chinese dialect (which was in fact his native language) was considered by other Chinese to be especially uncouth and comic. He had a rare gift of clowning in this language, to attract laughter and sympathy. With an incomplete education he had drifted about Northwest China for a good many years, although still a young man. He had driven cars for Chinese merchants, Chinese warlords, and the Sven Hedin Sino-Swedish Expedition in Inner Mongolia and Sinkiang. He had an incredible knowledge of the seamy side of frontier life—brothel slang, drinking slang, folklore, bandit lore.[24]

Lattimore and Effie hit it off immediately, spending several long nights singing over beer, with selections in Mongol performed by both of them.[25] Effie was amenable to transporting the party to Yenan. He had a battered old Dodge and access to gasoline, and he was known around Sian for taking foreigners on touristy trips to local shrines. The party left June 18, traveling three days and spending four days in Yenan.[26] Mao, Chou, Chu Teh, and the rest of the Communist functionaries spoke with them freely. The visitors found the Communist operation fascinating, as had Edgar Snow, and all but Mrs. Jaffe published accounts of their trip. Lattimore, though, was somewhat frustrated with his opportunities to investigate Communist operations. His major interest being Communist relations with Mongols and other minorities, he requested permission to visit the school maintained outside Yenan for non-Han peoples. As he told it later, "I was not allowed to, and the best I could manage was to meet a group of them who were brought into town for the purpose. The interview was not successful. The Communists had an interpreter present, and were obviously upset when I started talking to a couple of Mongols in their own language, which the interpreter did not understand; and as I did not want to make trouble for anybody, I gave up the attempt."[27]

When the Lattimore party was ready to leave, Mao tried to persuade Effie Hill to stay behind and take charge of the maintenance and repair of what passed for a motor pool in Yenan. Lattimore thought this effort

> most revealing of Chairman Mao's mind. . . . Effie, in spite of his fantastically complete understanding (in certain ways) of his special Chinese milieu, had also a kind of racist contempt for it. His attitude was, "this is a world of skulduggery and crooked dealing. I know the way these Chinese think—but with my extra margin of being a white man, I can always out-doublecross them." Socially, I think he would have to be called a lumpen-bourgeois. He knew little of politics except on the level of "who gets away with the boodle," but he had a destestation of communism. He must have had a deep instinct that it would ruin his raffish way of life.
>
> It is interesting that Chairman Mao, while he was polite, considerate, and patient with us Americans, really tried as hard as he knew how to retain this declassé Swede in Yenan. And why not? American intellectuals come a dime a dozen. There is a new crop every generation. But a European motor mechanic, with an earthy command of a genuinely peasant dialect, able to show what you do with machinery and explain how you do it—that would be a treasure. I am glad to be able to record also the opinion of Effie Hill, the gut-reaction anti-Communist. On the way back from Yenan I asked him, "Well, now that that's over, what do you think of Mao Tse-tung?" His answer was, "I've been with all kinds—merchants, warlords, intellectuals, Kuomintang political big-shots. But this is the only Chinese I have seen who could unite China."[28]

Lattimore wrote two stories for the London *Times* when he returned to Peking, sending copies of them to IPR headquarters in New York and to the American embassy in Nanking. The embassy promptly forwarded them to the secretary of state with a cover letter summarizing Lattimore's conclusions. From a later vantage, two of Lattimore's judgments stand out.

The first is that if Japan continued to encroach on China, "a large part of
both the Chinese army and Chinese people will go over to the Communists." The second judgment, less prescient but more probative as to Lattimore's candor about Communist aims, is worth citing in full:

> The Communists had appealed for a United Front long before the cap-
> ture of Chiang Kai-shek at Sian last December. That was only the in-
> cident which gave them a chance to intervene, to demonstrate that they
> really wanted a United Front more than they wanted the Generalissi-
> mo's head and that they were prepared to make concessions even when,
> temporarily, they held the kind of advantage that terrorists would have
> used ruthlessly.
>
> Does this mean the abandonment of the Revolution? It seems to me
> as foolish to think so as to suppose that the Soviet Union is on its way
> back to capitalism. Primarily, the Communists must have felt that the
> United Front as a rallying cry against Japan would have a wider popular
> appeal than the demand for revolution; while secondarily, a democratic
> phase in China would mean a filtering down of political education among
> the common people, making it possible to renew Communist demands
> in the future.[29]

One will find nowhere a more accurate assessment of Chinese Communist
strategy or a more vigorous assertion that Mao and followers were committed Communists, not "mere agrarian reformers" or "so-called Communists" as some journalists were then saying.[30]

On July 7, 1937, after Lattimore was back in Peking, the Japanese used
an incident between Japanese and Chinese troops at the Marco Polo Bridge
as an excuse to capture Peking and extend their invasion of China. This
incident brought on large-scale fighting, but the Lattimores missed most
of it. Their son David was ill with dysentery, and the Lattimores went to
a seaside resort for the summer. When they came back to Peking in September, the Japanese occupation had become stifling. The mails were being
monitored, and Lattimore knew that publishing a journal from Peking
would be impossible under the circumstances. Nor would he be free to
travel as before in Manchuria and Inner Mongolia. He decided to return
to the United States.

Before he left, one incident impressed on him the fallacy of the Japanese
claim to have Mongol support. Lattimore and a journalist friend visited
the Japanese Office for Mongol Affairs in Peking and spoke with a young
Mongol in Japanese uniform. At first they spoke Chinese, which yielded
nothing but official Japanese propaganda. Then Lattimore started speaking in Mongol, and the whole atmosphere changed. The young Mongol

"asked me where and how I had learned. I told him. 'You must be Lattimore,' he said. I told him I was. 'In that case,' he said, 'I will talk with you, but not with your friend. Don't pay any attention to this Japanese uniform. All of us here are the same. We are working for the Japanese because we have to. But we are not really working for the Japanese. We are Mongol nationalists, and we work for Mongol nationalism if, as, and when we can.' "[31]

In December 1937 the Lattimores boarded ship to return to the United States. Until then Lattimore had been almost totally absorbed by events in Asia. This absorption led to a distinct "Asia first" orientation toward the global struggle developing between the Axis powers and the West. From Lattimore's viewpoint, aggression had started in Asia, and Japan's success had set the precedents for Italian and German activities in Ethiopia, Spain, and Czechoslovakia. As he explains in his 1953 autobiographical sketch for Senator Joseph O'Mahoney,

> I left China hotly anti-Japanese, and ready to argue with anybody, in print or on the platform, that the whole trouble in the Far East was the fault of the Japanese and not the Chinese. I was particularly bitter about the Japanese propaganda—the most successful propaganda they had— that Japan was "saving" China from the Russians and the Chinese Communists. I put it the other way round, and argued that if the Japanese cracked up the regular armies and regular government of China the Chinese would go on fighting, but the leadership would pass to the Communists; that it was the Japanese by their aggression, and not the Chinese by their patriotic resistance to a foreign invader, who were promoting the danger of Communism.[32]

Lattimore left China with more than burning convictions about Japanese aggression. He had used his time to publish several important books. A new edition of *Manchuria, Cradle of Conflict*, came out in 1935, incorporating an updated account of Japanese activities, and *The Mongols of Manchuria* was published in 1934. Both became standard works. In addition he produced a dozen or so articles, one of which, "On the Wickedness of Being Nomads," is a ringing defense of the nomadic life and a biting commentary on those, especially Marxists, who stigmatize nomads as backward. In this article Lattimore condemns not just Chinese and Japanese for chauvinism but also the Soviet Union for "ruthlessly subjugating" Mongol practices to the "alien ideas" stemming from Moscow. He notes that "Soviet influence in Outer Mongolia is, apparently, much more indirectly and circumspectly exercised than Japanese control in Manchuria."[33] But the clear message of the article was hostile to all three Asian powers.

Lattimore spent the first six months of 1938 in California, editing *Pacific Affairs* and writing *Inner Asian Frontiers of China,* a book that solidly established his scholarly reputation and continues as a classic to this day.

Pacific Affairs remained troublesome. Lattimore went far to include articles and letters representing all points of view, even those he personally rejected. One significant instance involved Edgar Snow. W. E. Wheeler II of San Francisco wrote a letter to the editor that Lattimore printed in the March 1938 issue. Wheeler was incensed at a favorable account of the Chinese Communists by Snow carried in a previous issue.

Snow found, as had Lattimore, that the Chinese Communists' temporary suspension of revolution in favor of land reform and rent control might win over many Chinese peasants to their cause. Wheeler could not believe this scenario. His own studies of Chinese history had led him to believe that the importance of the family, the power of the scholar-aristocracy, and the disreputability of the "vagabond" class from which the Communists came all combined to make it inconceivable that Mao and colleagues could ever come to power: "As an aim and a principle, Communism in China is doomed." Wheeler's contempt for Snow, and for the editor who accepted Snow's article, permeates his two-page diatribe.[34]

Lattimore could not reach Snow for a rebuttal, so he made a few comments on Wheeler's letter himself. He was the soul of moderation. He observed that the consensus of those who had actually visited the Communist areas was that these were neither marauders nor vagabonds, nor were they insincere, and that the hold of the scholar-aristocracy was passing. Further, the Communist insistence on fighting Japan, which accounted for the moderation of their ideology, was a highly successful tactic. It capitalized on "the most passionately held ideal of the whole Chinese people—its claim to survival among the free nations."[35] In the face of Wheeler's armchair theorizing, one might have expected a more vigorous response from an empiricist like Lattimore.

Lattimore still hoped to get manuscripts for *Pacific Affairs* from the Soviets, but an incident in 1938 scotched that possibility for good. Lattimore sent an article he wanted to publish by the British economist L. E. Hubbard to Motylev for Soviet comment, as was the usual practice. Hubbard had written that economic conditions in Russia were deteriorating, and Motylev was furious. Nevertheless, there was no official Soviet response to Hubbard, so Lattimore published the article in the June 1938 issue, giving editorial footnotes and also carrying a companion piece with a more favorable view of the Soviet economy.[36] Motylev was not mollified. There were no further Soviet contacts with the IPR, and in 1939 the Soviets even stopped paying their former two or three thousand dollar contribution to IPR. They had paid a total of $12,000 during their brief membership, a fraction of IPR's annual budget of more than $100,000.[37]

CHAPTER THREE

At Johns Hopkins

Before Lattimore left China in 1937, he wrote Isaiah Bowman, then president of the Johns Hopkins University, inquiring if Bowman knew of a university that needed a China specialist. Bowman wrote back that Lattimore "must not think of any place except the Hopkins" and offered him a job. Lattimore took up residence in September 1938 as a lecturer in the Walter Hines Page School of International Relations. This was a half-time appointment, allowing him to continue editing *Pacific Affairs*. Within a year he was made director of the Page School.

Taking the appointment at Johns Hopkins had one unfortunate consequence. Robert LeMoyne Barrett, who had helped the Lattimores financially during their Asian travels, was dead set against the new allegiance. Lattimore called Barrett's attitude "crankiness" and said, "He despised the Hopkins only a little less than he despised Harvard. He thought I was betraying my true role as the free-roaming traveler." Relations became so strained that Lattimore felt he had to decline any more help from Barrett. The estrangement lasted until 1950.

Settling down in Baltimore was not easy for Lattimore. He had spent little of his life in the United States and now had to learn a whole new culture. Baltimore was not the easiest place to begin his education, for strangers were not welcomed with open arms. Here Eleanor's gift for friendship was of great value to him, as was her superior knowledge of American folkways. Still, the Lattimores made few close friends outside the Johns Hopkins community.

Lattimore attended meetings of the American Philosophical Society in Philadelphia during his first year at Hopkins and there met a fellow adventurer who was perhaps his most intimate friend for twenty-four years:

the Arctic explorer Vilhjalmur Stefansson. "Stef," as he was commonly known, soon married Evelyn Baird, and the Lattimores and Stefanssons spent many holidays together. In her introduction to *Silks, Spices, and Empire*, which the Lattimores edited, Evelyn Stefansson Nef (her name after her second marriage) describes the

> special kind of dialogue that Owen and Stef engaged in when conditions were right. Quiet was required—it didn't matter how many other people were present if they were good listeners—and something to hold in the hand, a glass of wine or a cup of coffee. Then these two exceptional men, each expert in his chosen field and interested in everything that related to it directly or peripherally, would begin. In comparing Eskimo and Mongol ways, no detail was too small to be recited and followed by evaluation, comparison, and speculation. Both brought marvelous but different linguistic accomplishments to the discussion. Each could stir the other intellectually and bring out his best. Humor was not omitted, a satiric, tart sort in Stef's case and an earthier, more boisterous, punning kind in Owen's. Throughout 20 years we spent many evenings in this kind of exchange.[1]

Mongols and Eskimos, however, were not topics of academic concern at Johns Hopkins when Lattimore started teaching there. By the fall of 1938 Hitler had annexed Austria, and Chamberlain had capitulated at Munich. Even American undergraduates were beginning to sense the menace of the Fascist powers, and Lattimore's geopolitical approach to politics made sense to many of them. But he had the wrong hemisphere; they were Eurocentric, and his pleas for support of China against Japan made little impression.

Lattimore's opinions on European events were somewhat heretical. He thought that England and France had "precipitated an era of dirty politics by the attempt to appease Hitler and turn him against Russia." There was therefore some justification for Stalin's pact with Hitler, even for the Soviet attack on Finland. But on the Russo-Finnish War he equivocated. The Russians had no "moral justification" for the attack; hence he supported a Baltimore group called Fighting Funds for Finland. But he rejected the right-wing position that the United States should declare war on the Soviet Union because of the Finnish invasion.[2]

It was during his first year at Johns Hopkins that Lattimore made the most serious error of his career. A manuscript was submitted to *Pacific Affairs* by Mary van Kleeck, a pro-Soviet writer whom Lattimore did not know, praising Stalin's purge trials because they strengthened the Soviet Union for the coming battle against Germany and Japan. In reaching this conclusion van Kleeck tossed a bouquet to the Russian masses: "It was the masses who made the revolution. It is the masses who have developed and saved the Soviet Union. It is the Soviet Union today, made strong because of its firm base among the same masses, that alone among all the great nations has been able to check any of Hitler's declared plans. The Soviet Union has won a victory for the democratic nations."[3]

Lattimore had heard similar comments on the purge trials from journalists in Moscow, especially his friend Demaree Bess. Since Lattimore identified with the masses of China, or any other country, against the bureaucrats who bedevil them, he decided to publish van Kleeck's article, which appeared in the June 1938 *Pacific Affairs*.

Now *Pacific Affairs* had a tiger by the tail. Among protesters, the ferocious anti-Stanlinist William Henry Chamberlin, who had been Moscow correspondent for the *Christian Science Monitor*, was the most insistent. His comment on the van Kleeck analysis reached Lattimore soon after the June issue was off the press. Here indeed was the kind of public airing of controversial issues to which Lattimore was committed. Chamberlain noted the absence of documentary evidence in the Moscow trials, ridiculed the Soviet claim that the conspiracies against Stalin could have been so important and yet produced such meager results, noted discrepancies in the confessions, and claimed that the behavior of the defendants did not ring true. Lattimore printed Chamberlain's rebuttal in September.[4]

He also added an editorial comment. On his 1936 trip to Moscow, he had met Radek and Rakovsky, two purge victims. He found their trial testimony to be in character and psychologically convincing. In addition, overbearing Soviet bureaucrats were getting their comeuppance: "The accounts of the most widely read Moscow correspondents all emphasize that since the close scrutiny of every person in a responsible position, following the trials, a great many abuses have been discovered *and rectified.* A lot depends on whether you emphasize the discovery of the abuse or the rectification of it; but habitual rectification can hardly do anything but give the ordinary citizen more courage to protest, loudly, whenever he finds himself being victimized by 'someone in the Party' or 'someone in the Government.' That sounds to me like democracy."[5] It was a statement he lived to regret. The purges merely strengthened Stalin's control, consolidated the bureaucracy, and, as Lattimore later learned, wiped out the China specialists for whom Lattimore had great respect.[6]

Lattimore's misjudgment of the purge trials was undoubtedly influenced by his generally favorable evaluation of Soviet foreign policy, which emphasized collective action against the Fascist powers, and his knowledge that Soviet minority policies in Asia had been far more enlightened than those of other nations. He was nonetheless wrong.[7]

Far more important to Lattimore than argument about Stalin's purges was what he thought to be the craven British-French appeasement of Hitler at Munich. He was convinced of the interrelationship of European events with the scene developing in Asia. In the December 1938 *Pacific Affairs* he wrote a brief comment, "Can the Soviet Union Be Isolated?" It concerned the possibility that Britain and France would continue appeasing Hitler "as a necessary preliminary to the isolation and encirclement of the Soviet Union." Should this isolation happen, and should Hitler line up with Japan against the Soviet, Soviet aid to China, which was the most important source of war material used by Chiang Kai-shek against the Japanese, might dry up. But Lattimore did not think this eventuality likely. Stalin had shown no disposition to back down from engagement in Asia and had already tangled with Japan in Siberia. In fact, as Lattimore saw it,

> The Soviet Union holds a stronger strategic position than ever. Against Germany, the Red Army no longer has to plan for the defense of the awkward salient of Czechoslovakia, but can dig in on its own territory. To attack the Ukraine, Hitler's "pure" Germans will have to cross a belt of Slavic populations, who may for the moment be subservient, but have already been taught that the Germans will always despise and abuse them. Against Japan, the Soviet position is even better. The Japanese have been thrown back from Siberia with great loss of prestige, and forced to involve themselves more inextricably than ever in a war with China which is more hopeless than ever.[8]

Most pundits at that time believed that the Soviet army had been "demoralized by purges"; Lattimore's position was heretical.

Sensing the coming war, Lattimore spent a six-week vacation in Europe during the late summer of 1939. He tried again to get clearance from Moscow to visit the Mongolian People's Republic, but without success. Most of his time he spent in Sweden, paradoxically in the company of Sven Hedin, a celebrated Asian explorer but also, so Lattimore heard, an honorary member of the Nazi party. Lattimore said that his affinity with Hedin was based on professional interests; on other matters they vigorously disagreed, as they did about the Soviet Union.[9]

Hedin foresaw the Hitler-Stalin pact, which astounded Lattimore. He soon realized, however, that it made sense geopolitically. Sworn enemies could make a deal when each stood to gain something, and Stalin did gain something from the pact. Lattimore shared his view of the nonaggression pact with that British master geopolitician, Winston Churchill. In *The Gathering Storm* Churchill writes, "It is a question whether Hitler or Stalin loathed it most. Both were aware that it could only be a temporary expedient. The antagonisms between the two empires and systems were mortal." Churchill goes on to note that the Russians had "burnt into their minds" the disasters of 1914, when their frontiers were more favorable than in 1939. They had to "be in occupation of the Baltic States and a large part of Poland by force or fraud before they were attacked. If their policy was coldblooded, it was also at the moment realistic in a high degree." [10]

But Japanese aggression, not the Hitler-Stalin pact, was uppermost in Lattimore's mind, and no issue of *Pacific Affairs* failed to touch on that topic. However, Lattimore did not confine discussion of Japan to those in sympathy with his views; for instance, the September 1939 issue carried an apology for Japan by one of its foremost supporters, Elizabeth Boody Schumpeter. Her eighteen-page article, "The Problem of Sanctions in the Far East," capitalized on her work with three other economists at Harvard on the recent economic development of Japan. Concerned with heading off strict economic sanctions, Schumpeter argued that Japan was only securing in China the same raw materials that the colonial powers had secured "in the past by methods which now shock us." An embargo on what little the United States still exported to Japan would be a hostile act: "once you deny countries access to food or raw materials on any scale, you are warring on civilian populations; you are employing the very tactics you deplore." [11]

In his editorial comment Lattimore refrained from direct attack on Schumpeter's argument, instead suggesting that *Pacific Affairs* readers who had opinions should send letters for inclusion in the December issue. Seven of his readers responded, and he quoted from their letters in December. One agreed with Schumpeter, five disagreed, and one waffled. Lattimore again stayed out of the argument.

The Institute of Pacific Relations had scheduled its seventh major conference for Victoria, British Columbia, in late November 1939. The outbreak of war caused some changes. Instead of the usual full-scale conference, IPR held a more modest "study meeting" at Virginia Beach. Only six countries managed to send official delegates: Australia, Canada, China, New Zealand, the Philippines, and the United States. Great Britain and France sent observers only. Japan refused to send anyone, as did the Soviet Union. William L. Holland, who edited the study meeting report, attributed the Soviet absence to transportation difficulties.[12] The truth was that the Soviet's seven-year flirtation with the IPR had simply come to an end. In the Soviet view, the bourgeois imperialists who dominated the IPR had finally shown their true colors, retreating and compromising when confronted with Fascist aggression. Collective security had finally and disastrously failed. The Soviets, who had been willing to support France and Britain had those countries defended Czechoslovakia against Hitler, now knew they were on their own. To add insult to injury, the British and French, in an agreement signed at Tientsin on June 19, 1939, gave in to Japanese demands that Japan's occupation currency be accepted as legal tender in British and French concessions, on a par with Chinese currency. This agreement was appeasement in Asia, and the Russians fumed. Carter's continued letters to Soviet officials begging their participation in the IPR went unanswered.

The talk at the Virginia Beach meeting, in which Lattimore participated, was all of the war in the Pacific. Every conceivable point of view was presented. Perhaps the most amazing speech was given by "a leading member of the Chinese group" who said that Japanese warnings to China about "the Communist bogey" from which Japan could save them were nonsense. The Chinese Communist party was no threat to the Chinese Nationalists, "for neither the political nor economic structure of China as a whole reveals any trace of inclination toward Marxism, and, in the strict sense of the term, China has no Communists. What groups there are under this name certainly cannot be regarded as such as understood in Europe, or elsewhere."[13]

Lattimore cringed at this statement: he knew Mao and his followers to be genuine Communists. Other Chinese delegates were more realistic, but the uttering of such fantasy by a high-ranking Nationalist was not a sign of candor at the top.

CHAPTER FOUR

"China Will Win"

Lattimore returned to Johns Hopkins from Virginia Beach to find a welcome invitation. A letter from the prestigious *Virginia Quarterly Review* asked him to submit his thoughts on American responsibilities in the Far East for publication in spring 1940. It was an opportunity to speak his mind free of the multinational constraints imposed on *Pacific Affairs*. He eagerly set about composing his personal credo for American policy in Asia, which appeared as the lead article in the spring issue of the quarterly.[1] There were few surprises in the article. As expected, his number one antipathy was to Japanese aggression in Asia. "Japan has gone on an utterly unjustified rampage. . . . The average American has an uneasy conscience about the amount of help that America has been giving Japan by supplying the raw materials of war. He would like to see that stopped."[2] America's premier task should be to cut off supplies to Japan.

As to China, Lattimore held that Chiang Kai-shek was now determined to reclaim Chinese sovereignty, free of domination by any outside power. The United States should absolutely endorse this objective, since only U.S. support "would give the Chinese regular army and the Kuomintang the degree of help they need to maintain their ascendancy under Chiang Kai-shek. It would guarantee that the Chinese Communists remain in a secondary position, because it would strengthen those Chinese who are opposed to Communism—the very Chinese whom we are now helping Japan destroy." Lattimore admitted that the "detonative ideas" of Soviet Marxism were present in China but argued that they could be contained if we cut off support to Japan and aided Chiang.[3]

One unexpected thrust of Lattimore's advice was his insistence on preventing Soviet domination of China. As editor of *Pacific Affairs* he could not display opposition to Soviet aims in Asia. Here, in a different forum, he directed his argument to precisely this point:

> Above all, while we want to get Japan out of China, we do not want to let Russia in. Nor do we want to "drive Japan into the arms of Russia." . . . We are disturbed by the thought that Russia might get control of China. We are alarmed by the possibility that Russia and Japan might agree on a partition of China. . . . the savagery of the Japanese assault is doing more to spread Communism than the teaching of the Chinese Communists themselves or the influences of Russia. It supplies the pressure under which the detonative ideas can work. At the same time it destroys Chinese wealth of every kind—capital, trade, revenue from agricultural rent—thus weakening that side of Chinese society which is most antagonistic to Communism. The smug pseudo-neutrality of the great powers, among which America is the most important, has no weakening effect whatever on the Chinese Communists, but has a very destructive effect on the progressive middle classes who would naturally draw on the ideas and resources of the democracies if they were not shut out in this way.[4]

While the *Virginia Quarterly* article was in press, another quite different document emerged from the New York Office of the South Manchurian Railway Company (SMR), a sprawling conglomerate that Japan used for the exploitation of Manchuria. Dated February 15, 1940, the document, "The Institute of Pacific Relations: Trends and Personnel of the American and Pacific Councils," antedates by years other attacks on the IPR as pro-Communist. The author is not given, but from various syntactic infelicities one can assume that it was written by a Japanese employee of SMR. The document was never publicly released, but copies of it no doubt reached Japan's apologists in the U.S. The report uniformly interprets any anti-Japanese sentiment on the part of IPR personnel as pro-Communist. Thus, at the very time Lattimore was making vigorous policy recommendations for keeping the Soviet Union and the Chinese Communists from dominating China, the Japanese railway people were beginning to attack him as pro-Communist. The SMR writer denied "the adverse press and radio reports from the Orient, such as those of the Japanese troops brutally raping, pillaging, and terrorizing the Chinese civilians—accounts at least exaggerated and often completely false." Nor had Japanese troops slapped or stripped British and American women.[5]

The IPR, according to the Japanese railway writer, was influenced by a number of "German Jewish refugees" on the research staff who were trying to tie Japan in with the "nazi structure." The article classified twenty-five IPR staff members. Most of them were labeled anti-Japanese, hence pro-Russian, with E. C. Carter and Fred Field the worst and Lattimore coming in third.[6] At the end of the report the writer admitted that some IPR members were pro-Japanese and hence unobjectionable; they were identified as "Professors Treat, Fahs, Gowen and Schumpeter." "Schumpeter" was no doubt Elizabeth Boody, rather than her economist husband Joseph. When Elizabeth Schumpeter volunteered information about Lattimore to the FBI in 1945, she made the same analysis of his procommunism that the SMR report had made five years earlier.[7]

Lattimore, teaching and writing at Johns Hopkins, was blissfully unaware that the South Manchuria Railway was poised to assault him and the IPR. Nor was he aware that in the early months of 1940 he was inadvertently making of Freda Utley a bitter opponent. As noted above, when Lattimore met Utley in Moscow in 1936, she had been impressed by his willingness to stand up to Soviet experts on the Mongols, contrasting Lattimore's independence with Carter's sycophancy. Traveling to England later that year, Lattimore met Utley on a channel steamer, helping her and her infant son get ashore and through British customs. In early 1937, when Lattimore was in London and saw Utley several times, she was again grateful for his helpfulness. As she told the story, "They were very kind to me and my son. They sympathized with me for the loss of my husband. They deplored the mass arrests, imprisonments without trial, and other tyrannical features of Stalin's Russia."[8]

When Utley came to the United States in 1938, Lattimore arranged lectures for her in Baltimore, where she addressed the American Committee for Non-Participation in Japanese Aggression. The friendly relations continued into 1940, when she settled permanently in the United States, staying for a while with the Lattimores in Baltimore. But the friendship began to sour in the same year, commencing with an incident during a dinner at a Washington restaurant. As Lattimore recalled in 1977:

> She heard that through IPR I met the then-Soviet Ambassador in Washington. So she twisted my arm to telephone him and beg for an interview with him. So very reluctantly I did so. Oumansky was his name. I said, "Do you know Freda Utley?" and he said, "Yes, I do, and I don't want to have anything to do with her." "Well, she wants very much to be granted an interview with you." He said, "I will not have anything to do with that woman." He may even have said, "that bitch." From that moment she was convinced that I had sabotaged her request, and if I had really wanted to I could have arranged it. And eventually, when she gave up all hope of getting her husband loose, she became

openly anti-Stalin, anti-Moscow, and anti-Soviet Union, and she became one of the active people feeding material to the China lobby.

Lattimore did not worry overly much about Utley's husband in 1940. Hitler was conquering Western Europe. The pace of events outran *Pacific Affairs*, even had Lattimore wanted to deal with the Asian consequences of the defeats of France and Holland. But he did deal with one controversy in an editorial comment about the Dutch colonies in the Pacific. How would the Netherlands deal with them at the end of the war? Lattimore supported freeing them entirely, a position offensive to Britain, France, and the Netherlands alike.[9]

Again he sought a channel for his ideas less constricted than *Pacific Affairs*, this time in Philip Jaffe's *Amerasia*. The thesis he argued in the August 1940 issue was simple: China would win against Japan and kick out the colonial powers from their Chinese concessions. This example would inspire the Indochinese to throw out the French, the Indonesians to throw out the Dutch, and the Indians and Malays to demand independence from the British.[10] There was nothing ideological about this prediction: it was simply the inevitable consequence of a Chinese victory.

Most Americans did not realize that these events would happen. As Lattimore pointed out, many of them wanted to forget what was happening in Asia and to leave Asia "to one side for the moment, until the situation in Europe has cleared up." To Lattimore, the Asian situation was reasonably clear no matter what happened in Europe, since Germany and Italy could not rescue Japan even if they were to defeat Britain. His blunt conclusion: "What America must decide is whether to back a Japan that is bound to lose, or a China that is bound to win."[11]

Lattimore had by now achieved scholarly stature sufficient to cause the prestigious Council on Foreign Relations (CFR) to seek his services. President Bowman of Johns Hopkins was again his sponsor. Lattimore was commissioned to prepare a memorandum for discussion by CRF's Territorial Group on the topic "Alternatives of United States Policy in the Western Pacific"; interested members of the CFR could read his memorandum and then discuss it at a meeting on October 5, 1940. Lattimore's five-page memorandum began by summarizing U.S. options in Asia:

There are four main alternatives for a policy of protecting and stabilizing American interests in the Western Pacific, with the minimum commitment of America to imperial or protective responsibilities.

1) Conciliation of Japan, and acceptance of a New Order in East Asia in which Japan will be dominant.

2) Stronger support of Britain and British interests . . . on the assumption that the British will eventually be able to return to the Far East with full power and prestige.
3) Cooperation with Russia, intended to create a new balance of power in the Far East. . . .
4) Acceptance of a New Order in East Asia, to be based on the assumption that China must be completely and genuinely independent of both Japan and America, with China dominant on the mainland and Japan dominant on the seas of the Western Pacific.[12]

One knows without further reading which alternative Lattimore prefers. The first alternative would be popularly known as appeasement; there was nothing wrong with this approach on moral grounds, but it just would not work. China would be demoralized, Japan would be certain to expand into Southeast Asia, and the policy "would not create a dependable barrier against Russia."

The second policy might have had some virtues if British victory in Europe could be assumed, but it was not certain. Even if Britain won and eventually reclaimed most of its Asian empire, the United States would still be saddled with burdensome commitments in the Pacific.

The third alternative, cooperation with Russia, was just not practical. It would have a very bad public reception in the United States, and Russia was so "morbidly suspicious of American motives" that we could never negotiate suitable areas of influence. Soviet ideology was not the barrier; rather, geopolitical realities intervened.

Dismantling the other three arguments brought up "clear American commitment to the establishment of a fully and genuinely independent China." The questions Lattimore raised about this policy were (1) would it risk war with Japan? and (2) would it be stable in the postwar world? On the first question, Lattimore seriously underestimated the power of Japan. He acknowledged that all-out commitment to China might trigger a declaration of war by Japan but predicted that we could withdraw our fleet to Hawaii and rapidly strangle Japan by a total economic blockade. Major advantages of this policy would be stiffening Chinese determination to fight Japan and improving Chinese morale. It was a theme he would hammer at until Pearl Harbor settled the matter.

But would Chinese hegemony in Asia be stable? He thought it would be stable if China won without having to call in Soviet troops to help. China would have to keep "warily out of political commitments to Russia, while at the same time making business deals, on business terms, with the nations which have the most free capital to export—notably America."

Presumably the CFR elders approved Lattimore's geopolitics: they asked him to lead similar discussions twelve more times in the 1940–48 period. In his 1984 history of the CFR, Robert D. Schulzinger concluded that "Lattimore's memoranda for the Territorial Group were remarkable principally for their anti-Soviet outlook. . . . Lattimore loved China, despised Russia, but only mildly disapproved of Japan."[13] Schulzinger is correct about Lattimore's attitude toward China, but Lattimore was less hostile toward Russia and more hostile toward Japan than Schulzinger's reading of the CFR minutes contends.

In the December 1940 *Pacific Affairs* Lattimore reviewed Motylev's *Pacific Nexus of the Second Imperialist War*. The number of copies of this book printed by the Soviets (twenty thousand) and Motylev's scathing analysis of British and American "imperialist" motives indicated to Lattimore that the book was designed for internal Soviet consumption rather than as propaganda abroad. Nonetheless, Lattimore found the book significant because of its clear hostility to Japan: "It does not in the slightest degree prepare the public for a Soviet 'deal' at the expense of China."[14]

The *New York Times* noted Lattimore's review in an editorial of December 11, 1940. Motylev's book, said the *Times* writer, was welcome: "At a time when it is increasingly clear that the war in Europe and the war in Asia are at bottom a single war, China's capacity for continued resistance to Japanese ambitions is becoming more and more important." Pro-Chinese opinion from Russia was as happy an omen to the *Times* as it was to Lattimore.

The "China will win" theme had constant exposure in Lattimore's increasingly frequent speeches: at a Public Affairs Forum in Baltimore, January 21, 1941; at a meeting of American Military Engineers on the Johns Hopkins campus later that month; at a large gathering of the Washington Committee for Aid to China on February 11. The Washington speech, however, contained an infelicitous remark. Lattimore said that the U.S., "although pledged to become the arsenal of democracy, has in fact been the arsenal of aggression."[15] To the extent that the U.S. had shipped oil and scrap iron to Japan, he was quite right. Conservatives would later claim that the phrase proved Lattimore subversive.

In April 1941 Lattimore reached his widest audience with a three-pronged geopolitical analysis. For the foreign policy elite of the CFR he discussed

the possibility that Japan would propose a nonaggression pact to the Soviet Union. Such a proposal, he thought, might be made, and he was
persuaded that the Soviets might accept. If so, the U.S. had to respond
with vastly increased aid to Chiang.[16]

His second audience was the readership of *Foreign Affairs*, in which he
published an article analyzing the failure of Japan to bring sufficient force
against China to deal a knockout blow. It was then, he thought, too late
for Japan to mobilize the great resources required to defeat China. Nevertheless, we could take no chances: Chiang still needed all the support we
could send him.[17] A *New York Times* editorialist endorsed Lattimore's
article on March 20.

But Lattimore still had more to say, and in the April 1941 issue of *Asia*
he looked into the future of Asia with a prescience sufficient to wipe out
any debits accumulated elsewhere. He emphasized that the Chinese were
bitter about U.S. ambivalence toward Japanese aggression and about our
neglect of Asia to concentrate on Europe. Years later the Asia-first wing
of the Republican party would excoriate Lattimore for many imagined
transgressions, but in April 1941 he could hardly have put the Asia-first
case better.

> It is quite true that we shall not have an easy time with an Asia headed
> toward emancipation. We shall not have an easy time in any case. We
> shall have the worst time of all if we simply try to defer making up our
> minds about Asia until we set Europe straight. A time in which Europe
> desperately needs to set itself straight is not a time in which Asia will
> consent to be smothered. . . . Already there is evidence of demorali-
> zation in China—even to the point of talk about civil war. What we do
> not sufficiently understand is that this is largely because of the bitter-
> ness of Chinese disappointment in the democracies. The most potent
> friends of the Anglo-American kind of democracy have been the most
> deeply shocked by our rallying cry—"This way to the lifeboats. White
> men first!" Their voice is that of Madame Chiang Kai-shek, who has
> said that, if China goes down, it will not be for lack of Chinese courage,
> but because China has been strangled by a noose fashioned of "British
> appeasement, American profiteering, and French fear."
>
> If we are to have chaos in China, then, it will be of our own making.
> . . . Apart from the fact that this chaos would spread all over Asia, civil
> war in China would mean, in the end, the triumph of the Chinese Com-
> munists. This would be a magnificent irony, seeing that unless they are
> forced into a civil war the Chinese Communists are bound to remain a
> minority. They themselves could not start a civil war with any hope of
> success, for that would turn a great part of the army against them, and

many of the peasants. If, on the other hand, a civil war should be forced
on them, while they themselves continue to demand a united front and
a clear victory over Japan, most patriots would rally to them, including
many moderates who would in no other circumstances follow Communist leadership. . . . It would be a tragic folly, and the culminating
folly of two decades, if American vacillation and failure to support the
patriots in China—the hard-pressed guardians of the American stake in
evolutionary democratic progress—should let loose defeatism, civil war
and revolution. [18]

The Chinese civil war in 1946–48 was indeed such a tragic folly. It was
won by exactly the forces Lattimore predicted would win, and for his
reasons.

The CFR, having heard on April 3 Lattimore's warning of the possibility of a Soviet-Japanese pact, called him back to lead another discussion
after such a pact was signed on April 13. His memorandum this time,
dated May 6, 1941, was far more elaborate than his earlier document and
was designed as background for understanding relations between Moscow, Tokyo, Chungking, and Yenan. Emphasizing the tenuous connections between Moscow and Yenan, Lattimore lay the groundwork for his
later prediction that a Communist-led China would not be subservient to
Moscow.

> The Chinese Communists, although members of the Comintern, differ
> from all other Communist parties in their relations to the Comintern.
> . . . The territory they control, the population they administer, and the
> war in which they are engaged force on the Chinese Communists all
> kinds of decisions which they must make on their own responsibility.
> It can easily be understood that in minor decisions of detail it would be
> absurd to refer to distant Moscow; but even in major decisions of policy
> the Chinese Communists must often have to work first from the merits
> of the case, doing whatever they can later to square their decision with
> the "general line" of the Comintern. . . . It is therefore probably not
> an exaggeration to say that *the Chinese Communists have perhaps more
> influence on the Comintern than the Comintern has on them.* If this is
> true, it is so significant that its importance can hardly be overempha-
> sized. (Lattimore's italics) [19]

Lattimore therefore concluded that since Moscow-Yenan ties were weak
and since Stalin did not fully trust Mao, the Russians would continue to
support Chiang as the only Chinese leader capable of holding his country
together against the Japanese. His essential point: "To preserve satisfactory relations between the Russians and the non-Communist, right-wing

Government of Chiang Kai-shek, it is worth making very serious efforts
to improve American relations with Russia." Lattimore's line was finally
adopted—after the Japanese struck Pearl Harbor.

German strategists began to note the advice coming from Lattimore.
Paul Wohl translated the comment on Lattimore by Major General Professor Karl Haushofer, Germany's master strategist and Hitler's mentor,
as carried in Haushofer's *Zeitschrift für Geopolitik:* "We consider Lattimore as the spiritual guide of America's trans-Pacific cultural policy and
geopolitically as the most remarkable personality of highest political and
scientific caliber opposing the old world."[20] Wohl's translation is not idi-
omatic, but Lattimore's talents were clearly appreciated in the Third Reich.

There is no evidence in any of Lattimore's writings prior to the summer
of 1941 that he was a danger to American internal security. But there was
a trap that ensnared him nonetheless: guilt by association. The first notice
the FBI took of Lattimore was based on his association with a group that
three years later was declared subversive. Serial 1 of the FBI headquarters
file on Lattimore, dated May 16, 1941, at Baltimore, Maryland, tells the
tale:

MEMORANDUM

The following name is submitted for consideration for Custodial Detention in case of a national emergency.

> Name—OWEN LATTIMORE
> Address—210 Chancery Road
> Nationalistic Tendency—Communist
> Citizenship Status—Unknown

SUMMARY OF FACTS:

OWEN LATTIMORE is Vice-Chairman of the Maryland Civil Liberties
Committee according to correspondence which among other things criticized the FBI and the Dies Committee and on other literature obtained
in the Enoch Pratt Library, Maryland Room, Verticle [*sic*] File, under
the title, "Maryland Civil Liberties Committee, Baltimore, Maryland."

NOTE:

The Baltimore Field Division is presently conducting active and vigorous investigation of the above named individual.[21]

Unlike most FBI documents, this one does not give the author or the
addressee.

Baltimore FBI agents worked on the Lattimore investigation for ten days in June and July. We do not know whether they concluded that the Maryland Civil Liberties Committee was harmless or whether Lattimore was to be included on the Custodial Detention list because of his membership. On September 3, 1941, when the Baltimore agents reported to FBI headquarters, Lattimore was off the hook—not because the investigation found nothing against him, but because he was no longer in FBI jurisdiction. Serial 3 of that date disclosed where he had his office and quoted an unnamed informant as saying "that he would trust subject with his life and knows that everyone in Baltimore felt the same about the subject" and that he was "shocked at the idea that the subject was even remotely considered as a person involved in subversive activities." The report went on to state that Lattimore's credit rating was good; that all his previous addresses in Baltimore were checked; that he was listed in the city directory; that the Supervisor of Elections had no record relative to the subject (this was important to the FBI; a suspected subversive might have registered as a Communist or Socialist); and that neither the Baltimore City Police nor the Maryland State Police had records on Lattimore. However, there were newspaper stories, one of which announced that Lattimore had arrived in Chungking to become special adviser to Generalissimo Chiang Kai-shek. This article ended the investigation:

> Due to the fact that the subject is now located in China, it is believed no further investigation is necessary and it is requested that his name be dropped from the Custodial Detention List.
>   —C L O S E D—[22]

Closed? The Lattimore FBI file would grow to 38,900 pages.

However, one segment of Lattimore's life was closed in 1941. The June issue of *Pacific Affairs* was his last. He did not know of the sea change impending in his life when in April he wrote his editorial for the June issue, but it served well as a valedictory. "After Four Years" took twelve and a half pages and covered much the same ground as his CFR–*Foreign Affairs*–*Asia* trilogy. He included his standard castigation of the Western democracies for appeasing the Fascists and hanging on to their empires, but with some new phraseology. "In short, the problem of empire could be casuistically presented, up to September, 1939 as no more than a problem in opening up to imperial rule a few more areas in a world already committed to the principle of empire. This could be quite simply done by issuing licenses to be imperial to three more master-races. 'We shall grow, but you will not be diminished,' said the fascist rulers to the democracies. With the outbreak of war between the established master-races and the claimant master-races all this was changed."[23]

The "master-races" terminology was incendiary. It was seized on by later detractors such as Irving Kristol, quoted contrary to context, and used to show that Lattimore, by opposing imperialism, was following the Communist party line and was against Britain's struggle with Germany.[24] Nowhere did Lattimore ever oppose the Allied war effort, during the Hitler-Stalin pact or after Hitler tossed it aside. All he was saying by this colorful "master-races" language was that the Allies had to give up their colonies and support self-determination in Asia.

CHAPTER FIVE

Adviser to Chiang

After Stalin signed the nonaggression pact with Japan on April 13, 1941, Chiang could no longer count on Soviet aid. He was forced to step up his efforts to get supplies from the United States. The Roosevelt administration, though, was torn by conflict over Asian policy. The president, Secretary of War Stimson, and some of the military wanted to support China in every way possible without precipitating war with Japan. Ambassador to Japan Grew, his chief assistant Eugene Dooman, and other pro-Japan officers wanted to avoid any appearance of a major commitment to China.

Even the strong China supporters, however, were uneasy about Chiang's reluctance to commit all his forces against the Japanese invaders and his determination to crush the Chinese Communists. Chiang did not pretend that the supplies he wanted were for use against the Japanese; as he told Ambassador Nelson Johnson in October 1940, "It is not the Japanese army which we fear, because our army is able to deal with it, but the defiant Communists. American economic assistance plus the aid of the American Air Force can stabilize our unsteady economic and social conditions, thus making it impossible for the Communists to carry out their schemes." [1]

Johnson and U.S. Naval Attaché James McHugh were not alarmed at Chiang's attitude. McHugh especially was a bitter opponent of the Chinese Communists, whom he blamed for most of China's problems. Against the advice of such figures as Edgar Snow and U.S. Marine Captain Evans Carlson (an old China hand), McHugh argued that the United States should stay clear of the Communists. Talk of giving Mao military aid was abhorrent to McHugh; such support would only weaken the Nationalists. [2] In the coming battles over aid, Lattimore sided with McHugh; Lattimore was committed to the belief that all-out support of Chiang would "keep the Communists in a subordinate position."

These clashing opinions became highly salient with passage of the Lend-Lease Act by Congress on March 11, 1941. Roosevelt could now transfer war supplies by executive decision to nations whose defense he considered vital to the defense of the United States. No more dependence on bureaucratic inefficiency and infighting, no more roadblocks from the reactionaries in the State Department; the reins of *this* program were in the White House.

Though Congress's motive in passing Lend-Lease was primarily to aid the British, the Chinese saw its potentialities at once. T. V. Soong, Chiang's primary agent in Washington (Chinese Ambassador Hu Shih was a figurehead), immediately urged Roosevelt to send a special envoy to Chungking to survey China's needs.[3] Soong wanted Harry Hopkins, Roosevelt's chief troubleshooter, but Roosevelt would not send him; instead, he made Hopkins overall Lend-Lease administrator. But the idea of a personal presidential envoy to China appealed to Roosevelt; special emissaries were prominent in his administrative style. This way he could bypass the notorious bureaucracy of the State Department, establish personal relationships with foreign leaders, and better control relations with China.[4]

Roosevelt sent as his envoy a brilliant and ambitious young White House economist, Lauchlin Currie. Sensing the developing importance of China, Currie welcomed the opportunity. He spent four weeks in February and March 1941 in Chungking, conferring with Chiang, Madame Chiang (who charmed him completely, as she did all high-level American visitors except General George Marshall), and James McHugh; he also talked to Ambassador Johnson, but Johnson was about to resign and took a jaundiced view of the whole process. Nevertheless, Currie's extensive report on his mission played up to Roosevelt's global ambitions. Chiang, he said, did not want to liberalize and broaden his regime. War between the Nationalists and Communists was possible, but Roosevelt could use the lever of Lend-Lease to push Chiang toward reform. Why not send a team of Americans to supervise aid, with technicians supplying know-how and a liberal political adviser to push Chiang in the proper direction? Chiang had in fact asked for a political adviser, though his motive was to use that adviser to bypass the embassy and get maximum possible aid. Currie also recommended that Roosevelt boost Chiang's stock in the United States by public statements of admiration and support.[5] Currie's scenario may have impressed Roosevelt, but its naïveté about Chinese politics has been forcefully analyzed by Michael Schaller:

[Currie] twisted the Chinese experience to fit his own vision of reform. As the New Deal had attacked the bastions of the old economic order, Americans could train Chinese Keynesians to smash the legacy of rural poverty and political oppression. Currie seemed completely unaware of the fundamental class and land struggle which underlay China's crisis. He possessed no sense of what forces the KMT represented, or why the Communists could successfully appeal to the peasantry. Moreover, to expect any political group in China to accept the indignity of subordinating themselves to foreign advisors was to totally misunderstand the direction of Chinese nationalism since the 1911 revolution.[6]

No understanding of China appeared in the White House of early 1941. Roosevelt gave quick approval to the dispatching of advisers to China, instructing Currie to come up with the name of a political adviser. Currie's first choice was George S. Messersmith, then ambassador to Cuba. Messersmith pleaded ill health and declined.[7] Currie was shortly visited by John M. Gaus, professor of political science at the University of Wisconsin and formerly one of Currie's instructors at Harvard. Gaus, known as a recruiter of New Deal personnel, had obtained for Currie his job with the Roosevelt administration. When Gaus appeared in Currie's office, Currie immediately solicited him for the job as Chiang's adviser. Gaus also declined: he knew too little about China. But on the train down from Wisconsin Gaus had read and admired an *Atlantic Monthly* article by one Owen Lattimore. Why didn't Currie recruit Lattimore?[8]

Currie was reluctant at first. Lattimore had never been a government employee and had irritated the State Department by criticizing U.S. policy as too soft on Japan; also, neither Currie nor Roosevelt had ever met him. Nonetheless, Currie called Lattimore down from Baltimore for an interview and was impressed. He asked if anything Lattimore had ever written would be embarrassing; Lattimore mentioned an attack he had once made on Chinese Chief of Staff Ho Ying-ch'in, but Currie did not think this article important. Since the Treasury Department, and not the State Department, was the most important agency dealing with China, Currie arranged a briefing for Lattimore at Treasury, chaired by Harry Dexter White. (Lattimore later sneered at the investigative prowess of the witch-hunters, who never uncovered this connection with White.) White and his colleagues, satisfied that Lattimore understood the importance of economic factors in U.S. China policy, approved the appointment. On April 29, 1941, Currie wrote a memorandum headed "Political Adviser to Chiang Kai-shek": "Ever since our discussion on this matter I have been looking for the right man, as the position is of enormous importance."

He had found the right man. Lattimore had extensive language skills and experience in Asia, was not associated with any group or faction in China, and had "New Dealish political attitudes." Roosevelt would need to consult Lattimore before making the appointment, if only to add to Lattimore's prestige in China.[9]

Roosevelt responded to the memo by asking Currie to contact Johns Hopkins President Bowman and Rear Admiral Harry E. Yarnell, recently retired commander of the U.S. Asiatic Fleet. Both were enthusiastic about Lattimore, Bowman noting Lattimore's leadership of Council on Foreign Relations meetings with effusive praise.[10]

Currie repeated the suggestion that Roosevelt personally interview Lattimore, as "it is most important that he be thought to possess your confidence." Roosevelt did so, apparently liked Lattimore, and on May 19 sent a casual note to Secretary of State Hull: "What do you think of having the Chinese Government appoint Owen Lattimore as political adviser? It sounds good to me."[11]

Hull despised the whole idea, seeing it as one more Roosevelt stratagem for bypassing State. Stanley Hornbeck, chief of the Far Eastern division and Hull's primary adviser on Asian matters, also abhorred such an appointment. Neither objected to Lattimore as a person, however, and Hull yielded to his superior with a restrained note on May 21. He said that since the Chinese government had had various American advisers in the past and since Lattimore was "well and pleasantly known by a number of my associates," there was no objection to the appointment. However, it should be clear that Lattimore would serve as a private American citizen, not as a government official.[12]

Then the wheels began to turn. Currie cabled Chiang on May 29 that the president "suggests for consideration Owen Lattimore . . . as a person admirably equipped for the post." Chiang wired approval June 1, stating that T. V. Soong, his liaison for Lend-Lease matters, would make arrangements. Soong and Lattimore met on June 3, when they agreed on a six-month tour of duty with a salary of $10,000 plus expenses. Soong confirmed this offer in a letter June 11, Lattimore formally accepted June 18, and the news began to spread on the Washington cocktail circuit.[13]

Neither party was sure who should make the announcement. Currie wrote Roosevelt on June 20, suggesting that Soong issue a statement emphasizing that Lattimore was going to China "on the nomination of President Roosevelt."[14] Roosevelt wrote "O.K." on Currie's proposed announcement.

But nothing was released for eight days. Hitler scuttled his pact with

Stalin and ordered the German army into the Soviet Union on June 22. This world-shaking event absorbed the Washington community for at least a week. Every factor in the world power equation had now changed. China was confronted with a complete cessation of Soviet aid and a complete dependence on the United States. Lattimore's mission was thought to be crucial.

On June 28, 1941, the Lattimore announcement was released in Washington and Chungking. Most American dailies carried the story the next day; the *New York Times* headline read, "Lattimore Named Adviser to Chiang. Appointment of Widely Known Writer on China Evokes Praise in Chungking. Held Token of Esteem. Author's Immediate Task Will Be to Facilitate Aid from United States." Chinese Ambassador Hu Shih complained later to the FBI that the whole thing had been done clandestinely and that he had learned of the appointment from one of his subordinates, who met Currie at a party.[15]

Lattimore now had to resign as editor of *Pacific Affairs*, but E. C. Carter continued to take an interest in his doings and arranged several conferences for Lattimore with persons knowledgeable about China. One of them was Soviet Ambassador Constantine Oumansky, from whom Lattimore was anxious to learn about Russia's probable future course in Asia. A luncheon with Oumansky proved enlightening. The Soviet Union, said Oumansky, would continue to support Chiang Kai-shek just as it had in the past; all Soviet arms went to his Nationalist government. The Russians did not want any split in the shaky Chinese United Front; Japan had to be kept tied down. Lattimore remembered one cynical remark about the Generalissimo: "I suppose you know what kind of a son of a bitch you'll be working for?"

Lattimore was to leave from San Francisco July 8. Sadly, this time he had to leave Eleanor behind. His only public appearance in the U.S. before his departure was at a dinner meeting of the San Francisco IPR on July 7. His speech, according to the *San Francisco Chronicle*, "rang with faith and confidence in the China he is to serve." On his new superior, he went overboard: "Among the handful of great world leaders, Generalissimo Chiang Kai-shek is conspicuous for the fact that he is not only a great leader, but a leader who has steadily grown in strength and stature in the last four years, a growth commensurate with that of the country itself."[16]

Lattimore arrived in Chungking July 19 to take up residence in a house belonging to T. V. Soong, which had earlier housed Lauchlin Currie. It was a far cry from Mongol yurts in the Gobi. Chungking was not the world's most livable city, but Lattimore's house had one big attraction: there was room for the Dilowa, his old friend from North China, to stay with him. The Dilowa was still working for the Nationalists; Lattimore said Chiang kept him as a hostage to ensure the good behavior of the Inner Mongolians.

Lattimore's reception in the Chinese capital was by all accounts warm and approving. Unlike previous emissaries he kept a low profile, which, according to McHugh, contrasted sharply with that of the flamboyant and dogmatic Manuel Fox, a Treasury representative in China. Lattimore, said McHugh, benefited from his "quiet and open-minded approach to his task." [17] Despite the general approval, there were detractors of the Lattimore appointment. One of them, a Chinese professor then in Kunming, wrote to various American friends that Lattimore was a tool of the leftish *Amerasia* group and of such unreliable intelligentsia as Lauchlin Currie. [18] However, this was a minority opinion.

Chiang began conferring with Lattimore immediately. They could talk without an interpreter, despite the Generalissimo's provincial accent. Chiang's first question was "What does Roosevelt think about the war in Russia?" Lattimore answered, "President Roosevelt thinks the Russians are going to come out on top," to which Chiang replied, "Good. All my generals are telling me that the Russians are all washed up, but I agree with President Roosevelt. The Russians are going to win."

Then Lattimore raised the question of his contacts. Whom should he see? "Call on all the embassies," Chiang said, "but call on the American embassy last or nearly last." Lattimore then asked whether he should take the initiative in calling on the Soviet embassy, to which Chiang replied, "Yes, of course. You must be in touch with them." Then came the sticky question of the Chinese Communists, who maintained a liaison office in Chungking. Should he call on them? "No, don't call on them. Let them call on you."

On July 21 "administration officials" in Washington told the United Press that one of Lattimore's major missions was to make a firmer peace between Chiang and the Communists so that American aid would not be used in a civil war. The *New York Times* carried this story the next day. Sumner Welles, acting secretary of state, immediately denied it. [19] Welles was right. Lattimore had no such charge. He was there to advise Chiang, not to promote American policy.

One early report on Lattimore's mission came from McHugh in a letter to Currie dated July 22. Lattimore had made an excellent impression during a layover in Hong Kong and had handled "the flood of callers and appeals which descended on him" very well. He was doing equally well in Chungking. Chiang had already spent half an hour alone with Lattimore. McHugh felt that Lattimore "has an opportunity to get in behind the scenes as no one before him whom I have known. He said he intended to see all who call, seek information wherever he can get it, but do as little talking as possible."[20]

Lattimore was true to his word. Richard Watts, in a perceptive story from Chungking appearing in the *Baltimore Sun* of August 24, 1941, noted the high level of speculation about Lattimore's mission, speculation fueled by Lattimore's reticence: "Since his arrival Mr. Lattimore has been exceedingly close-mouthed, even to his newspaper friends of long standing, and has been interested in hearing views, rather than expressing any of his own."[21]

Lattimore's major utility for the Chiangs was his skill at drafting and revising Chiang's many appeals to Roosevelt. These appeals went to Currie, who had the president's ear; it soon appeared that the Lattimore-Currie channel to the White House was as useful as if Lattimore had himself been a presidential confidant. The cable-drafting session of July 31, a transcript of which showed up in Lattimore's FBI file, shows how the channel worked.

Generalissimo saw Mr. Owen Lattimore between 5:50 and 6:50 p.m. on July 31st, 1941. The following took place.

Generalissimo: I am deeply interested in the questions concerning Sinkiang, Manchuria and Mongolia and would like to discuss them with you again in the future. Meanwhile, I have something else to take up with you.

China has been engaged in four full years of war of resistance to Japanese aggression only to find that her position still remains one of isolation. Despite the fact that America has been generous in her expression of sympathy and friendship for her and has given her material assistance as have Britain and Soviet Russia, China enters the fifth year of war without an ally. What guarantee would there be when the war comes to an end that the other democracies would not keep holding her off at arms length and would not treat her on the basis of equality? This is something which has been troubling the minds of the Chinese people.

Simultaneously the Japanese and their puppets have been exploiting this anomalous situation by conducting an intensive propaganda to the effect that white men are still treating China as a colony and would not hesitate to sacrifice her interests for the purpose of insuring their continual domination in the Far East. For their own prestige, the Japanese strongly emphasize that they are treated as equal members of the Axis Alliance, which had recognized their puppet regime. They warn that China despite her four years of war and still having not received similar treatment from the democracies, should look out. Such propaganda has caused much vexation to the Chinese masses although they have not yet given expression to their painful feelings. If not stopped, this would weaken the force of Chinese resistance. President Roosevelt is in a position to remedy the situation. I have two proposals in mind for his consideration.

One proposal is that the President suggest to Great Britain and Soviet Russia that they form an alliance with China. The other proposal is China's participation in the joint Pacific Defense Conference of America, Britain, Australia, and the Dutch East Indies, which has been going on for some time. . . . In the circumstances, if President Roosevelt doesn't take the initiative, neither of these proposals would materialize. . . . I would not have mentioned this matter to any other foreign friend.

Mr. Lattimore:	Does the American Ambassador know anything about it?
Generalissimo:	No, he does not know it. I wish you to convey this to President Roosevelt direct either by wire or by airmail.
Mr. Lattimore:	I will do so as you wish. . . .
Madame:	It is better for Mr. Lattimore to wire to President Roosevelt because it will take nearly three weeks or one month to airmail a letter by clipper.
Generalissimo:	(having agreed to Madame's proposal) Please make a draft and let me read it over.
Mr. Lattimore:	(on parting) Am I right to say that should both proposals prove unacceptable the Generalissimo would be prepared to hear a third one?
Generalissimo:	Do not refer to a third proposal, but merely confine yourself to one of the two proposals I have mentioned.[22]

Here we see Chiang's intent in asking for an American adviser. He did not just want more aid; he wanted equality for China. Could even Franklin Roosevelt have delivered it?

Acting on these instructions, Lattimore drafted a cable to Currie. The first draft included Chiang's negative comments about British and Russian treatment of China, but on reflection Lattimore suggested that these comments be omitted.[23] Chiang agreed, and the cable was dispatched August 2. Currie forwarded it to Roosevelt and summarized it for Acting Secretary of State Sumner Welles, suggesting that the White House merely "acknowledge receipt and say that the President has the matter under advisement."[24] However, the proposals were not acceptable to the Americans. Roosevelt knew that Churchill thought China unworthy of Great Power status equal to Britain, Russia, and the United States and would never agree to such a British-Chinese-Soviet pact. Roosevelt also knew that China leaked like a sieve and that the Pacific allies would not allow Chinese representatives to participate in their defense plans. But Lattimore had done his best.

McHugh wrote Currie another long letter on August 3 after a luncheon meeting with Lattimore, Manuel Fox of Treasury, and Captain Joseph Alsop, aide to General Chennault. McHugh was now even more impressed with Lattimore's discretion and diplomacy. Lattimore, for his part, was impressed with the Generalissimo, whom he believed to be sincere. Mayling (Madame Chiang) had warmed up to Lattimore, and Lattimore "had been present with some of Chiang's inner circle when really confidential matters were being discussed." The way in which Lattimore dealt with the rumor that he had been commissioned to mediate between the government and the Communists also impressed McHugh. Lattimore "emphasized that there is an essential difference between the way Japan looks upon China and the way the United States views China. Japan takes the point of view that she is entitled to dictate and regulate the internal affairs of China. The U.S. on the contrary emphasize that they wish to aid China, but do not consider China's internal politics to be their business. Naturally, however, it is easier to aid a united country than one which is split and we would therefore like to see the differences between the Communists and the Government adjusted."[25]

Despite Lattimore's belief that he was not under surveillance, Chiang's secret police head, Tai Li, described by American observers as a combination of Heinrich Himmler and L. P. Beria, kept a watch on him. In the 1950s Tai Li's files were searched for evidence that Lattimore had been secretly conspiring with the Chinese Communists and sending messages to Moscow. No such evidence was found.[26] Lattimore had, on Chiang's orders, talked to Chou En-lai and had sent secret messages to Currie via Madame Chiang, who held the code. But Lattimore was extremely security conscious. Not until Chiang died did Lattimore even begin to write about what had passed between them or about the reports he had made to Chiang.

On August 12, 1941, Lattimore was guest of honor at a dinner party given by the Chinese People's Foreign Relations Association. In a brief ceremonial speech he sounded all the pro-China and pro-Chiang themes he had consistently held for several years. His address, "America and the Future of China," was printed in the September issue of *Amerasia*. It was also widely distributed by the Chinese propaganda ministry; E. C. Carter, in New York, hailed this approbation as evidence that Lattimore had "made good with the Generalissimo."[27]

Lattimore's reception by the Chinese thoroughly irritated the new American ambassador, Clarence Gauss, who was the top-ranking American foreign service officer in Chungking. Gauss normally declined social invitations from the Generalissimo but yielded to his staff and agreed to attend a reception hosted by the Sino-American Association on the birthday of Confucius. To Gauss's dismay, Lattimore was also a guest of honor at this reception, and Gauss had to stand with Lattimore while H. H. K'ung, finance minister and a descendant of Confucius, made obeisance at the altar of his ancestor. McHugh duly reported this incident to Currie, along with an additional instance in which Lattimore was honored by being seated at the ambassadorial table at a large tea given by the Generalissimo. Both gestures had infuriated Gauss, "but neither was in any way the doing of Owen. He is being given the greatest respect by all hands in the Government and I think it speaks highly for the tact and ability he has displayed. If they violate the dictates of protocol by ranking him with Ambassadors, it is no fault of his. I have never seen it accorded to any other foreigner."[28]

Life in wartime Chungking was not all teas and banquets. August 1941 was a month of relatively good weather, and the Japanese took advantage of it to bomb the Chinese capital unmercifully. Lattimore spent many days in air-raid dugouts. These experiences underground were more informative than most of his above-ground interviews. As he recalled these sessions in 1977:

> I used to go to a dugout of a high political figure. It was a deluxe dugout, very safe, and other high figures would come. I was the only foreigner present, the conversation was entirely in Chinese, and in the

dark people forgot there was a foreigner present, much less an American. They were sure, as Chiang was sure, that Japan was not going to go against Russia, but would turn against the European empires in Southeast Asia, and this would bring in America. They didn't precisely foresee Pearl Harbor, but they thought America would be in before the end. And they were already talking about the long-term future, with Japan defeated and the colonial countries weakened. The most powerful country on the scene is going to be the United States, and anything that's not nailed down tight the Americans are going to get away with. Now, how do we prepare to confront and deal with postwar American imperialism? And not once in any of these conversations did I hear any talk about long-range defence against Soviet imperialism.

When not conferring with Chinese officials, sitting in air-raid shelters, or attending banquets and teas, Lattimore worked on various projects Chiang set for him. Several of these projects dealt with China's unruly frontier provinces. Lattimore wrote an extensive paper recommending ways for Chiang to consolidate his hold on Manchuria after the war. He thought the Generalissimo should select young Manchurians who hated their Japanese occupiers, bring them to Nationalist centers, train them in administration, and promote them in the Kuomintang hierarchy. After the war they could represent the government as authentic Manchurians, not as carpetbaggers from South China.[29] The proposal was rejected, though, as the pressure in the Kuomintang to give jobs to henchmen and relatives of existing party officials was too great. At the end of the war Chiang was represented in Manchuria by southern troops who lacked familiarity with the territory they were occupying and wanted nothing more than to be demobilized and go home. As Lattimore explained, the way was thus left open for the Communists to say to the Manchurian Chinese, "Why should Chinese be ruled by outsiders? We Communists are Manchurian born and bred. How about an alliance?"

When Chiang later analyzed the failures of Nationalist armies in the civil war, he gave no hint of understanding Lattimore's earlier advice. Corruption and military incompetence were his themes: "It cannot be denied that the spirit of most commanders is broken and their morality is base," he declared in June 1947.[30] This was no doubt true; it was also true that Nationalist efforts were hampered by the lack of indigenous leadership in the occupying armies.

Lattimore was very conscious that the recommendations he forwarded to Currie for bolstering Chinese morale (such as Chiang's request for a Sino-British-Russian alliance or Chinese participation in Far East military councils) were not acted on. As a geopolitician he understood that Roosevelt had good reasons for neglecting them, but he kept trying. On August 25 he cabled Currie suggesting that "it would have excellent effect" if Currie were to attend Allied discussions about to take place in Moscow, traveling via Chungking "in order to coordinate aid to China and Soviet."[31] Roosevelt discussed this suggestion with Currie, but again the answer was evasion.

Currie and Lattimore both wanted China to have a larger share of Lend-Lease armaments. They won a battle in September: diversion of a group of bombers from Britain to China. Currie's description to Lattimore of how he "put the fear of the Lord" into British Lend-Lease officials reveals an infighter of great skill. The British, he told Lattimore, "regard me as Public Enemy Number One. However, I do have some friends among them and I intend to do my best to get them to adopt a better attitude toward China."[32]

Both Lattimore and Currie fought the Europe-first versus Asia-first battle with all the resources at their command. Of course, they lost most of the time. Lattimore, in Chungking, had to keep the Chinese "on board" despite Washington decisions. In a note to Madame Chiang on October 13, 1941, he acknowledged, "The majority view in Washington is that Hitler must first be defeated via the Atlantic and Europe, and after that it will be relatively easy to deal with the Far East. Neither Currie nor I agree with this view; but so long as it is the predominant view in Washington circles, it must affect the policy which the President is able to follow."[33]

During the last two weeks of October 1941 Chiang and Mayling were to tour battlefronts and hence be away from Chungking. During this period Chiang dispatched Lattimore to Yunnan to learn the situation there and to evaluate the management of the Burma Road. Yunnan's capital, Kunming, was the Chinese terminus for truck traffic still reaching China from the south. The Japanese seemed about to attack Yunnan. The governor of Yunnan, Lung Yun, was not Han Chinese but from a local mountain tribe and was not firmly under Chiang's control.

Lattimore was in Kunming October 14 through 30; he interviewed extensively, keeping detailed notes of what he learned. Much of it was technical, but one ninety-minute interview with Lung Yun impressed Lattimore immensely. It was toward the end of Lattimore's stay, and while earlier interviews had been perfunctory, with Lung Yun evading Lattimore's questions, on October 30 Lung opened up. This interview was private; Lattimore recorded, "He evidently decided that I was all right." Lung, worried about the possibility of a Japanese invasion, asked Lattimore to intercede with Chiang for more supplies to Yunnan. Lung also wanted Lattimore to pry out of Chiang some acknowledgment of the heroic work Yunnanese people had done building the Burma Road; the Nationalist government had never mentioned their great sacrifices, which included thousands who gave their lives in the construction. But the most interesting aspect of the conversation was Lung's questioning Lattimore about Russia. He "kept asking questions about the war there. I mentioned casually Stalin's not being a Russian, & his ears pricked up. What, then? I said he came from a 'small minority mountain tribe & that one reason for his early rise in the communist party was because Lenin had picked him to draft a nationalities policy.' Lung tickled to death."[34]

Lattimore cabled his impressions of the Yunnan danger to Currie immediately. He also held a rare news conference: the *New York Times* of November 4, 1941, reported his opinion that Lung Yun would cooperate in repelling a Japanese attack.[35]

Ironically, the November issue of *Asia* carried Paul Wohl's article about Haushofer's praise of Lattimore as America's "geopolitical masterhand" and the source of the "ice-cold strategy of the Anglo-Americans."[36] Whatever label might have been appropriately applied to the Roosevelt administration's improvisations, "ice-cold" was hardly the one, and Lattimore was not calling the shots.

Chiang, however, began to feel that the Lattimore-Currie channel was about as effective as he was likely to get, and he entrusted that channel with increasingly important messages. On November 11 Chiang sent a new request through Lattimore, one that a U.S. Treasury representative had refused to send. The request was for economic support and had the usual warning that "economic collapse would affect whole country simultaneously and might be sudden and overwhelming." Lattimore was sympathetic; when Chiang approached him, he cabled Currie immediately.[37] Action took a while, but Lattimore and Currie did expend considerable effort on this request.

Lattimore absorbed a vast amount of information during the fall of 1941. One of the topics on which he became well informed was the Communist problem. Among his informants was Roman Catholic Bishop Paul Yu-pin, with whom Lattimore talked on October 13. Yu-pin believed that the Communists were a big problem in China but not an insuperable one. Chiang should defer dealing with them until after the war because a victorious China would have no trouble with them, and they would then have no appeal to the Chinese masses. Therefore, the bishop opposed Chiang's talk of open attacks on the Communists: "If they are not attacked, they themselves cannot resort to arms because the whole nation would turn against them."[38] With much of this analysis Lattimore agreed. Whoever started a civil war would indeed incur the wrath of the whole nation.

On November 11, Chang Han-fu, editor of the Communist newspaper in Chungking, called on Lattimore. In the course of a long and revealing session Lattimore brought up the demand of the Communists not only to organize a legal political party but to maintain their own army. How could they justify this demand? Chang replied, "This is a practical question of democracy. At present, when they have arms, they are frequently attacked & individuals arrested. What would happen to them if they had no army & still advocated the things they at present advocate, which are far short of communism? They would not fear to surrender their arms if the govt were actually practicing the modest degree of democracy which is all that they themselves are advocating. I did not pursue this question, as it only leads to the old 'you first' argument."[39]

As anticipated by Chiang, Chou En-lai and Lattimore met about a dozen times in 1941. Some of these were casual conversations at parties, but some were intense discussions in private. Lattimore found Chou to be every bit as discreet and diplomatic as his reputation painted him, yet blunt on matters that did not require secrecy. Surprisingly, only one report of a meeting with Chou, that of November 24, 1941, remains in Lattimore's files. Most of what they discussed concerned the details of Nationalist-Communist relations, but toward the end Chou came to grips with China's future.

> He said the great need in China is for a little visible progress in democratization. Said the Gimo naturally thinks in military terms of discipline & authority. Does not bend easily to the give & take, "bargaining" aspect of the democratic process. At the same time, he wants democracy, wants to start China toward democracy. Trouble is, it is easy to be in favor of a future democracy, because the phrases and concepts are simple & admirable. . . . Asked him what I should say to Gimo as representing Chou's idea of a program. He said, politically: a few steps in democratization. Not too much, not too fast. The Communists do not expect democracy in a week, but they feel there must be enough actual progress forward so that the mass of the people have the sense of moving forward. Militarily: use the Lease-Lend program to bring in not only arms but arsenal material. Get fuller arsenal production, at same time build up a mechanized force for an effective, heavy counteroffensive against Japs. Communists are quite content to have all this done by Government, as they have been quite content to

have all Soviet supplies sent solely to Govt. The Govt will then obviously have nothing to fear from them.[40]

By November 1941 Lattimore's utility to the Generalissimo and Mayling had been clearly established. Mayling took him on long walks and
consulted him on many matters, including a worldwide radio broadcast
she was to make. She asked Lattimore to draft an appropriate text pleading China's case to other nations. He did so, and she thanked him for a
"useful" script that "contain[ed] many excellent ideas."[41]

Lattimore had signed on for only six months; in November Chiang
asked him to accept a year's extension of his contract. Lattimore agreed,
provided he could take home leave for three months to get treatment for
dysentery. Chiang thought this leave appropriate, especially since Lattimore could talk up China's cause while in the United States more effectively than anyone else could. As originally planned, Lattimore was to fly
to Baltimore in mid-January 1942, then return to China in mid-April with
his wife and son. Lattimore cabled this plan to Currie November 14.[42]

Departing from his usual practice of responding to requests from his
chief but not volunteering advice, Lattimore on November 13 suggested
to Madame Chiang that the cable being prepared for Currie include this
statement: "YUNNAN SITUATION AM CONVINCED IF UNITED STATES ATTI-
TUDE UNEQUIVOCAL JAPAN WILL NOT INVADE STOP IF ATTITUDE HESITANT
INVASION MAY BE PRECIPITATED STOP IF BARGAINING ATTEMPTED AND
CONCESSIONS LIKE OIL OFFERED THREAT WILL BE RENEWED WHEN AND WHERE
MOST FAVORABLE TO JAPAN."[43] The Chiangs agreed to this addition.

Chiang now spent a great deal of time with Lattimore, discussing his
plans and fears extensively so Lattimore would be prepared to put the best
face on China's needs in Washington. Lattimore's notes on dinner at the
Chiangs' on November 14 reveal clearly how these two saw the war. Both
agreed that unless Hitler achieved a major breakthrough in the Middle
East and stabilized the Russian front, Japan could not count on any help
from her Axis partners. To Chiang, the lack of German support meant it
was time for the United States to declare war on Japan and "break" her;
it would then be easy "to move to the counteroffensive against Germany." Lattimore then sounded a note of caution:

> Told him that I entirely agreed with him as to the feasibility & ad-
> visability of finishing off Japan now, but warned him that neither Lon-
> don nor Washington yet ready to admit this. The European orientation
> still prevails. . . .

He said: If they stick to that, they'll eventually lose the war. I said,

They're still sticking to it, very tenaciously . . . you forget India. It is because of India that the British will never allow the war to be ended in Asia first. And very influential people in Washington will back the British in this very tenaciously.

He said: But there is no trouble in India now. The question is not pressing. (I think he was testing me.)

I said: That's not it. The victory of China . . . would be the liberation of China from semi-colonialism, & that would start a great tide of liberation in the colonial world (chieh-fang ti ta ch'ao liu). He threw back his head & laughed. Madame backed me strongly. . . .

Told me he is preparing a speech which will analyze & urge the defeat of Japan first and promptly. Will send me an advance copy for suggestions.[44]

The Lattimore-Chiang-Mayling seminar on the state of the world convened again on November 16, 17, 24, 26, 27, 29, and on into December. Lattimore's notes and Madame Chiang's correspondence show continuing mutual respect and complete candor. On November 16, Chiang, looking ahead to the postwar period, asked Lattimore to come back to China about every six months.[45] Lattimore was agreeable. He had come to like Chiang. For all Chiang's faults, Lattimore believed him to have China's best interests at heart, and he was not a dictator. The uneasy coalition over which he presided made that impossible. Lattimore stated repeatedly that Chiang could not have been authoritarian in the usual sense since he did not have the power to issue orders as he thought best. Chiang, said Lattimore, always had to ask when making a decision, "What orders will my generals accept from me?"

On November 21 Lattimore's timetable for home leave changed. The Generalissimo wanted him to take leave immediately, returning correspondingly earlier. Accordingly, Lattimore cabled Currie, "In order return before spring developments, Generalissimo suggested I make trip now, returning end January. Please change reservation to clipper nearest December 10, Hongkong. Ask wife get ready."[46]

Shortly after Lattimore's travel plans were made, Madame Chiang wrote one of her many intimate and friendly letters to Currie. One paragraph of her letter of November 29, 1941, was noteworthy: "Mr. Lattimore will tell you everything that has been going on. He works very closely with us, and I am so glad that it was he whom the President chose. He is a man with whom one can feel perfectly relaxed, and in these days of strain and stress that is the only type of person whom we personally can bear to have near us. His enthusiasm in his work and happy spirit is also a good tonic."[47]

Unfortunately, Lattimore was not able to tell Currie everything that was going on, at least not yet. There was no December 10 clipper from Hong Kong.

Japanese-American relations had been tense for years. American opposition to Japanese expansionism had grown steadily, and in July 1941, as a result of the Japanese takeover of southern Vietnam, the United States, acting with Great Britain, imposed an embargo on trade with Japan, shutting off much of their supply of oil. The oil embargo was particularly damaging to the Japanese navy and convinced the Japanese military that war with the United States and its allies was inevitable. Oil supplies could be had from the Dutch Indies, but attacking them would provoke war with the United States.[48]

In Washington, Secretary of War Stimson, hostile toward Japan, argued for maintaining the embargo; he was joined by pro-China officials in the State Department. American military leaders, especially Chief of Staff George Marshall and Chief of Naval Operations Harold Stark, knew the United States was not prepared for war; they wanted to postpone any further move against Japan until early 1942.

During October and November 1941 the Japanese pressed Washington for a relaxation of the embargo. They talked peace and equal opportunity in Asia, but they were willing to yield none of their territorial gains to secure this relaxation. On November 16 Japanese Ambassador Nomura presented Secretary of State Hull with a proposal that glossed over long-term problems but sought to restore oil supplies for Japan. This proposal was firmly rejected by the Roosevelt administration. Since American cryptologists had broken the Japanese codes and knew that Japan had scheduled further military moves, Americans had no faith in Japanese proposals to decrease the number of troops they had stationed in Vietnam or to make peace with China. Hull thought the Japanese demanded "virtually a surrender."

Marshall and Stark still insisted that more time was needed, that conflict with Japan had to be postponed. Accordingly, Hull began work on a modus vivendi proposal, with suggestions from Roosevelt, the military, Treasury, and his own diplomats. By November 22 tentative drafts of this proposal were shown to representatives of Britain, Australia, the Netherlands, and China. This proposal was to remain in effect for three months, during which time the two parties would continue seeking "a peaceful settlement covering the entire Pacific area'' on the basis of a longer attached document calling for fundamental changes in Japanese activities. The modus vivendi itself only required Japan to cancel further military advances and to withdraw its troops from southern Vietnam; the problem of Japanese troops in China was not addressed. In return the United States would release Japanese accounts and allow limited exports to Japan of food, drugs, and other supplies, including a monthly allotment of oil for civilian use only.[49]

When Chinese Ambassador Hu Shih heard the proposal, he was apoplectic. This offer was appeasement; it left Japan free to continue her operations in China and to continue threatening the Burma Road to China from bases in Vietnam. It would supply Japan with oil. Hu Shih informed his government that the American proposal would be disastrous for Chinese interests.

On November 25 Chiang Kai-shek's full wrath descended on Washington. Chiang used every channel available to express his outrage at the modus vivendi proposal. Hu Shih bore a vigorous cablegram of protest, and T. V. Soong carried an even stronger version to Secretary of the Navy Knox and Secretary of War Stimson. But probably the most powerful message came through the Lattimore-Currie channel:

> After discussing with the Generalissimo the Chinese Ambassador's conference with the Secretary of State, I feel you should urgently advise the President of the Generalissimo's very strong reaction. I have never seen him really agitated before. Loosening of economic pressure or unfreezing would dangerously increase Japan's military advantage in China. . . . Any *Modus Vivendi* now arrived at with Japan would be disastrous to Chinese belief in America. . . . Japan and Chinese defeatists would instantly exploit the resulting disillusionment and urge oriental solidarity against occidental treachery. It is doubtful whether either past assistance or increasing aid could compensate for the feeling of being deserted at this hour. The Generalissimo has deep confidence in the President's fidelity to his consistent policy but I must warn you that even the Generalissimo questions his ability to hold the situation together if the Chinese national trust in America is undermined by reports of Japan's escaping military defeat by diplomatic victory.[50]

Hull reeled before this avalanche, but there was more to come. At 12:55 A.M. November 26, a cable arrived from Churchill. Normally skeptical of Chinese motives and capabilities, Churchill now told Roosevelt that he knew negotiations with the Japanese were for the United States to handle, but in regard to the modus vivendi proposal he protested, "There is only one point that disquiets us. What about Chiang Kai-shek? Is he not having a very thin diet? Our anxiety is about China. If they collapse, our joint dangers would enormously increase. We are sure that the regard of the United States for the Chinese cause will govern your action. We feel that the Japanese are most unsure of themselves."[51]

On November 26, as Hull deliberated, he knew there was a slim chance the Japanese would accept the proposal. Intercepted Japanese messages to Nomura revealed that if no Japanese agreement were signed by November 29, "things are automatically going to happen." Hull thought it unlikely that such a rigorous Japanese timetable would be cast aside for the meager provisions of the modus vivendi. Consequently, Hull decided to throw the whole thing out. On November 26 he wrote the president, "I desire very earnestly to recommend that at this time I call in the Japanese Ambassadors and hand them a copy of the comprehensive basic proposal for a general peaceful settlement, and at the same time withhold the *modus vivendi* proposal."[52]

Roosevelt promptly agreed. The outcome was the attack on Pearl Harbor.

Was Lattimore's cable instrumental in Hull's decision? Hull does not say so in his memoirs. Charles Callin Tansill and Percy Greaves emphasize the impact of the Lattimore cable, and perhaps they are right.[53] But the weight of a protest from Winston Churchill must have been greater than an alarm from Chiang's personal adviser.

Would the modus vivendi proposal have caused the Japanese to call off the Pearl Harbor attack? In *Infamy: Pearl Harbor and Its Aftermath* John Toland cites a postwar conversation in which Tojo allegedly told General Kenryo Sato that "if he [Tojo] had received the original Roosevelt *modus vivendi*, the course of history would probably have changed."[54]

Toland does not press the point. A more crusading historian in 1950 was quite willing to press several points, blaming Lattimore and Currie for the outbreak of war:

United States Senate
June 28, 1950

Senator Bourke Hickenlooper
Senate Office Building
Washington, D.C.

Dear Bourke:

During the present anti-Communist fight, from time to time matters are brought to my attention which I feel should be brought to the attention of the Senate and the country. . . .

I presently have in my files considerable information dealing with the activities of Owen Lattimore prior to Pearl Harbor. As you know, a tentative *modus vivendi* had been worked out between the United States and Japan prior to Pearl Harbor. At that time, Laughlin Currie was the President's advisor. Laughlin Currie has been named by Elizabeth Bentley as part of her spy ring. The Pearl Harbor Hearings indicate that Currie got in touch with Owen Lattimore, who was in China at that time, and who thereupon cooperated with Currie in bringing all possible pressure to bear upon the Administration to suppress any peace agreement with Japan. Lattimore's wire is reproduced in the Pearl Harbor Hearings in full.

In 1948 when Currie was accused by Bentley as being a Communist spy, he was represented by Dean Acheson when he appeared before the committee. This was while Acheson was temporarily out of the State Department. Complete documentation is available for any one of the Senators who care to handle this subject.

With kindest regards, I am

Sincerely yours,

Joe McCarthy

P.S. This letter is being sent to five Republican Senators.[55]

CHAPTER SIX

War

Lattimore's cable of November 25 evolved from much discussion with Chiang and Mayling the night before. Lattimore made the first draft; Madame suggested changes and additions over dinner; the final draft, according to Lattimore's notes, "was made by my taking the first two versions and dictating a third to her." Chiang then joined them to discuss what Chinese reaction would be if the United States agreed to let Japan keep the Northeast (Manchukuo), forcing withdrawal only from the rest of China. Chiang thought such a compromise would "undermine the whole victory"; Lattimore agreed. Madame Chiang was pessimistic and later asked Lattimore " 'between ourselves' whether I thought China could get Northeast back entirely. I said can, and must."

Also during this conversation Lattimore reported his most recent talk with Chou En-lai, whereupon Chiang observed, "Chou only Communist who is a Chinese at heart. Madame added, He means the rest all think like Russians."[1]

Chiang called Lattimore in again on November 26 "to discuss Hu Shih's summary of America's suggested terms to Japan. Madame more worried than Gimo, who said genially, as we went in to supper, This is just what politics is. After supper, drafted another cable; but it was not sent until middle of next day."[2]

This cable of the twenty-seventh was even sharper than the previous one. Lattimore said that the Generalissimo was "shocked by suggestion that an agreement would be no worse than Britain's closing Burma Road. He wishes President understand that fundamental question is not wording of terms but departure from principle involving sacrifice of China, callousness of which impossible [to] hide." China was now entering her fifth winter of war, and hardships were appalling. The concessions in the proposed modus vivendi would have immediately revived Japan; if they were offered, "Defeatism in China will become an avalanche." This comment, and more, came from Chiang and Mayling. But the last three sentences of the cable were pure Lattimore: "Personally convinced after five months widest contact China cannot remain isolated. Must seek association. National preference is associate America now and future but if increasing danger of American desertion must seek re-insurance."[3] Seeking "re-insurance" meant turning to the Soviet Union.

Late in the day on November 27, as Lattimore wrote in a memo dated three days later, "News began coming through that American appeasement called off." Chungking collectively breathed a great sigh of relief. Whatever doubts Chiang had about the utility of the Lattimore-Currie channel were now swept away. Rejection of the modus vivendi was worth a great deal to Chiang, and Lattimore had apparently played a major role in it. Lattimore had dinner at Chiang's again November 29, writing afterward that Chiang "showed me letter, extremely flattering to me, which I am to take to President."[4]

Madame Chiang's favorite charity was a fund for war orphans. Lattimore contributed three hundred dollars on December 1, and Madame thanked him effusively on the third, also inviting him to lunch the next day.[5] Lunch grew into a long weekend. Lattimore stayed at their residence, usually talking with Chiang or Madame or both, December 4–7. Nine pages of closely typed notes, prepared by Lattimore shortly afterward, record their conversation.

They began by discussing Lattimore's memorandum on how Chiang could handle the problem of reintegrating the Northeast after Japan was forced to disgorge it. At the conclusion of this discussion, "[Chiang's] comment was brief: 'Nothing to add & nothing to change.' "[6] They then moved into the problem of countering Chinese Communist propaganda. As Lattimore recorded it, Chiang began:

> Hongkong & the U.S. are the main centers of the propaganda of the Chinese Communists against the Chinese Government and the Kuomintang. . . . At the present time all the subversionists . . . are concentrated in Hongkong. Quite clear that time after time correspondents who have visited China get, as they leave through Hongkong, a dose of propaganda which distorts what they have been able to learn for themselves in China. Main field in which propaganda issuing from Hongkong takes effect in U.S. China needs a counter-propaganda in U.S. How is this to be managed? Wants me to look over the question while

at home. This weakness may partly be that those in Chungking in charge of propaganda for U.S. not in sufficiently close contact with U.S. & may be missing chances on what they should distribute. How about finding some good, trained men in U.S. to handle job? I said I should be glad to look into question. However, certain difficulties. Practically every trained anti-left propagandist in U.S. is under strong influence either of extreme right or even fascists, & hence Axis. This would never do for China. He laughed & agreed. I said what we all need is propagandists & publicists who are real democrats, & he agreed again.[7]

The third topic of conversation December 4 was the "fundamental question of the Pacific area," a matter on which Chiang apparently delivered a monologue. Germany, Japan, and Russia were "eternally aggressive." About Britain, Chiang was equivocal; he discussed India extensively, maintaining that "if the British endeavor to keep India in subjection, they will destroy themselves and their Empire." He thought the British might give up India gracefully. He concluded: "In any case, American participation in the economic development of China is a natural postwar development. America and China . . . will form an enormous block out of the total world population, with common economic interests & consequently fundamental agreement in political outlook. Gradually India will tend to become a part of this block."[8] Lattimore did not comment.

The final topic on December 4 was economics. Chiang was unhappy with the Sino-American agreement establishing China's Stabilization Board. This agreement was negotiated and signed by T. V. Soong. Chiang did not realize how faulty it was until H. H. K'ung pointed out the clauses giving U.S. Treasury representatives all the power. Chiang concluded that he "would like me [Lattimore] to see, without pressing matter at all, whether these clauses could be modified to be more equitable to China."[9]

Discussion continued the morning of December 5, beginning with the military situation. Chiang was confident that his armies could hold unless the Japanese managed to "concentrate overwhelming air forces on any front." He thought U.S. help to build his air force was needed more than any other military aid. Lattimore's record of this discussion is only half a page.[10] What came next required three crowded, single-spaced pages to report. Lattimore begins:

> As we were coming home from a walk, the Gimo asked me if I would make that evening criticisms of what I thought the most serious shortcomings I had noticed during my stay. . . .
> After supper I led off by saying that after only 5 months I could not yet consider myself authoritatively informed on any one subject. . . .

China after all is still going through political revolution, economic revolution, social revolution—all uncompleted, & all in face of a war for survival against an enemy better equipped for aggression than China is for defense. To understand China's real progress & achievements, you have always to take a larger time-bracket than a few months: over 5 years, 10 years, etc, you can see amazing progress.

Again, I am a foreigner & a newcomer to political life. It is much easier for me to hear complaints than to understand in its full complexity the whole process of Revolution & the War of Resistance. Moreover, I can never be sure of the exact authority or integrity of my informants, or the relative accuracy or completeness of their facts. Therefore I wished the Gimo to "criticize my criticisms."

Lattimore then dealt with military affairs. China, he said, could not ease up on the military front and let others save her. The Chinese must take initiative, if only politically, as Chiang had done in regard to the necessity for regaining the Northeast. On economics, he suggested that China utilize the know-how of small units, producing goods for local consumption that would not strain the inevitably weak transportation system and would not require massive amounts of capital. "Politically, the most criticism that I have heard has been against the [Kuomintang] Party. Widely said, especially by younger men, that Party controls the people too much and represents them too little. Too much appetite for rule, too little spirit of service." He also argued that "the iron methods of the Russian Revolution are inappropriate to China." Chiang should emphasize Sun Yat-sen's program.

Toward the end of his account Lattimore noted: "This long discourse not as unbroken or prosy as notes sound. Gimo frequently put in suggestions or questions, which is why it went on so long. He made a number of written notes. At end, he asked if I would criticize 'the weak points I had noted in him personally.' Here Madame came in, remarking it was hardly a fair question to ask me. He relented, & I let it go. I think I missed a big chance. I have no opinion on his weak points, because I think he is an amazingly rounded character; but I could have commented on his *situation*—how his great power tends to surround him with yes-men." After a paragraph of Chiang's complaints about the Communists, and a repeat of the remark about Chou being the "only one who even looks [sounds?] reasonably like a Chinese," Lattimore concluded: "Said after I come back, wants me to go into economic & social questions, both subject by subject & region by region."[11]

There was more of the same the next day, and the next, as Chiang and Mayling monopolized Lattimore's time for four full days.

McHugh wrote Currie December 3, noting that Lattimore was returning to the states early at Chiang's request and that it was a good thing "because he will be able to give all concerned an intimate and accurate picture of the situation here." [12]

Lattimore was scheduled to take a plane from Hong Kong to San Francisco on December 9, which meant leaving Chungking for Hong Kong several days before. The weather was bad in Chungking that first week of December, and Lattimore's plane could not take off. Only this happenstance prevented Lattimore from being in Hong Kong when war broke out. The Japanese struck Hong Kong as well as Pearl Harbor, disabling the plane on which he had been scheduled to fly. It was a full month before he was able to leave China, and by that time a Pacific crossing was no longer possible.

The intervening month in China was frenetic. With the beginning of the American involvement in the war the whole atmosphere of Chungking changed. Since the Americans were fighting, the Chinese no longer feared appeasement of Japan, but they had other fears. Lattimore's cables to Currie reveal Chiang's new perceptions of the war. In a message on December 9 Lattimore reported that the Generalissimo strongly urged

> prompt simultaneous Soviet-Chinese declaration of war on Japan following American declaration. Coordinated Chinese-Soviet land action essential because only Soviet can attack both by sea and air and thus is key to joint land, sea, air war by all democracies whereas if Soviet hesitates Japan can fight democracies piecemeal. . . . Generalissimo anxious to use every approach to Soviet, including Washington, in order to insure undelayed Soviet participation. Soviet Military Attache hinted that if Soviet fights Japan America might not concentrate main effort in Pacific. Clear indication that America will give priority to Pacific over Atlantic until Japan settled would undoubtedly bring Soviet in. [13]

Recognizing this proposal as wishful thinking, Lattimore added no endorsement to the cable.

On December 11 Lattimore forwarded a new set of Chiang requests. All Pacific fronts should be coordinated; there should be a military pact among the Pacific allies, including Russia if possible; Chungking should be the headquarters of this Inter-Allied Pacific Military Commission; and an American should head it. Again, Lattimore added no personal opinion. [14]

With the United States now at war Chiang asked Lattimore to evaluate
the new situation for him and recommend actions to adapt to it. Lattimore
accordingly submitted a three-page memorandum on December 14. He
acknowledged that early Japanese successes would decrease Allied prestige
in China, stimulating pessimism and tendencies to collaborate with the
Japanese. These tendencies would be strongest among landholders and
followers of local warlords, especially in Yunnan, Sikang, and Szechwan,
where scarce supplies were already being hoarded. The government should
deal sternly with hoarders, as it had recently in Szechwan, and it should
press for a large, morale-building loan from the U.S. Treasury, which
would both alleviate China's economic situation and demonstrate American determination to support China.

Lattimore had many other specific recommendations for improving
China's prospects, the most noteworthy of which dealt with the Communist problem. Surprisingly, for once he gave Chiang no lectures about
improving the lot of the peasants. Instead, he emphasized Chinese relations with Russia and the United States: "Increased cooperation with Soviet Russia is militarily a necessity, and politically it will mean that during
the immediate future the Communists will not dare to make trouble. For
the longer future, cooperation with America, especially through the proposed loan, will be a reinsurance against Communism. While America
has no interest in interfering in internal questions in China, she certainly
does not want to see a Communist China and does want to help establish
a China that will both be completely independent and in its domestic government completely stable."[15]

The "proposed loan" part of this agenda was warmly received by Chiang,
but Lattimore now ran afoul of U.S. Ambassador Gauss. Gauss strongly
opposed such a loan, believing it to be inflationary. Given this opposition,
Chiang preferred to promote the loan by sending Lattimore personally to
Washington with his request. Unfortunately, Japanese depredations in
the Pacific had closed all transportation routes. By December 21 Chiang
could no longer postpone transmission of the loan request to Washington,
and Lattimore was instructed to cable the request to Currie so that Currie
could start working on it. The full argument backing the loan would be
available when Lattimore was able to get out of China.

For political and psychological reasons, Chiang wanted a "really big
Treasury loan"—$500 million. On the face of it, such a request seemed
hopeless. Demands for American resources and money were massive, and
despite the fact that the United States had been attacked in the Pacific,
defeating Hitler remained Roosevelt's first priority. Lattimore's cable of

December 21 succinctly stated the case for the loan. Because China was virtually deprived of external supplies, a "big psychological economic move [was] required [to] offset serious prestige damage [of] early Pacific setbacks." The loan would back Chinese bond issues, encourage entrepreneurs interested in China's future reconstruction, and generate small loans for agriculture and industries.[16]

Lattimore had barely gotten off the loan cable when he was called to attend a meeting Chiang was having with Field Marshal Lord Wavell, Viceroy of India, who was in Chungking to discuss Anglo-Chinese measures for stopping Japanese advances. Chiang's smoldering resentment of British arrogance burst forth at this session, and he excoriated the British roundly. They had not listened to him when he warned them years earlier that surrendering to Japan the silver hoard belonging to the Chinese government, but stored in the British Concession at Tientsin, would be like "feeding raw meat to a tiger," only whetting the Japanese appetite. The British had been similarly stupid in Hong Kong, where they refused to incorporate more than five or six thousand Chinese into their armed forces; yet "neither Kowloon nor Hongkong itself could have been defended without the arming of every available able bodied Chinese." Britain was wholly indifferent to Chinese interests in the Far East and was trying "to settle all issues primarily from the point of view of restoring the British position."

In matters of finance, said Chiang, "there must be a fundamental revision of attitude." The British Treasury representative, Sir Otto Niemeyer, had proposed a £10 million British loan, and a matching $50 million American loan, both to be secured by revenue from Chinese customs. Chiang laid out his contempt for British shortsightedness in language that Lattimore recorded as follows:

> Such a proposal altogether ignores the political realities. The question involved is not one of banking operations to be handled in terms of commercial investments, security, annual interest, and amortization. China cannot consider bartering pledges like this to Britain and America, any more than she would contemplate the hiring of a mercenary army to Britain for the defense of Burma. Any question of a loan cannot be regarded as an end in itself, but merely as a technical operation in the pooling of resources for a common purpose, representing British mobilization of economic resources and Chinese mobilization of manpower resources. For such purposes, the required loan to China should be on the scale of 100 million Pounds, not ten million, and there can be no question of security. Victory is the security.[17]

Chiang's tirade was first translated for Lord Wavell by Hollington Tong. Lattimore says that Tong thought Chiang was too harsh and toned it down a bit. Madame, however, thought her husband had not been vehement enough; she gave her own, more stinging version. As Lattimore recalls, "The Generalissimo, watching rather than listening, knew exactly what was going on. He turned to me and said: 'Mr. Lattimore, will you please give the correct translation?' That was the toughest interpreting assignment I ever had." Wavell listened politely, then defended British actions as best he could. That night Lattimore put a mild version of the conversation in an aide memoire that he submitted to Madame, dated December 21, 1941.[18]

Lattimore's induction into the intimacies of the Chinese ruling dynasty was accomplished at Christmas. The Soong family had embraced Christianity at their father's knee; hence, Christmas was always celebrated by the three Soong sisters (Mayling, Chiang's wife; Ai-ling, Mrs. H. H. K'ung; and Ch'ing-ling, Sun Yat-sen's widow) and the Generalissimo. Lattimore was invited to the family Christmas dinner in 1941. He was the only foreigner present. Despite tensions between the leftish Madame Sun and the rest of the party, Lattimore said they were "perfectly correct" toward each other.

No cables to Washington were composed over Christmas dinner, but two days later the Generalissimo's wrath at the British came to boiling point again, this time fueled by British delay in Burma of Lend-Lease cargo destined for China. Lattimore's December 28 message to Currie carried Chiang's castigation of the British for "bungling highhandedness." They were also "incompetent, arrogant," and several other choice adjectives. The whole problem was a racist, imperialist mentality; there would be "further unpardonable blunders unless American pressure forces realization China not extension their colonial empire." Currie was to report these comments to Roosevelt and T. V. Soong.[19]

There was a reprise on January 1, 1942. Chiang instructed Lattimore to say that the British refused to admit "any essential Chinese-British equality. This furnished enemy with deadliest propaganda everywhere in Asia. . . . Should China [be] unable cooperate, British must bear entire responsibility. . . . In view all above Generalissimo . . . asks immediate assurances British will put situation right and guarantee no repetition. . . . Generalissimo attitude very firm." Two similar cables went out on January 4. Lattimore inserted a personal opinion in one of them: "My information from British source is British incompetence, confusion in Burma hard to exaggerate."[20]

Initial White House response to this flood of cables was, as Chiang saw it, bittersweet. Washington was willing to talk about a big loan, but Treasury suggested that it be issued "on basis of schedule of particulars," which was not what Chiang wanted at all. Lattimore was instructed to respond on January 7: "Only possible method is 500 million loan purely political with no restrictions or conditions, at least as broad and generous in terms and conception as lend lease."[21] Lattimore wrote cables almost every day during the first two weeks of 1942.

By mid-January Pan American had established routes over the Hump of the Himalayas into Burma and from there westward; Lattimore was scheduled to leave Chungking January 15. Chiang, K'ung, McHugh, and other Americans loaded him with letters to deliver in Washington. Chiang's letter to Roosevelt, dated January 12, contained fulsome praise for Roosevelt's recommendation of Lattimore and concluded, "Mr. Lattimore will personally convey to you my views on some important matters upon which I have not touched above. If there are messages you wish to send me, I should appreciate you entrusting them to Mr. Lattimore to be conveyed to me upon his return to China."[22]

Lattimore left on January 15 as scheduled. At a stop in Calcutta he wrote Chiang thanking him for "your generous treatment of me during the first period of my service under you in China."[23] On January 17 he was off to Karachi, Iran, Egypt, Gambia, Brazil, and the United States, where he arrived February 8.[24]

The Chinese loan was debated in Washington in early February. Despite the misgivings of Ambassador Gauss and skeptical State Department officials, who thought China could not use such a loan effectively, Roosevelt supported it. The bill authorizing $500 million for China passed Congress while Lattimore was recuperating from his travels. Roosevelt signed it February 13 and on the same day received Lattimore for a report on conditions in China.[25]

As instructed by Chiang, Lattimore set forth the Generalissimo's concerns about the British. All of Chiang's recent contacts with British officials had alarmed him; they seemed not to realize that the Chinese and other Asians were determined to throw off the yoke of colonialism and assume status in international affairs equal to that of the Western nations. Roosevelt was sympathetic to Chiang's position, but he also had to deal with British, French, and Dutch officials who did not think the same way. And Roosevelt's immediate problem was to win the war; postwar problems of sovereignty in the Pacific had to be put on hold. Lattimore was instructed to calm Chiang's fears without promising anything specific.

Lattimore sweated over the cable he now composed for Chiang. The copy in his FBI file is undated but was probably sent February 15. It is diplomacy personified:

> FOR GENERALISSIMO HAVE LAID BEFORE THE PRESIDENT THE VIEWS YOU DISCUSSED WITH ME JUST BEFORE I LEFT CHINA STOP HE RECEIVED THEM VERY CORDIALLY WHILE THE TIME HAS NOT YET COME TO INITIATE DISCUSSION OF DETAILS THROUGH FORMAL CHANNELS HIS BROAD UNDERSTANDING OF PROBLEMS OF WESTERN PACIFIC IS VERY SIMILAR TO YOURS AND VERY SYMPATHETIC AND HE FEELS THAT IN DUE TIME DETAILS CAN BE WORKED OUT SATISFACTORILY STOP IN THE NORTHWESTERN AREA IT WOULD BE NECESSARY TO CONSULT A THIRD PARTY STOP IN THE SOUTHWESTERN AREA THE PRESIDENT FINDS THAT CHURCHILL IS RECEPTIVE TO THE IDEA OF HANDLING BY MEANS OF TRUSTEESHIP COMMA A LARGE NUMBER OF COLONIAL PROBLEMS IN A WAY THAT WILL SHOW A MARKED AND RAPID ADVANCE OVER PREVIOUS CONCEPTS OF COLONIAL SOVEREIGNTY AND OVER MANDATE METHODS AS APPLIED UNDER LEAGUE OF NATIONS (LATTIMORE) [26]

Chiang could not have been happy to hear this, but his satisfaction with the loan must have mitigated his distaste for Roosevelt's waffling about colonialism.

On February 16 Lattimore wrote Madame Chiang a long letter about his activities in support of China, about his approval of the appointment of General Stilwell to command American troops in the China-Burma-India theater, and about the assignment of John Paton Davies as advisor to Stilwell. His visit with Roosevelt had gone well, and he had seen T. V. Soong, General George Marshall, and, of course, Lauchlin Currie. All this work was enabling him to push the Chinese cause of making the war in Asia a higher priority. The letter was not all business. On the personal side he remarked, "It has been perfectly wonderful to be with my wife and son again. You and the Generalissimo were always so considerate of me; but your concern that I should bring my wife back with me is the most wonderful thing of all. You will be amused to hear that my son, aged not yet eleven, is already giving lectures on the Burma Road with my photographs as illustrations." [27]

During his time in the United States Lattimore engaged in dozens of activities promoting the welfare of his patron in Chungking. On February 21, 1942, he joined Pearl Buck in endorsing a plea of United China Relief to raise $7 million in private funds for war victims and refugee rehabilitation. At a later banquet of that organization, at Radio City in New York, he joined Clare Boothe Luce and Wendell Willkie in praising Chinese war efforts and expressing confidence that Japan would be defeated.

On February 24, speaking off the record to the Washington Press Club, Lattimore scored a major hit. Creighton Hill, of *Babson's Washington Reports*, took the trouble to write Lauchlin Currie about it: "It was the unanimous opinion of a group of members of the Press Club, in the wake of Mr. Lattimore's talk, that under no circumstances should he be allowed to return to China. The Generalissimo doesn't need him half so much as he is needed right here. In fact, his nomination as Secretary of State was offered and seconded." At the bottom of the letter Hill wrote in pencil, "He's a marvellous guy—and did a magnificent job."[28]

A week later Lattimore and Manuel Fox of Treasury were questioned informally and off the record by the Senate Committee on Foreign Relations. Lattimore wrote in a letter to the Generalissimo the same day (March 4) that the session lasted two and a half hours, that there were many questions about the loan, and that it "went very well indeed."[29]

The Council on Foreign Relations took advantage of Lattimore's presence to invite him to report on the topic "Chinese Opinion on Postwar Problems." This discussion with the Territorial Group on March 18 was lengthy; since it was also confidential, Lattimore was less inhibited in expressing his opinions of America's European Allies than he was in his public statements; the Allies do not come off well. But the heart of his message was that colonialism was dead in Asia. Self-determination had become a "fighting creed" there, and many Asians were "determined to realize their democratic aspirations no matter what the cost may be. In a true sense, they are barricade democrats." Lattimore referred to a recent statement of Secretary of the Navy Knox that in fighting the war, the western front had primacy. The Chinese were suspicious of that statement: "They argue that no matter in what part of the world the war may be fought out, the important thing is the political outcome in Asia."

When the U.S. role in postwar China came up, Lattimore was optimistic:

The Chinese have neither the intention nor the power to keep the white man out of the Orient. They want the white man there, and they want his advice and money, but they do not want his political control. They know they will have to behave well if they want his investments. They realize that at the peace conference they will be comparatively weak. There will be an enormous job of reconstruction to be done in China, and if it is not done quickly there will be chaos. . . . But Americans should not look upon this as an opportunity for charity or condescension. For we ourselves will have a tremendous job of making the transition from an expanded wartime basis to peacetime levels. One of the biggest single remedies for United States industry might be the Chinese market. We should, therefore, think of how China might aid the United States as well as the reverse.

Lattimore also argued that the United States should strengthen China as much as possible "to act as a balance against the Soviet." Even though Russia would be faced with vast reconstruction tasks, it would be tempted to expand into an Asian power vacuum. This brought up the question of the Chinese Communists: "The strength of the Chinese Communists is not increasing. In 1937, the Communists had from 150,000 to 200,000 well-trained troops. Some of these troops are now engaged in guerrilla warfare, and allowing for extensive casualties and replacements, their numbers probably do not exceed the figure of 1937. . . . Chungking observers object to the Chinese Communists on two grounds: (1) the alien loyalties of the latter, and (2) the fact that the Communists represent a challenge to national unity—or to the dominant position of the Kuomintang."[30]

Lattimore had no doubts that Chiang and his Nationalists could, and should, retain control of China's destiny. Some of his longest letters to Chungking were to Hollington Tong, Chinese minister of information, with whom Lattimore had worked closely. Tong was upset with the anti-Chiang bias of Edgar Snow's writings, especially an article in the *Saturday Evening Post*. Lattimore discussed Snow at great length, explaining to Tong how he was trying to "set the record straight" and counteract Snow's partiality to the Chinese Communists.[31]

Not only the CFR but also the army's Military Intelligence Division (MID) wanted to probe Lattimore's insights into what was happening in China. On April 7, 1942, a MID officer interviewed him extensively, recording some specific recommendations. China should have a full representative on the Combined Chiefs of Staff to "offset political cleavages within the framework" of the Allies. The United States and the Soviet Union should jointly proclaim a policy of independence for Korea. The Atlantic Charter was a psychological mistake, especially since Churchill had stated that it did not apply to India; the charter should be downplayed in propaganda directed toward Asia. Finally, the United States should not attempt to run China's war effort. There is no indication of what MID thought of these comments.[32]

During the spring of 1942 Lattimore was a whirlwind of activity. Every conceivable forum was open to him, and he used them all to promote the cause of China. He gave at least three public lectures in Baltimore, the last of which had to be moved from the Hopkins campus to a large public theater. He spoke to a select group of Yale alumni at the Yale Club in New York. He spoke to an overflow crowd at the Cleveland Foreign Affairs Council and delivered one of the featured speeches at the American Council on Education convention in Chicago May 1. There were many more.

The texts of some of these addresses survive. Probably the most compelling was the speech he gave in Ottawa to the Canadian Club meeting of May 7. Prime Minister Mackenzie King was in attendance, as were many other senior Canadian officials. The high point of Lattimore's speech was his statement of the "Asia first" position.

There is a natural tendency among all of us in North America to think of Europe as the center of the world. Our traditions, our history, our education, all lead us to think of Europe as the approach to all international problems. . . . But can the problems of the world as it is constituted today be settled in Europe? If you settle Europe, does the rest of the world automatically fall into place?

We Chinese—if the Chinese Minister will allow me to use the expression—do not feel that way. The war did not start with Pearl Harbor. It did not start in September 1939. It did not start even in 1937 with the Marco Polo Bridge incident. The nearest date that you can set as an accurate date for the beginning of this war was the invasion of Manchuria on September 18, 1931. From that aggression with which we, the democracies in and out of the League of Nations, failed to cope, started a degeneration of the whole world system, not simply of collective security, but of all our standards. It spread from Manchuria to Abyssinia, from Abyssinia to Spain, to Czechoslovakia, and only then to Poland and the present phase of the war.

From the Chinese point of view it is unreasonable to think that when the prime causes of the war lay in Asia the issues of the war can be settled in Europe. If you stop to think for a moment, supposing the Axis were to win, you will see that the main loot for the Fascists would lie, not in Europe, but in Asia to a very large, perhaps, I think, to a preponderating extent. Asia is what we are fighting about.[33]

Lattimore felt his reception in Canada had been very warm indeed. The Chinese minister in Ottawa no doubt communicated to Chungking about Lattimore's impact there. One week later Currie received a cable from

Madame Chiang. The cable does not survive, but Currie's memo to Roosevelt about it does: "I have received a cable from Madame Chiang for Owen Lattimore, asking him to remain here for the next three or four months to emphasize to our people the necessity of supporting China and regarding her as an equal partner in war and peace."[34] Lattimore was quite willing to stay home for a while longer.

Periodically Lattimore reported to the Generalissimo. In a letter of April 22 he explained that he and Currie had worked out the matter of announcing American support for Korean independence; the president had agreed that we should follow the lead of China rather than making a unilateral declaration. About Chiang's desire for a formal Sino-American alliance, he carefully explained that Americans were inclined to avoid such long-range commitments and that since an alliance would have to clear Congress, it was best "to work for every possible kind of common action" without alliances.[35]

In the April 22 letter Lattimore also dealt with his contacts in State, Treasury, Army, and other agencies. There was great confusion in wartime Washington, and many requests from China fell between the cracks of competing agencies. For getting China's interest attended to, the most important man was Currie: "If it were not for his tireless energy in personally following the course of every order and shipment for China, through bureau after bureau, the actual shipments would be both smaller and slower."

In addition to the lecture circuit, Lattimore was asked to write for mass-circulation magazines, including *American Magazine* and *National Geographic*. The articles he wrote for those two magazines are undisguised tributes to China and Chiang; the *American Magazine* piece of June 1942 was alone worth what Chiang paid him for the entire year. Entitled "How to Win the War," it begins by noting the pettiness of American complaints about war-caused shortages compared with the tribulations of the Chinese after five years of Japanese assault. Yet Chinese morale remained excellent, and Chiang's armies had stopped Japanese armies by sheer willpower. "If we can look on the Chinese with intelligence and imagination, if we can learn from them how they work miracles by teamwork, by self-sacrifice, by a proud new spirit of fighting for a better country and a better world—then we, too, can work miracles. We can win a quicker victory and a greater peace. If you want to know how to win the war, study China. . . . The individual Chinese may be only breaking stones with a hammer or carrying earth in a basket, but by the thousands they built an airport in the mountains as well as we could build it with our elaborate machinery. Each knows that he, with hammer or basket, is fighting in a great cause."[36]

The whole article is similarly laudatory. It was no doubt necessary in the early months of the war to convince Americans that China would not be a drag on the Allied war effort. Lattimore was fulfilling this function diligently. But the total effect was oversell, and he vastly exaggerated the genius of Chiang. The claim that "a land long torn by inner dissension and local prejudice has, under Chiang Kai-shek, become united, just as our thirteen colonies once became united" ignored the realities of warlord power and Communist separatism, neither of which Chiang had overcome and both of which emerged to frustrate American hopes for China. Nor was Chiang as eager to "help [his] new allies" as Lattimore claimed.[37] The major long-range Chinese objectives were (1) to defeat the Communists and (2) to destroy any trace of European imperialism. Lattimore emphasized the latter but ignored the former. His emphasis on China's role in the war was incompatible with the views of Marshall, Hull, and the rest of the Eurocentric American officials.

During Lattimore's absence from China, severe problems arose between Chiang and the commander of American troops in the China-Burma-India (CBI) theater, Lieutenant General Joseph W. Stilwell. Stilwell, like Lattimore, knew China well. Unlike Lattimore, he had a clear command responsibility and needed Chiang's cooperation; when he didn't get it, he developed a visceral dislike for Chiang, as Barbara Tuchman demonstrates.[38] The confrontations between the two led, in May 1942, to Chiang's request that Harry Hopkins be sent to China to see firsthand how Stilwell was misusing his authority and how much more amicable Sino-American relations would be if only General Claire Chennault replaced Stilwell.[39] Both Chennault and Naval Attaché McHugh were in constant communication with Currie, and the White House decided that something had to be done. Roosevelt still refused to send Hopkins to China, so Currie volunteered for the mission.

Unlike Lattimore, Currie assumed he could perform miracles. His memo to Roosevelt suggesting that he be sent to China implies that he could learn how to solve all outstanding Sino-American problems, including Stilwell's many difficulties. Since Stilwell denigrated the Generalissimo, Stilwell had to go. And since Chiang was the indispensable leader, the Chinese Communists were not to be encouraged. Currie refused to see Chou En-lai, instead using John Paton Davies, an advisor to Stilwell, to communicate with the Communists.[40]

When Currie returned to Washington, his solutions were simple: re-

place Stilwell with Chennault, replace Ambassador Gauss with John Carter
Vincent or Owen Lattimore, and promise Chiang the airplanes he wanted
as soon as they were off the assembly line. The first of these solutions
Roosevelt partially agreed to, sending Currie to General Marshall with
word that he wanted Stilwell relieved. Marshall stood his ground, refused
the suggestion, and forced Roosevelt to back down. Roosevelt took no
action to replace Gauss; he did promise Currie more planes.[41]

Since Lattimore and Currie were both heavily involved in Chinese affairs, Lattimore frequented Currie's office during 1942, looking after correspondence and making telephone calls. As Currie told a Department of
State investigator in 1952, "I cannot now recall how much use he made
of it. My impression is that he dropped by frequently for a few months
but that he did not regularly occupy a desk." While Currie was in China,
Lattimore checked the mail for China matters that needed handling.[42]

The Office of Strategic Services sought Lattimore's opinions on June
10, 1942. Captain Ilia Tolstoy and Lieutenant Brooke Dolan quizzed Lattimore at length about the situation in China. In a four-page report to
their superior, Colonel Preston Goodfellow, they noted that Lattimore felt
that "the Communist Chief *Chu Teh* imposes his form of gov't on the
people of the provinces across which his War area cuts. This is a great
source of uneasiness to the Generalissimo and the Kuo Min Tang which
naturally object to any different philosophy of gov't being imposed on a
large section of the Chinese people. For this reason O.L. believes that Chu
Teh is careful not to destroy the Landlord system in his area; O.L. believes that Chu Teh is running a Democratic rather than a Communist
Regime in North China." Lattimore went on to say that Chu Teh was not
indoctrinating his troops "to nearly the same degree as the early communist die-hards who made the great retreat [the Long March] in 1935 to
Shensi."[43]

Lattimore continued writing during the summer of 1942; one of the
products was a monograph for the Foreign Policy Association, published
as their Report Number 12 on September 1. Titled *Asia in a New World
Order*, the report is orthodox Lattimore, talking about the virtues of Chiang,
the sacrifices and determination of the Chinese, the death of colonialism,
the importance of the Sino-Soviet border areas, the impossibility of
American control of China's political and economic development, the necessity of China recapturing sovereignty over Manchuria. Lattimore also
attempts to answer those critics of Roosevelt who deplored American alliance with China or Russia, neither of which were democracies in the
Anglo-American sense.

This discussion brought Lattimore to the problem of communism in Asia, and his treatment of this topic is both fair and, in hindsight, accurate.

> Rapid but orderly emancipation, in order to incorporate in the growing and developing body of democracy that half of humanity which lives in East Asia, brings up inevitably the problem of the degree of violent revolution and the possibility of the spread of communism. The overwhelming majority of Americans are opposed to communism by long established social habit and by emotional and intellectual response. It would be well if we were to recognize more generally that a similar majority of the Chinese are opposed to communism in the same ways, and that communism has few roots in India and little power to grow there. We in America certainly do not realize, and just as certainly ought to realize, that the question of whether and how far communism will spread will probably depend more on us than on the Russians.
>
> Criticize communism as we may, we ought also to be prepared to criticize ourselves. To prepare ourselves for the right things to do, we must first see clearly the wrong things that have been done. We must be ready to admit that the blame for Manchuria, Ethiopia, Munich, and Spain falls primarily on the Western democracies, as condoners and sometimes even compounders of aggression, as we are ready to criticize Russia for the pact with Germany, which failed in the same way that the pact of Chamberlain and Daladier with Germany failed.[44]

The Columbia Broadcasting System put Lattimore on their popular "Symphony Hour" July 26, and he made the most of this opportunity to further the Chinese cause. The Chinese, he said, "are the only troops of the United Nations who have been able to recover territory once occupied by the Japanese." He also praised General Chennault and the American fliers fighting for China, called for planes to be sent to China as fast as we could produce them, and lauded the Generalissimo for his wholehearted war effort.[45]

By July 1942 Lattimore had been in Chiang's service for a year. It was a challenging and exciting tour, but Lattimore was beginning to tire of his role as spokesperson of a foreign government. He had had no word from Chiang as to when he would be recalled to Chungking. He told Currie to suggest to the Chiangs that perhaps it was time for him to return to Johns Hopkins. He could advance the Chinese cause as well from there as he could on Chiang's payroll.

Currie passed this suggestion on when he arrived in Chungking. The response was quick.

Headquarters Of The Generalissimo
China

Chungking, Szechuan
5 August 1942

Dear Mr. Lattimore,

The newspapers here have contained frequent references to the
good work that you are doing on behalf of China in America. All
your letters to the Generalissimo and myself have been received,
and we have been greatly interested in your delineation of the
present state of feeling among the American people.

We fully realize that, as an American, you can say a great number of things, that it would be difficult, if not impossible, for a
Chinese to say with good grace. When they are said by an American who has lived most of his life with us and who speaks with evident sincerity, they sink deeper and have a profound influence.

Dr. Currie has spoken to us regarding your feeling that possibly
you might be of more use to China if you returned to John [*sic*]
Hopkins. While we appreciate the value of your suggestion, we feel
that if you could return to China for the time being and help to
establish more cordial and closer relationship between the American
Military Mission and China and the Embassy and us, you would be
rendering an even more direct and much needed service. And so the
Generalissimo wishes you to return to China as soon as you can get
transportation. . . .

With all good wishes to yourself and Mrs. Lattimore,

Yours very sincerely,

Mayling Soong Chiang[46]

Sensitive to Chinese ways, Lattimore realized that he could not simply
refuse to honor the Generalissimo's request. But now that the United
States was at war, being on Chiang's payroll was awkward. As he later
said to Joseph O'Mahoney, "There would soon be an official channel for
everything, and even if I avoided getting into people's hair, a lot of people
would imagine that I was getting into their hair."[47] An important assignment for his own government seemed the best way of gracefully leaving
Chiang's service.

Elmer Davis approached him during the summer of 1942 about directing the Pacific Bureau of the Office of War Information (OWI). This bureau was mainly producing radio broadcasts to the Pacific region and Asia,
and Lattimore was eminently qualified. He accepted. Lattimore therefore

decided to extend his service with Chiang to the end of the year and arranged a diplomatic way to resign at that time.

A cable now went from Roosevelt to Chiang: "Lattimore will return as you suggest for temporary duty Chungking under your orders however if acceptable to you President would appreciate it if you would allow him to resign after short visit to return to America to take over news and propaganda supervision for entire Pacific area under Office War Information. If you agree this can be announced from either Chungking or Washington when Lattimore leaves here."[48]

In late September, Lattimore flew back to China carrying a letter to the Generalissimo from Roosevelt. It explained why the United States could not immediately fulfill most of the Chinese requests Currie had delivered.[49]

Chiang did not want to cut his ties with Lattimore permanently. Chinese protocol dictated that a faithful retainer not be allowed to *resign*; consequently, when the announcement of Lattimore's OWI job was finally made by Chungking October 30, the Associated Press carried the following story:

CHIANG KAI-SHEK PREFERS TO LEND AIDE TO OWI

Chungking, China, Oct. 30 (AP).—Generalissimo Chiang Kai-shek has granted a leave of absence to his American political adviser, Owen Lattimore, who will return to the United States as director of the Pacific Bureau of the Office of War Information, with headquarters in San Francisco.

"Rather than accept a resignation from Mr. Lattimore, who was appointed his adviser last year on the recommendation of President Roosevelt, Chiang Kai-shek preferred to lend him to the OWI," an announcement said.[50]

Lattimore found Chungking, in early October 1942, more strife-ridden and rumor-plagued than before. The Stilwell controversy raged. Despite Madame's letter instructing Lattimore to return in order to help establish more "cordial" relations between Stilwell and Chiang, Lattimore played no role in solving that problem. He was inactive largely because Stilwell was not available to him, but he also sensed that it was a hopeless task.

By this time the optimism engendered by Currie's visit had dissipated. Chiang was full of complaints. Why was China still not incorporated into the mainstream of Allied military councils? Why was Secretary of the Treasury Henry Morgenthau so hostile? Why were American Lend-Lease supplies being diverted to the Middle East? Why did Chennault not have the confidence of the American high command? Lattimore was as candid as tact permitted.

There were the usual interviews, dinners, press conferences. Typically, on October 23 Lattimore spoke to a dinner of fifteen Chinese cultural societies. According to the *New York Times*, Lattimore said the Allies were planning to open new fronts in Europe and Asia and that they would eventually wage a knockout offensive against Japan from Chinese bases. "When the final victory is won, he said, China will emerge as one of the world's great democracies, unfettered by Western imperialism, with a future of progress that will make the next 100 years a 'Chinese century.' "[51] This reference competed with Henry Luce, whose "American Century" article in 1941 had staked out a different claim to world leadership.

Chiang knew before Lattimore arrived in China that this was to be a farewell visit. As Lattimore recorded in the O'Mahoney manuscript: "The Generalissimo was very cordial about my resignation, but would not let me go at once; and when I did go, he very handsomely insisted that I must still consider myself in his service, free to return at any time, and, as he put it, 'on reverse lend-lease' from him to President Roosevelt." In 1943, in appreciation of Lattimore's services, Chiang (or possibly Madame) directed H. H. K'ung to send Lattimore a gratuity. The amount K'ung's American agent sent him was five thousand dollars. Lattimore was gratified but could not accept the gift as he was then an employee of the U.S. government.[52]

Shortly before Lattimore was to leave China, he had a chance to talk to Chou En-lai. "I asked him, 'What do you think of my mission here? Have I just been wasting a couple of years, or was it worthwhile from your point of view?' He said, 'Very worthwhile. We think you've done a very good job for Chiang Kai-shek. Because it was absolutely essential to maintain contact with Chiang Kai-shek. If it weren't for Chiang, there would be a half-dozen Wang Ching-wei's going over to the Japanese. Chiang Kai-shek is essential to the national resistance and you have served him well.' "

The most touching farewell letter in Lattimore's files is from the finance minister, H. H. K'ung. That crusty banker's admiration seems genuine: "Though one must accept the parting of friends as something unavoidable in life, I cannot help feeling reluctant to see you leave China. During the period of your service as Political Advisor to the Generalissimo, your knowledge in Chinese has been a great asset. . . . Hence, even your temporary transfer from China is a great loss to us."[53]

This time Lattimore's trip to the United States was deluxe. In the fall of 1942 Madame Chiang was beset with various ailments; Sterling Seagrave gives an impressive catalog of them in *The Soong Dynasty*. She and the Generalissimo decided that this was the time for her to go to the United States both for medical attention and to exert her charm on those who dispensed American funds. The normal military transport would not do for Madame. Thus, a Boeing 307 Stratoliner named *Apache*, piloted by Cornell Shelton, was flown from the United States to pick her up. Lattimore and Madame's niece, Jeanette K'ung, and a party of retainers were to accompany her. They met Shelton's plane at 4:00 A.M. November 19 at an airfield near Chengtu and took off for the westbound route to the United States. After landing at Mitchell Field in New York on November 27, Madame was taken by Harry Hopkins to Columbia Presbyterian Medical Center and registered under a false name. She spent eleven weeks there and emerged healthy.[54]

Lattimore went on to Baltimore and Washington. On December 7 he briefed Roosevelt on the China situation, telling reporters as he left the White House that " 'final, decisive victory against Japan can be won only on land in China.' Beating the Japanese Navy will not be sufficient, he said, for Japan's major strength is her army, which is still strong and in China. The defeat, he asserted, will have to be accomplished 'by land-based aircraft in China.' "[55]

The Institute of Pacific Relations was holding its eighth conference December 4–14, 1942, at Mont Tremblant, Quebec. Lattimore was able to attend only the last few days, but his views were very much present. His Foreign Policy Association report, *Asia in a New World Order*, was one of several documents distributed to all the conferees; the issues it discussed were prominent in conference deliberations. The Mont Tremblant conference was later prominent not because of what was said but because of who attended and who suggested them as participants. This was the first IPR conference at which government officials of the IPR countries were permitted to take part in discussions.[56]

Lattimore left Mont Tremblant to rush down to New York on December 15 for another discussion with members of the Council on Foreign Relations. Before that eminent group he propounded this warning: "If the partial solutions [to the colonial problem] put forward by the United Nations at the close of the war lack cohesion, the victors may drive into Soviet arms the small peoples bordering on Russia. Sovietization would thus be due to our failure."[57] He added that Chinese morale was still strong despite a deteriorating economy; that Chiang's stock was still very high; and that the Chinese should be better integrated into military councils.

After the CFR meeting Lattimore had a week to relax at his Baltimore home. There was only one other official duty before he reported to OWI in San Francisco: Roosevelt wanted him to draft a letter to Chiang explaining that total independence might not be immediately granted after the war to all the colonial areas. The new concept was "trusteeship," which Roosevelt informed Lattimore was "an advance over the mandate of the League of Nations." This message, Lattimore knew, would infuriate the Generalissimo. In the letter that Lattimore drafted, the "trusteeship" concept was softened by a promise that "after the war we shall have to think of China, America, Britain and Russia as the four 'big policemen' of the world." There were several other sops to Chiang's vanity, including the statement that "the President is delighted by the friendship that has sprung up between his wife and Madame Chiang and is looking forward eagerly to Madame Chiang's visit to the White House." [58] Roosevelt made minor changes in Lattimore's draft, then informed the astounded Currie that the letter was to go out over Lattimore's signature. Lattimore by then had gone to San Francisco to take over the OWI job. Currie now had to inform Lattimore that he was to be saddled with Roosevelt's obnoxious (to the Chinese) views on colonialism. Apparently, Currie telephoned to break the news gently, then sent the final draft to Lattimore with a cover letter: "I am afraid the enclosed puts you on a bit of a spot. It was the President's own idea that the bulk of the letter be represented as being your views rather than his. I thereupon suggested that there was really no need of a letter, but he disagreed with that. Unless, therefore, you want me to go back and tell him that you object to having these views ascribed to you, I am afraid you will have to take a deep breath and be prepared to accept paternity." [59]

Lattimore took a very deep breath. He had no use whatever for the trusteeship idea. Perhaps, had he been in Washington instead of San Francisco and had he been going back to Johns Hopkins instead of starting on the OWI payroll, he would have told Roosevelt what to do with this letter. But he wrote Currie on January 1, 1943, "It certainly does require a deep breath to accept paternity of that little job in *fait accompli*. However, here goes. I am sending the letter back to you, airmail registered." [60] It went to China over Lattimore's signature, carried to the Generalissimo by a new naval attaché replacing James McHugh. Lattimore was not to communicate with Chiang again until he returned to China in 1944.

CHAPTER SEVEN

OWI, San Francisco

In late December 1942 Lattimore arrived in San Francisco to direct the Pacific bureau of the Office of War Information. OWI's objective was to further the war effort by broadcasting news and commentary encouraging our allies and discouraging our enemies. In the Pacific, Japan was the only enemy.

By the time Lattimore arrived, the San Francisco office consisted of some five hundred writers, broadcasters, analysts, and support personnel. Overall policy was made in Washington, where the Department of State and Joint Chiefs of Staff (JCS) collaborated on comprehensive directives, one for Atlantic operations, another for the Pacific. Lattimore was responsible for applying these directives through the seven section chiefs: Japanese, Korean, Philippine, Chinese, Indonesian, Malay, and Southeast Asian. Lattimore held daily staff conferences, and according to Charlotte Riznik, his office manager, presided over them with "a light hand." [1]

Each of the sections had its own peculiar problems. The Japanese section was the most important: OWI wanted to break Japanese morale and stimulate disaffection from the Tojo regime. The "Joint Anglo-American Plan for Psychological Warfare for Japan," promulgated on March 16, 1943, by the JCS, devotes three pages to how these objectives were to be accomplished. Section (c) of the Japanese directive lists these goals: "(1) to create amongst the people of Japan a feeling of distrust of their present regime by calling attention to its usurpation of power and its departure from 'Imperial Way.' (2) to create fanatical opposition by individuals and by secret groups. Note to (1) and (2): This theme is as delicate as it is important and requires very careful handling by methods to be determined in advance. All attacks upon the Imperial family must be avoided." [2]

Finding personnel to handle such delicate themes was difficult. Obviously, the whole Japanese program needed educated, Japanese-speaking writers and broadcasters who were completely loyal to the United States. But in the wartime hysteria of 1942 all persons of Japanese ancestry living in California had been evacuated to detention centers. The commander of U.S. forces on the West Coast would not allow a single Japanese to reside in San Francisco, no matter what the needs of the OWI. Consequently, all the Japanese-language programs had to be prepared east of the Rockies and flown to San Francisco for broadcast.

When Lattimore took over, the head of the Japanese desk was Clay Osborne, a journalist described by *American Mercury* in 1939 as "born in Indian territory and raised in the Oregon backwoods. He now lives and writes in Gardena, California."[3] That is about all we know of Osborne's background; libraries are singularly lacking in any trace of his career. He probably achieved his most important status with the OWI job. Lattimore's FBI file has extensive material about Osborne, but it is heavily censored. The FBI files show that Osborne had been a Japanophile before the war and that he despised his new boss. It is impossible to tell from the available records what caused this hostility, but Osborne gradually became determined to dislodge Lattimore from the directorship of Pacific operations.

Accordingly, Osborne began to accumulate documents that he thought would show that Lattimore was violating directives from Washington, placing sycophants in OWI posts, slanting broadcasts to show the Soviet Union in a favorable light, and so forth. These documents included the secret policy directives from Washington, which Osborne thought Lattimore covertly rewrote; local directives authored by Lattimore; transcripts of dozens of OWI broadcasts; clippings of newspaper columns by isolationists and archconservative writers such as David Lawrence, George Rothwell Brown, and various Hearst columnists attacking OWI; complete programming schedules for two full days of OWI broadcasts; and extensive personal notes Osborne himself made explaining how Lattimore was deviating from the "master plan."[4]

In March or April 1943 Osborne went to the FBI office in San Francisco with his story of Lattimore's subversion. The agents were not sympathetic. Next he tried the Office of Naval Intelligence. Since the ONI people were regularly consulting with Lattimore and admired him, they were even less impressed with Osborne's charges. Bruised, Osborne began to believe that the whole U.S. government was honeycombed with Communist conspirators; obviously, he would need more and better evidence to break through the conspiracy. He continued collecting what he felt to be incriminating documents in his office.

Osborne found his smoking gun on October 13, 1943. The Chinese government broadcast a speech by Sun Fo, president of the legislature in Chungking, in which Sun gave the standard Chinese line on postwar Japan: "Unless a republic replaces imperialism in Japan in the postwar period another world conflict is inevitable. Japanese imperialism, if not totally destroyed once and for all during the present war, would form a permanent menace to the safety of China and Korea. The Mikado must go."[5]

Since the directive on China called for rebroadcast of important statements by Chinese government officials, Lattimore ordered Sun Fo's statement to be put on the air in all languages except Japanese and Korean. He did not see this as a violation of the Japan directive forbidding attacks on the emperor, since the Sun Fo statement was a Chinese rather than American position and was not available to Japanese listeners. Osborne saw it otherwise; this was "an attack on the Imperial family," forbidden by OWI directives. Osborne was now positive that Lattimore was a Communist, working to subvert American interests in Asia.

Sometime in the fall of 1943 George E. Taylor, an Asian specialist in the Washington OWI office, visited San Francisco. Osborne knew Taylor, thought Taylor to be hostile toward Lattimore, and unburdened himself of his suspicions. A decade later, Taylor reported that Osborne had "so seriously taken [the Lattimore matter] to heart and was so emotionally overcome that he ended up crying on Taylor's shoulder." Osborne's emotional state grew steadily worse. In 1954, when Justice Department attorneys interviewed him in a mental hospital, they concluded that he could not be allowed before a jury.[6]

In November, shortly after the Taylor visit, Osborne decided he could not stand working under Lattimore any longer. He assembled his documents and engaged an army friend (whose name he never revealed) to provide a military vehicle to haul his documents from the OWI office to his apartment. This done, he resigned from the OWI without revealing his real reasons.[7] Lattimore had no knowledge of Osborne's theft or of its purpose.

In early 1944 Osborne's wife, thinking her husband weak for not taking further action and having no faith in the San Francisco FBI agents, took the documents to the Los Angeles FBI office. The agents there were equally unimpressed with Osborne's case against Lattimore and were instead upset with the theft. Instead of impaling Lattimore, Osborne's wife got Osborne in trouble. The Los Angeles FBI referred Osborne's theft to Washington, but in the last year of the war the Department of Justice had no time to take a former OWI employee to court. In a memo dated August 24, 1944, Assistant Attorney General Tom C. Clark advised that "prosecution was not warranted and that further investigation was not requested."[8]

Osborne's determination to bring Lattimore to justice was not lessened by his second rebuff at the hands of the FBI. He clung to his outrage and his documents until the inquisition burst on the scene six years later. Even then he was odd man out; others who had worked for Lattimore praised both his leadership and his fidelity to government directives.[9]

The Chinese operations of OWI were complicated because there were three Chinas: the National government in Chungking, the Japanese puppet state under Wang Ching-wei, and the Communist would-be government in Yenan. Broadcasts to China had to take them all into account. The Nationalists had to be encouraged and praised, the Japanese subjects had to be reassured that the Allies would not neglect their interests when the war was over, and the Communists had to be nudged to continue cooperation with Chungking not only to fight Japanese armies in 1943 but also because the JCS assumed the Allies would mount an invasion of the Japanese homeland from bases in Communist-controlled areas. Lattimore, whose admiration of Chiang Kai-shek remained strong, had no trouble maintaining good relations with Chinese Nationalist officials. His rapport with Yui Ming, head of the Chinese News Service in San Francisco, was excellent. Yui Ming was invited to attend OWI policy meetings and expressed pleasure that someone with Lattimore's understanding of China was in charge of OWI.[10] Hollington Tong, still Chinese minister of information, regarded Lattimore's tenure as head of the Pacific OWI operation as productive of cordial, mutual understanding, and in April 1944 he found Lattimore's successor far less satisfactory.[11]

Despite these cordial relations with the Chinese government, Lattimore was careful to avoid hiring Chinese who might be on the Kuomintang payroll. He wanted fully independent Chinese. After some hiring and firing, he thought he had them. Then in late spring 1943 he heard that Chew Sih Hong, one of the two Chinese language specialists working under his jurisdiction in the New York office, had been declared ineligible for employment because of suspicion of Communist leanings. Lattimore did not know the source of the information about Hong; a Civil Service Commission document released in 1980 reveals that the accuser was in the Washington office of the Chinese News Service.[12]

Hong was a brilliant linguist. The U.S. army had hired him in 1942 to teach Chinese to 224 American officers who were preparing to work with Chinese troops; Hong got rave reviews. But he was also president of the *China Daily News* in New York, a paper not under Kuomintang control; Hong's accuser said it followed the Communist line.

Anticipating trouble with the Hong appointment, on June 15, 1943, Lattimore wrote his friend Joseph Barnes, head of the New York OWI office, explaining why Hong and another employee, Dr. K. C. Chi, should be kept on. The letter explained in great detail how Chinese living in the U.S. were subject to competing claims on their loyalty. The Japanese puppet, Wang Ching-wei, was a veteran of Chinese politics and knew how to exert pressure on the many Chinese whose families still lived in areas controlled by the Japanese. The Nationalists in Chungking operated a vigorous overseas bureau that kept tabs on every Chinese community in America: "Thus there is a very intense conflict going on every day in every Chinatown in America between the Wang Ching-wei agents and those of the Kuomintang."

But there were also unaffiliated Chinese, and Lattimore insisted that OWI employees should come from this group, assuring loyalty to OWI rather than to Wang or Chiang. There were some Chinese Communists in the United States, and OWI needed to avoid hiring them also. Lattimore knew that old Dr. Chi, who had been a wealthy landlord in Shansi Province, was not a Communist, and Dr. Chi vouched for Chew Sih Hong; this assurance was sufficient for Lattimore. "There will be no difficulty with either man, no irresponsible playing with Chinese politics, and no leakage to any faction." Two months after Lattimore wrote Barnes, the Civil Service Commission sent an investigator to San Francisco to interview Lattimore about Hong and Chi. After a two-hour conversation in which Lattimore provided greater detail about the politics of Chinese communities in the United States, the investigator reported that "he would go along with Lattimore and in favor of Mr. Hong's retention in the service."[13]

This recommendation did not satisfy the Civil Service Commission, which requested that Admiral Richard P. McCullough, head of OWI security, and Frank March and E. Newton Steely of the security staff interview Lattimore again to decide whether the outcome of the San Francisco interview was correct. Lattimore was scheduled to visit New York on August 31, 1943; the three OWI officials then went over the Hong and Chi cases with him. They emerged with a divided verdict: McCullough and Marsh supported Lattimore; Steely opposed him.[14] Hong continued in his post at OWI.

The demands for security investigations during the war were so great that extensive backlogs developed; many investigations took place months after an official assumed his post. This was the case with Lattimore himself. The Federal Works Agency (FWA) was charged with checking out high-level civilian appointments but didn't get around to Lattimore until he had served five months in the OWI. Finally, in May 1943, an FWA representative interviewed him.

FWA did not possess the FBI report of May 1941 in which the Baltimore FBI office recommended that Lattimore be put on the Custodial Detention list because of his membership in the Maryland Civil Liberties Committee; nor did the agency possess the later report that canceled this recommendation. FWA did possess a Dies Committee (House Un-American Activities Committee) report showing that in 1940 Lattimore had been a member of the Maryland Association for Democratic Rights, which, according to Dies, was a Communist front. The investigator interviewed Lattimore and demanded an explanation.

Lattimore acknowledged the membership but protested that the very respectable Baltimoreans who had invited him to join were anything but Communists and had appealed to him on the grounds that the organization supported China and opposed the sale of war matériel to Japan. There was nothing Communist about the organization or about him. He then cited his support of aid to Britain and of Lend-Lease and his opposition to the Communist-inspired American Peace Mobilization during the period of the Hitler-Stalin pact. When asked about his attitude toward the Chinese Communists, "He advised that he tolerated but did not approve of the Chinese Communists who supported China against Japanese aggression, explaining that his toleration was based solely on the purpose of unifying China against the enemy."[15]

The rest of the FWA file was sweetness and light. Five prominent individuals (names withheld by the FBI) who were interviewed about Lattimore reported favorably. Investigation of his employment with the IPR and Johns Hopkins University "developed no derogatory data." Finally the FWA went to the Chinese embassy to inquire about Lattimore's service with Chiang. There an official, again name withheld, reported "subject was well considered by the Chinese Government and had performed his duties in a satisfactory manner. ——— was reported to have commented that CHIANG would be happy to utilize subject's services again."[16] Lattimore was cleared.

Despite the demands of administering the Pacific bureau of OWI, Lattimore continued to write and publish. The April 1943 *Foreign Affairs* carried his article "Yunnan, Pivot of Southeast Asia," which argued that

China would not dominate Southeast Asia after the war unless she felt hemmed in by a restored European colonialism. In June, Lattimore submitted a memorandum, "Mongolia and the Peace Settlement," to the Council on Foreign Relations. The main thrust of this article was that Russia would not try to annex Inner Mongolia. [17]

The National Broadcasting Corporation also sought Lattimore's services as commentator on a radio series entitled "The Pacific Story." Mrs. Inez Richardson of Stanford University and Jennings Peirce of the NBC studio in Hollywood conceived and produced the series. Scripts were written by Arnold Marquis on the basis of research done by Eleanor Lattimore. The first "Pacific Story" broadcast aired from Los Angeles July 11, 1943; the Lattimores continued with the series for thirteen weeks. Lattimore had been reluctant to assume the task of preparing a weekly commentary in addition to his other activities, and since NBC felt that his radio voice "lacked warmth," the series was turned over to a succession of different commentators after the Lattimores' contract expired. [18]

This brief foray into broadcast journalism convinced Lattimore that the written word was still his best medium. In 1943 he published his seventh book, *America and Asia,* notable for heaping even more praise on Chiang than had his previous publications. The Generalissimo was "a world statesman, of real genius." [19] Even before *America and Asia* was off the press, Lattimore and his wife were beginning *The Making of Modern China,* a brief history of the Kuomintang. Published a year later, this work too includes lavish praise of Chiang. Russian reviews were scathing, dismissing Lattimore as a "learned lackey of imperialism." [20]

Even though he was no longer on the Generalissimo's payroll, Lattimore kept in touch with his Chinese patrons during his residence in San Francisco. After she recovered her health, Madame Chiang toured the United States, speaking of the needs of the Pacific war and dramatizing China's great sacrifices. Lattimore wrote to her several times. On March 30, 1943, he sent her recordings of all her American speeches to that date. He told her, "These statements of yours have been of unique value. Traveling around the country you must of course be aware of the great impact they have had on the way Americans think about China; but perhaps you have not yet realized how wide the range of your speeches has been. Our office has been translating them into all the languages that are spoken from Korea to Australia and from Honolulu to Burma; thus your words have been steadily at work spreading the consciousness throughout Asia and the Pacific that China is not only one of the United Nations but is setting the moral standard and the standard of political thought in Asia." [21]

A month later Lattimore wrote Madame urging her to visit Canada before she went home. Canadian pressure, he said, had influenced Britain's belated renunciation of the Anglo-Japanese alliance. If Madame were to stimulate Canada's interest in the Pacific war, this interest would increase pressure on Britain to cooperate more fully with China.[22] Madame Chiang took this advice, speaking to the Canadian Parliament June 16.

Despite referring to the Generalissimo as a "coalition statesman of genius," Lattimore began to worry that Chiang was now appearing to ease off China's prosecution of war against Japan, counting on American forces to win in the Pacific and saving his strength to fight the Communists.[23] He put these worries in a confidential letter to Currie July 20, adding a comparison of Nationalist and Communist policies:

> *Dangers of the situation.* In China, the Communists are officially regarded as "the extremist party," and the information filtered through to the Generalissimo is intended to maintain this view. It should be frankly recognized that in the China of today the Kuomintang are much more nearly totalitarian than the Communists. Since the Communists are in opposition, one of the things they oppose is the totalitarian tendency of the Kuomintang. This makes them in fact *the party of moderation.* (Lattimore's italics)
>
> *The problem of American policy.* While it would obviously be inadvisable for America to appear as the protector of a foreign Communist party, it would also be incautious for American policy to appear to sanction the use of force for removing from politics, in an allied country, a party which is more moderate in its political program than the party in power.
>
> Perhaps it might be advisable for the State Department to seek an opportunity for a statement comparable to one which was made in the case of India in 1942. In the Indian case, a statement was made that the American troops in India were to hold themselves entirely aloof from and neutral to Indian questions.[24]

This was Lattimore's first clear acknowledgment of a major worry about the Generalissimo and of his belief that the United States should not intervene in a Chinese civil war, whatever the stature of the Kuomintang leader.

Lattimore made his final wartime appearance before the CFR Territorial Group December 14, 1943. His title was "Russia and China in the Far East." Most of his presentation was a repeat of the theme that Soviet minority policies had been very effective, much more so than China's, and that people in the border areas "are bound to do Russia's propaganda for her, by saying that things were better under Russian influence." In fact, were a plebiscite to be held in Outer Mongolia (as it later was), the people "would vote 100% to keep free of Chinese control." Lattimore did not gloat over this Soviet prowess; he pointed out ways in which the Chinese government could counter it.[25]

Returning to San Francisco from his New York appearance, Lattimore stopped off in Chicago to talk to Kenneth Colegrove, an Asian scholar at Northwestern University to whom Lattimore offered the job as head of the Japan desk vacated by Clay Osborne. Lattimore did not remember this meeting with Colegrove, but Colegrove claimed in 1951 to recall it in great detail: "I was opposed to liquidating Dutch imperialism in Indonesia after the war. Then I mentioned something about the Chinese Communists, and this surprised me a great deal to have Lattimore, whom I thought by this time had lost some of his control, claim that he had more information on China than I had, which was, of course, true. He went so far as to say that Chinese Communists under Mao Tse-tung were real democrats and that they were really agrarian reformers and had no connection with Soviet Russia." Colegrove also said that Lattimore advocated the murder of the Japanese emperor and his family.[26]

Lattimore never believed that the Chinese Communists were "real" democrats, or that they had no connection with Russia, or that the Japanese emperor and his family should be murdered. Colegrove, when the inquisition came, made similar damaging statements about other prominent scholars; to a man, they called him a liar.[27] It is clear why Colegrove was not hired as head of OWI's Japan desk: Lattimore could never have tolerated anyone who approved of Dutch rule in Indonesia.

After more than a year in San Francisco, Lattimore was becoming restless, as was Eleanor. They missed their Baltimore home, and Lattimore wanted to be free to comment publicly on postwar policy. In March 1944 he asked to be relieved of the Pacific job. Elmer Davis agreed if Lattimore would remain on call for consultation and special assignments.

Lattimore had hardly gotten unpacked in Baltimore when Davis frustrated his plans. Davis thought the OWI broadcasts had been very effective and wanted to see if army and navy commands actually fighting the war would set up mini-OWIs in their field headquarters. Lattimore was handed this mission and by mid-March was flying to Honolulu and Australia to spread the OWI gospel to two of America's crustiest military moguls: Admiral Chester Nimitz and General Douglas MacArthur. The success of this mission was in doubt. The military had long believed the Japanese would rather die than surrender and were thus immune to propaganda. There was also resistance to civilian ideas and "Roosevelt agencies."

Nevertheless, Lattimore convinced Nimitz that a mini-OWI in his field headquarters was at least worth a try. As he told it,

> That left me with my mission to General MacArthur half-successful in advance, since an Army theater of command would only with reluctance turn down facilities already accepted by a Navy theater of command. Moreover I took with me to Australia, as prospective head of OWI operations under General MacArthur, an American newspaperman who had previously, as an editor of a paper in Manila, enjoyed the General's confidence. Nothing was really left except to assure the General that the OWI man under him would be paid by Washington and supplied with materials by Washington, but would do nothing except under the General's control and orders. The General then embarked on a fascinating discourse, and after an hour or so I left, mission completed.[28]

So Lattimore headed home once more, hopeful that he would finally be able to reenter private life.

CHAPTER EIGHT

Mission with Wallace

Roosevelt was not quite ready to let Lattimore settle down. The president was about to send Vice President Henry Wallace on a three-month trip to Siberia and China, and Lattimore's presence was required.

There are as many explanations of the genesis and purpose of the Wallace mission as there are chroniclers of it. Roosevelt, as noted earlier, had a compulsion to send special envoys everywhere he wanted to go but couldn't: fact-finding missions, troubleshooting missions, promise-the-sky missions, even plain goodwill missions such as the round-the-world trip of Wendell Willkie in 1943 or the cultural mission of playwright Lillian Hellman to Moscow in 1944. Roosevelt's envoys were expected to establish rapport with foreign leaders and convince them that if he were not fighting a war from a wheelchair, the president would be there himself.[1]

Despite Roosevelt's habit of dispatching emissaries, Secretary of State Cordell Hull thought the Wallace mission originated with Wallace, who was concerned that the strained relations between the Chinese Nationalists and Communists made it impossible for China "to assume a position of influence alongside the three big Western powers. . . . Vice President Wallace went to China in 1944 with the idea of converting both parties to this point of view. This was his own idea." But Hull considered Wallace a bull in a China shop and opposed the trip. Publicly, Wallace said that Roosevelt wanted him to preach the necessity of Chinese unity to the Generalissimo. Barbara Tuchman's view was that "the selection of Wallace had more to do with domestic politics than with China." Roosevelt simply wanted Wallace out of the country so he could select a more popular running mate for the fall election.[2]

Among other things, Wallace was to meet with Averell Harriman, U.S. ambassador to the Soviet Union. But Roosevelt did not want Wallace in Moscow, where he might meet Stalin. Instead, Harriman would go to Tashkent to meet the vice president. "The President," Harriman later wrote, "was perfectly willing for Wallace to see Chiang Kai-shek. Indeed, he thought that the Vice President's liberal influence might do some good with Chiang. But he was taking no chances of confusing Stalin about American policy."[3]

About one facet of the mission FDR was not uncertain in the slightest. As Wallace reported a conversation with the president, "He urged me to take Owen Lattimore with me, who, he said, was one of the world's great experts on the problems involving Chinese-Russian relationships. President Roosevelt had long been fascinated by the tribes which for many hundreds of years have wandered back and forth across what is now known as the Russian-Chinese boundary. He wanted me as an agriculturist to observe how they lived on both sides of the boundary and to form some opinions [with, presumably, Lattimore's guidance] as to how possible future causes of conflict between China and Russia might be minimized. He asked me specifically not to see the Chinese Communists because he thought that might belittle the importance of the special message which he asked me to convey to the Generalissimo."[4] This special message was one of complete support for the Nationalist government of China.

Wallace was to have a small staff: Lattimore, because of his knowledge of the Sino-Soviet border areas and his ability to speak Mongol; John N. Hazard, an economist fluent in Russian; and John Carter Vincent, China specialist in the State Department who had Hull's confidence and who was to keep Wallace from giving away the store. The Skymaster flight crew was the best that could be assembled; Colonel Richard T. Kight had piloted Willkie around the world.

News of the Wallace mission, and of Lattimore's participation, reached Chungking by late April. Madame Chiang wrote Lattimore April 28, 1944, telling him that if he were indeed coming with Wallace, "I should be very happy if you will be our house guest during your visit to Chungking."[5] He was pleased.

Both Roosevelt and Wallace issued public statements before the trip. Roosevelt's was brief, laconic, unrevealing. Wallace's was lengthy, impassioned, apocalyptic: "The President has asked me to visit Asia. The President is a symbol of hope for millions of people throughout the world and I am proud to serve as one of his messengers. . . . The object of the trip is to let our Asiatic friends know the spirit of the American people and the beliefs and hopes of their Commander in Chief."[6] The statement continued in this maudlin vein for nine more purple paragraphs.

The Wallace party took off from Washington May 20, 1944, following the great circle route via Minneapolis, Edmonton, Fairbanks, Whitehorse, and Nome; they arrived at Velkal in the Soviet Union May 23. Wallace's account of the Soviet leg of the journey, *Soviet Asia Mission,* is a minimally competent travelogue deficient primarily in its political judgments. Lattimore also wrote about the Russian visit for the *National Geographic.* Both accounts enraged the Soviet-haters because of their upbeat tone.[7]

Lattimore later explained why he and Wallace wrote favorably about their Russian experiences: "We were in Siberia at the period of Russia's most cordial willingness to cooperate with America. The news of the landing in Normandy arrived while we were there, and the Russians overflowed with goodwill. We were allowed to visit places that had been visited by no other mission, and I am sure that the benefit to America in 'background intelligence' was of great value."[8]

Despite the aura of good feeling about D day, the Soviets carefully prepared for their high-level visitors. They had learned well from the czars how to create Potemkin villages and how to disguise slave labor camps. In 1944 little was known in the outside world about the extent of the gulag or the conditions of the prisoners' life and work. Elinor Lipper's book on Kolyma was still six years off, and Robert Conquest and Alexander Solzhenitsyn yet further in the future. The Russians went to great lengths to hide the gulag from Wallace and company; since Wallace was a fitness fanatic, this deception was not easy. The vice president seized every opportunity to stride off into the countryside for an invigorating walk and on at least one occasion was barely prevented from stumbling across an undisguised slave labor camp.

What the Russians showed Wallace, however, was impressive, so Wallace's book, *Soviet Asia Mission,* glamorized Soviet accomplishments in Siberia much as the American press glamorized the heroic achievements of the pioneers who opened up the American West. Wallace and party were actually taken to Magadan, a new mining center in the Kolyma Valley, where thousands of prisoners extracted precious metals for Soviet industry. Wallace's description of this visit was enthusiastic: "At Magadan I met Ivan Feodorovich Nikishov, a Russian, director of Dalstroi (the Far Northern Construction Trust), which is a combination TVA [Tennessee Valley Authority] and Hudson's Bay Company. . . . We had to work hard to get this place going, said Nikishov. Twelve years ago the first settlers arrived and put up eight prefabricated houses. Today Magadan

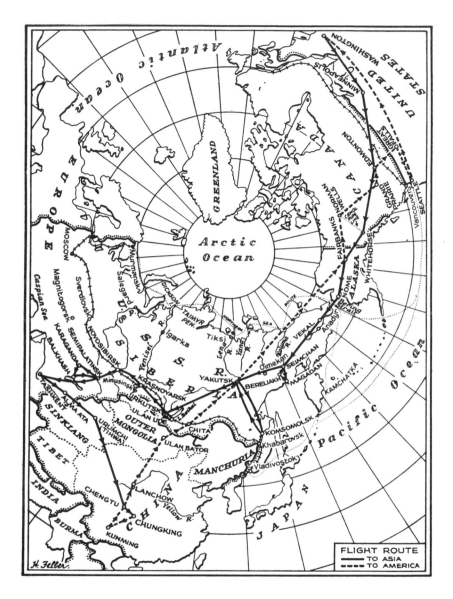

Route of the Wallace mission, 1944. From Henry A. Wallace, *Soviet Asia Mission* (New York: Reynal and Hitchcock, 1946).

has 40,000 inhabitants, and all are well-housed."[9] What Wallace did not realize was that General Nikishov had been ordered to remove all signs of prison labor, including guard towers and barbed wire.[10]

That evening the Wallace party saw the film *North Star*, which was then popular in the Soviet Union. Mrs. Nikishov thought it "marvelous that Americans would produce such a picture about us." Wallace did not know that the Russians were laughing at *North Star* for its idealized picture of Soviet life, nor did he know that Lillian Hellman, who had written the original screenplay after her usual thorough research, was so disgusted with what director Lewis Milestone did to it that she bought out her interest and refused credit for it.

Wallace's superlatives went on and on, about Velkal, Seimchan, Yakutsk, Chita, Krasnoyarsk, Semipalatinsk, Karaganda, Balkash, and Tashkent. At Tashkent, Wallace met with Harriman. The crux of Harriman's message was that Stalin still expressed his firm support of Chiang Kai-shek, a message that Wallace was to pass on to Chiang. Wallace did, by all accounts, register this message, but it hardly diluted his single-minded attention to farming. Harriman reported later to Hull, "All his life, Wallace had been trying to get American farmers to accept science. In the Soviet Union he saw scientific methods being forced on the farmers, and it was heaven for him."[11]

Lattimore's perspective was broader. Here he was finally able to visit the other side of the fascinating Sino-Soviet border, to compare this culture with what he knew of Sinkiang, Manchuria, and Inner Mongolia, and to see some of the priceless artifacts of prehistoric and ancient times. Yakutsk was particularly enjoyable for Lattimore; there he met the renowned A. P. Okladnikov, the archaeologist-anthropologist. Okladnikov had been given the whole of the Lena River watershed as his province. Even in wartime Okladnikov could commandeer transport and other services for his archaeological digs. He had already worked out the history of the migration of the Yakut people from the Altai up to the Arctic, with excavations and serious attention to rock carvings. Lattimore observed, "Okladnikov did a marvelous job. I was the only man in the party who was interested in this, so Okladnikov took me personally through his museum and exhibits." A bond was created between the two men that lasted until Okladnikov's death thirty-seven years later.

When the Wallace party stopped at Minusinsk, Lattimore was determined to see the museum, which had a famous display of Stone Age and Bronze Age artifacts. Historians had used these artifacts in reconstructing the history of ancient contacts between the Black Sea peoples and the Chinese of the Great Wall. Wallace relates with amused tolerance what happened in Minusinsk:

> We arrived in Minusinsk late in the afternoon with only an hour to spare before going down-river and leaving, perhaps forever, this famous site. Now, the mayor of Minusinsk is Grigory Averyanich Murop, an obliging person in his way but not too well informed about the small town where he was the big man of affairs. . . .
>
> Murop really didn't know very much about a certain small wooden house on the edge of his town. Why not come up to his office in the hour we had to spare? Why make such a fuss about seeing a "little old museum"? "It's a world-famous institution," Owen Lattimore exclaimed in mild exasperation. Murop's eyes opened in a quizzical look, as though he thought it just couldn't be true. "Well," he said slowly, "if that's how you feel about it, let's see the place. It's a long walk," he warned us. "To get back in time we must start at once."
>
> The urbane official strode briskly with regained self-assurance, setting us a stiff pace all the way to the museum door, where he stopped in evident embarrassment. The door was locked and nobody responded to his urgent knocks. Having no key, Mayor Murop looked about for some familiar subordinate on whom to vent an order. His eye lighting upon a small boy leaning against the nearby wicket fence, the mayor demanded: "Where's the old woman?"
>
> "Granny, you mean? She's gone home to eat."
>
> "To eat! Go fetch her, immediately."
>
> "Seichas," said the boy, dashing off through a broken fence and across the open field. In a few moments he came running back, with "granny" hurrying behind him. She was breathless and almost tongue-tied with excitement. When she opened the door, we all trooped inside to view the famous relics of prehistoric agriculture—bronze rakes, farm implements, stirrups, etc. The curator was so scared and stuttered so badly that John Hazard could hardly understand what she said in Russian. Owen Lattimore, knowing the international language of archeology, plied her with questions. She had all the answers, and her inscriptions on displays were all in English. "An expert curator," Lattimore remarked as we departed. "She knows her archeology of the Copper and Bronze Age." [12]

Thus, both Wallace and Lattimore were entranced by their Siberian odyssey and published glowing accounts of what they saw and did. Wallace's book did not approach the prominence or sales of Wendell Willkie's millennial *One World*. Ironically, *Soviet Asia Mission* achieved notoriety during the inquisition because of Wallace's unfortunate language describing the gulag as a TVA–Hudson's Bay Company.

Lattimore, lacking Wallace's personal fortune, sold his travelogue to the highest bidder—*National Geographic.* Since the first requirement of such magazines is that their articles capture the attention of subscribers, Lattimore wrote accordingly. His correspondence with the editors shows that they appreciated his "fast-moving and vivid narrative." When the cold war came, this vivid narrative was not so well appreciated. Nor was the analogy he shared with Wallace, comparing Dalstroi with TVA–Hudson's Bay.[13]

After their tour of Siberia the Wallace party flew to Urumchi, the capital of Sinkiang in western China. For Lattimore this was a spiritual journey of the most moving dimensions. He began keeping a diary, and his surviving diary notes begin as he approached Urumchi. It was June 18, 1944, almost two decades since he had been there on his honeymoon. "About two hours to follow the route Eleanor and I rode in 17 days from Urumchi to Talki. I thought of her all the time. It was amazing how much I remembered & recognized after 18 years—even with different appearances from the air."[14] The rest of his forty-five-page diary, carrying him through three weeks of China and the Mongolian People's Republic, is low-key.

The streets from the Urumchi airport into town were lined with people. Such a high-level group had never landed there. Lattimore was surprised by the numbers of White Russians (refugees from the Soviet Union) and their children, all "reasonably well dressed." At lunch that first day with the governor, Wallace controlled the conversational agenda: "soybeans, strawberries, fruits, rainfall, irrigation." Lattimore made a marginal note for this entry: " A hint at my low opinion of Wallace's topics of conversation with highly-placed Chinese."

That evening at a state dinner Wallace made a speech without notes that Lattimore had to translate, phrase by phrase. "What a job! I was far from perfect, but it was a wry comfort to note how eagerly Chinese dodged the job." The next day they spent inspecting: the cadet school, whose commandant was a protégé of Ho Ying-ch'in; the Women's Academy, established and supervised by the governor's wife, and according to Lattimore a first-rate operation; an animal-breeding station on the Turfan Road, "rather poor work"; and a Uighur farm, irrigated but with a low yield. They had dinner with American Consul Horace Smith, and Lattimore had a chance to encourage Governor Sheng to keep up his enlightened minority policies, since the Chinese could not compete with the neighboring Russians by force and had to win over the Kazakhs, Uighurs, and other minorities by favorable treatment.

June 20 found Lattimore once again in Chungking, once again with Chiang and Madame. The Generalissimo met Wallace's party at the airport, then took Lattimore to see Madame and on to the American embassy for dinner. The next morning Lattimore inspected the OWI office, writing no comment. The party lunched with Ho Ying-ch'in, Wallace went off on an inspection trip, and Vincent and Lattimore rested at Chiang's. That evening was a state dinner, but Lattimore comments only that he did not have to translate. There were more inspections of schools and agriculture stations on June 22, and in late afternoon Chiang called for the vice president to come for a conference. Lattimore was excluded at Wallace's specific instruction. According to protocol, this treatment was correct; Lattimore had not attended sessions with Harriman in Tashkent. Here, though, the situation was somewhat different. Vincent did not speak fluent Chinese, and at this first high-level conference he was dependent for translation on Madame Chiang, who was notorious for misrepresenting what her husband told foreigners, and on T. V. Soong, who had his own agenda. Thus, there is some question as to the accuracy of the record of this conference as provided by Vincent.[15]

As Vincent recorded it, there were two main topics: Chiang's lecture about how the United States should remain "cool" toward the Chinese Communists, who were really not much help against the Japanese but were a serious threat to the Chinese government; and Wallace's inquiry about sending an army intelligence group to Yenan soon, which Chiang rebuffed by saying "please do not press; please understand that the Communists are not good for the war effort against Japan."[16]

That evening T. V. Soong hosted a small dinner; Wallace, Lattimore, Vincent, and Hazard were all present. Lattimore particularly enjoyed talking with Wu T'ieh-ch'eng, once mayor of Canton, where he had put down a Communist insurrection, and later in 1941 ranking official of the air-raid dugout to which Lattimore had been assigned.

Back at the Generalissimo's residence after dinner, the four Americans talked late with Madame. Lattimore was startled when Madame Chiang "passed a remark, cryptic enough to slip by others, about my return of gift." He had thought, when he refused the five thousand dollar "bonus" Chiang had directed be sent him after his final months on Chiang's payroll, that his letter of refusal was "as grateful and tactful as I could make it." Now to have Madame Chiang refer sarcastically to his ingratitude was very puzzling. After mulling it over for a while, he decided that, in the standard Chinese way of doing things, the original amount set by the Generalissimo (or Madame) had been ten thousand dollars, and along the way somebody had squeezed off half of it. This would have meant that his reply, which named the amount, had to be suppressed, and Madame never received it. No wonder she was caustic.

In his diary entry for June 23, Lattimore notes: "Called early for unexpected interview with Gimo. He made some friendly chit-chat, then asked me pretty bluntly what VP trip all about. He obviously meant, in particular, was VP going to make a real drive to bring him & Communists together. Having discussed this in advance with JCV, I wanted him to take onus of any initiative in Communist rapprochement. Therefore I went into quite a long speech."

In this speech Lattimore dealt first with Soviet-American relations. Soviet resistance to German armies had turned American opinion around on the viability of the Russian government. Since postwar reconversion would require expanded markets for American production, and since Russia would need our machinery and techniques, "U.S. big business, finance, industry are pressing for an understanding with Russia good enough to allow economic confidence on both sides. There is not a whit of ideology in this."

He turned next to China, telling Chiang that "China will always be a main pillar of U.S. Pacific-Asiatic policy," but he warned that economically China would be a long-term proposition. Chiang should not expect too much from America. Then Lattimore talked about China's postwar dealings with her turbulent frontiers. His diary records:

> At various points during this discourse—the longest uninterrupted speech I had ever made to the poor Gimo—he would nod agreement or indicate that I should go on. Then I asked him several questions:
>
> 1. Will the Russians enter the Pacific War?—Yes, as soon as they are assured of their position in the West.
> 2. What form will their intervention take? Are they likely to attack straight through Mongolia-Manchuria?—Undoubtedly.
> 3. When they do attack, are they likely to win important & rapid victories?—Yes.
>
> I then shifted from question to statement. If the Russians win important victories as soon as they come in, it will change the whole map of the Pacific war. Therefore it is better for both America and China to have a clear understanding with them on cordial terms *before* they come in.

We then had breakfast. Afterwards I went into Gimo's room to phone.

He sat reading a paper and read out to me headlines of Nimitz' communique claiming a victory over the Japs at sea, east of Philippines, June 19. . . .

Then the morning's talk with VP. Finishing my phone call, I just casually entered the room & was present, without Wallace saying anything about it. . . .

At this interview were present Holly [Tong], Wang Shih-chieh, VP, JCV & myself. Holly did most of interpreting, with Wang or myself occasionally taking over. Holly, in interpreting a longish passage, is inclined to leave gaps. When he did, I boldly filled them in. Gimo nodded approval, & occasionally turned & asked me specially to interpret instead of Holly or Wang.

Evidently at this interview Gimo had made up his mind to show an attitude of generous cooperation, without waiting for pressure. He offered to give the US Army right to send observers—intelligence officers—into North China, including Communist territory. This is something Army has wanted a long time, & in itself would make VP's trip a success.

Linked not too obviously with this concession Gimo made a maneuver typical of him, in a way typical of him. He made a long, detailed & reiterative complaint that American critics—diplomats, the Army, the press—are forever urging *him* to make terms with the Communists. Nobody ever tells the Communists they ought to come to terms with him. Nobody ever brings up such minimum requisites as the submission of the Communists to unified command & military discipline.

To my mind, this is Gimo at his most Chinese. He wants desperately to have us mediate between him & Communists; & he will accept almost any real terms if in the outward bargaining we will save his face by making a noise about the degree to which the Communists ought to yield. VP completely fails to get this—understandably. Have urged JCV to hammer it home to him.

After the long morning session Lattimore went back to the OWI office in Chungking, where he met the Dilowa. His old friend was low in vitality and morale, but the U.S. navy doctor had given him a thorough examination and found him healthy. The Dilowa found conditions in Chungking deplorable, but he was very "positive" on events in the Mongolian People's Republic; the premier, Choibalsan, was a "good and decent man." The Dilowa told Lattimore that the Inner Mongolians were now leaning toward unification with the MPR and against both the Chinese and Japanese. Lattimore spent all afternoon with the Dilowa; he left reluctantly for supper at the Chiangs'.

The morning of June 24 Wallace and his group left for Kunming. Chiang asked Lattimore for his "last words of wisdom which I for once had gumption to avoid giving." But he did make a suggestion: the Generalissimo should send men such as Ch'en Li-fu, "calumniated by the Communists," to the United States so Americans could see what they were really like. This was an amazing suggestion. Ch'en Li-fu and his brother Ch'en Kuo-fu headed one of Chiang's vicious secret police organizations.[17] They were a cut above Tai Li, who was known as China's Himmler; Ch'en Li-fu had studied English under Lattimore's father and took a degree in mining engineering at the University of Pittsburgh. But he was known to be ruthless, and John Carter Vincent reported to the State Department that if Chiang were to create a viable and popular government, "the Chens and the Tai Lis must go."[18] Chiang did not respond to Lattimore's suggestion about Ch'en Li-fu.

Chiang did tell Lattimore that he "wanted me to come out on a trip at least once every six months. Found chance to put Madame straight on why I had refused gift (she said she never received letter). Out to plane, where I dodged farewells." It was, all things considered, a great visit. But if Wallace's respect for Lattimore's translating abilities went up, Lattimore's respect for Wallace did the opposite. Agriculture, nothing but agriculture, seemed to occupy the vice president's mind. Even in Chungking, nerve center of the most tortured nation on earth, all Henry Wallace could get excited about was crops, farming, and volleyball.

Leaving Chungking, the Wallace party flew to Kunming, one of China's loveliest towns and Chennault's headquarters. Lattimore noted the activities of their first nights in Kunming: "Paroxysms of volleyball, badminton, ping pong. I gave up and went to bed. Staying with Chennault, who very friendly." He stayed in bed the rest of the time there, as this diary entry indicates: "Kunming, June 25–26. Pretty blank for me, as diarrhea all the time. Would have been lovely chances for rural photos, too, if only could have stayed a couple of 100 yards from can safely."

Though Lattimore was sidelined, the others generated more than enough activity. In conference with Vincent and Captain Joseph Alsop, Wallace expressed concern about Chiang's request that Stilwell be replaced as commander of U.S. forces in the China-Burma-India theater. Vincent and Alsop were also sympathetic to Chiang's wishes: Stilwell's often-expressed contempt for the Generalissimo made Sino-American cooperation exceedingly difficult.

After extensive discussion all three agreed that they should recommend to Roosevelt that Stilwell be replaced. But who should succeed him? Wallace suggested Chennault, who got along well with Chiang. Vincent concurred. Both Wallace and Vincent knew that Chennault was strongly opposed to the Chinese Communists, who reciprocated the feeling. Recommending Chennault, therefore, was an anti-Communist act of major import.[19] At this stage Alsop intervened. He believed that no one could replace Chennault as air force commander in China and that General Marshall and other military figures would vigorously oppose his appointment.

There was a reasonable compromise: Lieutenant General Albert C. Wedemeyer, who was well received by the Generalissimo and his staff. Wedemeyer was not well known to the Communists; he was brilliant; and he was acceptable to the American high command. Alsop won the day. A cable went out from the vice president of the United States, to the president of the United States, recommending that Stilwell be fired and replaced by a far less charismatic leader.[20] Lattimore knew nothing of the deliberations or the cable.

Eight years later, when Pat McCarran ran amok with his Senate Internal Security Subcommittee, John Carter Vincent, as anti-Communist as any good Southern Baptist, was accused of serving the Communist cause by concurring in Alsop's suggestion that Wedemeyer, rather than Chennault, replace the irascible Stilwell.

The Wallace party left Kunming June 27, landing at Chengtu in Szechwan Province. There Lattimore saw a good Air Force doctor and learned that he would survive. He was particularly anxious to do so; the governor of Szechwan was Chang Ch'ün, a friend from Chungking's air-raid shelters, a man whom Lattimore liked and trusted. Wallace, true to form, divided his time between volleyball and agriculture. Lattimore had abundant opportunity to talk to Chang. Lattimore also wanted Wallace to talk to Chang away from one of the Gimo's agents, Huang, dubbed the Grand Eunuch. Candid conversation was impossible in Huang's presence.

Lattimore's activities in Chengtu were so extensive that his diary barely covers them; when he got back to Baltimore, he wrote additional notes that tell more of the story:

> At Chengtu Chang Chun talked to me in great detail about politics when there were just the two of us. Chang wanted to make sure the Americans understood that he wanted a revived United Front with the Communists, negotiated earlier, while the Communists were still weak, rather than later, when they certainly would be much stronger. Chiang Kai-shek's argument was that it was he, not the Communists, who had been getting Soviet supplies and that at the end of the war it would certainly be he, not the Communists, who would get American supplies. Therefore he was justified in toughing it out. Chiang's guns-and-

bullets arithmetic led him to underestimate the immense potential of peasant support of the Communists. To the peasants, the Communists didn't talk about "communism." They talked about "land." Chang Chun understood this much better than Chiang. After the war, when Chang Chun visited Washington, he found that my name was not on the guest list for a reception put on for him by the Department of State. He insisted that it be added—to the chagrin of the Department. . . . Quite unabashed, Chang Chun, in the presence of Department personnel, asked me to stay behind, for a personal talk, as the reception was breaking up. During the talk, he asked me if I would act as his personal, confidential advisor and consultant, writing to him about whatever I thought was important and dealing with any questions that he might raise in writing to me. I replied that it would be a privilege to work with him, and it was an honour to be asked, but that a question of seemliness bothered me. I had been an employee of Chiang Kai-shek, and he was still a subordinate of Chiang's. Would not a moral problem arise? A former employee and a present subordinate, working together independently of the man who had been the boss of one of them and was still the boss of the other? Chang Chun was enough of a Confucian to accept my evasion gracefully.

But at Chengtu, there was no private chat between Chang Ch'ün, Lattimore, and Wallace. The Grand Eunuch had also learned about Wallace's proclivities for strenuous exercise. Lattimore relates three separate incidents when he thought he had sequestered Wallace so that Chang could talk to him; volleyball or a race to the top of a nearby hill always intervened. One particular incident irritated Lattimore. On June 29, the party was to inspect the Min River Irrigation District, China's most famous and ancient irrigation scheme. Lattimore and Chang Ch'ün were down to breakfast early, hoping to talk with Wallace before the Grand Eunuch appeared. No luck. The Grand Eunuch was lurking nearby and challenged Wallace to a game of volleyball. Wallace accepted, and they played for an hour. When the trip to Min River started, Chang Ch'ün managed to exclude the Grand Eunuch from the car in which he, Lattimore, and Wallace were riding, but Wallace, tired from volleyball, slept all the way.

When they arrived at the foot of a hill from which the whole Min River operation could be seen, Wallace challenged everybody to race him to the top. From Lattimore's diary:

> Everybody followed him, trudging as fast as they could. The Governor and I looked at each other and stayed behind. We got back into the car and chatted. By the time the retinue got to the top, Wallace had got his breath back. He charged back down again, with the others not quite so

far behind him as they had been going up. Wallace's attitude toward this 2,000 year old feat of engineering can be summarized: He congratulated the Chinese on their enterprise far back in the days when there were not yet any Americans; but today, of course, it would have to be done with bulldozers, dredges, and all the rest of it. The Chinese could learn to do it, under American planning and supervision.

We then went on to a pleasant lunch, in a room which did not look out on the irrigation. Chang could not talk to VP, because too public, especially with the Grand Eunuch sitting as close as he could, listening with the bland intentness of a tape recorder.

One can understand why, when in 1948 Wallace posed as the great presidential hope of liberals, Lattimore stayed far away.

The party spent June 30 to July 2 in Lanchow. Lattimore wrote extensively about the inspections, dinners, personalities; but the highlight of his stay there was another meeting with the Dilowa. Since the Wallace party was to go next to the Mongolian People's Republic, Lattimore extracted from the Buddha every bit of current information he could get.

For a Mongolist who had tried so often to get to Ulan Bator and failed because the controllers of access, the Russians, would not cooperate, Lattimore's notes on the Mongolian stay of two days are remarkably low-key. He did record the topography during the flight and the condition of the fields and livestock, but there was no recorded exhilaration comparable to his first view of the Heavenly Mountains in 1927. Instead there was a torrent of political and sociological data.

When the Wallace plane landed July 2 at a field east of Ulan Bator, Lattimore descended first. Recognizing Choibalsan from photos, Lattimore greeted him by name. The response was immediate and warm. Lattimore wrote in his diary, "Choibalsan speaks very clearly, so I got off to a good start interpreting in Mongol."

Lattimore saw "many big, fine, new buildings, but quantities of [yurts] & whole quarters of rather poor, Chinese style courtyard dwellings." There was a huge hospital, much more impressive than anything he had seen in Inner Mongolia. His general impression was that the Mongols were running their own show and that they knew what they were doing. Russian influence was "very strong, but the kind of influence is 'how to do it' rather than 'what you must do next.' " He was told there were about fifteen hundred Russians in Ulan Bator, a city of one hundred thousand.

Surprisingly, there was still considerable private wealth in the MPR. The richest individual was said to be a woman in Kobdo who owned five thousand sheep and one thousand head of other stock. Her possessions meant she must have a large number of employees and therefore "exploitation of man by man." But the factories, such as the textile mill he saw, were easily nationalized from the beginning because they were something new.

Mongol nationalism showed strongly. So far as he could learn, the constitution, which borrowed from many countries, had not been translated into either Russian or Chinese. The "main stream of political thought, however, undoubtedly flows from Lenin-Stalin. . . . Seems to be no Mongol Sun Yat-sen. In the State theater, there is a small medallion each of Sukhe Bator & Choibalsan over the stage; but at each side of the stage a large medallion of Lenin & one of Stalin, each with a long quotation."

On July 3 Wallace and party got "the tour." The presentation consisted of a factory making serums and vaccines for animal husbandry, where "competent Mongol veterinarians and technicians" showed them around, with Russian "consultants" staying in the background. Then they saw three agricultural camps. The camps swarmed with healthy children, in contrast to what Stilwell had seen when he was there in 1923.[21] Lattimore inquired about the scourges of syphilis and gonorrhea, whose effects he had seen in Inner Mongolia. His guide said these diseases were under control except in a few remote areas. Lattimore believed it. At one camp he met a man who owned more than one thousand head of animals and whose family "pullulated with children." Lattimore regretted the vice president's presence on this tour. He found people talked more freely in their own tents, "but it's the devil to get VP into a tent. Only got him into one, & he was out again like a bat out of hell."

Lattimore noticed that most tents had Buddhist shrines "in their due place of honor"; but the only operating temple in Ulan Bator was a kind of "junk heap temple, with gear obviously salvaged from a number of temples. Only 10 lamas. Head man grizzled, portly, genial. No boy lamas. . . . As near as I can make out, policy is to prevent reincarnations of Living Buddhas & to swing people over to religion expressed in form of family shrines & attendance at public lama prayers at which the ceremony continues, but without the worship of living, human, ruling 'reincarnations.' "

That night they were entertained by the Minister of Livestock, who "turned out to be quite a fellow, well-read in structure of US Govt. He looks like a burly ox of a back country Mongol whom you would not suspect of intellectual activity. The whole crowd detailed to look after us are a fine lot. Average about 30."

The party left Ulan Bator on July 4. Dick Kight managed to celebrate

that most American of holidays by firing a volley from his pistol at day-
break. There was some alarm among the Mongols, but Lattimore easily
put their fears to rest. There seems to have been no ceremony on departure, nor did Lattimore express regret at having so few hours in the country he had so long wanted to visit.

They had one more stop before crossing the Pacific: Chita in the Soviet
Union. There Lattimore met a Soviet general who impressed him almost
as much as the Soviet general who bought Agnes Smedley milk on the
Trans-Siberian impressed her. This General Kozlov was "genial, tough,
confident." He had fought two years on the western front and was now
in Soviet Asia to train troops. He could not say they were preparing to
fight Japan; Lattimore wrote in his diary that Kozlov said, "We have
neighbors here who bear watching," meanwhile "unwinding a wink that
creaked like stage machinery. He admires our landing operations on the
Western Front."

The evening of July 4 in Chita the Russians showed a movie of Wallace's party beginning in Yakutsk and ending in Alma Ata. Lattimore
wrote, "VP now realizes that as far as movies go, cucumbers & alfalfa
have their limits."

This was Lattimore's last notation in his diary. There was not much
talking with Wallace on the way back; the vice president busied himself
with the speech Roosevelt had instructed him to give in Seattle shortly
after their return. Lattimore made no contribution to the speech or to the
report Wallace later sent to Roosevelt. If Wallace followed the "Party
line," as assorted ex-Communists later proclaimed, he discerned it all by
himself.

CHAPTER NINE

"Who Lost China?" Begins

Lattimore returned home from the Wallace mission July 10, 1944, just in time to follow the 1944 Democratic convention as it discarded Wallace and selected Harry Truman as vice presidential candidate. Roosevelt maneuvered Truman's nomination, knowing that conservative anti–New Deal forces were building in the electorate and that Wallace was a prime focus of their hostility. Truman was from the border state of Missouri and hence acceptable to Southerners; more conservative than Wallace, he was also a loyal party man. As usual, Roosevelt calculated accurately; he went on to swamp his opponent, Thomas E. Dewey, in November.

His successful campaign meant four terms to one man; no other president in the history of the republic had served more than two. It began to look to Republicans as though the Democrats had a stranglehold on the White House, and the intensity of anti-Roosevelt feeling increased again. At the time, few could see the coming rejection of so many of Roosevelt's policies, especially his efforts to build with the Russians that edifice of peace to be called the United Nations. In the euphoria of the last years of the war, isolationism seemed to be dying. When the New Isolationism (as Norman Graebner calls it) later emerged, it was built around concern for Communist triumphs not so much in Europe as in Asia.[1]

With his travels in wartime Asia behind him, Lattimore now turned to geopolitical concerns in a major way. Building on lectures he had given at the University of Omaha in 1944 and on the lecture "The Cause of Freedom in Asia," sponsored by the Mayling Soong Foundation at Wellesley College, he wrote his first book designed for a popular audience. *Solution in Asia* was published in February 1945; two chapters of it were carried by *Atlantic Monthly* in January and February. Judged by sales and prominent reviews, it was an immediate success.

Most of the themes in *Solution* had been sounded in earlier Lattimore articles. He continued, for instance, to emphasize the importance of the war in Asia, going back to the Japanese invasion of Manchuria in 1931 as the precedent for all that followed: Fascist aggression, democratic appeasement. He continued to regard Chiang as a coalition statesman of genius, not a dictator but a nationally revered symbol of resistance to the Japanese. Japanese occupation of China's industrial areas had weakened the Kuomintang coalition, making it increasingly a party of landlords. This trend he deplored, but he still assumed that Chiang had the capability of remaining China's leader and that the Kuomintang would dominate the coalition government he thought might emerge after the war.[2]

As to the Chinese Communists, he gave them credit for having a more nearly democratic structure than the Kuomintang, despite their doctrinaire base. And they were not, he argued, mere tools of the Kremlin. Lattimore did not believe that the Communists should be allowed to keep a separate army. "Once there is uniformity of political rights throughout China, under a government elected by the people, that government should enforce unity of military command and uniform conditions of military service."[3]

The Soviet Union would increasingly be a power in Asia, whether we liked it or not. Lattimore cited Wendell Willkie's argument with a Soviet factory superintendent who claimed Russia was democratic because he himself was infinitely better off than his father and grandfather. This economic interpretation of democracy, said Lattimore, gave the Soviets a "great power of attraction" to the subject peoples of Asia. This attraction did not mean other countries were going to go Communist; the United States still had "the clearest power of attraction for all of Asia" because, among other things, we had set a definite date for freedom of the Philippines, we safeguarded the rights of workers, and we gave our businesspeople "unlimited opportunities."[4]

When it came to the "solutions" of Asia's problems, Lattimore pulled no punches. He strongly endorsed the profit motive as the most effective stimulant to develop Asian economies: "an important step toward the solution of the problem is a policy of encouraging the development of independent local capital and industry in colonial territories. . . . the businessmen among the subject peoples are in the forefront of progress. They want political independence not only for itself, but as a step toward economic freedom of opportunity." The industrial nations should allow the new states of Asia to set tariffs allowing them to accumulate capital and build up industry.[5]

America's interests also demanded expansion of the free enterprise system. "We need political stability and economic prosperity in China so that we can invest our capital there safely and sell our products in an expanding market." What about the Russians? "Britain and America can successfully support their legitimate capitalist interests in China, and at the same time work in co-operation with the Russians for democratic harmony in a country in which the second-largest party is Communist." The Bretton Woods economic conference had set up the right machinery; we needed only to use it to obtain "the maximum volume of private investment."[6]

When Lattimore wrote a preface for a reprinting of *Solution* in 1972, he acknowledged error in assuming that the United States would have to invade the Japanese islands to win the war; he did not know about the atomic bomb. He also acknowledged overoptimism about the effectiveness of the forthcoming United Nations.[7] But his fundamental analysis of Chinese politics had stood the test of time. The Chinese Communist party *was* isolated and not a mere creature of the Kremlin. The Kuomintang *was* coming increasingly under the control of landed gentry. Where he went wrong in China was in his continuing faith in the ability of Chiang Kai-shek to reform his government, unite China, and render Mao impotent.

Other people were writing in 1944 and 1945 also. The most important one in the Lattimore story was Alfred Kohlberg, wealthy New York importer of Chinese embroideries. Kohlberg had been active in both the IPR and the American Bureau for Medical Aid to China (ABMAC). Hearing from Lauchlin Currie and others of widespread corruption in the distribution of ABMAC's shipments to China, Kohlberg decided to look for himself. In June 1943 he went to China as a representative of ABMAC. Not speaking Chinese, he was dependent on what his Chinese hosts told him and showed him; since his hosts were affiliated with ABMAC, none of what he heard justified charges of corruption. Toward the close of his Chinese visit Kohlberg met Edward C. Carter in Chungking. Carter was an officer of United China Relief, ABMAC's parent group. Kohlberg tried to convince Carter that ABMAC was doing a good job; Carter listened passively, promised nothing.

Kohlberg was now convinced that Currie, Carter, and other ABMAC critics were lying about the organization. He returned to the United States angry at what he had heard. As he told his biographer, Joseph Keeley, "To me it smelled like treason because I couldn't see anyone benefitting from these lies but the Japanese. The possibility of Communist motivation had not occurred to me."[8]

That deficiency was soon remedied. Kohlberg discussed his distress at the China situation with Dr. Maurice William, an ex-Socialist who had written a book exposing the fallacies of Marxist thinking. William believed the IPR was riddled with Communists and was behind the attack on ABMAC. Kohlberg determined to explore this accusation for himself.

His first effort was at the IPR offices, where (according to Keeley) he tried to buy back issues of *Pacific Affairs* and *Far Eastern Survey*. Allegedly he was rebuffed by IPR officials: the issues he wanted were no longer available. He turned to the New York Public Library, where he found his back issues and spent a year reading everything about China. Then he read the *New Masses* and the *Communist* for the same period. Kohlberg concluded that Dr. William was right: IPR and the Communists zigged and zagged together.

By November 9, 1944, Kohlberg was ready to clean house in the IPR. He sent a "rambling, confusing eighty-eight-page document consisting of quotations from *Far Eastern Survey*, *Pacific Affairs*, and various Communist publications" to IPR General Secretary Carter.[9] A cover letter said:

> Three or four years ago, you may recall, I resigned after a dozen years membership in the IPR. You asked me the reasons for my resignation and I told you frankly that I thought you had too many Communists on your staff. You asked me if I thought you were a Communist, to which I, of course, replied "No." You then told me that you did not question your staff as to their political beliefs: whether they were Democrats, Republicans, Socialists, Communists, or what not; that you investigated their qualifications and judged them by their work. This seemed to me at the time a very business-like attitude and I withdrew my resignation.
>
> After reading [a booklet by Maxwell S. Stewart] I decided to look into the IPR publications further. . . . As a result of this reading, I now attach hereto a lot of clippings from your publications, along with clippings from "The Communist" (Official organ of the Communist Party in the USA) and "New Masses" (another Communist organ), also a few other clippings that seem to bear on the same issues. If you will go through these, I think you will find that your employees have been putting over on you a not-too-well-camouflaged Communist line. . . .
>
> If you agree that a housecleaning in the IPR is long overdue, I will be happy to help. My suggestions would be:
>
> 1. Fire all the Reds, because the truth is not in them.
>
> 2. Adopt a policy of presenting facts rather than opinions. Identify the sources of your information.
>
> 3. Name a responsible body to determine policy. . . .

> I am sending a copy of this letter and the accompanying extracts to other members of, and contributors to the Institute, in the hope that many will read through the material and form their own conclusions.
>
> Very truly yours,
>
> *Alfred Kohlberg*[10]

Kohlberg's charges fell on unsympathetic ears. The prominent financier Thomas Lamont, for instance, "realized that the charges were perfectly silly."[11] Kohlberg's rebuff by Carter and the IPR trustees set a course for the rest of his life: until he died in 1960, he conducted a running crusade against the IPR and its alleged influence on American China policy.

IPR held its ninth conference January 6–17, 1945, at Hot Springs, Virginia. Lattimore was an active participant, registering his opinions in three familiar areas.[12]

First, he was clear that European colonialism was outmoded and wrong and that if the Western democracies waffled on this issue, only the Soviet Union would gain. Raymond Dennett, in 1945 secretary of the American Council of IPR, thought that Lattimore was a bit too vigorous in his attack on colonialism. It "did not sit very well with the British, French, or Dutch, who thought he overstated his case somewhat."[13]

The second area of Lattimore's comments at Hot Springs dealt with postwar Japan; his views were the same ones he included in *Solution.*

The third topic, his views on China, put him, for the first time, in conflict with his old friend Admiral Yarnell. Lattimore wanted the conferees at Hot Springs to press the Chinese about liberalization; Yarnell disagreed. An agenda-setting meeting before the conference proper shows this exchange:

Admiral Yarnell: But if criticism leads to the overthrow of the Chungking government, what will take its place? No other party is strong enough at present to assume control.

Mr. Lattimore: The more reasonable Chinese feel that Chiang's Government is the only hope for a continuing and stable government in China, but that it will be continuing and stable only if it modifies its policy; otherwise it will be overthrown.[14]

Here was the crux of the Chinese problem. Could the "more reasonable Chinese," the Western-educated liberals who were powerless in Chiang's uneasily balanced congeries of warlords, Whampoa generals, landlords, secret police empires, the Soongs, K'ungs, and Ch'ens—could these reasonable types actually gain any power without upsetting some delicate structure? It was a question answered by history in the negative. But as to the Hot Springs agenda, Lattimore won out. Chinese internal politics was discussed.

Much worry was expressed at Hot Springs about the ability of the Allies to hold together after the war, especially about relations between the Western nations and the Soviet Union. This worry was rapidly dissipated. Shortly after Hot Springs, at Yalta on February 3–10, 1945, the Big Three met in conference, and the publicity following that historic meeting swept all skepticism before it. Americans of all political persuasions rejoiced that Churchill, Roosevelt, and Stalin seemed to agree on a postwar program that would achieve what the Versailles conference after World War I did not: a permanent mechanism for keeping the peace.

But the euphoria following Yalta was short-lived; within a month Ambassador Harriman in Moscow believed that the Yalta accords were being brushed aside by Stalin. Steadily during 1945 the tensions between the Big Three began to grow. Roosevelt's death on April 12 accelerated the process. Lattimore especially was saddened by Roosevelt's death; obtaining peace was now going to be much more difficult.

On the day the Yalta conference convened the *Nation* carried an article by "Pacificus" entitled "Dangerous Experts."[15] The article attacked two Japanophiles who were instrumental in Allied diplomacy and whose views Pacificus believed had in the past and would in the future lead to disaster. One of those Pacificus attacked was Eugene Dooman, at the time of Pearl Harbor counsellor of embassy to Ambassador Joseph Grew in Tokyo. Pacificus claimed that Dooman "was primarily responsible for the execrable mistake in judgment which minimized the threat to the United States represented by Tojo's appointment in October, 1941." Dooman believed Lattimore was Pacificus; Lattimore now had a new, bitter, and powerful enemy.

Dooman not only believed in retaining the imperial system in Japan but also thought that the only elements the United States could rely on were business leaders, court-circle aristocrats, and bureaucrats. Pacificus ridiculed this belief: "If the policies of these minor Neville Chamberlains are put into effect, American and British influence will be found in support of the discredited imperialist ruling group of Japan." This was a mortal assault on Dooman.

The FBI ultimately spent thousands of hours attempting to determine the identity of Pacificus (and another pseudonymous writer, Asiaticus) to no avail. But his real identity did not matter. What mattered was that Dooman, at the close of a brilliant career, expecting to be among the top policy makers for the American occupation of Japan, was sidelined by the State Department; and Dooman blamed Lattimore.[16]

Dooman's suspicion was plausible. Lattimore did not write the Pacificus article, but he agreed with most of it. He also agreed with I. F. Stone, writing in the *Nation* of July 14, 1945, under the title "Pearl Harbor Diplomats." Stone carried the attack on Dooman to greater lengths, concluding that "Grew and Dooman were suckers to the end." Dooman no doubt believed Lattimore to be behind the Stone attack also. Both Grew and Dooman now became active in the American Council on Japan, carrying their anti-Lattimore views to other foreign service people, to the FBI, to right-wing journalists, and ultimately to the Senate. When Grew resigned as undersecretary of state in mid-1945 (to be replaced by Dean Acheson), Lattimore's enemies were sure that Lattimore had engineered the resignation and had wrested control of Asian policy from the Japanophiles.[17]

One does not think of 1945 as a year in which blacklisting of media talent was taking place, yet in May of that year, when the NBC Blue Network was looking for a commentator on Asian affairs, they considered Lattimore. To check him out they went to the FBI. The story is told in a memo from Clyde Tolson to Hoover, May 28:

RE: OWEN LATTIMORE

Mr. William Neal, of the Blue Network, WMAL, telephoned stating that an official of the Blue Network Headquarters in New York had asked him to see whether he could secure any information concerning the above-named individual who is under consideration for employment as a commentator as an expert on far eastern matters. Mr. Neal stated that the Blue Network had gotten into trouble because of securing the services of another individual who later developed to have radical tendencies.

After a check was made of the file I told Mr. Neal that while the FBI could not be quoted in any manner I would tell him very confidentially that certain connections and background of this individual were such that it was believed the Blue Network would want to be very cautious before utilizing his services as a far eastern expert commentator. Mr. Neal stated he understood the situation and was most appreciative of our helpfulness.[18]

So far as present FBI releases show, there had been no addition to the Lattimore file since 1941, when Lattimore was briefly put on the Custodial

Detention list because of his association with the Maryland Civil Liberties Committee. Nevertheless, the "check of the file" Tolson mentions shows that the bureau had recorded somewhere the following: Lattimore had appeared on a program with Frederick Vanderbilt Field; had attended several receptions at the Soviet embassy; was an honorary chairman of Indusco, Inc. (an American group supporting Nationalist China's industrial cooperatives); had spoken at an organizational meeting of the Maryland Citizens Council, a group supporting the United Nations; and was an associate of Pearl Buck in the East and West Association. These activities caused Tolson to warn the Blue Network against hiring Lattimore. Lattimore never knew of the network's interest in his services.

In 1945 Lattimore became increasingly concerned with the probability that Britain, France, and the Netherlands would attempt to reassert their control over their colonies. The Indonesians and Indochinese, as he saw it, would die to a man fighting the reimposition of European rule, and Britain's writ in India had also expired. He was fearful that any attempt at regaining these colonies would so embitter Asians that they would turn to the only alternative source of support: Russia.

Accordingly, Lattimore wrote his most powerful statement to date against a return to colonialism, which was published in the May 28, 1945, *New Republic* as "The International Chess Game." His fulcrum for moving American opinion into a vigorous anticolonialism was the reception given American troops returning to the Philippines. That country already knew precisely when it would become fully independent: "We had, in the Philippines,—and we alone had it—something politically much more important than 'loyal natives' fighting under American officers. We had Filipinos and Americans fighting side by side, for different countries but for the same loyalties. We had, in our period of defeat and suspended government, guerrillas who were both a military arm and a political movement. We had, when we came back, a welcome both as deliverers *from* the Japanese and deliverers *of* the Filipinos. We are having *from the Filipinos*, a demand for closer association, rather than clearer dissociation, which may prove actually embarrassing to certain aspects of our policy"[19] (Lattimore's italics).

Again, Lattimore's position was overwhelmingly pro-Western, anti-Communist: "What we have done in the Philippines is to show that colonial liberation can be moved forward at the instigation of the sovereign power, and that it can be made evolutionary instead of revolutionary." We should, Lattimore said, firmly reject the pleas of our European allies that reasserting control in Asia was "sound," while arguments in favor of freedom were "sentimental." And the Russian role in all this? The Soviets could gain strength in Asia neither by "Moscow guile nor Moscow gold"; they could succeed only if the European democracies were stupid.[20]

Lattimore's impassioned plea for a wise colonial policy probably made few converts. The leaders of the European powers were generally committed to restoring the status quo. And eventually, in Vietnam, the United States found itself financing a French effort to recapture that colony and ultimately fighting in the jungles against Ho Chi Minh.

Kohlberg was getting nowhere in his private attacks on IPR in 1945, but he scored a big victory by proxy in the public domain. Early in 1945 Max Eastman came to Kohlberg for material on the Chinese Communists.[21] Eastman was a former Trotskyite who in his old age turned to red-baiting. He had good credentials: two years in Russia, fluent in the language, nine years as an editor of *Masses* and the *Liberator*. As William L. O'Neill says in his sympathetic biography, "Russia was his greatest adventure, and explaining communism to the world became the great mission of his life."[22] In 1945 Eastman (along with J. B. Powell, a former journalist in China) turned to the arena where he feared the next great Bolshevik triumph.

Eastman and Powell put their call to arms, "The Fate of the World Is at Stake in China," in the June issue of *Reader's Digest*. The problem, as these authors saw it, was Communist propaganda weakening support for Chiang Kai-shek. Since the future of the world depended on the fate of China, China had to be kept out of Communist hands. Only Chiang could do this. Theirs was one of the earliest tocsins sounded in the "Who lost China?" debate:

> A flood of books, articles, reviews, news dispatches, lectures and radio broadcasts is pouring across our country dedicated to the sole purpose of confusing American public opinion about the situation in China. There are four main points in this deception now being practiced upon us—all equally false and all aimed at persuading us to abandon another 450 million people to the totalitarian infection spreading from Russia. *Deception 1. That Russia is a "democracy" and that China can therefore safely be left to Russian "influence."*
>
> OWEN LATTIMORE is perhaps the most subtle evangelist of this erroneous conception. Mr. Lattimore appraised the net result of the Moscow Trials and the blood-purge by which Stalin secured his dictatorship in 1936–39 as "a triumph for democracy." He now urges our government, in a book called *Solution in Asia*, to accept cheerfully the spread of "the Soviet form of democracy" in Central Asia. His publishers thus indicate the drift of his book on its jacket:
>
> "He [Mr. Lattimore] shows that all the Asiatic peoples are more interested in actual democratic practices, *such as the ones they can see in*

action across the Russian border, than they are in *the fine theories of Anglo-Saxon democracies* which come coupled with ruthless imperialism. (Italics in original)[23]

It was a cheap shot at Lattimore, who did accurately claim that Central Asian peoples were impressed by the advances of ethnic minorities in Russia. But the statement about "leaving China safely to Russian influence" was diametrically opposed to Lattimore's advice.

Deception number two, according to Eastman and Powell, was that the Chinese Communists were not really Communists and had no connection with the Soviet Union. Lattimore did not believe that and never said it. He always said that Mao was an ideological Communist, albeit an independent one. Eastman-Powell attacked Harrison Forman and Edgar Snow here; they could not attack Lattimore.

Deception number three: "That the Chinese Communists are fighting the Japs, and that the Chinese National Army is not." In hindsight this comment was not a deception. Both sides fought, as they saw fit, against Japan. The Communists fought more effectively.

Finally, deception number four: "That Chiang Kai-shek is a fascist, and that his totalitarian regime is preventing the Communists from establishing a democracy." Eastman and Powell never say who was peddling this last deception. They did not quote Lattimore; he did not believe it.

O'Neill, in his biography of Eastman, comes down hard on the *Digest* article:

> Here in a single article one finds almost every important error and prejudice that was to cripple Sino-American relations for years to come. Almost everything was wrong with it. The Kuomintang was not only undemocratic, which the authors admitted, but hopelessly corrupt, authoritarian, and incompetent. The "people's welfare" was the last thing on its mind. China did not have to choose between the United States and Russia. It was perfectly clear at the time not just to Edgar Snow but to most informed journalists that the Chinese Communists were genuinely independent, though of course genuinely communist as well, which not all wanted to admit. Snow, Lattimore, and the rest were not the molders of America's China policy. This article's attack on them foreshadowed the myth that America "lost China" partly because of evil journalists. . . . This unfortunate article, the worst Eastman ever put his name to, was a sad omen. Max was losing touch with reality.[24]

Perhaps. But the "reality" of future American policy was precisely the "error and prejudice" that Eastman and Powell set out to establish. Lattimore was outraged. He wrote to the *Reader's Digest* asking for an opportunity to reply but was curtly rejected. Edward C. Carter then suggested to Lattimore that the *Digest* be rebutted by a letter to the *New York Times;* Lattimore was to draft such a letter, and the IPR would edit it and try to get Thomas Lamont to put his name to it. This project failed; Lamont deplored the Eastman-Powell article, but felt himself too ill-informed to pose as an authority on China.[25]

Thus, the Eastman-Powell article was not contradicted by any equally prestigious source. Lattimore now stood publicly indicted as accepting cheerfully the spread of Soviet power in China. This indictment was a triumph for Kohlberg.

June 1945 was significant to Lattimore in other ways. On Sunday, June 3, the Lattimores hosted a cookout at their home in suburban Ruxton, Maryland.[26] As far as Lattimore knew, it was an ordinary weekend event, with three friends visiting him from Washington and two Johns Hopkins couples joining him and his family for hamburgers, conversation, and country atmosphere.

One of the Washington guests was Foreign Service Officer John Stewart Service. He had recently returned from China, and the Lattimores wanted to see him. Since they had invited Service to come up from Washington, Lattimore decided they might as well invite two others to come along. Lieutenant Andrew Roth, of the Office of Naval Intelligence, whom Lattimore had met once, had just completed a book about Japan and wanted Lattimore to look at the galley proofs. Rose Yardumian was in charge of the Washington IPR office and an old friend of the Lattimores. The three drove up to Ruxton together.

The guests from Johns Hopkins were invited casually; Lattimore, crossing their paths on campus, suggested they might be interested in meeting his Washington friends. The local guests were Professor Malcolm Moos and his fiancée and Professor George Carter and his wife. Moos was in political science, Carter in geography.

Lattimore did not know that Sunday that the FBI was tailing Service and Roth and would arrest them three days later in what became, to the China lobby, one of the most enduring symbols of treason: the *Amerasia* case.

Amerasia was Philip Jaffe's left-wing magazine; Lattimore had once been on its editorial board. By 1945 *Amerasia* had become strongly anti-Chiang. Jaffe was anxious to obtain the latest reports from China and had contacted Service on the latter's return to the United States, asking if he had any material that might be available for background use. Service, in accord with a common government practice then and now, loaned Jaffe seven or eight of his own reports on China. Service had himself classified these reports and requested Jaffe to return them after reading. Service had never met Jaffe before 1945. Jaffe and Roth, though, were old friends. Roth had written for *Amerasia* and was one of Jaffe's most reliable leakers of government information.

The incident that triggered FBI surveillance of Service and Roth was the discovery by the Office of Strategic Services (OSS; predecessor to the CIA) that *Amerasia* had printed large portions of one of their classified reports in its January 1945 issue. OSS officials were startled at this leakage of their documents and broke into the *Amerasia* office one night without a search warrant to see if other government documents were in Jaffe's possession. They found several dozen. The matter was then turned over to the FBI. Bureau agents trailed Jaffe, finding him and Kate Mitchell to be in touch with Service, Roth, and two others. Because of Jaffe's friendship with Earl Browder and other American Communist party officials, the FBI assumed that Jaffe was passing the classified documents to the Soviet Union. On June 6, three days after the Ruxton cookout, Roth, Service, Jaffe, Mitchell, Emmanuel Larson (also with the State Department), and journalist Mark Gayn were arrested on espionage charges. (No evidence of espionage was ever found, and the charges were reduced to illegal possession of government property.)

There are basically two versions of what happened at Ruxton. One version is agreed to by the Lattimores, Service, Roth, Yardumian, and Professor Moos. According to them, most of the party spent the day enjoying the Lattimore yard, admiring the Chinese objects in the house, eating hamburgers, and chatting; Service and Roth, though, spent much time reading and discussing the proofs of Roth's book. Lattimore also looked at the proofs for a while, and he and Service disappeared upstairs at one point, for, as Lattimore recalled, "a very interesting thing. Jack had been working on a quotation from Mao Tse-tung in that period containing some bitter indictments of the United States as an imperialist power, and he used an expression which baffled Jack Service. So he said, 'Can you make this out?' I couldn't. So we went up to my study to our dictionaries to see if we could chase it down. We finally came to the conclusion that it was peasant dialect from his own province, not current in standard Chinese. It probably meant something like 'rotten stinking of blood.' And this was the subversive problem on which we had our heads together."

In an affidavit submitted to the Senate in 1950 Professor Moos added that at some period during the afternoon Lattimore went out in the backyard to cut weeds with a scythe. Moos remembered talking to him during the weed cutting.[27]

A quite different version of the Ruxton picnic came from the Carters. George C. Carter was fanatically anti-Communist, and when the *Amerasia* arrests were announced, his imagination began to work overtime, as did his wife's. Though the FBI documents are partially sanitized, and though the claims of Carter and his wife show discrepancies, both of them reported clandestinely to Senator McCarthy after he got on Lattimore's case that Lattimore, Service, and Roth conferred for a long time over some documents. When asked what they were doing, Lattimore allegedly replied that they "were declassifying certain documents in favor of some friends." But the Carters remained in the shadows, willing enough to report secretly to McCarthy and the FBI but unwilling to testify openly or provide an affidavit.[28] Carter became a pariah on the Johns Hopkins campus and in the 1950s moved to Texas.[29]

After the *Amerasia* headlines on June 6, 1945, the case disappeared from the news until August. In the Far Eastern division of State presided over by Joseph Grew, however, Japanophiles such as Eugene Dooman and Joseph Ballantine continued to work against Service, John Paton Davies, and John Carter Vincent, all of whom were regarded as insufficiently anti-Communist. When the *Amerasia* arrests were announced, Dooman gloated to Vincent, "We're going to get bigger fish than that. Isn't it too bad about Jack Service?"[30]

Lattimore, stimulated by what he had heard from Service and Roth, became increasingly concerned about American policy in Asia. Chiang did not seem to be liberalizing his government, civil war in China seemed more likely, and the undesirability of leaving Hirohito on the emperor's throne in Japan was not acknowledged in Washington. Had Roosevelt still occupied the White House, Lattimore would have had little difficulty making sure that the views he and like-minded Sinophiles held got through to the top. Truman he did not know. After some deliberation Lattimore decided to confront the issue head-on. He wrote Truman June 10, 1945:

Dear Mr. President:

When Generalissimo Chiang Kai-shek, on the recommendation of President Roosevelt, appointed me his political advisor in 1941, the policy of the United States was to support a united China. There appears now to be a major change in our policy, which may invite the danger of a political and even a territorial division of China, and the further danger of conflict and rivalry between America and Russia.

Until quite recently, great care was taken to avoid any inference that America, in aiding China as a nation, was committing itself to all-out support of one party in China's domestic affairs. There now appears to be a fundamental change. Public statements by men regarded as spokesmen for American policy encourage many Chinese to believe that America now identifies the Chinese Government with one party and only one party, commits itself to the maintainence of that party, and may in the future support that party in suppressing its rivals.

Such a belief among Chinese may make Russians feel that America has led the way in committing itself to one party in China, and that Russia would be justified in following that lead and committing itself to the other major party. . . .

In the eyes of many people such a development would mean that America itself, long the supporter of China's political and territorial integrity, had initiated a new policy identified with the political and territorial partition of China. . . .

With the utmost earnestness, I venture to urge you to have America's policy toward China impartially reviewed by advisors who are not associated with either the formulation or implementation of that policy as recently practiced.

Respectfully yours,

Owen Lattimore[31]

Truman's answer four days later was typically brusque: "The Chinese situation is developing alright. The policy has been definitely outlined to the Chinese. The Russians and the British and ourselves have reached an agreement which I think is in the best interest of China. I would be glad to discuss it with you sometime, if you feel inclined."[32] Lattimore quickly accepted this lukewarm invitation, and a date was set: Tuesday, July 3, 1945, at eleven-thirty. Suspecting that the session with Truman would be perfunctory, Lattimore carried with him two one-page memoranda to leave with the president, hoping that Truman would endorse them and pass them on to the State Department.

Lattimore's assumption about the brevity of his conference with Truman was accurate. Truman was curt, just as in the letter. Things were under control. Lattimore remembered that he was in and out in a matter of minutes. He suspected that no residue of his argument remained with Truman. The memos Lattimore left were saved for posterity in the White House records, but there is no evidence that they had any effect. Compared with his visits to Roosevelt, Lattimore's session with Truman was inconsequential. It is no wonder that five years later it slipped his mind.

In view of McCarthy's later claim that Lattimore was the chief architect of our China policy ("as any schoolboy will tell you," added the senator), the Lattimore advice is worth inspecting. His first memo was headed "China Policy":

There are two alternatives in China:

1. Division of the country between Chiang Kai-shek and the Communists. This would mean, for Chiang, a permanent policy of getting American support, for which he would give anything America wants; and for the Communists, a similar policy of getting Russian support, with similar results. The eventual consequence would almost inevitably be war between America and Russia.

2. A unified China. To unify China, there must be a settlement between Chiang and the Communists and simultaneously an agreement between America, Russia, and Britain to build up China as a whole. The Communists would have to accept minority standing as a long-term status; but Chiang would have to give them real power within a coalition government, proportionate to their real strength—not just token representation.

In other words, we can have either a divided China, with Chiang having dictatorial power in his territory, subject to acting as an instrument of American policy; or we can have a whole China, at the price of pretty drastic political change, including limitation of the personal power of Chiang.

Unless he is certain of American policy, Chiang would rather have unlimited power in a small China than limited power in a larger China. He still thinks that America is on the fence, but will be stampeded into jumping down on his side, against Russia, if he hits the right timing in a civil war against "the Bolshevik menace." Influential advisers tell him that America is headed for a long-term conservative trend, with Republican ascendance, and that Henry Luce, Walter Judd, etc., have guessed the trend correctly.

The basic American interest is represented by policy No. 2. It can be successfully worked. Chiang is tenacious, but has shown in the past that he knows when to give in and try a new policy. But he will only play ball if America and Russia, with British approval, make it plain that they are going to be joint umpires. America, alone, cannot either coax or bluff Chiang into a settlement with the Communists involving real concessions; but if Washington and Moscow agree, both Chungking and Yenan will carry out the agreement.[33]

Notice that a China unified by Communist victory in a civil war was not within Lattimore's conception. He believed that even if Chiang failed to liberalize his government, the Communists were not a viable alternative—unless Russia came fully to their aid and the United States stayed out. The ultimate horror was not therefore a Communist-dominated China but a war with Russia into which the United States would be drawn.

The second memo, "Japan Policy as Related to China Policy," voiced his opposition to a "soft" peace for Japan and to the influence of the Japanophiles:

> Japan, politically, now banks everything on the hope of peace terms that will make possible a comeback and another war. The only possible comeback is as leader of an Asiatic coalition, under the racial battle-cry of "down with the white man." Therefore unlike Germany, where the principal Nazi underground will be in Germany, the Japanese underground must be largely in other parts of Asia. China is the key to this problem.
>
> Like Germany, Japan must also do its best to pit the Western Allies against Russia. China is also the key to this problem.
>
> Therefore, in China the Japanese problem is not WHETHER they are going to be defeated, but HOW to manage the process of being defeated to their own future advantage. The Japanese have already begun to handle this problem by seeing to it that their defeat contributes to both the political and the territorial disunity of China. Where they can manage to retreat in favor of Chiang Kai-shek and not in favor of Communist guerrillas, they do so. Where there are no Communists, they try to retreat in favor of provincial, regional, or warlord troops, instead of Chiang Kai-shek troops, so as to contribute to territorial disunity. They hope that if China can be led into both "ideological" civil wars of landlords against peasants, and regional civil wars of provinces against the Central Government, Japan will not be eclipsed during its years of postwar weakness.
>
> To counteract this Japanese policy, the American policy in China must work steadily for peace, unity, and modern political forms.
>
> At the same time Japan hopes that fear of Russia will induce Britain and America to be "soft" with "anti-revolutionary" Japanese big business, and to wink at the fact that big business in Japan is as militarist as the militarists.
>
> To handle American policy in the new phase, it is necessary to make adjustments to the fact that China, rather than Japan, is now the key to Far Eastern policy as a whole. In most government agencies at the present time the tendency is to find Japan-trained men in higher policy-making posts than China-trained men, simply because Japan used to be a more important Great Power than China.[34]

Could Lattimore's arguments have conceivably influenced American policy toward China? Certainly not the first one. Chiang was adamantly opposed to giving the Communists "real power in a coalition government," and when General Marshall went to China at the end of 1945 on his mission to mediate the impending civil war, he was instructed that in the event of failure the United States would back Chiang.

Lattimore's advice may have been unwise. Mao was not about to "accept minority standing as a long-term status." It is doubtful that even Russian pressure could have forced Mao to relinquish the autonomy of his army, as Lattimore believed he should be required to do.

The second memo, about Japan and the influence of the Grew-Dooman-Ballantine axis, provided some rationale for believing that Lattimore might have influenced personnel changes in the State Department. Within a short time all three of the senior Japanophiles were out of the department. But post hoc is not propter hoc; all of them had reached retirement age, and not even Grew claimed that he had been pushed out. Certainly American policy toward Japan did not conform to Lattimore's formula.

On July 3, 1945, James F. Byrnes was sworn in as secretary of state. The installation of Byrnes triggered changes all down the line. The *New York Times* of August 6, 1945, headlined "Byrnes Expected to Drop Four Top Aides. Grew, Rockefeller, MacLeish and Holmes Likely to Go in Wide Reorganization."[35] The forecast was accurate.

John Carter Vincent, head of China Affairs at the time of the Byrnes appointment, recommended Lattimore for a State Department job. The same *Times* article that forecast Byrnes's shakeup reported, "Also mentioned is Owen Lattimore, Professor of International Relations at Johns Hopkins University and an authority on the Far East. Mr. Lattimore, however, has had no diplomatic experience. A possibility also is that Mr. Lattimore will be named a special adviser on Far Eastern Affairs." It never happened. Grew, though about to retire, still had clout and vetoed Lattimore.[36]

Unfortunately, Byrnes's memoirs do not deal with the Japan versus China dispute among departmental personnel or with the liberal versus conservative positions on the treatment of Japan. Byrnes notes casually that Grew asked to resign in the summer of 1945, and he accepted the resignation "with regret."[37] Byrnes thereupon appointed Acheson to replace Grew as undersecretary.

Byrnes had no ideological agenda in wanting Acheson; they were friends and had worked together amicably. Byrnes simply wanted someone in whom he had confidence to take charge of the department when he was away. But Acheson was a hardliner on the issue of the emperor; he thought the whole concept of a head of state as deity to be anachronistic and took the same position as Lattimore that the emperor was part and parcel of the Japanese war group. This agreement was purely fortuitous; Acheson had never met Lattimore and was in no way influenced by him.

For conspiracy theorists the Byrnes reshuffling was a highly significant event. When Vincent was made director of the Office of Far Eastern Affairs a mere month after the Acheson appointment, the personnel changes recommended to Truman by Lattimore had been made. This coincidence was later held to prove Lattimore's power.

CHAPTER TEN

Kohlberg and the Pauley Mission

On August 6, 1945, the first nuclear bomb was dropped on Hiroshima, and questions about the effectiveness of psychological warfare against Japan became moot. The Japanese rushed to surrender; on September 2 General MacArthur presided over the official ceremony on the deck of the *Missouri*. One cosmic watershed had been crossed.

Less newsworthy but nonetheless highly salient to the political wars shaping up in the United States was the failure of a grand jury on August 10 to indict three of the six persons arrested in the *Amerasia* case. The jury did indict Andrew Roth, Emmanuel Larson, and Philip Jaffe; but John Stewart Service was unanimously cleared, and Mark Gayn and Kate Mitchell were let off on a divided vote. The failure to indict these three stuck in the craw of the China lobby for the next thirty years.[1] To use the vernacular, Chiang's supporters believed that the fix was in.

The case of Service was particularly galling. Service had written some of the most trenchant criticism of the Chinese Nationalist government and some of the best-documented praise of Mao and the Yenan Communists. How could he have been exonerated by a grand jury unless the government attorneys deliberately fudged the evidence against him?

From an objective viewpoint, the unanimous exoneration of Service is easy to understand. What had he done? He had simply loaned documents *he* wrote and *he* classified to a journalist. The practice of leaking such documents to journalists (frequently on background) was as well established then as it has been ever since. Service explained to the grand jury that what he had done with his documents was common throughout the government, and the jury believed him. Harvey Klehr and Ronald Radosh, using transcripts of FBI taps on the telephone of Tommy Corcoran, a lawyer assisting Service, show that Corcoran influenced government attorneys not to grill Service before the grand jury; this agreement, they claim, constituted a fix.[2] This is a peculiar conclusion since Radosh and Klehr acknowledge that "Service probably wouldn't have been indicted anyway." So what was fixed? The most that can be said is that "Corcoran's intervention spared him tough questioning in front of a grand jury."

Other developments in the *Amerasia* case intensified China lobby paranoia. Emmanuel Larson learned from his building superintendent that federal agents had been let into his apartment without a warrant. On September 28 he filed a motion to quash the indictment because the evidence had been obtained illegally. The Department of Justice was alarmed; Jaffe, the main culprit, could also file such a motion, which was certain to succeed. If he did so, the whole case would evaporate.[3]

The Department of Justice decided to act the same day that Larson filed his motion. They contacted Jaffe's lawyer, who had already suggested a plea bargain for his client. The government offered to let Jaffe off easy if he would plead guilty simply to unauthorized possession of government documents. The lawyer accepted. It was Friday. James McInerney, assistant attorney general in charge of the Criminal Division, found a judge who would work Saturday morning. On September 29, 1945, in an unusual weekend session, Jaffe came to court, pled guilty, and was fined $2,500, and the Department of Justice was spared the embarrassment of having a notorious case thrown out of court because of illegally obtained evidence.[4]

To hardline anti-Communists, this outcome was a perversion. *Amerasia* festered in the cold war years until they believed, as George Sokolsky put it in a broadcast of July 17, 1949, that "the *Amerasia* case was bigger, more important, and historically more significant than the Alger Hiss case."[5]

With the war over in 1945, Lattimore assumed that his government service was finished, and he settled down at Johns Hopkins to plan postwar programs for the Walter Hines Page School, of which he was still the head. Only minor provocations intruded on his academic activities; among these provocations was the Kohlberg article in October's *China Monthly*.

Alfred Kohlberg's "Owen Lattimore: Expert's Expert" is not as virulent as most of the Kohlberg corpus. Kohlberg acknowledges that Lattimore backed Chiang Kai-shek during the war and that he praised Chiang as a "world statesman, a real genius"; Kohlberg even gives Lattimore credit for giving Chiang's industrial cooperatives a pat on the back. But dominating the article are Kohlberg's usual slanders: Lattimore was a "great admirer of the Communist system" who wanted to "lock China into the Communist world system," and *Solution in Asia* does not "clearly reveal" what Lattimore recommended for Asian economies.[6]

Lattimore protested the article, and unlike *Reader's Digest, China Monthly* agreed to carry his response. "Reply to Mr. Kohlberg," in the December 1945 issue, argued that Kohlberg was so inaccurate as to be completely unreliable and set forth "what my attitude really is toward Russia, and toward Russian influences and interests in China." Lattimore wrote: "I do not believe that a spread of Communism anywhere in Asia (or indeed in Europe or America) is either inevitable or desirable. I believe that throughout Asia the desire of ordinary men and women for a democratic order which includes private enterprise and private profit is more important than the desire of minorities in each country for a Communist or Socialist order of life. More than that, I believe that the country which most people in Asia would like to imitate and emulate is America rather than Russia."[7]

After noting numerous inaccuracies in Kohlberg's account, Lattimore suggested that Kohlberg's quotations from *Solution* might "lead some readers to consult that book as a whole and form their own opinions" of his views. *China Monthly*, however, was not about to give Lattimore the last word. Lattimore's article ended on page seventeen of the December issue; several pages later Carmac Shanahan began a new and more virulent attack on Lattimore in an article entitled "False Solution in Asia." Shanahan had been a Roman Catholic missionary in China, and he had heard about atrocities committed by the Communists. The Chinese couldn't be gravitating toward communism, as Lattimore thought would happen if Chiang failed to liberalize his rule.[8] In Shanahan's three pages no single sentence acknowledges Lattimore's solution: private property, the profit motive, encouragement of small business, evolutionary development rather than revolution, and in China the continued leadership of the Generalissimo. Lattimore did not reply to Shanahan.

In October Lattimore got another call from Washington. The predator nations were defeated, and now justice had to be done for their victims. All of Asia had been savaged by the Japanese, and the victims were clamoring for reparations. Truman gave the task of deciding who was to get what from the Axis to Edwin W. Pauley, a prominent Democratic oil magnate.

Pauley's first task was to set reparations goals for Europe; this task he completed by September 14, 1945. Truman then instructed Pauley to lead a reparations mission to Asia.

Pauley had probably never heard of Lattimore, but on October 5 J. R. Parten of the United States Commission on Reparations wrote Pauley a memorandum: Lattimore was an outstanding Far East authority and should be invited to serve on the mission, selecting whatever assistants he wanted.[9] Pauley thereupon contacted Lattimore to see if he were available. Lattimore's response was lukewarm. Certainly he was interested in the project; foremost among his personal beliefs was the conviction that Japan had treated the Chinese brutally and should make whatever amends were reasonable. But another lengthy trip away from home, family, and job was not inviting. Pauley sweetened the offer by arranging for Eleanor to come along as part of the support staff; she had considerable experience administering IPR projects and worked closely with her husband on his professional tasks.[10] Mrs. Lattimore was placed on the Pauley mission rosters and received her travel authorization, but it was canceled because of the housing shortage in Tokyo.

The Pauley mission personnel (twenty-two including support staff) went on active duty in Washington on October 15.[11] There were briefings and a general staff meeting, and Lattimore took every opportunity to interview experts on Japan during this period. Before the mission left for Tokyo Pauley was confronted with unfavorable publicity about Lattimore that upset him. Walter Trohan's article in the *Washington Times Herald* of October 26 was headlined "State Department Sends MacArthur Soviet Sympathizers as Aides." Trohan did not seem to understand that Lattimore was working under Pauley on reparations matters, not as an aide to MacArthur, but Kohlberg and Eastman had done their work. Trohan wrote "Another Red sympathizer, if not a Communist, Owen Lattimore has been named a special economic adviser to Tokyo." Other members of Pauley's staff assured him that Lattimore was not a Communist, and the mission went forward; but seeds of suspicion had been planted.

The first contingent of the mission left for Japan November 1, 1945. Lattimore had been preparing a "Forecast" memorandum on the problems they would face. The memo was ready for presentation to H. D. Maxwell, chief of staff, when they landed in Tokyo.[12] The occupation, as Lattimore saw it on the basis of what he learned in Washington and from news reports, was going well; MacArthur had managed it with "great skill." The Japanese power structure was not monolithic, and MacArthur had kept competing groups off balance, exploiting conflicts between them in order to find those groups that he could use to support American policy.

All power holders in Japan, however, wanted to preserve their own privileges. Demilitarizing Japan and breaking up the Zaibatsu cartels would not be easy. In his memorandum to Maxwell, Lattimore fleshed out the ways of promoting entrepreneurship that he had first mentioned in *Solution*:

> Each negative step taken in demilitarizing Japan should be accompanied by a positive step which permits the formation of an anti-militarist interest group. It is no use trying to indoctrinate Japan with a democratic ideology based on words and arguments, unless the people who hear the words and study the arguments can see that they fit their own interests. Examples: Break-up of the Zaibatsu will be only temporary unless other ways of doing business are deliberately encouraged and given the edge, in such a manner that the Zaibatsu, when they try to recombine, will find that their principal obstacle is not an American decree, but the resistance of newly formed Japanese small-scale and middle-sized enterprises with interests of their own to defend. Possibly a start could be made by setting up tax scales with incentives for smaller enterprises and deterrents for cartels and associations.[13]

It is not likely that this memorandum had much influence. What Lattimore recommended was in line with established American policy for the occupation, but the Pauley mission was specifically charged with considering reparations.[14] Lattimore's role was primarily to relate possible reparations to the needs of Japan's victims, not to show how small businesses could be encouraged.

Two areas of Japanese industry were assigned to Lattimore for analysis: machine tools and aluminum. Both areas had been expanded for war production far beyond any possible domestic needs. By the time he finished his investigations, Lattimore had found the Japanese to possess approximately 850,000 machine tools, compared to the 1930 prewar stock of 150,000. The interim report of the Pauley mission (January 12, 1946) slated half the machine-tool hoard for reparations. In aluminum, the war-induced production was even greater. No aluminum whatever had been produced until 1934, when Japan was already deep into Manchuria. By 1944 nine major plants produced annually 152,200 metric tons of aluminum, all of it for the war effort. Japan had no bauxite, the civilian economy used little aluminum, and there was excess capacity in the copper industry that could be devoted to aluminum should civilian demand increase. Lattimore—and Pauley—finally recommended that only a plant or two be retained to process the estimated two and one-half years' supply of scrap.[15]

Aside from his assigned industries, much of Lattimore's attention was devoted to China. Here he locked horns with another commission member, Arthur G. Coons. Toward the end of November Coons gave Pauley a memorandum on reparations policy as it affected China. Lattimore disagreed with much of Coons's memo. On November 26 Lattimore presented Pauley with a document "in modification or amplification of Coons' interpretations." One of Coons's assumptions was that the United States should accept as a given that "Russia is pledged to support of Chungking." Coons apparently based this assumption on the terms of the recently signed Sino-Soviet Treaty.

Lattimore exploded: "Russia is NOT pledged to support of Chungking. Article V of the Russo-Chinese Treaty pledges non-interference in internal affairs. This has always been a thorny point with any country that negotiated a treaty with Russia." Russia had agreed to moral support and assistance to the Nationalist government, true, but in the context of the war with Japan. That war was now over. International lawyers could argue interminably about whether the Soviets were obliged to support Chungking against domestic enemies.[16]

If it were not enough to have caught Coons trusting the Russians, Lattimore found fault with another Coons conclusion: "We dare not leave Jap troops (or, for that matter, Jap civilians) in North China, if we wish to consider the victory over Japan complete." To this Lattimore responded, "I disagree. With the fall of Japan, the Japanese in North China are like a tank with no gas. The Japanese were powerful in North China because they were hooked up with Japan as a power base." The only way they could now have power would be to hook up with the Americans. Lattimore thought we should get our military out of China; then the Chinese would expel the Japanese quickly.[17]

Coons claimed, when interviewed by the FBI in 1950, to remember a controversy among members of the Pauley mission over reports that Soviet troops were stripping Manchuria of its industrial facilities. Coons believed these reports to be true; Lattimore allegedly refused to accept them because he was pro-Soviet.[18]

Lattimore did not recall a controversy over the accuracy of reports that Russia was stripping Manchuria. He did recall discussing probable Russian strategy with Martin Bennett, an engineer with the mission whom Lattimore much respected. Bennett was assigned to visit Manchuria for purposes of estimating Manchuria's suitability as a recipient of Japanese reparations. Bennett, as Lattimore remembered in 1979, reported that the Russians had indeed removed many industrial plants from Manchuria. But they had been amazingly inconsistent in their actions: "He said that some of the machinery had been crudely stripped, so much so that it was probably more damaged than useful by the time they got it up to Siberia. Others, he said, had been done with surgical precision and delicacy."

Bennett told Lattimore about a visit to one large, Japanese-built hydroelectric-irrigation dam. The Russians had left the dam intact but had carefully removed the turbines, which were engineered for that dam only and could not be used elsewhere. Bennett's conclusion as Lattimore recalled it: "Looking at where those turbines had been lifted out, the job was so beautifully done, those turbines are probably sitting nearby in Siberia, waiting for the Chinese Communists to win, and they will be put back." This incident reinforced Lattimore's skepticism about the Soviet commitment to sole support for Chiang.

Lattimore wrote another memo to Pauley on November 28, this one about "American public opinion on China and Manchuria." Many observers of the Asian scene were talking about a United Nations trusteeship for Manchuria as the only way to counter Soviet influence there. Lattimore felt that while Americans would object to Manchuria becoming a Soviet puppet state, they would also object to assuming responsibility for a trusteeship.[19]

Yet a third memorandum, written in anticipation of Pauley's trip to China, is headed simply "Situation in China," and it puts succinctly Lattimore's advice on that tangled matter. Lattimore begins, "You know already that I think our policy in China [intervening on the side of the Nationalists without requiring Chiang to reform] has been heading for calamity, so you can apply your own discount to the following." He then gives Pauley a preview of various proposals for aid to Chungking that Pauley would confront in China, all of them aimed at military defeat of the Communists. Lattimore knocks all of them down as unrealistic.

> Japan held North China for eight years occupying all strong points and the communication lines between them. This was not enough. Extensive field operations were undertaken. Still not enough. The Communists continued to increase, in numbers and still more in influence, right up to the end of the war.
>
> Into this area we are now helping to move Government troops. These troops, except for a few units, are inferior to the Japanese in arms, training, and morale. They were never able to advance against the Jap-

anese in large scale operations. . . . And yet, just because they have the prestige of American policy behind them, they are expected to defeat the Communists whom the Japanese were never able to crush. This is utter nonsense.

The intervention policy in North China could only succeed if we committed really large numbers of American forces to active field operations against the Communists. Politically, I do not see how we could get away with this. The reaction at home would be too strong. . . .

The whole history of civil war against the Communists in China proves clearly that every attempt to cure Communism by killing Communists only results in breeding more Communists than can be killed. Why? Because more and more middle-of-the-road people are pushed into the Communist ranks. Most of the people in the Communist ranks today are there not because they read a book or heard a speech, but because they were brutally treated, callously overtaxed, and denied elementary rights. . . .

In the Far East, we have got to hold up our end against Russia. We can't do it unless we stop pushing into Communism people whom the Russians themselves couldn't lead into Communism.[20]

And in that claim, Lattimore was assuredly right.

Pauley had now come to regard Lattimore as knowledgeable and perceptive; he put Lattimore in charge of preparing the official mission statements on treatment of the crucial Japanese machine-tool and light-metals industries. Likewise, the other members of the mission remembered Lattimore as competent and knowledgeable when the FBI interviewed them in 1950.[21]

The final Pauley commission report was based on the conviction that the Japanese had built up an industrial plant far in excess of civilian needs in order to arm their military for conquest of Asia. And despite the devastation of parts of Japan, Pauley found that "Japan still retains, in workable condition, more plant and equipment than its rulers ever allowed to be used for civilian supply and consumption even in peaceful years. That surplus must be taken out. To complete the demilitarization of Japan by taking it out will not mean the complete deindustrialization of Japan. I want to be very emphatic on that point." Pauley also found that the Japanese were not starving and in fact had a standard of living, even with war devastation, higher than that of other countries in Asia.[22] These were all positions that Lattimore wholeheartedly supported.

Pauley agreed with Lattimore that the Zaibatsu cartels had to be destroyed if Japan were to be set on a peaceful course.[23] Nor was the emperor to be exonerated; he was to be "deprived of the ownership or control of any assets located outside Japan proper." This was not a Carthaginian peace. As to the specific areas handled by Lattimore, the final commission report called for removing half the capacity for the manufacture of machine tools and for shipping any transferable facilities for producing aluminum and magnesium (which were then primarily used in aircraft) to countries Japan had invaded.

Lattimore was chosen to present two of the eight sections of the report to the Far Eastern Commission on January 12, 1946. The only other member to present more than one section was his friend Bennett.

However high Lattimore ranked with his colleagues, he ranked even higher with MacArthur's counterintelligence chief, Brigadier General Elliott R. Thorpe. Thorpe's job was to investigate all foreigners entering Japan. In Lattimore's case, the visitor made an impression on Thorpe sufficient to generate a personal friendship. Five years later Thorpe was vigorous in his support of Lattimore's patriotism.[24]

Six days after its presentation to the Far Eastern Commission, the Pauley group left for Washington, a final general staff meeting, and demobilization. There was some grumbling among Japanophiles, but the report as a whole was widely praised. Pauley commended Lattimore for his good work.

But there were journalists in Tokyo who were not so convinced. One of them, Dennis McEvoy of *Reader's Digest*, noted that Lattimore kept suspicious company: Jack Service and Edgar Snow. This bit of intelligence was passed on to Major General Charles A. Willoughby, who succeeded Thorpe as counterintelligence chief. Willoughby was a fanatic who dug out records on every New Dealer sent to Tokyo during the early years of the occupation. Three years after the Pauley mission, Willoughby's people gathered reports on Lattimore's contacts.[25] In addition to the McEvoy item, Lattimore was rumored to have seen Thomas A. Bisson, to have met with former Japanese IPR activists, and even to have interviewed some Japanese Communists. But Willoughby could not connect Lattimore with any known subversives.[26]

Elizabeth Boody Schumpeter could. She was still feeding the FBI her analysis of how Lattimore was helping the Russians. On January 5, 1946, the Boston FBI office reported to Hoover that Schumpeter had been to see them again, agitated by Lattimore's membership on the Pauley mission. She reminded the FBI that Lattimore was friendly with Andrew Roth of *Amerasia* fame, that he was a pal of poet Archibald MacLeish, that he was acquainted with Charles Siepman (whose sin was that he was a friend of the left-wing Clifford Durr of the Federal Communications Commission), that *Solution in Asia* was a pro-Soviet book, and that the Lattimores had joined the East and West Association sponsored by the subversive Pearl Buck.[27] FBI headquarters did not react to this latest from Boston.

Closer to home, but also unknown to Lattimore, reactionary trustees of Johns Hopkins, inspired by Kohlberg, began a campaign to get Lattimore fired. The opening salvo came from trustee James R. Young of Pawling, New York, in a letter to Provost Stewart Macaulay on December 1, 1945. Young noted that contributions to the IPR were drying up after Kohlberg's "remarkable job of research," and Johns Hopkins should expect the same as long as Lattimore was there. Young and many of his friends were intensely interested in Far Eastern affairs and "would like to see the Johns Hopkins take the lead but this cannot be expected if you have Lattimore on your hands. . . . I would most certainly recommend that from 1946 you clear yourselves of any connection with Lattimore. He is away now from your staff which might be a splendid opportunity to make the absence permanent."[28]

Provost Macaulay responded extensively, debunking Kohlberg and defending Lattimore. No beleaguered academic could have asked for a better defense. The most telling sentence: "It is my firm belief that Lattimore's presence at the University will bring us a great deal more money than will be lost, but even if that were not the case I would have no hesitancy in saying that a university, if it is to be worthy of the name, must continue to support scholars whose work is honest and original even though those scholars may have views which are not shared by—for example— the people who hold the purse strings."[29] It was the beginning of a fifteen-year controversy.

Also while Lattimore was in Japan with Pauley, Washington was startled by the fiery resignation of Ambassador to China Patrick Hurley.[30] Hurley believed that his attempt to bring the Chinese Nationalists and Communists together had been sabotaged by Service, John Paton Davies, and the rest of the foreign service China hands. It was Hurley's resignation blast that caused Truman to send General George C. Marshall to China to mediate the incipient civil war, thus bringing Marshall within the sights of the demagogue from Wisconsin in 1950.

CHAPTER ELEVEN

The Triumph of Ideology over Politics

The public sniping at Lattimore begun by Eastman in *Reader's Digest* and by Kohlberg in *China Today* grew steadily. Lattimore became the arch-heretic on what was now the most sensitive subject in American politics: China. He insisted that Chiang had to reform his government in order to merit additional American aid; he promoted a united front government in which Chiang would give up some of his power and the Communists would give up their independent army; and he bucked the conventional wisdom by insisting that Mao was not a puppet of Moscow and that Sino-Soviet conflicts would count for more than ideological affinities.

Lattimore did not realize at the time the extent to which geopolitics had lost ground to ideology in the United States. He had always been non-ideological, more pragmatic than crusading. He was not in the United States during the Red Scare of 1919–20 and had not experienced the blind fury of anticommunism that lay beneath the surface of American society.[1] He had been well schooled in ways of capitalist firms during his years with Arnhold and Company and knew that the bottom line was profit or loss. Lattimore extrapolated this hardheaded attitude to international relations; Haushofer was correct in talking about Lattimore's "ice-cold strategy."[2] Self-interest, to Lattimore, would always triumph over ideology.

He had good company in this belief. After the German attack on Russia in 1941 American ideological opposition to the Soviet Union began to give way to support of Soviet efforts to destroy Hitler. Even the right-wing press and some Catholic authorities came to approve Lend-Lease to Russia and full cooperation with the Soviet military. In this change of mood Americans were following the lead of Winston Churchill, who was as strongly opposed to bolshevism as any but who feared the power of Hitler even more. The American Legion supported aid to the Soviet Union; and in 1943 speakers representing the National Council of Soviet-American Friendship were invited to some American Legion and Veterans of Foreign Wars meetings.[3]

Many American business leaders also dropped their anti-Soviet attitudes to contemplate postwar sales to the Soviet Union. That country was in shambles; who but the United States could sell Russia what she needed to rebuild? Where but in Russia were the markets that could guarantee full employment for American industry and avert another depression? When Lattimore told Chiang in 1944 that the desire of American business to have an understanding with the Soviet Union in order to export American products "had not a whit of ideology in it," he was again correct. As late as March 1945 *Nation's Business*, published by the U.S. Chamber of Commerce, salivated over Soviet orders to General Electric, ITT, and Newport News Shipbuilding.[4]

American acceptance of the Russians as allies, however, was never monolithic. As the euphoria following Yalta dissipated, the Catholic church, the right-wing press, the American Legion, and the business community began an anti-Communist crusade supported by the FBI that by midcentury swept all before it.[5]

Bonnie Sharp Jefferson, in a study of the right-wing press during the period August 1945 through March 1947, found extensive and vigorous anti-Soviet coverage in the Hearst papers, the McCormick Patterson papers, *Reader's Digest, Time, Life, Catholic World,* and *America.* The Catholic papers were particularly incensed at Russian actions in Eastern Europe; the secular press was more concerned about events such as the Gouzenko spy case, the secret Yalta agreements, and the Soviet presence in Iran.[6]

And even as much of the business community was anticipating significant trade with Russia, the conservative wing of the U.S. Chamber of Commerce took an opposite course. Peter H. Irons describes the Chamber operation in some detail; here it need only be noted that in December 1945 the Chamber of Commerce Board authorized a propaganda campaign against Communists in American labor. Francis P. Matthews, an insurance man from Omaha who had been national head of the Knights of Columbus (and was decorated a papal chamberlain), was named chair of this effort. Matthews secretly hired Father John F. Cronin to prepare the first Chamber pamphlet on communism.[7]

The whole Chamber campaign was securely in the hands of zealots. It proclaimed that not just American Communists but also their bosses in the Soviet Union were mortal enemies. Matthews, appointed Secretary of the Navy by President Truman, was fired in 1950 for a bellicose speech advocating preventive war against Russia; the tenor of his ideology was shown by his claims that the United States was "the repository of the Ark of the Covenant" and that we were "the custodians of the Holy Grail."[8] Cronin was right with him; after investigating Communist infiltration of labor unions for his employer, the National Catholic Welfare Conference, Cronin made headlines by claiming, on March 10, 1946, that Communists had penetrated the federal government so deeply that there were 2,000 in federal jobs in Washington alone, 130 of whom were in policy positions. The next day five congressmen, including Edward Rees, Republican of Kansas, and John Rankin, Democrat of Mississippi, seized on his remarks to agitate for an investigation.[9] This was the beginning of the postwar resurgence of the House Un-American Activities Committee (HUAC).

Cronin welcomed the Chamber assignment. Eight days after his alarmist speech he wrote Matthews, "There are reasons to believe that Soviet armies may be on the march in but a few weeks. Christianity through much of the world is threatened. Within the nation, the Communist fifth column is functioning smoothly, especially within the ranks of government and atomic scientists."[10]

On October 7, 1946, Matthews released the Chamber of Commerce document, *Communist Infiltration in the United States*, over his signature, not wanting the public to suspect "there was any Vatican influence on it."[11] Although the Chamber's major concern was the unrest caused by Communists in labor unions, the newspapers emphasized claims of government subversion and the "cynical" betrayal of China to the Soviet Union at Yalta. Pro-Soviet foreign service officers were said to be responsible.

The Chamber report reinforced successful Republican efforts to capture Congress in the 1946 elections by using the Communist issue against Democrats. By the end of October more than two hundred thousand copies had been distributed, including one to every Catholic bishop; in November copies were sent to eighty thousand Protestant ministers. The report was instrumental in persuading Truman that he had to tighten government security; his establishment in March 1947 of a Federal Employee Loyalty Program was one outcome of the Chamber crusade. Subsequently the Chamber published two more anti-Communist tracts to which Cronin contributed.[12]

The beginnings of the inquisition were fueled not just by Cronin and other prominent Catholic leaders such as Bishop Fulton Sheen and Cardinal Spellman; Hoover and the FBI surreptitiously fed information to Cronin, and the FBI director himself took to the hustings to evangelize his own alarmist beliefs about domestic Communist power.[13] The American Legion joined in, as did the right-wing newspapers. An anti-Communist obsession ruled the country for more than a decade. Lattimore and other "realist" geopoliticians were inundated in the process.

Shortly before Lattimore left on the Pauley mission, he signed to write a weekly column for the Overseas News Agency (ONA), a small, British-backed purveyor of opinion about foreign affairs located in New York. He wrote only one column before departing with Pauley; beginning in February 1946 when he returned from Japan, he wrote his weekly commentary without a break until the end of November 1949. The ONA articles provide a comprehensive picture of his thought during this period; when the Justice Department in 1953 engaged four bitter enemies of Lattimore to "analyze" his writings for a Communist slant, 195 entries in the analysis they produced were drawn from ONA columns. ONA did not have a large clientele, but articles did appear in such major outlets as the *New York Herald-Tribune*.[14]

When Lattimore started regular production of ONA commentary in February 1946, the Marshall mission to China was under way. Lattimore approved of it. He admired Marshall, though he had never met him, and believed that the contending forces in China could be reconciled. As he put it on February 23, "One major aspect of that policy [U.S. China policy] has improved immeasurably since General Hurley went over the hill with an Indian war-whoop and General Marshall, with dignity and silence, took his place in Chungking." But changing the flamboyant Hurley for the sober Marshall was not enough: "There are too many Americans in China right now, running too many kinds of things. . . . Nothing goes on in China without an American advisor attached to it, or an American mission poking into it. Pretty soon the Chinese Communists are going to become the symbol of straight nationalism in China, because they are the only people in China who don't have Americans looking over their shoulders every time they make a decision" (February 23, 1946).

Lattimore had initially been worried about the continuing Soviet presence in China. On March 8 he complained about the "Russians swarming all over Manchuria." By the end of May the situation had changed. The Russians were out of Manchuria. Now the Chinese Communists were free of the "biggest handicap" they had among their countrymen, the "accusation that they were really not a Chinese political party but the agents of a foreign power. Today, the Americans are in danger of running into the same kind of bad public relations that the Russians had before" (June 3, 1946).

Lattimore sounded this theme repeatedly. On August 9 he claimed that the U.S. presence was "rapidly draining the 'reservoir of good will' which Wendell Willkie called our greatest asset." Lattimore considered this loss of goodwill a real tragedy, for despite his continuing belief that Soviet policies toward Asian minorities had been generally successful, and had created a "power of attraction," he had no illusions about *Chinese* attitudes toward Russia. In a long essay on Manchuria (May 7, 1946) he reviewed the history of Sino-Russian relations, noting that

> it is important to remember that fear and dislike of Russia are older and more established in the Northeast than anywhere else in China. The feeling is not primarily political or ideological. It is just plain anti-Russian. The first Cossack raiders, after overrunning Siberia, penetrated to the Northeastern provinces a little earlier than the landing of the Pilgrim Fathers in New England. Ever since then, the Russians have been regarded as a violent, uncontrollable and unpredictable people. The Chinese term hung-hutze, now a generally used name for bandits, literally means "red beards" and was originally applied to Cossack freebooters in the Amur region. The deeply ingrained fear of the Russians has, I hear, been added to by the recent behavior of Russian troops.

Chiang was beginning to squander this Chinese anti-Russian feeling. At the start of 1946 Lattimore still upheld the Generalissimo as a statesman with vision. As late as July 13 Chiang was following Lattimore's recommendation about policy toward Inner Mongolia and the vital frontier province of Sinkiang. There was to be a substantial degree of autonomy for these groups; and, reasoned Lattimore, if Chiang were easing authoritarian control over important minority groups, surely he would liberalize his regime as a whole, thus undercutting the demands of the Communists.

A column on July 19 emphasized Chiang's flexibility for maneuvering within the Kuomintang, where right-wing forces were pushing for military conquest of Communist-held areas and liberal forces were pushing for negotiation. Lattimore believed Chiang was too wise to yield to the war forces, knowing that were he to bring on a civil war, most of China would turn against him.

By August 24 he was no longer optimistic. John Leighton Stuart, who for fifty-two years had been a missionary and then president of Yenching University, was now U.S. ambassador to China and was pushing accom-

modation between Nationalists and Communists. But the government was
not listening. Lattimore observed, "The Kuomintang Government's insistence that 'he who is not with us is against us' has led to serious losses.
China's most important labor leader, strongly rightist for twenty years,
has now turned against the government. And a growing group of modern-
minded men and women, largely Western-trained, while refusing to go
over to the Communists, is also refusing to support or work for the
Kuomintang."

This was all grieving Stuart, and it grieved Lattimore.

By September civil war in China loomed large. Marshall's mission had
failed, Stuart was failing, and hostilities were imminent. Lattimore's analysis
on September 27, 1946, was prophetic but no longer favorable toward
Chiang:

> Both the Kuomintang and the Communists have to avoid, if they pos-
> sibly can, the responsibility for breaking off negotiations utterly and
> finally, and forcing a real showdown, but for different reasons. The
> Kuomintang want to make the strongest appeal they can to American
> public opinion; the Communists want to make the strongest appeal
> they can to Chinese public opinion.
>
> The Kuomintang are the war party in China. They have had monop-
> oly control over the Chinese Government, and they do not want to
> negotiate, because real negotiations would lead to a compromise, and a
> compromise would mean surrender of some of their monopoly privi-
> leges. They would rather fight, but they know they cannot fight suc-
> cessfully without continuing American aid. Therefore they must try to
> see-saw between pretended negotiations and experimental use of mili-
> tary power until, if possible, they have persuaded American public opinion
> that the Communists are a stiff-necked generation of vipers who have
> no intention of ever being reasonable. Then, they hope, the Americans
> will finally get mad and tell the Kuomintang to go the limit, with full
> American backing.
>
> The Communists are the peace party in China. The Chinese who are
> actual Communist party members, together with the regular Commu-
> nist military forces, are not strong enough to fight a civil war on their
> own. They survive only because they have the support of millions of
> people who are not Communists. These people do not want civil war;
> they long for peace. They will not fight to protect the Communists.
> They will fight only to defend their own rights and interests. They are
> backing the Communists only because they fear the Kuomintang more
> than they fear the Communists.

In 1946 such an analysis did not attract lightning. By 1950 it was proof of
subversion.

Things continued to get worse. As the Chinese national holiday on October 10 approached, Chiang, against American military advice, threw all his forces into an attempt to capture Kalgan (Changchiakow) in northern China. This was, according to Lattimore, a ploy to convince the United States that the Nationalists were going to win, so we might as well send them additional aid and speed up the process. Lattimore thought it was time to make a decision. Disillusioned as he was with the drift of Chiang's policy, he could not bring himself to say simply, "We should cut our losses and get out." That would open the way for Russian influence. His October 12 column was a long, agonizing statement of the pros and cons.

Staying behind Chiang was throwing good money after bad. Getting out would make us look like we were retreating under fire. Stalin was rubbing salt in our Chinese laceration, claiming that we were not "contributing to world peace in China." What to do? "There are two courses open to us. We can frankly ask the Russians for an undertaking that they will not come flooding in if we get out; or we can announce, as a purely American decision, that we have set up a definite calendar for getting out," but with a proviso that we could change our minds if the Russians did not cooperate. "Either alternative could be managed in such a way as to show dignity and a sense of responsibility, instead of the panic of a green gambler who has lost a foolish bet."

Despite his belief that the Communists were capturing an increasing support from suffering Chinese peasants and the disillusioned middle class, Lattimore did not believe that the Communists could win a civil war. He thought there would be a stalemate. This was his worst judgment during 1946, probably influenced by his lingering belief in Chiang's ability.

Throughout his 1946 commentaries on China, Lattimore never lost sight of his basic beliefs about the only way in which China could develop economically: private enterprise in a stable and peaceful environment. He made this point on August 14: "For us what counts in China is the future. To big business and little business, to Roosevelt and Henry Wallace New Dealers and N.A.M. conservatives alike, it is plain that no American policy in China can pay dividends unless the Chinese themselves make China safe for loans, investment, and trade." On November 16, appalled at the reactionary forces building in both China and Greece, he pled for support of the middle classes in those two nations:

> It is to these people in the middle that the attention of statesmanship urgently needs to be directed. Economically, they stand for private initiative, private enterprise and profit, and the responsibility of the individual. Politically, they stand for the integrity of the individual as the unit of society. . . . They are all the more important because, in coun-

tries like Greece and China the losses of war have largely wiped out
individual savings, which means private capital. In such countries, a
large percentage of postwar enterprise will have to be supported by the
State—and what the State supports, it will also inevitably direct and
control, at least to a certain extent. If, in these countries, we wish to
keep alive the element of private enterprise, and eventually bring it
back to health and vigor, then we must support these people in the
middle.

We are not doing so in China. Our aid and our money are going into
the hands of men who are in cahoots with monopolies which profiteer
on scarcity, with rings of speculators, and with black marketeers. Recent dispatches from Shanghai and Tientsin, China's two greatest cities,
tell the tale of independent businesses going bankrupt by the score. The
business men who are thus put out of business will not welcome their
sudden excess of spare time as an opportunity to rally round and help
the government prosecute the civil war.

Eloquent, but too late.

Other Lattimore columns during the year sustained themes he had already expressed. One was anticolonialism. He deplored Dutch and French
determination to retain sovereignty in Indonesia and Indochina and thought
Churchill's "Iron Curtain" speech little more than a plea for American
help in retaining the British Empire. Later in the year when the Attlee
government decided to free India, he applauded. He continued his distrust
of the Japanese emperor and industrialists and praised MacArthur consistently for reining them in.

And a continuing major concern was for the welfare of the Mongols in
China. Early in the year, as we have seen, Lattimore thought Chiang
would deal with them generously. His contacts with Mongols in China
now led him to believe that they most wanted home rule in a nonexploitive China; they would not opt for union with the Mongolian People's
Republic unless the Chinese repressed them (March 29). Chiang's statements to the contrary, what Lattimore learned from returning observers
was that the Chinese had behaved as conquerors and carpetbaggers in
Inner Mongolia. He became increasingly pessimistic about the outcome.
As to the Mongolian People's Republic, he strongly urged U.S. recognition and admission to the United Nations. This approach, he felt, would
decrease Mongolian dependence on Moscow (September 6).

Lattimore's interest in the Mongols led to a major project of the Page
School. Working through the American embassy in China, he contacted
two young Mongols who had fled their homes when the Communists

took over and who in 1946 were working for the Nationalist government. Both were fluent in Mongol, Mandarin, and Japanese; both feared that opportunities for professional study of the Mongol language and culture would be minimal under the Nationalists, and they were both on the Communist list of traitors. Lattimore applied to the American Council of Learned Societies for a grant to bring them to Johns Hopkins. Eventually he succeeded, and in 1948 John (Gombojab) Hangin and Peter (Urgunge) Onon left China just ahead of the Communist forces sweeping into Nanking.

But the Page School, and Mongol scholarship, were not high-priority items in 1946 America. The highest priority was already anticommunism. Lending credibility to the Chamber of Commerce crusade was the announcement on February 15 by the Canadian government that a cipher clerk in the Soviet embassy in Ottawa, Igor Gouzenko, had defected, bringing with him extensive files that proved a Soviet espionage ring operated successfully in Canada; more important, the ring had links to similar rings in the United States and Britain. Twenty-two persons were arrested in Canada.[15]

The Gouzenko revelations built on the foundation of the *Amerasia* case. Frank C. Waldrop, a Hearst columnist whose article "How Come?" appeared in the *Washington Times-Herald* on June 6, 1946, quickly linked Lattimore to *Amerasia* and to the State Department. State was using Lattimore as an "instructor" in its lecture series for young career diplomats. (Lattimore lectured for the State Department precisely once.) Lattimore, said Waldrop, was a "bosom pal of Henry Wallace" and had been on the editorial board of *Amerasia*.

The day after Waldrop's column appeared, a House subcommittee under Sam Hobbs of Alabama, charged with investigating *Amerasia*, picked up Waldrop's challenge. It would now add to its agenda, according to the *Baltimore News-Post*, "an inquiry into reasons why Owen Lattimore, Hopkins University school director, former member of the *Amerasia* editorial board, is a current instructor of budding young diplomats in the State Department."[16] The *News-Post* also publicized for the first time a HUAC finding on Lattimore: he had "five listings in the index of Communist front organizations issued by the former Dies House Committee on Un-American Activities." Lattimore responded that this was the first he had heard of any such HUAC listing and commented that the "notion that I might be a Communist is utterly ridiculous. Of course, I am not." The same charges appeared again a month later in the *Chicago Journal of Commerce*.[17]

HUAC, under the nominal chairmanship of Representative John S. Wood of Georgia but really run by Representative John E. Rankin of Mississippi and J. Parnell Thomas of New Jersey, scored an unrecognized triumph in 1946. It had achieved permanent status as a regular committee of the House at the beginning of the Seventy-Ninth Congress and was receiving hefty appropriations to carry out its investigations; nevertheless, it seemed to be floundering until October 1946. In that month, as Walter Goodman describes it, the committee

> reached out and grasped the life buoy of Louis F. Budenz. Budenz, preeminent example of the fervent Communist turned fervent Catholic anti-Communist, was like a tourist who is drawn to the shabbiest sections of all the towns he visits. As a Communist, he was managing editor of the *Daily Worker*; as an anti-Communist since his break in 1945, he became a star performer for the passionate right. It was his inclination to melodrama that brought him to the Committee's attention in the fall of 1946. On Sunday, October 13, he delivered a radio talk in Detroit, in which he said that American Communists took their orders from a secret agent of the Kremlin. The disclosure was made in the language of *The Shadow:* "This man never shows his face. Communist leaders never see him, but they follow his orders or suggestions implicitly." On Tuesday Thomas announced that Budenz would testify before the Un-American Activities Committee.[18]

Until then Budenz had confined his attacks on his former comrades to the occasional speech and to debriefing by the FBI. He was at first nervous about entering the hurly-burly of congressional hearings; he requested, and was granted, a delay in his appearance until after the congressional elections.

The midterm elections of 1946 demonstrated that the tide was running strong for any who pursued anticommunism. Republican National Chairman B. Carroll Reece set the election theme in June: the choice that confronted Americans that year was between "Communism and Republicanism." The Democrats, said Reece, "were committed to the Soviet Union." House of Representatives Republican leader Joseph W. Martin of Massachusetts claimed the night before the election, "The people will vote tomorrow between chaos, confusion, bankruptcy, state socialism or Communism, and the preservation of our American life."[19] In California an unknown Richard M. Nixon defeated the Democratic incumbent, Jerry Voorhis (who had resigned from HUAC in disgust), by red-baiting. Voorhis was alleged to follow the Moscow line.

None of these politicians approached the anti-Communist venom of a

Republican candidate for the Senate in Wisconsin. Joseph McCarthy, and the newspapers supporting him, fraudulently attacked his Democratic opponent, Howard McMurray, as a Communist fellow traveller. McMurray had been endorsed, to his horror, by the Wisconsin Communist party, an endorsement that he promptly repudiated. The repudiation made no difference. McCarthy took the endorsement and ran with it, losing no opportunity to portray McMurray as disloyal. Joe McCarthy did not discover communism as a political issue in 1950. He had used it four years earlier.[20]

The Republicans swamped the Democrats that November. For the first time since Hoover was president, they controlled the Congress. The number of Democrats in the House fell from 242 to 188, in the Senate from 56 to 45.

HUAC, though still controlled by the Democrats in the fall of 1946, lost no time in capitalizing on the new respectability of red-baiting. J. Parnell Thomas, slated to become chair, and his South Dakota colleague Karl Mundt, took the lead in pressing their new mandate when Louis Budenz appeared before the committee November 22. As Walter Goodman tells it, Budenz

> reviewed his ten years in the Communist Party, apologized for his infatuation, and discussed, in an informed way, the C.P.'s subservience to Moscow and the tactical disbanding of the Communist International early in the war. Rankin, Mundt, and Thomas, like handlers of a skilled but insufficiently bloodthirsty boxer, did their best during most of their three and a half hours together to free him of what inhibitions he may have had over turning the hearings into an anti-Communist rally. "I think the distinction you are trying to make, Mr. Budenz," Mundt drew him on gently, "is that what they actually have in Russia is not the Communism of Marx and Engels, but a dictatorship, and Communism under which people are denied a great many things under the concepts of Communism."[21]

Budenz obliged. As the hearing went on, he became less cautious. And he learned two things on November 22. He sensed first that an appearance before Congress was an attractive medium in which to display his newfound righteousness, and second that he would find a sympathetic audience. And he learned that he need not pull his punches in this protected environment, where he was shielded from libel. In fact, the congressmen who queried him wanted every bit of melodrama he could provide.

Harry Truman issued his order creating the Temporary Commission on Employee Loyalty on November 25. It was too little and too late. The

day after Truman's order, Parnell Thomas announced that the election
results had given Congress new marching orders: *they* were to uncover
and expose Communists of all hues in government, unions, Hollywood,
education, and the atomic establishment. The New Deal was a Communist project and New Dealers were intrinsically subversive. HUAC set off
in what Goodman accurately describes as a "frenzy."[22]

CHAPTER TWELVE

Cold War Declared

Lattimore did not welcome the increasing hostility between Russia and the West. He thought opportunities for improving the life of the world's downtrodden decreased as unsettled political conditions interfered with economic development. He was convinced of the truth of the peasant saying "When elephants fight, the grass gets trampled." The minority peoples on the Sino-Soviet border, especially the Mongols, stood to lose by conflict between the great powers. As to China, its welfare could only be assured by Soviet-American cooperation in preventing civil war. In 1947 he thought that the United States could induce Chiang, and the Soviets Mao, to moderate their ambitions.

The failure of the Marshall mission to dampen the flames in China, signaled clearly in the report issued by the general January 8, grieved Lattimore. The worst characteristics of both the Kuomintang and the Communists seemed to be ascendant. But he gave Marshall credit for trying and approved Marshall's appointment as secretary of state. Marshall was a far-sighted statesman, and, in Lattimore's opinion, "He has never succumbed to either the tradition of contempt for the British or the tradition of implacable hate for the Russians which are characteristic of many of our professional Army and Navy men; but there is not the slightest danger that he will be taken into camp by either the Russians or the British."[1]

Lattimore did not approve of the call to arms that publicly signaled the breach between East and West: the Truman Doctrine speech of March 22. It was largely negative, phrasing George Kennan's containment thesis in military terms. In a dozen different ways Lattimore deplored any policy

that was merely anti-Soviet. In the Asia he knew, such a policy was bound
to fail.

The Marshall Plan, in contrast, offered opportunities for the little nations on both sides of the East-West divide to benefit. Lattimore was hor-
rified when Molotov was instructed to pull the Soviet and East European
delegates out of the Paris conference to implement the Marshall Plan.
This withdrawal left economic reconstruction to competing and hostile
blocs (July 12).

Even worse was the demand of the colonial powers (especially France
and the Netherlands) that the colonies over which they exercised a shaky
sovereignty be integrated into European Economic Community plans. Their
proposal, that each European country and its colonial possessions should
be considered as one unit for the use of American credits,

> implies an important modification of the United States policy of secur-
> ing free circulation and unlimited competitive opportunity for the
> American dollar. Under it, most American dollars would not enter a
> colonial country directly. They would first enter an imperial country.
> There they would be taken up by banks and industries, which would
> then draw on the raw materials of the colonial possessions to revive
> European production and trade. Thus in the long run the colonial peo-
> ples would foot the bill for the revival of Europe. . . . [This proposal]
> implies confirming and stabilizing all the surviving institutions of co-
> lonial rule. (August 8)

But it was not possible to perpetuate colonial rule. Its time was past.
As Lattimore foresaw, neither the glamorous French Foreign Legion nor
the stolid Dutch conscripts were a match for the crusading nationalisms
of Asia. Hence the diversion of aid to suppress colonial rebellion was intrinsically counterproductive.

Here the United States faced a dilemma. France's strategic location, and
the rhetoric of the Truman Doctrine, affected the conditions under which
Marshall Plan aid could be dispensed. The United States had to have France
on board, and probably Holland too.

> [Yet] by being too eager-beaver about the anti-Communist and stop-
> Russia aims of our policy (which in themselves are perfectly sound and
> statesmanlike aims), we have got ourselves stuck with the support of
> governments which are more and more undisguisedly governing not
> only against the Communists but against most of the people. . . . In
> Western Europe we still have a chance to support governments that
> govern with the people instead of against the people. . . .

But France, in Indochina, and Holland, in Indonesia, are trying to slug it out against the nationalism of their unwilling subjects. The colonial military expenditures of these two countries are dangerous ratholes in the Marshall Plan for Western Europe. Through them, millions and even billions of the American dollars intended to restart the wheels of economic life in Europe may leak away in futile slaughter in Asia. (December 20)

The Indonesians eventually repelled Dutch attempts to reassert sovereignty and massacred a threatening Communist party. The French held out in Indochina until after the Battle of Dien Bien Phu in 1954. By then the United States had sunk so much into France's war in Indochina that it could not break itself of the habit; unable to cut its losses, it kept wasting money and blood for two long decades. In 1947 nobody foresaw the consequences of this perversion of the Marshall Plan better than Lattimore did.

In China things were quite different from Europe. The dollar aid that Lattimore saw as helping to revive Europe would do no good in China, where Chiang's regime was rapidly losing the mandate of heaven. There was no alternative non-Communist group for the United States to support. The Chinese Communists were not so much winning as Chiang was throwing his control away. During 1947 and 1948 the reality of Nationalist rule was too painful for Lattimore to contemplate. The world-class leader whom he had once praised now presided over a regime whose weaknesses were lethal. Here is how things looked to one observer: "To tell the truth, never, in China or abroad, has there been a revolutionary party as decrepit and degenerate as [the Kuomintang] today; nor one as lacking spirit, lacking discipline, and even more, lacking standards of right and wrong. . . . This kind of party should long ago have been destroyed and swept away." Officers were indifferent to the condition of their men:

> They so ignored such basic elements in their training as aiming, firing, reconnoitering and liaison that the soldiers' combat skills are so poor that they cannot fight. Nor did they provide the troops with adequate food, clothing or medical care, even embezzling supplies meant for the men. . . . the spirit of most commanders is broken and their morality is base. High-level officers [have] become complacent in their high posts, encumbered by family members, and acting like warlords. As a consequence, their revolutionary spirit is almost completely dissipated, and they are concerned only with preserving their military strength and resources. . . . But the chief reason, which cannot be denied, arose from the paralysis of the party: the membership, organizational structure

and method of leadership all created problems. Thus, the party became a lifeless shell; the government and military also lost their soul; with the result that the troops collapsed and society disintegrated. . . . And especially, [the troops] were ignorant of the need to protect and unite with the people, even unrestrainedly harassing them.[2]

Not a pretty picture—*but it is not Lattimore's picture.* Both quotations are drawn from *Chiang Kai-shek's condemnation of his own regime,* as found in the Taiwan archives during the 1970s by Lloyd Eastman. Eastman's 1981 article in *China Quarterly* was the first to explore what Chiang himself thought in the late 1940s about the reasons for the downfall of his regime. As reluctant testimony, this is of the highest order: *Chiang lost China.*

Stories of incompetence, corruption, low morale, and plundering by Nationalist soldiers were only beginning to filter out of China in 1947. Lattimore searched avidly for information that would justify his continuing hope that Chiang would be able to carry out the reforms that alone could stave off Communist conquest; such information was not there. His ONA articles during 1947 document his increasing disillusionment.

In January, Lattimore commented on the significance of recent student demonstrations against the Nationalist regime; Chinese students had always been harbingers of change. In February, Lattimore pointed out the great advantage Mao had because he was independent of foreign support, whereas the Chinese believed Chiang to be propped up by Americans. (There was a long statement of how the Russians had "lost" China in earlier years by too obviously supporting Chinese Communists, a theme that Lattimore had developed before and one that Harrison Salisbury brilliantly articulated in 1971.)[3] On March 1, Lattimore commented on discontent among Chinese air force officers, a group that should have had the highest morale.

Also in March, Lattimore emphasized Mao's skill at capturing the allegiance of peasants, a class that Chiang unfortunately neglected. On March 28, he noted that "of all the Communist movements in the world the Chinese Communist movement is the most independent of Moscow," a conclusion that most Americans would not accept for many years. On April 11, he noted with sadness the condition of Taiwan, where Nationalist forces massacred thousands of native Taiwanese who were protesting Kuomintang policies. He also deplored the situation of small businessmen, both Chinese and American, in Chiang's China: "if you want to get the deepest, most malodorous dirt on the corruption of the Kuomintang in China today, and want to be sure it is not from an ideologically tainted source, you should go to an American businessman from one of the kinds of business that is getting the squeeze put on it." The plight of minorities was Lattimore's theme on March 24: Chiang "saw the wisdom" of a policy giving the Mongols and others a high degree of autonomy but was unable to carry it out because of powerful warlords.

An article published June 4 presents perhaps the best summary of what Lattimore believed Chiang was up to.

> The seriousness of the civil war crisis in China is beyond all concealment. Indeed, the Chinese Government is not trying to hide it, but is hoping that Washington will be stampeded by the seriousness of the situation into renewed and large scale intervention. What would suit Nanking best of all would be to have the Americans again bring Kuomintang troops by air and sea into Manchuria, to circumvent the Communist-led forces which have cut the railways.
>
> Nanking hopes for a dramatic move like this in the belief that it would provoke a crisis between America and Russia. The Kuomintang wants an American-Russian crisis because the civil war in China has become completely unjustifiable unless it can be re-dramatized as a "Spanish" war, with America backing one side and Russia the other.

This outcome was what Lattimore had warned Truman about in 1945.

Manchuria was again his subject on July 8, 1947. Southern Chinese carpetbaggers had totally failed to secure the support of Manchurians for the Chiang government. In August, Lattimore talked with Ch'en Chiak'ang, a Chinese Communist delegate to the World Youth Festival in Prague. Ch'en described how the Communists were subverting Nationalist troops sent north to conquer Manchuria.

> "It is quite simple," Chen said. "We isolate the officers. Then we assemble the men in mass meetings and invite anybody who feels like it to describe 'How I came to be in the army.' One story after another describes how the poor are dragged away from the villages by the Kuomintang while the landlords' sons escape service. Pretty soon they are all so sore that they come over to our side. Or, if they feel like it, we give them some money and food and tell them to go home—if they can escape the Kuomintang conscription gangs. It's wonderful advertising." (August 29)

By November 1, Lattimore could title one of his ONA articles "Aid to Kuomintang Is Blind Alley": "The fact that the Kuomintang just doesn't have what it takes is, incidentally, the answer to the threadbare argument that we have to try and stop Russia with the Kuomintang. This is too much like arguing that, in order to stop Russia, we had better start equipping the Army with plenty of muzzle-loading, flint-lock, smooth-bore guns. Even a weak coalition government in China would be better for us than the Kuomintang."

But Lattimore's disenchantment with the Nationalist government was not as complete or as vigorous as that of observers who had been in China more recently. One such observer, Professor Nathaniel Peffer of Columbia University, was the featured speaker at a CFR discussion that Lattimore attended on March 5. Peffer "felt that for the first time in thirty-two years the situation in China showed no hopeful signs whatever. . . . The Kuomintang government is the rottenest and most corrupt that China had experienced in a thousand years. . . . The presence of American troops in China adds fuel to the fire of anti-American propaganda. Russia would like nothing better than that our forces remain indefinitely."[4]

Peffer was not plugging the Communists. It was very difficult to judge their character. "Compared with the Kuomintang political thugs and leeches, the Communist leaders, taken man for man, are physically, intellectually, and morally superior. On the other hand, their word is not to be trusted. In one breath they profess to be truly democratic, and then go on to proclaim their complete faith in Marxist ideology. They look for a dictatorship of the proletariat after passing through a necessary transitional period of semi-capitalism." Peffer saw no possible course for the United States but to pull out of China, completely and at once. Lattimore would not go that far. He "pointed out the danger that the vacuum left in China by American withdrawal may be filled by the Russians," but Peffer replied that we must take that obvious risk.[5]

In September 1947, General Albert C. Wedemeyer, who had just returned from a fact-finding mission to Asia, delivered his report to General Marshall and the public. Though a friend of Chiang, Wedemeyer was also an astute and careful observer. His remarks at the end of his mission, delivered to the Chinese State Council on August 24, were as stinging a condemnation of Kuomintang incompetence and corruption as were the conclusions coming privately from Chiang Kai-shek himself. Since Wedemeyer's remarks were public, they received a great deal of publicity; the Chinese pretended to be shocked. Chiang's supporters in the United States, still clinging to the wartime belief that Chiang was a great and effective leader, were appalled. Lattimore was not; Wedemeyer's testimony moved him closer to the Peffer position. In his first column after gaining access to Wedemeyer's report, Lattimore concluded:

We have yet to face the full consequences of our mistaken policy in China. It is not just that we have lost money on the Kuomintang. The Chinese Communists have been enormously toughened by their successful resistance to an American-backed Kuomintang. Their popular, non-Communist following has incalculably increased. They have won a prestige that it would be dangerous to underestimate, by defying the strongest country that has ever intervened in China, and getting away with it.

It is doubtful, however, whether our China policy planners have yet resigned themselves to the prospect of closing out our disastrous deal at such a heavy loss. They are still likely to try throwing a little more good money after bad. (September 27)

Anxious as Lattimore was to avoid statements that could contribute to Soviet hostility, events in 1947 caused him to use harsh language. He did not like Soviet refusal to participate in the Marshall Plan, and on October 18, he castigated the Russians for preventing East Europeans dealing with the West: "These people are 'pro-Marshall Plan,' and the signs are that the Communists intend to keep them squashed with one hand while they build up a 'Molotov Plan' with the other."

On December 6, Lattimore discussed the growing American economic and political influence in Iran, on Russia's border. The Russians were complaining bitterly. Lattimore dismissed such claims. U.S. gains were the result of our superior economic aid, rather than, as the Russians said, "sinister economic imperialism." The Russians were simply jealous.

Korea was another area where Soviet machinations were not to Lattimore's liking. The Russians were trying to bar any pro-Western Koreans from voting in the upcoming all-Korea elections. Lattimore agreed with Lieutenant General John R. Hodge, commander of American forces in Korea: the Russians were pretending that only communism was democratic (October 25). However, Lattimore did not believe that we could have our way completely in Korea. To make an American satellite of that unhappy land would obviously menace Russian security; Korea was too close to Vladivostok. Compromise was needed.

Lattimore also commented extensively on Japan during 1947. MacArthur, he believed, was doing a fine job. Politically, MacArthur was reining in the "war group," and there had been "amazingly little political turbulence." Economically, the results had not been as impressive, but this was understandable: political control was relatively easy to implement; economics were more complicated (May 3 and 7).

In hindsight, Lattimore's observations about the state of the world in

1947 are hard to fault. He was still somewhat optimistic about what could
be accomplished by the judicious use of American power, and he relin-
quished his faith in Chiang painfully and reluctantly. But the fact of cold
war he now acknowledged.

Lattimore wanted to visit the Mongolian People's Republic in 1947. He
had only been there once—in 1944 with Henry Wallace. Since the United
States did not recognize the MPR and direct communications were not
available, he had to send his request via the Soviet ambassador in Washington. His letter of February 11 to Marshal Choibalsan, the Mongolian
premier, reviewed his interest in Mongol scholarship, reminded the premier of the friendly reception accorded him in 1944, and asked to study
there from June to September. His cover letter to Ambassador Novikov
presented an alternate plan: if the MPR did not welcome him, he would
like to visit the Buryat-Mongol or Kazakh republics of the Soviet Union.
Neither of these letters was answered.[6]

As weeks went by and no answer came from Choibalsan or the Russians, Lattimore decided that since he could not visit a border state in Asia,
he would try Europe. Czechoslovakia would be appropriate; a group from
Putney School, where his son David was enrolled, planned to attend the
World Youth Festival in Prague during July and August. It could be a
family outing.

Czechoslovakia was still a free state in 1947. Visas were easy to get,
and there were no restrictions on the movement of foreigners. The Lattimores were able to circulate freely, talk to Czech Asian specialists, and
spend a day touring with Foreign Minister Jan Masaryk. Lattimore found
Czech minority problems fascinating and the people friendly. His geopolitical observations were less than prescient; he thought the East European
countries under Soviet control would be able to work together to moderate Soviet rule, and he did not anticipate the Soviet takeover of Czechoslovakia in 1948. At the time of his visit, Communists (40 percent of the
electorate) and non-Communists were working together effectively. Lattimore expected this cooperation to continue (August 2).

Three years later, when the inquisition peaked, the anti-Communist
fanatic J. B. Matthews found in David Lattimore's attendance at the World
Youth Festival, held under Czech Communist auspices, proof of his father's "Communist connections." The Prague gathering, said Matthews,
had been a "raucous anti-American, pro-Soviet affair." David Lattimore
and other Putney participants had not found it that way, though there
was a vigorous exchange of opinions among those present. Matthews held
the older Lattimore responsible for the sins of the younger, noting that

young David "has no independent income, and must, therefore, have gone to the Communist meeting with his parents' consent and at their expense. His conduct as a minor was both legally and morally a matter of his parents' responsibility."[7] A dozen copies of this attack on the Lattimores are still in Matthews's Lattimore file.

The Lattimores went to England after the Czech trip; Owen attended the IPR conference held that year at Stratford-On-Avon. He described this conference in an ONA column of October 4, noting that there were few Asians in attendance, the only sizable delegation being from Kuomintang China. This absence brought a reflection on IPR's history: "Once criticized for having anything to do with such a subversive crowd as the Kuomintang, it is now criticized by others because only the Kuomintang Chinese are represented in it, not the Chinese Communists." Lattimore deplored French and Dutch refusal to allow Indochinese and Indonesians to attend. The British had made their peace with Indians and Pakistanis, several of whom were then active in IPR.

While Lattimore was pursuing these professional interests, the domestic cold war steadily intensified. HUAC started on a major program of investigating Communists in government, unions, media, science, the armed services, and Hollywood. The new Republican leadership of the House promised full support and an expanded budget.

The National Industrial Conference Board, aping the Chamber of Commerce, commissioned a report on communism in the Department of State, to be written by labor specialist and former Marxist Benjamin Stolberg. This report was released in February 1947 and circulated to newspapers. Lattimore was prominently featured as "the most important adviser to the State Department on Far Eastern Policy." William Loeb (later publisher of the Manchester, New Hampshire, *Union-Leader*) sent a copy to the FBI; they were not impressed.[8] Unlike Father Cronin, who had written the Chamber's pamphlets after considerable research, Stolberg did practically none. He gleaned most of his material from Alfred Kohlberg's writings and the *Reader's Digest*. The FBI was aware that Stolberg had a credibility problem: Jerome Davis, prominent teacher and labor leader, had won a substantial libel settlement from Stolberg and the *Saturday Evening Post*.[9] Apparently the National Industrial Conference Board pamphlet aroused little interest. Lattimore never heard of it until his FBI file was released in 1980.

He had heard of Executive Order 9835, however. This was Truman's order, issued March 12, 1947, establishing a loyalty program for federal employees. Lattimore was not a federal employee, but EO 9835 was aimed at some of his friends. The publicity given to heretical opinions was escalating. HUAC hearings, the alarmist *Reader's Digest*, Hurley's charges against the China hands, the continued sniping at the *Amerasia* people by Hearst, Scripps Howard, and McCormick Patterson newspapers, plus the massive Catholic attack on Russia—all made it clear that heresy was about to become an offense for which an employee could be fired.

And there was still Kohlberg, whose crusade against the IPR continued unabated. His 1944 letter to Edward Carter demanding a housecleaning in the IPR had been rejected by the trustees, and in 1945 the institute issued a formal response. Kohlberg's next move was to ask the IPR for its mailing list, so he could distribute his charges to the membership. This request was refused. Kohlberg then went to court to force the IPR to provide him its membership list. The IPR finally agreed to hold a general membership meeting on his charges and allowed him to solicit proxies for that meeting. The meeting was held on April 22, 1947. Kohlberg's call for an outside investigation was defeated 1,163–66.[10]

One outcome of the Kohlberg ruckus was concern in the State Department about whether foreign service officers could afford to belong to the IPR and whether IPR publications were reliable sources of information. Consequently, in the summer of 1947 State Department Special Agent Daniel H. Clare, Jr., was assigned to investigate the IPR and *Amerasia*, which Kohlberg asserted was its twin sister.

Clare worked on the IPR-*Amerasia* investigation "intermittently" from August 15 to September 10, when he submitted his report. Apparently he did little more than summarize Kohlberg's writings, adding a few errors of his own. Kohlberg's study of IPR publications was attached as an appendix to Clare's report. The FBI, which first saw the Clare report in April 1950, noted, "There are many inaccuracies in the report."[11]

Clare ranked IPR personnel according to their presumed influence. Lattimore appeared fourth in his discussion but was introduced in these words: "By far the brightest star of the big four of the Institute of Pacific Relations is Owen Lattimore, familiar of former President Roosevelt, confidant of State Department higher echelons, and 'subtle evangelist' of the Union of Soviet Socialist Republics. In 1941, Mr. Lattimore was appointed by President Roosevelt as an advisor to Generalissimo Chiang Kai-shek, and at that time he was characterized by the former President as 'an expert's expert.' "[12]

Clare did some digging on his own. He apparently interviewed Louis Budenz, who "is aware that he [Lattimore] is a sympathizer, but is unable to recall at this time any incidents which definitely indicate that he was a member of the Party." Max Eastman was also quoted on Lattimore, but not from an interview; Clare picked up the "subtle evangelist" phrase from Eastman's *Reader's Digest* article. Most of the rest of Clare's material derived from Kohlberg.[13]

Since Clare's superiors had a special interest in diplomats, a major section of his report deals with persons who had served the State Department in some way. There are thirteen of them, and again Clare saves the most important for last: "These associations, however, shrink to insignificance in comparison with the ties between the Institute of Pacific Relations and John Carter Vincent. On May 21, 1947, an editorial in the New York World-Telegram flatly charged: 'The policies of this branch (Office of Far Eastern Affairs) have been consistently pro-Soviet and pro-Chinese Communist. The clique headed by John Carter Vincent reflects the views of the Institute of Pacific Relations. A complete break with this propaganda organization is required.' "[14]

Vincent was under attack at the time by Senator Styles Bridges. Vincent's promotion to career minister and his nomination as minister to Switzerland were argued in the Senate from May until his confirmation July 23. Bridges, Kohlberg, and Clare lost this battle too. It remained for John Foster Dulles finally to force Vincent out six years later.[15]

Lattimore was disturbed by the struggle over Vincent. From the Wallace mission he knew Vincent to be a superb diplomat, loyal and discreet to a fault. And Vincent was anything but pro-Communist. Thank God, Lattimore thought, *he* wasn't subject to the calumnies thrown at sinologues on the public payroll.

CHAPTER THIRTEEN

Europe Up, Asia Down

Lattimore had been a student of Asia all his life. His professional concerns were centered there, on China and its problems, on the Mongols whom he greatly admired, and on Japan as the major threat to both of them. The focus of his journalistic commentaries was always, What policies should the United States follow in Asia?

In 1948 this emphasis shifted. The struggle with Russia was important in Asia, but the most important pressure points were in Europe. It was there, rather than in Asia, that Western-style democracy had to be saved. Western Europe was the cradle of democratic practice; if that area could be strengthened and democracy there invigorated, the United States would not face alone a hostile world of totalitarians.

These beliefs were articulated in Lattimore's writing from the beginning of the cold war, and in 1948 they came to the fore. To Lattimore, the Marshall Plan represented an absolutely vital effort to strengthen our most important salient. A reading of his output during this period shows that the success of the European Recovery Program (ERP) was the measure against which he judged policy in Asia, the Middle East, and Africa.

And there were threats to the Marshall Plan. First and foremost was the danger that the lingering isolation of conservative Republicans would hamstring if not defeat Marshall Plan appropriations. Eastern internationalist Republicans were not the problem; rather, Lattimore feared the conservative, anti–New Deal, "fortress America" thinking of midwestern and western Republicans, who had much power in the Senate. They were dangerous, he thought, not just because they were reluctant to appropriate money for "decadent" Europe but because they insisted on squandering precious aid money on lost causes in Asia. This money would be better spent on allies who could use it effectively. The Republican blend of isolationism toward Europe and interventionism in Asia was called "neo-isolationism" by Norman Graebner; a neo-isolationist was one who wanted to fight in China.[1]

George Marshall proposed the ERP at the Harvard commencement June 5, 1947. Britain and France thereupon called a meeting in Paris; Molotov attended briefly, then stormed out. A second meeting was called, to be attended by representatives of all European nations west of Russia except Spain. The Soviet satellites did not attend, but sixteen nations did; between July and September they hammered out an integrated program for restoring the economies of Western Europe. Truman accordingly presented legislation to Congress in December 1947 calling for expenditure of $17 billion over four and a quarter years. Debate then began in Congress.

As Thomas A. Bailey describes the opposition, "Critics of the Marshall scheme charged that it was just another 'Operation Rathole.' 'Uncle Santa Claus' had already poured too much money into the pockets of ungrateful Europeans—about $12 billion in various loans and handouts since mid-1945. America had better make herself strong at home, conserve her resources, and help her own needy people. Otherwise she would offend the Soviets (who were already offended), divide Europe (which was already divided), and lay herself open to the Russian charge (which had already been made) of 'dollar imperialism.' "[2] Perhaps Congress would have passed the ERP without stimulus from Russia, but the Soviet coup in Czechoslovakia in February 1948 strengthened Truman's hand. Finally, by early April a one-year appropriation of $6 billion passed, and Truman signed the bill April 3.

Lattimore commented on the congressional fight over ERP in an article on January 17. Congressional supporters of Chiang were pressing for aid to China; Truman appeared to be yielding to their demands. Lattimore thought Marshall and the congressional supporters of aid to Europe would bargain with the "fanatics who are for all-out intervention in China" in order to get the funds for Europe. He was correct.

Not only congressional Republicans were giving Marshall trouble; Asia-first generals were also causing problems. Lattimore's sympathies were all with Marshall, not Truman; the president, he thought, was not exercising appropriate leadership. Without Senator Arthur Vandenberg, Republican of Michigan, the Marshall Plan would have gone down the drain (March 13).

The second great threat to the Marshall Plan came from the colonial powers. Both the Netherlands and France were waging full-scale war in their Asian colonies. The Dutch were spending a million dollars a day in an attempt to reclaim Indonesia, the French in Indochina probably even more. These expenditures would represent a drain on whatever would be appropriated for European recovery (March 19).

On April 9, Lattimore went back to the threat of siphoning off money to a moribund China. The administration had agreed to a substantial appropriation for China to assure the passage of ERP. Lattimore was aghast; he thought that Washington was in the grip of "such intense emotions that people are hitting out in all directions without stopping to make sure what they are hitting at. . . . The hysterical House vote on inviting Franco Spain into the Marshall Plan [later rescinded] shows what the emotion is about and the state it has reached. Congress has worked itself up to a point where the only standard of measurement for a foreign policy proposal is one question: How anti-Russian is it?"

Aid for Korea was akin to aid for China. Neither was cost-effective. In May, Lattimore compared Israel and Korea as prospective recipients of American aid. The Israelis were people like us, staunch individualists, solidly middle class, endorsing collectivism only through labor unions where it was necessary to get a living wage. Korea, by contrast, did not "have the even texture and the large measure of social equality" that Israel had. Korea, therefore, "is incompetent to use intelligently either economic or military forms of aid. . . . It will waste American aid even more incompetently and corruptly than the Kuomintang in China" (May 21).

By June the American presidential campaign was heating up. Unhappy as he was with Truman's rhetorical belligerence, Lattimore still supported the president. Dewey was handicapped by the power of the Republican neo-isolationists, who were interventionist toward Asia; they demanded a statement on increased support for China in the party platform. The Progressive party candidate was Henry Wallace, of whom Lattimore had seen enough in 1944. Wallace the politician was "a first class disaster." Wallace was against the Marshall Plan, holding that any foreign aid should be given through the United Nations. Lattimore supported the UN but knew that that cumbersome, strife-ridden organization could not save Western democracy. And, as Lattimore wrote for ONA on June 26, Wallace was an appeaser: "Appeasement of Russia will not do it. The Henry Wallace campaign has already shown that Mr. Wallace gets a large part of his support from the desire for peace with Russia; but the strength that he draws from this feeling is undermined by the fear that his only notion of peace may prove to be the appeasement of Russia."

Seven more times in 1948 Lattimore wrote in his weekly column of the dangers facing the Marshall Plan. In the months before the election, when Dewey appeared sure to win, Lattimore emphasized the hemorrhaging of foreign aid into Asia that a Republican victory would bring. After Truman's startling victory he worried still about the drain into French and Dutch colonial wars. In his wrap-up column at the end of the year he rejoiced that "the Marshall Plan really got rolling." But the plan did not solve all our problems: Americans seemed not to know whether the ERP was a preparation for war with Russia, which Lattimore opposed, or a mobilizing of human and other resources to strengthen democratic forces in Europe, which he supported (December 30).

And Israel still hung in the balance. Truman had not yet extended formal recognition, and Israel had not yet been admitted to the United Nations. Lattimore thought the United States should move more vigorously: "Israel is not merely a new state but the only democratic state in the Near and Middle East. If it survives, the effect will be revolutionary: growing political movements among the neighbors of Israel will demand that their governments yield to them some of the democratic rights that are the very essence of the society of Israel" (December 30). The prophecy was questionable, but the value judgment was not. Lattimore supported aid to *democracies.*

If the prospects for strengthening democracy in Western Europe went up in 1948, the prospects in Asia went down. China was the greatest disaster area.

Lattimore had a chance to argue his views of the Chinese situation on the prestigious "Town Meeting of the Air" on January 6. He and Richard Lauterbach, a journalist who covered Asia, paired off against two Republicans: former ambassador William Bullitt and Representative Walter Judd.[3]

Bullitt led off with a call for defending the United States by underwriting the Chinese Nationalists. His speech was cast in apocalyptic terms: "we face today the possibility that the Soviet Government, using the Chinese Communists as tools, will conquer China. And everyone in the Far East from General MacArthur down, knows that a Communist China would eventually mean a Communist Japan and that the American people in the end would face attack by combined Communist forces of Russians, Chinese, and Japanese. . . . We must act instantly and effectively or we shall betray into the hands of Stalin not only China but also the greatest adventure in human freedom that this earth has known—our own America."

Lauterbach spoke next, politely but firmly denying that Chiang represented a viable or worthy force. Judd followed, claiming that the Nationalists were not too far gone either to use aid effectively or to reform themselves. The stage was now set for vintage Lattimorean sarcasm:

> Mr. Bullitt, you seem to think that we ought to fight the Russians with cheap coolie labor because the average Chinese lives on less than $40 a year. Mr. Judd, you are trying to dodge the fact that the Chinese Government is a gangster with a gun on one hip by professing a childlike faith that it will turn into a Boy Scout if we give it a gun on each hip. I disagree. (Applause.)
>
> I don't think you can stop communism on coolie wages, and I don't think you can reform gangsters by giving them more guns. (Applause.) I agree with you, Mr. Lauterbach, that for every Communist the Chinese Government is killing with American guns, it is creating four new ones by its cruelty and corruption. (Applause.) . . . I don't know how stupid the Russians can be, but I do know that if they are stupid enough to try to take over China, they will have a hundred times more trouble than they are having right now. The present government of China has definitely proved one thing: it is the most expensive instrument we could possibly use to try to stop Russia and the spread of communism.

Bullitt was wounded. In the discussion period he asked Lattimore a long and tendentious question. Lattimore began his answer "Mr. Bullitt, for a question, that's quite a speech." Things went downhill from there. Lattimore had acquired another enemy.

Lattimore's 1948 ONA articles presented his conviction that Chiang could not then reverse his fortunes and that the only hope for a non-Communist government was in a new coalition. This coalition would be composed of "men who, in crisis after crisis during the last 20 years, have proved that they are not dupes of the Communists, but who have also earned popular respect by their steady opposition to one-man dictatorships." Rapid advances toward the Yangtze River by the Communists were encouraging this "third force" movement (January 3). It took the form of a Revolutionary Committee of the Kuomintang, and its aims were to "clean out the corruption of the later years of the Kuomintang and to go back to the traditions that gave it vigor when Sun Yat-sen was still alive" (January 30).

Lattimore held some hope for the Revolutionary Committee. It was in vain. Chiang's armies were disintegrating so rapidly and the Communists were sweeping south so swiftly that the third force never had a chance.

As the American elections approached, Chiang and his supporters counted on a Republican victory to bail them out. This also was a vain hope. Even had Dewey won, the momentum of Communist advances would have continued. As Lattimore saw it, China was effectively Mao's (August 13).

But if Lattimore's lingering hope for a coalition government in which non-Communist elements would have real power was unrealistic, his prediction in July that Mao would eventually be another Tito was right on the mark. This was not a popular doctrine. Diehard American supporters of Chiang resisted it well into the 1960s. To Lattimore, the parallels with Tito were abundantly clear. Mao, like Tito, was gaining power on his own and was not put in power by Soviet armies: "Similarly, the Chinese Communists are deeply rooted in nationalism. They have supported Russian policy, interests and moves everywhere outside of China, but within China they have consistently pursued policies of their own and have developed methods of their own which are based squarely on Chinese conditions" (July 3).

Lattimore was also right about the "ladder" theory (a forerunner of the domino theory). Some Americans believed that if the Russians, with Mao as their stooge, took over China, the Chinese Communists would "take over the revolutionary and nationalistic movements in Indo-China, Burma, and Indonesia. This is a ladder of absurdity, not of cause and effect. There are important Chinese minority communities in Indo-China, Siam [Thailand], Burma, Malaya, and Indonesia: but in every one of these countries there is a phobia against the Chinese" (December 3). He was right. Indochina did go Communist, but Ho Chi Minh fell out with his Chinese sponsors. The others were saved for democracy. Communism proved no more monolithic than Christianity.

Lattimore was chair of a CFR session on Japan in January 1948. The discussion leader was James Lee Kauffman, who had taught and practiced law in Tokyo. CFR records do not reveal who selected Kauffman as the discussion leader; certainly it was not Lattimore. Kauffman supported a program to rehabilitate Japanese business leaders who had manned the war industries, precisely what Lattimore opposed. This view also put Kauffman at odds with General MacArthur, whose initial directives broke up the business combines (Zaibatsu) and taxed the profits of large enterprises heavily. Kauffman was explicit about MacArthur's economic policy: "this policy does not conform with our ideas of the rights of property, or with the organization of the American economy. It will lead to socialism in Japan, despite the fact that General MacArthur feels it will save Japan from socialism by promoting free competitive enterprise."[4]

If this were not enough to agitate Lattimore, Kauffman defended the wartime record of Japanese business leaders: "United States investigation since the war has failed to turn up any evidence connecting the Zaibatsu with responsibility for the war. None of their leading figures are being tried in the War Crimes Trials." It is difficult to imagine Lattimore remaining silent when confronted with such statements, but his only response was to ask Kauffman if General MacArthur had ever challenged the directive to break up the Zaibatsu; Kauffman said no.[5] Perhaps Lattimore felt that as chair he should not engage in controversy with the guest. But he got back at Kauffman in his ONA columns and thereby attracted another dedicated interest group in opposition to him.

The American Council on Japan (ACJ) was a small, loosely knit group organized in 1948 to reverse American policy in the Japanese occupation. Its spearhead was Harry F. Kern, foreign editor of *Newsweek*; James Lee Kauffman, Eugene Dooman, former Ambassador Joseph Grew, and former Undersecretary of State William R. Castle were the organizers. Until Howard Schonberger's incisive study of the occupation, little attention was paid to the ACJ. Unlike the China lobby, ACJ never attracted much attention, but many prominent officials worked quietly with it. And where the China lobby failed to secure all-out American aid to Chiang's armies on the mainland, ACJ succeeded brilliantly in reversing American policy in Japan.[6] Along the way, Kern and others spread the Elizabeth Boody Schumpeter charges that Lattimore opposed the emperor and the Zaibatsu because he was a Communist.

Thus in the United States, the prewar alignment of forces, with Sinophiles opposing Japanophiles, had now completely collapsed; both of them now concentrated on undermining Lattimore, T. A. Bisson, Vincent, and the IPR.

In China, however, committed Nationalists still opposed the strengthening of Japan. Lattimore noted their protests. In an ONA article on April 3, 1948, he quoted Chang Hsin-hai, biographer of Chiang Kai-shek and Kuomintang spokesman, as saying that the Zaibatsu should be prosecuted as "war criminals of the first order" and that the new U.S. effort to build up Japan was detrimental to Chinese interests.

On July 2 Lattimore again endorsed the views of Wang Yun-sheng, editor-in-chief of the major Nationalist newspaper in Shanghai. Wang was also apoplectic about American policy in Japan; it was not really concerned with reconstruction, but with using Japan as an instrument against the Russians. And the United States was preparing for a new war. Wang thought this policy might force China to side with Russia since the Russians also opposed an "American bastion" in Japan. Lattimore agreed that it might.

Japan then disappeared from Lattimore's columns until November 19. Results of the first Japanese war crimes trials were available then, and while Lattimore was pleased that a number of civilians who had been close to the emperor were convicted, the Zaibatsu had largely escaped. Not only that, but the occupation policies Kauffman supported were now being adopted. The early MacArthur directives designed by liberal New Dealers were being replaced by regulations encouraging a rapid return of Japanese industrial power. William H. Draper, an investment banker serving as undersecretary of the army, led a mission to Japan in early 1948 that signaled and accelerated the shift in occupation policy. Japan was to replace China as the anchor of U.S. policy in Asia. Lattimore thought this policy to be not only wrong but counterproductive. He thought the Japanese would now feel we wanted them as a satellite: "The day they begin to feel that way, the combination of anti-Emperor and anti-American feeling will provide the two sides of the entering wedge of Communist infiltration and Russian influence" (November 24). Lattimore's judgments of the wisdom of our Japanese occupation grew steadily more negative.

Surprisingly, Lattimore had little to say about the Czech coup in February 1948. It was a great disappointment to him; he had assumed that the Czechs would be able to continue their mixed economy and coalition government, providing a continuing example of a state (like Finland) in the Soviet shadow but not under Communist control. The coup proved this assumption wrong. But he had also noted that the Czechs were disturbed by the American plan for the restoration of German heavy industry, which was as much a threat to them as was Soviet domination. On March 3 he speculated that the Czechs were disturbed at American "organizing" of Germany, which made them more willing to be "organized" by Russia.

Lattimore did not return to a discussion of Czechoslovakia until September 9. In that article he wrestled with the puzzle of the recently deceased Eduard Benes, who had cooperated with, but not endorsed, Czechoslovakia's Communists. Why had Benes not "openly denounced" the Communists? Lattimore thought it was because Benes either wanted to avoid a civil war or could not agree "with the ruthlessness of the Communist way of doing things."

Since "Communist ruthlessness" had now triumphed, Lattimore was left with only gloom. Western Europe might still be saved. The Marshall Plan was lifting democratic spirits significantly. But Eastern Europe, except for Yugoslavia, was now firmly under Russian control.

One moral emerged from all this turmoil: the "great powers," the United

States and Russia, were not omnipotent. Each suffered limitations on the reach of its power. This limitation was nowhere clearer than in the crisis brought on by the Soviet blockade of Berlin in June. The United States mounted a massive airlift to supply Berlin, testing whether the Russians would risk war by interfering with our planes. We won that test, and Berlin was saved. But at what cost? The bottom line, for Lattimore, was still gains versus costs. He used the Berlin airlift to illustrate the limits of power in a column of July 15.

> The changeability of power haunts those who hold it. The Soviet kind of power has clearly run into diminishing returns, at least for the time being in Yugoslavia. The American kind of power is putting on a demonstration in Berlin that is awe-inspiring but at the same time has overtones of absurdity. The quick mobilization of planes to shuttle supplies to a city of two million was a show of a kind of strength that no other nation could muster. . . .
>
> Yet this great operation has overtones of absurdity because we have gone so far that we are actually air-lifting coal into Berlin. What is the economic sense of a policy which depends partly on the ability to carry coal around in the air? It is like the mountain giving birth to a mouse: technologically a good stunt, if you want to use so prodigious an effort for so small a result.

There were suggestions from some Russia-haters that we should go beyond the Berlin airlift to close the Suez and Panama canals to Russian ships and to blockade the Dardanelles. This strategy Lattimore did not approve. He agreed with James Reston that Russian setbacks were substantial: heavy losses in the French trade unions, defeat in Italian and Finnish elections, Marshall Plan successes strengthening non-Communist governments throughout Western Europe, the startling independence of Tito. To initiate anti-Soviet moves in Suez, Panama, and the Dardanelles might "set up a terrific backfire of sympathy for Russia throughout the world and even in this country—and that would be the end of the American way of life" (July 24). Apocalyptic, this; it was one of the few times Lattimore gave way to thorough pessimism.

Kohlberg, Lattimore's sworn enemy, stirred no great fuss in 1948. Having been beaten down in his crusade to reform the IPR he withdrew from it and concentrated on the open letters he sent to a mailing list of eight hundred persons: journalists, politicians, businessmen, clergy, anyone who attracted his attention. The message was still the same: we were losing the war against communism in Asia because of traitors in our midst. One major Kohlberg effort failed; he and like-minded Chiang supporters forced an audience with Thomas Dewey, hoping to persuade Dewey to hit China policy hard in his campaign. Dewey brushed them off.[7]

But Kohlberg did score in one arena. On a trip to Japan he was received cordially by General Willoughby, who put him up in the Tokyo headquarters of Army Intelligence. One evening Kohlberg found a large document marked "Confidential" on his bedside table. It was Willoughby's manuscript on the Sorge spy ring, which had supplied information to the Russians before the war. Kohlberg read it until 2 A.M. While he was out to breakfast the next morning, the manuscript mysteriously disappeared.[8]

The Willoughby manuscript provided Kohlberg with new ammunition. Two of Sorge's associates were connected with Lattimore: Guenther Stein and Agnes Smedley. Lattimore had published Stein in *Pacific Affairs*, and Smedley had been in Yenan when Lattimore was there in 1937. Kohlberg went home and wrote an article on the Sorge ring for the May 1948 issue of his magazine *Plain Talk*. It attracted little attention except from the army, which denied that Smedley had been a Soviet spy.[9]

HUAC attracted the most attention in 1948. Walter Goodman called it a "Vintage Year" and began his chapter this way: "Nineteen forty-eight stands as the most celebrated year of the Committee on Un-American Activities, a year of threat and counterthreat to which the Committee responded with enormous gusto. . . . It was an election year, filled with decisions that would define the limits of the cold war in Europe and the extent of our reaction to it at home. . . . It tended the spy fears of the day, producing a record number of sensational headlines as its contribution to the Republican Presidential campaign. And with its presentation of the Hiss-Chambers drama, it touched a generation of liberals to their very souls."[10]

Americans who lived through the 1950s, and many who came of age later, appreciate the significance of the Alger Hiss case. Every witness or scholar, right or left, who deals with the inquisition attests to its salience. (Ronald Reagan revived it in 1984 by giving the Medal of Freedom posthumously to Whittaker Chambers.) On August 3, 1948, Chambers publicly accused Hiss of serving the Russians; Hiss denied it and was indicted for perjury December 15. Richard Nixon, then a member of HUAC, rose to the vice presidency and ultimately the presidency largely on the basis of his prominence as the chief pursuer of Alger Hiss. Two years after the Hiss indictment Joseph McCarthy, flailing about for spectacular charges to advance his own anti-Communist crusade, chose the single most damning indictment he could find: he claimed Lattimore was the boss of the whole ring of which Hiss was a part.

But it was not just the discovery of an alleged Communist at one time high in the government that made 1948 a vintage year. Republican outrage at losing yet another presidential election to the Democrats was a powerful incentive to find a set of issues that would turn the voters around.

Why did the myths about the loss of China obtain their stranglehold on the American psyche at midcentury? When one identifies the first act in the selling of these China myths, one is forced to conclude that China became an obsession because the Republican party, prior to Franklin Roosevelt the majority party, had by 1948 been shut out of the White House for sixteen long years. It was then robbed of its certainty of recapturing power by a Missouri haberdasher, whose major error while in office was the loss of China to the Communists. The Republican party, having lost with a moderate, bipartisan, me-too campaign in 1948, was desperate to find an issue—any issue—with which to return to power. After the 1948 election, China was that issue.[11]

It is hard to imagine an issue that could have served the party better. Republicans had been unable to overcome Democratic candidates running against the Hoover depression. With the cold war going strong, with spies and traitors everywhere, with our friends in Asia going under, it was time to concentrate on foreign policy.

One wing of the Republican party had always put Asia first. World War II in Asia was the Republican's war, commanded by a great Republican general with presidential ambitions. Democrats had emphasized a war against Hitler that many Republican leaders felt we had no business prosecuting, since the Axis was the only bulwark against the true menace to America—the Soviet Union. Now the Asia-firsters came into their own. In 1948 Dewey was a shoo-in; he could not lose. When he did lose, the sober, statesmanlike approach of his campaign lost with him. From then on, with exceptions such as Vandenberg, Republicans concluded that bipartisanship in foreign policy and rational discussion of campaign issues—in short, Marquis of Queensberry rules—were out. Nice guys finished last. If Truman could win by raising hell about Republican domestic policies, perhaps a Republican could win by raising hell about Democratic foreign policies. Especially China policy.

The "loss" of China was the best thing that ever happened for the Republican party. It answered a politician's prayer for a rebuttal to what they saw as twenty years of socialism, New Dealism, and treason. The bitter, unexpected, and undeserved blow of Truman's victory enraged the Asia-firsters, emasculated the moderates, and led American politics into an orgy of scapegoating and witch-hunting.

CHAPTER FOURTEEN

Barmine

Until January 1949 the FBI file on Lattimore was thin. It contained only twelve documents, half of which concerned Lattimore's activities in the Maryland Civil Liberties Committee and the Maryland Citizens Council. The other documents were mostly reports from the Boston FBI office occasioned by Elizabeth Boody Schumpeter's visits, when she complained that Lattimore's stance against Japanese aggression was motivated by pro-communism. None of this struck the bureau as warranting additional investigation.

On January 12, 1949, Boston wrote headquarters again. There was a new angle: Boston had a report of the testimony of an informant in the Hiss investigation who identified Lattimore as a Russian agent. Boston wanted to make sure this item caught Hoover's attention. It succeeded.[1]

The new witness was Alexander Gregory Graf Barmine.

Barmine, a defector from the Soviet Union, was born of a noble family in 1899. He wrote that when the revolution broke out, he was "filled with hope and enthusiasm for the new Russia and the new world we were going to create. I left the university and engaged as a volunteer in the new army. At the same time I joined the Communist party. Six months later I was named political commissar of the battalion and later of the regiment, after taking part in the fighting in the Ukraine. After a course at military school I served as an officer in the war against Poland. Since then I have served in the Soviet Government in many posts and have given all my force and strength to the workers' cause, which I espoused in 1919."[2]

Barmine's accounts of service to the Soviet government in his various autobiographical writings differ from the account he gave the FBI, but he was consistent in claiming that he was for many years a brigadier general in military intelligence and that when he defected in 1937 he was chargé d'affaires of the Russian embassy in Athens. The immediate stimulus for his defection was Stalin's purging of former colleagues; he sensed that his time was coming.

From Athens he went to Paris, claiming status as a political refugee; in 1940 he came to the United States, where he worked in a metal factory. Like many defectors, he now gave to anticommunism the same "force and strength" he had once given to the revolution. In 1942 he entered the U.S. Army as a private. Apparently his former skills as a Soviet brigadier general were no longer with him, as he was still a private in 1944 when he left the army to join the Office of Strategic Services.[3]

OSS seemed to appreciate his talents even less. Barmine does not discuss his work with OSS, but admits he was fired. He says the stated reason was repeated absence from the job because of illness, but that the real reason was his extracurricular activities.[4] By 1944 he had made contact with various publishers and was busily turning out exposés of Soviet perfidy and subversion. The publication to which he gravitated was *Reader's Digest*.

Barmine's article "The New Communist Conspiracy" appeared in the *Digest* in October 1944. It is a typical warning of how the American Communist party was merely a tool of the Kremlin, far more dangerous after Earl Browder "dissolved" it and formed the Communist Political Association. The Communists had penetrated American labor unions and used their agents in the army and navy to defeat counterintelligence efforts.[5] Barmine had not yet discovered China policy, the IPR, or Lattimore.

But the FBI discovered Barmine. On February 14, 1945, the New York office interviewed him. If he was so knowledgeable about how the Soviet network operated in the United States, they expected that he would know some of the key operatives. Barmine disappointed them. He could not name any Americans working for the Soviet Union.[6]

However, Barmine's contacts at the *Digest* soon provided him with names of Soviet apologists, if not with names of spies. He became friends with Max Eastman, shortly to publish the anti-Lattimore article with J. D. Powell; in March 1945 Eastman wrote a glowing preface to Barmine's book *One Who Survived*. Eastman had gotten the anti-Lattimore corpus from Kohlberg and now passed it on intact to Barmine. Barmine also became close to *Digest* staffer Bill White, son of the famous editor William Allen White. Bill White and Barmine collaborated to dissuade the *Digest* from publishing a condensation of Lattimore's allegedly pro-Soviet

Solution in Asia.[7] Barmine subsequently wrote a hostile review of *Solution* that appeared in the *New Leader.*[8] Paraphrasing (if not plagiarizing) the Kohlberg review of *Solution,* Barmine ignored the last three chapters, in which Lattimore argued for free enterprise in Asia, and instead attacked the misleading publisher's blurb.

Despite getting an article in the prestigious *Digest,* Barmine's career as a writer did not flourish. He was out of work from late 1944, when the OSS fired him, until October 1948, when he joined the Russian section of the Voice of America. During this period of unemployment the State Department told the FBI that Barmine was alleged to have seen a list of Soviet agents in the United States that included the name of Alger Hiss. The bureau thereupon contacted Barmine again, on October 23, 1946, when "he was closely questioned as to whether he knew of any Soviet agents in the United States or even if he suspected any individual. He denied knowing anything definite and added that he was merely suspicious of some things."[9] The Bureau was again disappointed; this was just another bad tip from State.

Barmine had lied to the bureau. To Bill White and other former *Digest* associates he had already suggested that Lattimore might be a Soviet agent,[10] but his suspicion did not become public knowledge until the McCarthy ruckus four years later.

In 1948 Barmine watched fascinated as HUAC had its "Vintage Year." In July, Elizabeth Bentley soared to stardom as she named a score of persons whom she claimed had been serving in her espionage ring. In August, Chambers unleased the spectacular charges against Hiss.[11] (Neither Bentley nor Chambers named Lattimore.) Here, Barmine surely reasoned, was a formula for advancing the anti-Communist cause: bring charges of treason, not just of fellow-traveling, against specific Americans. Then the naïve would sit up and listen.

His opportunity came before the end of the year. Despite two earlier disappointments the FBI went back to Barmine on October 26, 1948, to see if he could add to the testimony against Hiss. Apparently he said nothing about Hiss, but he had a new story: Owen Lattimore and Joseph Barnes had been "working" for the Soviets in 1933.[12] (Barmine later "corrected" this date to 1935.)

The story was confused, but it concerned an incident Barmine now remembered from his years as head of the Soviet Auto-Motor Export Corporation in Moscow. In this position he was responsible for one overt activity, shipping cars and trucks abroad, and for a covert activity, furnishing arms to pro-Soviet groups in other countries, including China's

Sinkiang Province. For the latter operation he needed experienced "military men" to organize delivery of the guns, tanks, ammunition, and supplies he was to position in China.

Where were these experienced military men to be found? Barmine claimed that during this assignment he worked closely with General I. Berzin, head of Soviet military intelligence. General Berzin told Barmine not to worry: the Soviets had two Americans working for them in China, Owen Lattimore and Joseph Barnes of the IPR. They would handle his need for experienced men in Sinkiang.[13]

Berzin was a major Soviet figure who headed military intelligence from 1924 to 1935 and was senior Soviet adviser to Loyalist forces in the Spanish civil war in 1936–37. Barmine claims that while he held the export job, he conferred with Berzin—his boss—three or four times a week.[14] This claim is strange. Berzin was running so many agents in so many countries (including superspy Richard Sorge) that it is difficult to envisage his taking so much time with the mundane business of exporting.[15] Even more difficult to believe is that in his autobiographies written well before 1948, Barmine mentions Berzin not at all. Barmine writes about some 315 of his colleagues and superiors in the Soviet Union, from Stalin on down, paying special tribute to those who were caught up in Stalin's purges.[16] Berzin was liquidated in 1937, as were many other associates of Barmine, yet Barmine had not a word to say about Berzin.

Nor does Barmine mention Lattimore, Barnes, or the IPR in his autobiographies. In any case, the improbability of Barmine's scenario is staggering. For one thing, Barmine admits that he never contacted, met, or used Lattimore and Barnes. Within a short time of his "learning" from Berzin that Lattimore and Barnes were Soviet agents, Barmine asked to be relieved of the Auto-Motor Export job. He was then transferred to the diplomatic service.

Furthermore, to describe Lattimore and Barnes as experienced military men is ridiculous. Lattimore had always been a businessman-scholar-journalist. Barnes was a pure journalist and by the late 1940s was foreign editor of the *New York Herald-Tribune*. Neither ever had military service. And there was a problem with dates. In 1933, the date Barmine first mentioned, Lattimore was in China, but nowhere near Sinkiang, and his affiliation with the IPR did not come until the end of the year. Nor was Lattimore near Sinkiang in 1935. Barnes was in China for a while in 1933, but not in Sinkiang; in 1935 he was not even in China.

If the IPR was furnishing such stellar personnel for Soviet military intelligence, it is hard to see why that country attended only one IPR conference and ceased to pay dues after 1939. Nor does it make sense for the Russians to have consistently denied Lattimore permission to enter their country, other than for the 1936 trip he made to meet Carter in Moscow.

Barmine clearly appreciated the flimsiness of his story. In later retellings he embellished, contradicted, and disparaged it to the point of farce. He even said of his own tale that he was not sure it could be called "evidence." The FBI eventually wrote off his testimony as "uncorroborated," noted that he told contradictory versions, and doubted his credibility.[17]

But in March 1948 J. Edgar Hoover took Barmine's testimony seriously enough to order the Baltimore office to start a "thorough and complete investigation" of Lattimore, with telephone taps and physical surveillance. (He also ordered that a microphone be hidden in Lattimore's home if the agents could install it secretly; it is not clear that they were able to do so.) The object was to find out whether Lattimore "is presently or has been in the past engaged in espionage activities." Now the Lattimore file began to grow rapidly, and his classification was upgraded, in bureau nomenclature, from an "Internal Security" case to one of "Espionage." A request for permission to tap his telephone went to the attorney general on March 24, 1949, and on April 3 the tap was installed.[18]

Physical surveillance began toward the end of March. A lecture tour Lattimore made to New England was followed closely. He, his wife, and the recently arrived Dilowa Hutukhtu (noted as traveling incognito) stayed overnight with writer Richard Lauterbach in New York, then journeyed to Springfield, Massachusetts, on March 30. Both Lattimore and Lauterbach spoke to the Springfield Adult Education League that evening, calling for recognition of people's governments in Asia and saying that we might be able to deal with the Chinese Communists.[19]

The next day Lauterbach returned to New York, and the Lattimore party went on to Cambridge. There they stayed for three days with Professor John King Fairbank. Fairbank gave a dinner party at the Buena Vista Restaurant in honor of Lattimore on April 1, and Lattimore addressed Fairbank's seminar in History of Far Eastern Civilizations that evening. The surveillance report filed by Boston also noted that Lattimore was a friend of Andrew Roth, Clyde Kluckhohn, Charles Siepmann, Michael Greenberg, and Harriet Moore.[20]

The telephone tap provided advance notice of Lattimore's movements for the next nine months. Agents shadowed him everywhere he went. His lecture schedule for 1949 was extensive, and the faithful FBI kept watch on each appearance; in Philadelphia April 21, New York May 5, the Army Chemical Center May 9, the Council on Foreign Relations May 10, an NBC broadcast from New York June 7, and then on vacation.

Surveillance reports on these engagements show the FBI at its dogged best. The cable to the Washington field office (WFO) and Baltimore from New York on May 5 is typical:

OWEN LATTIMORE DASH ESP [espionage]—R. [Russia] RE BALTIMORE TEL MAY FOUR AND WFO TEL MAY FIVE LAST. SUBJECT ARRIVED NYC SEVEN TWENTY A.M. EST. MET DUDLEY FRAZIER OF LITTLE BROWN AND COMPANY AT BARCLAY HOTEL . . . THEN PROCEEDED TO CBS WHERE SUBJECT APPEARED ON TELEVISION PROGRAM TWELVE NOON TO TWELVE THIRTY P.M. SHOW ENTITLED "VANITY FAIR." SUBJECT, BRUNO SHAW AND ANNALEE JACOBY GUESTS OF DOROTHY DOAN ON PROGRAM. TRIP TO NYC APPARENTLY TO PUSH SALES OF SUBJECTS NEW BOOK. SUBJECT LEFT NYC ONE THIRTY P.M. EST AND ARRIVING BALTIMORE FIVE P.M. EST.[21]

Entirely unaware of being followed everywhere, the Lattimores, Dilowa Hutukhtu, and the Onons went to Bethel, Vermont, for a vacation at the end of June. They were to occupy Stoddard farm, belonging to Vilhjalmur Stefansson, who was then in Iceland. This created a bit of a problem for the FBI. A mail cover was easy (the Bethel postmaster gladly allowed the FBI to intercept and steam open Lattimore's mail), and it was easy to tap the telephone, but physical surveillance was not easy.

The nearest FBI office was in Albany, New York, three and a half hours' drive away. The gung ho Albany Special Agent in Charge (SAC), A. Cornelius, Jr., was more than prepared to drive that far to maintain surveillance of a suspicious character like Lattimore. But once the agents were near the Stoddard farm, there was no cover. In a city or town, agents could pretend to be eating in a restaurant, drinking in a bar, or simply waiting in a parked car. Rural Vermont did not offer such opportunities. As Cornelius plaintively put it, "The farm itself consists of several hundred acres on top of the mountain, and there are no buildings in which one could stay to observe any activities on the farm."[22]

So Cornelius read the mail, listened to the telephone recordings, and sent photographs of letters in Chinese and Mongol to Washington for translation. Unfortunately, Cornelius or one of his associates was not highly skilled at photography. A shipment of exposed film mailed from Albany to bureau headquarters on August 4, 1949, drew this response on August 10: "This is to advise you that the roll was too far underexposed to print, it being loaded in the magazine with the emulsion side away from the lens so that the exposures were made through the back of the film. There is attached hereto, an instruction card with the correct method for unloading and also the correct exposure guide. Film is being returned herewith."[23] Some film, however, turned out clearly. Hundreds of letters to and from Lattimore were put in bureau files. Vital facts about Lattimore's activities were learned, such as that he had managed to install an indoor bathroom in one of the buildings at the Stoddard farm.

What SAC Cornelius lacked in photographic skills he made up for in geopolitical imagination. Now that the Albany district had been blessed with a world-famous suspect, he rose to the occasion. He read up on Buddhism so he could place the Dilowa in a monastic hierarchy (he was comparable to a Roman Catholic cardinal); he studied the history of Mongolia and of Tibet and the interrelations of the Buddhist authorities in those countries. He referred to the recent *China White Paper* and the appointment by Secretary of State Dean Acheson of a committee headed by Philip Jessup to review Asian policy, a committee that would undoubtedly seek Lattimore's advice. He followed Reuters and Associated Press dispatches about unrest in Tibet and about the dispatch of an emissary from China to Lhasa to reaffirm Chinese sovereignty there. All this and more SAC Cornelius put in a three-page letter to Hoover on August 9.[24]

Nor was this an idle show of erudition to impress the boss. There was a conclusion:

> In view of the above factors, it would be quite possible that LATTIMORE by influencing his Mongolian associates (and they influencing their superiors and/or constituents in Tibet) is in a position to assist in bringing about the inclusion of Tibet in the Soviet or Chinese Communist sphere of influence, which country today, is not in either sphere. It is even possible the Communist forces would desire to see the tenth Lama replaced by a new Buddha if it would better suit their cause. It is then possible that LATTIMORE'S guest, the Dilowa (Living Buddha) may possibly be that person. It may be that continued investigation of LATTIMORE will tend to confirm or disprove this conjecture.
>
> It is suggested that possibly this may be of assistance to the newly formed advisory committee, and it is believed they should be so advised prior to negotiations they may undertake with OWEN LATTIMORE.[25]

We do not know if Hoover read the Cornelius memorandum. Two months later, however, D. M. Ladd wrote to Hoover about the Jessup committee having consulted Lattimore. Ladd quoted, without acknowledgment, from the Cornelius memo and concluded that "Lattimore could be of immense

importance to the Russians" as an adviser to Jessup. Hoover did read this
memo and commented below Ladd's signature: "This is shocking. Press
vigorously investigation of Lattimore."[26]

The FBI investigation spilled over into the fledgling CIA. Many of Lattimore's alleged transgressions occurred abroad, out of the bureau's jurisdiction. Hoover thought the CIA might be able to furnish some information. On June 22, 1949, Hoover wrote the CIA, asking if that agency
could verify Barmine's claim and also check out some fourth-hand gossip
(source deleted) to the effect that Lattimore had divulged information to
the Soviets.[27] Robert A. Schow, CIA assistant director, answered the bureau on August 10, hardly a speedy response; the CIA blacked out the
substance of his letter when it was finally released in 1986.[28]

By contrast, the bureau moved rapidly and included in their investigation the mysterious Mongols Lattimore now had with him. Until Lattimore began the Page School Mongol program in 1947, there was little
academic study of that exotic land and people. The Foreign Service Institute (State Department), American Council of Learned Societies, and the
Carnegie Corporation all agreed to underwrite his project. It was to be
multidisciplinary; Lattimore hired American linguists and social scientists, but his major effort was to obtain native speakers of Mongol. John
Hangin and Urgunge Onon came to Johns Hopkins in 1948, barely getting
out of Nanking before the Communists arrived.

Lattimore wanted the Dilowa also. Periodically he had letters from his
friend, by 1948 in a Tibetan monastery and planning to live out his life
there. Homesick as he was for his native Mongolia, the Communists there
would not tolerate his presence. He plaintively explained this in a letter
to Lattimore: "Though I am not against them, they must be against me.
The old can sometimes forgive the new, but the new can never forgive the
old."[29] By the end of 1948 Tibet too seemed an insecure refuge, and the
Dilowa contemplated a move to India. Lattimore persuaded him instead
to come to the United States. He arrived in Baltimore early in March
1949.

Despite State's clean bill of health to all three Mongols, the FBI was
suspicious. The Dilowa's baggage came by ship, arriving May 6. Every bit
of it was searched. There were numerous letters written in Mongol; it
took almost a year for the FBI to get these translated. They apparently
showed no evidence that the Dilowa had Communist thoughts, but one
very suspicious enclosure raised a warning flag with SAC McFarlin in
Baltimore: "The following described letters, made available by the same
highly confidential source referred to above [the search of Dilowa's bag-

gage] were in sealed and addressed but unstamped envelopes. . . . Baltimore exhibit #51—letter and envelope bearing what appears to be Mongol script. It will be noted that folded in the letter were two dried flower petals, which appear in the photograph. The Bureau is requested to advise, if possible, whether these dried flower petals are of any known significance."[30]

Four rolls of film were also confiscated from the Dilowa's luggage. When developed, they also must have been innocuous. Later FBI documents show no incriminating evidence coming from the Dilowa's baggage. But agent Cornelius in Albany had planted the seeds of suspicion: the Dilowa might yet be the Communists' chosen agent to take over Tibet. This fear endured in bureau files.

The bureau missed one high-level attack on Lattimore in early 1949. John F. Kennedy was still only a congressman, but he knew what to feed the then-hawkish citizens of Salem, Massachusetts. On January 30, seeking to explain the "tragic" decline of Chiang Kai-shek, for whom we had gone to war against Japan, Kennedy borrowed liberally from Bullitt, Hurley, and other Asia-firsters: "Our policy in China has reaped the whirlwind. The continued insistence that aid would not be forthcoming unless a coalition government with the Communists was formed was a crippling blow to the national government. So concerned were our diplomats and their advisers, the Lattimores and the Fairbanks, with the imperfections of the diplomatic system in China after 20 years of war, and the tales of corruption in high places, that they lost sight of our tremendous stake in a non-Communist China." Kennedy later regretted this indiscretion. Fortunately, in 1949 he did not command the rhetorical heights of the presidency.[31]

The March 19, 1949, *Collier's* brought a surprise from Louis Budenz. When he first started writing about the Soviet threat in his 1947 autobiography, *This Is My Story*, he portrayed the Soviet Union as operating directly through American Communists. The takeover of America would come after the collapse of the American capitalist economy. In this first Budenz call to arms there was no mention of Asia, China, Japan, or the IPR. Budenz listed eighty-seven Americans who were working with the Soviets to hasten America's collapse; Fred Field and Owen Lattimore were not among them. By the time he wrote for *Collier's* in 1949, the Soviet threat had assumed a quite different dimension. His title was "The Menace of Red China": "The Communist conquest of China, now dangerously near completion, long has been planned as a major milestone in Moscow's road toward creation of a Soviet America. Japan and Korea are next on the schedule, then Indonesia and the Philippines. Once in control of the western Pacific's vast manpower and vital rubber, tin and oil resources, Russia hopes to be ready for the final showdown with the United States. That is the blueprint, at least, of Soviet world conquest. . . . Since 1927, every American Communist has been inculcated with the Soviet tenet that China is the master key to a Red White House."[32]

This "master key," as Budenz suddenly remembered, was first activated in 1937, when Earl Browder called a "China conference" at Party headquarters. Ten American Communist party leaders attended. Budenz says: "Browder announced that he had received word that 'the followers of Mao Tse-tung have to be presented in a new dress.' With a sarcastic grin and Kansas-imitated twang, he said our new objective was to picture them as a mild variation of Plains states agrarian reformers. Up to that point they had been known simply as Chinese Communists."[33]

At this China conference Fred Field allegedly suggested the idea of working through "legitimate" organizations such as the IPR. "This is not a Communist organization," writes Budenz, "but Field later succeeded in becoming secretary of the American Council. . . . Browder masterminded the new China policy. Having served two years in China as a Communist International representative, he was an authority on that country." Budenz also identified five writers who took part in Browder's project: Philip Jaffe, Lawrence Salisbury, T. A. Bisson, Harrison Forman, and Guenther Stein. Thus, China became Russia's "steppingstone to world domination. . . . It took nearly a quarter of a century to reach the goal, which only proves that while the pattern of conquest may deviate, it never dies."[34]

One would be tempted to suspect that Budenz had bought Kohlberg's conspiracy theory in toto except for one thing: Lattimore and all his works are missing from the *Collier's* account. It took another year for Budenz to adopt the full Kohlberg agenda.

Meanwhile, Lattimore was putting out an agenda of his own. It was *Situation in Asia*, requested of Lattimore by Little, Brown in late December 1948 and completed by Lattimore in three weeks. Publication date was April 4, 1949.[35] Naturally, this was not all new material; some of it came from Lattimore's ONA columns, one chapter came from a paper he had delivered to the American Historical Association in December, and two chapters had been prepared for the *Atlantic Monthly*. There were no surprises.

Since the Communists had all but taken over China, and the Soviet Union stood to gain by this takeover, the Russian menace figured strongly in *Situation*. Lattimore does not equivocate about this menace. "The spread of direct Russian control over Asia would be disastrous for the countries of Asia as well as for America and Europe. To replace one kind of empire with another kind of empire would make things worse, not better." And while Russian propaganda painted Marxism as "modern and progressive," this description was erroneous; "according to this theory, to be 'progressive' in politics means to be on the side of that which is coming up and against that which is going down." Lattimore believed that we had to adopt policies that would "demonstrate that there can be progress and democracy—democracy for Asia, in forms acceptable to Asia—without Marxism."[36]

Such policies did not mean we had to go to war with Russia. The Truman Doctrine was still too provocative. Our defenses already in place were sufficient to protect our own territory; in the Third World, our superior economic capabilities would tip the balance of influence in our favor. "The fundamental adjustment will then require the Russians to concede that capitalism is not withering or collapsing, while we shall have to concede that Communism cannot be extirpated by war. On our side, we shall have given a fresh impetus to both capitalism and political democracy."[37]

As with his earlier book, *Solution in Asia*, Lattimore consistently argues the superiority of capitalistic productive power and the inferiority of Soviet communism. "America is the strongest private-enterprise country in the world, and there are all kinds of jobs, all over the world, that can be done better by American private enterprise than by any other agency." As to the former colonial areas, "The American interest in these countries is to cultivate the maximum field of legitimate operation for American private enterprise in trade, in contracting and engineering, and in supplying and installing machinery."[38]

Lattimore was still convinced that Mao was not under the thumb of the Kremlin, that China would go its own road internally. MacArthur had done a great job in Japan, despite the 1948 reversal of policy, but Japan still could not be counted on in the future. And on the nascent revisionist thesis that Truman ordered use of nuclear weapons only to intimidate the Russians, Lattimore was emphatic: there was "no justification whatever" for believing it. With no exceptions, throughout *Situation* Lattimore advocates democracy and free enterprise.[39]

One influential force in American opinion paid no attention to *Situation*: the American Legion. On May 5, 1949, Kenneth R. Hammer, chairman of the Maryland Legion's Americanism Commission, released a list compiled by the commission of 102 prominent citizens who were "un-suitable for Legion sponsorship" as speakers or entertainers. It was largely a roll call of Hollywood and Broadway personalities, but there were a few professors, among them Lattimore. When the *Baltimore Sun* asked Lattimore about it, he responded with "complete surprise." "The only person on the list with whom I'm acquainted," he said, "is William L. Shirer. I'll always be glad to be on any list with him."[40]

Underneath the sangfroid there was concern. When Lattimore learned that Richard E. Lauterbach was also on the list, he wrote Lauterbach, "If you know of any proposal for action by a group of us who are clearly libeled by the 'guilt by association' listing please let me know. Since actual loss or damage as the result of such a story is one of the most important things in bringing a libel action, and since you have already had an article turned down, I think your case is clearer than mine. It makes me furious to see you get this kind of treatment, and I want to do anything I can to help."[41]

Nothing came of it. Buried in Lattimore's FBI file is a wiretap report made by the FBI on two prominent Communist party functionaries. Part of what the FBI overheard concerned Lattimore and the Legion list.

> Baltimore Confidential informant T-15 [the wiretap] of known reliability, advised on May 6, 1949, that PHIL FRANKFELD, Chairman, District No. 4 of the Communist Party, with headquarters in Baltimore, and GEORGE MEYERS, Labor Secretary, District No. 4 of the Communist Party, discussed a HENRY WALLACE rally. . . . Near the conclusion of their conversation, according to the informant, MEYERS referred to the American Legion's "Honor Roll" and that the Legion had listed in the newspapers over a hundred names to "tip people off that they are traveling under false colors." MEYERS made the statement "they even got OWEN LATTIMORE on there, and WALTER DURANTY." According to the informant, FRANKFELD seemed puzzled and responded with the following one-word inquiry, "LATTIMORE?" The informant stated that MEYERS laughed, repeated both names and thereafter told FRANKFELD that he, MEYERS, guessed he would have to start writing with his "right" hand. . . . MEYERS seemed to ridicule the implications the Legion list might suggest insofar as LATTIMORE and WALTER DURANTY are concerned.[42]

While the American Legion was compiling its list of un-American speakers, Lattimore was probing a Russian weakness that few others saw and that would not be fully visible for four decades. His ONA article of April 19, 1949, "Nationalism in Russia's Back Yard," commented on a

chauvinistic piece "written for Bolshevik highbrows"in the Moscow magazine *Questions of Philosophy*. Lattimore had always given the Russians
high marks for their easy assimilation of Asian ethnic groups, but this
article, "Against the Bourgeois Ideology of Cosmopolitanism," indicated
growing arrogance on the part of the Russians.

Cosmopolitanism was wrong, said the writer, because it implied that
there was a body of universal ideas equally valid for all peoples at all
times. Such a notion is un-Russian, for the Russians "are the outstanding
people" of the Soviet Union, with the richest history and the richest culture. Lattimore observed, "In the headstrong Russian way, they are now
overdoing the whole business by laying claim to having invented practically everything." The *Questions of Philosophy* piece was patronizing,
inaccurate, and offensive. Lattimore predicted that if the Russians maintained this attitude, they would face nationalistic hostilities throughout
their vast territory.

The FBI wiretap on Lattimore picked up another interesting item in
May. On May 10 Lattimore received a telegram from the Office of Naval
Research in Washington inviting him to attend a meeting of the Arctic
Research Laboratory in Point Barrow, Alaska, May 17. The FBI immediately went to Naval Research to ask why Lattimore was going on this trip.
Navy replied that Dr. Detlev Bronk, president of Johns Hopkins and a
member of the Arctic Research Laboratory Board, was unable to make
this meeting; Lattimore was a substitute nominated by Bronk and cleared
by the navy. The navy also supplied the itinerary and names of other
persons attending. The bureau decided this trip was legitimate and no
surveillance was necessary.[43]

Despite Lattimore's heavy involvement in writing, lecturing, and the
Mongol project, he was interested in branching out into other activities:
capitalist-style activities. In July 1949, while he and his family were living
at the farm in Vermont, Lattimore wrote a business friend of his, Owen
Roche, on Long Island. There were several things he wanted to talk to
Roche about, not the least of which was making money.

Among other things, why shouldn't you and I pool our experience,
yours in Latin America and mine in the Far East, and go into business
as consultants on foreign trade under Point Four, or simply as opportunity offers. I once gave a large corporation some sound advice on
their investments in Shanghai under Japanese occupation. They took
the advice, and liquidated their investment before Pearl Harbor. It seems
to me that a couple of men who know their way around in the field of
foreign trade and investment ought to be able to give equivalent advice

today; only under present conditions, of course, it would be primarily a question of giving advice on where to undertake new ventures rather than on the liquidation of old commitments.[44]

Roche's response does not survive, and Lattimore did not remember how this project turned out. If it had gotten started, the force of the inquisition would have aborted it shortly.

When the famous *China White Paper* (formally titled *United States Relations with China*) came out on August 5, 1949, Lattimore was an avid reader. It was, he thought, a tremendous mistake. His analysis of the motives behind the *White Paper*, and of the probable consequences of issuing it, was the most incisive to be found.[45] In an ONA column of August 13 he noted the struggle between Truman's administration and the Asia-first Republicans over whether to try to revive Chiang Kai-shek. Truman was right on this point: Chiang could not be rescued. Lattimore concluded with two points, the first that the *White Paper* highlighted the "two-billion dollar bankroll that was squandered" in China, making the Democrats look bad.

> On the second point, that of emphasizing the redness, ruthlessness, and Russianness of the Chinese Communists, the *White Paper* commits what will in time be revealed as a serious diplomatic blunder. Secretary of State Dean Acheson, in his statement accompanying the *White Paper*, speaks of the Russian influence in China as a "foreign domination masking behind the facade of a vast crusading movement," and even suggests that American policy should now encourage the Chinese to "throw off the foreign yoke."
>
> Such language is a diplomatic mistake because, while a Russian yoke on the necks of the Chinese may be one of the possibilities of the future, it is not an actuality of the present. The insinuation that the United States is ready at any moment to encourage a new civil war in China is a grave error. The main body of the *White Paper* will support the belief, already prevalent in China, that American intervention has been much greater than Russian intervention. The suggestion of a new kind of American intervention will drive the Chinese closer to the Russians.

Mao took precisely this line in a series of four articles using more invective and sarcasm than he had ever before displayed.[46] Nor did the Nationalists like the *White Paper*. It pleased nobody.

Four months after the Point Barrow trip another public attack on Lattimore's loyalty appeared. The September 1949 issue of *Columbia*, the magazine of the Knights of Columbus, carried an article, "Disaster in

China," by Father James F. Kearney, S.J. Some of the material was similar to the Eastman-Powell *Reader's Digest* article, but most of it came straight and undiluted from the source: Kohlberg. The "disaster" was of course the Communist triumph: "For Communism it is the greatest triumph since the Russian Revolution; for us, though few Americans yet fully realize it, it is perhaps the greatest disaster in our history; and the end is not yet. Who is responsible? It wasn't a one-man job; short-sighted Chinese officials contributed some fifty percent of the catastrophe, we the other fifty percent. There are those who believe, though, that no Americans deserve more credit for this Russian triumph and Sino-American disaster than Owen Lattimore and a small group of his followers. Owen Lattimore, confidant of two U.S. Presidents, adviser to our State Department."[47]

Surprisingly, the FBI did not acquire this article until November 28, and it was January 30, 1950, by the time two agents from the San Francisco office interviewed Father Kearney at Santa Clara University. After discovering that Kearney had never met Lattimore, could not identify his "followers" or associates, did not know who in the State Department associated with Lattimore, and had no knowledge of Communist party activity on Lattimore's part, they hit pay dirt: Kearney "advised that ALFRED KOHLBERG, 1 West 37th Street, New York City, had been his principal source of information concerning LATTIMORE, other than LATTIMORE's books and articles."[48]

Kearney described for the FBI agents Kohlberg's "open letter" operation, stating that in 1948 Kohlberg had informed him that Lattimore screened applicants for positions in the Far Eastern Division of the State Department; however, Kearney could not name any of these individuals. Kearney then added what was, in light of his claimed dependence on Kohlberg, a peculiar reservation about the man: "He expressed the belief that in view of KOHLBERG's hatred of Communism, KOHLBERG may be indiscreet, and that he would hesitate to recommend an interview of KOHLBERG by this Bureau."[49] This was fine with the bureau Lattimore specialists; they had long regarded Kohlberg as unbalanced and had no desire to interview him. Not until McCarthy quoted Kohlberg before the Senate did they change their minds.

When President Truman announced on September 23 that the Soviet Union had exploded a nuclear bomb, America's virile self-image took another beating. For most observers the trauma was military; Lattimore took a different view. The Russians may have had a bomb or two, but we had a stockpile. The real danger, as Lattimore wrote in an October 3 ONA article, was in what the bomb represented by way of advanced technology. We could no longer afford the complacent assumption that all the fingers of Russian technologists "are nothing but clumsy peasant thumbs." We now had to revise our estimate of Russian competence, period. Now "Russia's possible industrial application of atomic energy is of even more importance than atomic bombs."

But an equally significant development did not receive from Lattimore the attention it deserved. On October 1 Mao Tse-tung declared the existence of the People's Republic of China (PRC). Lattimore knew this was a milestone, but having been raised abroad and having had little contact with the Protestant mission support system in the United States, he did not appreciate the symbolic significance of this triumph of atheistic communism. He saw the creation of the PRC as primarily a geopolitical problem, to be dealt with on the international stage. It was in fact far more a domestic political problem.

To many Americans, the atheists defeated the Christians in 1949. The inquisition could never have achieved its virulence without the massive grassroots devotion to Christian missions. In 1936 there were at least six thousand Protestant missionaries in China, and each of them had a built-in constituency back home.[50] As Sherwood Eddy, prominent chronicler of China missions, noted of his youth, "China was the goal, the lodestar, the great magnet that drew us all in those days."[51] John Hersey's *The Call* recreates this Sinocentrism vividly. China was also the lodestar for Henry Luce, who was born in China of missionary parents and who developed a lifelong attachment to the cause served by his father, to the country where his father served, and to the great captain who, until 1949, ruled that country. In the Luce theology, which all of his publishing empire promulgated until his death, missions and righteousness, Republican politics, and Chiang and Americanism were all inseparable.[52]

The psychological significance of Mao's victory lay not just in the fact that the American missionary enterprise suffered a defeat but in the fact that the heathen Communists beat them at their own game. The Communists won the *theological* battle, the battle for souls. Mao, with his rigid moral code, his strict standards of service and self-abnegation, his overwhelming creed of devotion to duty, had captured the spirit of the Protestant ethic and turned it against them. For many missionaries the triumph of the Communists caused intolerable dissonance. *Their* China, the Kuomintang, was riddled with "graft and greed, idleness and inefficiency, nepotism and factional rivalries," in the words of missionary-ambassador John Leighton Stuart. Stuart was overtly envious of the discipline and abstemiousness of the Maoists, qualities which he admitted were "no mean achievement, especially in the perspective of Kuomintang shortcomings."[53]

For several decades American religious circles simply could not cope with the idea that any kind of Communist regime could achieve the popular devotion Mao had in his early years. In 1972 E. Gray Dimond, provost of the University of Missouri at Kansas City Medical School, toured China with a team of fellow doctors. When he gave a series of lectures in the Midwest after his return, he began to get letters: "My pastor has told me to write to you. I told him I was not able to understand how godless, Communist China could not have alcoholism, drugs, venereal disease, and prostitutes. How can this happen in the absence of the Bible? Surely the explanation must be that Christianity is alive and operating behind the scenes. Please write and assure me that this is true." "Your reports about Red China and what you saw there do not do your scientific training justice. It is obvious that you were shown only well-selected areas which had been prepared for you. My minister told me so."[54]

American Catholics, though with less investment in China than Protestants, were also appalled when "China, in the end, rejected Christianity and chose Marxism." Richard Madsen, in the *Holy Cross Quarterly*, explains why Mao's triumph was so traumatic: "The Chinese Communists succeeded in doing what the churches always claimed to want to do, but never succeeded to any great degree. they fed China's hungry, provided medical care for her sick, eliminated the great gap between China's few rich and many poor, made China into a self-reliant nation, and helped bring new meaning and hope into the lives of great masses of Chinese people."[55]

Lattimore believed that the professional Kuomintang supporters in the United States were in it for money or power or both, but he was in error. Shirley Stone Garrett, in "The American Churches and China," had it right. "With the Communist takeover . . . the collapse of the missionary era left a deep sense of betrayal. . . . It is certain . . . that China's repudiation of the missionary gift worked like a disease in the consciousness of many Americans."[56] The significance of that disease for Lattimore was not yet clear.

In the summer of 1949 SAC Cornelius had warned FBI headquarters about the dangerous possibility that Lattimore would be consulted by Philip Jessup and his committee to review China policy; this threat materialized when Jessup wrote several dozen pundits for their suggestions on August

18; Lattimore replied within the month. His six-page letter digested his book *Situation in Asia* and concluded, "The major aim of United States policy in the Far East . . . should be to enable the countries of the Far East to do without Russia to the maximum extent. This is a much more modest aim than insistence on and organization of hostility to Russia; but it is an attainable aim, and the other is not."[57] One wonders if Cornelius would have worried so had he actually read this letter.

The Jessup committee talked privately to a number of State Department and other Asian experts during the summer and held a roundtable discussion on American policy toward China on October 6, 7, and 8, 1949.[58] Twenty-five "outsiders" attended the discussion. Five of them vigorously opposed even considering diplomatic relations with the People's Republic; Lattimore advocated waiting a while but thought that Titoist tendencies in Peking could be enhanced if recognition were granted after a reasonable wait. This advice put him at odds with the leader of the nonrecognitionists, Harold Stassen, at that time president of the University of Pennsylvania.

Lattimore also opposed Stassen's proposals for heavy support of the rump Nationalist government in the south of China and later attacked Stassen by name in several of his ONA columns for this proposal. At the conference Stassen came loaded with charts and graphs in the custody of an assistant; the charts showed how we could still save half of China by expeditious aid.[59] It was an impressive performance. As Lattimore remembered it, "Stassen was busy showing how important he was; he kept popping out to get messages from his assistants." But Stassen and his supporters lost the argument. Most of the academic participants, and many of the business leaders, agreed with Lattimore: nonrecognition made no sense as a long-term policy. Stassen had his revenge before McCarran's Senate Internal Security Subcommittee two years later. It was the familiar charge: Lattimore had "lost" China to the Communists.

Lattimore had, of course, played a part in "advising the State Department" about China policy at the roundtable conference. But despite the near consensus of the participants in favor of eventual recognition, the U.S. government did not act on the majority opinion. Perhaps it is still arguable whether recognition would have been a wiser policy, but it is not arguable that Lattimore influenced policy. The roundtable was ignored.

On November 8, 1949, Lattimore spoke to the students of the National War College. It was his only appearance as an official lecturer before this group. His topic was "The Situation in Asia." Much alarm was raised in the Congress some years later when it was learned that Lattimore had "infected" the military, but his message that day was as anti-Communist as was his book of the same title: the Russians would not be able to control China; nationalism in Asia would be most effectively captured by free enterprise ideas; the United States was superbly placed to promote political democracy in Asia so long as our models were not the Kuomintang and Syngman Rhee. The one weakness of his analysis was again Japan: he said the Japanese were unreliable. Lieutenant General H. R. Bull, commandant of the National War College, said the response to Lattimore's lecture was "most gratifying." [60]

On November 25, 1949, Lee Nichols of United Press interviewed Lattimore about Mao's threat to invade Tibet. The FBI apparently talked to Nichols, since a two-page report on Lattimore's opinions about Tibet includes direct quotations from him and Nichols. Lattimore explained in some detail the status of the Dalai Lama as the ruler of Tibet, determined to maintain Tibetan autonomy. There were, however, two rival Panchen Lamas, of lesser rank, one of whom appeared to be speaking for the Chinese. Nichols asked if the Chinese Communists were interested in taking over Tibet. Lattimore answered:

> The only thing that I have seen is that story off the Communist radio some weeks ago more or less denying that it was the business of the authorities in Lhasa to declare the political status of Tibet. I rather pricked up my ears when I saw that because it indicated that regardless of general Communist protestations about the right of self-determination and self-government and all the rest of it, in this case they were putting the emphasis on China's national claims. . . . They might be able to do something by interfering in the internal politics of Tibet but from the point of view of sending an army of their own to conquer the country—well, they may be bullheaded enough to do it but I can't see what the percentage would be. [61]

We do not yet know whether the "bullheaded" Chinese Communists gained or lost by invading Tibet. We do know where Lattimore's sympathies lay: as always, with the ethnic minority.

As if the other events of 1949 had not kept Lattimore fully occupied, he agreed at the urging of a prominent Indian official to attend a conference in New Delhi December 4, expecting to return within ten days. When he landed in New Delhi, a personal aide of Jawaharlal Nehru was waiting for him and whisked him off to confer with the prime minister. Nehru was anxious to have Lattimore's observations on several problems confronting India; one of them was the situation in Kashmir, to which Lattimore was sent for five days. When he returned to New Delhi, Nehru,

Ambassador to China Panikkar, Foreign Secretary Menon, and other Indian officials debriefed him extensively. Nehru's partiality toward Lattimore elevated the latter's prestige with the IPR delegates considerably, but it irritated Loy Henderson, the American ambassador, who believed Nehru too inclined toward socialism, which was but the first step toward communism.

Lattimore reported extensively on his Indian trip to Roger Evans of the Rockefeller Foundation, which had financed his air travel. In his long letter to Evans the only mention of the conference itself was a glowing appraisal of one of the participants, W. F. Rivers, the Delhi representative of Standard Oil. Rivers he found to be the ideal "business diplomat." This was probably an indirect criticism of the official American diplomatic staff in India, which did not have Rivers's "extraordinary range of friendships among both Indians and foreigners."[62]

Because of the Kashmir trip and many conferences with government people, Lattimore did not get back to Baltimore until December 26, 1949.

In Lattimore's absence, J. Edgar Hoover reached a decision. The public attacks on Lattimore were extensive enough, and the FBI file was thick enough, that prosecution was possible. That being the case, since evidence obtained through the use of illegal wiretaps was not admissible in court, the technical surveillance of Lattimore was to be discontinued. Removal of the wiretap was ordered December 20, 1949.[63] From now on, anything obtained by the bureau was to be available for court use.

PART TWO

The Inquisition

CHAPTER FIFTEEN

Top Soviet Spy

Until 1950 Owen Lattimore was a typically inner-directed, iconoclastic scholar. The constraints on his independence were self-chosen and only mildly inhibiting. No organizational bureaucracy stifled his creative thought, neither the Institute of Pacific Relations, nor Johns Hopkins, nor even the Chinese Nationalist government. He said what he thought, and it was often unconventional.

In 1950 all this changed. He found his life taken charge of by lawyers, his privacy invaded by reporters and government sleuths, and his formerly freewheeling discourse forced to conform to the end of proving that he was not a tool of the Kremlin. For five and a half years the inquisition ran his life. The Lattimore story became a part of America's anti-Communist pathology.

The year began happily enough when President Truman announced disengagement from the struggle in China on January 5. The *White Paper* had exacerbated Republican dissatisfaction with China policy; Asia-first senators were pressing for a commitment to the remnant Nationalist regime on Taiwan. Truman wanted to put a stop to this talk. Disregarding the advice of his staff and of Secretary of Defense Louis Johnson (but agreeing with Secretary of State Dean Acheson), Truman read a statement at his morning press conference January 5: the United States had no predatory designs on Taiwan and would not establish military bases there, nor would it interfere in the Chinese civil war.[1]

Lattimore was pleased. He knew that American policy in Asia had to be built on the reality of nationalism and that continued support of a discredited regime could only increase Asian resentment at American meddling.

A week later, in Acheson's famous "defense perimeter" speech, the administration clarified its Asian policy further. Military authorities, including MacArthur, had drawn a defense line in the Pacific that included Japan, Okinawa, and the Philippines, but excluded Taiwan and Korea. This defense line had been reported in the world's press; the Russians already knew well what American plans were. Acheson merely restated them on January 12 in a speech to the National Press Club; but in the heightened tension of 1950 his speech attracted a great deal of attention.[2]

Lattimore also approved of the defense perimeter. He thought South Korea was a loser under Syngman Rhee, who was as out of touch with his people as Chiang had been. He believed, as did the Department of State and the Joint Chiefs of Staff, that South Korea was not a viable government and could not defend itself against a Soviet-supported attack from the north. And, like official Washington, he felt that American defense dollars were better spent elsewhere.[3]

Republican pique at Truman's hands-off stance toward China was intense. The China bloc in Congress, egged on by General Chennault, William Bullitt, the right-wing press, and Chiang's various representatives in the United States, began a long and powerful campaign to support Chiang for an effort to retake the mainland. This campaign was reinforced on January 21, when Alger Hiss was convicted of perjury.

The Hiss case had dragged through the courts all during 1949. A first trial, ending in July with a hung jury, was followed by a second. In both trials Whittaker Chambers was the crucial witness against Hiss. The second jury believed Chambers; and the conspiracy theories of Alfred Kohlberg, up to then generally ignored, received powerful reinforcement. There *were* traitors in the government conspiring to promote Soviet plans for world conquest. Hiss had been at Yalta, where China was "sold down the river." Hiss had been the assistant to Stanley Hornbeck, head of the Far Eastern desk at the State Department. Hiss had been general secretary of the United Nations Founding Conference at San Francisco. Now it was proved to the satisfaction of a jury that Hiss had been a Communist, working all along to deliver China into the hands of the enemy.

It is hardly possible to exaggerate the importance of the Hiss conviction to the developing witch-hunt. If this pillar of the foreign policy establishment could be a traitor, treason could be anywhere. Worse still, Secretary Acheson, who presided over the whole conspiratorial apparatus, refused now to disown Hiss. At a press conference January 25 Acheson was asked if he had any comment on the Hiss case. He refused to discuss legal aspects of the case but said friends of Hiss had to make a personal decision.

His own decision had been made: "I do not intend to turn my back on Alger Hiss." The standards that impelled him to this position "were stated on the Mount of Olives and if you are interested in seeing them you will find them in the 25th Chapter of the Gospel according to St. Matthew beginning with verse 34."[4] Congress, according to Acheson, flew into a tantrum. However motivated Acheson was by Christian charity, his words served as gasoline to the fires of Asia-first resentment.

All writers on the McCarthy years acknowledge that the Hiss verdict convinced a vast constituency that treason in the New Deal of Franklin Roosevelt was widespread. It also showed that ex-Communists such as Whittaker Chambers were perceived as credible, and it demonstrated that politicians pursuing subversives could achieve national status, as Nixon did. All of these outcomes were salient for Owen Lattimore.

The tempo of traumatic events early in 1950 continued unabated. It was front-page news for every paper in the country when President Truman announced on January 30 that the United States would develop a hydrogen bomb. And on February 3 Klaus Fuchs, who had worked on the American atomic bomb project during the war but was now in England, confessed that he had passed atomic information to the Russians. Three days later the Republican National Committee announced "Liberty against Socialism" as the major issue of the 1950 congressional elections. The party statement declared: "We advocate a strong policy against the spread of communism or fascism at home and abroad, and we insist that America's efforts toward this end be directed by those who have no sympathy either with communism or fascism."[5] No one realized, that early in the campaign, how many thousands of people would be charged with sympathy for communism.

Lattimore's attention to these events was distracted by a request from the United Nations that he head a technical assistance mission to Afghanistan, exploring the kinds of economic aid appropriate for that country. The timing of this request was awkward. His lecture schedule in 1949 had kept him away from Baltimore more than normal, he had just returned from a three-week trip to India, and the Johns Hopkins Mongol project needed his attention. On the positive side, he strongly supported the UN, and Afghanistan was a part of the Sino-Soviet border he had never visited.

The Afghan mission would require that he be gone the month of March on an exploratory trip and then for the period from June to September to negotiate final agreements with the Afghan government. This was a big chunk of time. He was uneasy about accepting the assignment and wrote

John W. Gardner of the Carnegie Corporation, which supplied the major funding for his Mongol project, that he would not go if Carnegie thought he would be slighting the Mongols. Gardner replied that he thought the Mongol project well enough organized that it could safely be left in the hands of Lattimore's associates while he went to Afghanistan.[6] Lattimore therefore accepted and prepared for this new venture. He was to leave March 6.

There was another project to be attended to before he left. The rapid advances of the Chinese Communists into Tibet suggested that that area would be under their control in a year or two. Lattimore believed this overthrow would mean loss to the scholarly world, perhaps permanently, of the priceless manuscripts in Tibetan monasteries. Lattimore talked about prospects for rescuing these manuscripts with Dr. Arthur Hummel of the Library of Congress. Hummel, an orientalist, was convinced that Lattimore was right and suggested that the matter be put to Luther Evans, the Librarian. Lattimore wrote Evans on February 26, 1950: "As country after country comes under communist control it is cut off from the scholarship of the world, as well as from other contacts. There usually follows a scramble in which a few refugee scholars are brought to the United States or other countries and a few books, manuscripts, and other materials are salvaged. Such salvage is, however, just that—unplanned salvage. Tibet is clearly doomed to come under control of the Chinese Communists. There is, however, time for a planned salvage operation. . . . a wealth of material never yet worked on by Western scholars could be brought out during the next few months."[7]

Lattimore then described to Evans the major sources of manuscripts and what might be found; recommended that the Dilowa Hutukhtu be used to negotiate with Tibetan authorities; explained how Indian cooperation could be obtained; and urged prompt action before the curtain was rung down on Tibet. It was a prescient effort. Perhaps, had the United States not contracted inquisition fever, Luther Evans and the Library of Congress might have acquired the treasure trove of Lama Buddhist lore later destroyed in Mao's Cultural Revolution. As it happened, doctrinal purity took precedence over any kind of scholarship, especially esoteric orientalia.

While Lattimore was wrestling with a decision on Afghanistan, the FBI was wrestling with the problem of keeping up with Lattimore. Lacking a wiretap, the Baltimore office had trouble knowing where and when he was traveling. His home in Ruxton was like the farm in Bethel, Vermont: poor cover for spies. As SAC McFarlin complained to Hoover on February

16, "The peculiar location of the LATTIMORE home eliminates any possibility of successful physical surveillance without the aid of a technical surveillance."[8]

The Baltimore office had other troubles. McFarlin was worried about the local vigilantes. After the American Legion put Lattimore on its blacklist, ultrarightists in Baltimore began their own "investigations." Two of them were serious threats to the bureau.[9]

One of the vigilantes was a woman whose name the FBI will not divulge. She had been to the Baltimore FBI office several times, alerting them to Lattimore's subversive influence on impressionable Hopkins students and protesting his alleged role in formulating American China policy. McFarlin told headquarters in his February 16 letter that there was "the ever-present possibility that she will present the matter to the House Committee on Un-American Activities or other persons placed in high political positions in Washington, D.C., in which event there might be undesirable repercussions on the Bureau."[10]

Subsequent serials in the Lattimore file show that the bureau had trouble deciding how to handle the female informant. The matter was serious enough to wind up in the hands of Assistant Director D. M. Ladd. Writing to Hoover on February 17, Ladd recommended that the woman not be contacted again; her charges against Lattimore were trivial. But Hoover reversed Ladd; he did not want HUAC to get potentially important information from an informant directly. His embarrassment at Nixon's getting information from Chambers still rankled. Baltimore was therefore instructed to contact the woman, make sure that she had no new information, and convince her that the bureau was on top of the case. Baltimore found nothing new, and the woman apparently did not go to HUAC.[11]

A more serious private crusade against Lattimore was conducted by Kenneth Hammer, Maryland American Legion commander and chair of its Americanism Commission. According to Daniel H. Burkhardt, who was closely associated with Hammer as adjutant of the Maryland department of the Legion, Hammer was an attorney-investigator who had learned the trade as a military intelligence agent during the war.[12] Burkhardt thought Hammer brilliant; the bureau thought him dangerous. Hammer's activities included efforts to get the Baltimore police to tap Lattimore's telephone, amateur surveillance of Lattimore and the Mongols, and frequent calls to SAC McFarlin. The bureau wanted none of this freelancing. Headquarters Security Division dispatched Lee Pennington, a midlevel bureau official, to dampen Hammer's vendetta against Lattimore.

Pennington and McFarlin called on Hammer at Baltimore headquarters of the Legion February 23, 1950. As Pennington reported to Ladd, "It was pointed out to [Hammer] that we were very much perturbed concerning —————— activities in the Lattimore case and hoped that all information would be referred to us instead of being disseminated to a number of agencies and a policeman. It was pointed out to [Hammer] the activities of over zealous individuals might undo considerable work on the part of the Bureau and result in individuals under suspicion becoming aware that their activities were being scrutinized."[13]

Hammer agreed to back off, though it must have been hard for him. By the time of the Pennington visit McCarthy was riding high, Lattimore had been named as a dangerous subversive before the Senate, and Hammer's sedulous work was getting him no credit at all.

Joe McCarthy was now getting all the attention, and attention was what he wanted most. His ruthlessness was not channeled, as was Nixon's, to gain him higher office. McCarthy learned early that careful and constructive work, such as he did on the postwar housing problem, had no headline appeal. His publicity improved when he charged into the Malmedy investigation, attacking the U.S. army and defending German SS troops who had massacred American soldiers.[14] In 1949 McCarthy generated considerable notice by red-baiting the *Madison Capitol Times*. But he was still in the minor leagues. Nixon's coup with the Hiss case was the kind of promotion he needed.

McCarthy selected communism as the theme for his famous Wheeling speech on February 9, 1950, and his use of the issue caught fire. He did not content himself with generalized charges of subversion or treason or Communist sympathy. He gave numbers and claimed that his numbers represented current traitors, still working and making policy in the State Department. They were all known as risks to Secretary Acheson, who was protecting them. When the Democrats demanded that he put up or shut up, he named names. That was all it took.

McCarthy stepped up the tempo of the anti-Communist crusade far beyond any other evangelist. We know much about the character of the senator, of his devotion to the scabrous and scatological, from two extensive biographies by Thomas Reeves and David Oshinsky. Daniel Bell and his collaborators in *The Radical Right* show how McCarthy appealed to the status insecurities of both ethnic and religious groups. Richard Fried, Nelson Polsby, and Michael Rogin emphasize the part played in the McCarthy saga by Republican politicians for straightforward political rea-

sons. Edwin Bayley has shown McCarthy's consummate skill at anticipating news deadlines and manipulating the media.[15]

But an adequate account of the McCarthy power must deal with his
instinct for reaching the dark places of the American mind. His "proof"
was vacuous. Even though he bought the Kohlberg agenda, he did not
really address the issues of China policy. He alluded to and presupposed
these arguments. His direct appeal was to fear and conspiracy. Robert
Griffith's classic book on McCarthy is aptly titled *The Politics of Fear*.

McCarthy sensed the country's need for simple answers to the challenges of the cold war, and he provided them. Clean out the conspirators
(Acheson, Jessup, Lattimore), jail the traitorous dentist (Dr. Peress), fire
the disloyal military (Marshall, Zwicker), and fortune will again smile on
the United States.[16]

He came along when the climate was ready for this message, when
many of America's military and masculine self-images had been bruised
and battered. He had a technique that his colleagues could only view with
awe. Without the McCarthy genius to underwrite the China lobby, the
China myths could never have taken such powerful hold. William Knowland may have deserved the disparaging title "Senator from Formosa,"
but he was an honorable and decent man. Kenneth Wherry may have
exaggerated a bit when he told a cheering crowd, while it was still conceivable that Chiang Kai-shek might endure, that "with God's help, we
will lift Shanghai up and up, ever up, until It's Just like Kansas City," but
Wherry would not have descended into gutter politics without Mc-
Carthy's guidance.[17] Styles Bridges, Homer Capehart, Bourke Hickenlooper, H. Alexander Smith—these were vigorous partisans, but they were
not without honor. It was McCarthy who engineered the descent into
diabolism. Senator Arthur Watkins, the ultraconservative Utah Mormon
who chaired the McCarthy censure committee, said that McCarthy took
us into "depths as dark and fetid as ever stirred on this continent."[18]

For a while it appeared that McCarthy's crusade would abort. The
Wheeling speech and his subsequent addresses at Denver, Salt Lake City,
and Reno contained nothing substantial, and Democrats were outraged.
He did name specific "security risks," citing Hiss, John Service, Harlow
Shapley, and two unknowns, but he had little to back up his charges.
When he went before the Senate on February 20, he was still talking
about these same people and dealing with others who were only numbers.
He had no evidence. Senator Robert Taft, called "Mr. Republican" by the
pundits, said it was "a perfectly reckless performance."[19] But McCarthy

had gotten attention, and the Democratic leadership established a committee under conservative Maryland Senator Millard Tydings to investigate the loyalty of State Department employees; now McCarthy had a center ring in which to stage his circus. On March 8, two days after Lattimore left for Kabul, the Tydings hearings opened.[20] For Lattimore, these hearings were an affront to many of his State Department friends, but no personal threat. He had never worked for State.

McCarthy was now a magnet for all the Soviet haters and most of the China lovers in the country. Naturally Kohlberg was among those who unloaded their files on this new spokesman. Keeley, Kohlberg's biographer, writes that Kohlberg and McCarthy did not meet until March 23 or 24, after McCarthy had fingered Lattimore before the Senate.[21] But McCarthy had obtained the Kohlberg materials well before that; they had metastasized throughout the fanatical right wing. He got them from J. B. Matthews, from Willard Edwards and Walter Trohan of the *Chicago Tribune*, and from George Sokolsky, Westbrook Pegler, and Howard Rushmore of Hearst, all of whom were primed to provide the China sellout story.

McCarthy's first efforts to give Tydings a comprehensive account of government security risks centered on Judge Dorothy Kenyon, whom he falsely claimed held a prominent State Department appointment and belonged to twenty-eight Communist fronts. But as Oshinsky notes, "McCarthy's verbiage outran his evidence."[22] It developed that Kenyon's only connection with the State Department was as an unpaid delegate to the UN Commission on the Status of Women. For this she did not even need a security clearance. And only one of the subversive connections he charged against her had any cogency. When Kenyon appeared before Tydings, she gave a most convincing account of her loyalty. The case against Kenyon dissolved in short order.

McCarthy then moved on to Philip Jessup, who was a high State Department official but who also came before Tydings fortified with powerful evidence of his patriotism. Then McCarthy took potshots at seven other people, resurrecting the Service case and adding, for the first time, Owen Lattimore. This was on March 13. But it was hit and run, without substantial payoff, and McCarthy continued to lose ground.

He now saw that he needed a flagship case such as Nixon had had. On March 21 he claimed to have found it. Since Hiss had become such a symbol of subversion and had been judged guilty by a jury of his peers, why not top the charges against Hiss? Why not produce the very top of the spy ring, the "boss" of Alger Hiss?

It is not clear how McCarthy settled on Lattimore. Kohlberg would be the most likely source for the idea of making Lattimore into a Soviet spymaster, but if Keeley is correct, and McCarthy did not meet Kohlberg until two days after he promoted Lattimore to the exalted position of "top Soviet spy," Kohlberg could not have talked him into it.

The FBI was bereft of any explanation. Their files contained nothing even suggesting such a role for Lattimore. But they were concerned. Nixon had stolen a march on them in pressing the attack on Hiss. Were McCarthy now to sell a bill of goods on Lattimore, Hoover would indeed look bad.

One explanation of how McCarthy settled on Lattimore made the rounds of the State Department. Francis Sayre, who was in the State Department at the time, attended a conference in Geneva where he heard that McCarthy was going to name him as a spy. Sayre, a past president of the National Council of Churches (NCC), went for help to his old friend John Foster Dulles, also a former NCC president. Dulles allegedly went to see McCarthy and told him to lay off Sayre. McCarthy just laughed. "Sure, why not, we have lots more names in this file," he replied, and without looking, reached into a drawer and pulled out the Lattimore folder.[23] The story has this much plausibility: McCarthy's methods were that haphazard and reckless.

But McCarthy had a brilliant sense of timing and a sure instinct for what an uncritical press and a disillusioned public would buy. He passed the word to newsmen that he was about to name "the top espionage agent in the United States, the boss of Alger Hiss." This announcement got everyone's attention, and he let it simmer for several days. Then he told Jack Anderson, with whom he was on good terms, that "Mr. X" was Owen Lattimore, but this information was not for attribution. He also told Anderson "a Gothic tale about Communist spies who had been landed on the Atlantic coast by an enemy submarine and who hastened to Lattimore for their orders."

Shortly thereafter McCarthy named Lattimore in a secret session of the Tydings committee, and as Anderson puts it, "named him with a finality that was awesome in its bridge-burning: '. . . definitely an espionage agent . . . one of the top espionage agents . . . the top Russian spy . . . the key man in a Russian espionage ring.' Propelled by the gambler's bravura, he raised the bid even higher: 'I am willing to stand or fall on this one' " (Anderson's ellipses).[24]

McCarthy made his executive session charge against Lattimore on March 21. It leaked immediately. Peyton Ford, assistant to the attorney general, called the FBI late that afternoon to request a summary of the Lattimore file. Attorney General McGrath reported to President Truman, who was vacationing in Florida; in turn, Truman asked that the whole Lattimore file be sent him.[25]

Hoover balked at this request. He could not let the complete file get out of his hands. The White House might blow the anonymity of some of the informants, and illegal and compromising activities by the bureau would be revealed. The bureau had been partly responsible for the collapse of the *Amerasia* case because of illegalities; such a debacle could not be allowed to happen again. So Hoover told Truman that the bureau could not part with the Lattimore file, which by now consisted of ten volumes and several thousand pages. He told McGrath that the case was active; the files were in constant use and "if released would seriously impair our investigative work. . . . As an alternative, I am having prepared a complete summary of the information developed . . . which I am transmitting to Mr. Peyton Ford."[26] This was the "complete summary" that was later shown to the Tydings committee; it was also sent to the president.

But Hoover covered all bases. In case he was ordered to release the complete file, he put a crew to work making photocopies of the whole thing. Ladd, in a memo to Hoover of March 24, reported, "(1) The complete Lattimore file has been photostated in accordance with your instructions. (2) The brief on the Lattimore case is being worked on. Supervisors will work Saturday and Sunday and have it ready Monday." Hoover responded, "I must have this Sunday afternoon."[27]

Just to make sure the director realized how compromising the Lattimore file could be, Supervisor A. H. Belmont instructed the compilers of the "complete summary" to make a list of compromising items. Belmont reported the results to Ladd March 27: "In connection with the preparation of the brief on Owen Lattimore, the volumes of the Lattimore file and the loose mail connected therewith were examined for possible embarrassing or objectionable material contained in each serial for consideration in the event this file is released outside the Bureau." Outcome: 167 items were found to be objectionable or embarrassing.[28] There were wiretaps and intercepted mail involving wholly innocent persons; the luggage search of the Dilowa's belongings; mentions of custodial detention; the warning to Blue Network not to hire Lattimore; the charge that Atlantic–Little Brown was a "Communist tinged" publishing house; unverified information; letters to and from the CIA; names of dozens of informants; bureau derogation of Barmine's credibility; acerbic comments by the director; and records of many illegal surveillances.

Hoover won this battle; he was not required to produce the complete file.

Lattimore found his time in Afghanistan, March 12–29, 1950, both profitable and fascinating. The mission dealt primarily with the Afghan minister of economics, who had a colorful background and was a good negotiator. Shortly after Lattimore arrived, however, he received disturbing cables from Washington. One, arriving March 14, was from Reuters: "SENATOR MC CARTHY IN SENATE FOREIGN RELATIONS SUBCOMMITTEE TODAY SAID YOU HAD COMMUNIST SYMPATHIES AND ADDED 'THIS MAN'S RECORD AS PRO-COMMUNIST GOES BACK MANY YEARS.' WE WOULD APPRECIATE ANY REPLY YOU CARE TO MAKE FOR PUBLICATION WORLD-WIDE AND ESPECIALLY IN AMERICA. WE HAVE ARRANGED FOR PRE-PAID REPLY UP TO 100 WORDS ADDRESSED PRESS REUTERS NEWS AGENCY LONDON."[29]

Lattimore did not answer Reuters. A second cable, from Bert Andrews of the *New York Herald Tribune,* arrived the same day. "SENATOR MC CARTHY HAS MADE SERIOUS CHARGES AGAINST YOUR LOYALTY STOP COULD YOU CABLE ME FIVE HUNDRED WORD STATEMENT COLLECT."[30]

This one Lattimore did answer. "UNKNOWN HERE JUST WHAT MC CARTHY SAID THEREFORE DETAILED REPLY IMPOSSIBLE UNTIL RETURN IN FEW DAYS TIME WHEN WILL CONTACT YOU MEANTIME HOPE PUBLICITY WILL RESULT IN WIDE SALE MY BOOKS AND REALIZATION THAT COMMON SENSE IS POSSIBLE IN UNITED STATES FAR EASTERN POLICY."[31]

Nothing further arrived until March 24. By then McCarthy's "top Soviet spy" charge was circulating in Washington. No one had yet published it, but the Associated Press figured they could at least get Lattimore's reaction to use when it was safe to do so. AP cabled him on that date; he received the message in Kabul March 25. "SENATOR MC CARTHY SAYS OFF RECORD YOU TOP RUSSIAN ESPIONAGE AGENT IN UNITED STATES AND THAT HIS WHOLE CASE RESTS ON YOU STOP SAYS YOU STATE DEPARTMENT ADVISOR RECENTLY AS FOUR WEEKS AGO STOP HAVE CARRIED MRS. LATTIMORE'S AND DR. BRONK'S DENIALS OF MC CARTHY CHARGE AT PUBLIC SENATE HEARING THAT YOU PRO-COMMUNIST STOP PLEASE CABLE YOUR OWN COMMENT MC CARTHY'S ACCUSATIONS. BEALE ASSOCIATED PRESS."[32]

Lattimore knew then that he was in a dirty fight. None of his enemies or opponents had ever made such a charge: neither Schumpeter, nor Kohlberg, nor Eastman, nor Kearney, nor anyone else he was aware of. He talked to the members of his mission and to the Afghans; all were of the opinion that he should not break off the mission even two days early because of this nonsense. They were appalled at this new evidence of anti-

Communist hysteria and expressed full confidence in Lattimore. He therefore sent an answer to AP: "MC CARTHY'S OFF RECORD RANTINGS PURE MOONSHINE STOP DELIGHTED HIS WHOLE CASE RESTS ON ME AS THIS MEANS HE WILL FALL FLAT ON FACE STOP EXACTLY WHAT HE HAS SAID ON RECORD UNKNOWN HERE SO CANNOT REPLY IN DETAIL BUT WILL BE HOME IN FEW DAYS AND WILL CONTACT YOU THEN."[33] One of the myths about the Lattimore case is that Lattimore cut short his stay in Afghanistan to deal with the McCarthy charge. In fact, he stayed until the negotiations were completed on March 27.

When Lattimore passed through Karachi on the way home, the public affairs officer in the U.S. embassy there, Merritt N. Cootes, talked to him several times. Cootes reported these conversations to the State Department, and his report wound up in FBI files. (Cootes had the distinction of giving Lattimore a new middle initial. Lattimore had no middle name or initial, but people were always giving him one. Mostly it was "J.," sometimes "M.," and Cootes tried "Owen L. Lattimore.")[34]

During the course of his conversations with Cootes, Lattimore commented on the many predictions in diplomatic circles that the Chinese Communist regime was doomed to an early demise; he thought, to the contrary, that it was solidly entrenched and that it would be "dangerous if America underestimated this new force."[35]

Ambassador-at-Large Philip Jessup had just been through Karachi on a fact-finding tour, and one of his major topics of inquiry had been Indochina. Cootes asked Lattimore what he thought about the American decision to back Bao Dai there; Lattimore said he "thought that the United States had made another mistake in recognizing Bao Dai, just like we did with Chiang." Cootes then noted that Jessup approved of Bao Dai but disparaged Ho Chi Minh; the latter was a shadowy figure who had "not actually been seen by any reliable person since December 1937." Lattimore said one would expect Jessup to say that, but the evidence in French reports indicated that Ho was getting steadily more powerful. Lattimore told Cootes he planned to return to Pakistan in May or June to do the same sort of broad survey he had just done for Afghanistan.[36]

Lattimore's prediction about Indochina was accurate; his assumption that he could continue in the service of the UN was not. The inquisition had already claimed him.

If the FBI, the Justice Department, and the White House were in a turmoil over McCarthy's sudden elevation of Lattimore to top Soviet spy, unofficial Washington was even more agitated. Everybody knew about it, but nobody could put the charge on the record until McCarthy made it publicly. Nobody, that is, but the intrepid Drew Pearson. Pearson hated McCarthy. He realized the riskiness of being the first to broadcast the story, but he decided that McCarthy was bluffing and hoped he could squelch McCarthy's gamble by a vigorous defense of Lattimore. Accordingly, on March 26 he opened his national radio broadcast as follows: "I am now going to reveal the name of the man whom Senator McCarthy has designated the top Communist agent in the United States. Senator McCarthy has stated that he would rest his entire charge of State Department communism on this case. The man is Owen Lattimore of Johns Hopkins University."[37] Pearson continued with a ringing defense of Lattimore. Overnight Lattimore became a household word.

McCarthy's "gambler's bravura," as Jack Anderson called it, compelled the senator to assemble a detailed case against Lattimore. For this he needed all the help he could get. It was easy to come by. To his existing coterie of Hearst, Scripps Howard, and McCormick Patterson reporters he quickly added Kohlberg, who later claimed to have furnished most of the material McCarthy used in attacking Lattimore. The two met for a long dinner either March 23 or 24. Kohlberg wrote in his personal notes, "Joe asked me to give him the story of the China sellout step by step and in chronological order. This I did during a two-hour, leisurely eaten dinner. Jean Kerr took brief notes, not in shorthand, yet the following week in a speech on the Senate floor the Senator told the story of the sellout of China just as I had told it to him there, almost without error."[38]

Kohlberg exaggerated slightly; some of McCarthy's material came from Freda Utley. McCarthy had a crew of thirteen assembling, organizing, and writing, among them Jean Kerr, later his wife; Charles Kersten, former congressman from Wisconsin; Ed Nellor, a reporter formerly with Hearst; Joe's chief investigator and right-hand man, Don Surine.[39]

McCarthy's dependence on Surine for the first two years of his crusade (Roy Cohn elbowed Surine aside in 1952) was symptomatic. Surine was everything a good investigator should not be: impulsive, inept, cocky, careless. He had been with the FBI for ten years; it was a miracle that he lasted so long. Hoover fired him in 1950 for involvement with a prostitute during an FBI investigation of a white slavery ring. Surine always lied about this, claiming that he had resigned from the bureau. Eventually, Hoover was forced to write a letter to Senator Mike Monroney disavowing responsibility for the former agent.[40]

Surine compounded McCarthy's recklessness and mendacity. He was instrumental in the attack on Anna Rosenberg, a prominent New York labor lawyer whom George Marshall nominated as Assistant Secretary of

Defense for Manpower. Surine almost single-handedly got McCarthy embroiled in the fraudulent activities of Charles Davis, a psychotic who fabricated documents intended to discredit John Carter Vincent and who falsely charged Edward R. Murrow with having been on the Soviet payroll in 1934. Davis was denied security clearance by the Department of Defense, yet he was McCarthy's "contact man" in collecting classified documents from McCarthy's loyal underground in the military, the CIA, Justice, and State.[41]

In the sleazy 1950 Maryland senatorial campaign, which saw the defeat of Millard Tydings, Surine played a prominent role, including a kidnapping and threats of violence against a mailing contractor. He wrote McCarthy's attack on Adlai Stevenson as pro-Communist in the 1952 presidential campaign.[42] Dan Burkhardt, Maryland American Legion adjutant and a member of a group of former intelligence agents active in the anti-Communist field, says that his group rejected Surine's application to join. He was "too wild."[43]

Hoover's contempt for Surine was total. Time after time he warned agents to be careful in dealing with Surine. At one stage of the Lattimore investigation, in March 1950, Baltimore agents were told that "they should not have any further contact with SURINE."[44] Reports of adventures in which Surine went astray over some crackpot would-be informer invariably carry a sarcastic notation by Hoover. To some extent, the cretinous nature of McCarthy's speech on Lattimore was due to Donald Surine.

One of the potential witnesses about Lattimore who came to Surine's attention was Alexander Barmine. The FBI, already suspicious of Barmine, interviewed him again on March 27. Barmine now had a new charge against Lattimore. As reported by SAC Scheidt in New York, "BARMINE SAID THAT IN FORTY NINE THE PANCHEN LAMA COMPETITOR OF THE DALAI LAMA OF TIBET VISITED THE US AND WAS RECEIVED BY THE SUBJECT [Lattimore]. UPON LEAVING THE US THE PANCHEN LAMA ARRIVED IN COMMUNIST CHINA AND CLAIMED HIS TITLE FROM THAT POINT." Bureau naïveté was sufficient to cause them to investigate this howler. They checked it out with State. The Panchen Lama had never visited the United States and could not have been "received" by Lattimore.[45]

Surine did not know of this latest evidence of Barmine's hyperactive imagination. Charged by his boss to gather any dirt that could be flung at Lattimore, Surine determined to extract an affidavit from Barmine for McCarthy to use in addressing the Senate. His channel for approaching Barmine was Barmine's old friend from *Reader's Digest*, Bill White. On March 28 White telephoned Barmine, telling him that McCarthy would like to talk to him and that one of McCarthy's agents would contact him shortly. Barmine said he did not want to talk to McCarthy or his agent. This refusal did not deter Surine, who telephoned Barmine at Barmine's Voice of America office, invoked status as a Senate employee, and induced Barmine to meet him in a nearby bar. At the bar, Surine asked for an affidavit McCarthy could use against Lattimore. Barmine refused, said he would have nothing to do with McCarthy, and stalked out.[46]

Failed mission? Not for the intrepid Surine. He went to the nearby apartment of Eugene Lyons, another professional anti-Communist journalist, asked to use a typewriter, and typed up what he had heard from various people as Barmine's story about Lattimore. Surine headed his production "Expected testimony from Alexander Barmine." At the bottom of the page he wrote in longhand, "Above facts related to me by Alexander Barmine at Schrafft's Bar 57th St. N.Y.C. 5:30 p.m.–6:10 p.m.—3/29/50," and signed his name. Lyons, somewhat uneasy about this procedure, nonetheless was persuaded to add his bit. He countersigned the document: "I have read the above statement. Eugene Lyons." It was this flaky concoction that McCarthy flourished before the Senate the next day. After the McCarthy speech, Barmine was furious. He told the FBI that the McCarthy "affidavit" was a forgery and vowed that if he was ever confronted with the document he would accuse Surine of perjury.[47]

But McCarthy thought it was wonderful, and it came at the right moment. He had asked for time to address the full Senate on March 30. He was now confident that he had the goods on Lattimore. He sent telegrams to Republican friends: "Would like to have you share some pumpkin pie with me this afternoon on the Senate floor."[48] His flagship case was about to be launched; the pumpkin allusion was to the evidence Whittaker Chambers supplied about Hiss.

McCarthy also notified the FBI to have someone on hand after the speech to get the documents he was going to use. The bureau declined. They would be happy to have him send any documents over to the FBI building, but the attorney general did not want McCarthy to "mousetrap" the bureau by "having a photographer take a picture of him handing over the 'documents.' "[49]

The Lattimore speech did not represent the nadir of McCarthy performances; that honor must be reserved for his scurrilous attack on General George C. Marshall a year later. But the Lattimore speech was nonetheless unique in some ways. It was, for one thing, probably the only time

McCarthy came close to an apology and a retraction. Midway through the speech he stated, "I fear in the case of Lattimore, I may have perhaps placed too much stress on the question of whether or not he has been an espionage agent. In view of his position of tremendous power in the State Department as the 'architect' of our far eastern policy, the more important aspect of his case deals with his aims and what he advocates; whether his aims are American aims or whether they coincide with the aims of Soviet Russia. Therefore, forgetting for the time being any question of membership in the Communist Party or participation in espionage, I would like to deal briefly with what this man himself advocates and what he believes in." But it was a hollow retraction. McCarthy's whole effort was to brand Lattimore as a loyal Soviet servant, not in spying on the American government, which would only lead to loss of some documents, but in influencing American policy, which led to the loss of China. This charge required McCarthy to claim that Lattimore had "tremendous power" in the State Department; in truth, he had none whatsoever. One infelicitous remark on this theme brought sardonic laughter from the audience. Said McCarthy: "I believe you can ask almost any school child who the architect of our far eastern policy is, and he will say 'Owen Lattimore.' "[50]

The law firm of Arnold, Fortas, and Porter, engaged by Eleanor Lattimore, issued an analysis of McCarthy's speech, pointing out more than a hundred errors. There were at least that many.[51]

McCarthy's handling of the *Amerasia* case was typical. Hoover never claimed that the FBI had a "100% airtight case" of espionage and treason in *Amerasia*. When Hoover heard this claim, he caused a search to be made to see if he had gone overboard in 1945; he had never said anything like it.[52] Nor did the Justice Department prosecutor say that "he could cover all the facts in that case in less than 5 minutes," as McCarthy claimed. Nor did *Amerasia* have a "large photocopying department"; John Stewart Service was never "in communication from China with Jaffe"; no member of the grand jury voted to indict Service, who was unanimously no-billed; Service never wrote reports "urging that we torpedo our ally Chiang Kai-shek"; Joseph Grew was not "forced to resign" because he wanted Jaffe prosecuted; Service and Roth were not at Lattimore's home the night before the *Amerasia* arrests, but three days before, on an entirely innocent visit.[53] Contrary to McCarthy's claim, a congressional committee had upheld the Justice Department handling of *Amerasia*: on October 23, 1946, the Hobbs committee reported that Service had not "stolen" any documents; instead, he loaned some to Jaffe that he himself had written and had army permission to retain. Jaffe did not get any of Service's reports before the State Department did.[54]

McCarthy had, despite his statement to the contrary, gotten information from the FBI. Lattimore was in no way "responsible" for Stilwell's activities in China. McCarthy did not have an affidavit from Barmine. Lattimore did not control the magazine *Amerasia*. Lattimore did not have two cameras with him on the Point Barrow trip, and the inference that he gave photographs of secret installations to the Russians was false.

Lattimore's statement that "the Communists were destined to win" applied only to China in 1948, not to anyplace else; McCarthy's extrapolation of it to all subsequent Soviet-American rivalries was wholly illegitimate. Jessup was never editor of *Pacific Affairs*; neither Jessup nor Lattimore "pioneered the fictional idea that the Communists of China were not Communists at all." The State Department did not send Lattimore to Afghanistan; the UN did. Roosevelt did not "appoint" Lattimore as adviser to Chiang; Roosevelt could only nominate him, and it was not on the recommendation of Henry Wallace. Wallace did not recommend the "torpedoing" of Chiang Kai-shek. Lattimore did not head the Pauley reparations mission to Japan; Pauley did. The list of falsehoods, great and small, is almost endless. Some of them McCarthy got from Freda Utley, though most came from Kohlberg.

The whole thing was typical paranoid rhetoric. Historian Richard Hofstadter was right in denoting McCarthy as the paradigm paranoid. The very fantastic character of his conclusions led to "heroic striving for 'evidence' to prove that the unbelievable is the only thing that can be believed."[55] Calling McCarthy's striving "heroic" is perhaps too complimentary. One incident during the McCarthy address foreshadowed the personal contempt for any opponent that steadily brought McCarthy into disrepute even with his early Republican backers.

When McCarthy quoted parts of Lattimore's letter to Barnes about hiring Chinese personnel for OWI, Senator Charles Tobey of New Hampshire questioned him as to why he did not place the whole letter in the record. McCarthy replied that the letter was classified secret. Tobey knew McCarthy's "quotation" was false, but McCarthy refused to release the whole document.

Senator Herbert Lehman of New York took over the questioning:

> *Mr. Lehman:*   When charges are made against the loyalty of a man
>   he should be given an opportunity to answer those
>   charges in the same forum in which the charges are

made. I should like to ask the distinguished Senator
why he is so delicate in refusing to yield to the request of the distinguished Senator from New Hampshire to give the full text of the information, when
the Senator from Wisconsin has no hesitation whatsoever in coming before this body and before the
American people and attempting to damn and blacken
the reputation of many people who may be innocent.

Mr. McCarthy: If the Senator would like to know why some of these
documents are not being made available to the press,
if he will step over here I will show him part of a
document which will make very clear to him why it
would be completely unfair to make them available.
Does the Senator care to step over?

Mr. Lehman: I am delighted to.[56]

Lehman then walked down the aisle and stood with his hand out. The
two men stared at each other. Stewart Alsop observed this tableau from
the press gallery, and his account tells better than the *Congressional Record* what happened next:

McCarthy giggled his strange, rather terrifying little giggle. Lehman
looked around the crowded Senate, obviously appealing for support.
Not a man rose.

"Go back to your seat, old man," McCarthy growled at Lehman. The
words do not appear in the *Congressional Record,* but they were clearly
audible in the press gallery. Once more, Lehman looked all around the
chamber, appealing for support. He was met with silence and lowered
eyes. Slowly, he turned and walked . . . back to his seat.

"There goes the end of the Republic," I muttered to my wife, whom
I had smuggled into the press gallery to see the show. It was a poor
imitation of Lord Grey, but it did not seem exaggerated at the time. For
at the time this triumph of the worst Senator who has ever sat in the
Senate over one of the best did seem a decisive moment. . . . Thus old
Senator Lehman's back, waddling off in retreat, seemed to symbolize
the final defeat of decency and the triumph of the yahoos.[57]

Not many observers of the McCarthy performance thought the yahoos
had triumphed. McCarthy's "evidence" was noticeably shoddy. The Luce
publications, fervently pro-Chiang and anti-Communist, panned the speech.
According to *Time,* the senator was in trouble; "McCarthy had promised
to stand or fall on his case against Owen Lattimore, and he clearly had
little left to stand on."[58]

But McCarthy's ultraright newsmen stood by him. Willard Edwards praised his speech in both the *Chicago Tribune* and the *Washington Times-Herald*. The *Tribune* article described McCarthy's output as "weighty new evidence . . . an extraordinary demonstration of what a one-man investigator of state department communism could disclose in a brief period." Edwards's *Times-Herald* article went beyond praising McCarthy to rub salt in FBI wounds. Edwards claimed, "A somewhat embarrassed FBI agent listened as McCarthy produced a series of documents which he said were being turned over to the FBI. Although FBI director Hoover has made no official statement on the Lattimore case, he has not denied reports that his agents have uncovered no evidence warranting criminal prosecution."[59] Indeed, the bureau had no such evidence. Neither did McCarthy.

Several months after the McCarthy speech, the bureau did have an analysis of the trash McCarthy had paraded before the Senate. This analysis was muted and, as released in 1980, heavily censored; but on those points not censored McCarthy came out losing. Hoover had not, as already noted, described the *Amerasia* charges as 100 percent airtight. The bureau did not accept the McCarthy "affidavits" about Lattimore and Roth declassifying documents "in favor of their friends" as true.[60]

The bureau knew Wallace had not recommended Lattimore to President Roosevelt and that Lattimore had not headed the Japanese reparations mission. As to the Barnes letter, the bureau noted, "Intensive investigation has failed to reflect corroboration of the charge that Lattimore loaded the OWI with Communists."[61] Only the claim McCarthy got from Freda Utley that Lattimore's writings followed the Communist line had any support from the bureau.

McCarthy gave a number of documents to the bureau. By the end of June 1950 there were fifty-nine documents in McCarthy's donation. Most of them the bureau already had. The final disposition of most of them can be traced in the files. Twenty-six of the fifty-nine were discarded as false, meaningless, irrelevant, fraudulent, or hopelessly vague. Four were discarded because the informant was known to the bureau as unreliable or mentally unbalanced. One was impossible to check, and one contained useful information from a reliable informant.[62] The disposition of the rest is unknown.

By September 1950 someone on McCarthy's staff had begun to worry that their investigative batting average was low. Surine was dispatched to the FBI's Washington field office, where he told the agents that McCarthy wanted a copy of the bureau's current summary report on the Lattimore case. The reason, as reported by agent Guy Hottel: "Senator McCarthy, in the future, would not make any further allegations without being able to support such allegations by an investigative report. He [Surine] said that if he could get the report, he would attribute the information contained therein to a different investigative agency," thus maintaining Hoover's cover story about never releasing reports outside eligible agencies.[63] This was a familiar charade, but Surine did not get the FBI summary that time.

CHAPTER SIXTEEN

Out of the Woodwork

Perhaps not every schoolchild could identify Lattimore as the architect of American policy in the Far East, but by the end of March 1950 every scoundrel in the country, and some abroad, knew that Lattimore had been targeted as another Hiss. Would-be informants came crawling out of the woodwork, drawn to McCarthy as moths to light, each peddling a new version of Lattimore's evil deeds.

Abe Fortas did his best to warn Lattimore that he was "operating in a situation characterized by insanity" and that "it may be necessary that you get down in the gutter in which we are now operating as a result of Senator McCarthy's personal attack on you."[1] But not even the worldly-wise Fortas fully appreciated the depravity of some of those who now sought fame as accusers of Lattimore. The "respectable" witnesses (Utley, Chambers, Barmine, George Carter, Budenz) were only the visible part of the problem. The underclass of kooks and winos, drifters and opportunists, many of whom would never be named publicly but all of whom were eagerly embraced by McCarthy and the zealous Surine, added a dimension to the problem that no rational argument could deal with. Lattimore could hardly have gotten down in the gutter with *them* even had he wanted to.

Here there was a paradox. While J. Edgar Hoover was preeminent in stirring up the midcentury scare about domestic communism, and while he hated Lattimore with a passion, it was the ability of Hoover's agents to discern flakiness in those clamoring to sell their testimony against Lattimore that prevented things from being even worse. The bureau made mistakes; there were illegalities aplenty; but only the bureau cut the crazies down to size. The right-wing press, the House and Senate inquisitors, even the Justice Department tended to believe the most implausible tales about Lattimore. Hard-bitten FBI agents knew the difference between evidence and trash.

Lattimore was still in Afghanistan when the accusations began. To understand the intensity of the onslaught he faced on his return, it is necessary to sample this underclass attack and note the willingness of McCarthy and his supporters to believe the unbelievable.

Some of the fantasies spun about Lattimore were predictable. If Lattimore were a Soviet spy, he might well have been associated with the most famous Soviet spy ring operating in the Far East, that of Richard Sorge. Sorge worked from 1930 to 1941, first in Shanghai, then in Tokyo, sending brilliant reports on Asian events to the Kremlin. The imagination of several would-be informants followed precisely this path.

On March 23, exactly two days after McCarthy named Lattimore as the top Soviet spy, the first of the Sorge informants appeared. A report of that date from the Washington field office (WFO) of the bureau is heavily censored; all that comes through is an anonymous informant's claim, second- or third-hand, that Richard Sorge kept a diary and that "the name of OWEN LATTIMORE appeared therein with the indication that he was a 'friend who could be used.' "[2] This caused a flurry of bureau activity. By the next day bureau files had been searched, and this informant was found to have a record. He had talked about Lattimore six months earlier but had not mentioned Sorge. Orders went out immediately to locate and reinterview this individual.

On March 27 WFO caught up with this informant. He was vague. He had not actually seen Sorge's diary. He had been a friend of the late secretary of defense, James Forrestal, and perhaps Forrestal had told him about it. He was sorry he could not be of more help.[3]

So the bureau went to the Office of Naval Intelligence and the Intelligence Division of the army to see if they knew about Sorge's diary. By March 28 both had denied ever hearing of such a document. On March 30, as McCarthy was speaking to the Senate, SAC Scheidt in New York reported that records of the Sorge case maintained in his office showed a 1947 document from General Willoughby, MacArthur's intelligence chief (G-2), listing "The Members of the Sorge Spy Ring." Lattimore was not among them. The informant was written off by the bureau.[4]

A month later the Sorge rumor cropped up again. In this set of documents the FBI released names. The channel for this canard was Frank Tavenner, general counsel of HUAC. Tavenner's tale: "One of the Staff Investigators for the HUAC named Owens is alleged to have seen the original of Sorge's confession, wherein Sorge named several American Communists, it being stated that he, Sorge, then furnished a list of names of individuals who could be depended upon by Communists to cooperate and that Lattimore headed this list." Easy to check. The bureau got to Owens, and he backed down from his tale. Someone else had seen the Sorge confession and told him about it. Tavenner, humbled, put his staff to searching their Sorge papers: there was no mention of Lattimore.[5]

There was one more Sorge story, this the most irrational of all. It began when Hoover and McCarthy received identical letters from a German soldier of fortune, Willi Foerster. Foerster had lived in Japan before and during World War II but was expelled as an undesirable alien and shipped to Europe in 1947. In May 1950 Foerster was living in Agno, Switzerland. His English was a bit unruly, but the meaning of his letter of May 9, 1950, is clear:

Sir:

From press reports I learned the controversy of Senator MacCarthy contra Lattimore and, that the FBI has orders to re-investigate the whole question carefully, therefore I wish to inform you as follow:

1. I do not know whether or not camerade Lattimore belonged to the US Communist party or any US underground organisation. But I know exactly that Lattimore was intimately connected with Dr. Richard Sorge, the master-spy of the Kreml who worked in Tokyo (Japan) until he was catched by the Japanese secret police and, after a court trial and a stated open confession sentenced to hang. This verdict was executed in 1944. Before Dr. Sorge was hanged I had the unpleasant chance to see and talk with him several time in the Sugamo prison, Tokyo (Japan).

2. A certain Max Clausen, who turned out to be the first assistant of Dr. Sorge and who also was convicted in connection with Dr. Sorge's spy work to life-prison ———— asked [Foerster's wife, on her] vacation trip from Japan via America to Germany to take along a private letter from Dr. Sorge to America, and buy in San Francisco post-stamps and then mail said letter ordinarely. This letter, Clausen said at that time, contained private family matters Dr. Sorge did not want to be known by the Japanese secret police, who censored secretly foreigners mail.

3. [My wife] took this letter along to America and mailed the same as requested. Said letter, as I clearly remember, was addressed to a certain schoolteacher Owen Lattimore. I thought "Owen" was the calling name for a female.[6]

There followed a page and a half of colorful prose about how he, Foerster, had been mistreated, how Americans were stupid to "liberate" Max Clausen, and how the State Department was leading the world into "disaster and confusion."

This letter did not impress the FBI, and Hoover did nothing about it. McCarthy and his excitable investigator Surine, however, jumped on it immediately. On May 18 the *Washington Daily News* carried a story headed "Global Private Eye Probes State Dept. for McCarthy."

> Sen. Joseph R. McCarthy (R., Wis.) has an international investigator in Paris helping him uncover evidence against State Department officials, it was disclosed today.
>
> The agent was said to divide his time between his Paris attic office and traveling on the famed Paris-Istanbul Orient Express.
>
> Sen. McCarthy refused to identify him, but the agent is said to be an American with contacts in U.S. intelligence circles and the French Surete General.
>
> It was revealed the agent has already visited Switzerland to obtain affidavits which Sen. McCarthy hopes will link a Soviet spy ring to one of the major targets in his charge that the State Department is harboring Communists.

Surine, fired with enthusiasm about this new development, appeared at the WFO May 24. Off the record, he told agents there

HIS OFFICE NOW HAS REPRESENTATIVE EN ROUTE JAPAN IN EFFORT TO SECURE DOCUMENTARY PROOF OF THIS INCIDENT FROM INDIVIDUAL HE DECLINED TO IDENTIFY BECAUSE IF STATE DEPARTMENT LEARNED OF THIS HIS REPRESENTATIVES LIFE WOULD BE IN DANGER. SURINE ALSO CLAIMED HIS TELEPHONES ARE BEING TAPPED, HIS MAIL TAMPERED WITH, AND HE BELIEVES THAT HE IS UNDER CONSTANT SURVEILLANCE. INDICATED THAT STATE DEPT IS RESPONSIBLE FOR THIS. . . . SURINE'S PURPOSE IN FURNISHING INFO RE SORGE NOT KNOWN. HE HAS STATED THAT QUOTE THEY ARE INTERESTED IN BEATING THE BUREAU UNQUOTE ON THIS CASE.[7]

Hoover, on hearing this tale, ordered the legal attaché (an FBI man) at the U.S. embassy in Paris to go to Switzerland to interview Foerster. On May 30 the attaché's report reached Washington. McCarthy's "global private eye," one John E. Farrand, had already seen Foerster. Foerster had provided Farrand with an affidavit stating that Lattimore was working with Sorge and that Sorge had sent a letter to Lattimore in the United States via Max Clausen and Foerster's wife. Further, Foerster knew where hard evidence was: (1) he had a file on Max Clausen, with a penciled notation made in 1937 about the letter to Lattimore; this file had been turned over to Lieutenant Root of the Army Counterintelligence Corps in Japan in 1946. (2) His former wife, Martha Ann Foerster, now residing in Nagano, Japan, had made a notation about this letter in her diary.[8]

Hoover wrote General Willoughby, asking him to check out the Foerster story. Willoughby replied June 6:

> Ref Hoover request. . . . no papers of interest are in Root file except 10 Sep 46 ltr and a business agreement of no current interest. . . . No notes of any kind or in pencil on margin of papers sent Lt Root. Mrs Foerster interrogated Apr 49 and again 31 May 50. Her statements ref Sorge ltr carried by her to USA in both interrogations are similar. She remembers ltr given to her by Clausen thru W. R. Foerster was addressed to Miss or Mrs Sorge. She states on 31 May 50 that "She has never heard of Owen Lattimore, never kept a diary, has no documents or papers concerning Sorge or Lattimore and that Willi Foerster is an habitual and current liar." Our experience with Willi Foerster over period of several years suggest that he is an unreliable opportunist of questionable veracity attempting use of uncooperative ex-wife as stooge for vague repts made to high levels to secure his obj of returning to Japan. It is significant that in 1949 his statement centered on our interest in Sorge, now he has substituted the name of Lattimore, and no doubt will change his stand to coincide with whatever issue is of importance at the time.[9]

That, one would think, would end the matter. But truth rarely catches up with rumor, and the McCarthy crew tried to connect Lattimore with Sorge for the next three years. On August 1, 1950, McCarthy gave the Senate a story based on the Foerster affidavit his agent had obtained in Switzerland, claiming that the story was supported by an army report about the Sorge case released in February 1948. The army report was alleged to be significant "in connection with the Foerster affidavit mentioning Lattimore." Willard Edwards, McCarthy's most gullible journalistic collaborator, wrote up this story in articles appearing in the *Chicago Tribune* and other papers. The headline over the *Tribune* story screamed, "M'Carthy Links Lattimore to Slain Red Spy." Edwards did acknowledge, in the last line of his story, that "Lattimore's name was not mentioned in the Army report."[10]

By the time of this revelation the Korean War was dominating the news, and Edwards's story got little response. The Sorge connection disappeared.

Surine resurrected it in 1953. In July of that year, still chasing phantoms, he told the bureau that he had "located a witness who will identify

Lattimore as a member of the Sorge Spy Ring and the Soviet espionage apparatus." The bureau knew his witness, believed him to be of "questionable credibility," and ignored the whole thing.[11] McCarthy never produced the witness.

Another rogue informant came from the ranks of the U.S. navy. On April 4, 1950, the WFO informed headquarters that a potential witness against Lattimore was Navy Commander Milton M. "Mary" Miles, then stationed in Rhode Island.[12] As American coleader of the Sino-American Cooperative Organization during the war, Miles had worked closely with, and become deeply attached to, Nationalist secret police chief Tai Li.[13] When Tai Li died in 1946, Miles moved heaven and earth (and the naval bureaucracy) to be allowed to go to China to the funeral. Miles's wartime experiences in China had been debilitating; he suffered a nervous breakdown at the end of the war and was hospitalized for many months.[14]

Less than twenty-four hours after FBI headquarters learned that Miles had interesting information, two Boston agents were talking to him in an office at the Naval War College in Newport. What they heard was indeed spectacular. Much of this interview is still denied by the FBI, since Miles demanded that "under no circumstances should his identity be made known." (FBI censors did not realize, when they released a sanitized version of this interview, that describing this secret informant as "the American who during the recent war was closest to Tai Li" would positively identify Miles.)

Miles began his interview with the Boston agents by acknowledging that he "dislikes heartily OWEN LATTIMORE." Though he never had any "affirmative proof" that Lattimore was a Communist or a Russian agent, everything Lattimore did while in China "was designed to subvert the Chinese National Government and to facilitate the seizure of power by the Chinese Communist Party." And, as reported by the Boston agents, there was one specific action that damned Lattimore:

> When HENRY WALLACE came to China on his "good will mission," LATTIMORE acted as interpreter. WALLACE made some comment concerning collaboration between the Nationalist and Communist forces before CHIANG KAI-SHEK. LATTIMORE wilfully and falsely, [according to Tai Li] translated this comment to the Generalissimo so that it read in substance: "Unless you permit American military men, press representatives, OSS representatives and State Department officials to immediately establish liaison with the government at Yenan, President ROOSEVELT will deny you any further Lend-Lease aid and we will permit your country to fall into the hands of the enemy."

CHIANG KAI-SHEK was alleged to have been shocked by this threat because he could not exist at that particular moment as the head of a living nation without such aid. He thereupon responded in the following language: "The only reason that I have barred Americans from visiting Yenan is because any government which issues a visa should do so with a guarantee that the person's life and property will not be molested. I can make no such guarantee with reference to the territory occupied but not governed by the forces at Yenan. If you wish to assume the burden of protecting your own life and property, you certainly have my permission to go there. I cannot suffer you to refer to Yenan as a government. It is like your telling me that if I wish to visit the Government of the United States, I must not only see Mr. ROOSE-VELT at Washington, but also FRANK HAGUE of Jersey City.[15]

Here was another ludicrous scenario. Neither Miles nor his alleged informant, Tai Li, attended the conferences with Chiang where Kuomintang-Communist relations were discussed. T. V. Soong, not Lattimore, was the translator according to the official records. Lattimore at the time was still a strong supporter of Chiang and had Chiang's full confidence. And, had Lattimore mistranslated something vital, Soong, Madame Chiang, or Wang Shih-chieh would have corrected it immediately.

But the Boston agents were not skeptical of Miles's tale, and their acceptance of his statements was reinforced when he told them that he had "thirteen and a half tons of material in his confidential file and safe" in Washington. This material consisted of "diaries and personal notes concerning the political activities, black market activities and illicit sex life of the individuals named above [Lattimore, Vincent, Davies, Service]. . . . This safe has been sealed under the cover 'Top Secret' and ——— he is the only living person who has the combination."[16]

The Boston agents were ecstatic. Miles obviously had the smoking gun needed to convict Lattimore. Their report showed a most positive evaluation of Miles: "He is a direct, forceful individual, given to carefully weighing his words. He indicated that he would say no more about the above-named persons until he could refresh his memory from his notes and prove his statements."[17]

One can imagine the excitement at FBI headquarters. Unfortunately, Commander Miles was unable to come to Washington immediately to produce his thirteen and a half tons of documents; the best the bureau could do was to instruct WFO to see him as soon as he was in town.

Miles was finally available May 5, when two WFO agents interviewed him at his home. The outcome was startling. Far from producing the "proof" that he had promised a month earlier in Boston, he stated that there was a possibility that there might be information in these files concerning OWEN LATTIMORE and others whose names are mentioned in the reference Boston letter. [Miles stated] however, that he did not remember any particular document in the files which contained any information concerning OWEN LATTIMORE or the others mentioned. He stated that if he were to search all of his files he would probably be on a "wild goose chase." ——— He stated that he had apparently been misunderstood by the interviewing agents of the Boston Office, for he advised that . . . he had no files in his possession. ——— further, he also stated that he had no diaries or personal notes concerning the political activities, black market activities, and the illicit sex life of the individuals mentioned in the reference Boston letter.[18]

Reeling from this unanticipated setback, the Washington agents pressed Miles specifically on the other charges he had made in Rhode Island. He backed down on all of them.

The bureau was now greatly embarrassed. Hoover had already informed Assistant Attorney General James M. McInerney of the Miles revelations, which now had to be retracted. The Baltimore office of the bureau was even more upset; they wrote Hoover requesting that Boston and Washington agents be asked to "advise whether there was anything [about Miles's behavior] to indicate that he expected or experienced any pressure from any outside source to tone down his very definite statements regarding the subject [Lattimore] and his possession of documents to corroborate such statements."[19]

Baltimore also wanted a follow-up on Miles to see whether the inconsistencies in his statements could be resolved. So the Boston and WFO agents who had interviewed Miles were probed as to whether they thought he might have been subject to pressure. All responded negatively; Miles was a tough, independent individual, a "man of action" who "would not stand for pressure from any source." They advised dropping the whole matter. The Boston office was particularly opposed to confronting Miles with an agent from each office: he would only be alienated and embarrassed. Anyway, said the Boston response, "It would appear ——— that few of the records in his possession were composed under his direct supervision or by agents employed by him. It is exceedingly doubtful that he has access to the original sources and therefore the evidential value of such material is extremely questionable."[20]

Hoover did not let the matter rest there. There had to be *something* to the original Miles account other than complete hallucination. Who else might have been witness to the mistranslation? The Chinese participants,

Chiang, Madame Chiang, Wang Shih-chieh, and T. V. Soong were out of his jurisdiction. There was no point in asking Lattimore. Vincent, however, was in Switzerland; the legal attaché in Paris could be sent to interview him. This was done, and on June 1 the Paris FBI man saw Vincent at the Berne Legation.

Vincent was incredulous. The story made no sense at all. There had been too many Chinese present who had a perfect understanding of English for any such fraud to have occurred.[21] This was enough to sour even Hoover on Miles as an informant. There is no further mention in bureau files of the "Wallace mistranslation" charge.

In mid-April 1950 a Japanese mischief maker went to the San Francisco office of the FBI with the unlikely story that Lattimore had directed the Strategic Bombing Survey (SBS) sent to Japan in the fall of 1945 and that he had hired at least four Nisei Communists for the survey. SBS was an operation of the U.S. Air Force, then still under Army. The FBI had close liaison with Army. A few telephone calls could easily have located an air force officer with definitive knowledge of who ran SBS. The bureau should also have recalled that Lattimore had been an active member of the Pauley reparations mission, which operated at the same time as SBS. Lattimore could not have directed SBS while devoting full time to Pauley. Somehow, these commonsense observations were never made.

The informant report that made the charge appears in a letter from the San Francisco office to Hoover dated April 25, 1950: "Regarding OWEN LATTIMORE group worked under the name of the Strategic Bombing Survey included three known Japanese Communists who are presently in Los Angeles. They are SHIRO TAKEDA . . . NOBUYOSHI . . . and TEIJI KOIDE. . . . They flew in Tokyo by the Strategic Bombing Survey group immediately after the surrender under LATTIMORE direction. When they came to Tokyo, I was very much surprised. Many of us who knew their commie reputation could not understand why such boys were sent there. It was rumored that the communistic encouragement might be introduced."[22] This letter started a full-scale search. WFO, Baltimore, Los Angeles, and other offices were instructed to determine who directed SBS, who selected personnel, what the records of these Japanese Americans were, and what role Lattimore played in it all.

It was not until August that WFO provided the names of those in charge of SBS. The list of thirteen included Paul Nitze, John Kenneth Galbraith, George Ball, and Rensis Likert. Likert was alleged to have "had quite a bit to do" with recruiting personnel. The WFO sources "advised that at no time during the bombing survey did the name of LATTIMORE come to their attention as having recommended persons to be employed. Both stated that at this time they had never heard of LATTIMORE."[23]

That should have settled the matter, but it did not. The FBI now set about to interview all or most of the thirteen persons named as directors of SBS. Accordingly, requests for interviews went out to Detroit, New York, Baltimore, Los Angeles, and elsewhere; when reports came in from these interviews, the universal answer was that Lattimore was not involved. Not until November 15 did WFO tell headquarters, in effect, "Enough. There's nothing to this."[24]

But a late report came in November 29 from San Francisco. That office had finally connected with a former Office of Strategic Services (OSS) officer who was one of the directors of SBS. He gave a bit of background to the survey that showed that even as early as 1945 anti-Communist fanaticism was interfering with professional judgments of government officials. This informant told the bureau that the SBS official responsible for hiring "based his selection of individuals upon their qualifications, competency and willingness to accept assignment to an overseas post." The SBS informant remembered that there had been a challenge to the loyalty of SBS personnel. Representative Andrew May alleged that several of the fifty SBS staffers were Communists and threatened to "expose" the survey as Communist infiltrated. Army authorities were annoyed at the delay caused by May and devised a brilliant strategem; they "randomly removed the names of approximately 20 men from the list of selected personnel. May and his council [committee] were then satisfied and the group departed for Japan."[25]

The end was not yet. Incredibly, as late as December 1951 the bureau was still interviewing former SBS personnel because "LATTIMORE is charged with using his influence in the hiring of Communists for the U.S. Strategic Bombing Survey."[26] It was one of the worst performances in bureau handling of the Lattimore case.

McCarthy got hundreds of calls from people who claimed to be able to identify Lattimore as a Communist. One of them came on April 17, 1950, from a seaman named Sidney Troster in Memphis. Troster claimed that he had met in Memphis two persons with significant knowledge of Communist affairs. One was a fellow seaman. This seaman told Troster that "while unloading the *SS Bayside* in Shanghai, China, one Colonel Tsing of the Nationalist Army ——— that he and many others in the Nationalist Army were Communists. ——— should not be surprised because the United States Government also has Communists in it, adding that the

US has its Lattimore." Troster had other tales. One of them was about a trip through the Panama Canal during the war when a crew member took photographs of the canal, later giving them to a Russian spy in Shanghai.[27]

The day after getting these stories from Troster, McCarthy phoned Ladd at the bureau. Ladd immediately contacted Assistant Director Alan Belmont, ordering "that a memorandum be submitted to the Department advising of the additional information received from Senator McCarthy and that this investigation is being conducted."[28]

Ladd also phoned SAC Hostetter in Memphis, instructing Hostetter to interview Troster and his two friends and cable results to the bureau.[29] It is doubtful that Ladd thought this story credible but the bureau could not allow McCarthy to steal a march on it.

The day after Ladd's call to Memphis, Hostetter wired a six-page report to Washington.[30] A full page of it is still denied for "national security" reasons, and all names are denied, so the exact sequence of events is hard to determine. The clear parts of Hostetter's cable, plus later reports from Knoxville and WFO, provide a biography of Troster that does not inspire confidence.

Troster was from Toronto. In 1945 he joined a Canadian maritime union, which turned out to be Communist controlled. Troster became a Communist, worked as a seaman for several years, and served as a courier for the Party, taking sealed messages to ports all over the world. About 1940 he became disillusioned with communism, left the Party, was beaten up by Communist goons, and came illegally to the United States. After various unfortunate adventures in Toledo and New York, he went to Memphis, where the Immigration and Naturalization Service caught up with him. On April 7, 1950, INS sent an agent from Washington who questioned Troster for seven hours but did not take him into custody. Troster then decided to contact Senator McCarthy, according to an FBI cable, believing that "HE WOULD BE IMMEDIATELY TAKEN TO WASHINGTON, WHERE HE WOULD HAVE AN OPPORTUNITY TO TALK TO HIGH GOVT. OFFICIALS CONCERNING HIS IMMIGRATION STATUS."[31]

The telephone call to McCarthy, however, did not yield a ticket to Washington; instead, Troster was interviewed by Hostetter in Memphis. This result did not satisfy Troster; the next day he started hitchhiking to Washington. The FBI put out a bulletin to have Troster apprehended, but to no avail. When he arrived in Washington, he telephoned a friend in Memphis, learned that the FBI was looking for him, and decided to go to the WFO. There he was interviewed on April 27 by Supervisor E. M.

Gregg, who proved to be a hard-nosed interrogator. After going over his life story, Troster confessed to Gregg that he had no information about Lattimore, nor did his friends in Memphis. He had made it all up. When Gregg reported on the interview, he noted that Troster was "extremely nebulous when queried concerning dates, stating 'I don't want you fellows pinning me down on dates because I don't recall them.' " At the conclusion of the interview, Troster asked Gregg for a sleeping pill.[32]

Gregg turned Troster over to the INS; presumably he was sent back to Canada. The bureau had once again followed one of McCarthy's leads to a dead end.

Some of Lattimore's enemies in Baltimore were also hallucinating in April 1950. On the eighteenth a woman active in countersubversion phoned McFarlin with a new story that she had gotten from an anonymous source. McFarlin's telegram to Headquarters reported "A REUTERS, BRITISH NEWS AGENCY, DISPATCH FROM KABUL, AFGHANISTAN DATED ON OR ABOUT MARCH EIGHTEEN [said that] OFFICIALS OF THE AFGHANISTAN GOVERNMENT HAD A SOCIAL FUNCTION AT KABUL IN HONOR OF THE RUSSIAN AMBASSADOR TO PAKISTAN AND HIS NINETEEN ADVISORS. THIS FUNCTION WAS ATTENDED ALSO BY SUBJECT [Lattimore] AND THE OTHER MEMBERS OF THE UN COMMISSION WHO WERE THEN ON A MISSION TO AFGHANISTAN."[33] This informant also noted that the Russian ambassador would have gone out of his way to meet Lattimore in Kabul.

McFarlin, whose office usually grasped each new lead eagerly, showed a bit of skepticism at the end of his message. "IT COULD BE REASONED THAT IT WOULD BE PERFECTLY NORMAL SHOULD THE AFGHANISTAN GOVERNMENT HOLD SOME OFFICIAL SOCIAL FUNCTION IN HONOR OF THE RUSSIAN AMBASSADOR AND HIS ADVISORS TO INVITE SUBJECT AND THE OTHER MEMBERS OF THE UN COMMISSION WHO WERE THEN PRESENT IN AFGHANISTAN AS FOREIGN DIGNITARIES. HOWEVER, NY IS REQUESTED TO CONTACT REUTERS IN NYC TO ASCERTAIN IF THE ABOVE DISPATCH ACTUALLY EXISTS, AND, IF SO, TO FURNISH COPIES OF SAME TO THE BUREAU AND BALTIMORE." FBI headquarters seemed more impressed with the story than was McFarlin, since they quickly passed it on to Assistant Attorney General McInerney. Meanwhile, Reuters was put to work tracking down the incriminating dispatch. By April 25 the New York office of Reuters reported that they had heard from London and that no such dispatch existed.[34]

That would probably have been the end of it, except for Don Surine of McCarthy's office. The Baltimore informant believed that the FBI was showing insufficient zeal, so she took her story to McCarthy. McCarthy turned it over to Surine. On May 19 Surine phoned WFO, asking that a Lattimore case officer contact him. The meeting was held three days later. Surine's story had some new embellishments; whether the Baltimore source had provided them or Surine thought them up himself is unknown.

The affair in Kabul was no longer a "social function" but a "most important meeting." And there were some new participants:

> In conjunction with the meeting in Kabul, SURINE said that he had also learned that ANDREW ROTH, the subject in the Amerasia investigation who is now serving as an Advisor to Communist HO CHI MINH in Indo China, had also attended this meeting along with MINH. SURINE identified MINH as a Communist who had been employed at the Russian offices in Boston from 1931 to 1933 prior to the United States recognition of Russia. He also advised that in 1937 MINH had visited at the LATTIMORE home in Baltimore.
>
> SURINE believed that the foregoing could be verified by the Central Intelligence Agency or by reviewing dispatches issued by the Reuters News Agency, which had issued releases concerning (1) LATTIMORE'S presence in Kabul and (2) the Russian group in Kabul en route from Moscow to Karachi.[35]

One has to assume that renewed FBI attention to this implausible tale was caused by lack of internal coordination. McFarlin in Baltimore cabled headquarters requesting that WFO "attempt verification" of Surine's account through the CIA. Headquarters followed through not only with the CIA but also with the State Department.

The CIA, never inclined to exercise itself about requests from Hoover, took its time about answering. Most of its reply of June 19 is denied, but the bottom line was skepticism. Ho Chi Minh had tuberculosis: "it is considered doubtful that he could have undertaken a trip requiring arduous physical exertion. . . . it would appear reasonable to conclude that it is improbable that a meeting took place between these individuals at the time and place mentioned."[36]

The State Department was more positive. Their embassy in Kabul knew of no such meeting. Ho Chi Minh could not have been in Kabul, and Ambassador Louis G. Dreyfus observed, "It is interesting to note that Professor Lattimore in paying courtesy calls on the Chiefs of Mission of countries which are members of the United Nations, was not received by the Soviet Ambassador. His requests for an interview were either not replied to or the false statement was made that the Ambassador was out of the city."[37]

If the Reuters and Dreyfus responses were not definitive, McFarlin added an observation from Baltimore. Since Lattimore did not move to Baltimore until 1938, he could hardly have entertained Ho Chi Minh at his home there in 1937.[38]

This was the end of the "meeting in Kabul" flap. Even Surine had to give up on it. But there were dozens of other equally risible stories in his repertoire; it was a veritable encyclopedia of hallucinations.

One of the most bizarre stories concerned Leon Trotsky's murderer. This story came from an adventurer whose name the FBI documents deny. The informant, who had spent time in Mexico, wrote McCarthy sometime in April 1950 claiming to know much about communism in Latin America. McCarthy passed this information to the bureau.[39]

The bureau took it up. Dallas FBI agents interviewed the informant on April 21, at which time he elaborated on the claims he had made to McCarthy and "indicated that he had other information which he did not wish to disclose," but he would be in Washington during the first week of May and would tell Ladd about it. As was now routine in bureau interviews with informants on communism, the agents asked him if he knew anything about Owen Lattimore. He did not. The agents described him as "one of those persons with a detective complex and he made a most unfavorable impression."[40]

By the time he reported to the bureau on May 5 in Washington he knew something about Lattimore, connecting him now with the 1940 murder of Trotsky by Frank Jackson. He had a female acquaintance who "had occasion to talk with TROTSKY'S murderer and the latter said 'Don't worry about me, I won't hang or be executed as I have a contact in the United States who is highly placed in the United States Government.' He then identified this contact as OWEN LATTIMORE."[41]

The informant was unable to give the FBI much time in Washington; he had to leave for New York, but the bureau could contact him again there. This they finally did, on September 7. He repeated the Frank Jackson story but had no further details. He would, however, be happy to provide the name of his source in Dallas, and the bureau could tell her that he had given them her name.[42]

The bureau did not follow up this lead, probably because they found it too fantastic to pursue. On December 2, however, the New York office called headquarters to say that the female source of the story about Jackson and Lattimore had been investigated by them previously because of her Communist connections. She was then in New York and was likely to be subpoenaed soon by HUAC, which intended to hold hearings on Trotsky's murder. Shouldn't the bureau get to her first, so they would not be caught short if she told her story publicly? Headquarters agreed, and New York agents interviewed her the next day.

As with almost all of the leads that came from McCarthy, this one too vanished into thin air when it was finally tracked down. The woman had indeed talked to Frank Jackson, but she had "NEVER HEARD FRANK JACKSON MAKE ANY STATEMENT AT ANY TIME THAT HE HAD AN IMPORTANT CONTACT OR FRIEND IN US GOVERNMENT. [She had never heard] OF OWEN LATTIMORE BEFORE RECENT NEWSPAPER PUBLICITY."[43]

Of all the charlatans clamoring for the spotlight and claiming knowledge about Lattimore during 1950, few were as resourceful as Paul Walters (this seems to have been his real name; the FBI documents have a long paragraph about his several aliases, but most of it is denied). Not only did Walters lead McCarthy, Surine, Robert Morris, J. B. Matthews, and the FBI on a merry chase; he also extracted money from both Alfred Kohlberg and a fanatic anti-Communist in Baltimore, Virginia Starr Freedom, to carry out a wild mission to Cuba.

On April 20, 1950, Walters called McCarthy from New York. He had information proving that Lattimore was a Party member, but he would give it to no one but McCarthy. It is not clear how much of his story he told McCarthy over the telephone, but it was enough for McCarthy to promise Walters that one of McCarthy's trusted agents would contact him immediately.[44] McCarthy then instructed J. B. Matthews to get in touch with Walters. Matthews invited Walters to come to his apartment that same evening, and he complied; he was there from 7:00 P.M. until 2:00 A.M. Matthews was impressed. Walters could name Communist party officials whom he had known in Baltimore during the 1930s, such as Al Lannon and Tommy Ray. Matthews called Robert Morris, at that time in New York for the Republicans on the Tydings committee, and Morris also heard the story by telephone.

Before Walters would talk, he demanded that the FBI not be informed; Matthews agreed to this request. Then Walters began a tale that outdid even Louis Budenz's story of Party instructions on tissue paper to be flushed down the toilet. Walters had seen a list of contributors to the Communist party in the handwriting of Roy Hudson, a list now stored in Mexico City; it contained the name of Owen Lattimore as a contributor. Walters could get this list in forty-eight hours. He also recalled two times when Lattimore addressed the Baltimore Waterfront Section of the Party in 1932 and 1933. And shortly before the Seaman's hunger march on Washington in 1932, Lattimore had signed a receipt for $1,380, which was money collected to finance the march.[45]

In 1934, Walters said, the Party ordered that all records in possession of the Baltimore Waterfront Branch be gotten rid of. The records were to be eliminated in one of three ways: (1) buried in a box under the cellar of the union hall at 1629 Thames Street; (2) sent by courier to the town of Taxco, Mexico, where the records were buried in caves in a hillside outside of town; or (3) taken by courier to a building operated by a Party sympathizer in Mexico City, which was occupied exclusively by Communist artists. Whenever it was Walters's turn to destroy records, he would collect them in an old sea bag, then dump them in a container to be buried beneath the union hall.

This sea bag was to become Walters's passport to fame and fortune. Shortly after 1934, he said, he quit the Communist party, left Baltimore, and bought a string of racehorses. He kept racing equipment in the old sea bag. In 1940 he got out of the racehorse business, sold his horses to a Florida agent named Jose Gomez, and included the sea bag with the deal. A month after this sale, he received a letter from a horse trainer in Cuba who had purchased the horses and sea bag from Gomez. There were some papers, including a receipt, in the bottom of the sea bag. Were these of any value? Walters did not answer the letter.[46]

Now, in 1950, he knew what had happened. On some occasion when he dumped the Communist documents out of his sea bag, "a couple of them apparently stuck in the bottom of the bag and remained there unnoticed until found by the Cuban trainer in 1940." If he could just get to Cuba, he could locate the horse trainer, recover the papers in his sea bag, and produce documentary proof of Lattimore's Communist party activity.[47]

Not only that, the Roy Hudson list of Party contributors was probably at the repository in Mexico City. He had friends there who could obtain it and bring it to New York. Or perhaps he could go get it himself. The latter proposal later appealed to Surine, who told the bureau on April 28 that he and Walters were going to Mexico City the next day.[48] (Apparently this trip did not take place.)

Walters had other tales: about an American consul in Italy who was a Communist, about a company he worked for that was acting for the Party, about Communist lawyers in Baltimore. But it was the promise of documents about Lattimore that attracted Matthews and later his friends Kohlberg and Virginia Freedom. Walters made several telephone calls while he was at Matthews's apartment, saying that he was calling collect to Mexico and Havana.

The next day Matthews and Morris discussed Walters's claims extensively. They concluded that despite their promise to Walters not to involve the FBI, there was sufficient doubt about his credibility to get the bureau to check him out. Accordingly, on April 22 Morris requested the FBI to send agents to talk to him and Matthews. When the agents appeared at Matthews's apartment that evening, they heard the Walters story and were requested to check it out quietly. All this was reported to Ladd the next day.[49]

Ladd's reaction was to inform Matthews and Morris that the bureau would do no investigating unless they could talk to Walters. Two days later Morris said they could talk to Walters after a week had gone by. Meanwhile the bureau did routine name checks. New York showed nothing, but Baltimore found some interesting items. Walters had not been active in the Communist party there in 1931–34. (Nor had Lattimore been in the city at that time; he was in China.) In 1947 Walters had been arrested by the Baltimore County Police for obstructing justice and withholding information relative to the commission of a crime. He was a "heavy boozer," and his "FORMER EMPLOYER ADVISED THAT HE WAS A MAN OF MYSTERY AND TOLD WEIRD TALES."[50]

This information should have been enough to kill FBI interest, but McCarthy was involved. So on April 27 Hoover asked the legal attaché in Havana to check out the places to which Walters had allegedly made telephone calls from Matthews's apartment. This investigation produced nothing.[51]

McCarthy was now going strong on the Walters story. Surine had been put in charge of it. An incident in New York April 30 stirred up some bad blood between McCarthy's henchman and the FBI. SAC Scheidt cabled the bureau on that date that he had located Mrs. Walters, learned that she and her husband were checking out of their hotel very soon, and put a tail on them. His cloak-and-dagger report:

SPOT CHECK INSTITUTED AT APPROXIMATELY NOON OF THIS DATE. UNKNOWN MAN OBSERVED LOADING PACKAGES AND BABY CARRIAGE IN CAB, IN FRONT OF HOTEL ———— UNKNOWN MAN GLANCED UP IN DIRECTION OF BUREAU CAR AND IMMEDIATELY PROCEEDED THERETO, OPENED THE DOOR OF THE CAR AND IDENTIFIED HIMSELF AS FORMER AGENT SUR-

INE. HE DISPLAYED HIS TEN YEAR KEY HANGING ON HIS TIE CHAIN. HE
STATED "I RECOGNIZE THIS CAR AS A BUREAU CAR AND I ASSUME YOU
ARE A BUREAU AGENT. I WISH YOU WOULD CLEAR OUT OF THE AREA. I
AM WORKING IN COMPLETE COOPERATION WITH THE BUREAU. MY
MAN MADE A MISTAKE LAST NIGHT ——— PLEASE DO NOT CHECK THIS
——— FOR IT MAY MEAN THIS MAN'S LIFE." HE THEN INDICATED THAT
HE WAS GOING TO WASHINGTON THIS WEEKEND AND WOULD SEE MR.
LADD AND THE DIRECTOR AND GIVE THEM THE WHOLE STORY. [Hoover's
comment in the margin at this point: "He will never come near the
Bureau."] HE THEN RAN TO AN AWAITING TAXICAB AND ENTERED WITH
——— AGENT IN BUREAU CAR COULD NOT DISCREETLY TAKE UP THE
SURVEILLANCE IN THE AUTOMOBILE AND WAS UNABLE TO LOCATE A CAB.[52]

But the agents traced Surine's cab, learning that it had gone to Newark
Airport and that Surine had given the driver a seven-dollar tip.

McCarthy was uneasy when he heard that Surine had been tailed by a
bureau agent. Jean Kerr, McCarthy's secretary, called Hoover and arranged an appointment for herself and another McCarthy staffer (not
Surine; Hoover was right, he never came near the bureau) to see the
director. On May 1 Hoover wrote a long memo to Tolson about their
visit. They had come to smooth ruffled feathers. Hoover's memo said that
according to Kerr, Walters had promised McCarthy that he would "produce the documents" that weekend to prove Lattimore a Party member.
But the next day Kerr telephoned Hoover to say that Walters had produced nothing.[53]

Walters then disappeared from FBI files until May 11, when he surfaced
at the Miami FBI office and told a sad tale to SAC Carson. He had originally hoped to testify before the Tydings committee, but when Tydings
did not call him, Surine put him in touch with Virginia Starr Freedom of
Baltimore and Alfred Kohlberg of New York. They believed his story and
agreed to finance a trip to Cuba to retrieve his sea bag and the Lattimore
receipt. Kohlberg sent a former Office of Naval Intelligence agent with
him on this trip, but the ONI man "kept him in a drunken condition from
time of departure until arrival back in Miami last night." The ONI man
also "tried to dope him" in Miami. Sadly, he did not find his sea bag.[54]

Walters arrived back in New York May 22, when FBI agents there talked
to him. His whole tale now unraveled:

SUBJECT CLAIMS ALL OF THE MATERIAL AS SET FORTH IN REF MEMO IS PURE FABRICATION. ALLEGES THAT WHEN QUESTIONED BY SENATE COMMITTEE INVESTIGATORS THEY AND HIMSELF WERE DRINKING HEAVILY. AS A RESULT OF INTOXICATION, HE IS NOT SURE WHAT HE TOLD THEM BUT NONE OF IT TRUE. . . . IN ORIGINAL STORY TO J. B. MATTHEWS AND ROBERT MORRIS, SUBJECT ALLEGED ATTENDING CP MEETINGS AT WHICH LATTIMORE LECTURED. NOW STATES THAT HE NEVER TOLD THIS STORY AND THAT HE HAS NO KNOWLEDGE OF ANY CP ACTIVITIES ON PART OF LATTIMORE OTHER THAN SEEING HIM IN OFFICE OF ADES IN BALTIMORE. . . . STATED THAT IN ALL INTERVIEWS WITH SENATE COMMITTEE INVESTIGATORS THEY ALL ATTEMPTED TO "BLOW UP" HIS STORY AND HAVE HIM TESTIFY TO FABRICATION. MAINTAINS HIS ONLY MOTIVE IN ORIGINAL CONTACTS WITH COMMITTEE WAS PATRIOTISM. ADMITS PRESENTLY DEALING WITH NY JOURNAL AMERICAN NEWSPAPER THROUGH [former FBI agent] LARRY E. KERLEY TO SELL STORY AND TO INVESTIGATE CP ACTIVITIES. . . . UPON REQUEST BY INTERVIEWING AGENT, SUBJECT REFUSED TO EXECUTE SIGNED STATEMENT. NO FURTHER INVESTIGATION CONTEMPLATED BY THIS OFFICE. [55]

After this memo, Walters disappeared from bureau files. The only missing detail provided by a bureau summary was that Kohlberg had supplied $520 to pay Walters's wife's expenses while he was in Cuba. On July 13 Hoover notified Assistant Attorney General McInerney that the Walters investigation was a dead end. [56]

One of the ingenious former Communists who wanted to jump on the anti-Lattimore bandwagon was from Cleveland; his name is blacked out in the FBI files. This man went to the bureau office there May 9 with the claim that a Communist writer who used the pen name B. T. Lo was really a collaboration between Lattimore and Thomas A. Bisson. B. T. Lo represented these men's initials reversed. Farfetched? Not in the climate of 1950. The FBI machinery began to track down this possibility. [57]

B. T. Lo was found to have signed his name to only two articles. One appeared in the June 1940 issue of the *Communist,* the other in the July 1946 issue of *Political Affairs.* Both articles contained phrases indicating that the author was a Party member. The Cleveland ex-Communist claimed that the style of the 1946 article, "U.S. Imperialist Intervention in China," was similar to Lattimore's style in *Solution in Asia*.

There were several avenues the bureau could use to check out this hypothesis. One was a straightforward search for somebody who knew the author of the B. T. Lo articles. Accordingly, twenty-six leads were put out to bureau and army offices requesting file searches and ordering interviews of ex-Communists who might know B. T. Lo and of anti-Lattimore China specialists who would be familiar with Lattimore's publications.[58] (One lead was later canceled: "John K. Fairbank should not be interviewed at this time.")

The results were disappointing. No biographical directory, government bureau, or library had a listing for B. T. Lo. None of the ex-Communists interviewed knew who he was, though several said he did indeed write like Lattimore. One ex-Communist said that Lo might have been one of two Chinese associated with the Committee for a Democratic Far Eastern Policy; the bureau checked out this suggestion, with negative results. The *Daily Worker* index, *New York Times* index, Library of Congress, and other similar repositories yielded no information.

The Baltimore FBI office, always more zealous and optimistic than headquarters, refused to admit defeat. On July 6 Baltimore wrote Hoover pointing out that Louis Budenz had said Lattimore was charged with changing the Party line on Chiang Kai-shek, that this task was carried out by Bisson in the July 14, 1943, *Far Eastern Survey*, and that Lattimore and Bisson had been to Yenan together in 1937. Q.E.D. Baltimore therefore had a new avenue of investigation to suggest: "The Bureau Central Research Desk is requested to compare the style and expression of articles written by B. T. LO with the known writings of OWEN LATTIMORE and THOMAS ARTHUR BISSON, aka T. A. BISSON." Baltimore also wanted federal income-tax records searched to see if Lo had ever filed a return.[59]

FBI Inspector Carl Hennrich supported the IRS search. Hoover, always sensitive about bureau relations with other government agencies, shot it down on July 19; it would require an immense search by IRS. "This is an unreasonable request and might injure our present excellent relations."[60]

Hennrich also supported Baltimore's request to the FBI Central Research Desk. The head of that office, F. J. Baumgardner, objected in a letter to Belmont on August 9: "Such a comparison will require extensive research and can not be expected to produce conclusive results. The B. T. Lo articles are alleged to be the production of Lattimore and Bisson and, therefore, the style and expresssion of either would be altered in such a joint article. A further limitation is the availability of only two specimens of the B. T. Lo writings."[61]

Baumgardner got his way.

Then there was a discouraging report from Seattle. A bureau informant there, probably George Taylor, read the B. T. Lo articles and decided that Lo was less sophisticated than Lattimore was. As for Bisson, he was a "dull, factual writer" whose style was different from both Lo and Lattimore. Further, Lattimore held opinions different from those stated by Lo.[62]

The bureau then went back to the original informant in Cleveland. Presumably, Cleveland agents told him that little support could be found for his tale. He then changed his ground: B. T. Lo's similarity to Lattimore-Bisson was one of substance, not style: "he feels the same author may have written both articles since similar conclusions are reached."[63]

Other informants were still skeptical. A Washington, D.C., authority frequently consulted by the bureau on China affairs said the B. T. Lo language would not have been used by Lattimore.[64]

By the end of November, headquarters had cooled on the whole topic. Hoover wrote Baltimore telling them that most of the leads had been run out; since nothing of consequence had been obtained, "No comparison will be attempted by the research desk at the Bureau at this time."[65] The matter appears to have died at this stage.

But Baltimore filed it away for future reference. In November 1952, when the Justice Department was about to take the Lattimore case to a grand jury, Baltimore raised the B. T. Lo matter again. There were "a number of new high-level Communist Party defectees who might now be in a position to give information concerning this matter." Why not interview these defectors in Denver, Miami, Los Angeles, and New York? Hoover gave his approval, but the new "high-level defectees" knew nothing about B. T. Lo. This was the end of the line.[66]

There is almost no end to the series of improbable tales and unreliable informants in the Lattimore FBI file. They become wearisome. They were all seeking to ride the wave of hysteria unleashed by McCarthy. Ultimately the FBI rejected them all.

Most of the tale bearers peddled their fictions through Senator McCarthy. One seaman who shipped on the United States Lines *General Lee* told McCarthy that Lattimore had boarded this ship in Manila in July 1936 and had created a disturbance on deck that delayed the ship's sailing. The FBI obtained logs for the *General Lee*, found no reference to Lattimore (who was nowhere near Manila at the time), and noted that the informant often overindulged in wine.[67] Another informant claimed Lattimore had worked for the Williams Drug Company in China, selling tiger's-blood pills; these pills were much desired by the Chinese, and their purveyors had access to "a wide coverage of the Chinese provinces." This also the bureau checked out; Lattimore had no connection with the Williams Drug Company.[68] Still another informant, an officer of Naval Intelligence in San Diego, claimed that Lattimore had been a "friend and associate of Nicholas Roerich," who was alleged to have been a Soviet spy. The Japanese claimed Roerich had traveled widely in Mongolia locating sites for Soviet air bases. Again the bureau conducted a major investigation; Lattimore was found to have had no connection with Roerich.[69]

There is no adjective adequate to describe the insanity of the times, the corruption and unreliability of the informants, or the gullibility of senators and their staffs. It was this netherworld of fanatics, psychopaths, alcoholics, con artists, and demagogues that Lattimore confronted on April 1, 1950, when he landed in New York.

CHAPTER SEVENTEEN

A Fool or a Knave

Lattimore arrived in London from Afghanistan on March 30, the same day McCarthy addressed the Senate. One of Lattimore's worries was whether he would get a chance to read his mail and be briefed on all the happenings in Washington before he had to face the press. He need not have worried; the British had everything arranged. They took him to their VIP room, where his mail was waiting, as was a telephone call from the UN office in London.[1]

The mail of greatest import was from Eleanor and the lawyer she had engaged, Abe Fortas. Eleanor's letter was almost apocalyptic: "You are going to have an opportunity of a lifetime to affect the future of democracy in this country. McCarthy has staked everything now on this one case, so that if he is thoroughly demolished now his whole house of cards tumbles and his methods and all he stands for fall with them. I am too tired to express myself sensibly, but all your friends and all the decent people in America are backing you and counting on you to come out with flying colors. You will have saved the 81 people on his State Department list, and a lot of other people who will soon be on other lists if he gets by with this."[2]

It was an admirable pep talk, but the mood of the country was too angry, the number of liars willing to capitalize on the Red Scare too large, the need of frustrated Republicans and ultraconservative Democrats for a scapegoat too great for one lone professor to turn things around.

Abe Fortas was more realistic. In addition to warning Lattimore that the country was deranged and that Lattimore was facing a gutter fight, Fortas described what he had done to present Lattimore's case. He had requested Tydings to schedule Lattimore for an appearance before the

249

subcommittee and had arranged a press conference for the Mongols. Fortas also wrote McCarthy and enclosed a copy of the letter for Lattimore
to read in London:

> We write this letter to you at this time to give you an opportunity
> publicly to retract and repudiate your charges that Mr. Lattimore is
> a Communist or Communist sympathizer or the agent of a foreign
> power. We suggest that a decent regard for the welfare of your
> country, for the high office that you hold, and for elementary
> Christian values, require you immediately to put a stop to this
> fantastic outrage. We are required, however, to inform you that
> any withdrawal of your charges that you now make will not, as
> a matter of law, exonerate you from such legal liability as you
> may have in the event that Mr. Lattimore chooses to bring action
> against you for the statements that you have made concerning him,
> including your "off-the-record" identification of him as the person
> whom you libelously accuse of being the "top Soviet espionage
> agent."[3]

But Joe McCarthy was careful of his own neck, if not those of others.
He had restricted his actionable statements to the Senate; senatorial immunity would protect him. His caution became clear on April 8, when he
made an impassioned speech to the Marine Corps League in Passaic, New
Jersey. There he attacked Lattimore, Jessup, and Service for "following
the Communist Party line" and dared them to sue him. It was clever
semantics. How would one prove that he had never "followed the Communist Party line?" Everybody in the country had followed the "Party
line" during the war, when Russia was our ally. Even MacArthur had
uttered outrageously pro-Soviet statements. And even though Drew Pearson
offered to pay McCarthy's legal expenses if the senator made specific and
actionable charges outside the Senate, he never did.[4]

After Lattimore had digested his mail in London, he met the press. This
was encouraging. The doctrinaire American journalists who accepted
McCarthy's hallucinations were absent, and the group at the London airport was "quite obviously assuming that I was innocent until proven guilty."
Lattimore was particularly pleased to see Hamilton Owens of the *Baltimore Sun* among them; Owens flew to London to get an early story carrying Lattimore's reaction to the McCarthy charges.[5] This decision took
some courage. Owens was well aware of the sentiment against Lattimore
in Maryland and of the hostility of one of the *Sun*'s columnists. His story
was upbeat and fair.

Lattimore was scheduled to arrive in New York March 31, but the flight was delayed and did not reach Idlewild until the next day. Eleanor, Fortas, and the press were waiting. At the airport Lattimore made only brief remarks showing his contempt for McCarthy. He made a longer statement at a press conference later in the day. This statement had been carefully prepared by Fortas, and copies of it were passed out. It was a frontal challenge to McCarthy's integrity: Latimore called him a "madman" and said, "The Soviet Union ought to decorate McCarthy for telling the kind of lies about the United States that Russian propagandists couldn't invent."[6]

Lattimore also reviewed his few connections with the State Department: being on State's payroll during the Pauley mission, since Pauley had no payroll of his own; taking part in Jessup's China policy roundtable for three days in 1949; and lecturing once to State Department personnel on Japanese problems. He categorically denied membership in or sympathy for the Communist party, a statement he later repeated under oath before Tydings. And he defended his extensive writings, which, he said, never advocated or supported the cause of communism. What he had done was "to find out and state publicly not only the weaknesses of the Communists' position in Asia, but also the points that might increase the danger that they will make progress with the people of that part of the world." Anticipating McCarthy's promise to produce testimony proving him to be a member of the Party, Lattimore threw down a challenge: "If anybody has sworn that I have been or am a member of the Communist party he is a perjurer. He should be prosecuted to the limit of the law."[7]

The press received him well, and questions were friendly. If the Hearst people were present, they passed up this opportunity to heckle.

Before Lattimore and his family left for home, Fortas got his approval for one more operation: "a telegram to Budenz, asking him in the interests of fair play either to disavow the press rumor that he had signed an affidavit for McCarthy, or, if he had, to advise us immediately and to disclose its contents. No answer ever came."[8]

The Lattimores had a weekend at home before moving to Washington on Monday, April 13, where preparations for appearing before Tydings were already under way at the firm of Arnold, Fortas, and Porter. One of their first activities that Monday was to release Lattimore's memo on Far Eastern policy that he had furnished Jessup in 1949. This memo got good play in the papers; it was the lead story in the *New York Times*. The headlines were absolutely accurate: "Lattimore Bares His Memorandum on Far Eastern Policy. Professor Acts after McCarthy Challenges State

Department to Release the Document. He Opposed Aid to Chiang. But Urged Efforts to Convince Orientals They Should Turn to U. S. and Not Russia."[9]

Next to the *Times* story about Lattimore's memo was a startling revelation from Henry Cabot Lodge, one of the two Republicans on the Tydings committee. Lodge had submitted a bill in the Senate to take the investigation of Communists in the State Department out of the hands of the Senate, where partisan wrangling and public charges against people like Kenyon, Jessup, and Lattimore were proving to be "a very defective way of promoting loyalty, since it often besmirches the character of innocent persons, weakens the position of the United States before the world, fails to find the really dangerous individuals and, by putting the spotlight on others, can actually increase the security of the real Communist ringleaders. . . . Mistakes have been made in the past and they must be ruthlessly corrected. All we can learn so far shows clearly that none of the current charges have been proven."[10] It was a ringing condemnation of Joe McCarthy. Abe Fortas could not have put it better.

Lodge called for a bipartisan commission of twelve private citizens to take charge of the inquiry and to conduct it in confidence. Unfortunately, matters had already gone too far for his proposal to gain widespread support. The Senate Democratic leadership could not support Lodge, since calling off the public Tydings hearings would deprive Lattimore and others of a chance to clear their names. And since the Democrats believed McCarthy to be a liar, they wanted to expose him in public. Lodge was too late.

While Lattimore and his crew were getting ready for Tydings, the FBI was reversing its stance on interviewing Alfred Kohlberg. On March 30 the Washington field office, noting that McCarthy derived most of his anti-Lattimore speech from Kohlberg, recommended to headquarters that Kohlberg be interviewed. Two days later SAC Scheidt in New York supported this recommendation. Hoover, still mindful of Kearney's opinion that Kohlberg was not trustworthy, was reluctant. But fear that McCarthy would steal a march on the bureau prevailed; on April 3 Hoover reversed himself, and the next day New York agents called on Kohlberg.[11]

The interview yielded little. Kohlberg affirmed giving McCarthy most of the documents used in his Senate speech and provided the agents with copies of some new ones. One document not previously seen by the bureau revealed Kohlberg at his mendacious best: claiming that Lattimore went secretly to Moscow in 1944; claiming that an IPR writer named

Abraham Chapman had been dishonorably discharged from the military; and stating that Lattimore had advocated turning over half of China to the Japanese in 1938.[12] These falsehoods did not particularly agitate the bureau; Kohlberg's major debacle was yet a week off.

For three frantic days the Lattimore party worked on his statement for the Tydings committee. Eleanor Lattimore was chief of staff; Fortas was prime legal adviser, with help from Thurman Arnold and Paul Porter. Joe Barnes broke off a lecture tour to help, mostly as devil's advocate; Stanley Salmen of Little, Brown edited. Lattimore's students and associates from the Page School, including George McT. Kahin, Dave Wilson, John De-Francis, and Ruth Bean concentrated on an analysis of how McCarthy quoted Lattimore contrary to context. By the afternoon of April 5, a forty-two-page statement was ready.[13]

Thursday, April 6, 1950, the nation's spotlight was focused as never before on a lone professor, charged with being the top Soviet spy in the United States. He appeared before a subcommittee of the U.S. Senate determined not only to defend his loyalty and integrity but also to counterattack the senator who had maligned him.

The hearing room was crowded when Chairman Tydings called the subcommittee to order at ten-thirty.[14] Senators Theodore Green, Brien McMahon, Bourke Hickenlooper, and Henry Cabot Lodge flanked the chairman. Senator Tom Connally, chairman of the parent Foreign Relations Committee, sat with the members. Behind them were Senators McCarthy, Scott Lucas, Charles Tobey, Karl Mundt, and William Knowland. Lattimore sat at the witness table with Fortas. Tydings swore Lattimore to tell the truth and asked him to proceed. Lattimore began his statement:

> Mr. Chairman, and members of the subcommittee, I wish to express to you my appreciation for this opportunity to reply to the statements about me which have been made by Senator Joseph McCarthy of Wisconsin. The Senator has in effect accused me of disloyalty and treason. He made these accusations when I was in Afghanistan, and I did not hear of them until some days after they were first made. . . .
>
> The technique used by the Senator in making these charges is apparently typical. He first announced at a press conference that he had discovered "the top Russian espionage agent in the United States." At this time he withheld my name. But later, after the drama of his announcement was intensified by delay, he whispered my name to a group of

newspapermen, with full knowledge that it would be bandied about by rumor and gossip and eventually published. I say to you that this was unworthy of a Senator or an American.

As I shall show in detail, McCarthy's charges are untrue. As soon as I heard of the substance of the charges I denounced them for what they were: base and contemptible lies. In fact, as I recall, on several occasions I used somewhat more colorful words.

Gentlemen, I want you to know that it is most distasteful to me to use language concerning a United States Senator which, to say the least, is disrespectful. To me, the honor and responsibility of American citizenship carry with them an obligation to respect the high office of a Member of the United States Senate. But that office, the position of United States Senator, likewise carries with it a responsibility which this man Joseph McCarthy has flagrantly violated. As a citizen who holds no official position, it is my right and duty to list these violations which are illustrated by the Senator's conduct in my own case.[15]

Lattimore then listed McCarthy's main offenses: making the U.S. government the object of suspicion and derision throughout the world, instituting a reign of terror among employees of that government, using classified documents without authorization, accusing people of high crimes without giving them opportunity to defend themselves, refusing to submit alleged evidence to the Senate, and going back on his word. It was prime invective.

One thing McCarthy had done that pleased Lattimore was to make Americans conscious of the fact that Asia was important to American security. He had himself "been trying all my life to arouse interest in this area." Now there would be a public debate on Asian policy, which was all to the good. Where McCarthy and his China lobby allies were mistaken was in assuming that anyone who disagreed with them about supporting Chiang in his aim to retake the mainland was disloyal.

Then Lattimore reverted again to sarcasm:

I wonder a bit how a man so young as Joseph McCarthy, whose acquaintance with national and international affairs is so recent, can have become such a great expert on the difficult and complex problem of China and the Far East. My wonder on this score increased when I read his speech on the Senate floor. Some of his material is from Chinese and Russian sources. Or perhaps I should say that some of his exotic material on Mongolia appears to trace back to some Russian source of distinctly low caliber.

I did not know that the Senator was a linguist. But really, the material that the Senator read is so badly translated and so inaccurate that I am sure that I should not like to place the blame for it on the learned Senator. Indeed, I fear that the sound and fury come from the lips of McCarthy, but that there is an Edgar Bergen in the woodpile. And I fear that this Edgar Bergen is neither kindly nor disinterested.

In any event, the Senator has stated that he will stand or fall on my case. I hope this will turn out to be true, because I shall show that his charges against me are so empty and baseless that the Senator will fall, and fall flat on his face. I trust that the Senator's promise that he will retire from the arena if his charges against me fail is not as insincere as his twice-repeated promise to resign if he should fail to repeat his libelous accusations in a forum which would expose him to suit. I hope the Senator will in fact lay his machine gun down. He is too reckless, careless, and irresponsible to have a license to use it.[16]

Brave words, but they were too optimistic. The senator was never to lay down his machine gun voluntarily.

Lattimore took an hour and forty-five minutes to present his case against McCarthy. He covered the Point Barrow charge, the claim that the IPR was a tool of the Russians, and Kohlberg's attack on the IPR. "It is easy to understand the joy of Kohlberg and his associates when they found the willing hands and innocent mind of Joseph McCarthy. It is easy to imagine their pleasure when they observe a United States Senator creating an international sensation by regurgitating their own fantastic and discredited venom."[17] He explained his trip to Yenan in 1937, his nonconnection with the *Amerasia* case, his distaste for Henry Wallace, his connection with the Maryland Association for Democratic Rights, the OWI letter to Joe Barnes, and the Soviet attacks on him as a "learned lackey of imperialism" and a mad scholastic.

Then he moved into the substance of China policy and the options open for the United States. There were four, as Lattimore saw it. (1) Support Chiang in an attempt to reconquer China: this was impossible. (2) Support a middle-of-the-road, non-Communist group in China: this was no longer feasible. (3) Recognize the possibility of Titoism in China and encourage it: this was his preferred position. (4) Adopt a policy of unremitting hostility toward the People's Republic: this would drive Mao completely into the orbit of the Soviet Union. In regard to the last possibility, he had a warning. Nationalist air attacks then being made on the mainland would cause Mao to seek Russian planes to counter them. This strategy would lead to the Soviets establishing air bases in China. "I personally believe that if the Soviet Union establishes air bases in China they will not be dismantled when the Nationalist forces are defeated. To me, this is an appalling prospect."[18]

After this lecture on geopolitics, Lattimore said, "Now, gentlemen, my analysis may be partly or wholly wrong. But if anybody says it is disloyal or un-American, he is a fool or a knave." He then read two pages summarizing recommendations he had made that were not followed by the State Department, concluding with a plea for open debate on the issues.[19] The audience applauded vigorously, and Tydings declared a brief recess. The rest of the morning session was taken over with questions from Senator Hickenlooper about events in China. Lattimore fielded them easily.

McCarthy did not return for the afternoon session. It was relatively mild, with Hickenlooper again struggling through inept questions about Asian politics, Sino-American relations, Lattimore's opinions about Chiang, and so forth.

There was one bombshell at about four-thirty. It came from the chairman, Senator Tydings.

> Dr. Lattimore, your case has been designated as the No. 1 case, finally, in the charges made by Senator McCarthy. You have been called, substantially, I think, if not accurately quoting, the top Red spy agent in America. We have been told that if we had access to certain files that this would be shown.
>
> I think as chairman of this committee that I owe it to you and to the country to tell you that four of the five members of this committee, in the presence of Mr. J. Edgar Hoover, the head of the FBI, had a complete summary of your file made available to them. Mr. Hoover himself prepared those data. [He didn't; it was probably Supervisor Branigan.] It was quite lengthy. And at the conclusion of the reading of that summary in great detail, it was the universal opinion of all the members of the committee present, and all others in the room, of which there were two more, that there was nothing in the file to show that you were a Communist or had ever been a Communist, or that you were in any way connected with any espionage information or charges, so that the FBI file puts you completely, up to this moment, at least, in the clear.[20]

There was great elation in the Lattimore camp. Dozens of spectators congratulated him. Press comment, except for the Hearst, Scripps Howard, and McCormick Patterson group, was favorable. Lattimore says the exhilaration lasted for two days; strangers would stop him on the street to shake hands. His father, a classicist, told him that his statement compared with Cicero's oration against Catiline.

Lattimore was particularly heartened by the presence at the hearing of Robert LeMoyne Barrett and his wife. Barrett, an explorer-philanthropist living in California, had supported Lattimore's travels until he took the job at Johns Hopkins. Now, with Lattimore's strong response to McCarthy, Barrett decided he was a solid citizen after all. From then until Barrett's death in 1969 Lattimore was again the recipient of Barrett subsidies. McCarthy never knew that he had inadvertently furthered Lattimore's travels.

David Oshinsky accurately describes the score at the end of the first Lattimore hearing. McCarthy was the big loser: "By first overstating his case and then retreating to safer ground, he seemed unsure of his own evidence. And Lattimore had proved to be a tough adversary, someone more than willing to slug it out in public. The blood had begun to flow, but most of it was on Joe's face. One reporter noted that 'a majority of Senate Republicans are clearly, if silently, exasperated and alarmed. They are deeply disturbed over the injury to the country's prestige . . . and they are certain that, politically, McCarthy's blast is going to do more harm by its backfire than it is on the target.' "[21]

But McCarthy was not giving up. He had missed Tydings's claim that the FBI files cleared Lattimore. When he heard about it, he exploded. "Either Tydings hasn't seen the files, or he is lying. There is no alternative."[22] But there was an alternative. The Lattimore case summary that Hoover took to the Tydings committee showed no credible evidence against Lattimore.

Tydings nonetheless muddied the waters in a press conference after the hearing. Reporters asked him whether Hoover had questioned Lattimore's loyalty and whether Hoover would hire Lattimore for the FBI. Tydings denied to the reporters that Hoover had said anything like this, though Hoover had disparaged Lattimore's loyalty. When the Tydings interview appeared in the press on April 4, Hoover wrote a strong memo to Attorney General McGrath emphasizing the "absolute necessity of being circumspect in discussion of matters in executive session because apparently some member of the Senate who was in attendance at the meeting in your office has seen fit to report in substance the comments which I made about Lattimore."[23] Hoover cared about leaks from the bureau only when he couldn't control them.

Hoover also wanted, as much as did McCarthy, to get the goods on Lattimore. The investigation was ratcheted up a notch. One of the ways in which Lattimore might be impaled was by checking out his finances. If he had unaccounted-for income, or if his net worth was greater than his legitimate income warranted, he had to be getting paid by the Soviets. Thus, a separate investigation into his finances was launched. For the next two years the source of every penny Lattimore had deposited in a bank since 1937 was traced. More than three hundred pages of the Lattimore file report microscopic inspection of his income and investments. Every magazine he wrote for was queried about what they had paid him; since many of his articles were gratis for academic journals, this investigation did not lead far. Every job Lattimore had held for the previous fifteen years was checked out. The fee for every paying lecture he gave was uncovered. Book royalties were determined. Eleanor's income was also checked. The interest on every government bond the Lattimores cashed was calculated.

Since his publisher, Little, Brown, was itself suspected of Soviet connections, the FBI was especially careful in getting their figures. Since espionage was suspected, the bureau would need "to determine whether payments made to Lattimore were actually in keeping with the royalty earnings."[24] No progress there: royalties matched sales.

Some of the bureau's findings were trivial to the point of farce. One check Lattimore had deposited shortly after his summer at the Vermont farm was for $6.03. It was from the Eastern States Farmers Exchange, a rebate on the purchase of paint brushes. Equally absurd was the bureau's tracing of the royalties on the copies of his books sold abroad. Lattimore wrote the introduction to *Gateway to Asia: Sinkiang*, by Martin W. Norins. Three copies of this book were sold in Europe, with Lattimore's earnings less than a dollar.[25]

Some bureau inquiries revealed the narrowness of agent experience. One of Lattimore's monographs, "The Gold Tribe, 'Fishskin Tatars' of the Lower Sungari," had been published by the George Banta Company in Menasha, Wisconsin. Banta denied paying Lattimore anything, but the bureau found out that the National Academy of Sciences had subsidized the publication. Perhaps NAS had paid Lattimore directly? The Baltimore FBI office, collection center for this mass of information, wrote the Milwaukee office, in whose jurisdiction Banta was located, asking the agent there "to ascertain the address of the National Academy of Sciences, and thereafter set out an appropriate lead to determine any income which LATTIMORE may have received from this source." Milwaukee replied with just a slight tinge of sarcasm: the NAS was located on Constitution Avenue in Washington, D.C.[26]

The whole federal project came to nothing.

The day after Lattimore's Tydings appearance, Hoover approved a second avenue of investigation: interviewing Lattimore himself. The bureau was touchy about talking to possibly hostile persons. Hoover absolutely refused to let his agents talk to employees of the *Washington Post*, to journalists such as I. F. Stone, and to iconoclastic academicians such as Arthur M. Schlesinger, Jr. Initial approaches to Lattimore, however, revealed that he would cooperate. Consequently, agents Ralph C. Vogel and Frank Johnston were assigned this task and briefed extensively on how to act. Ladd's memo of instructions for the interviewers is detailed and sophisticated. The bureau was afraid that Lattimore would insist on one of his attorneys being present, which would cramp the agent's style. A telephone call to Abe Fortas secured permission to talk to Lattimore alone.[27]

Beginning on April 10 and proceeding intermittently through August 4, Vogel and Johnston spent twelve days with Lattimore, soliciting from him comments about every allegation from any informant the bureau thought even somewhat plausible. At the end of this process a 134-page transcript was prepared, Lattimore read, corrected, and signed it.[28] There was mutual respect on both sides; Lattimore had spoken candidly, and the agents felt that he had pulled no punches. The bureau did not, of course, assume that Lattimore always told the truth, but it found no significant weaknesses.

A third investigation examined the extent to which Lattimore's writings followed the Party line. This was a specialized task for the Central Research Desk, which was not overjoyed at getting the assignment. Bureau files at that time credited approximately 125 books and articles to Lattimore's pen; they had apparently no listing of his extensive ONA articles. But even 125 items scared Baumgardner of Central Research: as he wrote Belmont on April 12, "It is quite apparent that if a detailed review and analysis of all the written works of Owen Lattimore are desired it will create a project which will take six Supervisors three weeks. It is to be kept in mind that after the entire works of Lattimore have been studied and analyzed, they must be compared and contrasted with the Communist Party line relative to China and to any other nation to which Lattimore's books may refer." Baumgardner's plea: let's be sure we want this, and even if we do, let's confine it at first to his books. Tolson and Ladd took pity on the overworked Central Research Desk and on April 17 agreed to confine the research to books. This task, they thought, should take no more than a week.[29] Ten weeks later Central Research produced the report.

It was not favorable to Lattimore. Baumgardner and his staff had an easy time finding statements from Lattimore with which some Communist authority agreed. In one instance, the kidnapping of Chiang Kai-shek at Sian in December 1936, they found seven specific statements agreed to by both Lattimore and the Communist party:

1. There was a widespread popular demand in China for united resistance to the Japanese.

2. The Kuomintang was responsible for the lack of unity.

3. Chiang Kai-shek's Northeastern armies were on amicable terms with the Communist armies.

4. The Chinese Communists did not take vindictive advantage of the situation to kill Chiang.

5. The Communists contributed to the happy solution: Chiang's release.

6. The release put an end to civil war and created a united front.

7. Chinese Communist policy had beneficial results.[30]

Going about it this way, it was easy to rack up a big score against Lattimore. What Baumgardner undoubtedly did not know is now the conventional wisdom of historians of modern China: every one of these statements was substantially true. There is no significance in such a "comparison." Nevertheless, the bureau analysis did not approach the convoluted sophistry of later efforts.

Five days after Lattimore's appearance before Tydings, Hoover wrote a letter to the attorney general that revealed how shallow Hoover's understanding of the responsibilities of his office really was.

In connection with the charges that have been made in the Senate to the effect that Owen J. Lattimore is an espionage agent and the widespread public interest which has resulted, I am wondering if you have given any serious thought to the desirability of immediately convening a Grand Jury in order that it might hear any person who has or might have information indicating espionage violations on the part of Mr. Lattimore.

In this connection, should consideration be given to convening a special Grand Jury, the thought occurs to me that if the names of the witnesses were to be made public, regardless of the outcome of the Grand Jury deliberations there would be a wholesome public response.[31]

This incredible proposal was answered by Peyton Ford, assistant to the attorney general, two days later. The answer was calm and designed to give no offense; Hoover's power was such that not even the attorney general felt able to lecture the FBI head on his proposed exercise in punishment by publicity: "I have discussed this matter with the Attorney General and he feels that the proposed action is premature and that we should exhaust completely the investigative possibilities of this case. Such action would probably create the general impression that we have available evidence of the commission of a crime, since grand jury proceedings are not ordinarily started unless such evidence is available. As the situation now stands, the grand jury would be unable to take any action and its failure to act might possibly be construed as a "whitewash" proceeding."[32] Not a word about Lattimore's rights or the legal requirement for grand jury secrecy to protect the innocent—just a warning that this action might miscarry.

Tydings held no more hearings for two weeks. Speculation about what would happen when he brought on McCarthy's "mystery witness" occupied the press and the Washington cocktail circuit. The bureau was also concerned, as we shall see in the next chapter.

But the bureau had another hot potato on its hands. New York agents interviewed Kohlberg April 4, at his home, and he told them he had additional documents on Lattimore and the IPR.[33] If they called him later, he would have this new material ready for them. He was also scheduled to go to the New York FBI office for an interview April 7 about Philip Jessup. Kohlberg, always distrustful of the FBI, showed up on the seventh with Howard Rushmore of the *New York Journal-American.* The agents did not want an audience; they made Rushmore wait in a different room while they talked to Kohlberg.

On April 10, when the New York FBI called him again, Kohlberg said he was going to Washington and could not give them his additional documents until he returned. The genesis of Kohlberg's trip to Washington remains obscure; apparently it arose out of a letter he received from Miller Freeman, an ultrarightist in Seattle who had written Kohlberg complaining about an interview Freeman had with Seattle FBI agents. Since Kohlberg was also unhappy with his FBI interviews, he wanted to go to the top with his dissatisfactions. He apparently telephoned somebody in headquarters and somehow got the idea that he had an appointment with Hoover on April 13.

On the day before he was to go to Washington, Kohlberg talked to reporters James O'Connor and Philip Santora of the New York *Mirror*. He was, as Father Kearney had predicted, indiscreet. The *Mirror* edition of April 13 carried a lengthy story by O'Connor and Santora:

> Alfred Kohlberg, importer and anti-Communist who furnished much of the information on which Sen. Joseph McCarthy based his pro-Red charges against Owen J. Lattimore and Ambassador Philip Jessup, yesterday disclosed the FBI will photograph the documents in his files next week. He said the files contain additional charges against Lattimore.
>
> Kohlberg said he was notified by FBI agents that they were ordered by J. Edgar Hoover to "dig up whatever they could on Jessup right away." Later they were directed to photograph all of Kohlberg's papers.
>
> "I told the FBI I had tried to interest them in these documents for five years," commented Kohlberg. "Now they'll have to wait until I get back from Washington, next week. . . ."
>
> Kohlberg, a member of the IPR for 19 years, remarked at a press conference in his office . . . that Lattimore played a "very important part in the sellout of China." He pointed to what he considers one instance of Lattimore's alleged change in sentiment.
>
> From June, 1941, to Spring, 1943, said Kohlberg, the Red Party line favored the Chiang Kai-shek regime.
>
> Lattimore, in a book titled "America and Asia," published in 1943, paid tribute to Chiang Kai-shek as "a world statesman, a real genius." The Communist Party line shifted. In June, 1943, said Kohlberg, when Lattimore became political advisor to President Roosevelt, he recommended Chiang's ouster.
>
> The following year, continued Kohlberg, Lattimore, in a book called "Solution in Asia," attacked Chiang's government as corrupt, reactionary, and feudal.[34]

The story went on to describe Kohlberg's long struggle with IPR.

When Kohlberg called FBI headquarters from the Mayflower Hotel the morning of April 13, expecting to get directions to Hoover's office, he was instead connected with Alan Belmont. Belmont told him the director was unavailable, but he could see Belmont at eleven o'clock. When Kohlberg appeared at Belmont's office, the assistant director had the New York *Mirror* article prominently displayed on his desk. He was seething.[35]

According to Belmont's report, Kohlberg started off by relating the Miller Freeman story. Freeman said the agents who talked to him "were attempting to have Freeman make statements to their liking, rather than to get the facts." This triggered a lecture from Belmont about the bureau's objectivity; they were interested only in "accurate information," and Freeman was simply wrong.

Kohlberg then complained that different pairs of agents had conducted his interviews in New York. Why didn't the bureau use the two agents who were best informed on the subject for both interviews? Belmont explained that the two agents who conducted the first interview were specialists on Lattimore; the second interview concerned Jessup, and Jessup specialists were used.

Having listened to Kohlberg complain for a while, Belmont opened up with his agenda. Why had Kohlberg thought he was scheduled for an appointment with the director? All bureau contacts with him had specified that he was to be interviewed in New York and was not to come to Washington. This criticism threw Kohlberg into confusion. There had been so many inquiries from the press and from the bureau that he had simply gotten mixed up.

Then Belmont lowered the boom. Why had Kohlberg lied to the *Mirror* reporters about Hoover ordering agents "to dig up whatever they could on Jessup right away"? Kohlberg spluttered, waffled, and apologized for an "incorrect inference." And why, asked Belmont, had Kohlberg claimed that "he had tried to interest the FBI in certain documents for five years," when the FBI had considered the matter carefully, discussed interviewing him, and decided against it. Kohlberg snapped back, "Because you were afraid I would do what I am doing now," pointing to the *Mirror* article on Belmont's desk.

This response brought from Belmont a lecture on bureau procedure. They never made public comment on active investigations. "It was pointed out to him that publicity during a case is harmful to an investigation and that as a general rule persons contacted by the FBI respected this and did not publicize the activities of the FBI. After considerable discussion, Mr. Kohlberg advised that he would, if so directed, retain in confidence any contact by the FBI in this and other matters and would refrain from making any comment to the press."

Kohlberg then calmed down and discussed some of his conclusions about the IPR. He had no proof it was engaged in espionage, but it had nonetheless served the Communist cause. At the end of this discussion, Kohlberg "particularly mentioned that he had been in close contact with Louis Budenz."

Belmont's report concludes, "The above interview was handled on a

rather firm basis, inasmuch as it appeared definitely necessary to set Kohlberg straight. There is no guarantee that he will not run to the papers and
mention this interview. However, his attitude upon leaving indicated that
he would not do so." Hoover scrawled beneath this conclusion, "Right.
H."[36] Kohlberg kept his word—until the Tydings committee released its
report in July.

CHAPTER EIGHTEEN

Agony at the FBI: Louis Budenz

In his March 30, 1950, speech to the Senate, McCarthy did not unleash his full anti-Lattimore arsenal. Perhaps he calculated that the Kohlberg and Utley materials and his phony Barmine affidavit would be sufficient. If so, he was mistaken. The widespread skepticism about his performance necessitated using everything he could muster. None of his early witnesses was top drawer. Kohlberg was recognized even by McCarthy's staff as disreputable. Utley was more respectable but did not make a good witness. Barmine had only hearsay to offer and was reluctant to offer that. McCarthy needed a Whittaker Chambers. J. B. Matthews provided the connection to a witness far more voluble than Chambers—the former Communist Louis Budenz.

The FBI had followed the career of Louis Budenz since his graduation from Indianapolis Law School in 1912: assistant director of the Catholic Central Verein in St. Louis, secretary of the St. Louis Civic League, publicity director for the American Civil Liberties Union, ten years (1921–31) as editor of *Labor Age*. The bureau had reports on his strike organizing and many arrests in Kenosha, Wisconsin; Patterson, New Jersey; and Toledo, Ohio. They knew he had worked with agitator A. J. Muste, had flirted with Trotskyism, and in October 1935 had joined the Communist party. As a Communist he served as labor editor of the *Daily Worker* in New York, then as editor of a Communist paper in Chicago, and finally as managing editor of the *Daily Worker*, where he also served as American correspondent for the London *Daily Worker*. Hoover had copies of all Budenz's dispatches to London; these articles agitated Hoover greatly, and he pushed hard to get Budenz indicted for failing to register as a foreign agent.[1]

Budenz claims in *This Is My Story* that all through his Communist years he sought to reconcile Communist doctrine with Catholicism; by 1945 this reconciliation appeared impossible, and he contacted Monsignor Fulton Sheen about rejoining the Church. Sheen encouraged him. Without letting his Communist comrades even suspect his approaching defection, on October 10, 1945, Budenz was received back in the church at a ceremony in St. Patrick's Cathedral. The next day he took up a professorship at Notre Dame.[2]

Sheen tipped off Hoover in advance about this defection, so the bureau was ready to move rapidly in debriefing Budenz. Special Agent J. Patrick Coyne of bureau headquarters talked to Sheen, who in turn negotiated with Budenz and Notre Dame. Budenz was wary about talking to the FBI; he was afraid that if word got out to his former Party associates, his personal security would be jeopardized. If he agreed to talk, he wanted Catholic agents to interview him.[3] Sheen checked out this request and was assured that the bureau would maintain confidentiality. Two Catholic agents, Coyne and Winterrowd, were ordered to prepare questions to put to Budenz. They took two rooms in a South Bend hotel; technicians were in the extra room recording everything Budenz said from a hidden microphone. Budenz did not know for thirteen years that he had been recorded.

The bureau's Communist experts, working with Coyne and Winterrowd, prepared seven hundred questions to put to Budenz, grouped under twenty-one headings. Two of the headings, "Communist controlled and influenced groups" and "Communist propaganda and publications," required him to tell what he knew about the IPR. In addition, seven questions related to the Chinese Communists and their American supporters.[4] Coyne and Winterrowd interviewed Budenz December 6–12, 1945, from three to five hours each day, skipping only one day. At the end of the series Coyne telephoned a preliminary report to Washington. Budenz, Coyne said, was cooperative and sincere: "Mr. Coyne stated he is not, however, as well informed as expected and they have confronted him with that fact, and he said he realizes this and attributes it to the fact that during the last several years, with the exception of one other man, he has been the only American Communist connected with the National Committee. The rest of them have been Moscow-trained either at the Lenin or Wilson School. He believes, and Mr. Coyne stated he was also of the opinion, that they have not taken him into their complete confidence. . . . Budenz is strictly a Labor man and knows what it is all about."[5]

Not "well informed" about the Communist party that he had served so loyally for a decade? The slight to Budenz's ego from this disparagement must have stung him severely. His entire subsequent career can be read as an attempt to escape this stricture, to escape the narrowness of his labor specialty, to appear as a savant on communism in all its forms and variants.

The tapes of these South Bend interviews were transcribed, and Winterrowd condensed the substance into eighty-six pages. Budenz had actually covered a lot more than labor affairs. There was at least one gaping hole, however: his knowledge of Asia was thin. In regard to the question about "persons supporting the pro-Communist Chinese" he denied that Edgar Snow was a Communist, claiming instead that "Harrison Forman was considered closer to the Communist Party than [was] Snow" and that Philip Jaffe was clearly a member. No others were mentioned.[6]

When it came to the IPR, Budenz was hardly more expansive: "The Institute of Pacific Relations, he said, was Communist inspired '100 per cent.' He later changed this statement to say that it was controlled by the Communists. With regard to one of its main officers, Edward Clark Carter, he said that he could not say Carter was a Communist but that he was looked upon as a Communist by 'those of us who had to deal with him.' " No one else was worthy of mention.[7]

Budenz was expansive about the subservience of the American Communists to their Soviet masters. The shadowy characters who flitted in and out of Party headquarters in New York disturbed him greatly, as did the "conspiratorial" activities of the Party. And he "identified a number of prominent people who have been on the fringe of the Communist movement in the sense that he, as a member of the National Committee of the Communist Party . . . considered them in that light. . . . Among those he named in this category was Congressman Hugh DeLacy of the State of Washington." And Budenz was more than willing to testify in behalf of the government in cases involving Communists, though he wanted a period of time to reorient his life and refresh his memory before he was called on. Coyne and Winterrowd arranged for him to contact the Indianapolis office should he recall additional pertinent information.[8]

Budenz's stay at Notre Dame was not very satisfactory, and after a year he moved to Fordham University. There he came under the bureau jurisdiction of Alan Belmont, at that time assistant special agent in charge of the New York office. Belmont soon discovered that Budenz was intent on pursuing a career of professional witnessing. He began to make anti-Communist speeches for Catholic groups and to give interviews to journalists. In October 1946 Budenz talked to a reporter about Hans Berger (alias Gerhart Eisler), whom he described as the chief Soviet overseer of

American Party affairs. This information the bureau found "disconcerting": they were investigating Eisler quietly, but now they had to tie up personnel on surveillance. Belmont wanted assurance from headquarters that "the New York Office would not be held responsible for any control over Budenz and would not be held responsible for any statement or action by him without Bureau knowledge." He got this assurance, but the bureau did want advance word of any proposed statement or action by Budenz in the future.[9]

In November, after Budenz appeared before HUAC, Coyne and Winterrowd met with him in Washington. In a long report Coyne revealed that Budenz thought the HUAC members "were not fast on the pick-up" when he mentioned matters of importance; they seemed more interested in personal publicity than in promoting the security of the United States. This was one of the few matters on which Budenz agreed with the Left. Ernie Adamson, of the HUAC staff, had even asked Budenz to attack several congressmen, specifically Claude Pepper of Florida. Budenz declined. He also told the FBI men that his book *This Is My Story* would be out by Christmas 1946 and that Father Cronin had written him suggesting that he affiliate with *Plain Talk*, a new ultraright magazine financed by Alfred Kohlberg. At the close of the interview Budenz indicated that he would be happy to assist the bureau with a brief on the Communist movement.[10] It was a good interview. Budenz appeared to be under control.

Accordingly, the New York office began to consult Budenz regularly, averaging once a week. He was more than willing to talk about most of the questions they raised, and when he didn't have an answer ready at the first inquiry, he would think about it and refresh his memory for the next week.[11]

On March 12, 1947, New York agents spent several hours with Budenz, getting his views on William Z. Foster, Steve Nelson, Earl Browder, and other Party notables. During this interview Budenz volunteered a new source of information for the bureau: Alfred Kohlberg had been to see him and had told him about the IPR, its pro-Communist propaganda, and how Kohlberg was trying to reform it. Kohlberg had wanted to know if Budenz could "give him some information on the members of the Executive Committee relative to their Communist tendencies." Budenz could and did. He now knew four Communists on the IPR executive committee: Edward Carter, Harriet Moore, Fred Field, and Len DeCaux. Budenz told the FBI that Kohlberg was grateful for this information and that he and Kohlberg had become fast friends.[12]

Five months after his first talk with Kohlberg, Budenz was interviewed about the IPR by Daniel H. Clare, Jr., of the State Department. Budenz told Clare "that he was not prepared to pass judgment upon the degree of Mr. Lattimore's association with the Party. He is aware that he is a sympathizer, but is unable to recall at this time any incidents which definitely indicated that he was a member of the Party." The bureau thought Clare's report was worthless. Belmont noted that Clare depended primarily on Kohlberg and said the report contained "many inaccuracies."[13]

By 1947 Budenz was being used by the Immigration and Naturalization Service as a witness against various Communists in deportation proceedings. One of these proceedings was particularly painful. On September 17, testifying for the government *In the Matter of Desideriu Hammer, alias John Santo,* Budenz's credibility was challenged on the grounds that he had committed bigamy and violated the Mann Act. Under cross-examination by Santo's lawyer, Harry Sacher, Budenz took the Fifth Amendment twenty-two times to avoid incriminating himself.[14] The story that came out of the *Santo* hearing is best told by Jack Anderson.

> The transcript [of Santo] revealed a more colorful past than was hinted at by the austere comportment of the present Fordham professor. During those halcyon days before his conversion, when Budenz the Communist was plotting murder attempts on Trotsky and stage-managing a plague of labor disruptions for which he was arrested twenty-one times and acquitted twenty-one times, and even before he formally joined the party, the good doctor was sampling the one compensatory amenity which Communist discipline, that harsh mistress, permitted her disciples—sexual philandering. While married to one woman, Budenz had lived with a second for several years. A third female showed up with him on various hotel registrations in Connecticut, Pennsylvania and New York. In the wake of all this there were three illegitimate children, a trail of forged hotel registrations and a divorce on grounds of desertion. After Budenz reconverted to Catholicism and conventionality, he tried, naturally enough, to put the most decorous face possible on things for the sake of all concerned. He faked a marriage date in his self-penned *Who's Who* biography; stumbled lamely in the timeless manner of errant husbands who are ambushed, through interrogatories about his incontinent past; and even took the Fifth Amendment about some of his trysts. It was a document filled with the small personal confessions which our adversary system wrenches from witnesses to large conspiracies, yet it raised valid questions about a credibility that had assumed crucial proportions.[15]

Publicity from the *Santo* case grieved the bureau, which was depending on Budenz for continuing revelations about Communist functionaries and crimes and expected to use him in important prosecutions yet to come. If he were alienated by embarrassing cross-examinations in piddling deportation cases, the anti-Communist cause would suffer. Agent Coyne was particularly worried about this development. On October 1, 1947, Coyne conferred with a Justice Department attorney who had followed the *Santo* case; the attorney "doubted very much if Budenz would ever want to testify again in any Government case, in view of the derogatory publicity which appeared in the press concerning Budenz" after the *Santo* hearing. Coyne wrote Ladd recommending that the bureau pressure Justice to curb use of Budenz for such trivia, saving him for continued use as a bureau informant and for important future trials.[16] We do not know Ladd's response; Budenz continued to serve as a witness in relatively trivial proceedings.

The bureau was not happy with Budenz's increasing association with Kohlberg, whom they regarded as unstable. In December 1947 Budenz revealed to Coyne that he was considering establishing a relationship with *Counter Attack*, an ultraright magazine run by Theo Kirkpatrick, a former FBI agent for whom Hoover had a deep antipathy. Kirkpatrick was luring Budenz with access to a cache of "secret records" kept in the *Counter Attack* office. Coyne warned Budenz against Kirkpatrick, fearing that association with *Counter Attack* would further damage Budenz's credibility. The warning went unheeded. Budenz not only took up with Kirkpatrick but also became consulting editor of the magazine; he later had his own anti-Communist newsletter printed on the *Counter Attack* press.[17]

In 1948 the bureau had clear warning that Budenz was capable of serious exaggeration. The *New York Sun* of April 27 carried a story headlined, "Budenz Bares Communist Plot to Infiltrate National Guard." The article caused great consternation both in New York and Washington. Agents were immediately sent to interview Budenz about it. After this interview and an examination of Budenz's previous statements to the bureau Ladd sent Hoover a six-page analysis of the incident. On one of Budenz's more startling claims to the reporter, Ladd noted that "Budenz advised Bureau agents that he had no actual factual support for such a statement." Ladd's conclusion was the first explicit bureau challenge to Budenz's general credibility: "It should be borne in mind that Budenz apparently is inclined to make sensational charges which the press interprets as startling new information when, in fact, the information is old and not completely substantiated by actual facts."[18] This, like many subsequent warnings, went unheeded. The bureau investment in Budenz was already too great to permit open acknowledgment of his unreliability.

In August 1948 New York SAC Scheidt noted another disturbing development. Budenz had frequently mentioned his need for a set of old issues of the *Daily Worker* to use in "refreshing his memory" concerning the many persons and events he was giving testimony about. Now his friend Alfred Kohlberg had come to his aid. Kohlberg bought a set of the *Daily Worker* covering the period of Budenz's Party membership, 1935–45, and lent it to Budenz. Observed Scheidt: "Since Professor BUDENZ is using Mr. KOHLBERG'S set of 'Daily Workers,' he is to a certain extent obligated to Mr. KOHLBERG. This is not the most desirable situation."[19]

Perhaps it was not desirable for the bureau. For Joe McCarthy, anything furthering the Kohlberg agenda was eminently worthwhile. Should Budenz support Kohlberg, and hence McCarthy, in early 1950, it would be a godsend.

At the beginning of 1950 Budenz had not yet weighed in against Lattimore. So far as anyone knew, Budenz had never met the Johns Hopkins professor and knew nothing about him. The Soviet conspiracy in which Budenz had played a role, about which he testified so extensively to the FBI, to the Foley Square trial of the top Communist leaders, and to HUAC, did not even have a China connection. When Budenz wrote his first book in 1947, he was totally unaware that China was the master key to a "Red White House"; this geopolitical doctrine appeared for the first time in his *Collier's* article of 1949.[20] Even then Budenz had nothing to say about Lattimore; Earl Browder was the "mastermind" of Kremlin machinations to install a Communist government in China and thus to open the door to Communist conquest of the United States. And, according to Budenz, Lattimore was not among Browder's five accomplices.

In 1950 Budenz's flair for the dramatic burst wide open. His devoted wife knew about this tendency even better than the bureau. According to her, Budenz was a master at entertaining their children with marvelous "Pumpernickel tales" invented through the "magic of his imagination."[21] In 1950 he turned this imagination to inventing tales about Lattimore.

J. B. Matthews, who knew Budenz well, sensed that he might be ripe for a new arena of witnessing. Clearly HUAC, court trials, and deportation hearings were being upstaged by the flamboyant McCarthy. McCarthy had written Budenz March 14 asking if he knew anything about Lattimore; Budenz did not answer.[22] But Budenz could not turn down a call from his good friend Matthews. When Matthews phoned March 25, Budenz was cordial. Matthews recorded the conversation without Budenz's knowledge. Several days later Matthews gave a copy of the transcript to the FBI. It is startling. Had this transcript been public at the time, Budenz's credibility would have suffered immeasurably.

Budenz's public posture was that of a reluctant witness, similar to

Chambers, who testified against those he claimed to be Communists only under subpoena and with great anguish. Chambers, however, was sincere; the Matthews transcript shows Budenz to have been a hypocrite. The bureau regarded this transcript as so important that half a dozen copies are scattered through the Lattimore file, and one was sent to the attorney general. After casual preliminaries, the conversation got down to business:

> *Matthews:* Would you be able if called upon to identify Owen Lattimore as a party member by virtue of your position on the DAILY WORKER?
>
> *Budenz:* Ah, you mean if I were subpoenaed?
>
> *Matthews:* Yes, that is what I mean.
>
> *Budenz:* It would be hearsay identification.
>
> *Matthews:* It would be, as I understand it, from one of our mutual friends—you know whom I am talking about?
>
> *Budenz:* Yes.
>
> *Matthews:* It would be because you had to know in your job?
>
> *Budenz:* That's right. I know 400 concealed Communists, J. B. that I cannot mention.
>
> *Matthews:* I understand.
>
> *Budenz:* Because if I did, why there would be such a furor that I would be discredited.
>
> *Matthews:* Yes.
>
> *Budenz:* That's why I am taking the thing seriatim so to speak. . . . I have several irons in the fire. I am eager to expose Field and Jaffe and the whole set up.
>
> *Matthews:* Yes, that whole Far Eastern business?
>
> *Budenz:* Yes. The only thing is, I want to do it in such a way that I don't appear to be too partisan, you know.
>
> *Matthews:* Right.[23]

It is noteworthy that even at this late date, on March 25, 1950, Budenz still had not zeroed in on Lattimore. He would testify about Lattimore, but he was "eager to expose" only Field and Jaffe. With McCarthy's speech of March 30, when Lattimore was put dead center, Budenz's priorities shifted accordingly. He had now come full circle. Whereas in 1949 his litany of Soviet machinations did not even include Lattimore, two years later his recollections of Lattimore's misdeeds filled eleven single-spaced pages of an FBI summary.[24]

The FBI was late in learning of Budenz's sudden concern about Lattimore. On March 26, 1950, Hoover routinely instructed the New York FBI office to check with Budenz about his *Collier's* article. If the IPR had influenced China policy and Lattimore had been editor of the major IPR publication, perhaps Lattimore had "knowingly assisted Communists in such activity" during his editorship.[25] Scheidt sent an agent to see Budenz the next day. His report to headquarters set forth the new revelations.

CONCERNING LATTIMORE, BUDENZ ADVISED THIS OFFICE ON MARCH TWENTYSEVEN THAT HE HAD NEVER MET HIM BUT HEARD ABOUT HIM MANY TIMES, PARTICULARLY AT POLITICAL COMMITTEE MEETINGS OF PARTY WHEREIN FREDERICK V. FIELD MADE REPORTS. IN THESE REPORTS FIELD STATED THAT LATTIMORE WAS GIVEN CERTAIN ASSIGNMENTS, OR HE REPORTED ON WORK DONE BY LATTIMORE. THERE WAS NO QUESTION IN BUDENZ'S MIND THAT LATTIMORE WAS A COMMUNIST. BUDENZ KNEW THIS FROM THE WAY FIELD REPORTED ABOUT HIM. BUDENZ ALSO HEARD HARRY GANNES REPORT ON LATTIMORE. BUDENZ BELIEVES HE FIRST HEARD OF LATTIMORE WHEN LATTIMORE WAS WITH THE IPR PROBABLY AROUND NINETEEN FORTY. FIELD REPORTED TO POLITICAL COMMITTEE ABOUT WORKING WITH LATTIMORE AND JAFFE. BUDENZ CONTINUED HEARING ABOUT LATTIMORE AS A COMMUNIST UNTIL AT LEAST NINETEEN FORTY FOUR. BUDENZ RECALLED THAT IN NINETEEN THIRTY SEVEN FIELD WAS REPORTING ON CHINESE MATTERS AND THE POLICY OF PLAYING UP THE AGRARIAN REFORM MOVEMENT IN CHINA AND MAKING IT APPEAR THAT THE CHINESE COMMUNIST MOVEMENT WAS REALLY THE AGRARIAN RE-FORM MOVEMENT. THIS IDEA CAME FROM BROWDER. THE ACTUAL CAR-RYING OUT OF THIS POLICY TOOK PLACE LATER. LATTIMORE WAS GIVEN THE ASSIGNMENT OF CARRYING OUT THE CAMPAIGN OF PUTTING ACROSS THE IDEA THAT THE CHINESE RED MOVEMENT WAS REALLY THE AGRAR-IAN REFORM MOVEMENT. BUDENZ HEARD THIS IN A REPORT BY FIELD. BUDENZ STATES ONLY A TRUSTED COMMUNIST WOULD BE GIVEN THIS ASSIGNMENT.[26]

Rubbing salt in the wound, Howard Rushmore published an article in the *New York Journal-American* on March 30, 1950, headlined, "FBI Is

Probing Lattimore Here": "One witness who knew Lattimore in China has been living here for more than a decade. Yet he was never interviewed by the FBI until the McCarthy charge against the Far East 'expert' was made public."[27]

There it was, all laid out in cold print: the bureau competing with McCarthy to see who could get to witnesses first and the demeaning claim that the bureau was acting only after McCarthy had publicized Lattimore. When the Rushmore article got to Hoover, he forwarded it to Ladd with a peremptory question: "This is what I feared. Just why wasn't this case intensified sooner?"

The bureau still did not know for sure who McCarthy's mystery witness was. Ladd ordered Belmont to find out. On April 1 Jean Kerr identified Budenz. By April 2 the bureau high command had seen the Matthews-Budenz phone transcript and knew that Budenz would be called to testify before Tydings, that his testimony would be hearsay, and that he claimed that he could identify four hundred "concealed Communists." Hoover ordered New York agents back to Budenz. On April 4 they interviewed him again. His "new" information about Lattimore was from the old Kohlberg charges: Lattimore had "played a big part publicly" in the attack on Chiang in 1943. And his four hundred concealed Communists included fellow travelers already attacked by HUAC and Kohlberg: Lillian Hellman, Donald Ogden Stewart, E. C. Carter, Harriet Moore, Charlie Chaplin, Paul Draper.[28]

This "information" did not seem important enough to explain all the fuss. Agents were sent back to Budenz on April 5. This time Budenz elaborated on the role played by Field and Jaffe, describing Jaffe's demeanor at national committee meetings, adding detail to what he had told the bureau on March 27; but he could not remember that the *Daily Worker* had ever mentioned Lattimore.[29]

Hoover was still dissatisfied. He queried Ladd as to whether the new information about Lattimore was known when a memo on the Lattimore case was sent to the attorney general on March 22; Ladd said no, the first they heard of it was March 27, and Budenz had been "reinterviewed on April 3, 4, 5, and again on April 8." Budenz was to "endeavor to refresh his recollection concerning specific assignments of Owen Lattimore and will be interviewed again on April 10th."[30]

Hoover was unhappy with this answer. He wrote at the bottom of Ladd's report, "Why didn't we ask Budenz why he hadn't told us sooner? We have been in almost constant touch with him for months. Also, why haven't we taken the initiative in questioning him? It begins to look like another Chambers case where we didn't press for information."

At the April 10 interview Budenz provided a substantial part of his list of concealed Communists: 136 names. Scheidt cabled the same day that

BUDENZ STATED THAT THE INDIVIDUALS HE NAMED ARE CP MEMBERS AND NOT JUST SYMPATHIZERS. HE CALLS THEM CONCEALED COMMU-NISTS BECAUSE THEY DON'T ADMIT THEIR MEMBERSHIP IN THE CP AND NEITHER HE NOR ANYONE ELSE CAN EXPOSE THEM SINCE THEY ARE PRO-TECTED BY THE LIBEL LAWS WHICH PARTY MEMBERS ARE ENCOURAGED TO TAKE ADVANTAGE OF AND FURTHER A SECTION OF THE REPUTABLE PRESS REFUSES TO ANALYZE THE RECORDS OF THESE INDIVIDUALS AND CHARGES PERSONS ACCUSING THEM OF BEING COMMUNISTS OF FINDING THEM GUILTY BY ASSOCIATION. BUDENZ WILL NOT BE AVAILABLE DURING THE NEXT WEEK SINCE HE IS ON A SPEAKING TOUR THROUGH THE MID-WEST.[31]

Surprisingly, Scheidt's cable did not include the latest Budenz "reflec-tions" about Lattimore. One of the New York supervisors remedied this oversight in a telephone call to Duty Officer Hennrich at 9:20 P.M. Henn-rich promptly wrote a memo to Belmont, who was now at headquarters in Washington. Budenz's "further reflections" were that Lattimore spear-headed the attack against Chiang Kai-shek in 1942. "Budenz recalled that the magazine 'Pacific Affairs' of the IPR carried an article attacking Chiang Kai-shek before it was officially known that the line was to change con-cerning Chiang Kai-shek from a policy of passive friendship to hostility. Budenz recalled that Field reported to the Political Committee that Latti-more had information that the line was changed."[32]

Since there was no such article in *Pacific Affairs*, Budenz later had to correct his claim. The article attacking Chiang was by T. A. Bisson, and it appeared in *Far Eastern Survey*, with which Lattimore had nothing to do. Then there was a new absurdity in the report from New York: "Bud-enz stated that up until the Hitler-Stalin Pact the Party made a practice of furnishing all members of the National Committee with onion skin copies of the minutes of the Political Committee meetings. He recalled reading reports by Field in the minutes and Lattimore was referred to as either 'L' or 'XL.' He stated that names were never mentioned in these reports, and that individuals were referred to by symbols. These reports had to be destroyed, or returned to a responsible official."[33]

By the time he got to the Tydings committee, Budenz had elaborated this to claim that the onionskin reports had to be torn up and flushed down the toilet; burning wasn't good enough, since it left ashes. No onionskin reports ever showed up, and no other Communist or former Communist corroborated their existence. And nobody but Budenz ever claimed to have seen Lattimore referred to as "L" or "XL." Budenz's imagination was working overtime.

By the second week of April the FBI was engaged in that characteristic bureaucratic sport of damage control. It was not enough that Budenz was now telling them his new reflections about Lattimore; McCarthy, with his promise of a "secret witness" and the leaked knowledge that it was Budenz, had "captured" Budenz in the eyes of the press and attentive public. The FBI had to get Budenz back under control. Further, they had to explain their failure to extract from Budenz any information about one of their major cases despite an estimated three thousand hours of interrogation.

Assistant Attorney General Peyton Ford was pressing the bureau on this. Ford talked to Lou Nichols on April 11, saying Senator Tydings was now "out on a limb"; the bureau had better prepare a memorandum on Budenz's knowledge of Lattimore and when the bureau had obtained this information. If Budenz did testify, Ford said, the attorney general should know the background.[34] Hoover had such a memorandum in Attorney General McGrath's hands within hours:

> [In regard to Ford's inquiry] you are advised that the Bureau has conducted exhaustive interviews with Budenz over an extended period of time dating back to his initial break with the Communist Party at a time when he was in seclusion at Notre Dame University.
>
> Since that time we have had occasion to interview him off and on at periodical intervals. He has always been most cooperative and helpful, however, there was no occasion to direct specific inquiry to him pertaining to Owen Lattimore until recently. It would appear that had information occurred to him pertaining to Lattimore that he certainly would have mentioned it since he was interviewed, for example, on April 22, 1948, regarding ———— and in connection with the *Amerasia* case. There was no reason to believe that Budenz knew Lattimore or would have knowledge of espionage activities. As a matter of fact, when Budenz was interviewed on March 27, 1950, he specifically stated that he did not know Lattimore personally. He then furnished certain information which he has added to on an almost day to day basis since that time.[35]

Hoover's growing disillusionment with Budenz eventually resulted in outright skepticism. But the working-level agents were way ahead of Hoover. The New York agents, whipped into a frenzy of activity by Budenz's sudden discovery of Lattimore, called in a crew over the weekend of April 8–9 to search their transcripts of Budenz interviews.[36] This review was completed late in the day April 10. Agent W. M. Whelan telephoned bureau headquarters at 2:00 A.M. April 11 with the results: Budenz had never mentioned Lattimore.

Whelan was caustic. He reviewed the various times Budenz had been grilled about IPR, about *Amerasia*, and about his *Collier's* article and had never even hinted that he had anything on Lattimore. Whelan concluded that when Budenz was interviewed about Lattimore on March 27, 1950, he had furnished a "rationalization" of the "alleged" part played by Lattimore in painting the Chinese Communists as mere agrarian reformers; however, Budenz had furnished "no information or even allegations which tend to prove" McCarthy's claim that Lattimore was a Communist agent.[37]

Whelan's conclusions caught the eye of Belmont as soon as he got to the office that morning. He telephoned New York, but Whelan had gone home after his 2:00 A.M. report to Washington. Belmont spoke to an agent whose name is denied, demanding another immediate interview of Budenz to find out why he had held out on the Lattimore information so long and to impress on him the importance of having a good answer.[38]

New York had bad news: Budenz had already left for his Michigan speaking tour. Belmont then set out, with some asperity, several tasks for the New York office: check with Mrs. Budenz, get Louis's itinerary, find out if he had yet received a subpoena from Tydings, and get his day and time of arrival back in New York. An agent was to meet him at the plane and *get answers*.[39]

New York must have gotten the overworked Whelan out of bed, for Whelan called Belmont later on April 11 to report Budenz's itinerary and arrival time in New York on Saturday April 15 and to give the news that Ed Morgan of the Tydings committee had wanted to serve a subpoena on Budenz the day before, but Budenz had already left. Belmont reported this conversation to Ladd:

ASAC Whelan was advised that in the event no instructions are received to the contrary, Agent ——— should interview Budenz immediately upon his return along the lines indicated above, the purpose being to find out why Budenz didn't furnish us this information regarding Lattimore before when he had full opportunity to do so. . . . I think, during the contemplated interview, Agent ——— can plant the seed in Budenz' mind that he was fully cognizant that the FBI was keenly interested in any information concerning Communism or espionage, that he had full opportunity to furnish information concerning

Lattimore during questions by agents relating to associated matters such as the IPR ———— and that he, Budenz, was negligent in not furnishing the information to the FBI concerning Lattimore prior to March 27, 1950. Agent ———— was instructed by me to plant this idea with Budenz during the contemplated interview if it could be done gracefully.[40]

At midnight Scheidt cabled Washington. Mrs. Budenz had called. Louis had telephoned her and said he had accepted a subpoena by telephone from Tydings to testify April 20.[41]

At 7:00 P.M. on the twelfth Scheidt cabled Washington again. He had talked to Budenz by telephone in Michigan. Budenz was now backtracking on several things, including his knowledge of Andrew Roth and his statement that Lattimore was to spearhead the attack on Chiang. But the vital matter was this: "BUDENZ ALSO WANTED TO BE ASSURED THAT THE INFO WHICH HE WAS FURNISHING THE BUREAU WOULD NOT BE MADE AVAILABLE TO SOME PERSON WHO COULD CROSS EXAMINE HIM DURING THE SENATE COMMITTEE HEARING. HE WAS GIVEN THIS ASSURANCE. BUDENZ STATED THAT HE SAW ALFRED KOHLBERG FOR A FEW MINUTES DURING THE PAST WEEKEND, AND KOHLBERG ACTED AS HIS LIAISON MAN WITH MC CARTHY."[42]

When Hoover saw this cable the next day, he exploded. "Did NY Office ask him why he hadn't given us the Lattimore material sooner? If not, why not? It was a perfect opening." Scheidt answered that the telephone line was not secure, so he did not ask.[43]

Tension at the bureau was now high. Belmont spent several hours on April 14 composing a letter to Ladd answering Hoover's complaint that the bureau had not sufficiently grilled Budenz. Belmont reviewed the bureau's contacts with Budenz exhaustively, noting that "Budenz has been cooperative and thoroughly respects the Bureau. His attitude is good. However, I do not feel that we are in a position to sit him down as we did Chambers and interview him for three months to drain him dry. He has many commitments and we do not have the hold on him that we had on Chambers." Belmont had several recommendations for getting Budenz to confess his error.[44]

Hoover still wasn't satisfied. At the bottom of Belmont's report he wrote, "O. K. but don't ponder about it too long. All very good if it is kept alive. We missed the boat with Chambers & now Budenz. We can't miss many more without getting strong public castigation."

At 9:15 P.M. Saturday, April 15, Budenz was met at LaGuardia Airport by the two agents who had been interviewing him. They were armed with half a dozen cables from Hoover telling them to ask Budenz about several specific charges he had made about Lattimore that didn't check out; but mostly they were to find out why he hadn't leveled with them.

The agents got an earful. Scheidt cabled headquarters six hours later, at 3:15 the next morning: "BUDENZ . . . SAID HE NEVER MENTIONED WHAT HE KNEW ABOUT LATTIMORE BECAUSE HIS INFORMATION WAS FLIMSY. IT WAS NOT LEGAL AND HE HAD DEVOTED MOST OF HIS TIME TO FURNISHING LEGAL EVIDENCE TO THE FBI. HE KNOWS HE SHOULD HAVE FURNISHED THE INFORMATION BUT STATES IT WAS HUMANLY IMPOSSIBLE . . . IN THE TIME HE HAD AVAILABLE TO WORK WITH THE FBI."[45]

So it was flimsy evidence that the high priest of anticommunism was about to pass on to a Senate committee, slandering a professor whom he had never met nor read, escalating the inquisition to an even higher pitch—and rescuing Joe McCarthy. Had the bureau been fair, rather than a cheerleader in the hysteria, it would have summarily scuttled Budenz as a Lattimore witness.

Instead, the bureau entered into a conspiracy with Budenz and the Department of Justice to prevent truth from emerging in the Tydings hearings. The bureau knew three things about Budenz's testimony: he thought it was flimsy, it was laughably inconsistent, and he was unwilling to face a cross-examiner who was prepared for him. Instead of informing Tydings, the committee staff, or McCarthy about the weaknesses of their next witness, Ladd telephoned Ford at Justice: "I told him that we had assured Budenz that this material would not be made available to the committee for cross examination purposes and that I hoped the Department was not furnishing it to the committee until after Budenz had testified." Ford said Justice would go along with this approach.[46] The Tydings hearings were not a criminal trial. Had they been, the FBI and the Department of Justice would have committed an obstruction of justice.

April was Budenz month at the FBI. Hundreds of memos, telephone calls, letters, telegrams, and conferences were devoted to getting Budenz under control. The speeches he made in Michigan caused further trauma; Hoover cabled New York on the nineteenth, asking them to check out five new claims Budenz made in Michigan that the bureau was not privy to. All of them turned out to be false: IPR offices were not located in the same building as the pro-Communist *China Today*, and Lattimore did not place a Communist elevator operator from Indonesia with OWI as a translator. Other claims Budenz made to the bureau in confidence, which were checked out with apparently negative results, are still classified.[47]

New York also continued its round-the-clock Budenz operation. Agents saw him every day between his return from Michigan on the fifteenth and his departure on the nineteenth to testify in Washington. Scheidt was up all night the eighteenth, preparing an eight-page telegram to Washington reporting what they had learned from Budenz that evening; his telegram was filed at 5:12 A.M. on the nineteenth. Thomas Reeves heard from Charles Kersten that "agents grilled Budenz so intensely that when Kersten later visited him, he and his wife were in tears from the pressure."[48]

At one point Budenz was to prepare a statement for Tydings; he didn't have time to do it. It was with some relief that he boarded an American Airlines plane at 1:35 P.M. on April 19 for Washington; he would at least get a tension-free evening with his host, Fulton Sheen.[49] The next day was D day.

Lattimore and Fortas were of course unaware of the turmoil and bitterness inside the government. They did know that Budenz could be a serious threat. As Lattimore describes it in *Ordeal By Slander*, Fortas told him:

> McCarthy is a long way out on a limb. The political pressures that are building up are terrific. The report that Budenz will testify against you has shaken everyone in Washington. It is my duty as your lawyer to warn you that the danger you face cannot possibly be exaggerated. It does not exclude the possibility of a straight frame-up, with perjured witnesses and perhaps even forged documents. You have a choice of two ways of facing this danger. You can either take it head on, and expose yourself to this danger; or you can make a qualified and carefully guarded statement which will reduce the chance of entrapment by fake evidence. As your lawyer I cannot make that choice for you. You have to make it yourself.[50]

Lattimore chose to take it head-on. He never regretted it.

Since Lattimore and Fortas did not know what Budenz would claim, there was little they could do to prepare for his testimony. One rumor had it that Budenz would claim that Fred Field had somehow implicated Lattimore in Party activities. Fortas talked to Field, who responded with a letter saying that if Budenz claimed that Field had told him anything at all about Lattimore, then Budenz was lying. Fortas also got an affidavit from Bella Dodd, a former Communist who had outranked Budenz in the Party, to the effect that in all her time as a Party activist she had never heard one word about Lattimore. And Brigadier General Elliot Thorpe, who had been head of counterintelligence and a rival of General Willoughby in MacArthur's Tokyo command, was persuaded to state the results of his investigations of Lattimore during the Pauley mission: Thorpe

said Lattimore was unquestionably a loyal American. He later told Tydings the same thing.[51]

One encouraging development buoyed Lattimore's spirits five days before Budenz's appearance at the Tydings hearings: he was asked to give
the closing address to the fifty-fourth annual meeting of the American
Academy of Political and Social Science in Philadelphia. This address made
the front page of the *Times;* Lattimore was quoted as recommending that
the United States withdraw support from the Nationalist regime on Taiwan but not as yet recognize the People's Republic. He also thought the
Nationalist raids against the mainland were dangerous since they might
induce the People's Republic to call in the Russians to counter them. The
academicians gave Lattimore enthusiastic applause.[52]

On April 20, 1950, when Budenz appeared before the Tydings commit-
tee, the audience was quite different from the scholars Lattimore had faced.
Clergy in black cloth were much in evidence; so were members of the
Daughters of the American Revolution, in Washington for a convention.
To this audience, Budenz was a dragon slayer.

Nonetheless, Budenz's task that day was harder than the one he had
faced in the Foley Square trials of the top Communist leaders in 1949. At
Foley Square he needed only to describe the extent to which admitted
Party functionaries were manipulated by Soviet emissaries. He knew the
defendants from working with them; he had firsthand knowledge, so there
was no doubt about his standing as a witness. At the Tydings hearings, in
contrast, he was making charges against a man he had never met, and his
claims about Lattimore, as he had admitted to Matthews, were hearsay.

But the aura of the Party insider was still useful. Budenz began by
reviewing his testimony about the Communist party as a conspiracy, not
a legitimate party at all but an arm of the international Communist movement.[53] This testimony was irrelevant to the Tydings committee's concerns about whether there were Communists in the State Department—
but it was vital to Budenz's image as an informer. So was his public stance
as a reluctant witness. Three times during his testimony he emphasized
that he came only under subpoena, unwillingly, sacrificing his time and
privacy for the greater good of the nation. Thus, he began with an outrageous lie, and it was all downhill from there.

Since his biggest hurdle was overcoming the hearsay handicap, he used
a rhetorical technique based on the theme of editorial omniscience. The
Daily Worker, which he had edited, was the Party organ for informing
the faithful not only what they were to believe but who was authoritative
in telling them what to believe. As editor, Budenz said, he had had

to understand what was occurring within the Communist movement. I also received direct instructions, well, almost hourly, as a matter of fact, but certainly every day, from the liaison officer connected with the Politburo. We had a liaison officer appointed who gave me instructions from day to day and in addition to that kept refreshing me on a list of about a thousand names which I was compelled to keep in my mind as to their various attitudes toward the party, the various shifts and changes, whether a man had turned traitor or whether he had not, and things of that sort. This list was not put down in writing because of the fact that it might be disclosed, consequently I was compelled to keep it in my mind, and this representative of the political bureau, the Politburo, kept refreshing my mind on this list of names.[54]

Budenz had developed this claim of editorial omniscience to overcome the handicap first revealed in 1945 to the FBI's Pat Coyne during the South Bend interviews: that because he had not been trained in Moscow, Party leaders did not fully trust or confide in him. As the years went by, Budenz found that a plausible answer to skeptical bureau agents asking him "How do you know this?" was "I had to know it in my capacity as editor." The editorial omniscience ploy did not always work; in some matters, such as Budenz's claim that the IPR and *China Today* offices were in the same building, the FBI could force him to recant by independent investigation.

In the area of naming names, however, the tactic worked like a charm. Who could disprove the contention that Fred Field had reported to the Politburo that Lattimore had carried out the assignment to "change the line" on Chiang Kai-shek? Field could deny it endlessly, but Communists lie. Lattimore's denial was self-serving. Jack Stachel, Earl Browder, and other Politburo members either wouldn't talk or would lie. It was a foolproof scheme.

Well, not quite foolproof. If the government was prepared to spend several million dollars investigating Budenz's accusations against one individual, as it did with Lattimore, Budenz could be refuted. There had to be, if Budenz was telling the truth about Lattimore, some individual somewhere who had left the Party and who would testify that he or she had taken orders from Lattimore, or had written a piece to carry out the new policy, or knew firsthand that Lattimore had directed this campaign. There had to be some evidence that Lattimore had "been of assistance" in the *Amerasia* case. There was no such confirmation, anywhere in the world, of any of Budenz's charges against Lattimore, and both FBI and Justice eventually gave up hunting for it.

Unfortunately, not all the four hundred concealed Communists fingered by Budenz were cleared by massive investigations. Some of them may have been secret Communists, but who knows what damage was done to those who were not? At the very least, their FBI and passport files bear the stain of Budenz's accusations.[55]

Apparently nobody laughed when Budenz told Tydings that he kept in his head a list of a thousand names as a requirement of his editorial job. Nobody from the FBI warned Tydings committee members that James Glasser, managing editor of the *Daily Worker* when Budenz was labor editor and in 1950 a former Communist, told the bureau that "based upon his knowledge of the functions of the managing editor of the *Daily Worker*, BUDENZ was obviously fabricating 'smears' against LATTIMORE and others, in his Senate Sub-Committee testimony. He added that although he does not know anything regarding LATTIMORE, he would wholly discount BUDENZ's remarks as those emanating from a psychopathic liar."[56]

Nor did the bureau publicize the fact that when Budenz's recollections of "concealed Communists" ran out well short of the promised four hundred names, Budenz "refreshed his memory" from lists of officers and sponsors of left-wing organizations such as the American Artists Congress, Artists Front to Win the Peace, Independent Citizens Committee of the Arts, Sciences and Professions, Newspaper Guild of New York, People's Radio Foundation, and Win the Peace Conference.[57]

"Editorial omniscience" was by itself insufficient to ensure Budenz's credibility. He used a companion rhetorical ploy extensively before Tydings: *his* hearsay was better than garden variety hearsay: it was *official*. In his first day of testimony Budenz described what he claimed he was told by Party leaders as "official" twenty-three times. Phrases like "the instructions and directions I received officially," "according to the official reports made to me," "it was officially reported that Mr. Lattimore had received word," "official documents," and so forth appear on almost every page of the transcript. This tactic may not have convinced all of his listeners, but coupled with his claim that Communists never lie to each other, only to those outside the Party, it got him through the pallid questioning of the committee members when they heard Budenz in executive session five days after the public hearing.

Not surprisingly, Budenz decided against reinforcing his hearsay testimony by citing the anti-Lattimore statements of his good friend Alfred Kohlberg. Rather, his corroboration was the *Columbia* article of September 1949 by James F. Kearney, whom Budenz described as "an expert on the Far East." Budenz quoted Kearney's article to Tydings: "There are those who believe, though, that no Americans deserve more credit for the Russian triumph in the Sino-American disaster than Owen Lattimore and a small group of his followers."[58] Senator Theodore Green of Rhode Island was skeptical:

> *Green:* Do you know where Father Kearney got his information?
>
> *Budenz:* I do not know, sir.
>
> *Green:* Did he tell you, or did he not, that he got it from Alfred Kohlberg, of New York?
>
> *Budenz:* No, sir.[59]

Kohlberg was, however, Kearney's main source. Not until October 1950 did the FBI check out the Kohlberg-Kearney connection, to the disgrace of both.

Budenz made five charges before Tydings. (1) At a Politburo meeting in 1937 Field and Browder commended Lattimore for placing the works of Communist writers in IPR publications. (2) At another meeting in 1937 Field and Browder decided that Lattimore should be given general direction of a campaign to organize writers on China to portray the Chinese Communists as not Communists at all, but as agrarian reformers. (3) In 1943, at a similar meeting, "it was officially reported that Mr. Lattimore, through Mr. Field, had received word from the apparatus that there was to be a change of line on Chiang Kai-shek." (4) In 1944 Jack Stachel told Budenz to "consider Owen Lattimore a Communist." (5) In 1945 Stachel told Budenz that Lattimore "had been of service in the *Amerasia* case."[60] None of these things ever happened.

The committee treated Budenz gingerly. The Democrats (Tydings, Green, and Brien McMahon) were more skeptical than were the Republicans (Lodge and Hickenlooper). The press was skeptical, but following journalistic standards of the day, Budenz's assertions, like McCarthy's, were news and were reported uncritically.[61] Even the *New York Times*, no fan of McCarthy, carried Arthur Krock's gullible column the Sunday after Budenz's testimony under the headline, "Capital Is Disturbed by Budenz Testimony. Even Critics of McCarthy's Methods Now Take Anxious View of New Development in Inquiry."[62] Budenz had fulfilled his role; he had rescued McCarthy.

But out of public view, challenges to Budenz's credibility continued to mount. On April 26 an important Pennsylvania ex-Communist, whose name is still denied by the FBI, told agents that

he [had been] expelled from the Communist Party ———— but had attended numerous Party meetings in New York City during the preced-
ing twenty years, where Communist Party policy was discussed, but he
could not recall that OWEN LATTIMORE'S name was ever mentioned as
having any connection with the Communist Party. ———— that he had
been following the LATTIMORE case in the papers and was of the opinion
that LATTIMORE was not a Communist because the Communist Party
would never allow LATTIMORE to depart from the Party line and write
articles which would be critical of Russia. ———— that he knows LOUIS
BUDENZ slightly and believes him to be dishonest and a psychiatric case.[63]

This testimony never saw the light of day.

On April 28, 1950, Budenz was grandstanding again. In a speech at
Peekskill, New York, he stated that he knew "who arranged the theft of
the *Amerasia* papers. . . . Budenz said the investigation of the *Amerasia*
case and charges that Owen Lattimore is a Communist should be closely
linked and that the Lattimore and *Amerasia* cases are 'both interlocked
and cannot be separated. If fully investigated the cases will provide one of
the greatest scandals that American political history has ever witnessed.' "[64] The FBI discovered that Budenz had, as usual, no "actual
facts" to support this charge.

As the summer wore on, the FBI discovered that Budenz had few "actual facts" about anything. On May 25, reporting a recent interview designed to clarify what Lattimore had actually done about changing the
party line on Chiang Kai-shek, the New York office told headquarters that
Budenz "was unable to state" whether Lattimore knew about this change
in advance, nor did he know whether Lattimore was responsible for publication of the Bisson article. A New York FBI report of July 18 reveals
Budenz soaring far into fantasyland. In large Russian cities, he said, "nearly
every child is trained in the art of paratrooping." Why? Because Stalin
had no regard for the lives of his citizens and was planning "large scale
attacks of suicide paratroopers carrying bombs," like the Japanese kami-
kaze pilots who gave their all in the Pacific war.[65]

For all his appeal to the Catholic faithful, Budenz was beginning to lose
even some of his church supporters. In a memo to Hoover May 1, 1950,
Ladd reported:

> Mr. John Steelman, the Assistant to the President, mentioned to Mr.
> Roach this morning while discussing other matters that he was becom-
> ing highly suspicious of the activities of Louis Budenz. He stated that
> the activities of Budenz had also aroused the suspicions of other per-
> sons, whom he indicated were attached to Catholic University here in

Washington. His contact at Catholic University apparently gave Steelman the impression that they had a "hot potato" on their hands and did not know how to get rid of him. The undercurrent of feeling seems to be, according to Mr. Steelman, that they are sceptical of Budenz's so-called return to Catholicism. They view him as still a "good Communist." Mr. Steelman commented that some Church leaders, (names not mentioned) have told him that Budenz's testimony before the Tydings Committee certainly did not help the prestige of the Catholic Church, and although he, Steelman, has no information to prove or disprove that Budenz is still a Communist, he stated that he certainly has his suspicions. He commented, "I hope J. Edgar is keeping an eye on him."[66]

Hoover noted laconically, "Keep possibility in mind."

1. Owen and Eleanor Lattimore at their wedding, Peking, March 4, 1926. Courtesy of David Lattimore.

2. Philip Jaffe, Lattimore, Chu Teh, Agnes Jaffe, and Thomas Bisson. Yenan, June 1937. Courtesy of David Lattimore.

3. Lattimore and Chiang Kai-shek, Chungking, September 1941. Courtesy of David Lattimore.

4. Henry Wallace, Lattimore, John Carter Vincent, and John Hazard, China, June 1944. Courtesy of David Lattimore.

5. Vilhjalmur and Evelyn Stefansson. Courtesy of Evelyn Stefansson Nef.

6. Owen and Eleanor Lattimore at Tydings committee hearings, April 20, 1950. Courtesy of Acme Photo.

7. William D. and Suki Rogers, summer 1953. Courtesy of Suki Rogers.

8. The Dilowa Hutukhtu, about 1958. Courtesy of David Lattimore.

9.   Lattimore in morning dress on his way to interpret for Queen Elizabeth II, November 14, 1963. Courtesy of Diana MacLeish.

10.   A. P. Okladnikov, Ulan Bator, summer 1964. Courtesy of David Lattimore.

11. Michael Lattimore, Fujiko Isono, Lattimore, and Chou En-lai in the Great Hall of the People, Peking, October 1972. Courtesy of David Lattimore.

12. Lattimore, Robert P. Newman, and Dean A.ec Stewart, University of Pittsburgh, March 19, 1979. Courtesy of Dewey Chester.

13. Lattimore and Maria Lattimore on the Great Wall, summer 1981. Courtesy of David Lattimore.

14. Premier Tsedenbal of the Mongolian People's Republic and Lattimore, Ulan Bator, summer 1981. Courtesy of David Lattimore.

CHAPTER NINETEEN

Exit Tydings, Enter Kim Il-sung

Lattimore held a press conference April 21, 1950, the day after Budenz appeared before Tydings. He gave reporters a seven-page statement and answered questions. Invective flowed freely. According to Lattimore, McCarthy had descended to a "new low" with his attack on George Marshall the night before; McCarthy was serving as a "stooge" for the China lobby, which was out to destroy anyone who disagreed with Kohlberg as to why China went Communist. As to Budenz, his testimony was false from beginning to end. If it were not false, Budenz would give it outside of Congress, where he could be sued for libel. Lattimore was encouraged by the reporters' response: "Their questions soon showed that Budenz had flopped and that there was no 'hot Washington tip' of revelations still to come." This time Lattimore won the headline battle in the mainstream press. The *New York Times* story on page one the next day was headed, "Lattimore Derides Budenz as Gossip: Reply to Ex-Editor's Charges Demands an Investigation of China Lobby Group."[1]

The favorable reception of Lattimore's press conference did not discourage McCarthy. He *did* have another mystery witness coming on: John Huber (alias Tom Ward), a former FBI undercover informant in the New York City Communist party. Huber had none of the liabilities of Budenz: he was not a double defector, had no multiple arrest record, had not taken the Fifth before official inquiries, had not violated the Mann Act, had served the FBI loyally, and had not joined the Communist party out of conviction. Further, while Budenz's testimony was hearsay, Huber was an eyewitness. He claimed he had met Lattimore at two Party meetings.

Huber monitored the New York Communist party from 1939 until 1947, writing extensive reports.[2] None of them ever mentioned Owen Lattimore. When the FBI investigation of Lattimore intensified after McCarthy's charges, the bureau systematically called in all current and former Party informants to see if any of them knew anything about the Hopkins professor. Huber was interviewed on April 14, 1950. His memory had by then been "refreshed" by contemporary headlines. He recalled that he had seen Lattimore at two Party meetings, both at the home of Fred Field.

The first meeting, on November 16, 1945, was "a farewell affair for Comrade Tung Pi Wu, who was described by Huber as the fourth highest Communist in the Chinese Communist Party. . . . According to Huber, Tung Pi Wu spoke through an interpreter thanking all those present at the affair for the splendid cooperation shown the Chinese Communist movement. Huber recalled that Lattimore had a private conversation with Tung at this affair." Only Party members were present. The second meeting, on February 17, 1946, was a fund-raiser of the Committee for a Democratic Far Eastern Policy. Field was chair of this Communist group, and Theodore White gave the main speech. Lattimore was among the eighty-five people present.[3]

The bureau was skeptical of this revised reporting by Huber, but it was routinely incorporated in the Lattimore file. Huber, now alerted that his "information" about Lattimore might be a valuable commodity, went to Larry Kerley, a friend and former FBI agent working for Hearst's *New York Journal American*. Kerley immediately alerted McCarthy; on April 17 Huber told McCarthy the same story that he had told the FBI three days earlier. McCarthy then arranged for Tydings to subpoena Huber. Kerley was also subpoenaed; his function was to establish that Huber had been a bona fide FBI informant.

April 25, 1950, was to be the day of McCarthy's triumph: the appearance before Tydings of FBI informant Huber proclaiming to all the world that, with his own eyes, he had seen Lattimore at two Communist gatherings.

Huber was not the first to testify that day. Abe Fortas had arranged for Dr. Bella Dodd, a former Communist who had outranked Budenz in the Party, to appear before Tydings. Dodd disagreed with Budenz on everything. She had never heard of Lattimore associating with the Party in any way; she had read two of his books and they did not follow the Party line; she ridiculed Budenz's tale of onionskin documents to be flushed down the toilet as sounding like "dime detective stories"; and she thought McCarthy's "smearing of public citizens [had] become a greater racket" than horseracing or gambling.[4] McCarthy sat through Dodd's testimony glum but confident: his bombshell was due next.

The bomb was a dud. When Tydings called for him to take the stand, Huber was nowhere to be found. Neither McCarthy nor Kerley could explain his absence. Huber had come from New York to Washington on a plane with them early that morning and had checked into the Carlton Hotel. They had not seen him since noon. A flurry of telephone calls during a short recess produced nothing. After a desultory fifteen minutes examining Kerley, the committee adjourned.[5] Huber was the famous "Disappearing Witness" of the Tydings hearings.

Hearst papers had a field day with Huber's disappearance. Kerley put out a statement that Huber "had been stabbed and threatened" to keep him from testifying.[6] Washington was in an uproar. The FBI tried to locate Huber; it was a week before they found him. What the agents heard on May 2 could have come from a B movie. But before they got the story of his disappearance, Huber said he wanted to change his testimony about Lattimore: he had seen Lattimore at Field's house only once, in February 1946. As to why he had not appeared before Tydings, Huber described to Scheidt what happened at J. B. Matthews's house in New York the night before his scheduled testimony. Present were Matthews, Kerley, and McCarthy; all took for granted that he would testify, but they didn't tell him what it would be like. He got nervous and told Kerley he wouldn't testify, but Kerley insisted. As the hours went by, Huber "became extremely dejected and worried." The whole group spent the night at Matthews's place, then all but Matthews flew to Washington the next morning.[7]

In Washington, Huber "was left sitting alone in McCarthy's outer office." He was "completely worn out, tired, nervous, and hungry, as they had not fed him at all that day." He left McCarthy's office and went to the hotel where he was supposed to have a room, but he found that no reservation had been made. After much confusion he did get a room. When Kerley arrived at the hotel, Huber went out to get a haircut. Walking down Pennsylvania Avenue, he "blacked out. He next found himself on 44th Street and Seventh Avenue, New York City, soaking wet."[8]

Scheidt then reminded Huber that he had told the New York office over the phone that McCarthy and Kerley had tried "to get him to testify to things that were not entirely accurate." What had he meant by this? "HE IMMEDIATELY BECAME EXTREMELY EXCITED, STARTED TO SHAKE AND CRY AND IT WAS NECESSARY TO CHANGE THE SUBJECT BEFORE HE OBVIOUSLY

WOULD HAVE A COMPLETE COLLAPSE. HE WAS LATER QUESTIONED ABOUT THIS AND NOTHING MORE DEFINITE COULD BE SECURED. IT WOULD APPEAR, THEREFORE, THAT EITHER HUBER IS LYING AT THE PRESENT TIME OR IS HAVING A MENTAL RELAPSE."[9]

When Huber calmed down, he told Scheidt that he wanted to appear before Tydings to redeem himself. Since he knew so little, he wouldn't need to spend more than five minutes on the witness stand. But Scheidt was not sure that this was a good plan. Huber had failed to keep previous appointments with the FBI, was highly excitable, and told contradictory stories. Scheidt did not believe the truth was in him.[10]

FBI agents saw Huber again on May 4; he had meanwhile been interviewed by Tydings's agents. Huber said he had told the Tydings people yet a different story. As Huber now told Scheidt, "THE PARTY AT THE HOME OF FRED FIELD AT WHICH HE SAW OWEN LATTIMORE WAS NOT A COMMUNIST PARTY MEETING AS FAR AS HUBER KNEW AND THAT AS FAR AS HUBER IS CONCERNED HE HAS NO INFO OF CP MEMBERSHIP ON THE PART OF OWEN LATTIMORE."[11]

The bureau meanwhile had checked out Lattimore's whereabouts in November 1945 and knew that Lattimore was in Japan, so that Huber could not have seen him at Field's house. And they looked again at Huber's voluminous reports in 1945 and 1946: there was no mention of Lattimore anywhere.[12]

Tydings did not subpoena Huber again. Once was enough. McCarthy also washed his hands of Huber. Unfortunately, the press never carried the story of how Huber had been induced by his handlers, McCarthy, Kerley, and Matthews, to lie about Lattimore. Only the FBI knew why Huber got cold feet.

Budenz did not get cold feet. On April 23, 1950, before a supportive audience in New York, he escalated his apocalyptic rhetoric another notch. According to the *New York Times* of April 24,

> Soviet Russia's program for world revolution under the leadership of Joseph Stalin includes definite plants to threaten the United States West Coast, Prof. Louis F. Budenz declared yesterday. In a speech at the twenty-ninth communion breakfast of the New York Post Office Holy Name Society in the Astor Hotel, he warned against recognition of the Communist government in China.
>
> The Professor of Economics at Fordham University and former managing editor of the Daily Worker said there long had been a plot by Communists in the Philippines, China and Japan to drive the "Ameri-

can imperialists'' from the Pacific and then link forces with those of Harry Bridges in Hawaii.[13]

Earl Browder appeared before the Tydings committee April 27. Browder was predictably contemptuous of Budenz; every one of the charges against Lattimore was false. So, said Mr. Browder, were McCarthy's charges against Dorothy Kenyon, Haldore Hanson, John Carter Vincent, and John Stewart Service. But Browder, although he had been expelled from the Party in 1946, still regarded himself as a Communist and refused to answer questions put to him by Senator Hickenlooper. The committee voted to cite Browder for contempt.[14]

The next day, Fred Field took much the same line. He and Lattimore were often at odds politically, but they respected each other. Field said Lattimore was never a Communist or even a sympathizer. Like Browder, Field took the Fifth on questions about his own politics. He, too, was cited for contempt, but at his trial Judge T. Alan Goldsborough found him innocent. The Tydings committee was not a straightforward seeker of information, said the judge, but called Field to testify so he could be "grilled."[15]

Field's testimony, on Friday, April 28, coincided with Tydings's release of letters from all living former secretaries of state and the current secretary, Dean Acheson. All stated that they had never even met Lattimore and that he was anything but the architect of American policy in the Far East. This denial did not help Lattimore; Republican senators tasting blood were not about to accept anything from officials serving under Democratic presidents.

Monday, May 1, the last anti-Lattimore witness came before Tydings: Freda Utley. She had a new slant:

> I think that Senator McCarthy was wrong in his original statement that Owen Lattimore is the Soviet Government's top espionage agent in America. I think the Senator under-estimated Lattimore. Mr. Lattimore is such a renowned scholar, such an excellent writer, so adept at teaching the American people that they ought to stop opposing the great, good, and progressive Soviet Government, that it is impossible to believe that Moscow would regard him as expendable, as all spies are. To suggest that Mr. Lattimore's great talents have been utilized in espionage seems to me as absurd as to suggest that Mr. Gromyko or Mr. Molotov employ their leisure hours at Lake Success, or at international conferences, in snitching documents.[16]

After a lengthy and distorted review of Lattimore's writings, Utley got to her main accusation. Lattimore was dangerous, and serving the Soviet cause, by presenting the Chinese Communists as independent of Moscow. This claim Utley could not believe, and she said that Lattimore knew too much to believe it also, so he was lying. "The primary and most important fact which has determined recent victory in the Far East is the subservience of the Chinese Communist Party to Moscow, and this is precisely the fact ignored or obscured by Mr. Lattimore in all his writings."[17]

When I interviewed Utley in 1977, twenty-seven years after this testimony, the evidence of Chinese independence of Moscow was abundant. She acknowledged this fact and implied that she had been too hard on Lattimore in 1950. She also admitted somewhat ruefully that in 1945, Chou En-lai, "one of the most remarkable men [she had] ever met," had tried to convince her that the Chinese Communists were not agents of Moscow, but she had been unconvinced.[18]

Utley told Tydings the story of her acquaintance with Lattimore, but she omitted one salient incident, her effort to get an audience with Soviet Ambassador Oumansky through Lattimore's intervention. Had this incident been known, her explanation of why she was so hostile toward Lattimore might have been less convincing.

In *Ordeal by Slander* Lattimore says that Utley's testimony redounded to his benefit, since she got wound up in esoteric ideological arguments, could not find documents when she needed them, and got flustered, hence turning both the committee and reporters against her. He may have been wrong in this judgment. Tydings was unnecessarily sharp with Utley. The *New York Times* report of May 2 by William S. White treated her with respect.[19]

For the next two days, May 2–3, Lattimore was again before Tydings. He felt that he was under less pressure than he had been during his earlier appearance. As he says in *Ordeal,*

> McCarthy's big gun, Budenz, had misfired. Huber and Freda Utley had provided only ludicrous anticlimaxes. It was my turn at last to review the whole grotesque, brutal, and long-sustained attempt at character-assassination.
>
> Once more the Caucus Room was packed so tightly that there were people standing around the edges, against the wall. The batteries of newsreel cameras were there too, but I soon noticed an encouraging sign. Instead of the lights blazing and the cameras whirring all the time, they went on only occasionally. That meant, I thought, that the newsreels were not on tiptoe with expectation. The sensationalism of the charges against me had already been somewhat deflated.[20]

Lattimore began by reminding the senators that McCarthy had given up his original "top Soviet spy" charge and was now struggling to make some lesser charge stick. He brushed off Freda Utley's testimony, saying he would respond to it when he had a chance to see the transcript.

But Lattimore once more provided some harsh invective. Whether he was too sharp in attacking McCarthy is still a debatable question. Many observers think that had he simply said, "McCarthy is in error," he would not have incurred the implacable opposition of McCarthy supporters. But Fortas thought he should come out swinging, and so did Eleanor. So he told Tydings:

> Now, gentlemen, I of course do not enjoy being vilified by anybody: even by the motley crew of crackpots, professional informers, hysterics, and ex-Communists who McCarthy would have you believe represent sound Americanism. But on the other hand, I do not like to appear to rely upon the testimony of others to establish my own good character. My life and works speak for themselves. Unlike McCarthy I have never been charged with a violation of the laws of the United States or of the ethics of my profession. I have never been accused, as McCarthy has been, of income tax evasion, of the destruction of records that were in my official custody, or of improperly using an official position for the purpose of advancing my own fortunes, political or otherwise.
>
> Unlike Budenz and Utley, I have never been a member of the Communist Party, or subscribed to a conspiracy to overthrow and subvert established governments. Unlike Budenz, I have never been engaged in a conspiracy to commit murder or espionage. . . .
>
> I recognize, however, that so long as a reckless and irresponsible man like Senator McCarthy is in a position to abuse the privileges of the United States Congress, the quality of a man's life and activities, however impeccable, does not protect him from vile assault. Even our greatest living American, General Marshall, has been subjected to McCarthy's vicious, dastardly, and repeated insult.[21]

Lattimore denied Budenz's charges categorically. He had not sought to "place Communist writers" in the pages of *Pacific Affairs*. Budenz's only example, an article by James S. Allen, had been accepted on scholarly grounds. Lattimore did not know whether or not Allen was a Communist.

Lattimore did know that he had always believed that the Chinese Communists were hard-line Marxists, only temporarily modifying their ideological stance to appeal to Chinese peasants. How could he have led a campaign to represent the Chinese Communists as "mere agrarian reformers" when he did not believe it himself? (The only thorough study of the "mere agrarian reformers" line, by Kenneth Shewmaker, upholds Lattimore completely. Utley herself first used the phrase, and Patrick Hurley and several journalists used it subsequently; Lattimore never used it.)[22]

Lattimore expressed only contempt for the Budenz charge that in 1943 Lattimore, "through Mr. Field, had received word from the apparatus that there was to be a change of line on Chiang Kai-shek." Lattimore was fully employed with the Office of War Information then and still strongly supported Chiang, as he did until 1946. Budenz had nothing whatever to back up his claim; Lattimore said that it was "as fantastic as it is malignant."[23]

And could Jack Stachel have instructed Budenz in 1944 to "treat as authoritative" anything Lattimore said? If so, Budenz did not follow orders. The pages of the *Daily Worker* for that year, as Lattimore pointed out, were totally devoid of his extensive opinions on China and Chiang. Lattimore treated as equally ridiculous Budenz's claims about "onionskin documents" and "of service in the *Amerasia* case," calling them "pure moonshine, or rather impure hogwash."[24]

Lattimore's summing-up of Budenz matched his excoriation of McCarthy.

> The plain fact of the matter, it seems to me, is that Budenz is engaged in a transparent fraud. Whenever someone is conspicuously accused of Communist affiliations, Budenz hops on the bandwagon and repeats the charges, garnished with more or less impressive references to Jack Stachel and other Communist characters. And I suspect that the reason why he uses, as his silent witnesses, officials of the Communist Party is that he believes that they will refuse to testify in rebuttal. But he guards himself even against this contingency by saying that if they do testify, contrary to his own statements, they cannot be believed. This I submit is about as ingenious a boobytrap as has ever been devised. . . .
>
> The pressure on Budenz is obvious. When a new sensation breaks out in the press and a man is accused—even if the accusation is false— what is the temptation that is dangled before Budenz' eyes? It is the easiest thing in the world for his own memory to be convenient and obliging. He can then rush up and say "I remember him too"—and thus revive his reputation as a peerless informant.[25]

The lead story in the *New York Times* the next day was headlined, "Lattimore Calls Budenz 'Informer' Lying for a Profit."[26]

Tydings did not finish with Lattimore on May 2; he was called back on May 3, mostly for questioning by Hickenlooper, an ally of McCarthy. The Iowa senator had dozens of questions, many of them prompted by claims of the underworld informants who had been drawn to the Mc-Carthy crusade. Lattimore dealt with them matter-of-factly. He had never met or been associated with Richard Sorge. He had never met or been associated with Ho Chi Minh. He had not declassified, or even seen, secret government documents at the Ruxton picnic with Service and Roth. He was acquainted, slightly, with Alger Hiss. There were no headlines here; and since on the same day McCarthy became embroiled in a bitter debate with Tydings and other Democrats on the Senate floor, Lattimore's final appearance before Tydings went largely unnoticed.

Of course, the right-wing press continued to snipe at Lattimore, and McCarthy discovered some new malefaction every week or so. Of judicious comment there was very little. The conservative *Christian Science Monitor*, however, carried an article on May 12 by Marius B. Jansen, then a Harvard graduate student, later a distinguished Japanologist at Princeton. In his article, "Owen Lattimore and the China Policy," Jansen asked, "What can we learn about Owen Lattimore from his writings?" and noted that Budenz and Utley claimed those writings contained proof of Communist allegiance. Jansen did not think so. Lattimore was clearly a capitalist and often anti-Soviet, as on the Marshall Plan and Soviet activities in Iran. As to Budenz's claim that the Party "allowed occasional deviations from their line to allay suspicion," Jansen noted that "they would hardly allow those heresies on the very issues for which they were using a man." And even when Lattimore's views failed to contradict the Soviet line, they could "stem from his own area of special interest. To deny this possibility means that all loyal Americans must operate in a limbo devoid of thought and imagination until the Soviet line is apparent, at which point we take the opposite line. Surely this is a counsel of intellectual despair."[27]

Jansen concluded, "In short, if the case against Mr. Lattimore is to be based upon his writings, we are left with the fantastic theory that the fate of four hundred and fifty million human beings on the other side of the globe was sealed by the Machiavellian activities of a man who wrote one thing and meant another; a man who, by proposing theories which were not followed, ran a government in which he was not an official."

For the rest of its run the Tydings committee investigated the *Amerasia* case. All the principals were called, and John Stewart Service got a thorough grilling. Beginning on May 4 Truman allowed Tydings committee members to read the files of the eighty-one State Department employees McCarthy had accused. The three Democrats on the committee spent much time with these files, Tydings claiming to have read every one; Lodge read only twelve of them, and Hickenlooper nine. This was a sore point when the committee came to write its final report.

The most spectacular event of May was a fiery speech to the Senate on the twelfth by Dennis Chavez, Democrat from New Mexico. McCarthy's effectiveness at stirring up anti–State Department sentiment was beginning to intimidate many moderate Democrats; Tydings urged them to take a stand. Chavez responded. He began quietly by referring to his own political career and service to the people of New Mexico, then moved into a statement of concern for the "hysteria and confusion" of the current scene, "a course so dangerous that few dare to oppose the drift lest they be the next marked for destruction." This trend was receiving impetus from statements on the floor of the Senate:

> Mr. President, for the first time in my 19 years in Congress, I make the deliberate point of referring to my religion. I speak as a Roman Catholic. . . . [W]hen I feel that the church which I revere is being used by an individual as a shield and a cloak to protect the purveyor of un-American, un-Christian, dubious testimony, I am compelled to identify what is going on and protest not only as a Catholic but as an American.
>
> Recently congressional committees and the general public have been provided with information regarding the Communist conspiracy, in America, and particularly inside the United States Government, by the man Louis Budenz. He has been speaking not merely as a private citizen. Budenz has been speaking with special emphasis as a Catholic, investing his appearances and utterances with an added sanctity by virtue of the fact that he recently went through the forms of conversion to catholicism.
>
> My ancestors brought the cross to this hemisphere. Louis Budenz has been using this cross as as club.[28]

Chavez then reviewed Budenz's Communist record, including conspiracies to commit murder and espionage. "Typically," he said, "these admissions are made after the statutes of limitations have expired. Smart boy. Budenz is thus protected from any prosecution which he might otherwise face." But even while he was committing these crimes, Budenz was "planning his next move." And it was a profitable one. Now he was "reveling in every minute of his new-found prosperity and sudden respectability."[29]

Then Chavez analyzed Budenz's reluctant stance. His testimony before

Tydings showed anything but reluctance: "He was glad to appear there. He was eagerly and hopefully anticipating that call." It was an uncannily accurate thrust, as if Chavez had been listening in when Budenz told Matthews how eager he was to expose the China hands. Budenz was, to Chavez, "one of those witnesses who require the inspiration of an audience to tell his story."[30]

Chavez's speech was more than an anti-Budenz polemic. He delved into history, citing Tacitus on the "exalted position of informers" in the corrupt Rome of Tiberius. He described the career of the anti-Jesuit Titus Oates, "the Louis Budenz of his day," in seventeenth-century England. He deplored the tendency to believe that fanatical former Communists are the best source of information on communism.[31]

Homer Ferguson of Michigan was livid. He demanded to know precisely what testimony by Budenz was false. Chavez replied, "I think everything he has said is false." Budenz had been so warped by his Communist years that "I do not think he knows truth from falsehood anymore."[32]

Tydings, Lucas, and a few other Democrats asked supportive questions: Ferguson and Capehart challenged Chavez for the Republicans. Chavez had a six-point conclusion. (1) We were providing a platform from which every unreliable and discredited individual could proclaim to the world that the United States was rotting with subversives, when it was not. (2) The witch-hunt had demoralized the government, but it had caught no spies. (3) The rights and reputations of prominent individuals had been impaired. (4) Fear of thinking heretical thoughts had been implanted in the minds of teachers, researchers, scientists, civil servants. (5) We were establishing a situation where there could be only two opinions—the Communist and the anti-Communist—which played right into the hands of Moscow. (6) These staged public inquiries interfered with genuine, diligent counterintelligence.[33]

Chavez made the front page of the *New York Times*. His was the first prominent attack on Budenz's credibility. Surprisingly few McCarthy supporters came publicly to Budenz's defense; the president of Fordham was predictably among them. McCarthy, in a speech to the Catholic Press Association, accused a "communist lawyer" of helping to write Chavez's speech.[34] Budenz did not respond.

The Johns Hopkins faculty invited Lattimore to address them on May 16. It was his first chance to express his gratitude for their overwhelming support. He spoke of the dangers to independent thought arising from the "reckless, machine gun toting politician" and the embittered China lobby. Since his battle seemed to be going well, Lattimore indulged in what, for him, was unusual levity. About the "propaganda-created myth of a university professor who pulls the strings of a whole government," he noted, "It was taken for granted throughout the hearings that I must in fact have had a heavy impact on policy in China and the Far East, and that the best I would be able to do for myself would be to plead that I had got the State Department only a little bit pregnant." [35]

Early June 1950 was relatively quiet. Senator Margaret Chase Smith and six Republican colleagues issued a "Declaration of Conscience" as a mild rebuke to McCarthy; he snarled right back and went on sniping at Truman, Acheson, Jessup, and Lattimore. But fewer mainstream newspapers were trumpeting McCarthy's charges. As William W. Stueck puts it, "On the eve of the war in Korea, it seemed that the Democrats might emerge relatively unscathed by the furor created by Senator McCarthy's charges." [36]

Then, on June 25, 1950, Kim Il-sung, with the probably reluctant acquiescence of Stalin, launched North Korean forces across the thirty-eighth parallel against the government headed by Syngman Rhee. [37] This action took Washington by surprise. Truman and his advisors viewed Europe as the primary field of potential Soviet aggression; the Joint Chiefs of Staff, General MacArthur, and the State Department had all excluded Korea from the list of vital areas that the U.S. would defend.

Truman quickly decided to defend South Korea. MacArthur was instructed to use any forces available to him, and after a successful holding action at Pusan, he engineered the spectacular landing at Inchon that routed the North Koreans. The country responded positively to U.S. intervention; even Senate Republicans approved Truman's action. It seemed for a while that the opprobrium fastened on Truman for his indifference to Chiang Kai-shek would be lifted, that Truman would be seen for what he was: a vigorous opponent of communism who made the right decision when the chips were down. Across the country, Americans believed that Stalin had now shown his true colors, that the Kremlin-directed conquest of the world was under way, and that the administration had finally responded appropriately.

With the headlines now dominated by the Korean War, McCarthy's crusade against domestic communism lost its glamour. In order to be consistent, he, too, had to back the president's action. Tom Coleman, a close friend in Wisconsin, wrote McCarthy July 7 urging him to take it easy on the administration for a while. McCarthy seemed to agree. He answered Coleman July 15, acknowledging that his access to America's front pages was gone—temporarily. But in the long run, McCarthy wrote, the casualty lists would mount, the people would wonder what actually happened in Asia, and they would "realize there was something rotten in the State Department."[38]

Despite his promise to Coleman, McCarthy could not hold his tongue. Within a week of the outbreak of war he was blaming the Korean attack on Communist infiltration of the adminstration. In a speech to the Senate July 6 he said that "highly-placed Red counselors [were] far more deadly than Red machine gunners in Korea." On July 12 McCarthy sent an open letter to Truman, condemning Acheson, Jessup, and "super adviser Lattimore" for the Korean mess.[39] These were no longer front-page stories, but in the long run McCarthy sold his agenda. Few people paid attention to the fact that excluding Korea from the American defense perimeter had been the idea of MacArthur and the military and that Acheson and Lattimore had followed, rather than inspired, the official position.

Until Inchon things were touch and go in Korea. The country needed scapegoats. Acheson and Lattimore were favorites.

McCarthy had his usual allies. Walter Trohan's article in the *Chicago Tribune* of July 10, 1950, headed "Face Saving Tag Put on Acheson for Policy Shift; Catholic Paper Also Cites Lattimore, Dulles," quoted an editorial in the current *Catholic Review*, official newspaper of the Baltimore archdiocese, to the effect that while Lattimore had been responsible for "setting off" the Korean War, he now had a change of heart and supported Truman's actions in Korea. But Lattimore had "not yet arrived at the point of blaming Russia for pushing her henchmen."[40]

Lattimore addressed the Asian situation in a speech at Johns Hopkins June 28. He was, as always, concerned that U.S. policy in Korea should benefit the whole population, not just Syngman Rhee; and he emphasized that despite the current focus on Korea, which was on the fringe of Asia, our true area of interest was the Asian heartland: India, Pakistan, Afghanistan, Indonesia. "All of these countries can be made allies, and very reliable allies, but they cannot be made puppets. In all of them, the passion that runs through men's veins is a passion for freedom from foreign rule. All of them are repelled by any policy that looks like restoration of colonial rule."[41]

After this speech the Lattimores left Johns Hopkins for a month of vacation on Cape Cod. The *Baltimore Evening Sun* story reporting their summer plans was headed "Aftermath of a Cyclone: The Owen Lattimores Will Rest until Fall."[42]

On July 17, 1950, the Tydings committee released a 313-page report, signed only by the three Democrats. Lodge wrote a minority report partially agreeing with the Democrats; Hickenlooper released nothing. The Democrats condemned McCarthy in scathing terms, declaring that his charges of Communists in the State Department were "a fraud and a hoax perpetrated on the Senate of the United States and the American people. They represent perhaps the most nefarious campaign of half-truths and untruth in the history of this Republic. . . . For the first time in our history, we have seen the totalitarian technique of the 'big lie' employed on a sustained basis."[43]

The report got wide circulation—by Democratic newspapers because of its conclusions, by Republican papers as proof that the Democrats were still soft on Communists. Few read the report to see whether its excoriation of McCarthy was justified. With Communist armies trying to push MacArthur's troops off the Korean peninsula, many Americans felt they did not *need* to read it. Communism was a menace no matter what Tydings said. And the same day the report was released, the FBI arrested Julius Rosenberg, charging him with espionage for the Soviet Union.

The Senate "received" the Tydings report after a bitter debate and on straight party lines: forty-five Democrats to thirty-seven Republicans. McCarthy had a field day with it: "Tydings tried to notify all Communists in Government that they are safe in their positions."[44] It was a whitewash, he said, a partisan attempt to conceal the truth that he had struggled so laboriously to put before the country.

The Tydings report was not a thorough investigation of the loyalty and security of State Department employees as a whole: it was a reasonable examination of the evidence about the ten individuals publicly accused by McCarthy. All of them, especially Lattimore, were found to be loyal Americans. The report was essentially accurate. Only with the recent opening of FBI files has it been clear how accurate it was.

After his final appearance before Tydings, Lattimore wrote an account of his battle with McCarthy. It took about a month to produce *Ordeal by Slander*, which was published by Atlantic–Little Brown on August 1. Reviews were predictable: McCarthy's friends panned it, Lattimore's friends praised it. Lattimore intended *Ordeal* as a postmortem; he thought the battle was all but over. This assessment was an error; only the preliminary skirmish was over.

Ordeal presents the chronology of McCarthy's attack, beginning while Lattimore was in Afghanistan and carrying through to his Tydings appearance. It also describes Lattimore's reflections on the methods and significance of McCarthy's crusade and answers the more important charges McCarthy made.

There are some good lines in *Ordeal*. Deploring the necessity for targets of the witch-hunt to cite Communist attacks on themselves as evidence of their loyalty, Lattimore observes, "The whole idea of proving that you are not despicable by listing the people who despise you is deeply humiliating." And his "ball-bearing lies" metaphor was a favorite with reviewers: "I had yet to learn that McCarthy is a master not only of the big lie but of the middle-sized lie and the little ball-bearing lie that rolls around and around and helps the wheels of the lie machinery to turn over."[45]

The final chapter of *Ordeal* expresses Lattimore's beliefs about the dangers of McCarthyism and how Americans could counteract them. As one would expect from a scholar who had spent his formative years in Europe and Asia and had then joined the academy in the United States, Lattimore assumes the virtues of reason, facts, freedom of research and speech—the pantheon of the intellectual. What he does not acknowledge is the fluctuating but ineradicable strength of anti intellectualism in America and the amorality of partisan politics. *Ordeal* claims that "the witch-hunting of which McCarthy is a part is recruited from ex-Communists and pro-Fascists, America Firsters, anti-Semites, Coughlinites, and similar fringe fanatics of the political underworld."[46] There were such fringe fanatics in the McCarthy entourage, but Lattimore is silent about the political forces that took up the "Who lost China?" debate to recapture the presidency.

A deeper analysis would have shown how the China lobby was rooted in the American self-image as the chosen people, in Asia-first Republicanism, and in the hatred of Roosevelt and all his works. Absence of this political dimension in *Ordeal* was noted by Alfred Friendly of the *Washington Post*: "An unfortunate omission is Lattimore's failure to relate his ordeal to Republican political tactics in an election year. Without drawing such a connection, a writer of the McCarthy story cannot make it entirely comprehensible." Such fundamental analyses of the period were not to appear until Michael Paul Rogin's *Intellectuals and McCarthy* (1967), Robert Griffith's *Politics of Fear* (1970), and Ross Y. Koen's *China Lobby in American Politics* (1974).[47]

Ordeal by Slander describes some of the disruptions McCarthy caused in the Lattimore household, but the most traumatic event is missing. The

Lattimores had bought a half interest in Stoddard farm, adjoining the Stefansson's Dearing farm in Bethel, Vermont. Lattimore paid $1,000 in cash for his share of Stoddard and spent more than $1,000 on repairs and improvements during the summer of 1949. Stefansson and his wife, Evelyn, had plans to make the two farms self-supporting, and they looked forward to spending future summers adjacent to the Lattimores.[48]

When the inquisition erupted in March 1950 it became clear that Lattimore needed the $2,000 equity he had in the Stoddard farm to help meet the costs of his defense. By May the two families had decided to put Stoddard up for sale. Stefansson put ads in three newspapers, with a selling price of $4,500, which would just recover the investment of the two families.[49] On June 6 Ordway Southard came to look at Stoddard; his was the only serious response to the ad. Stefansson had met Southard in Alaska in 1945, and in the winter of 1948 Southard had used Stefansson's library in New York, which was headquarters for the *Encyclopedia Arctica* Stefansson was compiling for the U.S. Navy. As Stefansson wrote Lattimore just after the contracts were signed to sell Stoddard to Southard,

> I did keep hearing more and more that winter about Southard being a Communist; but my clipping bureau was then sending me cuttings from the Hearst and Scripps-Howard press saying that I was a communist; and Westbrook Pegler was calling a friend of mine, A. N. Spanel, President of International Latex, a Communist or communist tool, sympathiser and abettor. To me this sort of thing was Salem Witchcraft over again, and I perhaps leaned over backward not to appear to be afflicted with what was increasingly worrying me as mob hysteria. It goes against the grain with me, even now, to take such precautions as many are taking against situations that could involve guilt by association.
>
> Today it was pointed out to me that you are already a victim of a guilt-by-association frame-up and that I must not let my pooh-pooh attitude become dangerous to you. So I must give you what lowdown I have, mostly hearsay, because of twin dangers: That your selling Stoddard to a "Communist" may be used against you, and that your coming to visit Dearing, contiguous to Stoddard, the week after the Southards move in, may be interpreted as a suspicious coincidence.[50]

When Lattimore received this letter, he immediately consulted Fortas, who sensed disaster. He advised Lattimore to attempt to cancel the sale. It was too late. Southard had a valid contract and could sue if it were broken. The problem then was how to handle the inevitable explosion if

Southard did indeed turn out to be a Communist and the McCarthy forces got wind of it.

Stefansson again had a powerful homily—he called it a "sermon"— which he delivered to the Lattimores in a letter of June 17. "I have read the DEVIL IN MASSACHUSETTS and the newspaper accounts of the current witch hunt, and I do agree that in Cotton Mather's Salem of 1692, and in Joseph McCarthy's United States of 1950, those have proved to be in greatest danger who were so conscious of their innocence that they were unconscious of the danger of being suspected. So I agree it is dangerous, during a time of hysteria, to act as if innocent—I agree that, to this extent, it is wisest to 'prove' one's innocence by joining in the hysteria and running with the mob."[51]

Lattimore, Stefansson continued, had acted courageously and not run with the mob. His recent speech to the Johns Hopkins faculty showed appropriate "outraged disdain" for the whole inquisition, but this disdain would not keep him from unjust attack.

Stefansson's fears were well grounded. Thomas J. Riley, of the Hearst papers, was digging into the facts of the Stoddard sale and talked to Evelyn Stefansson by telephone. Southard and his wife, said Riley, were Communists; Southard had run as the Communist candidate for governor of Alabama in 1942 (he received a total of 402 votes). Riley and the pro-McCarthy press didn't have all the facts straight, however. One of the false charges that filtered through to the FBI, via J. B. Matthews, was that "Alger Hiss, John Abt, and Owen Lattimore held meetings at the Stefansson home in Bethel, Vermont."[52]

But the big splash was saved for McCarthy. On July 27 he told the Senate that revenue stamps on the deed indicated that Lattimore had bought a half-interest in the property for about $1,500 in 1949 and had sold it for between $4,000 and $4,500. "So we find a well known Communist giving Mr. Lattimore $3,000. The Communist party often handles pay-offs— contributions—by transfers of property."[53] McCarthy also claimed that this had to be profit since there had been no increase in property values in Vermont.

When reporters caught up with Lattimore in Wellfleet, Massachusetts, he explained that he had only received half the proceeds and hence had made no profit at all. He had sold the property through Stefansson "to a complete stranger about whom I knew nothing and of whom I had previously never heard." McCarthy's methods, he added, are "not less base and despicable than they have been right along."[54]

CHAPTER TWENTY

China Attacks

On August 1, 1950, McCarthy waved before the Senate the affidavit John Farrand had obtained from Willi Foerster in March; it contained the charge that Lattimore had worked with Sorge. There is no reason to believe that McCarthy had learned anything new from Foerster or any other informant; what he told the Senate was all stale stuff, and the FBI agents cringed. Willard Edwards reported in the *Chicago Tribune*, "McCarthy said this evidence, like that revealed last week connecting Lattimore with two known Communists in a real estate deal, was another connecting link in his charge that Lattimore was a Communist agent. The discharge of the Tydings investigating committee, after a report whitewashing Lattimore and all others accused of communism, forced him to take such evidence to the Senate floor, McCarthy said."[1]

The mainstream press ignored McCarthy; the AP did not even report his speech. This treatment McCarthy found intolerable. On August 4 he wrote the editor of every daily newspaper in the country, enclosing the Foerster affidavit, complaining about the AP's lack of interest and noting that "the press coverage of our fight to rid the State Department of Communists left much to be desired." The editors were largely unsympathetic; AP responded that "the senator's statement lacked news value."[2]

But Lattimore was making news in August. Traveling through New England, he accepted the invitation of a friend, William G. Wendell of Portsmouth, New Hampshire, to visit Portsmouth and speak to the guests of the Wentworth-by-the-Sea Hotel after that hotel's regular Sunday night concert on August 27. When this speech was announced, there was an immediate outcry from local McCarthy supporters. The regent of the local chapter of the Daughters of the American Revolution and the past president of the New Hampshire Congress of Parent-Teacher Organizations led opposition to the Lattimore appearance.[3]

The hotel president, James B. Smith, was taken aback. Not wanting to offend either his guests or the local citizenry, he polled the hotel guests: 121 opposed Lattimore's talk, 89 approved it. Smith canceled, telling the *New York Times*, "Like the food we serve, it must meet with the approval of the greater percentage of our guests." Mrs. William E. Travis of the local PTA was more assertive: "Just now, with the critical condition of this country, anyone about whom there is any question should not be allowed to speak. I'm just against Communism, that's all." Lattimore was hurt and angry: "I am very sorry that any group of Americans would allow themselves to be panicked into refusing an opportunity for free discussion of subjects that must be openly debated. . . . There is no other democratic process for the spread of information and the formation of opinion."[4]

Four days later McCarthy roused the faithful with a stinging attack on Acheson and his advisers at the Fifty-second Annual Encampment of the Veterans of Foreign Wars in New York. The audience "applauded wildly."[5]

Also in August, Alfred Kohlberg swung into action. He was reading the Tydings committee report and found a statement to the effect that Father Kearney, who wrote the 1949 *Columbia* article attacking Lattimore, had told the FBI that he, Kearney, "had no direct knowledge of Mr. Lattimore's activities and that the principal source of his information had been Alfred Kohlberg of the American China Policy Association." Kohlberg had met Kearney several times but did not remember discussing Lattimore. Kohlberg fired off an immediate letter to Kearney. Was this true? Had Kearney actually said that to the FBI? Kohlberg would like Kearney to put what he told the FBI in an affidavit and indicate if Kohlberg was free to use it as he saw fit.[6]

Kearney had left Santa Clara University and was on missionary duty in the Philippines. When he got Kohlberg's letter, he was much disturbed. He had been interviewed by two men who claimed to be FBI agents in January; he had thought that anything he said would be kept strictly confidential. He understood them to ask him if he "had any further information on Mr. Lattimore than that contained in the article." He told them no, that they should contact Kohlberg. As Kearney's affidavit reads, "At no time do I recall saying, or intending to say, that most of the matter in the article in question came from Mr. Kohlberg."[7]

Kearney put all this in his statement, had it notarized September 21, and sent it off to his Jesuit superior, Father John K. Lipman, assistant procurator for American Jesuits in China. Kearney's letter to Lipman reveals the dominant Catholic attitude toward Tydings:

> Enclosed is a copy of an affidavit I am sending to be censored by the editor of America before being turned over to Mr. Kohlberg. The question of the F.B.I. is curious. Was it a frameup? *Two* men came instead of one, which seemed a bit strange. They seemed very much interested in a bit of information I gave them from Bullitt, which I had intended to be, like the rest, strictly confidential.
>
> Could you make discreet inquiries, through Blake, e.g., and see if any real F.B.I. men contacted me in January at Santa Clara. If so, why the breaking of a confidential interview, and why was it done so stupidly? I have had a very high idea of the F.B.I., and this doesn't seem to fit in. We could make it hot for Tydings, if he faked the whole thing. And I suggested as much to Kohlberg. We *did* speak a bit about Lattimore, as I told K., and as you may remember at the dinner in S.F. But not much. . . . Is it possible to get a copy of that Tydings report in S.F.? If not, Freddy McGuire could get one. You might pass on this info to him, if he thinks it is useful. He might be able to blow those fellows up at close quarters better than I could do it here. (Kearney's italics)[8]

If Freddy McGuire blew up Tydings or any of those fellows, it has escaped public notice. The Reverend Robert C. Hartnett, S.J., editor of *America*, told Kohlberg to use the affidavit as it was. Kohlberg used it to challenge the FBI, sending it to Hoover on October 5 with a cover letter concluding: "It seems to me that your agents inaccurately reported their interview with Father Kearney. That they did so for any ulterior motive seems to be ruled out by the fact that their interview was in January, some months before the McCarthy charges against Lattimore were made. As I intend to make this matter public, may I suggest to you, Sir, that the original reports of your agents now be made public."[9] Kohlberg then notes that this might seem a small matter but that it was important to everyone who thought the Tydings report a whitewash.

The bureau regarded this challenge as serious enough to require the two San Francisco agents to write an expanded account of their visit to Kearney. They did, retracting not a word of their original report: Kearney had indeed claimed that he got most of his information about Lattimore from Kohlberg, and they repeated several concrete particulars Kearney had given them.[10]

Hoover referred the whole mess to Deputy Attorney General Peyton Ford. Ford wrote back on October 21: "I think the record should be straight—but I hesitate to start a running controversy with Kohlberg. If you have any thoughts I would appreciate them." Attached was a draft letter to Kohlberg, which Hoover approved; in it Ford said the two agents "confirmed the facts as set forth in my letter dated June 22, 1950, to Senator Millard E. Tydings."[11]

There is no record of a Kohlberg reply. There is, in fact, no further record of bureau contact with Kohlberg. His informer status with the FBI reached its zenith in June and died suddenly in October.

As for Father McGuire, it is doubtful that the Kearney suggestion reached him. He was one of the few anti-McCarthy Catholics, and he later became involved in a bitter feud with Fulton Sheen, Budenz's protector.[12]

Budenz was under heavy pressure from the bureau to complete his "four hundred names" project. By midsummer 1950 he had dictated to an FBI stenographer the names and all he could remember about 380 "concealed" Communists. The list was amazing. As noted previously, Budenz had trouble coming up with the promised number and "refreshed his memory" from lists of officers and sponsors of left-wing organizations. In July, HUAC agents came to Budenz, telling him that the committee was "interested in obtaining the names of the 400 concealed Communists." Budenz demurred. He wanted to leave the list in the hands of the FBI. HUAC was not to be put off; the committee issued a subpoena for Budenz to appear on August 29 with his list. He did appear, but something caused the committee to leave him sitting in an anteroom until they disbanded. Willard Edwards thought it was administration pressure.[13]

In 1987 the FBI still declined to release the Budenz four hundred file. Even in 1950 they were unwilling to encourage Budenz to release parts of it to a confirmed Communist hater, Cecil B. DeMille, who wanted it for his blacklist. The matter was referred to Hoover, who responded, "Since Budenz seems to talk to others freely & without clearance with FBI I don't see why he passes the buck to us in this particular matter. Pass it right back to him."[14]

Budenz did name many on his list before congressional committees, which gave him immunity from suit. Many of them had no Communist connections at all. Budenz got around to putting Lattimore on the list in September 1950. We will probably never know how many prominent citizens were refused passports, failed to get jobs they applied for, or were

turned down for grants or scholarships because they were on the Budenz
list.

Lattimore returned to Johns Hopkins in early September. There were
disturbing press reports waiting in his mail. One that particularly aroused
his ire was a *Chicago Tribune* story of July 21. Kenneth Colegrove, political scientist at Northwestern University, was now attacking Lattimore
publicly. Colegrove claimed that Lattimore was a member of "a pro-
communist clique in and out of the State Department that sold President
Roosevelt on the idea that Chinese Communists were only agrarian reformers; Lattimore has been an advisor of the State Department despite
Acheson's denials."

Lattimore exploded. He wrote Colegrove September 5: "It is a lie, and
you know it is a lie, that I ever belonged to any kind of 'pro-communist
clique'; it is a lie, and you know it is a lie, that I ever 'sold' or attempted
to 'sell' President Roosevelt on the idea that the Chinese Communists
were only agrarian reformers; it is a lie, and you know it is a lie, that I
was ever an advisor of the State Department." Lattimore asked for an
apology and a retraction.[15] It never came.

The fuss in Vermont calmed down somewhat in late summer. Stefansson, who had previously been inclined to give Ordway Southard the benefit of the doubt, had changed his mind. Southard came uninvited to visit
the Stefanssons, wanting a reduction in his mortgage if he paid it off
early. Stefansson refused and was outraged when Southard confirmed his
Party membership. In a blazing letter to the Lattimores, which Stefansson
titled "The Wretched Southards" as if it were an article for publication,
he wrote that he had forbidden Southard to set foot on Dearing farm
again. Evelyn Stefansson wrote Eleanor Lattimore on September 11; her
mood was upbeat. "Everywhere we hear words of praise for Owen's wonderful fight. Mrs. Bundy [local Republican attorney] met a group in Barre
last week of 6 women from all over the country. They were all eager for
details and all convinced that not only was Owen guiltless, but he had
struck such a fine blow for freedom of academic thought, etc."[16]

On October 16 Evelyn wrote again, still impressed by the sanity of
Vermonters and happy that she and Stef would be able to meet Owen and
Eleanor shortly at a conference in Philadelphia, which was the best they
could do since the Lattimores could not afford to be seen in Vermont.[17]

But sanity in Vermont did not cancel out the fact that the country as a
whole was in the grip of a growing hysteria. Passage of the Internal Security Act of 1950 (the McCarran Act) over Truman's veto on September

23 proved this hysteria. The major feature of the act was a preventive detention or concentration camp clause. This act was one of the most repressive ever passed by Congress, which rolled over the veto 248–48 in the House and 57–10 in the Senate. Senators William Benton of Connecticut and Hubert Humphrey of Minnesota later expressed shame that they too had caved in to the pressure. Humphrey congratulated Estes Kefauver for resisting it. [18]

Lattimore continued to have trouble on the lecture circuit. There was a furious row when Wellesley College invited him to speak under the auspices of the Mayling Soong Foundation. The press was filled with attack and counterattack, pro- and anti-Tydings, pro- and anti-McCarthy. One Wellesley trustee, Mrs. Maurice T. Moore, returned early from Europe to take part in a board meeting on the matter. Mrs. Walter Brookings, widow of the founder of the Brookings Institution, wired a protest to Wellesley's president. Unlike the New Hampshire hotel, Wellesley stood its ground. [19]

But the ground under freedom of speech was crumbling. Despite FBI knowledge of the shaky nature of evidence against Lattimore, and despite near-unanimous testimony of those who knew him that he was not a Communist, the bureau was forging ahead with its investigation, seeking—and retaining—whatever testimony it could find against him, discarding or ignoring the contrary evidence. Hoover, for instance, was never told that Budenz had described his own testimony as "flimsy"; this revealing adjective dropped out of FBI reports as they went up the hierarchy.

The Baltimore FBI office was always more suspicious of Lattimore than was headquarters. Perhaps active American Legion, Catholic church, Minute Women of America, and other local opposition to Lattimore had infected the Baltimore agents. Perhaps the suspicion was simply a desire on the part of Baltimore, the "office of origin" in the Lattimore case, to capitalize on what they hoped would be a successful prosecution. Whatever the case, on October 13, 1950, the Baltimore SAC volunteered to headquarters that his office was "in the process of preparing a report summarizing information available which will establish instances wherein LATTIMORE committed perjury in his testimony before the Senate Sub-Committee." [20] There was no mention of espionage. It took Baltimore until December 28 to put its perjury summary together. During this period the country went from agitation to full hysteria.

The November 1950 midterm elections stirred things up. Republicans, almost without exception, ran on a "Democrats are soft on Communism" platform. Acheson was the chief scapegoat, Lattimore a close second. Nixon, typically, rode them both: he challenged his opponent, Helen Gahagan Douglas, to state "whether she subscribes to the Acheson-Lattimore policy."[21]

Democrats had counted on Truman's quick response to the North Korean attack to defuse the Communist issue, but things didn't work out that way. McCarthy's analysis in June was correct; as casualties mounted, so did public anxiety. MacArthur's brilliant Inchon landing temporarily eased concerns about the war, but on October 25, just before the election, Chinese forces appeared in Korea. This disturbing event again heightened public uneasiness.

The election in Maryland was particularly salient: Tydings was running. McCarthy and his staff took an active part, and there were dirty tricks aplenty, some of them carried out by Surine.[22] At the time many respected observers credited McCarthy with Tyding's loss, and McCarthy was quite happy to accept this judgment. In retrospect, McCarthy's attacks on Tydings did not account for the outcome; but what appeared then to be the case was what really mattered, and belief in McCarthy's prowess was strongly reinforced. Scott Lucas, another foe of McCarthy, lost to Everett Dirksen in Illinois, and McCarthy claimed credit for that victory, too. Overall the Democratic vote was good for an offyear election, and the Republicans did not capture either house of Congress; but McCarthy, Nixon, Dirksen, and their friends declared victory and vowed to keep up the anti-Communist battle.

Lattimore lectured to the Maryland Furniture and Carpet Association November 14, mostly on his early experiences in China. During the question period he was asked, "In your opinion, why was Tydings defeated?" Lattimore disclaimed any expertise about Maryland politics but ventured the tentative opinion that the outcome might have been different if Tydings had fought the whitewash charge "offensively rather than defensively. The senator had nothing to be ashamed of and everything to be proud of."[23]

But Lattimore was in a losing battle. McCarthy and his political and journalistic allies were always attacking, Lattimore defending. November and December were not good months. Johns Hopkins was still behind him, but the country was steadily moving into McCarthy's camp. Lattimore threw himself into the academic concerns neglected during the spring. He worked particularly hard to secure an American Philosophical Society grant for Father Louis M. J. Schram, a Belgian Catholic expert on Mongolia who wanted to continue his studies in the United States; he also tried to help the Indian Council of World Affairs in New Delhi to obtain young Mongol scholars who were neither Communist nor Kuomintang.[24]

The seminal event of 1950, however, was yet to come. More than the Hiss conviction, the McCarthy crusade, the Rosenberg arrest, or the original North Korean attack, it was the defeat of the U.S. Eighth Army by Chinese forces beginning on November 26 that traumatized the country. The panic about Korea and what events there meant for the United States began, in *New York Times* coverage, on November 29, with a three-line scarehead. For twenty-two days Korean War headlines in the *Times* averaged five columns in width. On November 30 Truman threatened use of nuclear weapons if pushed to it. At the height of the rout, on December 3, the *Times* editorialized, "In the short space of ten days, the whole world outlook had changed." An editorial December 4 claimed that the situation was "reminiscent of the days when Hitler's armies started on their march of conquest." On December 8 New York Governor Thomas Dewey instructed his civil defense leaders to prepare for "a possible million evacuees" from urban areas in the event of a nuclear war. Truman declared a national emergency December 16, and one of the many alarmist stories the next day had the federal government preparing to disperse. The crowning touch was provided by skiers in the Pacific Northwest. On December 18, 1950, they organized as "defense guerillas" to protect western mountain passes during a Communist invasion. And on Christmas Eve the Very Reverend Edmund A. Walsh, vice president of Georgetown University, said the U.S. should consider a preemptive nuclear strike against the Soviet Union.[25]

The Chinese entry into the Korean War and the defeat of MacArthur's finest drowned out Tydings's report in a crescendo of fear and frenzy. If those State Department types were not serving the Communists, how could all this happen? America's virile self-image took a beating in Korea.[26] The disaster there, added to the already powerful anti-Communist atmosphere, seemed to make McCarthy's case: against Acheson, against Jessup, against Lattimore. Budenz and Utley also benefited from the Chinese attack; they had said all along that communism was a monolith and that the People's Republic of China would do Stalin's bidding.

Baltimore FBI agents continued to dig up new ways of nailing Lattimore. On November 16, 1950, that office wrote Hoover suggesting an investigation of possible use by Lattimore of a pseudonym. "Pacificus" and "Asiaticus" were pen names that appeared in periodicals dealing with China and Japan. Asiaticus was clearly pro-Communist and had written for *Pacific Affairs* when Lattimore was editor; but Baltimore's immediate concern was Pacificus; "The purpose of attempting to identify PACIFICUS as LATTIMORE is to determine whether it would be practical to run down articles written by PACIFICUS on the theory that LATTIMORE may have given more open expression to his pro-Communist leanings in writings under his pen name." [27]

The search for Pacificus hung around for months. Nobody was able to tell the bureau who Pacificus was—except, unfortunately, someone whom J. Edgar Hoover hated so much he forbade agents to contact the man. This was I. F. Stone, Washington correspondent for the *Nation*. Stone had been the channel for the Pacificus articles. But as Branigan wrote Belmont, "Stone [is] reportedly a Communist since the mid 1930's, has been most vituperative in attacks on Bureau and the Director and cannot be expected to be cooperative. . . . Recommendations made that (1) we do not interview Stone unless requested to do so by the criminal Div. and (2) that we advise Criminal Div. of this decision." Below this Hoover wrote, "We will not do so under any circumstances. If they want him interviewed, they will have to do so themselves." [28] They never found out the identity of Pacificus.

Baltimore was also suspicious of Lattimore's claim to have supported Finland when Russia invaded. One of Lattimore's letters in IPR files (which the bureau had thoroughly inspected in 1950) asked Carter if he had seen any plausible explanation of the Soviet attack. Baltimore thought this letter might mean that Lattimore supported the Russians. He hadn't. The bureau decided his support of Fighting Funds for Finland had been genuine. [29]

Two weeks later Baltimore had five more suggestions, one of which was astounding: "numerous rather reliable sources" had indicated that Lattimore had served on the Strategic Bombing Survey. They thought this report should be checked out further. Headquarters paid no attention. [30]

By December 28 Baltimore had prepared its 545-page perjury summary. There were sixteen charges against Lattimore that presented "the best possibility for successful prosecution," all derived from Lattimore's testimony before Tydings. Baltimore thought a case might be made that Lattimore lied when he

1. denied Communist party membership and/or support of Communist principles;

2. denied affiliations with organizations on the attorney general's list;

3. denied knowing that the Washington Committee for Aid to China was Communist;

4. denied saying that the Chinese Communists were agrarian reformers and non-Marxists;

5. claimed he supported Finland against Russia;

6. claimed that *Pacific Affairs* was not pro-Communist while he was editor;

7. denied knowing Fred Field was a Communist;

8. denied knowing Chi Ch'ao-ting was a Communist;

9. denied knowing Chew Sih Hong was a Communist;

10. denied knowing the *China Daily News* was Communist;

11. denied taking initiative in placing any person in U.S. government service;

12. described his relationship with *Amerasia*;

13. described his relationship with Dr. Walter Heissig;

14. described his contact with Soviet officials in 1936;

15. described his association with Alger Hiss;

16. described the circumstances of his appointment as advisor to Chiang Kai-shek.[31]

Of this long list, only items one and eight survived the following two years of investigation. None of them impressed FBI headquarters. They had no evidence of Party membership at all, and "support of Communist principles" was vague. As to Chi Ch'ao-ting, he had been chief aide to H. H. K'ung as Nationalist China's finance minister. If K'ung had thought Chi non-Communist, so might Lattimore.[32]

Baltimore was reasonably sure they had done a thorough job, and they thought there was evidence to prosecute Lattimore. Just in case Justice thought otherwise, however, the report concluded, "Should the Department after reviewing [this] report, conclude that no violation exists insofar as the Perjury Statute or other Federal statutes are concerned, then it is recommended that the case be closed."[33]

Baltimore did not anticipate the future interest in the Lattimore case from a powerful and unexpected source: Patrick Anthony McCarran.

CHAPTER TWENTY-ONE

McCarran

In December 1950 crusty old Patrick A. McCarran of Nevada, nominally a Democrat but bitterly at odds with Roosevelt and Truman most of the time, decided to upstage HUAC and establish a Senate mechanism to root out Communists. After eighteen years in the Senate, McCarran was sixth in seniority and arguably first in power as chair of the Senate Judiciary Committee, which handled 40 percent of Senate bills and all judicial appointments. As Alfred Steinberg said in a November 1950 *Harper's* article, McCarran "emerged as a greater threat to his party's program than the combined forces of the Dixiecrats and the Republicans. . . . He need play ball on no team but his own."[1] Where McCarthy was impulsive and disorganized, McCarran was methodical and a master of Senate procedures.

Long before McCarthy discovered the anti-Communist issue, McCarran had made it his ideological anchor. Like Freda Utley, whom he later hired, he believed as early as 1941 that the Soviet Union, not Nazi Germany, was the greatest threat to Western civilization. When the State Department ordered the closing of all German consulates in the summer of 1941, McCarran denounced the action and "argued that Roosevelt should have broken all ties with the Soviet Union instead." In the middle of the war (April 19, 1943) he wrote his friend Pete Peterson, "I am convinced that there is a group in full control of this administration that proposes to turn our government over to anything but a democratic form." The party to which he belonged called itself Democrat, but McCarran said that his colleagues "in reality are nothing but communists to the very core."[2]

By 1945 Roosevelt wanted very much to get McCarran out of the Senate and offered him a federal judgeship. McCarran considered it seriously, as Von Pittman discovered, but decided that the threat of domestic communism, especially in the person of Vice President Wallace, compelled him to continue to serve in the Senate.[3]

In foreign policy McCarran's anticommunism led him to strong support of Francisco Franco in Spain; some called him the "Senator from Madrid." He won most of his battles for increased acceptance of the Spanish dictator.

The other arena that drew his concern was China. McCarran was a latecomer to this cause, not speaking out on China policy until September 1948, but he quickly gathered momentum and by 1949 was sponsoring a bill to give a billion and a half dollars to Chiang Kai-shek's Nationalists. The China lobby forces in Washington welcomed him to their ranks. V. K. Wellington Koo, Chinese ambassador to the United States in 1949, gave confidential papers outlining Nationalist defense plans for Taiwan to four Americans: John Foster Dulles, Representative Walter Judd, Senator William Knowland, and McCarran. McCarran accepted the entire corpus of China lobby beliefs, including the most risible: "Everyone knows that captured Chinese Red generals have admitted that their orders came from the Kremlin," McCarran told the *New York Times* in January 1949.[4]

The intensity of McCarran's anticommunism was matched by his devotion to its conspiracy corollary. The "loss of China" did not just happen. His close friend Norman Biltz, a Nevada businessman, recalled McCarran's conspiracy beliefs in an oral history:

> Senator McCarran believed completely that there was one *being* in the United States who directed the operation of the Communist Party. He was completely convinced of this, and so was McCarthy. Patsy told me many, many times, he said, "Norm, I can't get through the cloud. I can't find that person. But I feel his influence all over Washington." And he said, "If I throw up a hundred false balloons, if I make a hundred efforts that fail, if I make a hundred mistakes, and do eventually find that one man, I will have served my country well." And he died believing it. I wouldn't dare tell you some of the people he suspected. (Italics in original)[5]

We know some of the people he suspected. Roosevelt was one, but he died in 1945. Wallace was another, but his disappearance from national politics after the election of 1948 took him out of the running. By 1950, when McCarthy identified Lattimore as the top Soviet spy, McCarran was thinking the same thing.

Thus, it was entirely fitting that McCarran should establish in December 1950 a Judiciary subcommittee charged with investigating the administration of the new Internal Security Act, appoint himself chairman of this Senate Internal Security Subcommittee (SISS), and look for the Communist mastermind. Senate Resolution 366, passed December 21, 1950, was his authorization.

This subcommittee was to have seven members. Its composition was no accident. McCarran was not about to tolerate on his board of inquisitors any senator who would dissent from what *he* knew to be true: treason had lost China, Lattimore was the mastermind behind it, and the Institute of Pacific Relations was the vehicle Lattimore had used to accomplish Communist ends.

McCarran needed three Democrats and three Republicans for SISS. The choice was easy. Of the six Democrats available on Judiciary, three were certifiable liberals, scoring high on the Americans for Democratic Action (ADA) scorecard for the 1950 session of Congress: Harley Kilgore of West Virginia, Warren Magnuson of Washington, and Estes Kefauver of Tennessee.[6] Of the three Democrats remaining, James Eastland of Mississippi was most in tune with McCarran; he had applauded McCarran unstintingly in a speech to the Senate on July 14, 1950, and was in complete sympathy with McCarran's views on foreign policy and internal security. McCarran delegated Eastland to introduce the resolution creating SISS on November 30 since McCarran himself was away from Washington at that time.

Only one other Democrat, Herbert O'Conor of Maryland, was a member of Judiciary in 1950; although he was less vociferous in his anticommunism, he was on record against Lattimore and against admission of the People's Republic of China to the United Nations. O'Conor would do. Recently elected Willis Smith of North Carolina had been appointed to Judiciary; he had a certifiable record in his 1950 election campaign, defeating the liberal Frank Graham by red-baiting and pandering to the segregationists. Smith was not a strong supporter of McCarthy, as were the others, but he bought the China lobby position without exception.[7]

The selection of Republicans presented no problem either. Alexander Wiley of Wisconsin was far too liberal, William Langer of North Dakota was ideologically unreliable, and Robert Hendrickson of New Jersey was soft on foreign policy. The other three Republicans were perfect for McCarran's purposes. Homer Ferguson of Michigan, William Jenner of Indiana, and Arthur Watkins of Utah were ultraconservative. In three years of voting, they accumulated between them 13 votes aligned with ADA positions, 102 against. All were China lobby supporters, two were on record against Lattimore, and the third (Watkins) could not abide any supporter of Roosevelt. Watkins later deserted McCarthy's cause, but he remained a fervent McCarranite.

On the salient issues of foreign policy and internal security, McCarran had an investigating group without a single deviant opinion.

Joe McCarthy was not a member of Judiciary, but he saw that SISS would be a wonderful vehicle for furthering his interests. The Tydings subcommittee had not been to his liking: the Democrats were hostile, Lodge was lukewarm, and the minority counsel, Robert Morris, was powerless; only Hickenlooper came to his support. SISS was something else entirely; he could not have asked for a more sympathetic crew. He set about to attach himself, and his most loyal staff, to SISS.

Surine was the first to see action. He stayed on McCarthy's payroll but was soon spending most of his time working for McCarran. In a conversation with Thomas Reeves on April 7, 1977, Surine claimed to have played a major role in SISS activities; he said he had attended all the hearings, procured the most incisive evidence, and helped write the major committee report, which, according to Surine, was "the best source on American foreign relations from 1925–52."[8] These claims are exaggerated, but Surine did play a role in a cloak-and-dagger escapade that started SISS on its way.

Edward Carter, former IPR secretary, had stored old IPR files in a barn on his farm near Lee, Massachusetts. Hundreds of letters to and from Lattimore were in the files. The FBI New York office had studied these files at Carter's suggestion, finding that only five of them were at all pertinent to the investigation of Lattimore and that "none relate[d] to pro-Soviet or pro-Communist sentiments or espionage." The SISS crew did not know the FBI had seen the files. When McCarthy got a telephone call December 21, 1950, from Thomas Stotler, the son (FBI version) or nephew (Jack Anderson version) of the caretaker at Carter's farm, McCarthy imagined that a great evidential treasure might be surfacing. Surine was detailed to follow up this call. In early January 1951 Surine arranged with Stotler to liberate the treasure; together they secretly carried the IPR files to J. B. Matthews's office in the Hearst Building in New York. A report to the FBI said that Hearst had purchased the IPR documents; this seems unlikely.[9]

As Jack Anderson tells the story, by February 3, 1951, the Matthews operation had made copies of eighteen hundred documents. The security of Matthews's operation was not good; news of it spread to HUAC, Senators Ferguson and Mundt, and Hearst columnists Sokolsky and Westbrook Pegler. When a HUAC agent came poking around the Hearst offices, Surine and Matthews got cold feet. The documents were smuggled back to Carter's barn.[10]

To Matthews, Surine, and other Hearst associates, the label "Institute of Pacific Relations" *meant* conspiracy and subversion. This collection of documents had to be retrieved. McCarthy arranged for SISS to issue a subpoena for all the "letters, papers, and documents" in Carter's barn. Surine was then sent back to Massachusetts with Frank Schroeder, a McCarran employee, and on February 8 Schroeder served the subpoena on the legally incompetent caretaker (it should have been served on Carter). Surine and Schroeder loaded the files in a truck and drove them through a blinding snowstorm to New York, where McCarran had arranged an armed Treasury escort for the rest of the journey to Washington. The files were stored in Judiciary Committee offices, locks on the door were changed, and guards provided. As the *New York Times* reported February 11, 1951, "Senators assigned to investigate subversive activities said today they expected 'sensational' results from a seizure of voluminous files of the Institute of Pacific Relations."[11] The *Times* account was relatively low-key, buried on page fifty-four of a Sunday edition. Hearst, Scripps Howard, and McCormick Patterson papers carried headlines screaming "Secret 'Lattimore' Files" and calling the operation a "Daring Raid."

McCarran kept up the tempo. He told the United Press on February 11 that his committee "would investigate 'fully' all matters involved in the records." By February 20 this initial enthusiasm had apparently died down. An FBI informant told the bureau that "the Senate Subcommittee and Senator McCarthy feel that nothing of any real importance is contained in these documents" and that "the primary aim of the Senate Subcommittee is to reopen the 'Amerasia' case."[12] This turned out to be a bad tip. The IPR was the primary fixation of SISS for a long run.

One of the reasons McCarran stuck with the IPR investigation was that Robert Morris, who had moved to McCarthy's payroll after the Tydings committee disbanded, now went to work for McCarran. Morris, a former naval intelligence officer, believed that Lattimore really was the evil genius behind American failures in Asia. In the October 30, 1950, *Freeman*, Morris published "Counsel for the Minority: A Report on the Tydings Investigation." Tydings had been a whitewash, and the Democrats had been solely concerned with scuttling McCarthy. "But the most serious delinquency of the Subcommittee was its steadfast refusal to look into the nature of the Institute of Pacific Relations. It was serious because Budenz had testified (and others were prepared to do so) that this very influential organization during a particularly strategic period had been controlled by the Communists."[13] Morris gloried in possession of the IPR files; along with Judiciary Counsel Julian G. (Jay) Sourwine and SISS Director of Research Benjamin Mandel, Morris set out to study the IPR records systematically. The study lasted for a year. Not until February 1952 was Morris ready to confront Lattimore in public.

McCarthy was ready with a new challenge to Lattimore much sooner. Under Kohlberg's influence McCarthy set out to obtain evidence from the Chinese Nationalists that Lattimore had contributed to their downfall. One potential source was a foreigner in the United States for whom McCarthy had helped obtain a visa extension. This person had spent about twenty years, including the war years, in China. The FBI was still protecting him in 1981, and we know only that he was informant T-7 in the relevant documents. In early 1950 Surine approached T-7 and asked him to obtain information about Lattimore and others from Chiang's files on Taiwan. T-7 was reluctant; he did not want to become involved in American politics. Nevertheless, Surine persuaded him that "securing such information would be of assistance to the United States Government and would be a blow struck in the war against Communism."[14]

T-7 therefore contacted his friends in Taiwan and procured for McCarthy a seven page report entitled "A Copied Document." It was a mishmash of rumor and invention. Its opening salvo claimed that when Henry Wallace was in Chungking in 1944 he had a "secret conference with Stilwell, Lattimore, Davies, Service, Vincent, and Ray Ludden, the purpose of which was to plot the downfall of the Nationalist regime." Such a meeting could not have taken place, as neither Stilwell nor Ludden was in Chungking at the time. Davies did not attend any of the meetings with Wallace, and Lattimore was still plotting the survival of the Nationalist regime.[15]

The document attacked two of Lattimore's books but offered only minor additional gossip: "When Lattimore was in Chungking he had frequent associations with the bandit [Communist] representatives, Chiao Mu [Hu Ch'iao-mu] and Kung P'eng, and secretly passed on important intelligency [sic] relating to our side to be carried back to Yenan."[16] The first part of this is true; Chiang did instruct Lattimore to confer with the Communist representatives in Chungking. The latter part was wholly malicious and, as the FBI decided, an invention of the 1950s.

Other documents from Taiwan surfaced during the SISS hearings. An unusual one began its journey in January 1951. General Charles Willoughby of the Far East Command in Tokyo, an intelligence aide to MacArthur, was trying to obtain information for his book about Sorge; he sent Lieutenant Thomas Malim to Taiwan to obtain anything in Chinese Nationalist files that might relate to the Sorge spy ring. Malim spent about three unsuccessful weeks in Taipei; "although the Chinese authorities appeared anxious to be helpful, they were able to turn up very little of what he was looking for."[17] Malim prepared to return to Tokyo empty-handed, but at the airport about an hour before his scheduled departure a courier came up to him with a document in Chinese. Malim was "unable to question Chinese officials about the documentation or sources of the allegations" contained in this document because of the shortness of time.[18] The document appears to have been entitled "International Red Conspiracy Undermines China," and while the cast of characters was somewhat different from that of "A Copied Document," it represented the same genre of postfacto inventiveness.

This time the headings within the document coupled the name of the enemy American with the name of a Communist Chinese "bandit." Section one dealt with "Owen Lattimore and Madame Sun Yat-sen"; others were headed "John S. Service and Kung P'eng," "Alger Hiss and Chang Han-fu," "John K. Fairbank and Liu Tsung-chi."[19]

Despite Hoover's many requests to Tokyo for information about Lattimore, and though this document appears to be precisely what Hoover had been requesting, Far East Command did not send a copy to the FBI. The bureau appears not to have found out about it until June 25, 1951, six months after Tokyo got it. Hoover then wrote Army Intelligence (G-2) in Washington asking for a copy of the materials given to Malim. This request was passed on to Willoughby, who sent a copy of the document to G-2 in Washington on July 7. G-2 notified the bureau that the copy was en route and "would be made available to the Bureau as soon as received." But there is no trace of the document in bureau files for five months, and G-2 did not actually get it to the FBI until December 21, 1951, almost eleven months after Malim received it.[20]

The section of "International Red Conspiracy" dealing with Lattimore contains little about his activities in China other than what was by then available from the Tydings hearings and from Lattimore's books. He is charged with having "eulogized" the Chinese Communists throughout the world as "mere agrarian reformers" after his trip to Yenan in 1937. During his service with Chiang he allegedly pushed Mao's views as expressed in a booklet *The New Epoch*. During his trip with Wallace he took Wallace to see Madame Sun Yat-sen, giving the Communists "considerable encouragement." A long section on his activities in OWI all derives from sources in Washington and in no sense represents Chinese "intelligence." Army described the whole document as of questionable value.[21]

This document too came to SISS and along with the T-7 document provided questions when Lattimore was called before McCarran.

There was much stir in Baltimore the second week of March 1951. Lattimore was asked to speak to the United Nations Youth Council at Baltimore City College on March 7. Acting at the request of the local American Legion, Baltimore City Council voted 13–6 to ask the school board to cancel the speech. The rationale was that the IPR was being investigated; Lattimore had been an officer of IPR; therefore Lattimore was subversive. The school board, however, declined. Lattimore spoke on schedule. There were no incidents, and all but about fifty of the two thousand students attended his lecture. His subversive message, according to the *New York Times*, was that the United States should have a "foreign policy that would work equally well in Asia and Europe."[22]

But other news dominated the headlines that spring. On March 29 a jury convicted Julius and Ethel Rosenberg of atomic espionage; this case joined the Hiss conviction in the pantheon of right-wing causes. A mere two weeks later Truman fired MacArthur, and the resulting furor lasted several months. MacArthur came back from Japan as a conquering hero, and Truman endured obloquy such as few presidents ever have. When MacArthur addressed a joint session of Congress April 19, Missouri Congressman Dewey Short, with no apparent damage to the presumption of his sanity, declared, "We saw a great hunk of God in the flesh, and we heard the voice of God."[23] Then there were the headline-making MacArthur hearings, commonly known as the MSFE hearings, jointly held by the Senate Armed Services and Foreign Relations committees. The official title was "Inquiry into the Military Situation in the Far East and the Facts Surrounding the Relief of General of the Army Douglas MacArthur from His Assignment in That Area."[24] From May 3 to June 25, 1951, the public was treated to a daily display of the Asia-first doctrines associated with Republican conservatives. McCarran and his followers were on the sidelines cheering.

The MSFE report agrees on thirty conclusions. Most of them deal with military matters, but some are political. Among the political conclusions: the identity of our real enemy was not North Korea but international communism; Soviet domination of the People's Republic of China was clear; and the United States should support the Republic of China on Taiwan, keeping the People's Republic out of the United Nations.[25]

A final section of the MSFE report dissects an official War Department publication entitled *Our Ally China*, which indoctrinated American soldiers during World War II with various subversive beliefs. *Our Ally China* emphasized the complexities of Chinese politics and always put the label "Communists" in quotes, implying that they weren't Communists at all. The MSFE report concludes: "American soldiers desiring to obtain more facts in regard to the problem of our Chinese ally were given a reference for further reading. That reference was *The Making of Modern China* by Owen Lattimore."[26] So Lattimore stood impaled by yet another group of senators.

One minor vindication of Lattimore appeared in FBI files during the spring of 1951. McCarthy, FBI agent Cornelius in Albany, and various informants had sniped at the Dilowa as a Communist agent in disguise. The FBI investigated the matter through army channels. Hoover requested Brigadier General John Weckerling, chief of Army Intelligence, to find out what he could about the Dilowa. Weckerling's contact in Taipei then went to his Nationalist counterpart for information. It came in a quite different shape from the T-7 and Malim documents: "The Dilowa Hutukhtu is thoroughly reliable and has a long record of anti-communist activity. He is also reported to be highly thought of by members of the Legislative Yuan of which he was at one time a member. I [Nationalist G-2] have known of the Dilowa Hutukhtu's activities over a period of about ten years and met him twice in Peiping in 1947 and 1948. From all I know of him I believe he would have no part of communism, particularly as the advent of communism into [Inner] Mongolia could have nothing but bad effects for him and his disciples."[27]

Reader's Digest reentered the ranks of Lattimore accusers in 1951. The June issue carried an article by Elinor Lipper (alias Elinor Catala, according to the FBI) entitled "Eleven Years in Soviet Prison Camps." This was a condensation and translation of Lipper's book of the same title, published in Germany in 1950.[28] In the German edition Lipper ridicules Henry Wallace for his naïveté in believing everything the Soviets told him during his 1944 visit to Magadan. Lattimore is not mentioned.

In April 1951 an English edition of Lipper's book was published by Henry Regnery. It contains a new section, headed "Owen Lattimore's Report," excoriating Lattimore even more than Wallace, since Lattimore had an "opportunity offered to an American scholar [that] was unique: no free foreigner had set foot in this NKVD country before, and no one has done so since." Lattimore's sin was that he, more than Wallace, should have known that what they saw at Magadan was all show put on by the

Russians; Lipper then quotes seven passages from Lattimore's *National Geographic Magazine* article, castigating his exuberant account of Magadan and of the Russians who entertained him. Lipper told friends that the attack on Lattimore was inserted in the Regnery edition without her knowledge.[29]

It is hard to believe that Regnery behaved so crudely. However this insertion in the American edition came about, it was incorporated in Lipper's *Reader's Digest* article, and Lattimore was again deluged with hostile mail. He answered many of these letters at length, acknowledging that what he and Wallace saw and described were Potemkin villages but also pointing out assumptions and errors of Lipper's that vitiated her polemic. But his response did not get a circulation in the millions.

Lipper came to the United States on a lecture tour in 1951, and the FBI interviewed her in October. She acknowledged knowing nothing about Lattimore, not even being aware in 1944 that he had accompanied Wallace.[30] That may be why SISS, which had invited her to testify on Lattimore, did not carry through with the invitation—at least publicly. When Wallace testified before SISS, he admitted that Lipper probably gave an accurate picture of the Magadan slave-labor camp—except for the hog farm, which he thought she knew nothing about.

Morris, Sourwine, and Mandel used the spring months of 1951 to prepare their case against the IPR and Lattimore. They had literally thousands of IPR documents to organize. And organize they did. The Tydings hearings had been haphazard and unpredictable, influenced by the tug-of-war between McCarthy and Hickenlooper on one side and the Democrats on the other. The pro-McCarthy witnesses had not been thoroughly prepared. Even Louis Budenz, by 1950 the most practiced professional witness in the country, bobbled the ball. When Tydings counsel Edward P. Morgan asked him why, if Lattimore were a Communist, the *Worker* had panned *Situation in Asia*, Budenz could only say, "Sir, I can explain to you that we had the policy in protecting people who are out beyond the party proper, to criticize them with faint praise—that is to say, to damn them with faint praise—rather, to praise them with faint damns, is the way I want to put it. Now I can give to this committee examples of that, but I just will have to have time."[31]

There was nothing haphazard or unprepared about SISS. Seven senators and three top staffers were of one mind: the IPR and Lattimore were to be pilloried with precision. This precision was accomplished (1) by extensive staff work in order that the interrogating counsel would know exactly what the IPR documents said and (2) by preparing anti-Lattimore witnesses. All the anti-Lattimore witnesses went through one-on-one staff interviews as well as executive session rehearsals. These rehearsals were designed to prepare them to make the best case and to screen out questions that might yield embarrassing answers. Thus, in one instance, the secret session with Nathaniel Weyl revealed that he was familiar with the IPR and was prepared to identify Fred Field as a Communist but that he would not similarly classify Lattimore. When Weyl came before SISS in public session on February 19, 1952, he was led through an elaborate identification of Field; no question was asked about Lattimore.[32]

McCarran's justification of executive session rehearsals did not acknowledge their real purpose. McCarran wanted to avoid being tagged with McCarthyism; hence, he wanted to limit public exposure of some witnesses. He controlled leaks from executive session testimony and bragged, "Our policy of taking a witness into executive session and finding out what he knows and what he is going to testify works as a safety valve so that innocent people will not be harmed."[33]

McCarran's public agenda was also carefully designed to load the dice against the Baltimore heretic. Only after seventeen anti-Lattimore witnesses had appeared in public session, with their accusations spread throughout the media, did McCarran consent to give Lattimore a rebuttal. McCarran's witnesses fell into two categories: the damned (IPR people) and their accusers. Only one of the approximately 170 prominent scholars who endorsed Lattimore's loyalty was called to testify; that was John King Fairbank, who "qualified" as a witness because he was associated with the IPR and was himself a target of McCarthy. The FBI had interviewed many former Communists on their roster of regular informants who said Lattimore was unknown to them; only four of them were called by McCarran, and they were not asked about Lattimore. It was a stacked deck.

Between April and July 1951, SISS in executive sessions laid the foundation for its public hearings. At least a dozen anti-IPR witnesses were prepared for the public show. Joseph Zack Kornfeder was typical. Kornfeder had been a Communist party member from 1919 to 1934. He attended the Lenin School in Moscow from 1927 to 1930 and held prominent posts with the Comintern in South America and with the American Party in New York and Detroit. In 1934 he broke with the Party but couldn't bring himself to testify against it until after World War II. In 1947 he was extensively interrogated by the FBI and went on to testify before many state and federal bodies, including HUAC. By the 1950s the

bureau had classified him as "A PROFESSIONAL WITNESS WITH NO EMPLOY-
MENT OTHER THAN HIS ACTIVITY IN CONNECTION WITH COMMUNIST AF-
FAIRS."[34]

Even after McCarthy began his crusade, Kornfeder knew nothing about
Lattimore; the bureau asked him about Lattimore on April 14, 1950, and
he "could furnish no information." Then Kornfeder offered his services
to McCarthy, went on McCarthy's payroll to do research, and suddenly
knew a lot about Lattimore. A thirty-eight-page speech Kornfeder wrote
for McCarthy to deliver to the Senate is in Lattimore's FBI file; it was so
bad McCarthy never used it.[35]

Kornfeder was called by SISS in executive session June 8, 1951. The
text of what he said about Lattimore is heavily censored, but it includes
the claim that "Lattimore was, in the early 1930s, a secret member of the
Communist Party." The bureau got transcripts of SISS executive sessions
and analyzed what Kornfeder had said. On August 2 Belmont wrote Ladd
that Kornfeder was "prone to put too much faith in hearsay evidence and
conclusions"; in his Lattimore testimony, "Kornfeder makes numerous
allegations which are apparently accepted by the committee at their face
value with no attempts made to ascertain Kornfeder's basis for these charges;
hence, it is difficult to estimate his reliability as far as this testimony is
concerned, and his reliability in this regard must be considered unknown."[36]

When SISS interrogated Kornfeder in a public session September 20,
1951, they simply refrained from asking him about Lattimore. Instead,
they asked him about Comintern activities in Latin America in the 1920s,
about which he knew something, and about Comintern China policy, about
which he knew very little. Robert Morris did ask him about an IPR pamphlet, *China Yesterday and Today*, written by Eleanor Lattimore in 1946.
Morris quoted this pamphlet as saying, "For not until China achieves a
government in which the Chinese people are adequately represented and
which brings about agricultural reforms designed to give her farmers enough
to live on will the underlying causes of communism be removed." That,
observed Kornfeder, was following the Communist party line. It was not
an edifying performance. Nor was Kornfeder a credible witness in general; he had admitted perjury about his place of birth a year before, and
shortly after the SISS appearance he admitted to Conrad Snow of the
State Department Loyalty Security Board that he had lied about John
Carter Vincent being a Party member. But witnesses like Kornfeder were
necessary to SISS.[37]

Elizabeth Boody Schumpeter testified in SISS executive session July 3.

A censored version of her testimony was released by the National Archives in 1987. She explained to the committee how IPR had worked to get the United States into war with Japan, thus strengthening the Chinese Communists.[38] As to Lattimore, she interpreted a letter from the IPR files as showing that he sought the triumph of the Chinese Communists, but other charges against Lattimore were deleted by FBI censors. SISS did not call Schumpeter for public testimony. This is surprising, as she told them what they wanted to hear.

SISS heard at least nineteen witnesses between April and July, most of whom were anti-IPR. On July 10 McCarran announced that Fred Field would appear in executive session two days later and that Lattimore would follow him. McCarran had nothing to say about what questions would be asked or what the committee expected to learn.[39]

Field faced the committee for two hours on July 12; Willis Smith and William Jenner conducted the hearing in New York. William L. Holland, executive vice-chairman of the IPR, presented himself and asked permission to sit in; he got no reply, waited for an hour, and left. Smith and Jenner were silent when reporters confronted them afterward, refusing to say whether Field was cooperative. Field and his lawyer were ordered not to discuss the hearing with reporters.[40]

Before Lattimore's six-hour executive session on July 13, Senator Ferguson told reporters that the questioning of Lattimore would be based on "fresh material" and that the committee "was interested in finding out if there were any 'Communist influences' in IPR, adding that he did not mean to imply that there were."[41] That may have been the last neutral statement to come from a committee member.

Lattimore's private hearing was relatively free of acrimony, but it was not based on "fresh material." Morris, Mandel, and Sourwine had digested hundreds of IPR documents in which Lattimore figured and absorbed all the latrine rumors that had come to McCarthy and Surine. Their purpose was to get Lattimore on record on all this information. He was not shown any of the relevant IPR documents, nor was he informed as to who accused him of what. He sensed that Mandel was sitting in front of him with definitive answers to the questions they were asking, all relating to events ten or more years old. When he asked to be shown documents that would help him refresh his memory, his request was denied. Eight months later, when he underwent his marathon twelve days of public testimony, he realized that he had been set up: the SISS method of questioning gave him "somewhat the feeling of a blind man running a gauntlet."[42]

But it could have been worse. There was no hectoring or badgering in executive session. McCarran did seem more restrained and moderate than did McCarthy. No headlines resulted from his executive session. Lattimore told his wife that it hadn't been so bad.

By July 30 this tinge of optimism had vanished. Carter and Field had been before the first public hearings of SISS, and Barmine was next. Lattimore wrote a Canadian friend on that date, "We are getting ready right now for another bout with the Sons of Belial." [43] He was still dead center, with McCarran's forces deployed on every side.

Robert Morris was busy preparing witnesses and interrogations during July, but not too busy to seize on rumors and try to make something of them. On July 18 Freda Utley told Robert Morris about a rumor she had picked up at J. B. Matthews's place in New York. Lattimore was not an American as he claimed but "a Russian child adopted very young in China." Also, St. Bees, where he went to school "was a school for problem children." The St. Bees allegation did not seem fruitful to Morris, but the birthplace did. Lattimore had said under oath that he was born in Washington, D. C., though he had no birth certificate and no evidence of his birth other than what his parents had told him. [44]

Here, to Morris, was a blockbuster with which to confront Lattimore later in public: Lattimore could not prove that he was an American, and witness X says he was born in Russia. Morris wrote Lou Nichols at the FBI, asking if this rumor were true. Nichols thought Morris was salivating prematurely; he sent an agent to the District of Columbia Bureau of Vital Statistics. When the agent returned with birth certificate number 105986, dated August 6, 1900, showing that Lattimore was born in Sibley Hospital July 29, 1900, Nichols sent a copy to Morris. No cover letter, no response. [45]

Despite putting a lid on publicity about SISS executive sessions, McCarran felt free to talk in public. On May 4 he told the Senate that Lattimore had started the ruckus that led to General MacArthur's dismissal. [46] Lattimore had attacked the Zaibatsu, the *Daily Worker* had reported this attack, and therefore Lattimore had scuttled MacArthur. A chain of causality leading from a *Daily Worker* article to Truman's firing MacArthur was not beyond McCarran.

McCarran also killed a high-level commission headed by Admiral Chester Nimitz that Truman had appointed to review loyalty-security procedures. The commission members could not serve unless exempted from the conflict-of-interest statutes. McCarran, as chair of Judiciary, bottled up the bill to grant exemptions. As the *New York Times* editorialized on

May 28, "It is difficult to avoid the conclusion that Senator McCarran and his friends, who are planning an investigation of their own, don't want competition, especially from a non-political and non-partisan body of distinguished citizens."[47] Nimitz and his commission promptly resigned, and Truman gave up the whole effort.

D day, for McCarran, was July 25, 1951. On that day his full subcommittee, plus the Mandel-Morris-Sourwine trio, the faithful Surine, and Joe McCarthy, were on hand for their first public hearing in room 424 of the Senate Office Building. So was Edward C. Carter. McCarran called the hearing to order at ten-thirty, regretting that the hearing room was too small to accommodate all who wanted to attend. After putting the resolutions authorizing the subcommittee into the record, McCarran set forth his operating assumptions and methods in a lengthy statement. It was a prospectus to reassure those who objected to McCarthy. This committee was making no charges: "We propose to let the evidence precede our conclusions." No hearings would be televised; the committee wanted "to make a record, not to make headlines." Witnesses could have counsel of their own choosing. No witness would be subjected to "undue publicity."[48] The liberal community listened in astonishment and applauded. Edward C. Carter was sworn as the first witness.

The Edward C. Carter who now stepped into the spotlight was not the "handsome, supercharged man who had built the IPR into the preeminent Asian studies organization," as John N. Thomas puts it. He was past seventy, failing in memory, confronting without the aid of documents a committee staff steeped in those documents and determined to make a fool of him. When Carter asked committee counsel to provide relevant dates of Fred Field's activities, dates in the papers on Morris's desk, he was simply ignored.[49] This tactic was used many times. Even worse, Carter's counsel, Edgar G. Crossman, was thoroughly browbeaten. Ten minutes into the hearings Crossman suggested to Carter that he go back to a question that he had not fully answered. The "fairness" of chairman McCarran was clearly revealed in the following colloquy:

> *Mr. Carter:* My attorney, as you noted, reminded me to follow up and clarify a question that I thought at the time I was speaking was left hanging in the air.
>
> *Sen. McCarran:* I do not propose to let you have anything hanging in the air. The Chair will see that you have an op-

> portunity to clarify anything you wish to clarify. I
> wish to say to the attorney, if you violate the rule
> of this committee we will remove you to the audi-
> ence, and we will do it very fast.

Mr. Crossman: May I have—

Sen. McCarran: That is all; I have said the last word and that is all
                  there is to it.

Mr. Crossman: May I have an opportunity to discuss that question?

Sen. McCarran: No, sir. I said no and that settles it.[50]

Several dozen times in the 5,712 pages of the IPR hearings one finds a
similar caustic rebuke from McCarran, but only to IPR witnesses and
their counsel. There are almost as many, and worse, from Eastland. This
first day, the committee toyed with Carter like a cat with a mouse. But it
was a surrogate mouse. The committee did not care about Carter, the
superannuated, bumbling former IPR head. Their real target was Lattimore.

Most of the attack on Lattimore during the Carter hearing was directed
against the "cagey" letter. In 1938 IPR was sponsoring a series of pamphlets on the issues of the Sino-Japanese War. Carter and Lattimore exchanged letters about the progress of this series. In a letter of July 10,
1938, Lattimore wrote Carter:

> I think that you are pretty cagey in turning over so much of the China
> section of the inquiry to Asiaticus, Han-seng, and Chi. They will bring
> out the absolutely essential radical aspects, but can be depended on to
> do it with the right touch.
>
> For the general purposes of this inquiry, it seems to me that the good
> scoring position for the IPR differs with different countries. For China,
> my hunch is that it will pay to keep behind the official Chinese Com-
> munist position [on land reform] far enough not to be covered by the
> same label, but enough ahead of the Chinese liberals to be noticeable.
> For Japan, on the other hand, hang back so as not to be inconveniently
> ahead of the Japanese liberals who cannot keep up whereas the Chinese
> liberals can. . . . For the USSR, back their international policy in gen-
> eral, but without using their slogans and, above all, without giving
> them or anybody else an impression of subservience.[51]

This semifacetious epistle enabled SISS to bully Carter extensively. Here
was a clear admission that the IPR, with Lattimore's approval, was backing Soviet policy and trying to conceal it. Of course, in that context Lat-

timore *was* backing Soviet policy, which was opposition to Japanese aggression. But it was Lattimore's policy too, and he didn't want the Russians to get sole credit for opposing aggression. He explained it seven months later when he had a chance:

> This period, 1938, was the period of maximum Soviet cooperation with the United States, Britain, France, and the League of Nations. It was the stated policy of the U.S.S.R.—almost universally credited at the time as in good faith—to support international unity and to resist Japanese and also German and Italian aggression. Even by 1938, however, I had learned through my experience in dealing with Russians as editor of *Pacific Affairs*, that it is a standard Soviet maneuver to try to make every act of agreement between equals look as if it were acceptance of Soviet leadership. I did not believe in any such subservience to the Russians, and I did not want the Institute to make the mistake of allowing the Russians to claim, or anybody else to believe, that agreement as to international unity and against aggression was an act of subservience to Russian policy.[52]

The fumbling Carter could offer no such justification of Lattimore's words. He did not even remember the letter. The effect of the SISS examination of Carter was fairly reflected in the *Times* headline over William S. White's page-one story July 26: "Senators Get Lattimore Note Backing Russian Policy in '38." One can understand how a headline writer, under the pressures of daily journalism, could get it so perverted. One can also understand the game plan of the committee. Two weeks earlier, when the committee had Lattimore in secret session, they could have asked him to explain the "cagey" letter but did not. There would have been no headlines then, no shock value, no beginning foundation for a future committee conclusion of "Guilty as charged."

The appearance of Fred Field the next day was guaranteed to give IPR a bad name. As a trustee of the bail bond fund guaranteeing the appearance of the top Communist party officials convicted under the Smith Act, Field had refused to answer questions about the fund. This refusal brought him a jail sentence for contempt of court.[53] Thus, Field was let out of jail for the day and escorted to the SISS hearing room by federal marshals. There he refused to answer more questions. He did admit that he had served as U.S. representative of four organizations in the People's Republic of China, that he had sought a commission in intelligence during World War II, and that he had given sixty thousand dollars to the IPR.

This was all page-one in the *Times* again.

After humiliating two IPR witnesses, McCarran's public statements became bolder. Contradicting the judicious "wait until the evidence is in" posture with which he began the hearings, on July 27 McCarran told reporters that "his subcommittee 'will show how certain individuals, working together, influenced Government policies out of which came the predicament we are in today.' The predicament he referred to, he told reporters, was the hold the Communists have obtained on China with the backing of Russia. 'You haven't seen anything yet,' Mr. McCarran said, adding that so far the subcommittee was just 'laying a foundation for matters I know are coming on.' "[54]

One of the witnesses coming on was Alexander Barmine, who was to testify concerning the phony "affidavit" attributed to Barmine that McCarthy had waved before the Senate in March. Barmine appeared before SISS on July 31. As in the case of Budenz, the FBI did not caution SISS that Barmine's credibility was in doubt. The bureau had been caustic about Barmine's sudden "discovery" of Lattimore in 1948 and noted, "Interviews have been conducted with numerous individuals in an effort to corroborate this allegation with negative results."[55] An FBI brief of January 16, 1951, said nothing about Barmine's absurd story of the Panchen Lama visiting Lattimore; this most damaging hallucination went down the bureau's memory hole.

So Barmine appeared before SISS untainted by the bureau's doubts, basking in McCarran's praise: "I want to express my gratitude to you for coming before the committee of the Senate and before the American people and giving us the facts as to the dangers that are here with us at home. . . . The committee is grateful to you, the country should be grateful to you."[56]

Barmine repeated what he had told the FBI and his various journalist friends: in 1933 General Berzin informed him that Lattimore and Barnes were "their men," with military expertise available to advance Soviet plans for influencing and controlling Sinkiang. Then Barmine added a new wrinkle: in 1938 General Walter Krivitsky, also a Soviet defector, told him in Paris that Lattimore and Barnes were still Soviet agents. Barmine had never told this to the FBI. (There is no other testimony that Krivitsky said anything like this, nor do his memoirs mention Lattimore, Barnes, or the IPR.) It took the bureau a while to react to this new story, but eventually the New York office was directed to "resolve the discrepancy in the testimony of ALEXANDER BARMINE before the Senate Sub-Committee on Internal Security with information he previously furnished this office."[57]

Barmine told SISS that he had previously advised the FBI of this charge, but he hadn't. His only excuse now was that he "evidently became confused before the Senate Sub-Committee" and thought he had given the information to the bureau. This lame explanation was passed on to the attorney general without comment.[58]

Lattimore had some comment. The day after Barmine's testimony he issued a statement: "Any suggestion that I was ever 'their man' is pure poppycock. In 1933 I had no contact whatever with Russia, and had never been to Russia."[59] Nor was he associated with the IPR at that time.

SISS was embarrassed by Barmine's 1933 date, which was obviously wrong even if Barmine were right about the rest of it. So in the final report on the IPR the committee said that in executive session Barmine had given a 1935 date for Berzin's statement. This claim cannot be verified, but in his statement to the FBI Barmine used 1933. Moreover, the text SISS issued containing his public testimony was not corrected; it still says 1933.[60]

But it is Barmine's alleged relationship with Berzin that creates the most compelling doubt of his truthfulness. As noted before, Barmine names and identifies his Soviet coworkers ad nauseam in his memoirs—except for Berzin, who is never mentioned. Could Barmine actually have been close to the head of Soviet army intelligence? In his SISS testimony Barmine never mentions Berzin's full name. To reporters, however, he said his close collaborator and source of the charge against Lattimore was General Ian Antonovich Berzin. There was a Soviet general by that name. A Latvian, he had been with Lenin at the famous Zimmerwald conference and held various diplomatic positions until he died in prison April 12, 1941. This Berzin rates two and a half column inches in *Who Was Who in the USSR*.[61]

There was a Berzin who from 1924 to 1937 headed Soviet army intelligence, with a year of that time as "senior adviser" to Loyalist forces fighting Franco in Spain. This was Ian Karlovich Berzin, who also rates two and a half inches in *Who Was Who in the USSR*. How could Barmine have made this elementary misidentification? Krivitsky, in his memoirs, gets the right Berzin. Deakin and Storry, in *The Case of Richard Sorge*, take pains to distinguish between the two Berzins. If Barmine "worked directly under" Berzin for fifteen years, "spent hours in long conferences" with him, and saw him "two or three times a week," is it even possible that he could not have known the man's name and could have confused him with another Soviet general whose assignments were entirely different? To compound the whole improbable business, the SISS staff secured, from the *Soviet Encyclopedia* of 1927, the biography of the wrong Berzin, had it translated at the Library of Congress, and inserted it in the IPR hearing record to prove there really was such a person. Even a casual reading shows that this Berzin could not have been Barmine's claimed boss.[62]

Barmine was the first of the anti-IPR witnesses before SISS. As with those to come, he got kid-glove treatment. To use the legal term, he was "led" by questions well prepared to elicit only what the committee wanted to hear. Often Barmine had only to say yes to a leading question from counsel Morris: there is an instance of this leading on almost every other page of the report. The whole routine had been rehearsed in executive session. And of course, no one asked him, "Why did you claim that the Panchen Lama secretly visited Lattimore in 1949?"[63]

Despite the extensive preparation and the mutual esteem of committee and witness, Barmine was less than perfect. Senator Ferguson asked him about other testimony he had given:

> Sen. Ferguson: But the FBI did have that evidence that you have told here this morning about Mr. Barnes and Mr. Lattimore; is that right?
>
> Mr. Barmine: Well, if you call it evidence—
>
> Sen. Ferguson: Well, your statements that you gave here.
>
> Mr. Barmine: Yes.
>
> Sen. Ferguson: You mean to count that as evidence, do you not? It is what happened?
>
> Mr. Barmine: I have to tell you that when I got this to the FBI, I just considered in the sense that I learned to understand the evidence, I was very reluctant that this thing should be used, because I think it is a very old story and since then many things could happen, and that was all that I knew, but it was after all not my direct knowledge from the workings.[64]

For SISS, it did not have to be "direct knowledge from the workings" if it was anti-IPR. Hearsay was good enough for them.

Barmine's testimony got full play in the media. As usual, the *Chicago Tribune* carried the most lurid headlines: "Ex-Red Tells of Lattimore Aid to Russia. Called Agent for Secret Police."[65] Other papers, including the *Times* and the *Baltimore Sun*, headlined a rebuttal issued by Lattimore.

The day after Barmine's testimony, Representative E. E. Cox (Democrat from Georgia) spoke to the House about the tendency of tax-exempt foundations to give subversives lucrative grants. " 'Owen Lattimore, who played such an important part in the betrayal of China and the delivery of that country into the hands of the Communists, is a past master in extracting money from the various foundations,' Mr. Cox said."[66] Cox wanted this practice looked into and eventually formed a committee to do just that.

Hede Massing, former wife of Gerhart Eisler, testified before SISS August 2, 1951. This former Soviet spy named dozens of individuals who, she claimed, had been involved in espionage; Lattimore was not among them. She had met him, she said, only once, at a social affair.[67]

Now SISS turned to Asian scholars for its witnesses. Thirty-seven prominent Asianists were on public record vouching for Lattimore's integrity, and according to a Justice Department document he could get support from 130 more.[68] McCarran called exactly one of Lattimore's supporters, John King Fairbank. Six conservative, bitter anti-Lattimore professors were called, probably the entire such population.

Karl August Wittfogel was the first Asian scholar to testify against Lattimore. Wittfogel was a former German Communist who specialized in ponderous tomes explaining "Oriental despotism": how irrigation in China and other areas necessitated the development of centralized and authoritarian governments. Wittfogel and Lattimore had once been friends. By 1950 this had changed.

Wittfogel had served nine months in Hitler's concentration camps. John King Fairbank observed, "He had not liked the concentration camps he had been in in Germany and was determined to stay out of those he expected to begin operating here."[69] There was one sure way to achieve this: join the crusade against Lattimore. This strategy proved one's patriotism.

Consequently, the scorn Wittfogel heaped on Lattimore for advocating a moderate stance toward Peking, in order not to "drive the Chinese Communists in[to] the arms of the Russians," was total. Wittfogel said, "In my opinion, this is one of the funniest remarks I have ever heard in my life. You don't have to drive them very hard. I think it is insulting the intelligence of this country to make that kind of remark. . . . To assume that Stalin will be so stupid to repeat the mistakes which he has made in Yugoslavia, to overplay his hand and to destroy all the enormous powers of attraction, is a marginal possibility. . . . Stalin will do everything not to overstrain relations and from Mao's point of view everything is to be gained by staying with Stalin."[70]

Wittfogel ticked off the clues to Lattimore's communism. Lattimore was friendly with Chi Ch'ao-ting, whom Lattimore knew to be a Communist. How did Lattimore know? Said Wittfogel, "I told him" (in 1935, in China). Also, Lattimore had listened with a smile when Wittfogel denied to Woodbridge Bingham that he had ever been a Communist; since Lattimore surely knew Wittfogel was lying and did not protest, Lattimore was covering up for Wittfogel. That made Lattimore a Communist. Wittfogel said Lattimore's trip to Yenan in 1937 proved him a Communist; Mao would "be very careful whom he would let in." Lattimore wanted Russia to take over Korea, which would be the "best solution." Lattimore adopted the Communist usage of "feudal," applying it to pre-Communist China. Wittfogel conducted a true vendetta against Lattimore; G. L. Ulmen, Wittfogel's authorized biographer, takes at least thirty-six pages to describe Wittfogel's Lattimore obsession.[71]

The FBI was noncommittal about Wittfogel. They were disturbed when he told the Lattimore grand jury in 1952 something he had not told them, and Supervisor Branigan wrote Belmont a letter about it. What Wittfogel said is still secret. Wittfogel was a thoroughgoing ideologue, first as a Communist, then as an anti-Communist. He fit perfectly the pattern described by Herbert Packer in *Ex-Communist Witnesses:* "It seems generally true that former Communists experience a strong reaction against their old allegiance, and, in many cases, manifest an intense desire to do everything they can to abjure it. One also suspects that many former Communists abjure one set of absolutes in favor of another, that what formerly was the purest white becomes for them the deepest black, and that this tendency renders their account of the past suspect."[72]

The witnesses following Wittfogel had little to say about Lattimore. Professor George Taylor, of the University of Washington, thought the IPR was infiltrated by Communists, of whom the most pernicious were Fred Field and Lawrence Rosinger. But Taylor thought the IPR could still be purged and serve a useful function. Morris pointedly did not ask Taylor about Lattimore.

General Charles A. Willoughby appeared next, and SISS conspicuously failed to ask him too if Lattimore were connected with the Sorge spy ring. They knew the answer would be no. The committee did, however, attempt to get from Willoughby a judgment on Lattimore's responsibility for the attack on Pearl Harbor because of the cable about the modus vivendi proposal; Willoughby did not rise to this bait.[73]

On August 14 Elizabeth Bentley testified. She was one of the more prolific namers of concealed Communists, and during her SISS appearance she lived up to expectations. The staff had prepared her well. All of the persons they asked her about were, she said, Communists, most of them also engaged in espionage. Clearly Robert Morris, who was in charge of the questioning, did not intend to raise Lattimore's name. But Senator Eastland blurted it out. "Do you," he asked, "know anything about Owen Lattimore?" Bentley replied that she did not. Eastland clarified, "You do not know whether he is a Communist or not?" Bentley responded, "No, I don't." Morris quickly changed the subject. Bentley's refusal to name Lattimore is curious. Lattimore was a prominent member of the IPR, and Bentley said her boss and lover, Jacob Golos, claimed the IPR was "red as a rose."[74]

Whittaker Chambers came on August 16, though the committee did not demand much of him. He identified several spies, discoursed about the operations of the Communist underground, mentioned a number of Communists who had been connected in some way with the IPR, and was dismissed. There were no questions about Lattimore.[75]

By mid-August 1951 SISS had established itself as a major actor in the hunt for subversives. Opinions of its probity varied widely. On August 19 an evaluation by Harold Hinton in the *New York Times* "News of the Week in Review" section saw McCarran's operation benignly; the headline read, "McCarran Shies Away from M'Carthy Label. His Committee Operates Like Court, Shields Witnesses from Publicity." Hinton quoted extensively from McCarran's remarks at the first public hearing, noting that SISS members "decline to number themselves among the 'scaremongers and hatemongers' whom President Truman castigated so roundly earlier in the week nor do they like to be told they are 'carrying McCarthy's load.' " Hinton did not comment on the way McCarran treated IPR witnesses and their lawyers.

An opposing view appeared in the *Reporter* of August 21, written by Alan Barth of the *Washington Post*. The *Reporter* headline was "McCarran's Monopoly: The Nevada Senator Has Become Judge, Prosecutor, and Hangman on Loyalty Cases." Barth noted, "The chairman of the Senate Judiciary Committee has, over the last six months, managed to establish himself as Grand Inquisitor and Lord High Executioner in charge of the extirpation of heresy. He has done this through his chairmanship of the Judiciary Subcommittee on Internal Security, known more familiarly as the McCarran subcommittee; with his surveillance of the Subversive Activities Control Board created under the McCarran Act; and with his frustration of the Nimitz Commission on Internal Security and Individual Rights." For Barth, what McCarran was doing was more important

than what McCarran had said SISS was going to do. "There are," said
Barth, "literally no boundaries to its jurisdiction, and no check upon its
power to punish. "[76]

The day after Barth's article appeared, McCarran turned his heaviest
artillery against Lattimore: Louis Budenz. Budenz came before SISS on
August 22 and 23, confident that this time, in contrast to Tydings, he
need not fear hostile cross-examination. He was right; there was none.
Instead, a carefully orchestrated mutual admiration society held forth for
two days. Many of the holes in Budenz's testimony before Tydings were
plugged. The hearsay nature of what Budenz had to say was carefully
justified by the committee; both McCarran and Ferguson took pains to
validate the acceptance of hearsay in "proving" a conspiracy.

Budenz's claims about the truthfulness of Communists when talking to
each other, and about editorial omniscience, came through loud and clear.
Ferguson led on the first point: "And [what you were told by Party bosses]
had to be accurate for you to carry on; is that correct?" Budenz replied:
"Communist information among themselves is absolutely accurate. It must
be. It is the foundation of their work. "[77]

Morris set up the claim of editorial omniscience:

> *Mr. Morris:* At the outset, Mr. Budenz, were you in a position in the
> Communist Party where you would have access to more
> secrets, to the identity of more people, than the ordinary
> Communist?
>
> *Mr. Budenz:* Most decidedly. Indeed, more than the normal members
> of the national committee.
>
> *Mr. Morris:* Why is that, Mr. Budenz?
>
> *Mr. Budenz:* As managing editor of the Daily Worker, it was essential
> that I know the various delicate turns and twists of the
> line; not only of the line but of the emphasis of the line
> in the particular period of time.[78]

The "line" on Lattimore had expanded somewhat since Tydings. There
was still the claim that in 1937 Lattimore was ordered to carry out a
campaign to paint the Chinese Communists as "North Dakota non-partisan
leaguers"; there was still no single instance of where Lattimore had done
this. In 1943, according to Budenz, Lattimore had gotten "information
coming to him from the international Communist apparatus where he
was located . . . that there was to be a change of line very sharply on
Chiang Kai-shek." Here Budenz, apparently feeling the absence of anything specific implicating Lattimore, did a side step: "The Politburo sug-

gested that someone, and the name T. A. Bisson was mentioned in this connection, be enlisted to write an article in connection with the Institute of Pacific Relations publication on this matter." But Lattimore still got the blame, even if Bisson did it.[79]

Then there was the Wallace trip, where "a great deal of dependence was placed on Owen Lattimore, whom I was told by Mr. Stachel at that time to consider a Communist"; and in the *Amerasia* case, Lattimore "had been of great assistance to the defendants." A new charge, which Budenz picked up from the Japanophiles and MacArthur supporters, was that in 1945 Lattimore had attacked the Zaibatsu, calling for a hard peace in Japan. The Party spread Lattimore's opinion "throughout the country." But Budenz did not claim that Lattimore was responsible for the firing of MacArthur.[80]

Forty-one pages of the printed transcript show Budenz dealing exclusively with Lattimore. Budenz had done considerable homework since his last testimony about the IPR. The rest of the hearing presented, in assembly-line fashion, the sins of other Communists associated with the IPR. The routine was simple. Morris would ask, "Do you know X as a Communist?" Budenz would respond, "Yes, by official reports . . ." Then Mandel would introduce letters from the IPR files to show how active X had been, or what IPR publications X had written. The case of Lattimore's friend Vilhjalmur Stefansson was typical.

Mr. Morris: Mr. Budenz, do you know Vilhjalmur Stefansson?

Mr. Budenz: I know from official reports that he is a Communist.

Mr. Morris: Do you know he was a member of many Communist-front organizations?

Mr. Budenz: That is where much of the discussion around him centers. He was a member of so many, I think the word countless can be used without exaggeration. . . .

Mr. Morris: Is it your testimony that in addition to being a member of many Communist front organizations, he was also a member of the Communist Party?

Mr. Budenz: That is correct. . . .

Mr. Morris: Mr. Mandel, will you put into the record letters that will indicate Mr. Stefansson's association with the Institute of Pacific Relations?

Mr. Mandel: I have here a letter dated January 26, 1939. . . .[81]

Forty-three persons were subject to this routine.

Reporters and editors did not make much of Budenz's testimony this time; the *Times* story on his August 22 appearance was subordinated to that of General Willoughby, then appearing before HUAC. The FBI was more attentive: agent L. L. Laughlin was assigned to analyze what Budenz said and was disturbed. As he reported to Ladd on September 25, "The reliability of Budenz in instant testimony must be classed as unknown. In this testimony there are at least seven instances in which Budenz either furnished information differing from that furnished previously either to the Bureau or before the Tydings Committee, or relative to certain occurrences gives testimony which he has never made known before."[82]

Laughlin found that Budenz had reclassified the IPR from an organization "infiltrated" by Communists to a "captive" organization. The Wallace mission was upgraded from one that the Party "followed with great interest" to one in which Lattimore represented the Party. Lattimore's Yenan trip of 1937 was now a "Communist project"; Budenz had never said this before. John Carter Vincent was now "under Communist Party discipline"; this was new. Budenz's date for considering Joe Barnes a Communist was shifted back four years to 1936. Budenz for the first time located Fred Field on the onionskin copies of official reports; and he now named two new Party members, Max Granich and Kumar Goshal. Each one of these discrepancies was written up to be presented to Budenz for an explanation.[83]

Budenz, however, was not as high a priority for the bureau as he had been in 1950. It took a month for New York to send a report to headquarters with Budenz's answers. A cable of October 20, 1951, summarized his explanations: "IN GENERAL, BUDENZ STATED THE FOLLOWING CONCERNING ANY DIFFERENCES IN HIS TESTIMONY BEFORE THE COMMITTEE AS COMPARED WITH THAT FURNISHED THE BUREAU: WHEN TESTIFYING BEFORE THE COMMITTEE, BUDENZ STATED THAT HE FURNISHES INFO WHICH HE KNOWS TO BE A FACT. HOWEVER, WHEN FURNISHING INFO TO THE BUREAU, HE FURNISHES ONLY THAT INFO WHICH IN HIS OPINION HE CAN PROVE TO BE A FACT. BUDENZ STATED THAT FOR THIS REASON, THE INFO WHICH HE FURNISHES THE BUREAU IS FREQUENTLY MORE CONSERVATIVE THAN INFO FURNISHED TO A COMMITTEE."[84] No bureau comments on this explanation have been released.

Two weeks after Budenz testified to SISS , his credibility took a beating from Special Agent M. A. Jones, assigned by the bureau to analyze the 545-page perjury summary compiled by the Baltimore office eight months earlier. Jones's fifteen-page analysis, which never became public, was submitted to Lou Nichols on September 6, 1951.[85] It was devastating. Point by point Jones set forth the instances of possible perjury and knocked all but one of them down. Hardest hit were the instances based on testimony of Louis Budenz.

Item one was "POSSIBLE PERJURY IN DENYING COMMUNIST PARTY MEMBERSHIP, AFFILIATION, OR CONSCIOUS PROMOTION OF COMMUNISM." Budenz's testimony on this matter was reviewed; so were all the other claims that Lattimore had been a Communist "stooge," that he had been "used" by the Party, that he was anti–Chiang Kai-shek, and so on. At the end of this review Jones was curt: "Budenz ———— and the majority of the other informants have no personal acquaintance with Lattimore. Their information appears to be hearsay and of no value as evidence." Also under item one Jones dealt with the massive IPR files. "The results of the review of the IPR files do not reflect a definite stand by Lattimore in support of Communism. This support can be assumed from some of the material, but is arguable, and does not appear sufficiently direct to controvert his sworn testimony. . . . The report sets out a number of comments from various individuals on Lattimore's books and writings. There is no indication that any of these individuals could be qualified as an expert to testify to matters of opinion in the Communist field."

Item two covered association with pro-Communist groups. Jones batted them down one by one. Lattimore may have belonged to, but certainly was not active in, the Maryland Association for Democratic Rights. He had addressed a meeting of the Washington Book Shop, but he did not deny this and did not know it was Communist-affiliated: no perjury. There was no evidence of membership in any proscribed organization. On the charge that Lattimore perjured himself in denying that he had ever said the Chinese Communists were mere agrarian radicals, Jones did not even consider the Budenz version of that charge worthy of comment. And the others who charged it were simply wrong.

The rest of the alleged perjuries were similarly rejected, except item eight: "POSSIBLE PERJURY IN DENYING KNOWLEDGE THAT CHAO-TING CHI WAS A COMMUNIST." On the basis of E. Newton Steely's Civil Service Commission report in 1943, Jones felt that Lattimore could hardly have forgotten what Steely said and hence might have lied.[86]

Jones drew no final conclusion. It was probably unnecessary. The Jones analysis, so devastating to the entire conduct of the SISS hearings, never left the bureau.

SISS took a three-week vacation after Budenz's appearance. On September 14, 1951, they heard their first Japanophile: Eugene Dooman. Dooman had hated Lattimore since the Pacificus article attacking him and

Grew; now for the first time he had an influential audience for his rancor. He reviewed the proposal to hire Lattimore as a State Department consultant in 1945, noted Grew's veto, and strongly agreed with Grew. He mentioned the Pacificus article ("Dangerous Experts") and claimed that it showed the writer to be subversive, but he did not publicly claim Lattimore had written it. He did claim that Lattimore was the most prominent proponent of a Carthaginian peace for Japan, since Lattimore wanted to eliminate the Zaibatsu and exile the emperor.[87]

As Dooman told the story to SISS, Lattimore's views on Japan were accepted at the beginning of the American occupation, and the results were disastrous: "a capital tax of from 60 to 90 percent of all property above $1,000" was applied, which "almost at one stroke wiped out the capitalist class." This was a program similar to that of the Soviet Union in Poland. Senator Eastland wanted it clear what Dooman was saying: "That was a Communist system, was it not?" Dooman agreed that it was. The outcome was horrendous, according to Dooman: "Their [the capitalists'] places have been taken by hordes of black marketeers and Chinese and Formosan thugs of various kinds who have been engaged in illicit trade of various kinds and then amassed this enormous fortune." The picture of Japan in 1951 as bereft of capitalists and dominated by thugs did not strike reporters as reasonable. Even Willard Edwards's story in the *Chicago Tribune* skipped that part of Dooman's testimony. The *Times* did not cover Dooman at all. Dooman apparently did not believe that Japan would ever recover from the Lattimore-induced destruction of its capitalist class, and his contempt for those who disagreed with him on occupation policy was total.[88]

On September 5, 1951, a new combatant entered the ranks against SISS, against witness Budenz, and against Robert Morris. This was Joseph Alsop, prominent Washington columnist, strong anti-Communist, and vigorous supporter of Chiang Kai-shek. Alsop had been present at the Kunming conference of Henry Wallace and John Carter Vincent on June 25, 1944, at which the three conferees decided that Stilwell should be replaced by Wedemeyer as American commander in China. By 1951 Alsop disagreed violently with Vincent and Lattimore, who advocated recognizing the Peking regime. But Alsop knew that the judgments made by the beleaguered China hands were and always had been made as loyal Americans. He was outraged at the SISS attempt to condemn them as servants of the Kremlin.

Alsop's first column attacking McCarran came on September 5, 1951; the *Washington Post* headlined it "Investigate Everybody." Alsop ridicules McCarran's attempt to "prove that the Communist victory in China was the result of a plot hatched in the Institute of Pacific Relations," defends Vincent and Wallace for their recommendation to fire Stilwell ("a profoundly anti-Communist document"), and even includes Lattimore in his exoneration: "The same rules apply to other poor wretches that McCarran is after. Prof. Owen Lattimore, a man of great learning and befuddled politics, also went along on the Wallace tour. He did not see the drafting of the report to Roosevelt, but he made no protest against it."

Now that McCarran was out to rewrite history, was he going to charge the *New York Herald Tribune,* the *New York Times,* and *Life* magazine with the loss of China? They had all carried dispatches from reporters who detested Chiang and sympathized with Mao. "Are they," Alsop asks, "or is Henry R. Luce, to be investigated now? And what about Maj. Gen. Patrick Hurley? Again, this reporter can personally testify that General Hurley used to say the Chinese Communists were not Communists at all, and even to boast that he had Stalin's and Molotov's assurances on this crucial point. Is Hurley to be investigated?"

This first Alsop attack did not mention Budenz's testimony on the Wallace mission. Alsop wanted to do a thorough job on Budenz, and by September 12 he was ready. "To suggest that testimony given under oath is specifically untruthful is a very grave thing to do. In all honesty, however, it is now necessary to ask whether the much-publicized ex-Communist, Louis Budenz, has not been untruthful in his testimony before the McCarran subcommittee of the Senate Judiciary Committee." What follows is a powerful attack on Budenz: his inconsistent claims, his eagerness to give Morris the expected answers, his dependence on "official reports" that were highly improbable, his absurd classification of the Wallace cable about Stilwell as in accord with Party wishes. Alsop concludes, "The contemporary documentary evidence refutes Budenz' late-remembered verbal evidence in implication and in detail. Every word he said about Vincent would surely be thrown out in any court in the land. The hard facts cannot be escaped."[89]

Alsop wrote another anti-Budenz article on September 14 that caught the attention of Senator Herbert Lehman of New York. Lehman told the Senate that there were "grave published charges" involving "demonstrably false" testimony before SISS and that they should be investigated. Lehman wanted to put the Alsop columns in the *Congressional Record;* Senator Herman Welker of Idaho objected, and they were not entered until September 24. McCarran thereupon exploded at Lehman: Lehman was accusing him of subornation of perjury.[90]

Alsop's newspaper onslaught, even with Lehman's backing, did not change the ways of SISS. But the war was not over, and SISS was eventually forced to give Alsop a public hearing.

On September 20 Kornfeder was brought before the public. As previously noted, that professional witness was on such shaky ground that Morris refrained from even asking him about Lattimore.[91]

Then it was Kenneth Colegrove's turn. He told SISS the story of his refusal to take the Japan desk at OWI, explained how he disagreed with Lattimore on the "benefits of Dutch rule in Indonesia" (Colegrove thought Dutch administration had been good for Indonesia), claimed that Lattimore told him the Chinese Communists were "real democrats," said Lattimore followed the Communist line on Japan to the letter, and jumped on the IPR with both feet. Under Eastland's solicitous questioning Colegrove affirmed that the "Lattimore group" at the 1949 State Department conference was indeed the "group largely that had betrayed the Chinese Government to the Communists." The FBI boggled at this accusation; Colegrove had been far left until at least 1946.[92] Within a year of his testimony he was to write a ringing defense of Joe McCarthy.

Next on the SISS agenda was Raymond Dennett. Dennett had been secretary of the IPR American Council during 1944 and 1945, but he was not an uncritical defender of that organization. He had "grave doubts" as to whether the IPR staff were "objective research workers."[93] Hence the committee's treatment of Dennett was totally different from the harassment of Carter, Field, Lattimore, and other IPR stalwarts.

Nowhere in the IPR transcript does the committee's flagrant use of leading questions show more clearly than in the Dennett hearing. Sometimes he allowed himself to be led, as when Morris questioned him about Lattimore's role in the Hot Springs IPR conference of 1944 (see chapter 8). Other times he rebelled, as when Sourwine said to him about an IPR pamphlet, "This pamphlet distorted the facts for the benefit of the Soviet Union, did it not?" Dennett balked: "You are putting words into my mouth which I don't think I put there."[94]

Dennett's major contribution to the committee's case against IPR lay in his description of how the IPR attempted to influence opinion by selling pamphlets to the army and navy, conferring with government officials, and inviting them to conferences such as Hot Springs. Although he had doubts about the objectivity of some IPR staff, he resolutely rejected attempts to get him to label Jessup, Lattimore, or Carter as pro-Communist.

On September 28 William M. McGovern testified. Unlike his Northwestern University colleague Kenneth Colegrove, McGovern had never flirted with the Left. He had been ultraconservative all his life and was, from the committee's point of view, the perfect witness. Among other qualifications, he had a doctorate from Oxford. McGovern proved his worth early in his hearing, when he was asked what he thought of the Chinese Communists: "By 1937–38 I was convinced they were Communists. And that they were in close cahoots with the Kremlin."[95]

Most notably, McGovern despised Lattimore. On almost every dimension of controversy McGovern claimed that in private conversations, Lattimore expressed opinions diametrically opposite to what he was writing at the time. On the allegiance of Mao and colleagues, McGovern claimed that Lattimore told him many times in 1937 that "they were not Communists." McGovern claimed that in a Far East Advisory Committee meeting in 1945 Lattimore wanted to "reduce Japan to beggary and impotence. . . . to reduce Japan back to an agricultural country and destroy all Japanese industry." McGovern alleged that Lattimore wanted the Japanese emperor murdered and that he seemed to advocate the same fate for the emperor's wife and children.[96]

Eastland and Ferguson, the only two senators present, were delighted. The *Times* ignored McGovern, and even Wittfogel described him as a "dwarf."[97]

The next witness was top drawer. Harold E. Stassen, "boy governor" of Minnesota, serious contender for the Republican presidential nomination in 1948, and in 1951 president of the University of Pennsylvania, came before SISS October 1. Stassen, a fire-breathing supporter of the rump Chinese Nationalist regime on Taiwan, had attended the State Department roundtable conference on Asian policy in October 1949 with an impressive entourage of assistants to present charts, graphs, and specific programs for reversing the Nationalist defeat.[98] Had Stassen prevailed at the 1949 conference, and had his plan succeeded in restoring Chiang, the nation would no doubt have been very grateful.

But Stassen did not prevail. Lattimore, Rosinger, and others who thought the People's Republic was in China to stay were in the majority. The course of argument during this conference, as explained by Stassen, would make a book in itself. It took more than one SISS hearing to get it all:

Stassen appeared again on October 6 and 12, each time with "new documents" which he claimed would show the "Lattimore group" advocating capitulation to the Communists.

After Stassen's first appearance Lattimore requested the State Department to release the transcript of the 1949 conference. On October 11, this was done. Stassen's charges evaporated. Most of what he charged to Lattimore was someone else's opinion, and the rest Stassen had garbled shamelessly. William S. White's front-page story in the *New York Times* the next day avoided explicit judgment but made clear how far Stassen's mythical conference departed from reality. Stassen struggled once again, in his final appearance before SISS October 12, to show that his attack on Lattimore (and on Jessup, who was in the middle of a Senate confirmation battle) held water. It was a pathetic attempt, a preview of the slide into ridicule and irrelevance that marked Stassen's subsequent quadrennial attempts at the presidency.[99]

On October 5 Budenz, wounded by the Alsop attack, was again given a chance to develop his version of the Wallace Kunming cable before SISS. However, he had little to say about Kunming; the committee moved on to Wallace's subsequent career, and Budenz recounted at great length how the Communist party had worked to get Wallace the Democratic nomination for vice president in 1944 and, failing that, to get him appointed secretary of commerce, at which they succeeded. En route to his condemnation of Wallace, Budenz named several more "concealed Communists" known to him through "official reports."[100]

Surprisingly, Budenz was not again called before SISS, and the later vigorous attacks on his truthfulness by Alsop, Wallace, Lattimore, and Vincent went unanswered. Perhaps growing FBI doubts about his credibility spilled over into Senate channels. In later years Budenz refused even to discuss his Lattimore testimony. Donald Crosby, S. J., author of *God, Church and Flag: Senator Joseph R. McCarthy and the Catholic Church, 1950–1957*, interviewed Budenz and asked him about discrepancies in his Lattimore testimony. Budenz said it "wasn't pertinent" to discuss.[101]

The committee now turned to William L. Holland, then secretary general of the IPR. Holland was determined not to accept meekly the kind of abuse Edward C. Carter had been subjected to. He succeeded. Calmly but firmly, he refused to answer Eastland's bullying, "When did you stop beating your wife?" questions. Holland, as contrasted with Carter, was in full command of his faculties.

Sen. Eastland: Did you know traitor Harry Dexter White?

Mr. Holland: May I ask, Mr. Chairman, if the Senator would state his question again?

Sen. Eastland: Did you know traitor Harry Dexter White?

Mr. Holland: I certainly cannot answer that question, Mr. Chairman, because I have no knowledge that Mr. White was a traitor.

Sen. Eastland: Did you know him?

Mr. Holland: No, I never met Mr. Harry White. I know he was invited to one IPR conference, but he did not come.

Sen. Eastland: The information is that he was at the head of an espionage ring in Washington. That is true, is it not, in the Government in Washington?

Mr. Holland: I have no evidence which would make me believe—

Sen. Eastland: You read that?

Mr. Holland: I have read the story, but do not consider it at all convincing, but, Mr. Chairman, may I say that the Senator said, "You know that is true, do you not?" I wish it to be understood that I do not know it is true.

Sen. Eastland: All right, Harry Dexter White was an active supporter of the institute, was he not?

Mr. Holland: Mr. Chairman—

Sen. Eastland: Look at me and answer my question.

Mr. Holland: No.[102]

Holland vigorously expressed the unfairness of months of anti-IPR publicity with no chance for the IPR to reply in the same forum. Despite the committee's reluctance to accept a prepared statement Holland had brought with him, he effectively maneuvered it into the record. Morris was particularly frustrated by Holland's stubborn defense of IPR. Morris's planned agenda for the day included fourteen points of inquiry. As adjournment approached, he complained that he had been able to cover only two of them.[103] The committee adjourned, expecting to call Holland back the next week. It was five months before they got to him again.

SISS now encountered heavy fallout from the revised Budenz testimony. Joseph Alsop was already in print furiously objecting to Budenz's claim about Vincent. Henry Wallace now joined the fray, demanding a chance to tell the committee that Budenz was a liar. The chance came October 17, 1951.

Alsop was afraid of what McCarran's crew of interrogators would do to Wallace, so he sought first-class counsel for the former vice president. Alsop explained what happened in a letter to Ben Hibbs of the *Saturday Evening Post* on October 10, 1951: "I and two lawyer friends of mine . . . called altogether 30 lawyers before we found one with guts enough to appear on Wallace's behalf. . . . I can hardly remember having been in a tighter spot; for without [George W.] Ball it was perfectly clear that Wallace would be destroyed by McCarran, and Wallace's destruction meant my own destruction, and the destruction also of the large group of in my opinion perfectly innocent men untruthfully accused by Budenz."[104] With George Ball's help, Wallace gave a good account of himself.

For all his volleyball mania and agricultural single-mindedness, Wallace knew something about world affairs. He may have been too trusting of the Soviet Union before the Korean War. He was too willing to let Communists staff much of his 1948 presidential campaign. But when Robert Morris began picking at him for pro-Soviet statements during World War II, when everybody from Roosevelt and MacArthur on down to the lowliest private fervently cheered Soviet resistance to the Wehrmacht, Wallace rubbed Morris's nose in the anachronism: 1951 was not 1944.[105] Goodwill toasts to Soviet arms were not subversive during World War II. Soviet toasts to American emissaries were not sly hints that those emissaries were covert Russian agents. Wallace, like Holland, stood up to SISS bullying and gave as good as he got.

One of the items Morris raised was Wallace's enthusiastic description of Magadan, a description that Elinor Lipper had ridiculed. Mandel read into the record some of Lipper's invective. Wallace did not quarrel with Lipper's claim that Magadan was part of the gulag, but he did quarrel with her castigation of him: "With regard to slave-labor camps in Magadan, she calls it Potemkin Villages . . . which is the correct name. She does not indicate any way in which I could have known that there was slave labor at Magadan. . . . I visited experiment station after experiment station, and collective farm after collective farm. Always it created a favorable and a free expression—well, Wendell Willkie testified in exactly the same way that they were a pioneer people just like the kind of people he had known in the Middle West back in the time of his boyhood; that Mike Cowles, who accompanied Wendell Willkie, testified they were a magnificent pioneer race."[106]

Before the Wallace party left Russia to return to the United States, the

Russians held a banquet for them, with many toasts. One of the Russians, S. A. Goglidze, offered a toast that Wallace reported in *Soviet Asia Mission:* "To Owen Lattimore and John Carter Vincent, American experts on China, on whom rests great responsibility for China's future." This remark, to SISS, established beyond a doubt that Lattimore and Vincent were serving the Kremlin. Wallace did not think so: "I may say Goglidze made three or four other toasts . . . it was one of those regular Russian situations where you toast everybody under the sun. . . . Incidentally, Goglidze did this very subversive thing. He toasted the reelection of Roosevelt. It was a terrible kind of thing to do, but he toasted his reelection."[107]

Mr. Morris:	Mr. Wallace, do you know what was meant by the expression "on whom rests great responsibility for China's future?"
Mr. Wallace:	I can't read his mind.
Mr. Morris:	You do not know what he meant?
Mr. Wallace:	Of course not. Who knows what anybody means at one of these toasting affairs?[108]

Morris went on and on about the toast; about an interview Wallace gave to the *Spotlight,* allegedly a Communist paper; and about the instructions Roosevelt gave Wallace.[109] When Morris wound down, Julian Sourwine began nitpicking. Wallace had made a speech in Seattle on his return from China. Did Wallace write out his Seattle speech by longhand? Was any of it written on a typewriter? Where? Was there a typewriter on the airplane? Did he have access to it? Did anyone else type any portions of this speech? Did Wallace give a copy to Roosevelt? Was it a clean copy or a messed-up draft? After twenty minutes of such trivia, Sourwine was getting nowhere. Wallace knew that neither Lattimore nor Vincent had anything to do with his Seattle speech, but he did not recall the stages of its construction.

Mr. Sourwine:	I don't mean to be unduly repetitious, but sometimes a memory will come back if you try to think about it. I am sure it must be as incredible to you as to us that you have no memory whatsoever of whether you saw a rough draft of the statement, or not.
Mr. Wallace:	I do not think it is incredible in the slightest, sir. I have been so active over so many years that with regard to a minor matter of this sort, I see nothing in-

credible about it. I would say it would be remarkable if I did remember. If you were in a similar position—I judge you are about the same age as I—and you were testifying, you would find yourself in the same situation.[110]

Finally the committee got around to Kunming. The fateful conference with Vincent and Alsop was discussed again, and Wallace now had a chance to express his opinion of Budenz and of SISS gullibility about Budenz's testimony. Wallace reviewed the background of the Chiang-Stilwell controversy, the setting of the Kunming conference, and the part played by Alsop and Vincent. He speculated that had Roosevelt followed his advice promptly, Chiang might have held on to power. As to the cable, Wallace said: "I refuse to believe that members of a great and powerful body, the most distinguished legislative body in the entire world, can possibly fall for testimony that it was following the Communist line to recommend that Stilwell be replaced by Wedemeyer in 1944. Never have I seen such unmitigated gall as that of this man [Budenz] in coming before a committee of the United States Senate to utter such nonsense. I say it is an affront to the dignity of a great and honorable body, over which I had the honor of presiding for four years."[111]

Wallace came out of this confrontation looking very good.

Alsop had also demanded a chance to appear before SISS. McCarran did not want to confront Alsop publicly and tried to confine him to an executive session, but the columnist insisted. He was scheduled the same day as Wallace. Since Morris and Sourwine took three and a half hours to grill Wallace, Alsop was postponed to the next day. Before the committee adjourned, Ferguson and Smith, the two senators present, agreed that Alsop would be permitted to "make a presentation of some length" to begin his hearing the next morning.[112]

Given the tenor of Alsop's attack on Budenz and the publicity coming from Lehman's use of Alsop's columns, it is not surprising that McCarran himself presided at the opening of Alsop's testimony October 18. The senator from Nevada was in an ugly mood. He still felt the sting of Lehman's accusation of subornation of perjury. And he had not been told that Alsop had permission to read a prepared statement. The fireworks started as soon as Alsop tried to explain how Stilwell had been such a friend of the Chinese Communists and how the Wallace-Vincent-Alsop recommendation that Stilwell be fired was a "profoundly anti-Communist act." Alsop began to quote Stilwell's anti-Chiang statements, but McCarran immediately interrupted. Why was he quoting Stilwell and reading a prepared statement? Alsop explained that Ferguson and Smith had told him he could. McCarran huffed and puffed:

Sen. McCarran:	Whether you are running this committee or the committee is running itself is a matter to be determined very shortly.
Mr. Alsop:	I am not trying to run the committee in the least.
Sen. McCarran:	I think you are. You are proposing to quote something now that isn't your statement at all. It is a hearsay matter. What are you going to do with that. Are you going to be cross-examined on it, and if so, how?
Mr. Alsop:	I am not going to quote anything that isn't a public document.
Sen. McCarran:	I understand you to say you are going to quote from someone who is not here.
Mr. Alsop:	I am going to quote from a series of public documents, Senator. [113]

McCarran's challenge clearly reveals the committee's double standard. Budenz's hearsay was quite acceptable, but when Alsop wanted to cite Stilwell's diary, that was illegitimate: "It is a hearsay matter." There was further fussing and fuming before McCarran finally gave in, not on the grounds that Alsop had any rights, but on the grounds that the Stilwell quotes were taken from a HUAC report. But the committee's invincible belief in Budenz continued. The hearsay nature of Budenz's testimony was forgotten, and phrases such as "if Mr. Budenz knew for a fact that he and Mr. Vincent were Communists" cropped up throughout the day.

Alsop's story of the Kunming cable got meticulous attention from Morris and Sourwine. SISS would not concede it even possible that Wallace and Vincent had acted to support Chiang. They did concede that Lattimore did not "guide" Wallace at Kunming (as, indeed, he could not have, having been disabled at the time). At the end, after Alsop had recommended that Budenz be indicted for perjury, Sourwine made one last effort to neutralize Alsop's testimony: "Mr. Alsop, do you see any difference between testifying that you do not believe a man and testifying that he is a liar?" Alsop replied, "The overwhelming evidence before the committee indicates he lied on this occasion." [114]

About an hour into the hearing McCarran had to leave and turned the gavel over to Willis Smith. Smith was a no-nonsense presiding officer, but he was not as hostile as McCarran was. The ugly confrontations ceased, and Alsop was able to present his case with some decorum. In fact, there is some evidence that Alsop began to persuade Smith that Budenz was indeed a liar. Alsop wrote Smith the day after the hearing thanking him for being fair, requesting a chance to discuss Budenz with him privately, and attacking Robert Morris as the éminence grise behind the committee's coddling of Budenz. This was the first of several exchanges of letters between Smith and Alsop. Smith responded cordially to Alsop's initiative, and in a second letter of October 23 Alsop again urged Smith to meet with him and talk the matter over face-to-face. He wrote Smith, "I find myself terrified by the new acceptance among us of these professional informers, with their unsupported and interested accusations. If honest men of every political coloring do not rise up to oppose this new tendency, I hardly know where we may end." [115]

In a third letter, dated November 1, Alsop stated that if Morris continued in the subcommittee's employ and Budenz continued in the subcommittee's good graces, "I shall consider it a serious reflection on the subcommittee." [116] Alsop and Smith did meet later in Washington. If Smith was persuaded, he failed to move the subcommittee: Morris continued as counsel; Budenz remained the paragon of truth.

In 1981, reflecting on his activities thirty years earlier, Alsop wrote, "I think back on the campaign of my brother and myself which began with the attempt to expose Louis Budenz, as one of the high points of my long career as a reporter. Although Budenz had been given the front page, my charging him with perjury and offering the strongest supporting evidence was held to deserve no more than three paragraphs in the *New York Times*. I also begged Reston of the *Times* to take over the hired perjurers story, with Stew and me merely supporting the *Times*. He told me solemnly that he did not think it 'timely.' But Stew and I kept after the hired perjurers all the same, and we got them dismissed in the end because Paul Crouch [a prominent ex-Communist witness] went too far in a Philadelphia hearing and was actually convicted of perjury." [117]

After its bruising confrontations with Wallace and Alsop, SISS took a breather. Admiral Charles "Savvy" Cooke, a close friend of Kohlberg and a Chiang supporter, came in for some mutual admiration society palaver on October 19. Then the committee recessed for three months. The next witness, on January 24, 1952, was John Carter Vincent.

While the inquisition was being organized in the halls of Congress during the summer of 1951, a powerful drama involving Lattimore and the

future of Tibet transpired out of public notice. Lattimore was not a Tibetan scholar, but the Mongols he championed were Lama Buddhists, and
Tibet was the seat of their religion. The Dilowa had lived in Tibet several
years after the war and was close to the Dalai Lama and the Dalai's elder
brother, the Takster Lama. From the Dilowa, Lattimore knew of the
manuscript riches of Tibetan monasteries, hence his 1949 effort to interest
the Library of Congress in obtaining these manuscripts before the Chinese
Communists took over that exotic land.

The fourteenth Dalai Lama was young and had assumed full powers
only in 1950 after a ten-year regency. The Chinese invaded in October of
that year, and the Tibetans were forced to sign an agreement with the
People's Republic in May 1951. But the situation was still obscure; the
Dalai Lama's advisers were divided over the prospects of retaining real
autonomy, some believing that the Dalai should go into exile, others believing that he should remain in Tibet and try to work under the Chinese.
It was this dilemma that motivated a trip by the Takster Lama to the
United States in summer 1951. The Dalai was living in a remote monastery on the Indian border; he wanted his brother, among other things, to
consult the Dilowa and Lattimore as to whether he should return to Lhasa
or flee to India.

The United States government was indifferent to the fate of the Tibetan
libraries but quite willing to embarrass the Chinese Communists by clandestine support of Tibetan independence. This was the CIA's province; its
newly created front, the Committee for a Free Asia (CFA), flew the Takster Lama to the United States.[118]

The Takster Lama had never been out of Tibet and spoke no English.
CFA obtained the services of Major Robert B. Ekvall, son of a missionary
who had served on the Tibetan border, fluent in Tibetan, and a former
Army Intelligence officer during and after the war, to take charge of the
Takster's American sojourn.

Ekvall was known to the Lattimores. He had contemplated leaving the
army to work with Lattimore's Central Asian seminar in 1946, and Ekvall
and his wife spent a weekend with the Lattimores in Baltimore. Lattimore
liked Ekvall and encouraged him to enroll at Johns Hopkins, but the army
persuaded Ekvall to reenlist.[119]

When the Takster Lama arrived in the United States, Ekvall brought
him immediately to Washington. The Dilowa, however, was then in
Berkeley, and Ekvall frustrated all of the Takster's attempts to see the
Dilowa or Lattimore. As the Takster reported in a letter to the Dilowa,
who in turn wrote Lattimore, Ekvall said, "It would be a good thing for

you not to talk to the Dilowa Hutukhtu about the affairs of the Dalai
Lama on which you have come. Also, Lattimore is no good." The Takster
was greatly upset; Lattimore was furious.[120]

On July 23, 1951, Lattimore wrote a long letter to Ekvall. It was restrained but firm. After reviewing the Dilowa's history, his flight from
Outer Mongolia after the Communists tried him, his wartime service with
Chiang Kai-shek, his residence in Lhasa, his coming to the United States
in 1949, and his frustration at being unable to see the Takster, Lattimore
wrote:

> The Dilowa Hutukhtu was recognized in Tibet as the head of the rather
> large community of Mongol exiles and refugees from Outer and Inner
> Mongolia. When the Chinese Communists invaded Tibet the Dilowa
> Hutukhtu was in correspondence (as he still is), with Mongol Lama
> disciples of his in Kalimpong, on the India-Tibet frontier. Through cor-
> respondence forwarded by them, he is also in unbroken contact with
> the Dalai Lama personally and with certain of the elder statesmen of
> Tibet, such as Tsarong Shape. His advice and counsel is valued by them.
>
> The Dilowa Hutukhtu's sole concern with Tibet and its politics is the
> preservation and continuity of his religion. He has feared that if a Chinese
> Communist "soft policy" should tempt the advisers of the Dalai Lama
> to urge the Dalai Lama to return to Lhasa, all would be lost. He is sure,
> from his own experience in Outer Mongolia, that it would only be a
> matter of time until the church would be dispossessed, the Dalai Lama
> deposed or disposed of in one way or another, and the "reincarnation"
> of a successor to the Dalai Lama prohibited. The branch of the Buddhist
> religion of which the Dalai Lama is head and the Dilowa Hutukhtu a
> distinguished prelate would then be extinguished in the world. Rather
> than let this happen, the Dilowa Hutukhtu is convinced that the Dalai
> Lama should go into exile, there to maintain at least a spark of the
> eternal flame of his religion. . . .
>
> It would be a tragedy if, because of his personal friendship with me,
> the Dilowa Hutukhtu should be involved in the personal vilification and
> denigration to which I have been subjected and if, as a consequence,
> there should be sown in the minds of the Tibetans doubts and suspi-
> cions that their pathetic national tragedy is being wantonly subjected
> to mishandling, through no fault of their own, by contamination with
> the most corrupt and shameful, and to them obscure and frightening,
> side of American politics.[121]

Ekvall responded the next day. The Takster's inability to see the Dilowa, he said, was due to ill health. The Takster was in the hospital but
would receive the Dilowa as soon as he was able.

Ekvall eventually made good on his promise. Unfortunately, by then
the moment of truth had passed. The Dalai Lama returned to Lhasa from
his mountain hideout near the Indian border and began the uneasy coexistence with the People's Republic of China that ended in 1959 with the
Tibetan uprising and the Dalai Lama's escape to India.

In December 1951, when the Dilowa was back in Baltimore, Ekvall let
the Takster visit Lattimore. Eleanor Lattimore reported the visit in a letter
to the Robert LeMoyne Barretts December 10:

> We didn't hear anything more for a long time, but a week or so ago we
> had a phone call from Ekvall saying that the Takster Lama wished to
> call on us. He and a disciple and a keeper (doubtless from Central In-
> telligence) turned up and we gave a luncheon for them. Then in a few
> days Dilowa told us Takster and his disciple would like to come for a
> weekend. So last weekend we had the three lamas here (two Living
> Buddhas in one house!) It was lots of fun. Dilowa says this means
> Takster has declared his independence. But of course it's too late now
> to make any difference. One could certainly argue that if it hadn't been
> for McCarthy the Dalai Lama might not have gone back to Tibet and
> the Lama Buddhist religion, and a link between Tibet and the West,
> might have been preserved.[122]

Nineteen fifty had been a disastrous year for the Lattimores. Abe Fortas, writing to a friend who had inquired about how things were going,
said, "The McCarthy charges resulted in a serious financial drain. We
were forced to get reimbursement from Lattimore for out-of-pocket expenses such as mimeographing and long distance telephone calls, and this
ran into a substantial sum of money. We did not, as you know, charge
him a fee. The Lattimores incurred expenses, on the whole, which for
them were quite staggering. . . . The most serious trouble has been the
spiritual and emotional drain upon these really fine Americans. . . . this
savage attack has caused both of them to age perceptibly."[123]

A year later they had spent more and aged more. Lecture invitations
had dried up: in 1949 Lattimore had more than a hundred; in all of 1951,
only three. There were now almost no social invitations in Baltimore since
people were afraid to be seen with them. With the hiatus in SISS activities
after October 1951, Lattimore began to think about accepting standing
invitations he had to lecture to the Royal Geographical Society and the
Royal Central Asian Society in London. As Eleanor wrote the Barretts,
"We thought that this Christmas would be a good time to get away and
get a breath of fresh air before McCarran started up again."[124] Lattimore

wrote the two societies in London, got enthusiastic responses, and applied for passports in late November.

Ruth Shipley presided over the passport barony. She was ferociously anti-Lattimore, convinced that Budenz and Barmine had told the truth, and determined to apply the McCarran Act of 1950, which had a clause saying, "It shall be unlawful for any officer or employee of the United States to issue a passport to, or renew the passport of, any individual knowing or having reason to believe that such individual is a member of such organization [World Communist movement]." On December 6, 1951, Shipley wrote an eleven-page letter to her superior saying that Lattimore's passport request should be denied.[125]

There followed a bitter battle within the State Department. Senior officers, including Chief of Security Carlisle Humelsine, Undersecretary James Webb, and Counselor Charles "Chip" Bohlen, disagreed. They thought Lattimore was not a danger to the security of the country and should be allowed to lecture in London. Shipley was overruled; the Lattimores got their passports December 17.[126] It was one of the few battles Shipley lost.

While waiting for their passports, and not anticipating that harassment from McCarran would last indefinitely, Lattimore indulged another fancy. In fall 1951 Delhi University invited him to lecture there during the next academic year. Delhi had no funds, but the Fulbright program had brought them many prominent American scholars. Wishing to avoid embarrassment, Delhi consulted the Fulbright committees in India and Washington; they were told that if Lattimore applied on his own, he might be turned down, but if the Indian government made an official request, it would be honored. Nehru himself wrote the letter on behalf of his government; the American embassy in Delhi endorsed the request. It was turned down by the State Department. Eleanor reported to the Barretts, "The Indians are furious and consider it an affront to them, and it's all very embarrassing. I suppose we should know better than to make these foolish plans. But the whole situation is so unreal and fantastic that we just can't make ourselves feel like lepers."[127]

But the British lectures were still on. Before the Lattimores left for London, there were two ominous developments. John Service was fired on December 13, and John Carter Vincent began yet another State Department loyalty-security hearing on December 17. Lattimore was connected with both men.

The Service dismissal sent shock waves throughout the State Department. He had been examined, and cleared, six times; now the Civil Service Commission Loyalty Review Board, considering the most recent State

Department clearance, recommended to Secretary Acheson that Service be fired. For the public record, the reason given for the reversal was a reconsideration of the *Amerasia* case. But the board was lying. Its decision against Service was based on the faked reports from the Chinese Nationalist government in Taipei. McCarthy partially gave away this lie in a speech on January 15, 1952, when he said that Service "was known to have shared living quarters with a 'Soviet espionage agent.' " William S. White, writing in the *New York Times* after Service was fired, concluded accurately that the Service firing had "a significant meaning in partisan politics: a kind of vindication for Mr. McCarthy." [128]

Owen and Eleanor Lattimore arrived in the refreshingly calm climate of the British Isles in late December. The British, who viewed McCarthy as insane and the accusations against Lattimore as hallucinations, received them warmly. Had he chosen to, Lattimore could easily have ignited British attacks on McCarthy and followers. The American embassy in London feared just such a development and followed Lattimore's activities. The embassy report on Lattimore's visit eventually reached the FBI, which in turn forwarded it to the Justice Department. One paragraph of this report was especially revealing:

> In general, Mr. Lattimore attempted to avoid discussion of current Far Eastern problems and preferred to confine his lectures to his field of specialization, the nomadic tribes of Asia. . . . [He] explained privately to English friends that he would prefer not to talk on China policy because he was critical of American policy (on grounds that it is tending to isolate the Chinese Communists and to force them into greater dependence on the Soviet Union) and he was loath, as an American citizen traveling abroad to criticize his Government's policy. He has stated that his embarrassment in this regard is the deeper because of the fact that, with this one exception, he is wholeheartedly in support of American institutions and American policies. Perhaps it would be well to report a specific question put to him at Chatham House by Sir John Pratt, the well-known British fellow-traveler, whose ardent support of the Communist cause in Korea has proven so embarrassing for the British Government. At the end of Mr. Lattimore's lecture Sir John rose from his chair from among the audience and asked the following weighted question: "Do you, Mr. Lattimore, know of a single intelligent and well-informed American who does not believe that the *South* Koreans began the fighting?" Mr. Lattimore is said to have hesitated a moment for emphasis and to have replied: "Sir John, I do not know of a single intelligent and well-informed American who does not believe that the *North* Koreans began the fighting." (Italics in original) [129]

By any standard, Lattimore's 1952 tour of England was restrained and judicious. This restraint was due partly to his belief that one does not wash the family linen before foreign publics, but it was partly because he did support American policy except in Asia. But there was another reason: the venue was conducive to moderation. Lattimore himself had not changed; the feisty combatant of the Tydings hearings still existed beneath the calm exterior. When he returned to an overheated Washington, where his good friend John Carter Vincent faced an SISS inquisition, Lattimore's outrage was rekindled.

CHAPTER TWENTY-TWO

Venom: Twelve Days with SISS

By the time SISS adjourned in the fall of 1951, the *New York Times* was among those observers skeptical about McCarran's boasts of fairness and objectivity. That paper observed, in an editorial, that it was one thing to criticize China policy but quite another to assert that Communists in the IPR were responsible for that policy: "Furthermore, the committee has permitted the loyalty of various individuals again to be impugned without giving them the opportunity to reply immediately and in public."[1]

William S. White, writing in the *Times* shortly after Senate Judiciary killed the Nimitz commission, observed of SISS, "That group has become incomparably the most powerful of all, as far as Congress is concerned, in raising the Communist issue against the White House." White gave the committee credit for some amenities, such as no leaks from executive sessions, but concluded, "It remains the opinion of many observers, however, that the subcommittee suffers in objectivity because all of its members are far to the right of the Administration, and therefore the ordinary interplay of different opinions and different interpretations is not at work here."[2]

The American Civil Liberties Union did not distinguish itself in the Lattimore case.[3] Nonetheless, the ACLU did protest McCarran's procedure. Patrick Murphy Malin, ACLU executive director, in a letter to the *Times* printed November 16, 1951, said, "As we informed Senator McCarran on October 26, his committee has, to date, refused to permit counsel for the IPR to cross-examine witnesses against it and to have access to the IPR files, which are now in the committee's exclusive custody. . . . The right to cross-examine one's accuser is essential to fair procedure and should cut across all political or partisan lines."[4]

These opinions hostile to McCarran did not lessen the atmosphere of fear and intimidation. Few of the many groups that had invited Lattimore to speak before 1950 were willing to have him now. He did get an occasional audience; when he opened the 1951 season at the Yale Law School Forum on October 22, the auditorium was packed to the doors, and a loudspeaker carried his address to an overflow room. Lattimore's talk dealt mostly with the substance of U.S. Asian policy, but in response to questions he commented on the McCarthy-McCarran crusade: "America is a country in which democracy is so sound, so deeply rooted, that in spite of the temporary hysteria and fear, we shall pull through because the people will pull us through."[5] It was a particularly inaccurate prophecy. The people, like the Congress, would gladly have thrown Lattimore to the wolves. The judicial system pulled him through.

At the time, however, Lattimore sought an opportunity to confront the witch-hunters. He had fumed through the testimony of a dozen hostile witnesses, answering their front-page publicity with press releases of his own, which, if reported at all, were buried in the back pages (except in the *Baltimore Sun*, which gave him good coverage). On November 6, 1951, he wrote McCarran:

> It has repeatedly been reported in the press that your subcommittee of the Senate Judiciary Committee has promised that I will be given an opportunity to refute publicly the false and slanderous allegations that have been made about me before your subcommittee. Months have now gone by without my being given this opportunity, and I am now informed that your subcommittee will hold no more public hearings until January. This long delay greatly increases the injury done to me.
>
> I trust that you will notify me at an early date when I can expect to have a public hearing. It will, of course, take me at least a week to make arrangements and preparation for the hearing, and I should therefore appreciate as much advance notice as possible.[6]

McCarran replied curtly that Lattimore would be heard "at the convenience of the committee" and that it would indeed not be before January.

SISS staff kept busy despite the abeyance of the hearings. One of the tipsters feeding Ben Mandel claimed that a highly revealing report on Lattimore had been written by a Brigadier Menzie of the British Army to the U.S. Army in 1943. Mandel tried hard to obtain such a report from the Secretary of Defense; that office searched extensively and denied that such a report was in its files.[7] Mandel thought Army was stonewalling. He called the FBI in on his search, hoping they could move the military bureaucracy. FBI agent L.L. Laughlin reported to FBI headquarters on

November 28, 1951: "Mr. Mandel stated that he had received information from an authoritative source, which he described as 'the best,' indicating that Brigadier Menzie delivered to the Pentagon in 1943 an elaborate report on Owen Lattimore. Mandel advised that according to his information, Lattimore originally had been working for the British but he double-crossed them and when they found out about it the British turned him in to the American authorities, at which time the elaborate report in question allegedly was furnished to the Pentagon. Mandel described this report as containing 'a gold mine of information' which he was quite anxious to get hold of."[8]

The bureau was puzzled. They had implored Army for *everything* in its files about Lattimore. They checked again and satisfied themselves that there was no Menzie report. Six of the eight pages of the Belmont to Ladd letter burying the Menzie phantom are still denied in the interests of national security.[9]

Don Surine and Robert Morris chased the next will-o'-the-wisp. In August 1950 Surine contacted the FBI about an allegation that Lattimore had once reported the theft of a pair of field glasses from his car while parked in New York City. These were no ordinary field glasses; they were Russian made, embossed with the hammer and sickle. The bureau had checked out this story in 1950; the New York Police Department (NYPD) could find no record of this alleged theft.[10] Surine turned the tip over to Morris when SISS started operations.

On August 30, 1951, Morris wrote NYPD asking for another check of their records. Sure enough, the incident was there, classified as a "loss" instead of a "theft." But Morris did not know what to do with this new intelligence. Plaintively, he wrote Lou Nichols on January 14, 1952, enclosing the NYPD report: "You probably have done some work on the within matter. If there is anything that we can learn on it I would appreciate it." Several Lattimore case officers considered the "loss" of Lattimore's field glasses and reported, "In view of the fact that he [Lattimore] has advised the Bureau that, on at least two occasions, he traveled in the Soviet Union, the last time in 1944, his possession of these field glasses seems to be logical and it is not believed that an interview with him on this point would be productive." The bureau told Morris to forget it.[11]

McCarran, before he went off to Nevada for a winter break, gave *U.S. News and World Report* an interview. Seven pages of that magazine for November 16, 1951, carried his ringing endorsement of SISS, his complete faith in Budenz and other friendly witnesses, and an interim report on what SISS had concluded about IPR:

McCarran: The IPR originally was an organization with laudable motives. It was taken over by Communist design and made a vehicle for attempted control and conditioning of American thinking and American policy with respect to the Far East. It was also used for espionage purposes to collect and channel information of interest or value to the Russian Communists.

Q: Was that during the war?

McCarran: During the war and before the war. It has always been the thought of the Kremlin to control Asia. They have the same thought with reference to India today. They are going to use many of the same methods on India that they used on Asia, and they're going to use some of the same people as much as they can. I take that as a fact, on the basis of information from a number of sources. They always intended to get into Asia. . . . That plan has been, to a certain extent, accomplished. Central Asia, continental China, is Communist today. You've got to come to the conclusion that today Communist China is the vassal of the Kremlin. There is no doubt in my mind at all as to that.[12]

This hardly sounded like an "interim" report. McCarran had made up his mind. the IPR was guilty as charged, and McCarran had already done his best to see that "the same people" who delivered China to the Russians were not going to be free to run around the globe as Communist agents and deliver India to the Russians. His Internal Security Act of 1950 took care of that.

When SISS got going again in January 1952, John Carter Vincent was the first witness. The committee heard him in executive session January 24–26 and in public session January 30–31 and February 1–2. Vincent was the assigned target of Senator Homer Ferguson; in four of Vincent's seven appearances Ferguson was the only committee member present. As SISS hearings for IPR-tainted witnesses went, Vincent's was mild. Ferguson and Sourwine divided the questioning and were gentlemanly and polite. Vincent was courteous and accommodating. Only one sharp exchange occurred, when Vincent accused Sourwine of knowingly making a false inference.[13]

The SISS objective was clearly to use State Department and IPR documents to trap Vincent into making false statements. Vincent's widow told

Gary May in 1971 that Ferguson said in her hearing during a committee recess, "Come along to the hearing today. We're going to get Vincent on perjury."[14]

There were no revelations, and no minds changed, during these seven days. Vincent, a conservative and dignified Southern Baptist, was as innocent of communism as was the angel Gabriel. But Ferguson thought otherwise, and the rock-bottom China lobby creed he took into the hearings was not shaken in the slightest by Vincent's testimony. Ferguson believed that the Chinese Communist party was irrevocably subservient to the Kremlin; that Service had committed espionage and that Vincent shared that guilt by contributing fifty dollars to Service's defense fund; that Henry Wallace, with Vincent's guidance, had attempted to bring down Chiang by foisting General Wedemeyer off on him; that Dooman was accurate in claiming that State Department directives to General Mac-Arthur had destroyed the capitalist class of Japan; and that Lattimore—always coming back to Lattimore, through hours of questioning—had always followed the Communist line, yet Vincent had wanted Lattimore appointed as a State Department adviser.

Sitting at the committee table with his stack of documents, Sourwine demanded that Vincent recall details of minor meetings, conferences, dinners, decision sessions, even the furniture in the room where he interviewed a Chinese personage eight years earlier. Vincent had had significant matters on his mind as he administered the China and Far Eastern desks, accompanied the vice president to Asia and the secretary of state to Potsdam, and carried out the duties of a Foreign Service Officer Class One. Yet Sourwine chastised him for not remembering whether he had sent his regards to Madame Sun Yat-sen via Mrs. Edward C. Carter in June 1944. Ferguson picked up this memory lapse:

> *Sen. Ferguson:* Mr. Vincent, do you have the same difficulty in your work in the State Department, advising with other officers, of remembering things that have happened as you have here on the witness stand?
>
> *Mr. Vincent:* If it is a matter of going back—
>
> *Sen. Ferguson:* Are you as uncertain in your work there about what has happened as you are here?
>
> *Mr. Vincent:* Senator, this all happened 7 or 8 years ago.
>
> *Sen. Ferguson:* Can you answer that question?
>
> *Sen. McCarran:* You better answer that question.

Sen. Ferguson:	It is necessary for a foreign officer and a diplomat, such as you are, to remember things for 7 years, is it not? You have to keep them all in mind?
Mr. Vincent:	These incidents here, as I say, I do not recall. . . .
Sen. Ferguson:	I am asking. Are you usually in as much doubt?
Sen. McCarran:	I think that is a simple question and easily understood. Why do you not answer it?
Mr. Vincent:	If they were matters which I considered of as little importance as some of these things brought forward here, I would be in the same degree of doubt.[15]

At the end, Ferguson, apparently with serious intent, asked, "Do you believe it was a fair hearing?" Vincent, for the first time, lied: "Yes, sir."[16]

After Vincent, the SISS script called for a run of "Fifth Amendment Communists." Not all of those now called had been Communists, but several invoked the Fifth Amendment on principle, believing that Congress had no right to inquire into their political beliefs. There were ten of these minor witnesses, only three of whom had any significant relationship with the IPR. The others had attended a conference, had written an article, or had been ordinary dues-paying members. Most of them had never met Lattimore.

SISS learned nothing from them. When the FBI reviewed these transcripts, Branigan found that "any pertinent data contained therein" was already in bureau files.[17] Most of these witnesses, possibly all, were heard first in executive session, so the committee knew it would learn nothing from them. But it did "establish a record": here were ten subversives, unwilling to admit their past (and present) misdeeds, all connected in some way with the IPR.

Interspersed in the series of Fifth Amendment takers was one significant witness, Nicholas Poppe, also brought in to skewer Lattimore.

Poppe had been professor of Oriental languages in Leningrad, 1925–41, and head of the Mongolian department of the Soviet Academy of Sciences. Though he claimed not to have been a Party member, he had been trusted enough to be allowed access to Mongolia. When Hitler invaded the Soviet Union, Poppe moved to the Karachai region in the Caucasus, teaching in a pedagogical institute. When German troops reached Karachai, Poppe defected and helped the Germans set up a quisling government.[18] This government immediately appropriated all Jewish property and soon rounded up the Jews in the area for gassing. Poppe's account has it that he was sympathetic to the Jews and that he saved the lives of a small mountain tribe (the Tats) who were ethnic Iranians but practiced the Jewish faith. Whatever his actions in the Caucasus, he was soon brought to Berlin to work in the infamous SS Wannsee Institute. Poppe claimed that at Wannsee he worked exclusively on Mongolian and Siberian intelligence and did not contribute to SS depradations in German-occupied areas.

After the war Poppe attached himself first to British, then to American intelligence units. He was a hot property; the Russians wanted him for war crimes. But by 1947 the United States was actively seeking former Nazi experts on the Soviet Union; Talcott Parsons of Harvard's Russian Research Center pressed the State Department to have Poppe brought to this country. In May 1949 Parsons succeeded, but Harvard administrators refused to hire Poppe. The University of Washington in Seattle took him on, and he spent the rest of his career there as professor of Far Eastern languages.[19]

When he was attempting to secure academic sponsorship for emigration to the United States, Poppe had sought the assistance of Owen Lattimore. Lattimore knew of Poppe's work for the Nazis and refused to endorse him.[20] George Taylor, Poppe's superior at Seattle and an early witness before SISS, introduced Mandel to Poppe. Mandel was delighted to learn of Poppe's animus against Lattimore and arranged to have him testify on February 12, 1952.

Poppe's testimony was somewhat disappointing to SISS. Poppe denigrated the *Soviet World Atlas* (about which Carter and other IPR officers had been ecstatic and which Lattimore had reviewed favorably) and claimed that all the Soviet officials who briefly joined IPR in the 1930s were espionage agents. As to Lattimore, Poppe praised *Mongols of Manchuria* and *Inner Asian Frontiers of China* but thought Lattimore's treatment of the Mongolian People's Republic (MPR) in *Solution in Asia* was wrong. The MPR was not a progressive country, and Lattimore downplayed the "internal troubles" of 1932, which Poppe said constituted an "overt revolt of the entire population." Thus, Lattimore's picture of the MPR was not scholarly.[21]

Senator Arthur Watkins, the only committee member present, drew him out:

Sen. Watkins: Then he would be putting into his books the Soviet line?

Mr. Poppe: Yes, of course, and even involuntarily.

Sen. Watkins:	Do you mean that he did not do it purposely?
Mr. Poppe:	No; I don't know how, but I only say that one who takes his information always from only those papers, he depends greatly upon the ideas expressed in them, so I don't know whether purposely or not.
Sen. Watkins:	It would give the American people, then, who read the books, a distorted, a completely distorted picture of what was going on?
Mr. Poppe:	Yes, a distorted picture.[22]

But Poppe refused to be pushed into saying that Lattimore was ideologically motivated; he was just ill informed. Watkins dropped the subject.

Poppe, in his 1983 *Reminiscences*, is ambivalent about Lattimore. He is bitter that Lattimore pointed out publicly his work for the Nazi SS, but he acknowledges that the Lattimore case "reminded me of what I had witnessed on a larger scale in the Soviet Union. . . . His case should never have happened because under the provisions of the Constitution of the United States, Lattimore had the right to express any opinions, even controversial ones."[23]

Having put into the record, and the headlines, a long series of anti-Lattimore testimony, SISS was finally ready for its chief target. Between February 26 and March 21, 1952, SISS engaged Owen Lattimore in twelve days of acrimonious interrogation. It was the longest appearance of a single witness before any congressional inquiry up to that time. And it was front-page news.

Whether McCarran at this time believed Lattimore was the "one being" he had told Biltz about as directing the whole Communist movement in the United States we do not know. Certainly Lattimore was the arch-heretic; as such, his appearance required the presence of the arch-inquisitor. McCarran himself was present for the entire Lattimore run, and there were no one-man hearings. A majority of the subcommittee was present each day; on six of the twelve days all members were present except Eastland. McCarthy attended seven times.

Writers who later held that the SISS hearings were "conscientious and productive" (H. Bradford Westerfield) or "sober and devastatingly factual" (James Rorty and Moshe Decter) cannot have read the transcripts. The Lattimore hearings were nothing but blatant harassment, what Victor Navasky calls a degradation ceremony.[24] Had the committee wanted to hear both sides fairly, they would not have held off giving Lattimore a public hearing to challenge Budenz for six months, nor would they have allowed twelve other hostile witnesses to appear without rebuttal in the same forum. The timing alone indicates bias.

So does the contrast between the committee's coddling of anti-Lattimore witnesses, the failure even to acknowledge challenges to their credibility, compared with its bruising confrontation of Lattimore. Lattimore himself put it well: "One of the most shocking things that has happened in the proceedings is that not one of the witnesses against me has ever been asked in examination or cross-examination a question that would test his motives or his reliability."[25]

Further, SISS ignored all the evidence favorable to Lattimore that had been developed in the Tydings hearings, much of which had been reported in the press. This evidence was known to Morris, who had been minority counsel during the Tydings hearings. The entire corpus of evidence on the basis of which Tydings concluded that McCarthy's charges were fraudulent was totally disregarded. The biased selection of Asian "experts" called by McCarran has already been mentioned.

For seven of Lattimore's twelve days of testimony, Abe Fortas accompanied him as counsel; on five days, Thurman Arnold substituted. Fortas and Arnold were two of Washington's outstanding attorneys; the committee treated them like dirt. McCarran had been hard on counsel for IPR witnesses from the beginning. He had warned Edward C. Carter's counsel on opening day in July 1951: "Any witness called here may have the privilege of being accompanied and advised by counsel of his choice; but witnesses' counsel will not be permitted to testify nor to ask questions. This is not a trial, but an inquiry, and we intend to proceed in an orderly way." But when Carter's counsel suggested a clarification to Carter, McCarran shut him up peremptorily. Fortas and Arnold got the same treatment.

On the first day of Lattimore's hearing a contretemps developed during which Willis Smith defended the committee's treatment of anti-IPR witnesses on an unusual basis:

> *Sen. Smith:* Do you understand that this is a trial or is it in the nature of a grand jury procedure? You know the difference?
>
> *Mr. Lattimore:* I am sorry I don't.
>
> *Sen. Smith:* You know that a grand jury proceeding is one in which you are trying to get facts on which to base a charge. This is a grand jury. In a trial you say, "This man is accused of being guilty. Is he innocent or guilty?"

> You see a distinction, I know, between these. You understand that this was an inquiry in the nature of a grand jury proceeding to see what are the facts on which charges might be based.[26]

Shortly after this exchange, Lattimore protested that his lawyer was unable to counsel him:

Mr. Lattimore: I am sitting here under conditions in which my own lawyer is not allowed to tender advice to me while I am asked rather complicated questions involving legal points which might be pitfalls for me, to which I have to reply to the best of my ability.

Sen. O'Conor: Mr. Lattimore, is that not begging the question? You were advised, and if you were not advised, you are now, that on any of these so-called complicated questions if you are unable to comprehend them you have the right to consult with your counsel. Why do you give the impression in the record that you are being deprived of the right to consultation with counsel?

Mr. Lattimore: Senator, my counsel is not allowed to intervene at any time.

Sen. O'Conor: You are allowed to consult him.

Mr. Lattimore: At any time he thinks I may need advice and I in my ignorance may be at the most need of advice at any moment—

Sen. O'Conor: It is evident that you know when you need advice, and you know better than anybody else when you need it. . . .

Mr. Fortas: I wish to address myself to this program that the distinguished Senator Smith raised—that is, about procedure. It is, after all, a legal question. It is very difficult for a lawyer to sit here and hear statements that affect the interest of his client and to be in a position where he can't say anything. I am sure that all of you distinguished gentlemen who are lawyers appreciate that.

Now as to Mr. Lattimore's consulting with me, he is sitting here under an intense barrage of questions from one, two, three, four, five distinguished gentlemen, and his concentration is intense upon those questions, and he obviously can't be expected to know

> when to consult counsel. Now of course I have a very
> fundamental difference of opinion with Senator Smith
> as to the purpose of a Senate investigation. I believe
> that the purpose of a Senate investigation is to de-
> velop the facts, both sides of the facts, impartially and
> fairly. . . . But it does seem to me that when Mr.
> Lattimore is confronted with a choice as to whether
> this is a grand jury or a petty jury proceeding he is
> obviously at a serious disadvantage. . . . I beg your
> pardon, Senator, for getting emotional about this, but
> I do believe that it should be said.[27]

Wasted effort. O'Conor simply reiterated that Fortas "has the right to
advise with [Lattimore] at any time."

Fortas may have rejected Smith's grand jury analogy, but it was in
many ways apt. And the committee held firm to its determination that
Fortas was not to intervene, to protest the wording of a question, or to
warn his client of a booby trap.

There was a further prohibition on Lattimore's counsel. On February
28 Ferguson asked Lattimore if he had "ever worked for any government
other than the United States." Lattimore had worked for Chiang Kai-
shek, but he was not sure whether that meant working for the government of the Republic of China.

Mr. Lattimore:	May I qualify that answer, Senator? I worked for Chiang Kai-shek.
Sen. O'Conor:	The question is as to any other government. It admits of a direct answer: You were or you were not. And if you were, and desire to make any explanation, that is perfectly in order. But you ought to answer the question directly first.
Mr. Lattimore:	I don't think I can, Senator. I want to ask for the opinion of you gentlemen on this subject. I was in the employ of Chiang Kai-shek, who was at the head—
Sen. Ferguson:	Please answer: Were you or were you not in the employ of any other government?
Mr. Fortas:	Point of order.
Sen. McCarran:	You have no right to ask for a point of order. Just a minute, Mr. Chairman [O'Conor was temporarily serving as chairman]. Just a minute. I object to that way of proceeding. This gentleman has no right to ask for a point of order, and he is no part of this body.

Mr. Lattimore:	Let me rephrase the beginning of my reply. I do not believe—
Sen. McCarran:	Just a moment.
Sen. O'Conor:	Just a second, Mr. Lattimore. The question is one which, in the opinion of the Chair, does admit of a direct answer. He either was or was not. Now, he can make any explanation he desires after he has answered the question.
Sen. McCarran:	Mr. Chairman, just a second, before that goes any farther. I advised this gentleman when he first came in here of what his province would be. Now, that was no part of it, your breaking in with any point of order. Now, if you do that again, you are going to be excluded from this committee.
Mr. Fortas:	That is up to you.
Sen. McCarran:	That is all right, and don't do it again.
Mr. Fortas:	That is up to you.
Sen. McCarran:	I will certainly do it.
Mr. Fortas:	You have the power.[28]

Neither Fortas nor Arnold was actually ejected, despite occasional protests at McCarran's constant bullying. McCarran simply slapped them down again.

But the full force of McCarran's spleen was directed at the witness. Lattimore began his appearance by reading a fifty-page defense of his career and attack on his accusers. "Senators, I have asked for this public hearing because your proceedings have resulted in serious damage to my reputation as an objective scholar and patriotic citizen, to the Institute of Pacific Relations with which I have been connected, and to our Government's Foreign Service personnel and the conduct of its foreign policy."[29] After this first sentence Sourwine interrupted, and the acrimony began. Sourwine was spelled by McCarran, O'Conor, Smith, Ferguson, Jenner, and Watkins. For three days Lattimore tried to read his statement; he was interrupted and challenged after almost every sentence.

One of Lattimore's caustic remarks was in response to a demand that he name the members of the China lobby, on which he blamed much of IPR's troubles. He named Kohlberg, William Goodwin, and William Knowland (Republican from California), whom he called "The Senator from Formosa." This remark set off howls of outrage. Ferguson blustered, "That is a Communist line, is it not, 'the Senator from Formosa?'" Lattimore said no: he had read it in the newspapers, but he did not read

Communist papers. There followed ten minutes of badgering for Lattimore to come up with a specific paper and issue where he had read it. Finally Fortas intervened, "Can you give this witness a rest, please?" McCarran for once obliged.[30]

When the committee resumed, it was back to the China lobby.

Sen. McCarran:	Let us name the Senators who belong to the China lobby, is that the question?
Sen. Smith:	The persons who constituted the China lobby, and among them he named one Senator, and I would like to have him name the others, because he said or he referred to the State Department victims of the China lobby, and I want to know who constitutes the China lobby, the personnel, and the names.
Sen. McCarran:	That calls for names, Mr. Lattimore.
Mr. Lattimore:	All right, Senator. Before naming any further names—
Sen. McCarran:	That calls for names, Mr. Lattimore.
Mr. Lattimore:	Senator, I'll mention any further names only with great reluctance—
Sen. McCarran:	Your statement in that regard will be stricken from the record. Name the names. That is what the answer is.
Mr. Lattimore:	I am naming these names with the greatest reluctance.
Sen. McCarran:	That is stricken from the record. Call the names.
Mr. Lattimore:	I have characterized people as being—
Sen. McCarran:	Call the names, Mr. Lattimore.
Mr. Lattimore:	. . . in the lobby as being different—
Sen. McCarran:	Do you want to answer the question or don't you?
Mr. Lattimore:	Senator, before—
Sen. McCarran:	I ask you to answer the question now.
Mr. Lattimore:	Senator, yes, I will answer the question.
Sen. McCarran:	Your other statements will be stricken from the record, and you are called upon to name names, and now do so.
Mr. Lattimore:	Very respectfully, Senator, you are—
Sen. McCarran:	Let's name the names and answer the question of the Senator from North Carolina.

> *Mr. Lattimore:*   Senator, I have mentioned Mr. Alfred Kohlberg. I
> understand that an employee of the China lobby has
> been a Miss Freda Utley. I understand there is a great
> deal of private Chinese money in this country—
>
> *Sen. Smith:*   Now that does not answer my question.
>
> *Sen. McCarran:*   The last part of the answer will be stricken from the
> record.[31]

Some things may have been stricken from the record, but in general it
appears that no one on the committee staff ever bothered. It was like this
for twelve long, bitter days.

McCarran at one stage decided to belittle Lattimore's educational at-
tainments.

> *Sen. McCarran:*   Mr. Lattimore, are you a teacher in Johns Hopkins?
>
> *Mr. Lattimore:*   That is right.
>
> *Sen. McCarran:*   Of what institution are you a graduate?
>
> *Mr. Lattimore:*   I am not a graduate of any institution.
>
> *Sen. McCarran:*   Are you a graduate of any high school even?
>
> *Mr. Lattimore:*   I finished my studies at a high school in England—
>
> *Sen. McCarran:*   Did you graduate from high school? Can you not
> answer that question?
>
> *Mr. Lattimore:*   Senator, I just want to make a point here that I went
> to school in England where they do not graduate.
>
> *Sen. McCarran:*   Please answer the question. Did you ever graduate
> from high school? You can answer that "Yes" or
> "No."
>
> *Mr. Lattimore:*   All right, Senator.
>
> *Sen. McCarran:*   What is your answer?
>
> *Mr. Lattimore:*   I didn't graduate from a high school. I went to school
> in England; I left school at the age of 19 and there
> was no such thing as graduation ceremonies or di-
> ploma or anything of that kind.[32]

An hour later Freda Utley came back into the discussion. Lattimore
expressed the belief that since she had been hired by SISS, she "undoubtedly aided in recruiting witnesses and in rehearsing their stories." Another explosion. Did he *know* this of his own knowledge?

Mr. Lattimore:	I don't know for a fact.
Sen. Smith:	Then you are making statements here under oath, that are not the truth, so far as you know?
Mr. Lattimore:	I am making statements of strong opinions.
Sen. Smith:	We do not want any more opinions. We want statements of fact. You are sworn. If you do not know a thing to be a fact, we do not want you to be sitting here quoting somebody else's opinion. You are just wasting the time of everybody.
Mr. Lattimore:	Senator, a great many statements of opinion against me have been entered into the record. Am I not to be allowed to state my own opinions?
Sen. Smith:	No; you state facts. That is what we want.[33]

As a matter of *fact*, Lattimore was right. The opinions of Budenz, Barmine, Wittfogel, Dooman, Kornfeder, Stassen, and all the rest of the IPR-haters were strewn throughout the record. SISS wanted to hear them and received them kindly. Lattimore's opinions did not fit the SISS ideology.

There were, of course, moments of sanity in the hearings when both committee and witness were on good behavior. But generally the hostility of the committee drew out the anger of the witness. When it came to the vital question, "Have you ever received any orders or instructions or suggestions, directly or indirectly, from any Communist or pro-Communist source?" Lattimore had again to qualify his answer. He had been in Yenan: naturally there were suggestions from Mao and Chou. He had tried very hard to get the Russians to participate in *Pacific Affairs,* and they had some suggestions as to how that would be possible. But the committee didn't want any qualifications; they wanted a yes or no. So they asked him the same question *five times.* Finally the committee accepted his answer: no orders, no instructions, suggestions only from Russians and Chinese.[34] They didn't believe it, of course, but they moved on to other things.

Time and time again he was instructed not to "give reasons," not to explain, even not to think, just to answer yes or no. Time and time again McCarran blustered, "That will be stricken from the record." Only once did McCarran backtrack. It was in a discussion of Lattimore's query to Carter as to where, if at all, he could find a plausible justification for Russia's attack on Finland. Morris was questioning. He asked Lattimore a convoluted question about whether he or Carter wanted to justify the Russian invasion.

Mr. Lattimore:	My answer is "No." May I explain.
Sen. McCarran:	I do not think it is necessary for an explanation. The answer is "No." That is all there is to it. It is a question of the construction of the language.
Mr. Lattimore:	I think I have something pertinent to say on the subject.
Sen. McCarran:	I do not think there is anything pertinent. When you say "No, it is not interchangeable," then it is not interchangeable. That is your decision.
Mr. Lattimore:	May I explain why the answer is "No"?
Sen. McCarran:	No. The language speaks for itself.[35]

But the senator had gone too far. There was a "disturbance" in the rear of the room, which McCarran at first sought to quell by threatening to clear the room. But the disturbance continued, and the senator relented. "Just a moment. I think the Chair ruled erroneously, and I want to correct my ruling. I refused to permit the witness to explain his view on the first two lines, or three lines of the letter. I think I ruled hastily and I want to correct that ruling. I want him to have that opportunity. You may have it now."[36] Noblesse oblige.

Harassment of the witness there was aplenty, but the attempted entrapment was worse. Arnold, in *Fair Fights and Foul*, evaluates the procedure accurately: "The most striking fact about these questions and the manner in which they were propounded is that they were *not* asked in order to obtain information, but for the purpose of entrapment, for the committee, having seized the voluminous files of the Institute of Pacific Relations, was armed with documents dealing with the details the witness was commanded to dig up from the recesses of his memory of events of ten to fifteen years before" (Arnold's italics).[37]

This judgment was not confined to friends of Lattimore. The most compelling evidence of entrapment comes from the testimony of Warren Olney III, assistant attorney general under Eisenhower, to whom fell the task of supervising Lattimore's prosecution in 1953. Olney was genuinely troubled by the Lattimore case, as he told an interviewer for the Earl Warren Oral History Project:

Lattimore was questioned in very, very great detail. He answered all of the questions completely. . . . I do believe that Lattimore's experience . . . where he answered every question, was one of the major reasons why later people who were called before those committees would take the Fifth Amendment. It was not because they necessarily felt they'd done anything wrong, but because the questioning was being used not just to pull out the truth, but to try to lay a trap by getting some kind of a wrong answer along the line where there was contradictory evidence on which they could base a perjury charge. Lawyers, of course, advising their clients who were called as witnesses in that predicament, very properly would advise them to take the Fifth Amendment, not answer any questions.[38]

But Lattimore did answer questions, for twelve days. And the entrapment sometimes worked.

At Carter's suggestion Lattimore had lunched with Soviet Ambassador Constantine Oumansky just before he went to Chungking as adviser to Chiang. When asked in executive session, he said the Oumansky luncheon was after the German invasion of Russia. IPR files contained a letter showing that he had misdated the luncheon; it occurred before the German invasion of Russia, and Lattimore was off by several days. To SISS, this misdating was sinister; before the invasion the United States and Russia were enemies; after the invasion we were allies. Lattimore was not told in executive session that the committee had a letter showing his date to be wrong.

On March 3, 1952, Morris confronted Lattimore with the text of his executive session testimony, where he misdated the luncheon. No hint was given that the committee possessed a letter showing a different date. But Lattimore was put on record again:

> *Mr. Morris:*   Now, Mr. Lattimore, I will ask you some questions on the basis of that transcript. Did you testify that your meeting with Mr. Oumansky was after the Hitler invasion of the Soviet Union?
>
> *Mr. Lattimore:*   Yes, I believe I did. I couldn't guarantee that, just to the best of my recollection.[39]

It was not just entrapment; it was sleazy entrapment. Lattimore did not pretend to certainty in his answer. FBI evaluations of the Lattimore case noted this disclaimer.

Lattimore's attitude toward SISS was one of injured innocence. He knew they were out to prove him guilty of something and had suborned perjury to do it. He displayed his outrage fully in his prepared statement. As Murray Marder of the *Washington Post* put it, the statement "poured on the subcommittee a rolling denunciation representing eight months of accumulated ire." The *New York Times* also commented on Lattimore's

truculence: "Occasionally an old hand who knows how far he can go—
John L. Lewis, for example—will talk back to the Congressmen, but most
witnesses watch their manners. On Capitol Hill last week there was a
series of hearings that produced such bitter exchanges between witnesses
and committeemen that veteran observers could not recall a precedent."[40]

Was Lattimore's disdain for the committee justified? No doubt it was.
But many of his friends thought it unwise. When speaking truth to power,
humility is often called for. However, a softer attitude on Lattimore's part
would have made no difference. He was dead center in the sights of the
inquisitors, and no substitute victim could have replaced him. And if the
confrontation with SISS produced nothing else, it produced some prime—
and often hilarious—invective.

When Ferguson asked him if Russia were dominating the war in Korea,
Lattimore snapped, "If I knew the answer to that question, Senator, I
would be in Wall Street making a lot of money." When Lattimore pointed
out the obvious bias against the IPR in McCarran's 1951 *U.S. News* interview, Sourwine attempted to justify that bias on the basis of the five
volumes of testimony SISS had by then accumulated. Lattimore responded, "I have no idea, Mr. Sourwine, of how much the committee had
scooped up or what it scooped it up in, but I am aware that the hearings
are not complete, that this is a prejudgment in a hearing that is still under
process where most of the accused have not yet been heard."[41]

Sourwine was also the butt of a jibe when Lattimore accused the committee of trying to beat up on him:

> *Mr. Sourwine:*   Does your ego, sir, compel you to the conclusion that
> this subcommittee is after you rather than investi-
> gating the Institute of Pacific Relations?
>
> *Mr. Lattimore:*   Not my ego; my epidermis.[42]

Then there was the attempt of the committee to pin the downfall of
Chiang on Lattimore because he had recommended that new persons be
put in charge of China policy in 1945. Shortly after Lattimore's recommendation, Grew, Dooman, Ballantine, and Hurley retired or were removed from the China scene and were replaced by Vincent, Acheson,
Butterworth, and others thought to be sympathetic to the Chinese Communists. Willis Smith caught the sarcasm this time.

> *Sen. Smith:*   Mr. Lattimore, it is a fact that at the time Mr. Grew
> and at least some of these other men were fired, we
> did not have the same situation in the Far East with

respect to the Communists being in dominant control that we have today?

Mr. Lattimore: I presume you are right. That was some time ago, wasn't it?

Sen. Smith: Yes, so that since these men who were known as anti-Communists were relieved of their duties and their positions communism has made great advances in the Far East?

Sen. Jenner: That is why they were removed.

Sen. Smith: I am just asking for the facts.

Mr. Lattimore: Is your argument, Senator, a post hoc, ergo propter hoc?

Sen. Smith: I believe you said you did not want to indulge in legal or technical language, so I am asking you in plain language if, after these men were removed, it is not a fact that there have been great advances by communism in the Far East?

Mr. Lattimore: Yes. Of course, the advances of communism since the death of Julius Caesar have been even greater.[43]

Harold Stassen came in for a full share of Lattimore's contempt. Stassen's ten-point charge against Lattimore's contribution to the State Department's 1949 roundtable on China was dissected point by point. Lattimore commented on point ten:

10.   That no aid should be sent to the non-Communist guerrillas, nor to the Chiang Kai-shek forces. I said nothing of the sort.

In his second hearing, after the full record had been released, Mr. Stassen backtracked. He did not, of course, admit error. That would have been out of character for a Presidential candidate. He attempted to cover up by quoting some member of what he had labeled the "Lattimore group" (who, he said, had "not differed" from each other) in support of each of his ten points. He quoted me in connection with only 1 of the 10, and that in a way to distort my meaning.

Confronted with the absurd discrepancies between the kind of conference that he had pretended to describe and the kind of conference that was revealed when the full transcript was finally published, Stassen tried to escape by doing acts on the flying trapeze, as if he were a road-show McCarthy swinging through the air with the greatest of ease from "205 names" to "57" names and all the rest of it.[44]

A few minutes later Lattimore said, "Mr. Stassen at that moment was fellow-traveling with Senator McCarthy, and I should say that Senator

McCarthy is a graduate witch burner."[45] The committee did not take kindly his challenges to its good faith. In the end, perhaps Lattimore's irreverence and sarcasm prodded McCarran to go to the extremes he reached in getting Lattimore indicted.

An interesting contrast in hearing room atmosphere occurred in a break between the tenth and eleventh Lattimore appearances. John King Fairbank was brought before the committee. Perhaps the faithful six who had attended most of the Lattimore hearings wanted a rest; for Fairbank, Smith presided, with only Ferguson and Watkins present. The tone of the Fairbank hearing was completely different from that prevailing for Lattimore. Fairbank thinks this difference may have been because McCarran, who was absent, was "cynical and innately evil like McCarthy," whereas Smith, Ferguson, and Watkins were not. But the latter three were as abusive of other witnesses as McCarran had been of Lattimore. More likely, Fairbank's approach was more to the committee's liking. He began with acknowledgment that "the subcommittee has been grappling with the problems posed by Communist subversion. We know today that this is a real and vitally serious problem." Smith observed that "Mr. Fairbank's statement does not seem to be of quite the flavor of Professor Lattimore's statement," and Watkins agreed: "I think it is entirely different, from what I have read of it." In addition, Fairbank's attorney, Richard Wait, went out of his way to ingratiate himself with Senator Smith. Wait "found a relative and other things in common" with Smith. Wilma Fairbank did not like this approach; she said to Wait indignantly, "Why do you butter up that man?" Wait replied, "You catch more flies with honey than with vinegar."[46]

But Fairbank's testimony was not at all honey. He flayed Budenz, Bentley, McGovern, and the other anti-IPR witnesses at every opportunity. What he did not do was rub the committee's hypocrisy in their faces. Smith began the hearing with a statement derogating hearsay. Lattimore would have thrown that back at Smith with asperity, since Budenz's only contribution was hearsay. Fairbank stood his ground but refrained from sarcasm and invective. He emerged from the hearing unscathed.[47]

The substance of the Lattimore hearings, like the rest of the SISS product, did not impress the FBI. On April 1, 1952, Branigan wrote Belmont that the transcripts "have been thoroughly reviewed insofar as they pertain to the IPR and Own Lattimore, and it has been found that the pertinent information appearing in this testimony was already in Bureau files and had been forwarded to the Department."[48] But the committee did put Lattimore on public record under oath about a number of items pointing toward a perjury indictment. He was led to repeat his executive session claim that he had never handled Lauchlin Currie's mail when Currie was out of Washington. He emphasized again that he had never published an article by a person he knew to be a Communist, except the Russian author. He repeated his statement that he did not know in the 1930s that Asiaticus was a Communist. He said that he didn't believe that Chi Ch'ao-ting was a Communist. He insisted that he had made no prearrangements for the 1937 trip to Yenan. He again misdated his luncheon with Oumansky but said he couldn't be sure.[49]

Dozens of the bizarre charges brought to McCarthy by underworld informers (discussed in chapter 16) came up in these hearings, along with the selling of the Vermont farm, the Moscow trials, and the modus vivendi cablegram. Lattimore fielded them all. But his explanations were not persuasive to the committee. At the end of the twelfth day McCarran declared that the committee had something to say.

> What I am going to say now comes from the unanimous committee that has heard this hearing. It has been the settled practice of this committee to reserve its conclusions, with respect to the substance of the testimony that is taken, until the conclusion of the hearings on the particular matter under investigation. After careful consideration, however, this committee feels it proper at this time to make a statement with respect to the conduct of this witness, as a witness, during the time he has been before us. . . .
>
> The committee has been confronted here with an individual so flagrantly defiant of the United States Senate, so outspoken in his discourtesy, and so persistent in his efforts to confuse and obscure the facts, that the committee feels constrained to take due notice of his conduct. . . .
>
> Suggestions have been made that the committee should seek to discipline Mr. Lattimore for his contumacious and contemptuous conduct. Clearly Mr. Lattimore did, on many occasions, stand in contempt of the committee. Clearly he took that position voluntarily and intentionally. Mr. Lattimore used, toward the committee, language which was insolent, overbearing, arrogant, and disdainful. He flouted the committee, he scoffed at the committee's efforts, he impugned the committee's methods, and he slandered the committee's staff. His language was frequently such as to outrage and offend both the committee as a whole and its members individually, and, apparently, with intent to do so.
>
> There has been no striking back on the part of the committee. The committee has employed no sanctions against Mr. Lattimore because,

through forbearance, it has been found possible to make progress without disciplinary action. Despite Mr. Lattimore's recalcitrance at many points . . . the committee has preferred to err, if at all, on the side of allowing the witness too much latitude, rather than on the side of allowing too little.[50]

Then McCarran reviewed a dozen instances where he believed Lattimore had lied. His whole oration came to twenty-five hundred words. The conclusion was muted but clear:

The precise extent to which Mr. Lattimore gave untruthful testimony before this committee will never be determined. Human limitations will prevent us from ever attaining the complete knowledge of all his activities which would make it possible to assess each statement he has made and to catalog fully whatever untruths he may have uttered. That he has uttered untruths stands clear on the record. Some of these have been so patent and so flagrant as to merit mention at this time, as illustrative of the conduct and attitude of the witness. . . . When, in the face of the record, he undertook before this committee a deliberate attempt to deny or cover up pertinent facts, this witness placed himself in a most unenviable position.

The hearing is closed.[51]

Pure Kafka.

Newspaper accounts of the last day of the Lattimore inquisition naturally played up McCarran's "2,500-word tongue-lashing." The anti-Lattimore press carried little else. Some papers acknowledged that there was another side to the story: the *Baltimore Sun* headlined the statement Lattimore made in response to McCarran: "Senators' Charge He Was Untruthful Is 'Savage, Unfair' Attack: Lattimore." The most thoughtful comment was also in the *Sun:* John W. Owens's article "The Committee versus the Professor." Owens noted that "scarcely anybody remembers that the original charges were not only that Professor Lattimore was Russia's 'top espionage agent,' but was the principal 'architect' of American policy in the Far East. Scarcely anybody remembers that Senator McCarthy said he would stand or fall on this, the 'most important' case in his campaign against the State Department."[52]

These charges, observed Owens, had long since disappeared. The McCarran committee had issued no significant "finding of fact." What was a concerned citizen to believe? Perhaps now it was appropriate to reflect on this unprecedented twelve-day confrontation between citizen and solon. Owens's reflection was that "the Lattimore manner and method apparently rest upon a decision that, in the United States, a citizen who is before a congressional committee has as much right to insult a Senator as a Senator has to insult a citizen. He kicked off the proceedings before the McCarran Committee by taking the hide off its members, quite as energetically as they removed his hide at the close of the proceedings." Owens wondered whether Lattimore had established a "new school of deportment before congressional committees."

He had done so, of course, and it was controversial. Lattimore believed that his confrontational style had affected the fainthearted who knew he was innocent but were afraid to say so. As he expressed it in a letter to Vincent, "Intimidation has spread widely and deeply. People find it more and more easy to take refuge in rationalizing. . . . 'of course, everybody knows he isn't a Communist, but he shouldn't have talked back to senators in a manner not becoming a scholar and gentleman.' Thus we have a new standard. Senators can hit a man below the belt and keep it up day after day; but if he hits back straight from the shoulder, that is not 'becoming.' "[53]

Of course, many supported Lattimore's stand. One of the more poignant letters he received was from Barbara Tuchman: "You can have no idea what a lift one gets from a statement such as yours to the McCarran committee yesterday. If enough people will take courage from your words & attitude to fight back against the creeping glacier of McCarthyism, perhaps we can hold off the ice age of personal freedom that seems to be descending on us."[54]

Another supporter was Vincent, then in "exile" at the U.S. legation in Tangier. "I have just read carefully and with great appreciation your statement before the subcommittee. It is a masterful work of fairness, intelligence, and righteous indignation. . . . [My wife] will join me in saying catch the next freighter for Morocco and visit us in Tangier, where such committees do not exist and free enterprise is rampant—(is this latter phrase pro- or anti-Communist?)"[55]

Johns Hopkins was no sanctuary. McCarran's blast at Lattimore was sent to all faculty members; the *Times* said the campus was in an "uproar." McCarran disclaimed any knowledge of the mailing. The Hopkins trustees discussed the Lattimore situation at a meeting on March 28; Carlyle Barton, chair, said that the publicity was embarrassing but that nothing could be done about it until "those fellows in Washington" came up with an answer.[56]

The Philosophical Faculty (arts and sciences) of Johns Hopkins deliberated in anguish about Lattimore's contretemps with the Senate. Their academic council produced a two-page report on the matter that fussed and fumed and got nowhere. Its conclusion: "It would seem suitable at a future date—when calm judgments can be reached—for an appropriate academic body to be requested to consider whether the evidence produced indicates his [Lattimore's] unfitness as a scholar." The copy of this document in Lattimore's files is undated, there are no names on it, and it is heavily edited, some changes obviously in favor of Lattimore, some opposed to him.

The date for calm judgments never came.

CHAPTER TWENTY-THREE

Matusow, Bogolepov, the CIA, and Other Liars

On March 13, 1952, during a break in the Lattimore series, SISS listened to another of the unstable personalities attracted to the informing business: Harvey Matusow. Matusow had joined the Communist party in 1947 but became disillusioned by 1950 and signed up as an FBI undercover agent. His actions were not discreet; the comrades began to suspect him and expelled him in 1951. His expulsion made him available to the government for public testimony. As he later explained his witnessing career, he invented whatever was needed to make the headlines. He testified before HUAC, worked for the Ohio Un-American Activities Committee, gave evidence to the Subversive Activities Control Board, and testified against various teachers and labor leaders.[1]

These appearances whetted Matusow's appetite for the big time. He wanted to testify in the IPR hearings. He was already in the "major leagues," but the IPR and Lattimore was the world series. As he later wrote,

> When testifying on youth activities before [another] McCarran committee, I had said, with seeming casualness, "While I was working in a Communist bookstore in New York, I sold Lattimore's book, *Solution in Asia*." I added that it was used as official Communist dogma on the subject.
>
> This immediately aroused Morris' interest and he asked me to testify. . . .
>
> On Thursday, March 13, 1952, the hearing room was full. No one but the committee members knew who the witness was slated to be. Senator Eastland of Mississippi was acting as chairman.
>
> I didn't come right out and attack Owen Lattimore. I first had to

establish myself as an expert on Communist activities relating to the Far East. I referred to the Committee for a Democratic Far Eastern Policy and its selling publications which were printed in China. I rattled off a list of authors who had written on the subject of China. My bait was taken.

I painted a picture of the operation of a "Communist bookshop network," stating that there were such shops in every major city in the country. I deliberately dropped big names, and I implicated Henry Wallace by saying I had seen and sold a pamphlet of his that was printed by the Institute of Pacific Relations. . . .

This was all part of the broad picture of "subversion" with which I attempted to surround Lattimore. . . .

I climaxed my testimony with the dramatic assertion that Owen Lattimore's books were used as the official Communist Party guides on Asia. Once again, I told a complete falsehood.

The results of my testimony were most gratifying to me when I saw the newspaper headlines:

"Matusow Says He Believes Lattimore Red," "Lattimore Book Had Official Red OK, Witness Says," "Lattimore Book Had Party Line," "Charge Lattimore Book Is Red," etc.

I made front pages across the United States, thanks to Owen Lattimore. . . . I had reached the top rung of the ladder.[2]

This 1952 testimony was swallowed whole by SISS; Senator Eastland received it eagerly. Even the FBI was taken in by Matusow, who was described as an informant of "known reliability."[3]

After the Lattimore testimony was finished on March 21, 1952, the hearings lost their luster. Headlines were fewer. Though IPR hearings went on until June 20, never again did a witness attract six of the seven committee members; most were attended by a single senator.

William C. Bullitt, who appeared April 8, brought out only three committee members. Bullitt was a heavyweight, and it is surprising that his testimony was not more highly regarded. He had been the first American ambassador to the Soviet Union (1933–36) and then ambassador to France (1936–41). In 1947 Henry Luce sent Bullitt to China; his "Report to the American People on China" in *Life*, October 13, 1947, is regarded by many as the most influential single broadside supporting Chiang. By 1952 Bullitt was a power in the China lobby.

Bullitt had met Lattimore in Moscow in 1936; Carter arranged for Lattimore to confer with the ambassador. The recollections of the two men about this conference diverge strikingly. Bullitt told SISS that Lattimore had claimed the Mongolian People's Republic was fully independent, that there was no Soviet control whatsoever, and that the United States should recognize the MPR.[4]

Lattimore's version is quite different. He did want to recognize the MPR, not because it was totally independent, but because recognition would increase its independence.[5] Furthermore, Lattimore wanted to give the proper Soviet authority a piece of his mind about Te Wang. As he told me in 1987, "Soviet officials had been bitterly attacking Te Wang, the non-Communist Inner Mongolian leader. They accused Te Wang of being pro-Japanese. I told Bullitt that Te Wang was a true Mongol nationalist and represented a better chance for the future of Inner Mongolia than the Soviet-supported puppets. Bullitt then suggested I tell that to the Vice-Commissar for Far Eastern Affairs."

Both men agreed that they did have a session with the vice-commissar. Bullitt does not say what happened at that session; Lattimore said only that the commissar listened. SISS never heard Lattimore's response to Bullitt's version. The Bullitt charge, however, is presented twice in the SISS final report.

There were other minor anti-Lattimore witnesses. One of them was David Nelson Rowe, a sinologue at Yale who appeared before Senator Watkins March 27. Rowe had resigned from the IPR board in 1950; his major disagreement with IPR leaders was the position they took against colonialism. He appears to have been one of the few Americans who thought the Europeans wrought well in Asia and should hang onto their colonies.[6]

Rowe also supported Kuomintang authoritarianism. Perhaps his most revealing statement was about a discussion he had after the war with John Paton Davies. Davies thought that the Nationalist government was incompetent and unstable and hence the United States should not support it anymore. Row told Davies, "Well, when old Chiang Kai-shek wants to restore a bit of order by shooting a few people, you people get revolted by the idea, but in some cases there is nothing else you can do." Davies did not like this idea, according to Rowe.[7]

Even more unusual, Rowe deprecated Chinese nationalism. The Chinese would not mind being satellites of the Russians. Their attitude, according to Rowe, would be "We don't care whether the Western world thinks Russia is dominating us. That word doesn't express it at all. This is a workable, happy, satisfactory marriage for mutual adjustment, mutual interest; that is all it is. Let us put it this way: The Chinese in their relationship of ideological subordination to the Russians feel privileged, they feel privileged."[8]

Could there be a greater contrast with Lattimore's beliefs? When Morris asked Rowe about his conclusions as to Lattimore's politics, Rowe was ready: "My subjective opinion, for what it is worth, in the light of my 20 years of study in the far eastern field, is that as of today among far eastern specialists in the United States Lattimore is probably the principal agent of Stalinism. Now, I use this word 'Stalinism' by design."[9]

Rowe hit the jackpot.

The Baltimore FBI office was also impressed. Agent Alden read a headline in the *Baltimore News Post* March 27: "Rowe Sees Lattimore Agent of Stalinism." Alden cabled headquarters suggesting that Rowe should be interviewed if he had not been already. Hoover's letter to Baltimore a week later said that Rowe's testimony "had little probative value."[10] There was no FBI interview. But Rowe had joined the pantheon of right-thinkers whose testimony was enshrined in the SISS final report: he gets fifteen listings in the index.

After Rowe, SISS was in the doldrums for a while. Fred Field appeared, took the Fifth, and enlightened no one. T. A. Bisson, a prominent IPR writer, testified and did not take the Fifth. He had much to say and gave a good account of himself. Only Ferguson was present; there was little probing of the witness, and nothing came of it. Then the committee called Eleanor Lattimore and Catesby Jones, a student of Lattimore's who had helped put together Lattimore's explosive opening statement. Only Senator Watkins was present. He wanted to know every movement Lattimore, his wife, Catesby Jones, Lattimore's attorneys, Lattimore's secretaries, Lattimore's other students, and any other participants on Lattimore's side had made during the twelve days of Lattimore's testimony. Mrs. Lattimore answered all the questions she could and was dismissed. Nothing came of this questioning either. Edward C. Carter was brought back before the committee; that session also was unproductive. SISS was only marking time.[11]

Enter Ivar Nyman, his real name, alias Igor Bogolepov, the name he used while working with SISS and the CIA.

Nyman was a double defector. Born in Siberia in 1904, he graduated from the University of Leningrad in 1923 and joined the Soviet foreign office. He was drafted into the army; worked for the general staff; participated in the Geneva Conference on Disarmament in 1927–28; returned to the foreign office; had a tour of duty with Soviet forces in Spain in 1937; and was arrested as a Trotskyite and imprisoned in Moscow, then rehabilitated in 1938. He was then, so he said, assigned to work with Foreign Commissar Maxim Litvinov as a counselor. In 1939 Litvinov was replaced by V. M. Molotov, and Nyman was assigned to head Soviet broadcast operations in the Baltics. When Hitler attacked Russia in June 1941, Nyman retreated with the Soviet army to Leningrad. In the fall of 1941 General Andre Vlassov got in touch with him. Vlassov, a disillusioned Soviet officer, defected to the Germans and tried to organize a "liberation army" of captured and defected Russians to fight with Germany; his aim was to establish a non-Communist regime in Russia. Vlassov solicited Nyman's help, and they defected together.[12]

Nyman had a hard time of it. The Gestapo at first imprisoned him. Interrogation established that he was neither a Jew nor a commissar, so he was released by the Gestapo and turned over to the Wehrmacht. Since he had had journalistic experience, he was for a year "leading a powerful transmitter for the German Government on the outskirts of Berlin, carrying out the anti-Communist propaganda." Nyman had intended to join Vlassov's army of liberation, but he became disillusioned with the Germans, and when his radio operation was shut down in 1944, he "retired to a German farm in Bavaria, working as a manual worker and waiting until the American troops came and the war was over, which was in April, 1945."[13]

Nyman and other Russian refugees greeted American troops warmly, he said, but as it became clear that most Russians in Allied zones were going to be sent back to the tender embraces of Stalin, he went into hiding. By then he desperately wanted to come to the United States. By 1947 the cold war was on and the U.S. Army was recruiting Soviet refugees; Nyman got a job with the Army Intelligence School at Regensburg. He was regarded as a significant source of information about his homeland. Both the CIA and the FBI debriefed him extensively. An FBI document says, "Nyman was interviewed on two occasions in 1950 relative to Owen Lattimore and the IPR. He made no concrete allegations against Lattimore but did mention that he had been told by a Soviet official, name unknown, that Lattimore was the most suitable man in the U.S. to promote pro-Soviet propaganda relative to Mongolia. Concerning the IPR Nyman could offer no information of an evidentiary value."[14]

How SISS learned about Nyman is obscure, but in the summer of 1951 Senator Willis Smith went to Paris for an executive hearing with him. Nyman was quick on the uptake. Whereas in 1950 he knew nothing about the IPR and very little about Lattimore, by the time Smith talked to him he knew a lot. Smith recommended that he be brought to the United States for public testimony.[15]

McCarran agreed. He prevailed on Major General Bolling, Army G-2, to bring Nyman stateside. As V. P. Keay wrote Belmont on June 15, 1951, "He [Bolling] stated that he had been telephonically contacted by Senator McCarran, at which time the Senator indicated to General Bolling that he would like to have the Army arrange to have one I. Nyman brought back to the United States from Germany. . . . He stated that Senator McCarran has apparently perfected arrangements whereby Nyman will not need a visa. He will be flown to Westover Field, Massachusetts, and then secretly brought to Washington, where the McCarran Committee has made arrangements to have Nyman and his wife quartered at a hotel."[16] It was a cloak-and-dagger operation to match the seizure of the IPR files.

But something went wrong. Nyman was not delivered to Washington until April 3, 1952, a full ten months after McCarran apparently had everything arranged.[17] Meanwhile, SISS staff had worked with Nyman in Germany, and his "information" about Lattimore had grown exponentially. When he testified on April 7–8, 1952, his discussion of the subjects SISS wanted to hear about filled thirty-nine printed pages.

Nyman (now called Bogolepov) was obviously a prime witness; five senators attended his first hearing. And while everything he had to tell about Lattimore was hearsay, he at least claimed to have seen Lattimore— in 1936 when Lattimore and Carter visited Soviet offices in Moscow. It was then, Bogolepov said, that he heard Soviet officials, in the presence of Lattimore and other foreigners, discuss the supersecret Soviet "route through Mongolia to Manchuria." Such a route may or may not have existed, but Bogolepov proclaimed his shock at hearing it discussed in the presence of foreigners. When Lattimore and his party left the office, Bogolepov quizzed Kara-Murza, chief Soviet Mongolian specialist, as to who they were: Comintern or not? Kara-Murza replied, "No, they are not Comintern, not Comintern people, not quite Comintern people, but that is quite all right with him." This alleged conversation transpired in 1936; Bogolepov was recreating it in 1952.[18]

Bogolepov said that just before he left for his Spanish assignment, he was reporting on the prospects for getting the Mongolian People's Republic into the League of Nations. At a meeting of the Board of Commissars of the Foreign Office, Litvinov said that "the situation is still not ripe. We have to prepare the terrain." Morris picked up this nuance:

> *Mr. Morris:* Prepare the terrain?
>
> *Mr. Bogolepov:* Yes; prepare the terrain for the action.
>
> *Sen. Eastland:* You mean you had to prepare public sentiment.

Mr. Bogolepov:	That is right. That is what I would like to say. "It is necessary," said Litvinov, "to mobilize the writers and journalists and other people, to describe for the Western World the progress which is achieved in Mongolian Popular Republic, to say how life is progressing," and so on and so on. This was the first decision which was taken after my report. The second part of decision, the second point, was considering who will make this in different countries, whom we have to charge with this—how do you say, sir?
Sen. Eastland:	You mean the man who will be placed in charge of mobilizing public sentiment in the west?
Mr. Bogolepov:	That is right, whom we have to ask to do the job.
Sen. Eastland:	Who was that man who was decided upon?
Mr. Bogolepov:	Litvinov asked the officer of Mongolian desk of the Foreign Office, who was present—
Mr. Morris:	What was his name?
Mr. Bogolepov:	Parnoch, P-a-r-n-o-c-h—whom he would recommend, and before Parnoch could give his answer he asked "Lattimore, perhaps?"
Sen. Eastland:	Litvinov said "Lattimore?"
Mr. Bogolepov:	"Lattimore, perhaps?" yes. And Parnoch answered, "Yes, we will try to do that."[19]

After this incident Bogolepov left Moscow for Spain and did not know whether Lattimore had actually been charged with this mission.

But he told SISS a lot more about the IPR. He painted a picture of Soviet eagerness to place articles in Western journals that was totally unbelievable. Soviet IPR writers were to send their own manuscripts to American colleagues, making IPR journals "media for infiltration of ideas favorable for Soviet foreign policy in the Far East."[20] Lattimore found this testimony risible. The one thing he had tried hardest to do, as editor of *Pacific Affairs*, was to pry articles out of Soviet writers.

Bogolepov told the senators about Western writers who published books taken wholly from Soviet propaganda handouts. Among such writers were, he said, Sidney and Beatrice Webb, British socialists, and John Hazard, the Soviet expert who accompanied Vice President Wallace. This revelation whetted SISS appetites. Weren't there others? Yes, said Bogolepov, but he had to be careful. Senator Ferguson then asked, "You are not rich enough to defend yourself in a libel suit?" Bogolepov agreed that was it. Then Ferguson pointed out that in testifying before a congressional committee he could not be sued for libel. That brought forth more examples: Frederick Schuman, former ambassador Joseph Davies, Michael Sayers, and Albert Kahn had all cribbed Soviet propaganda and put it out as their own.[21]

One of Bogolepov's claims has been contradicted by a CIA agent who knew him at Regensburg. Bogolepov told SISS that until 1939 members of the Russian bourgeois class were not permitted to be Party members. Since his father was bourgeois, he could not join the Party. Peer de Silva, a twenty-seven-year veteran of the CIA, writes of Bogolepov in *Sub Rosa: The CIA and the Uses of Intelligence*: "I did know that he had come from Leningrad and that his family had been high in the Party structure in the prewar years. They had had privileges granted by the Soviet bureaucracy to their senior officials—an apartment in Leningrad, a telephone, a car, and they were able to buy food and clothing at the well-stocked Communist Party stores."[22] By 1952 Bogolepov wanted to distance himself from the Party; thus, he told SISS a new and different story.

Despite the high hopes of SISS for major impact from Bogolepov's testimony, it rated only page sixteen of the *Times*, and even Willard Edwards could not get it on page one of the red-baiting *Chicago Tribune*. After SISS, Bogolepov stayed in the United States for a while, speaking at the Harmonic Club of New York on December 6, 1952, and testifying, along with Alfred Kohlberg, before the House of Representatives Select Committee to Investigate Tax-Exempt Foundations on December 17. Both these appearances were chronicled by the *Times*.[23] Then Bogolepov disappeared.

One of the most fantastic episodes of the Lattimore saga took place in Washington State during the closing months of the IPR hearings. On May 17, 1952, Harry A. Jarvinen, a Seattle travel agent who regularly reported the comings and goings of Seattleites to the CIA, attended a dinner party with CIA agent Wayne Richardson. Jarvinen, an immigrant from Finland, had had trouble with various government agencies and was anxious to ingratiate himself with his CIA friends. After a few drinks Jarvinen conjured up a scenario in which, aping the 1949 flight from the United States of Comintern agent Gerhard Eisler, Owen Lattimore was planning to flee to the Soviet Union. Jarvinen told Richardson that Lattimore had bought a ticket on Air France to fly to Paris on June 21, then on to political asylum in the Soviet Union.[24]

Richardson relayed this startling information to his CIA superiors in Washington, D.C. CIA headquarters seems not to have been particularly intelligent at the time. Without doing any checking whatsoever, the CIA

sent a cable to the State Department on May 26: "OWEN LATTIMORE WILL
LEAVE ON A TRIP TO THE USSR VIA AIR FRANCE JUNE TWENTY-ONE, NINE-
TEEN FIFTY-TWO, ARRIVING PARIS JUNE TWENTY-TWO, NINETEEN FIFTY-TWO.
DATE OF TRAVEL TO KIEV AND MOSCOW VIA AEROFLOT ARE OPEN. HIS TICK-
ETS HAVE BEEN PAID FOR AND HAVE BEEN FORWARDED TO HIM"[25]

One can imagine the turmoil in the State Department. If Lattimore
departed secretly for the Soviet Union, the escape would set off a roar of
anger from McCarthy and McCarran. The administration would be unable to defend itself from such embarrassment. Few public officials seemed
to notice that Lattimore had been convicted of no crime, was not under
indictment, and had the full rights of any American citizen.

State acted on this cable by requesting the Customs Bureau to place a
stop order at all ports of exit, detaining Lattimore should he attempt to
leave the country.[26]

The CIA also sent a message about Jarvinen's hot tip to the FBI. On
May 29 the bureau swung into action as Belmont prepared a message for
Hoover's signature instructing all appropriate offices to investigate details
of Lattimore's trip. Despite the fact that this request went out over the
Memorial Day weekend, within twenty-four hours the FBI knew (1) that
Lattimore did not have an Air France reservation to Paris on June 21 or
any other date; (2) that he did not have a valid passport; (3) that the CIA
claim (relayed to FBI by telephone) that he was to depart from LaGuardia
was false, since Air France did not fly from LaGuardia.[27]

Bureau knowledge that the Jarvinen tip was almost certainly a hoax
was not immediately transmitted to State and the CIA. In Seattle, Jarvinen got cold feet and told his CIA friend on June 6 that Lattimore had
canceled his trip. But the CIA did not pass this information along to State
either; the bureaucratic machinery ground on, and Customs issued its
stop order five days after the FBI and the CIA knew there was no trip
planned. On June 12 the CIA furnished the bureau with Jarvinen's name
as the original source. Hoover ordered an immediate interview with the
Seattle agent. Jarvinen affirmed his original claim and insisted Lattimore
had canceled.[28]

While the CIA and the FBI sat on their knowledge that Lattimore had
no trip scheduled, the press learned of the travel ban on Lattimore. The
person named was too prominent, the action taken against him too unusual, for the bureaucrats in Customs to maintain secrecy. Rumors began
to circulate in Washington and Baltimore. The *Baltimore Sun* and the
Scripps Howard chain began pestering State about Lattimore, and other
newspapers joined in. Finally, at 5:10 P.M. on June 20, the State Depart-

ment press officer, Michael J. McDermott, went before reporters with a formal statement. Major dailies across the country headlined Mc-Dermott's announcement in their next editions. Paul Ward's story in the *Baltimore Sun* was the most comprehensive. It began: "Governmental action to confine Owen Lattimore to the United States has been taken on receipt of information from an 'official agency' to the effect that the Johns Hopkins professor planned an 'illegal' sortie behind the Iron Curtain, the State Department disclosed late today. The action—first of its kind taken against any American citizen—was initiated June 3 and without querying Lattimore as to his intentions, according to a department spokesman. He added that it would be fair to call the action 'a precaution against his skipping the country.' "[29]

The reason McDermott gave for preventing Lattimore's departure was that Lattimore did not have a valid passport for travel behind the Iron Curtain. This point, as Ward noted, "raised more questions than it answered." The skeptical journalists did not believe a stop order would be placed against an unknown person who might attempt to leave for forbidden lands without a validated passport. McDermott's press conference illuminates the interagency battles that got under way. Several reporters questioned him about how the State Department knew Lattimore planned to go to Russia. Would State stop him if the information wasn't solid and bordered on the fantastic?

A. The State Department does not take action on fantasies or inanities. We had information from an official agency, and it had to be given credence.

Q. Would the booking of passage be considered evidence?

A. Yes.

Q. Did Lattimore book passage?

A. I haven't said so.

Q. You haven't answered the question.

A. I won't.

Q. Was the agency that made the allegation the CIA (Central Intelligence Agency)?

A. I don't hear you.[30]

One person who heard, and commented predictably, was McCarthy. As the *New York Times* reported on June 26, he claimed that "the State Department will use every bit of power at its disposal to get Lattimore out of the country within the next two or three months." His truth had to be hidden, conspiratorial, and manipulated by the Kremlin.

Unbelievably, no one had asked Lattimore about his plans until after the State Department briefing on June 20. The next day Attorney General McGranery instructed the FBI to interview Lattimore. Baltimore agents found him the same day; he had no trip planned and had not bought or reserved tickets to Paris, Moscow, or anywhere else. On the same day Seattle FBI agents called on Jarvinen again. This time he came clean: the story was a complete hoax, made up to enhance his prestige as an informant to the CIA. Now "he was considerably upset and chagrined at the amount of trouble, effort, and money expended on the basis of his original falsehood."[31] Thus, on June 21, the same day that the Lattimore escape story gained universal exposure, the FBI learned that it had always been a hoax.

The truth in this case struggled to get established in the nation's media. Powerful biases were at work, especially in the right-wing, pro-Chiang papers. Since they had defined Lattimore as the bad guy, he probably was up to something nefarious. And of course he was a heretic, whether or not McCarthy was right about his being a spymaster.

Hearst dispatches on June 22 probably had the highest error rate in their coverage of the Lattimore-Jarvinen affair. David Sentner's story in the (Hearst) *Seattle Post-Intelligencer* of that date stated that Lattimore's itinerary included England, where he would lecture to the Royal Geographic Society; that the stop order was tied in with SISS; that Lattimore had booked steamship passage from New York; and that the initial tip came to the State Department from the FBI.[32] It would be hard to be more wrong.

The McCarthy-McCarran forces in the Senate were also active in putting out false information. McCarran let it be known that his committee would discuss Lattimore's trip and possibly reopen its IPR investigation. Jay Sourwine shared the SISS stock of rumors with Lou Nichols at the FBI: the tickets had indeed been issued for Lattimore's trip; they had been issued by the World-Wide Travel Service; they were ordered by Seattle attorney Ben Kizer; they were picked up by Kizer's son-in-law. Nichols told Sourwine not to "get out on a limb"; Sourwine was grateful for the tip.[33]

With several agencies acutely embarrassed, the bureaucratic game of eluding blame began. The FBI was the easiest agency to defend. Even though some Hearst papers attributed the Lattimore escape story to the bureau, too many officials knew the truth for this version to take hold.

The CIA had more trouble. At first they defended themselves in whimsical fashion. Reporter Ed Guthman of the *Seattle Daily Times* attended a "not for attribution" session with a high official of the agency. The CIA spokesman stressed that his agency was prevented by law from having an internal security function within the borders of the United States but could solicit information: " 'We have been in the habit of going to this informant in Seattle and picking up a basket of oranges (collection of information). In this basket of oranges, there apparently was an apple (the tip on Lattimore). We don't know if it was wormy, since we only deal in oranges. So we picked up the apple and handed it to the F.B.I, which deals in apples. We also gave it to the State Department, because it, too, seemed to be concerned with this apple.' The 'apple,' the C.I.A. spokesman asserted, was handed on exactly as it came in, without comment or evaluation." [34]

This was a lie. The form of the CIA message was not that of a "raw and unevaluated" tip, as the agency claimed. If the claim's accuracy was unevaluated, the CIA would have used cautious phrasing such as "We were told that Owen Lattimore . . ." or "A usually reliable source asserts that . . ." Receiving such a message, the State Department would have been on guard.

But the CIA did nothing of the kind. "Owen Lattimore will leave on a trip," the message read. The recipient, State, was predictably outraged in the days after the story broke to be taking the brunt of criticism. This outrage was clearly expressed in a story in the *New York Times* headlined "Tip on Lattimore Called Unqualified": "A high State Department official said today that the Central Intelligence Agency had represented a false report that Prof. Owen Lattimore had planned to visit Moscow as a confirmed fact. He denied that the agency had relayed the tip with a warning that it was 'raw and unevaluated data,' as C.I.A. officials had asserted privately." [35]

There is no question about who was right here. The CIA passed the story to Edward R. Murrow with the same cocksureness: "Everything was fourteen-carat, Lattimore was going to skip, they had it from a reliable source." [36]

The rest of the story was also a comedy of errors. Jarvinen was indicted for giving false information to a government agency, but when he came to trial on September 18, 1952, CIA Director Walter Bedell Smith forbade the Seattle agents to testify. The FBI agents, to whom Jarvinen had also lied, testified willingly, but the defense attorney made Jarvinen into such a hero that FBI testimony was disregarded by the jury. Jarvinen's "speculations" about the subversive Lattimore were "fired by his long hatred of Communism incurred in his native Finland."[37] Jarvinen's wife and mother wept openly while testifying to his true-blue Americanism. The jury deliberated seven hours and found him not guilty.

This was a miscarriage of justice. FBI files show not only that Jarvinen was guilty but that he had come to the United States illegally, had been under a deportation order for several months, and even after entering legally had been in trouble with one U.S. agency or another for years. And the anticommunism pose was dubious. On March 7, 1942, when he was ordered deported by the Hartford, Connecticut, office of the Immigration and Naturalization Service, he asked to be sent to Finland or Russia.[38]

Cold war hysteria caused many malfunctions of the American judicial system, most of them unjust penalties imposed on innocent people. But there were cases in which guilty parties, pandering to the climate of the times, went free. Jarvinen was such a case.

SISS wound up its public hearings on May 29, 1952, with a bevy of six top-drawer witnesses: General Claire Chennault, Elizabeth Bentley, Whittaker Chambers, Admiral Roscoe Hillenkoetter, Herbert Philbrick, and Hede Massing. Despite the stars, they got little press. It was a mutual admiration society meeting. Four senators were present, but not McCarran. Morris led the questioning.

All six witnesses agreed that Stilwell was a bad man; that Marshall's restrictions on supplies to Chiang's forces, and similar actions, caused the fall of the Nationalist government; that the People's Republic of China was a Soviet satellite; that Service, Davies, and other China hands were insubordinate and subversive; that there were still, in 1952, Soviet agents in the U.S. government; that Lattimore's luncheon with Oumansky was damning, whenever it occurred; that it was very difficult for a Communist to break with the Party; that Frederick Field could not have acted as a loyal American; that it was difficult to get documentary evidence that a person has been a Soviet spy; that General Berzin knew for a fact that Lattimore was a Soviet agent; that hearsay evidence of Communist activity was probative; that Communists could not be objective; that witnesses who took the Fifth Amendment were still Communists; and similar cosmic revelations.[39]

One might say the hearings closed with a whimper.

The bang came when, on July 2, 1952, SISS released its 226-page report.

The hearings had been biased; the report was venomous. The report was as unrepresentative of the hearings as the hearings were unrepresentative of the facts about Lattimore and the IPR. The report was skewed in its portrayal of what the subcommittee had done, highly selective in its review of the "evidence," totally reflective of McCarran's paranoid view of the internal Communist menace. But it was cleverly written. The crudities, bullying, and partiality to ex-Communists displayed in the hearings by the seven SISS members and the Morris-Mandel-Sourwine trio disappear in the report. The report is nothing but a brief for the condemnation of IPR and the prosecution of Lattimore and Davies.

One of the many falsehoods about SISS enshrined in our tribal history is that its IPR report was approved by the entire Senate Judiciary Committee. William F. Buckley, Jr., is the foremost disseminator of this myth. We do not know the precise vote when the report was considered in full committee; however, the minutes of the meeting of Tuesday, July 1, 1952, show that none of the three liberals on the committee voted to approve it. Estes Kefauver was absent, and Harley Kilgore and Warren Magnuson each asked "that it be made a matter of record that he refrained from voting on approval of the report."[40]

For a document that was to have such extensive repercussions in the political world, the Senate itself treated its release with remarkable casualness. When McCarran presented it on the Senate floor, he was the only Democrat in the chamber. Ferguson suggested that the presiding officer, Senator Harry Cain, issue a quorum call so that if anyone thought there was "anything wrong with the report" they could ask questions. McCarran shot down this request: he knew press coverage and China lobby promotion would determine the ultimate impact of the report. Since the normal press run of congressional reports at that time was only fifteen hundred, McCarran got approval for an extra five thousand—and there may have been a reprinting.[41]

SISS came to thirty-two somewhat overlapping conclusions, the more notable being:

The IPR has been considered by the American Communist Party and by Soviet officials as an instrument of Communist policy, propaganda and military intelligence.

The IPR disseminated and sought to popularize false information including information originating from Soviet and Communist sources.

Members of the small core of officials and staff members who controlled IPR were either Communist or pro-Communist.

The effective leadership of the IPR often sought to deceive IPR contributors and supporters as to the true character and activities of the organization.

Owen Lattimore was, from some time beginning in the 1930's, a conscious articulate instrument of the Soviet conspiracy.

After the establishment of the Soviet Council of IPR, leaders of the American IPR sought and maintained working relationships with Soviet diplomats and officials.

John Paton Davies, Jr., testified falsely before the subcommittee in denying that he recommended the Central Intelligence Agency employ, utilize, and rely upon certain individuals having Communist associations and connections.

Owen Lattimore and John Carter Vincent were influential in bringing about a change in United States Policy in 1945 favorable to the Chinese Communists.

And there were two recommendations for "departmental activity": (1) "that the Department of Justice submit to a grand jury the question of whether perjury has been committed before the subcommittee by Owen Lattimore"; and (2) "that the Department of Justice submit to a grand jury the question of whether perjury has been committed before the subcommittee by John P. Davies, Jr."[42]

Television had not yet carried the flavor of a congressional inquiry into the nation's living rooms. Two years later, when the Army-McCarthy hearings exposed the Wisconsin senator's bullying to a wide audience, the public was appalled. The IPR hearings probably would have had the same outcome—but there was no television. Journalists who packaged the SISS report for their readers had not waded through the 5,712 pages of hearings and exhibits. McCarran planned it well. The public got *his* story, and almost nothing but.

The *New York Times* began a story on the front page, carrying over to page four; at the end the *Times* gave brief rebuttals by Lattimore, Davies, and William Holland of the IPR. The *Baltimore Evening Sun* gave the story a scarehead, with the Davies and Lattimore rebuttals featured early in the story.[43] This was uncommon. Mostly, the nation's papers presented pure McCarran. *Time* and *Newsweek* took the report at face value.

Face value in this case was totally misleading. The report carries no reply to complaints of IPR officers that they had been denied, for the first nine months of the hearings, access to their own files. There was no acknowledgment of failure to test the credibility of the former Communists and pro-Chiang professors. Unbelievably, the report claims that SISS made "the closest scrutiny of the qualifications of Messrs. Barmine and Bogolepov"; it did nothing of the sort. Joseph Alsop and his vigorous attack on Louis Budenz are never mentioned. Dennis Chavez's derogation of Budenz's credibility is not even hinted at, much less answered. The dozen or so "concealed Communists" named by Budenz who sent the subcommittee sworn statements calling Budenz a liar are not mentioned. A mere two pages discuss the crucial Kunming cable, totally distorting it.[44] The testimony of all anti-Lattimore witnesses is emphasized; the testimony of the few pro-Lattimore witnesses, when acknowledged at all, is belittled.

There is one clear indication that SISS did not want to rest its case to any great extent on the testimony of Budenz, its most prestigious witness. Of the 24 anti-IPR witnesses, the one who gets most space in the report is Nyman/Bogolepov, cited on 47 pages. Budenz comes in fourth, with 21 citations, behind Barmine (25) and Poppe (22). Stassen, for all his bluster and many appearances, rates a mere two citations.

The report does not respond to IPR Secretary Holland's complaint that several boxes of IPR publications he sent the subcommittee in March 1951 were sitting unopened on the floor outside Sourwine's office on October 10. There was, said Holland, "no evidence in the subcommittee's record to indicate that the Institute's publications have been analyzed."[45] Not one of the prominent business and academic figures who controlled the IPR and who were alleged to have been "hoodwinked" by a subversive IPR staff were called to testify, despite Holland's repeated calls for them to be questioned. Ray Lyman Wilbur, a cabinet member under Herbert Hoover and then president of Stanford; William R. Herod, president of International General Electric; Philo Parker, president of Standard Vacuum Oil Company; Robert Gordon Sproul, president of the University of California—all were active trustees, but none was called. Not a single colleague of Lattimore at Johns Hopkins was called. No liberal or centrist Asian scholar was called except Fairbank, but there were six ultrarightists.

Budenz, Bentley, and Chambers were called, but not the ex-Communists Bella Dodd or Earl Browder. SISS ignored the many former Communists the FBI had interviewed about Lattimore who said they knew of no Communist activity or connections on his part; as late as 1982 the names of these informants were still denied. McCarran did get an FBI report that he requested on the Dilowa.[46] It showed in the strongest language that the Dilowa was an enemy of the Communists and that Lattimore's sponsorship of the Dilowa was profoundly anti-Communist. This information never appeared in the report. Lacking most of the SISS files, we cannot know how much similar evidence McCarran suppressed.

Harry Truman was not fooled. On July 5, 1952, after digesting the news about the SISS report, he wrote Attorney General McGranery:

> Attached is a copy of an editorial from the Washington Post on the report of the McCarran Committee. It seems to me that this editorial has the right approach to the matter.
>
> I do not want to prevent anyone from being prosecuted who deserves it; but from what I know of this case, I am of the opinion that Davies and Lattimore were shamefully persecuted by this committee, and that if anyone ought to be indicted as a result of these proceedings they are not the ones. If you find anything in the record that seems to indicate that the case should be laid before a grand jury, I wish you would let me know before that is done.[47]

Though Truman wasn't fooled, many journalists and academicians were. Perhaps the most influential work coming from a scholarly press was a cold war tract by H. Bradford Westerfield, *Foreign Policy and Party Politics*, published by Yale University Press in 1955. Westerfield accepts many of the China myths: there was "much validity" in Hurley's charges against the China hands, and John Carter Vincent was very slow in reaching the conclusion that "the Chinese Communists were accepting guidance from Moscow."[48] Most damning, SISS had told the truth:

> No brief summary here can do justice to the massive weight of evidence accumulated by the McCarran Committee during its long investigation in 1951 and 1952. By the standards reasonably applicable to congressional probes, this one was conscientious and productive. Its 5,000 pages of testimony, with extensive and orderly documentation, deserve more respectful attention than they have received from most liberal critics, many of whom have not even bothered to read the committee's 200-page report. Unfortunately, there is room here only to state a personal conclusion: that a Communist solution for Asia was favored by a large enough proportion of the active participants in the American IPR to affect substantially the content of its publications and the character of its public relations work and contacts with government.[49]

Alan D. Harper, in *The Politics of Loyalty*, is more moderate but still finds that SISS "was able to discover evidence of a Communist cell within the Institute." He attributes the China hands' "tolerance of the Yenan group" to their "mistaken assumption that these were not real Communists," although not a single foreign service officer under attack ever took that position. As to Lattimore: "The subcommittee, working at its job as McCarthy never did, established a serious question about Dr. Lattimore." SISS did work at its job; but what was the serious question it established about Lattimore? Harper does not tell us.[50]

Among nonacademic intellectuals, the pro-McCarran opinion is much more pronounced. Perhaps the shoddiest polemic in the whole war over the "loss" of China is Irving Kristol's article on Lattimore in *Twentieth Century* magazine. It out-McCarrans McCarran. For Kristol, Lattimore was the quintessential Stalinoid apologist, and the IPR hearings caught him directly in the cross hairs.[51]

James Rorty and Moshe Decter, writing under the auspices of the American Committee for Cultural Freedom, denigrate McCarthy but accept almost the whole corpus of McCarranism. SISS had an "overwhelming weight of evidence."[52] And there are others. The public got McCarran's story.

As late as 1980 the McCarran picture of the IPR found its way into the best-selling novel *The Spike*, in which Arnaud de Borchgrave and Robert Moss set out their scenario for the Soviet Union to take over the world. They were a bit off in their target date: the Soviet conquest was to be accomplished by 1985. And the conquest was to be achieved not by force of arms but by disinformation, the peddling of disguised KGB propaganda, just as in McCarran's scenario the IPR had paved the way for Stalin's takeover in China.[53] *The Spike* is grounded on the historical comparison to IPR. Thousands of readers who otherwise never heard of the IPR have read McCarran's version as set forth in *The Spike*.

The right-wing literature supporting McCarran ranges from the extremes of Robert Welch and the John Birch Society to the more moderate *National Review* and the book on McCarthy by William F. Buckley, Jr., and Brent Bozell. None of it is probative. Buckley particularly is a font of misinformation. He dissociates McCarthy from SISS, whereas FBI files show that McCarthy worked constantly with SISS; indeed, McCarthy attended more SISS hearings (eighteen) than did any other nonmember. Buckley also attempts to paint SISS as ideologically balanced, claiming that liberals Kilgore, Magnuson, and Kefauver "voted unanimously" for the IPR report. As we have seen, this claim is false.

So McCarran triumphed: in the Senate, in the press, in academia. The next step was to be in court.

CHAPTER TWENTY-FOUR

Roy Cohn as Torquemada

J. Edgar Hoover despised Lattimore. In the early stages of the investigation Hoover scribbled notes on several reports such as "Press vigorously investigation of Lattimore." When McCarthy made his flamboyant charges, claiming that Lattimore was the boss of the Hiss ring, Hoover let his predatory interest in Lattimore and his impulse toward drama run away with him. As noted earlier, Hoover asked for a grand jury with witnesses announced in advance to secure a "wholesome response."[1] What he meant was an intensification of the inquisition. He failed to get the grand jury in 1950, but the right-wing press, McCarthy, McCarran, Budenz, and the China lobby provided as much intensification as he could have wished. Paradoxically, Hoover's FBI analysts gradually calmed down his eagerness to prosecute Lattimore.

Bureau investigation turned up nothing to support a Lattimore indictment. Budenz, the most spectacular witness, was a zealot and had only hearsay. Barmine and Bogolepov were no better. Utley did not impress the bureau as a potential witness. The IPR files had nothing incriminating; after each release of SISS transcripts, Supervisor Branigan wrote Belmont that there was nothing new in them.

The main push in the bureau for a Lattimore prosecution came from the Baltimore office, as witnessed by the 545-page report that office forwarded to headquarters December 29, 1950, listing sixteen possible instances in which Lattimore might have perjured himself before Tydings. Headquarters turned this report over to Agent M. A. Jones, who is not otherwise identified but appears to have been a lawyer specializing in perjury at bureau headquarters. Jones spent many months evaluating the Baltimore report; not until September 6, 1951, did he write Nichols giving his judgment. In fifteen pages he knocked down every potential charge except one: Lattimore might have lied when he told Tydings that he did not know Chi Ch'ao-ting was a Communist. Jones thought Lattimore must have seen E. Newton Steely's report on Chi in 1943: "This directly contravenes Lattimore's testimony, but appears to be the only evidence that directly does so." There is no conclusion in Jones's document, but it destroys every suggestion from Baltimore except the Steely incident.[2]

On April 25, 1952, Branigan wrote Belmont that despite the continuing intensive investigation of Lattimore, there was still no evidence of a crime. But the SISS testimony had not yet been analyzed, and there were still six witnesses to locate. Branigan did not have much hope for them. He ended his memo to Belmont, "It is anticipated that this investigation will be closed when the leads, at present outstanding, are covered, at which time the [Justice] Department will be furnished a closing summary report."[3]

Two weeks later D. M. Ladd reported to Hoover on "the background and status of the perjury investigation in instant case." Ladd repeated much of Branigan's earlier memo; the outstanding leads were now down to four; when these were covered, the case would be closed.[4]

On May 7, 1952, Budenz got another black eye within the FBI, which had obtained galley proofs of a new Budenz book, *The Cry Is Peace*. These proofs were analyzed both in Washington and New York. The bureau was pleased that Budenz praised the FBI, but the analysts were appalled at his errors. Whether at bureau instigation or not, printing was held up until some of them were corrected. Among other errors, Budenz "drew unwarranted conclusions" from SISS and HUAC hearings; misrepresented Hiss's status with the Communist party hierarchy; connected Agnes Smedley with the IPR; got the arrest of Judith Coplon wrong; and claimed that Philip Jaffe had been proved to be a Soviet spy.[5] *The Cry Is Peace* did see print in 1952, but not from the respectable New York publishers (Mc-Graw-Hill and Harper Brothers) who had handled his earlier works. *Peace* came out in Chicago from Henry Regnery Company, a right-wing house. Budenz never again had a book published by a major house.

By May 27 there were only two outstanding leads. Hoover instructed Baltimore that as soon as these were covered, "you place instant case in a pending inactive status at the same time submitting a report covering the results of investigation not already reported."[6] Despite McCarran, the FBI was clearly ready to be done with Lattimore. Any initiative now had to come from Justice. That Department turned the case over to Edward J. Hummer for evaluation.

Hummer, a former FBI agent, had worked closely with Father John F. Cronin, who had investigated Communists in trade unions for the National Catholic Welfare Conference in 1945–46. Hummer fed information from the bureau to Cronin, who in turn reported to Richard Nixon on HUAC. Hummer's anti-Communist credentials were impeccable. In 1981 Cronin told me that Hummer "might ultimately be credited with the indictment of Alger Hiss and (for better or worse) the rise of Richard Nixon." In analyzing the Lattimore case Hummer was working first with FBI reports, the Tydings transcripts, and press reports, and then with transcripts, as they became available, from the IPR hearings. He did not have the bureau's Budenz file and hence was not aware of the many derogations of Budenz's credibility. Hummer shared Hoover's dislike of Lattimore: Lattimore was too friendly with Communists, not hostile enough toward the Soviet Union, and too naïve about Soviet expansionism. However, in his forty-page evaluation of the Lattimore case dated June 17, 1952, Hummer did acknowledge that Lattimore could at least explain his association with Communists: "He himself attempts to justify these associations in his statement, 'For many years I have made every effort to keep in touch with as many people as possible who are informed about the Far East, and I have obtained as much information as I could, whether they were Communists, anti-Communists, liberals, conservatives, businessmen, politicians, Army officers, or scholars.' "[7]

Hummer knew a viable prosecution from a bunch of garbage, and his forty pages show overwhelmingly that taking this case before a jury would be a waste of time. He also realized how biased the McCarran witnesses had been. The FBI had at least gotten testimony from some acquaintances of Lattimore, the overwhelming majority of whom proclaimed his honesty and loyalty even when they disagreed with him. SISS, in contrast, had mostly hearsay, and what was not hearsay was from those few "experts" who despised Lattimore:

> During the course of this investigation, the FBI interviewed several hundred individuals who could conceivably prove or disprove the allegations of espionage or membership in the Communist Party on the part of Lattimore. As was expected, many had no personal first-hand information. The majority concluded, based on a review of Lattimore's writings, that he was a loyal American and generally took the view that he is an honest, intelligent man of liberal persuasions and therefore could not be a Communist; that at one time he obviously believed that the Chinese Communists were merely a progressive agrarian movement, as did many others who now know the Chinese Communists are

Moscow-directed. [Lattimore did not believe this; Hummer had obviously not read his writings.] A minority of those interviewed using the same standard, namely, a review of Lattimore's writings, came to the conclusion that Lattimore was a Communist or at least a Communist sympathizer and Soviet propagandist. . . .

Most of [this minority] have one thing in common: they are nationally known as staunch anti-Communists. From their pens have come numerous books and magazine articles warning of the dangers of the Communist conspiracy. However, since they do not possess first-hand personal information concerning the Communist Party membership of Lattimore, their statements that he is a Communist, based upon a review of Lattimore's writings, are inadmissible in a court of law. The only way to get their statements and conclusions before a jury would be to indulge in the novel but doubtful expediency of qualifying them as expert witnesses. By the same token Owen Lattimore could produce over 170 prospective witnesses, mostly college professors and scholars interested in Far Eastern studies who would testify that, based on a review of Lattimore's writings, they have come to the conclusion that he is not a Communist or pro-Communist.[8]

Hummer reviewed every one of the perjury counts being considered. None of them would hold up in court. Even the Chi Ch'ao-ting count would have to depend, in Hummer's view, on the testimony of Wittfogel, and it would be Wittfogel's word against Lattimore's. The new counts suggested by McCarran, which Hummer could not be certain of until he got SISS transcripts, did not impress him: "As indicated at first blush and again without attempting to prejudge the alleged 'untruths,' they do appear trivial and there is some doubt as to their materiality. The instance of meeting Ambassador Oumansky could be further developed."

Hummer's conclusion: no attempt to indict should be made. "It is my considered opinion that this should not be done at the present time." One of the reasons Hummer then summarized was that "to charge technical perjury to minor questions is to invite a full acquittal and thus place Lattimore on a pedestal and make him a martyr, a role he would relish but does not deserve." Furthermore, it would give him a chance "to write a new book, no doubt entitled *Ordeal by Trial*."[9]

Hummer updated his analysis when the McCarran committee transcripts were available and furnished the results to the FBI. As of September 18 he thought only two counts were viable: perjury in Lattimore's claiming he did not know that either Chi or Asiaticus were Communists.[10] This conclusion was communicated to Branigan, whose response is still denied by the FBI. It is not clear what Hummer thought of going to a grand jury with these two counts, but his earlier analysis would suggest that he still did not find an overwhelming case. Nor did the FBI.

However, Hummer and the FBI failed to take into account the immense power and zealotry of Senator Patrick A. McCarran and his ability to locate a hatchetman who would do his bidding. Roy Marcus Cohn, late of New York City, brightest of all the legal stars in the anti-Communist firmament, now followed the lure of power to the seat of government as the best man to nail the slippery Lattimore.

Roy Cohn was the son of a respected judge in the appellate division of the New York Supreme Court.[11] He was precocious as a youth, graduating from Columbia College and Columbia Law School by the time he was twenty. He had to wait until he was twenty-one to be admitted to the bar; the same day he was admitted, he went on the staff of the U.S. attorney in Manhattan. There he specialized in subversive activities. Nineteen forty-seven was a good year to take up that trade. Cohn assisted in the prosecution of Communist party leaders under the Smith Act, worked on the Remington and Rosenberg trials, and led a federal grand jury looking into "Fifth Amendment Communists" at the United Nations.

The latter was a runaway grand jury; Cohn led it to believe that since thirty-nine Americans working for the UN had refused to answer questions from the jury about their politics, the jury should issue a presentment declaring these employees to be subversive. The Department of Justice opposed this presentment; Cohn went ahead anyway. His first effort to get the presentment out was regarded by all officers of the Department of Justice as premature. At a conference in Washington Cohn told Department officials that SISS was about to open hearings on the loyalty of American UN employees, and he wanted to act quickly so "we can beat them to the headlines."[12] Cohn did not get the first headlines, but he made up for it later.

What he did get, when he went to Washington, was a chance to work on the hottest case around—Lattimore. Cohn had wanted to get the Lattimore case brought before his New York grand jury. He could connect Lattimore to the United Nations because of the mission in Afghanistan in 1950. As early as May 1, 1952, Jay Sourwine had picked up a rumor (this time correct) that Cohn planned to present "phases of the Lattimore case involving perjury" to his New York grand jury; Sourwine passed this rumor on to Lou Nichols, who didn't believe it.[13] But just to make sure, Nichols asked Agent W. M. Whelan in New York to talk to Cohn.

Mr. Whelan advised at 5:30 P.M. today [May 2] that he had talked to Assistant U.S. Attorney Cohn who told Whelan frankly that he had a "theory" that David Weintraub, and Irving Kaplan, who are presently United Nations employees, had participated in discussions having to do with the selection of Owen Lattimore. . . . Mr. Cohn told Mr. Whelan that he also had the idea that the Special Grand Jury now in session in the Southern District of New York was interested in the Institute of Pacific Relations and he thought perhaps he could work something into this Grand Jury on Owen Lattimore. . . . Cohn stated that he heard confidentially that his proposed action was turned down. Cohn said it was his understanding that Mr. Lane [Cohn's supervisor] was told to discontinue any action along this line by "McGranery or McInerney."[14]

May 5, just three days after the FBI learned Cohn wanted the Lattimore case, James P. McGranery appeared before McCarran's full Judiciary Committee for hearings on his confirmation as attorney general. Truman had fired Howard McGrath and nominated McGranery to clean up the Justice Department. McCarran knew all about the Cohn proposal; Robert Morris had lunched with Cohn the day before.[15] So McCarran was suspicious of McGranery. The committee badgered him about the Lattimore rumors and about *Amerasia*, with which he had been connected, for the first hour of the hearing. Eventually it came down to this:

Sen. McCarran: If it should be related . . . that you were opposed to presenting the matter of Owen Lattimore to a grand jury, would there be any truth in it?

Mr. McGranery: There would not be, sir. I would emphatically say, as I stated here this morning, Mr. Chairman, that I never discussed it with Mr. McInerney or anyone else.

Sen. McCarran: And you have not discussed the presentation of any case with Mr. McInerney since you were nominated?

Mr. McGranery: No, sir, I have not.

Sen. McCarran: And you are saying that under oath.

Mr. McGranery: Yes, sir.[16]

So the attorney general–designate of the United States had in effect promised the chairman of the Senate Judiciary Committee that he would prosecute Owen Lattimore.

McGranery was not yet home free. Senators Ferguson and Watkins were against him and filed a minority report opposing his confirmation. But McCarran led the floor fight over the nomination, and McGranery was confirmed.

McGranery was now in a bind. He knew the Lattimore case was a hot issue, but he had the July 5 letter from Truman bitterly attacking the McCarran committee's harassment of Lattimore and opposing an indictment. The Republican national convention in July intensified McGranery's discomfort: Joe McCarthy's friends paraded around the convention hall holding up large red herrings bearing the names Alger Hiss, Owen Lattimore, and Dean Acheson.[17] But McGranery knew what he had to do. Truman may have selected him, but Truman was a lame duck. McCarran's power would last indefinitely.

McGranery knew the Justice Department was honeycombed with people, like Hummer, who did not think there was a case against Lattimore; he had to get someone in Justice who felt differently, who was acceptable to McCarran. The impresario who cleared the way was the right-wing columnist George Sokolsky, a friend of both McCarran and McGranery. Sokolsky had watched Cohn propel himself into the front ranks of Communist hunters. Harvey Matusow says Sokolsky bragged that he had advised McGranery "to appoint Roy Cohn as a special assistant to the Attorney General to bring the Lattimore case before a grand jury. In this way, Sokolsky said he had told McGranery, McCarran could be assured that the Lattimore case would not be quashed. Sokolsky jokingly said he was lenient in not forcing the indictment to be brought forth prior to the 1952 election." Matusow appears to be accurate in this report. Nicholas von Hoffman, in his biography of Cohn, also credits Sokolsky with mediating the Cohn appointment.[18]

Thus, on September 3, 1952, McGranery "directed the transfer of Roy M. Cohn, Assistant United States Attorney for the Southern District of New York, to the Criminal Division of the Department of Justice in connection with internal security matters."[19]

Cohn was taking a vacation in August, recuperating from his strenuous labors with the New York grand jury. In December 1979 Cohn told me that he did not discuss the Lattimore case with McGranery before breaking off his vacation and going to Washington. This seems unlikely. McGranery needed him precisely for that case, and Cohn had certainly tried to get it for himself in New York. And he wasted no time after he got to Washington. The day after his formal transfer, he called Alan Belmont at the FBI, asking for current addresses of prospective Lattimore grand jury witnesses: Karl Wittfogel, E. Newton Steely, Louis Budenz, Freda Utley, Nicholas Poppe, George Taylor, Alexander Barmine, and David Nelson Rowe. Cohn wanted to interview them.[20]

Thus began a frenzy of activity such as Justice had not seen for a long time. It was bad enough that Cohn swept in with all his youthful vigor; it was worse that he owed no allegiance to any of his immediate bosses and reported to McCarran every time he had a fight with his colleagues.[21] Cohn was candid about his unpopularity with the Lattimore case team: "Here was I a twenty-five-year-old kid coming waltzing down from New York, being liked, openly liked by Attorney General McGranery, which liking I returned. . . . And here I come in, a twenty-five-year-old guy and people who were fifty, sixty or something like that were sitting around the Department reading newspapers for twenty years and here I come full of action, and you know my light was on hours after they had gone home in the afternoon and I was there hours before they got there in the morning. And I was just, as my friend Senator Jenner once put it, I was the kid who went to the party and peed in the lemonade."[22]

The FBI got tremors from Justice immediately. On September 4 Branigan was visited by an attorney working on the Lattimore case who described the tidal wave that had hit the department. (The attorney's name is denied, but the context indicates that it could only be Hummer.) Hummer was disturbed. He thought Cohn was going off half-cocked; he and his colleagues did not want "to take a case to court unless the facts are such that a conviction will be forthcoming and that a conviction will stick." Cohn was talking about using all the SISS charges against Lattimore, most of which Hummer thought weak.[23]

By September 19 Cohn had a ten-page memorandum prepared recommending a perjury prosecution.[24] This document has not survived, but it must have been close to the actual charges submitted to the grand jury. Cohn was in gear. Part of his unpopularity in the department was due not to his hyperactivity but to his arrogance. One flagrant instance recorded in FBI files was the interview of witness X in San Francisco.

Witness X had something to say about Lattimore's knowledge of Chi Ch'ao-ting. Cohn was determined to interview witness X himself. Assistant Attorney General Charles Murray called the bureau on October 1, explaining that Cohn "was insistent that the Bureau not conduct the interview" because X was the "type of individual who must be coddled and babied, brought along slowly to the point where he will be cooperative, ———— that Cohn insisted that only he, Cohn, could conduct a successful interview with ————." Murray overruled Cohn and wrote a letter to the bureau instructing them to conduct the interview. Cohn then protested to McCarran; McCarran intervened with Justice; Justice backed down and at 3:40 P.M. the same day telephoned the bureau asking them to return Murray's letter. Murray then apparently went to McGranery and got a reversal, for at 3:50 P.M. Justice telephoned the bureau again: keep Murray's letter and interview X. Belmont, reporting this imbroglio with just a touch of sarcasm, recommended that the bureau do the interview.[25]

Belmont got another earful from Murray on October 1. Fighting over the Lattimore case had been intense, and Cohn's memorandum recommending prosecution was not accepted by the department. SISS was pressing the issue; all seven members signed a letter to the Justice Department inquiring what was being done about Lattimore. According to Murray, the department intended to answer the SISS letter by sending the committee Hummer's recommendation against prosecution, or at least the "gist" of it. Belmont observed, "It must be anticipated that if the Department advises the McCarran Committee of the results of its analysis [the Hummer memo] the McCarran Committee, with widespread publicity, will claim that the Department has whitewashed the Lattimore case."[26]

The next day, Belmont got another call from Justice. There was then "a better than 50-50 chance that the perjury angles of the Lattimore case will be presented to a grand jury."[27] Cohn was winning, no doubt with an assist from McCarran.

There is then a gap in the FBI file as released, and we do not know either the course of the battle over the Lattimore indictment or McGranery's role in it. The next relevant document is dated October 24, 1952. Murray wrote the FBI asking that they conduct further investigation on three of the perjury counts: the Oumansky luncheon, Lattimore's testimony that he did not take care of Currie's mail when Currie was away, and Lattimore's claim that he made no prearrangements for his 1937 visit to Yenan.[28] Justice was now clearly preparing to go before a grand jury.

About McCarran's role there can be no doubt. On October 3 he released the letter SISS had sent to McGranery urging prosecution. The *New York Times* headlined its story "M'Granery Pressed on Lattimore case": "The Internal Security Subcommittee of the Senate asked the Department of Justice today what it intended to do about the group's recommendation that Prof. Owen Lattimore be prosecuted for perjury. A letter to James P. McGranery, the Attorney General, which was signed by all the members of the subcommittee, was made public by the chairman, Senator Pat McCarran, Democrat of Nevada. A spokesman for the Justice Department said no comment would be forthcoming at this time."[29]

McGranery kept his promise to prosecute Lattimore, but he got back at McCarran for the senator's bullying by cutting Cohn out of the action. Cohn told me in 1979 that he had presented the Lattimore case to the grand jury, but his memory was false. Ed Hummer handled the presentation. McGranery had finally had enough of the abrasive Cohn.

The decision to drop Cohn was made on November 28. W. V. Cleveland, duty officer that night at FBI headquarters, reported in a memo to Belmont:

> At 6:10 P.M. on November 28, 1952, former SA Ed Hummer, who is now with the Criminal Division of the Department, advised that he had just left a conference held by the Attorney General in connection with captioned case [Lattimore]. The Attorney General instructed that this case is to be presented to a Grand Jury commencing Thursday, December 4, and specifically designated Hummer to take charge of the presentation. According to Hummer the Attorney General has instructed that there is to be no publicity in connection with this matter until Wednesday, December 3. In addition, the Attorney General instructed those present (including William Foley and Assistant Attorney General Murray) that Special Assistant to the Attorney General Roy Cohn was not to be advised of this contemplated action prior to December 3, the day on which the press release is to be made.[30]

So Cohn was sidelined from the blockbuster case he most wanted to handle. It was a humiliation that by 1979 he had fully repressed.

Between mid-October 1952, when McGranery provisionally decided to go to the grand jury, and December 4, when the presentation began, there was much pulling and hauling. The first list of eight proposed perjury counts was given to the FBI November 3.[31] They were all specific items: the date of the Oumansky luncheon, whether Lattimore knew Fred Field to be a Communist, his handling of Currie's mail, and so on. Baltimore was instructed to prepare another report, including everything in FBI files tending to establish perjury on these eight counts.

On December 1 the bureau had its analysis of the eight counts. Ladd wrote a six-page memorandum to Hoover: "Five of these instances are considered weak because of lack of evidence and because Lattimore admitted before the afore-mentioned committee that he was wrong in his original statements which are now considered perjurious. In another instance Lattimore prefaced his statement with the phrase, 'To the best of my recollection.' It was later proved through the introduction of a document that Lattimore was wrong. No other proof is available and it is felt that this instance is also weak. In the remaining two instances, there appears to be sufficient evidence to obtain indictments."[32]

Ladd then reviewed each of the counts and summarized the evidence. He concluded, "The Lattimore case is an extremely controversial one and it is believed the Bureau should take the position that any decision as to the merits of the evidence to support a possible perjury case is one solely for the Criminal Division to make." Hoover, reflecting the general skepticism of the FBI at this stage, wrote at the bottom of Ladd's memo, "The A.G. has decided to have Lattimore case presented to the G.J. No views of Bureau were sought."[33]

While Ladd was telling Hoover what a weak case the department had, an attorney who had been on the Lattimore case earlier, taken off it, then brought back, submitted to Justice a long argument for a general "promoter of Communist causes" count as the first count in the indictment. The writer was C. George Anastos. Such a general count, according to Anastos, was the "gist" of the case against Lattimore and would add materiality to the specific counts, which by themselves were trivial.

Furthermore, said Anastos, this general count would enable the prosecutors to enter into evidence much testimony that would otherwise be irrelevant: testimony that Lattimore was pro-Communist. He recognized that the new count would involve difficult interpretation of documents and would raise "ideological questions of free speech," but these difficulties could be overcome. After all, he said, the proposed general count "is analogous to and no more difficult than a count demanding the banning of a book for obscenity. In both cases the tribunal is capable of making a finding of fact based on its interpretation of a publication."[34]

Anastos carried the day. Hummer and Murray agreed, and a general count was made the first count of the proposed indictment: Lattimore had lied when he denied that he had been a promoter of communism and Communist interests. Anastos was barely in time. On December 2, a day earlier than planned, McGranery issued the news release. Lattimore's case was to go to the federal grand jury sitting in Washington, D.C., on December 4. (The news release was a violation of the law on grand jury secrecy.) The press release finessed the question of who would actually present the case; it noted only that the presentation "will be under the supervision of Assistant Attorney General Charles B. Murray."[35]

So the *Times*, and probably every other daily in the country, carried the story on December 3 that Lattimore would be a subject of grand jury action. Cohn was not mentioned. The *Times* story was front page, but not the lead. The lead story that day, with a three-column headline, "Clearing of Spies for U.N. Laid to State Department by Defiant U. S. Jury Here," concerned Cohn's runaway grand jury. Cohn had upstaged the Justice Department and had gotten even with Murray and Malone, who had tried to suppress his presentment about spies in the UN; moreover, he had timed the release beautifully. Cohn's talent for getting headlines soon came to the attention of another publicity genius, Joe McCarthy. And were there any doubt about Cohn's ability at self-promotion, his remarks to the court when the presentment was handed up, quoted in the *Times*, dispelled it: this investigation, Cohn said in all seriousness, was "probably the most important investigation ever conducted in the entire history of the United States."[36]

Cohn's publicity coup unnerved McGranery and staff. Perhaps that was the reason for McGranery's draconian instructions to Hummer on December 4. Hummer was informed that "the presentation of the facts of instant case before the Grand Jury must be completed and an indictment returned by Christmas of this year."[37] One can understand McGranery's concern. With all the fuss over the runaway UN grand jury, heaped on top of "twenty years of (Democratic) treason," the Yalta sellout, the *Amerasia* case, the loss of China—what better talisman could a departing attorney general have than an indictment of the man who masterminded the loss of China?

When school began in fall 1952, Lattimore concentrated as well as he could on the scholarly programs of the Page School. His prestige at Johns Hopkins continued high. George Carter, who had run to McCarthy with his story about Lattimore declassifying secret documents in 1950, was silent. Johns Hopkins faculty who knew Lattimore could not believe that the scurrilous SISS report could be taken seriously by the Department of Justice or that the endless hearsay of McCarran's former Communist witnesses could lead to prosecution.

Lattimore was still, at least in the international scholarly community, a major figure. He corresponded at some length with Krishna Menon, Indian foreign minister, about the situation of the Mongol exiles from communism then living at Kalimpong. Lattimore recommended to Menon that India take advantage of the intelligence these Mongols had to offer about conditions in the People's Republic of China and particularly in Tibet. Menon replied, "These Mongol exiles certainly deserve our sympathy and respect; and we shall keep an eye on them. I do hope you will come to Delhi again before long."[38]

Max Beloff, a prominent Oxford scholar, wrote Lattimore in February 1952 soliciting Lattimore's opinions on several matters relating to Inner Mongolia and Sinkiang discussed in a book Beloff was writing. Lattimore's appearance before SISS kept him from answering Beloff until May, when he reviewed for Beloff the latest intelligence from Central Asia and noted that both Chinese and Russians wanted to prevent a "pan-Mongolian" movement from flourishing.[39]

At the Page School, Mongol studies continued as well as possible given Lattimore's absences and preoccupations. The Dilowa dictated his autobiography and wrote political reminiscences, which Lattimore translated. Working with David Eberle and Harold Vreeland, the Dilowa also "provided the material for an institutional and social description and analysis of the position of the Lama Buddhist Church in pre-revolutionary Mongol Society." John Hangin and Urgunge Onon, the young Mongols at Hopkins, worked with their wives to produce a linguistic description and grammar of Chahar and Daghor Mongol; they also provided material for sociological and cultural analysis of the processes of change in Mongol society. Father Louis Schram, the Maryknoll scholar associated with Lattimore, continued writing his description of the sociology of the Mongols of western Kansu.[40]

Even during the tumult of 1952 many of these efforts came to fruition. The Dilowa's description of his former domain, the Narobanchin monastery, was published in the *Proceedings of the American Philosophical Society*. Lattimore's American outlets were no longer available (with one exception, noted below), but he had an article on the Genghis Khan relics in the *Journal of the Royal Central Asian Society* in April; an article, "Mongolia's New Relations with Her Neighbors," in the *Manchester Guardian* of November 24; and "Red Chinese and Red Barbarians" in *Eastern World* (London) in December.

Before the McCarthy onslaught, Lattimore and other IPR writers were prominent as book reviewers for the *New York Times* and the *New York Herald Tribune*. This work ceased after 1949. Of American journals, only the *Nation* still welcomed Lattimore's contributions. The December 6, 1952, issue, which appeared the same week McGranery announced grand jury action, carried Lattimore's "Inner Asia: Sino-Soviet Bridge." This article represents Lattimore's best effort to explain once again, and in light of current political realities, the plight of a gallant Mongol race fighting for autonomy. The article is a lucid explanation of what was then happening in the Sino-Soviet border areas, events to which Lattimore thought the United States should pay more attention. He concludes:

> In his National Press Club speech of January, 1950, Secretary of State Dean Acheson declared that Russia is engaged in "detaching" from China and "attaching" to Russia the northern areas of China. "This process," said Mr. Acheson, "is completed in Outer Mongolia. It is nearly com-

pleted in Manchuria.'' He went on to include Inner Mongolia and Sinkiang, and to say that ''this fact that the Soviet Union is taking the four
northern provinces of China is the single most significant, most important fact in the relations of any foreign power with Asia.''

Mr. Acheson could hardly have been more wrong, and if American
policy should rest complacently on the belief that he was right, there
will eventually be another uproar when it is discovered that things have
happened in Asia that we have not been told to expect.[41]

But Acheson's was the conventional wisdom. Everybody knew the Soviet
Union had attached the northern provinces of China.

On December 5, 1952, while Hummer was preparing the grand jury
presentation, Cohn was in Miami with Senator Homer Ferguson. Ferguson was expected to be the next chair of Judiciary when the Republicans
organized the Senate in January 1953. Cohn called Hummer from Miami.
His main message: even if Hummer succeeded in getting an indictment
of Lattimore, Cohn would ''not be able to assist the Government in the
trial of the subject since he [would] then be Counsel for the Senate Committee on the Judiciary.''[42] Was this bragging? McCarran was (or had
been) fond of Cohn, but would McCarran not have enough clout to keep
the faithful Jay Sourwine on as counsel? Would Ferguson insist on his
own man? That may have been Ferguson's intention in December, but
William Langer of North Dakota, rather than Ferguson, took over Judiciary. Cohn did not go with Judiciary; he attached himself, portentously,
to McCarthy.

December 15 brought bad news for the foreign service: John Carter
Vincent, after yet another security investigation, was suspended.

The next day an announcement came from the Justice Department. The
grand jury had indicted Lattimore on seven counts of perjury. No one was
more surprised than the Lattimore case officers in the FBI. Precisely what
Hummer did to overcome all the difficulties he and bureau evaluators had
identified we do not know. Hummer was a professional, and despite his
doubts he clearly gave the presentation his best effort.[43]

The announcement gave credit to Hummer for presenting the case;
Cohn, Anastos, and John H. Davitt were also mentioned. The seven counts
were unanimously agreed to by the grand jury except for count seven, on
which the vote was 22–1. The grand jury said that Lattimore lied under
oath when he denied

1. that he had been a promoter of communism or Communist interests;
2. that he was told that Chi Ch'ao-ting was a Communist;

3. that he knew Asiaticus was a Communist;

4. that he had published any articles by Communists in *Pacific Affairs*;

5. that a meeting with Soviet Ambassador Oumansky occurred during the period of the Hitler-Stalin pact;

6. that he handled Lauchlin Currie's White House mail when Currie was away;

7. that his trip to Yenan in 1937 was prearranged with Communist authorities.

Front-page news again, all over the country. Lattimore promptly denied all the charges.

The day after the indictment, Hummer stopped by his old haunts at the bureau. He told Inspector Carl Hennrich, and probably others, that Lattimore would be arraigned December 19; that bail would be set at $2,000; that the judge would grant a continuance for filing appeals until February 15, 1953; that Thurman Arnold claimed he could not defend the case because of other demands on his time but would bring in "the outstanding criminal lawyer in the country"; and that the defense would attack the first count on the basis of vagueness and the remaining counts as not material or significant.[44] It all happened just as Hummer predicted. Judge James R. Kirkland of U.S. District Court in Washington deviated one day from Hummer's prediction about filing motions: the deadline was to be February 16.

The bureau now began to worry that the case might be thrown out on the basis of their illegal 1949 technical surveillance of Lattimore. Hoover wrote the Baltimore office December 19 requesting that it furnish a memorandum describing "all information obtained as a result of the tesurs [technical surveillances] utilized in instant case" and the location of the logs and recordings.[45] This information was never needed.

December was a terrible month for China specialists. Many predicted the Lattimore trial would equal that of Hiss for bitterness and sensation. And if the Lattimore trial failed to equal expectations, perhaps that of John Paton Davies would. Davies was suspended from duty the same day Lattimore was indicted. He had not yet been indicted, but SISS was pushing for it, and McCarran got what McCarran wanted.

The right-wing press had a field day with Lattimore's indictment. McGranery's alleged softness on communism was forgotten, and the attorney general received the kind of heartwarming letters from ordinary citizens that the temper of the times encouraged. Typical was a letter from a Brooklyn housewife:

> As the mother of a young man on the line in Korea, may I thank you for at last bringing to justice the case of Owen Lattimore through whose efforts the support of the United States was withdrawn from the legitimate Chinese Government?
>
> This man has the blood of twenty thousand young Americans on his hands. His only excuse is stupidity and forgetfulness, strange claims for an expert.
>
> God is not mocked. Those fine young men died through the plotting of Communists here. Your job is to get them all.[46]

Lattimore got letters too, most of them encouraging. Many of his former IPR associates wrote in a morale-bolstering effort that meant much to him and his lawyers at Arnold, Fortas, and Porter. One of the most philosophical tributes was from Miriam S. Farley, a major writer for IPR, who compared Lattimore's tribulations with those of Job. "The parallel of Job, though obvious, is not exact. Job was the victim of an apparently pointless persecution by his own God. The persecution of which you are victims is not pointless, and it does not proceed from God but from the devil. . . . Your public vindication is not a matter of concrete proof; hence it depends on the trend of opinion, and it can never be complete. . . . You will keep the faith, and by so doing you will help others to keep it.[47]

Arnold Toynbee was less lyrical, more optimistic:

> Veronica and I were much concerned to see that the thing has been reopened again. After you had been cleared by the first senate committee, we had so much hoped that it was all over, and that you would be free once more to give your mind to scholarship.
>
> The only consolation is a point made by the correspondent of the London Times: Now that the case is to come before a court of law, the result will surely be final, this time at least; and, as you will once again be able to prove that the charges are unfounded, I take some comfort in this. All the same, I do wish you had been spared this additional affliction, and I am very sorry about it.[48]

The indictment, like the original 1950 McCarthy charges that brought Robert LeMoyne Barrett back into the realm of Lattimore supporters, was not without its benefits. In December 1952 Lattimore became a hero of the intellectual establishment worldwide. The testimony of Arthur and Mary Wright, prestigious Stanford scholars of Asia who maintained an extensive program of "exchanges of books, ideas and personnel" with foreign countries, is perhaps most compelling. The Wrights knew Lattimore well, and Mary Wright was close to Senator Lister Hill of Alabama. She wrote the senator February 9, 1953, aghast at the "lunatics who are trying to wreck this country," hoping that Hill would be able to help restore the good name of an innocent scholar. Wright included in her letter a description of the impact of the Lattimore prosecution on her contacts abroad:

> I don't think many Americans realize that Lattimore has become a symbol of the last stand of the "old" America, the "good" America—in England, Indonesia, Japan, India—everywhere. On the Lattimore case, the rankest Tory and the most ardent Laborite, the staidest Japanese conservative and the most volatile Indian liberal are in agreement. We do not get this impression just from letters. It is my business to keep up with a wide range of newspapers and periodicals; those who distrust us are hammering away at the Lattimore case with great effect. Those who want to trust us are almost pathetically begging their readers to wait; pointing to the fact that there is another America, that in the end the American people will not tolerate this kind of thing. We have just got to prove that this second group is right about us.[49]

Whether "this second group" was right or not is a moot point. More important for Lattimore's ultimate salvation, intellectuals in Europe and Asia came to regard him as a hero. The payoff of this response was delayed, but significant.

Several indictments during the witch-hunt were obtained illegitimately; Lattimore's was just one of them. One other fraudulent indictment that we know about, of economist Val Lorwin in December 1953, was corrected. Lorwin was on McCarthy's hit list of eighty-one Communists. Assistant Attorney General Warren Olney III went before the U.S. District Court for the District of Columbia on May 25, 1954, and got the Lorwin indictment dismissed. The government prosecutor, William Gallagher, had lied to the grand jury on two substantial matters. Gallagher admitted to Olney that he had pushed the indictment through rather "than attempt to explain the case to a Senate investigating committee."[50]

Somehow a similar mea culpa never emerged from the Lattimore prosecutors.

CHAPTER TWENTY-FIVE

Youngdahl

On the face of it, Pat McCarran could celebrate the coming of 1953 with glee. The new Eisenhower-Nixon administration would be a vast improvement over Truman in its zeal to punish Communists. The candidate McCarran supported for the other Senate seat from Nevada, George "Molly" Malone, won a close election. (McCarran opposed the Democrat Thomas Mechling.) McCarran's power in Nevada politics held steady. John Carter Vincent had been suspended by the State Department, and it was just a matter of time before John Paton Davies would get his due. McCarran's immigration law took effect, and 269 French sailors on board the *Liberté* in New York harbor were denied shore leave over Christmas 1952 because they refused to answer questions about their politics. Best of all, Lattimore had finally been indicted.[1]

McCarran's satisfaction over the Lattimore indictment, however, ran aground on an entirely unanticipated shoal: the vindictiveness of Roy Cohn. Cohn had been McCarran's eyes and ears on the Lattimore prosecution team, and he reported loyally and regularly to his patron. On the testimony of Cohn, we must assume that McCarran supported him as the new counsel to the Judiciary Committee, which Cohn told Hummer he was accepting.[2]

But Cohn's vanity induced him to seek revenge on Hummer. As Cohn saw it, Hummer did not deserve credit for the Lattimore indictment, nor should he have been in charge of the grand jury presentation. Either in late December 1952 or early January 1953 Cohn went to Robert Morris with a proposal: they should together show McCarran the early Hummer analysis arguing that there was no case against Lattimore, claim that this was one of the briefs that Hummer had presented to the grand jury, and get McCarran to demand that Hummer not be put in charge of the Lattimore prosecution. They consequently visited McCarran and showed him the Hummer brief; predictably, McCarran believed them and was livid at Hummer.[3]

McCarran's chance to humiliate Hummer came on January 19, when Herbert Brownell appeared before Senate Judiciary for hearings on confirmation as attorney general. Senator William Langer of North Dakota was now chair, but McCarran was ranking Democrat with only slightly reduced clout. Ten minutes into the hearing McCarran got his turn to question the nominee.

> *Sen. McCarran:* There is now pending in the Department of Justice, or, rather, pending before the courts of the District of Columbia, the indictment of one Owen Lattimore. That indictment was effected by this committee having sent the record of the Lattimore hearings to the Department of Justice. There is now in charge of that case a lawyer by the name of Hummer. I happen to know from personal observation in one instance—that is, of his brief—that he filed with the grand jury two briefs against finding the indictment. He is now in charge of the prosecution. Query: Do you believe that a man who has evinced his attitude as against the indictment should have charge of the prosecution before a trial jury?
>
> *Mr. Brownell:* Senator, I have stated before, and I want to state to you and the other members of the committee, that I shall use the greatest care in the selection of personnel there and the assignment to particular jobs to see to it that we get men who are interested in rigid enforcement of the laws of this country. I shall select a person in this particular case that you refer to, other than Mr. Hummer, who will study the record with great care; and, if there is wrongdoing in that case, he will be equipped in every manner to give an effective prosecution on behalf of the people.[4]

A firestorm broke immediately. The press was all over McCarran's office, the Justice Department, and the FBI with questions. Within hours McGranery issued a denial; Hummer, he said, had initially opposed prosecution but after reviewing the SISS hearings had recommended prosecution. Hummer had done such a good job before the grand jury that the vote was 23–0 on six counts, 22–1 on the seventh.[5]

Hummer's friends began a campaign to vindicate him. Father Cronin led the charge. On January 21 Cronin conveyed his dismay to McCarran: "I have known Mr. Hummer intimately for seven years. There are few officials in Washington, elected or appointed, who surpass him both in first-hand knowledge of Communism and in all-out opposition to this menace. . . . Undoubtedly you were deceived by someone who was ill-informed, malicious, or both. In simple justice, you owe it to Mr. Hummer and to yourself to get the facts. Once you have them, I feel sure that you will publicly correct the injustice you have done."[6] Cronin sent copies to Attorney General Brownell and Deputy Attorney General William P. Rogers.

William N. Payne, Jr., foreman of the grand jury that indicted Lattimore, speaking for all the jurors, also sent McCarran a blistering letter, by registered mail, telling the senator that he was protesting to the attorney general and stating that "several members of the Grand Jury have expressed to me the possibility of an investigation and reopening of the Grand Jury phase of this case to discover the source of these unfounded charges."[7]

Hummer, of course, also protested to any and all who would listen. His friends in the bureau insisted that he go talk to someone in McCarran's office. On January 29 Hummer visited Chief Counsel Jay Sourwine. Sourwine was sympathetic. As Hummer told Branigan the next day, "Sourwine advised that he knows that Senator McCarran was wrong in his statements and, according to Hummer, Sourwine 'doesn't know what to do about him,' meaning Senator McCarran. . . . Hummer stated he intends to write a Departmental memorandum recommending that this matter be brought before a Grand Jury, since it is a violation of Federal statutes to furnish any unauthorized person classified information."[8]

There followed a bitter series of exchanges between SISS staff, Hummer, and the FBI. The best worm's-eye view of the brouhaha was that of Eva Adams, McCarran's personal secretary. She had observed the whole thing, from the visit of Cohn and Morris with the senator to Father Cronin's storming over with protests from the National Catholic Welfare Conference on February 5. Lou Nichols got her evaluation of how it all stood then: "Miss Adams stated Cohn and Morris are now trying to deny that they made certain statements to Senator McCarran. Miss Adams, incidentally, is not too happy with either Morris or Cohn and told me she was going to have some problems, as was everybody else with these two."[9]

McCarran had the biggest problem. He had offended a constituency very important to him, and everybody in Washington knew he had unjustly maligned Hummer. During early February 1953 McCarran was out of Washington. When he returned, Sourwine and Adams persuaded him to apologize to Hummer. It was a hard thing for the crusty old baron to do, but on February 16 he wrote Hummer a letter.

> Upon returning to Washington, I find that an interpretation which was never intended has been placed upon my remarks with respect to your memoranda concerning the Lattimore case.
>
> All I intended to convey was that you had written memoranda with respect to this case and the question of whether it should go to a grand jury, and that you had in one memorandum arrived at and expressed the conclusion that there was no case against Lattimore justifying taking the matter to the grand jury, on the basis of the Tydings hearings and all evidence made available by the Federal Bureau of Investigation up to that time. I am sure you will agree with me that this was in fact the case.
>
> I am sorry if you have been hurt by the interpretation placed upon my remarks. I had no purpose of injuring you, and there was nothing of personal vindictiveness in what I said.[10]

This was all a lie. No false interpretation had been placed on McCarran's remarks. He had been given false information by Cohn and Morris and had repeated it in the Brownell hearing, with plenty of vindictiveness. But Hummer was a gentleman. He replied, "I wish to thank you for your courtesy, and the fair-mindedness of your views. I look forward to meeting you someday. Since I was born and raised in your neighboring state, Utah, I am sure we have some mutual acquaintances."[11]

McCarran knew the real villain in the fracas. Cohn was not made counsel to Senate Judiciary but went instead to the Senate Permanent Subcommittee on Investigation, where his devotion to G. David Schine, and his flamboyant style, eventually brought McCarthy into public disrepute.

Hummer was left with the tainted shreds of the Lattimore case. Over and above Cohn's nastiness, Hummer was appalled at the fanaticism that had led McCarran to intervene so outrageously in the judicial process and to force through a shaky indictment. Hummer knew that his original recommendation against prosecution was right, that the SISS hearings had not changed the situation, and that his success with the grand jury would not be easily repeated in court, where government witnesses would be cross-examined by a skillful attorney representing Lattimore. But Hummer also understood McGranery's position and the need to ride with the prevailing hysteria. That consideration, plus Hummer's dislike of Lattimore, led him to get on board the bandwagon. Anyway, twenty-three solid citizens on the grand jury had voted to indict.

But Hummer knew he could not head the prosecution.[12] It would take a rock-ribbed, copper-sheathed eminence to do that. In addition to Brownell's promise to McCarran, the Eisenhower ethos would demand a prominent, no-holds-barred prosecutor.

This problem was put in the lap of Earl Warren's former assistant in the California attorney general's office, Warren Olney III. Olney was a blue blood, a renowned prosecutor, just right for assistant attorney general in charge of the criminal division. One of Olney's first jobs was to look into the Lattimore case, which he discussed in an oral history:

> We inherited that case in the form of an indictment already returned. . . . It was within my authority to dismiss that indictment. I read the testimony and I read the reports. If I had been able to read the grand jury testimony and read the reports prior to any action being taken, I would have recommended against an indictment because it didn't seem to me that it was a provable case. There was enough there perhaps to call for as complete an investigation as you could make, on the chance that something more definitive in the way of evidence would show up. But on the basis of what was at hand at that time, it seemed very weak to me.
>
> But I didn't discuss this. I didn't pass the decision on to somebody else. I concluded that I ought to take the load on myself and I decided that we ought to go ahead and try it. The reasons were: if we dismissed the case, there would be a tremendous commotion, claiming that influential people had stepped in and caused us to dismiss the motion against Lattimore, just because he was a well-known and well-connected person. And there would be a great many people who would continue to believe he was guilty and, in fact, would think that dismissal was just evidence that he was.
>
> On the other hand, if we went ahead and presented the case in public for what it was—one never knows what's going to develop in a trial. . . . So we decided to go ahead with it. . . .
>
> So I thought we should find an outside prosecutor who was experienced and who would approach the thing with an open mind to investigate, prepare, and further evaluate the case. We would inform him, when he took it on, that if he concluded that the case was not triable and that the proof was not there, we would dismiss. On the other hand, if he concluded that it was a triable case, and he so recommended, then we would expect *him* to try the case, and not somebody else.
>
> We got Leo Rover for the purpose.[13]

Leo Rover had been appointed U.S. Attorney for the District of Columbia by Coolidge and held that post under Hoover and Roosevelt until 1934. He successfully prosecuted the Gaston Means case in connection with the Lindbergh kidnapping, taught law at Catholic University of America and at Georgetown, and in 1952 was selected "lawyer of the year" by the District of Columbia Bar Association. Rover's views on Lattimore were compatible with those of the new administration. Olney to the contrary, it is hard to imagine that Rover could have decided not to prosecute.

At first Rover was confident of his case. By March, however, he was having second thoughts. Count four of the indictment was particularly troublesome, and on March 6 Rover conferred with Inspector Hennrich of the FBI about this problem. Count two, in which Lattimore was charged with lying about his knowledge of Chi Ch'ao-ting, and count three, about Asiaticus, could be handled. But count four charged that Lattimore lied when he said he had not published articles by other persons known to him to be Communists. Who were these other persons? Apparently nothing specific had been presented to the grand jury. Four hundred eleven different individuals had written for *Pacific Affairs* while Lattimore was editor. Could the bureau find a Communist among them? As Hennrich reported this conference to Belmont, "During our discussion, Mr. Rover acknowledged that in connection with this particular count, it is, in effect, a situation of having the cart before the horse, in that an indictment has already been returned and now it is necessary to bolster the indictment by having additional investigation conducted in order to try to substantiate it in the event the Chi Chao-ting and Asiaticus counts fail."[14]

After some carping, the bureau agreed to check out the 411 potential Communists who had written for Lattimore. But things did not improve for Rover. On March 17 Robert Morris telephoned Lou Nichols with another of his tips about an incriminating letter Lattimore had allegedly written that might be tracked down (it wasn't). Morris had other news: "Morris also told me in confidence he was somewhat disturbed about a statement which he had heard, allegedly made by Rover _____ that Rover had said, in commenting on the Lattimore case, he would much rather have a case in which he had some confidence. Morris further stated this is the line which Hummer has been taking and he had been informed Hummer had told Warren Olney this was a bad case."[15]

It was a bad case, and Abe Fortas knew it. As he recalled in 1981, "I told Lattimore with all the force I could bring to bear that he had to tell me the truth, that I didn't want him to tell me anything that was not the absolute truth about what he did and what he believed in. I had a feeling that what he was telling me *was* the absolute truth. I never, despite what seems to me to be the lifetime that I spent on this case, I never had a moment of doubt."[16]

But Fortas knew well the political pressures to make Lattimore a scapegoat. As noted earlier, Fortas had warned Lattimore of the "possibility of a straight frameup, with perjured witnesses and perhaps even forged documents."[17] By 1953 Fortas's pessimism was fully justified. Whatever gossip went the rounds about the case against Lattimore being weak, the massive resources of the Justice Department, the FBI, and the McCarran Senate bloc would guarantee powerful prosecution.

Since the prestigious Leo Rover was heading the prosecution, Thurman Arnold, the best-known figure in the firm of Arnold, Fortas, and Porter (AFP), assumed an increasing role in the Lattimore case. Arnold was fully supportive of Lattimore. Having substituted for Fortas during several days of the SISS hearings, Arnold knew the lengths to which McCarran would go. Arnold wrote a friend in March 1952, "Never in my life have I seen anything more vicious and contemptible than the way the Committee is trying to break Lattimore."[18] He drafted most of the briefs, taking ideas from several Yale law professors and members of AFP.

Paul Porter, the other senior member of AFP, was less prominent in the Lattimore defense but equally committed. Gene Gressley relates one of Porter's prime anecdotes. Porter met an acquaintance at a suburban Washington country club who yelled at him, "Paul, are you still representing Communists and homosexuals?" Porter fired back, "What's the matter, John, are you in trouble?"[19] To help with the political aspects of the case, AFP hired Joseph C. O'Mahoney, a senator from Wyoming until his defeat in the 1952 election.

AFP had lots of help in preparing the Lattimore defense. John P. Frank, later a prominent lawyer in Phoenix, was in the early 1950s a Yale Law School professor. Frank clerked for Justice Hugo Black in 1942, then worked as a "sort of personal assistant to both Abe Fortas and Harold Ickes." He wrote a section on vagueness in the first or "backdrop" count and spent several summers in Washington working with AFP. He recalled in May 1986:

> It was the most important case I ever worked on. What was particularly remarkable was the moral intensity of the defense. It was the forces of good combatting the forces of evil. The fact that I was commuting from Yale for no pay indicates its intensity. The intensity of the witch hunt for the victims was enormous. Only the very tough could survive. The

rest would cop a plea or run away. What got Lattimore through was he had a backbone of steel, and his wife was absolutely courageous. The most remarkable single feature of these clients was they never expressed weakness, never asked "My God why can't this go away." Whatever McCarran could dish out, Lattimore could take and return.[20]

Frank also called together a group of his Yale colleagues to help with the Lattimore defense. Among them were Thomas I. Emerson, an expert on First Amendment rights; Vern Countryman, a procedure specialist; and Richard Donnelly, a criminal lawyer.[21] Emerson says of his work on this project:

> I was assigned to write on the First Amendment problem involved in the broad first count [of the indictment]. I was particularly glad to do this because it gave an opportunity to bring before the court a case that would reinstate the First Amendment as a limitation upon congressional committees at least in one area. . . . I developed in the brief the point that Lattimore was really being asked about his opinions, had been asked and was being tried for the opinions which he held not related to any overt acts. It was a question as to what his sympathies were and that whatever else may be within the scope of congressional investigating authority certainly an inquiry into mere opinion apart from conduct was protected by the First Amendment.[22]

The major burden of the Lattimore case fell on a junior member of AFP, William D. Rogers (not to be confused with William P. Rogers of the Justice Department, later a Nixon cabinet officer). Rogers took the briefs of the Yale group and Arnold, added evidence dug up by Lattimore's associates at Johns Hopkins (including Elsbeth Levy Bothe, later a circuit court judge in Baltimore), and edited the final product. This was the beginning of a long relationship; Rogers handled Lattimore's affairs after Fortas left the firm.

Most of AFP's clients were corporations involved with the government.[23] AFP took considerable risks in defending people caught up in the inquisition in those days. Lattimore was the preeminent civil liberties case handled pro bono by AFP, and it absorbed vast amounts of time from the very beginning. Fortas recalled:

> At the time of the Tydings hearings, we were representing Unilever. The general counsel and director of Unilever came over to see me about a very critical matter involving Unilever. I had never met the man. His name was de Baat. When he arrived, I told him I just couldn't give him any time on this crucial matter which I was handling pretty much alone

for the firm. I told him the reason for it. I told him that with considerable concern because Unilever was a very large client. And I said, "The only thing I can do, Mr. de Baat, is to invite you to come over to the hearings." So he came over to the hearings and sat there and was appalled and amazed. I told Thurman Arnold and Paul Porter that this probably means the end of our Unilever retainer, but that's the way it was. They agreed without a moment's hesitation. It turned out to be a rather amusing situation, because it really solidified our connection with Unilever. Unilever has vast interests in the Far East, and had known about Lattimore. So instead of losing a client, we really gained their admiration. Some years later, Paul Porter and I were in the Netherlands and we went out to the de Baat's estate, and were having tea in the garden. Three geese came along, and de Baat and his charming wife pointed out the three geese to us and said they'd named the geese Arnold, Fortas, and Porter. And de Baat hastened to say to me that the goose didn't have the same connotation in the Netherlands that it had in the United States, that geese recalled to the people of the Netherlands the warning of the invasion of Rome. Geese were much admired in the Netherlands. So they had named these three geese for us for our actions in the Lattimore case. . . . [The Lattimore case] didn't damage our firm; one result was it attracted the best young lawyers.[24]

Rogers was one of the young lawyers and has a somewhat different perspective on the Lattimore case. AFP at that time was a small firm, only seven members including juniors, and struggling financially. When Rogers finished a clerkship with the U.S. Court of Appeals in 1952, AFP wanted to hire him but could not afford to do so. To make ends meet that year the senior members borrowed on their signatures. Rogers therefore clerked with Justice Stanley Reed of the Supreme Court for a year, and in 1953 AFP had enough money for a new member, so they hired him. And the Lattimore case *did* hurt the firm:

The partners paid for their courage with money from their own pockets. The $250,000 of time they invested in Lattimore meant a lot to them at the time. Time spent on Lattimore meant time lost on paying clients. And they lost clients as well. Joseph N. Pew and the Sun Oil Company walked out on the firm in retaliation for our taking on the Lattimore case. Lattimore did strengthen the reputation of the firm as an outfit of courage and decency, but it cannot be true that the senior partners did not lose a lot of money as a result. Nonetheless, neither Abe nor any of the others ever complained. The cost was never discussed. They did not go around wringing their hands at the long hours or the fees that were foregone. And, ironically, Sun is now again an honored client of the firm.[25]

Even before Rover's appointment, Hummer, Davitt, and Anastos were getting ready for the defense motions. Hummer wanted to "put pressure" on a witness (name denied) to corroborate Budenz's testimony; the FBI held aloof from this suggestion, and Branigan recommended that the bureau do nothing without "prior Departmental authority." Hummer was also on the track of John Huber, the "vanishing witness" of the Tydings hearings. Huber apparently wanted to wipe out the disgrace of his 1950 fiasco and get into the top ranks of anti-Communist informers. He hired Edward Bennett Williams and gave Williams a sworn deposition to pass on to Hummer. In the deposition Huber changed his story again. He now swore that he attended a Communist party meeting at which Mr. and Mrs. Lattimore were "honored guests." Hummer was excited about this new evidence and wanted the bureau to interview Huber again to check him out. Branigan agreed to the interview, but it took the bureau a month to locate Huber. Despite the effort, his new story did not impress the bureau, and they passed it on without comment to Warren Olney. Huber then disappeared from the Lattimore file for another year.[26]

On February 3, 1953, the Baltimore office wrote headquarters complaining that it was difficult to prepare a report on the seven counts of the indictment because the Justice Department had provided no definition of "Communist." This lack particularly affected the report on count four, charging Lattimore with lying when he denied publishing articles by persons he knew were Communists. How was this to be interpreted?[27] It was a good question; it went straight to Justice, which took three weeks to answer.

On February 6, 1953, Chief Judge Bolitha J. Laws of U.S. District Court for the District of Columbia heard preliminary arguments in *United States versus Lattimore*, Criminal Number 1879–52. The first defense request was for postponement. O'Mahoney and Arnold told Judge Laws that the defense had to examine all the IPR records, which would take two or three months. Rover, for the government, said he was "anxious to dispose of the case during the spring term." Judge Laws set a trial date of May 11. Arnold also said that the defense would file a motion to dismiss. The key count, he said, was "a very vague allegation." All defense motions were to be filed by February 16.[28]

Lattimore's answer to the indictment was filed with the court February 16 as required. There were numerous motions: for change of venue, for discovery of government evidence, for a bill of particulars, for postponement of trial, and for inspection of the grand jury minutes. But the major motion, supported by a 100-page brief, was to dismiss the charges in their entirety. The headline-catching argument for dismissal was that SISS had set out to entrap Lattimore, not to carry out any legitimate legislative purpose.[29] Further, the prosecution was entirely political, and McCarran had interfered outrageously in the judicial process by trying to "coerce" the judgment of Brownell in his confirmation hearings.

The brief argued that the major backdrop count—that Lattimore had lied when he said he had never been a sympathizer or promoter of Communist interests—was vague and ill defined. "What are these Communist interests? Did President Roosevelt promote communism when he approved Yalta? Did President Roosevelt promote Communist interests when he furnished lend-lease to Russia? Did General Marshall promote Communist interests when he criticized Chiang Kai-shek's Government? . . . Tito is a Communist, and whatever his interests, they are of necessity also Communist interests. Was the Government of the United States a promoter of communism and a sympathizer with Communist interests when by both legislative and executive action it came to the aid of Tito?"[30]

The brief claimed that the members of SISS could not even agree among themselves, much less with Lattimore, as to the meaning of *communism*. The issues here were matters of opinion and belief, not overt acts, and as such were protected by the First Amendment. If this case went to trial, it would be "the first time in American history since the heresy trials of early New England" that a person would "be tried before a jury in a criminal case for statements of pure opinion and belief." Since there was no evidence of disloyalty, the prosecution "has fallen back on a charge about Lattimore's beliefs and sympathies, a charge so vague that it could be made a basis for trying anyone in public life who advocated any policy or expressed any opinion with which any future committee or prosecutor might disagree."

The brief also dismissed the six minor counts as nothing but "flimsy wisps. . . . From the longest interrogation of a single witness in congressional history, the prosecution fishermen, unable to produce a whale, have come up with minnows." Each of these "minnows" was then dissected, showing that Lattimore was asked to remember trivial items with no access to documents or memoranda, that he usually qualified his answer, and that he acknowledged error when SISS produced documents contradicting his memory. Further, the matters of fact on which he allegedly lied were not material to the stated function of the McCarran committee. They were totally irrelevant to an investigation of the Internal Security Act of 1950 or any other laws or subversive activities. On count five, for instance, what did it matter when Lattimore had lunch with Oumansky?

Both Whittaker Chambers and Elizabeth Bentley, two of the committee's most revered witnesses, had said it didn't matter at all.[31]

So the issues were drawn. Rover and his crew now had to answer them.

One of the first matters Rover dealt with was the troublesome "cart-before-the-horse" fourth count. Baltimore's demand for a definition of *Communist* as used in this count was relayed to Rover by FBI headquarters several times. On February 20 he gave an answer. "It is the opinion of this Division that it is not essential to the proof of this count that evidence of Communist Party membership be adduced. . . . any information which indicates that the referenced writers followed the Communist Party 'line' in their writings, wrote for Communist Party publications, or openly advocated the principles of Marxism-Leninism, would be pertinent to the count." While this definition may have satisfied Baltimore's conceptual problem, it did not ease the bureau's work load. They still had to review the files for information on the 411 writers whose work Lattimore had published. On April 13 Branigan reported to Belmont that they had processed 33 of the names; the remaining 378, he estimated, would take 70 days.[32]

To the bureau, the most dangerous Lattimore defense motion was discovery. The Lattimore motion requested "all FBI reports, memoranda and communications relating to the investigation and prosecution of Owen Lattimore" that had been available to Tydings, SISS, and the grand jury. The justification for this motion was that these documents "may disclose extremely important exculpatory matter." The bureau knew the Lattimore lawyers were right in one sense; there was indeed powerful exculpatory matter in raw FBI files, but this matter had been omitted in the reports sent to McCarran and the Justice Department. Bureau fears of the discovery motion were based on two things: (1) if the amount of bureau information furnished McCarran ever became known, Hoover's carefully constructed pose of never releasing reports to unauthorized persons would be destroyed; and (2) if clever defense attorneys had access to bureau reports, they might sniff out some of the hundreds of "embarrassing or objectionable" incidents occurring during the investigation: illegal wiretaps, bag jobs, leaks to anti-Lattimore reporters, and the like. There were several conferences between FBI and Justice people during February and March to discuss the discovery problem. Rover shared the bureau's concern and promised to oppose the discovery motion vigorously. On three of the memos reporting these conferences Hoover wrote comments, such as the one on March 13: "This now raises greater concerns about our furnishing Congressional Committees with information from our files."[33]

The attention of the McCarthy-McCarran group was partially diverted from Lattimore during March by the furious fight over the nomination of Charles "Chip" Bohlen as ambassador to the Soviet Union. McCarran was not on the Foreign Relations Committee, which had jurisdiction over diplomatic appointments, but as the *New York Times* noted, "He is a hard-hitting foe." McCarran joined the chorus against Bohlen: "Mr. McCarran said that Mr. Bohlen's connection with the Yalta Conference was 'enough for me.' "[34]

On March 17 the government filed its answer to the Lattimore defense motions. Rover had two main thrusts. One was to counter the claim that Lattimore was being prosecuted for his beliefs: "It should be emphasized at the outset that the defendant is not being prosecuted for adhering to a belief or opinion, political or otherwise, but rather for giving false testimony. He was not specifically asked to answer as to his political beliefs, but volunteered to state his political position. His adherence to a belief, therefore, was and is inviolate. The offense with which he is charged is that he lied in not believing what he said."[35]

The other government contention dealt with entrapment. Lattimore could argue this point at trial, Rover held, but it was not proper in a motion to dismiss. As to discovery, the government opposed it; Lattimore would find out what evidence they had at the trial. Nothing surprising here, and the defense lawyers felt reasonably confident that Rover had not seriously damaged their position.

Three significant events occurred while these motions and countermotions made their way through the district court process to a trial judge.

First, Budenz was caught faking again. One of the IPR trustees Budenz fingered as a Communist was Benjamin Kizer of Spokane, Washington. Kizer had written book reviews for *Pacific Affairs*. Budenz had told SISS his standard story that Kizer had been identified as a Communist by Earl Browder and Jack Stachel. The bureau told its Seattle office to investigate Kizer. When the report came from Seattle March 20, it made mincemeat of Budenz's charge. Kizer was clearly anti-Communist, having worked in the Crusade for Freedom launched by General Lucius Clay to combat Soviet propaganda in Europe. The Seattle SAC considered the matter closed.[36]

Second, in late March, Roy Cohn got back into the attack on Lattimore. He and David Schine, reporting to a public hearing of McCarthy's Senate Permanent Investigations Subcommittee about their "research" into U.S. libraries in Europe, noted that these libraries had books by Lattimore. One of them was actually *Ordeal by Slander*, which had as its main target a senator of the United States.[37]

And third, the end of March saw Chip Bohlen win his fight and enter service as ambassador to Moscow; and Chief Judge Laws assigned the Lattimore case to Judge Luther W. Youngdahl.

In April 1951, when President Truman fired General Douglas Mac-Arthur for insubordination and torrents of obloquy descended on the White House, only one of the forty-eight state governors publicly supported the President. On July 5, 1951, Truman called that governor in and offered him an appointment to the U.S. District Court for the District of Columbia. The governor was Luther W. Youngdahl, Republican of Minnesota, fervent Lutheran and strong defender of the Constitution.

Luther Youngdahl was born in Minneapolis in 1896. He graduated from Gustavus Adolphus College, served in the Army during World War I, and earned a degree at Minneapolis College of Law in 1921. From 1931 to 1936 he was a municipal judge in Minneapolis, then a Hennepin County court judge until 1942. From 1942 to 1946 he was an associate justice of the Supreme Court of Minnesota. The appellate bench was not to his liking, so in 1946 he sought and obtained the Republican nomination for governor. He won handily and was elected to that office three times. The *Washington Post* described him as "the state's most popular political figure." He was a tough "law and order" governor, enforcing the Minnesota liquor laws and driving out organized crime. His Lutheran faith played a strong role in his political life; Robert Esbjornson subtitles his biography of Youngdahl *A Christian in Politics*. Youngdahl told a *Washington Post* reporter, "Not once—not once during the three terms that I was governor of Minnesota—did anyone ever approach me to ask a favor, not about a contract or anything else. Of course, they knew they would have been thrown down to the bottom of the steps of the Capitol if they had tried."[38]

Successful as Youngdahl was at politics, he grew tired of political battles and decided that he wanted to finish his career trying cases in a courtroom. Truman's offer of a district court appointment came just at the right time.

Youngdahl listened to O'Mahoney, Arnold, and Rover argue the defense motions on March 31 and April 1. O'Mahoney led for the defense and got most of the press. As recorded by the *Baltimore Sun*,

> O'Mahoney declared that the Bohlen incident showed to what extent "fear and hysteria have driven some senators. . . . Bohlen might have been in this defendant's shoes. We cannot give way to hysteria. We cannot give way to political indictments."

Should the charges against Lattimore be upheld, O'Mahoney contended, "many a citizen of the United States in the future will be made a victim of an intolerant committee of Congress."...

The former senator said he was not challenging Congress' right to investigate where it pleases, but he added it was a different matter when the court was asked to punish a man on a deliberately "vague" charge....

O'Mahoney pointed to Lattimore's testimony denying that he had ever been a Communist. The former senator maintained it was no accident that the Government skipped this Lattimore denial in its search for grounds for an indictment and that it ultimately decided on a charge the Baltimore professor had promoted communism. The Government, according to O'Mahoney, was deliberately seeking a vague indictment.[39]

For the Lattimores, the court was a welcome improvement over previous hearings, contrasting startlingly with the twelve poisonous days before McCarran. For the first time Lattimore's counsel were able to function as counsel normally do: presenting the defense case coherently without imperious and belittling interruptions, in an atmosphere where the presiding officer was required to assume the innocence of the accused until proven guilty. This time, too, Lattimore was a spectator, not a combatant.

Nonetheless, the hearing was stressful. Eleanor Lattimore told the Barretts, "This has been another one of those Alice in Wonderland performances which seemed so unreal that it was difficult to believe it concerned us in any way."[40] And while Arnold and O'Mahoney (Fortas could not attend) were unshackled, the presence of a battery of seven government lawyers dedicated to putting Lattimore in jail was unnerving. Rover himself, as Lattimore saw it, displayed a full measure of acrimony, snarling the name "Lattimore" in a tone more appropriate for Judas Iscariot, spitting out the words "professor" and "intellectual" as if he were before a jury of illiterates, insinuating that in defending himself Lattimore had been demanding special privileges.

This latter insinuation rankled especially with Lattimore: "One of the most outrageous things was his completely cynical accusation that I myself was responsible for the publicity about my case because of having published *Ordeal by Slander*. He seemed to think people would assume that loose and sensational slanders against me made with Congressional immunity that projected me into the headlines not only in my own country but all over the world were not 'publicity' but that anything I said to clear my own good name was self-seeking publicity for no other purpose than to get myself talked about, as if I enjoyed it."[41]

There were other prejudicial tactics from Rover, including a statement that Lattimore's conscience was "between him and his God, that is if Lattimore believes in God." Rover also claimed that Lattimore had held a press conference just before the McCarran hearings, which was false, and that Lattimore had given his statement to the press before he gave it to the committee, which was also false.[42]

O'Mahoney led off for the defense, startling the Lattimores with old-fashioned eloquence that reminded Eleanor of the evangelist Billy Sunday. As a Catholic and former senator, O'Mahoney could attack the McCarran committee as no one else could. Arnold, in contrast, was scholarly and deadly logical. He cited two recent precedents, the *Bowers* and *Rumely* cases, which were appellate decisions supporting the defense contention that McCarran had been illegitimately probing Lattimore's beliefs, not asking questions germane to the charter of the committee. Youngdahl questioned Arnold on these precedents, and the judge clearly understood Arnold's argument.[43]

On the first day of the hearing Youngdahl requested that Rover rephrase the first count of the indictment as if he were charging a jury. This rephrasing, Youngdahl said, was necessary because he believed that indictments that could not be rephrased in simple, nontechnical language were often flawed. Rover responded evasively to this request, saying that it could be done only after all the evidence had been presented. Youngdahl sat poker-faced through Rover's response. Arnold and O'Mahoney felt that Youngdahl would throw out this first count.

The defense team and Lattimore were less optimistic about the minor counts. It seemed to them inevitable that any judge would be influenced by the universal assumption of the time that "where there is so much smoke there must be at least some fire and not just the nefarious activities of incendiaries and throwers of smoke bombs." They expected that Youngdahl would strike the first count on vagueness and First Amendment grounds but yield to public opinion by ruling "let the jury decide" on the rest. And the government had been working on public opinion. From friends at Johns Hopkins, the Indian embassy, and various newspapers, they knew that Justice Department lawyers had put out the story that Lattimore was going to be convicted with the aid of "surprise witnesses from Asia" and that his defenders had better stay away from him for their own good.[44] This rumor was fraudulent: there were no surprise witnesses from Asia—or from anywhere else.

At the close of the hearing Youngdahl denied the defense motion for change of venue, took the motions for dismissal and a bill of particulars under advisement, and granted the motion for postponement. Trial was set for mid-October 1953.

Rover claimed during the hearing that the government was seeking not to persecute Lattimore but only to prosecute him for perjury; and he promised that "every scrap of admissible evidence that can be secured" would be offered at trial.[45]

The FBI was fully mobilized to provide Rover with his "scraps of evidence." Baltimore alone had twenty-five agents working exclusively on preparation of a full report on the seven counts of the indictment; this team did not include agents working in the field. There were probably another seventy-five agents assigned to the Lattimore case in headquarters, the Washington field office, New York, and other major cities. Crackpots were still coming out of the woodwork, taking agent time to check them out. Many of them were still approaching McCarthy and Surine. One of Surine's sources touted the potential testimony of a soldier of fortune named Dimitri Bourlin. Bourlin had allegedly dealt with Lattimore in Inner Mongolia. The FBI referred the Bourlin charge to Army. Army replied that they "assumed that the Bureau knew that Bourlin had been thoroughly discredited as an agent"; that there was no record of Bourlin ever having been in Mongolia; and that Bourlin was too young to have been in Mongolia when Lattimore was there. Finally, in May 1953 Army Intelligence located Bourlin in Pundu Jail, Kuala Lumpur: narcotics running. It was like that for hundreds of hot tips.[46]

But presumably respectable people were after Lattimore, too. In April, John T. Flynn's *Lattimore Story* came out from Devin-Adair, a right-wing publisher. A blurb inside the front cover shows how Flynn publicized the SISS findings:

> Asked to tell why he wrote this book, John T. Flynn replied: "As the weird story of Owen Lattimore unfolded itself in official documents and sworn testimony, I noted that it had one flaw. *It was unbelievable.* In a Dumas novel of intrigue at the court of Louis XV, it might be accepted. But in America—the America of the 1950s—it seemed fantastically out of place and utterly incredible. Much has been written about it, but now all the evidence is available. Few have the time or means of sifting the immense folios of testimony and incriminating documents, which were dramatically unearthed in an old barn, as might be done in a screen thriller.

"I have therefore tried to fit together in this small volume all the characters, episodes, intrigues and confessions buried in 14 large volumes of testimony and documents, out of which emerges the curious story of a conspiracy involving over four dozen writers, journalists, educators, and high-ranking government officials—almost all Americans—to force the American State Department to betray China and Korea into the hands of the Communists. Unbelievable as this strange enterprise may seem, the proofs are now all here—not assumptions and suspicions and tortured deductions, but proofs. That is why I have written this book."

And Flynn was not alone. On April 5, 1953, twenty-eight writers and public figures sent a statement to seven hundred newspapers around the country protesting that McCarthy had not been treated fairly by the media. "Hardly any" literary critics had reviewed the senator's book, *McCarthyism—The Fight for America*, whereas Lattimore's *Ordeal by Slander* received "the widest coverage" and "the most extravagant and uncritical support" when it was published. Among the signers of this protest: William F. Buckley, Jr., Adolphe Menjou, Kenneth Colegrove, George Creel, Ralph de Toledano, Eugene Lyons, Felix Morley.[47]

Budenz got another black eye in April. In checking bureau files of the 411 *Pacific Affairs* writers, Budenz's 1950 SISS executive session charge that Catherine Porter was a concealed Communist came to light. Headquarters asked New York what they had in their files about Porter. What came back was disconcerting. When bureau agents had interviewed Budenz about the Porter charge in late 1950, he "was unable to supply any identifying data concerning the person he named and was unable to recall how he came to the conclusion that she was a Communist." Another scrap of evidence down the drain. The New York report concluded, "In view of above, no further action being taken by NYO with respect to Porter."[48]

There was plenty of action in the national political arena. In the month after Youngdahl held the first hearing in the Lattimore case, McCarthy, Dulles, Stassen, and Eisenhower staged their running battle over whether the senator could negotiate with foreign ship owners to keep them from trading with China. Stassen waffled, Ike waffled, Dulles waffled—only McCarthy stood firm. Journalists and politicos began to snipe at Eisenhower's lack of leadership in his party's battles with McCarthy. The Rosenberg lawyers filed another unsuccessful appeal of the death penalty. The Supreme Court barred Abraham Isserman, attorney for the eleven convicted Communist party leaders, from practice before it. Cohn and

Schine went on their whirlwind tour of U.S. libraries in Europe, finding subversive literature everywhere. HUAC concluded hearing forty-five witnesses in Hollywood. National Commander Lewis K. Gough of the American Legion urged the United States to meet Soviet threats with Soviet tactics. Charlie Chaplin gave up trying to reenter the United States. John Paton Davies was moved from the exposed salient of Germany to a post in Peru. Patrick Hurley, making his second run for a New Mexico Senate seat against Dennis Chavez, got the backing of the Senate Committee on Elections for an investigation of the vote. The Subversive Activities Control Board ordered the Communist party to register as a group seeking the overthrow of the government. Brownell announced the first twelve organizations ordered to register under the Internal Security Act of 1950. Eisenhower issued Executive Order 10450, tightening regulations for assuring the security of federal employees. John Carter Vincent, forced into retirement by Dulles in March, returned to the United States with a blast at the China lobby. Senator Herbert Lehman of New York attacked "McCarthyism and Jenneritis." From reading the newspapers of the time, one could conclude that the most important business before the country was a hunt for domestic subversives.

And on May 2, 1953, Judge Luther Youngdahl stoked the fires of the flaming witch-hunt with an order making headlines from coast to coast. Four counts of the Lattimore indictment, including the all-important first count, were thrown out, and the remaining counts were held to be of doubtful materiality, a matter that could be challenged at trial. It was a startling, sweeping, powerful decision.

> Having in mind the necessity of weighing the balance between the broad power of Congress to investigate and the protections afforded individuals by the Bill of Rights, as pointed out in Douds, and applying the rule to the indictment here, the Court is convinced that the first count is fatally defective. Under this count the defendant is charged with lying in denying that he had ever been a sympathizer or promoter of Communism or Communist interests. It is a statement made by defendant to the Committee.
>
> First, this count is violative of the Sixth Amendment which protects the accused in the right to be informed of the nature and cause of the accusation against him. The test has been laid down in Sutton . . . where the Court held that the meaning of the Sixth Amendment was that the defendant: ". . . be so fully and clearly informed of the charge against him as not only to enable him to prepare his defense and not be taken by surprise at the trial, but also that the information as to the alleged offense shall be so definite and certain that he may be protected

by a plea of former jeopardy against another prosecution for the same offense."[49]

Further, this count did not meet the requirement of rule 7(c) of the Federal Rules of Criminal Procedure; it was not a plain, concise, and definite statement of the offense charged. The "sympathizer and promoter of Communist interests" language was so nebulous that a jury would have to "indulge in speculation" as to what it meant. And this count was fatally defective because it restricted Lattimore's freedom of belief and expression, both protected by the First Amendment. Youngdahl acknowledged the climate of the times in concluding his rejection of the first count: "Communism's fallacy and viciousness can be demonstrated without striking down the First Amendment protection of discourse, discussion, and debate. When public excitement runs high as to alien ideologies, is the time when we must be particularly alert not to impair the ancient landmarks set up by the Bill of Rights."

Counts three and four were also stricken as violating the First and Sixth amendments, and count seven was defective "in its plain inconsistency and indefiniteness." And on the remaining three counts, "The allegations in counts two, five and six are so indefinite that the Court feels the defendant is entitled to a bill of particulars giving him certain information as to enable him to defend." Lattimore refused comment in Baltimore, "but his voice reflected obvious jubilation." Rogers says there was indeed a "big celebration. But we knew it would be appealed. One was allowed 24 hours of celebration, then it was back to the case."[50]

Senator Arthur Watkins said on the basis of "reports he had of the decision Judge Youngdahl's reasoning appeared to be faulty." Senator McCarran had no comment. Overnight Youngdahl became the lightning rod for the wrath of the pro-McCarthy press and the recipient of the hate mail that always comes to heretics and defenders of heretics.[51]

Again the burden of response was on Rover.

CHAPTER TWENTY-SIX

Rover, Asiaticus, and BDPT

When Lattimore was indicted, Johns Hopkins put him on leave with pay. He continued to have use of his office and secretary but taught no classes. He appreciated the fact that he had not been fired; many teachers at other institutions were. Several of Hopkins's conservative trustees, however, wanted to be rid of him. At least two trustees resigned, allegedly because Lattimore was kept on. Detlev Bronk, then president of Johns Hopkins, was said to be "driven to despair by trustee pressure to fire Lattimore."[1]

One of the ways in which President Bronk eased trustee unhappiness about their notorious heretic was by abolishing the Walter Hines Page School, and hence the position of director that Lattimore held. Bronk announced this action April 16, 1953, attributing it to "a broad reorganization plan."[2]

Memories of Hopkins personnel as to attitudes toward Lattimore vary widely. Bowman, who brought Lattimore to Hopkins in the first place and promoted his work for the Council of Foreign Relations, lived to see Lattimore attacked by McCarthy. FBI interviews of Bowman, if they are among the documents released under the Freedom of Information Act, are so heavily censored as to be unidentifiable. But an evaluation of what Bowman told the FBI appears in Hummer's memorandum of June 17, 1952:

> One of the most honest and fair appraisals of Lattimore was given by his friend, the late president of John Hopkins, Isaiah Bowman, who told the Bureau that he believed Lattimore was not a Communist. Bowman has had since 1938, he stated, many conversations with Lattimore. He described Lattimore as one who "likes to play in the shadows" and has no sense about the company he keeps; that Lattimore has spoken to

some groups of a "questionable nature of a Communist tinge"; that Lattimore has no objection to people seeing him under compromising circumstances; that he is the type who would have no hesitancy in openly contacting a known Communist. Bowman was well acquainted that Lattimore has been branded a Communist on occasion and he can well understand why.[3]

To Hummer's credit, he adds Lattimore's rebuttal to such charges of keeping "questionable" company at times: "For many years I have made every effort to keep in touch with as many people as possible who are informed about the Far East, and I have obtained as much information as I could, whether they were Communists, anti-Communists, liberals, conservatives, businessmen, politicians, Army officers or scholars."

According to some sources, Bowman supported Lattimore until his death in 1950; others claim that Bowman became disillusioned and no longer trusted Lattimore. Neil Smith, who has studied the Bowman papers extensively, and David Harvey, who taught at Hopkins for nineteen years, think Bowman had turned against Lattimore by 1948, when Bronk took over the presidency. Former Dean Wilson Shaffer told me that he had seen a several-inch-thick file on Lattimore in the possession of then-Provost Stewart Macaulay. This file cannot now be found. Since Macaulay was a prime FBI contact on the Hopkins campus, his file might clear up the question.[4]

Most of the Hopkins faculty strongly supported Lattimore. The most striking effort on Lattimore's behalf was that of philosopher George Boas. Boas was particularly concerned with the sniping of SISS and various columnists at Lattimore's lack of a Ph.D., even of a college degree of any kind, and the fact that unlike most professors, Lattimore wrote for public consumption. Boas therefore compiled a list of the leading Asian scholars in this country, and some in Europe, and wrote them asking for their opinions of Lattimore's scholarship. Boas omitted, of course, the six professors who testified against Lattimore to SISS.

Thirty-seven of these prominent academicians responded, and Boas and Harvey Wheeler, also a Hopkins professor, published the letters in February 1953 in a pamphlet titled *Lattimore the Scholar*. Some of those who responded stated that they disagreed with Lattimore's political positions and foreign policy advice, but all of them found his scholarship worthy, and many regarded him as the world's preeminent student of Central Asia. To the ideologically committed, Boas's booklet was a provocation. To the Justice Department, it was a clue to probable defense witnesses. Olney wrote Hoover February 23 asking the bureau to furnish a copy of the pamphlet.[5] Every single one of the scholars represented was investigated by the bureau, including the Englishmen Arnold Toynbee and I. A. Richards, the Belgian priests A. Mostaert and Louis M. J. Schram, the Dutch scholar J. J. L. Duyvendak, and several Germans.

Boas had another project: a defense fund. In January 1953, with the encouragement of "several members of the faculty," he sent out one thousand letters to Hopkins professors asking them to contribute to Lattimore's defense. According to the *Baltimore Evening Sun*, Boas's goal was $40,000. The local solicitation did not reach this goal, so Boas expanded his mailings to Asian specialists, geographers, and others on campuses elsewhere. Eventually, eighteen hundred people contributed $38,000.[6]

Provost Macaulay told the *Evening Sun* reporter that the university took no position on the Lattimore defense fund, but they may not have been completely candid. Gwinn Owens of the Sun Papers stated that during this period he worked for the Hopkins Fund, which sought private contributions to the university and its hospital. Owens supported Lattimore and contributed to his defense. J. Douglas Coleman, director of the Hopkins Fund, told Owens, "It's alright for you to give money to the Lattimore defense, but I won't get involved. That guy's ruined too many breakfasts for me."[7]

Creation of the Lattimore defense fund opened new avenues of investigation for the FBI. Their check on his net worth had long since been dropped; his assets were consistent with his legitimate earnings and normal expenditures. But this new fund! The Justice Department prosecutors were sure that the Communist party would show its hand here. So the bureau began a new search, this time for the subversive connections of Boas, the three advisors to the fund, the treasurer, and all the contributors they could locate. Before it was over, the accumulation of paperwork was so massive the bureau was forced to set up a new title for the investigation, "Owen Lattimore Defense Fund—IS-C," and a new file number, 100-400471.[8]

It is not likely that the bureau managed to investigate all eighteen hundred contributors, but all of those who wrote letters for *Lattimore the Scholar* were on a priority list and thoroughly checked. This activity was under very tight secrecy because of the "risk of this type of inquiry becoming known to the defense and being used by them at trial, or in the press, or both, to the embarrassment of both the Department and the Bureau."[9]

On August 20, 1953, the Baltimore office summarized what it had learned about the Lattimore defense fund. The cover letter noted, "This report . . . contains no instances of Communist Party or Communist Party front group support, other than oral expression of approval. The report identifies _____ supporters to be, for the most part, educators, students, and other persons of left-wing liberal or individualistic attitudes." In December a bureau informant at the Johns Hopkins branch of the First National Bank of Baltimore noted that deposits in the fund account "have dwindled down to an occasional check now and then." One of the occasional checks was from Eleanor Roosevelt: $100. No incriminating contributions were ever found, and the late George Boas never knew how much trouble and expense he caused the United States government.[10]

While Boas and other senior Hopkins faculty survived their support of Lattimore without appreciable damage, some nontenured supporters were not so fortunate. John DeFrancis, later a respected sinologue at the University of Hawaii, was an assistant professor in the Page School. When it was abolished, he was out of a job and for ten years was unable to teach his specialty. He found employment teaching low-level mathematics in a private school until the stigma of association with Lattimore subsided.

DeFrancis worked on the Lattimore defense, checking out among other things the background of Lattimore's attackers. He discovered that Freda Utley was, unlike Lattimore, one of the people who *had* written that the Chinese Communists were mere agrarian reformers. Lattimore was able to use this information with considerable effect. De Francis also took over some of Lattimore's lectures during the SISS hearings before Lattimore went on leave: "I remember giving one lecture in which I enumerated the reasons for the collapse of the Kuomintang in China and the victory of the Communists; this was pretty much an historical essay. In each case I would remark sarcastically 'And this factor was more important than the role of Owen Lattimore.' A student came up to me afterward and said to me with a kind of fear and trembling, 'Do you realize that the FBI may have been there?' I said 'Goddamit, I was talking to the FBI.' "[11]

While most Hopkins faculty strongly supported Lattimore, George Carter continued to oppose him privately. The biblical archaeologist William Albright (and his wife) and Carl B. Swisher attacked Lattimore publicly. Swisher was a political scientist of strongly anti-Soviet opinions. He warned his graduate students that if they had signed a list on the department bulletin board to help with the Lattimore defense, they should take a razor blade and cut out their signatures. Crossing it off was not enough.[12]

George McT. Kahin, a prominent authority on Southeast Asia, was a graduate student in political science at Johns Hopkins when the Lattimore case broke, but he refused to be intimidated by Swisher and worked extensively for the Lattimore defense. In 1951 Kahin applied for a job at

Cornell. When the Cornell political science department asked for letters of recommendation from Kahin's professors, Swisher refused to write. Cornell telephoned him, and he talked vaguely about Kahin being "irresponsible." The Cornell caller pressed Swisher to be specific. What exactly had Kahin done? Swisher would not talk about Lattimore; he finally said, "Well, he worked with the American Friends Service Committee in helping the Nisei who were interned at the beginning of the war." This revelation, says Kahin, "turned the whole thing around." Kahin got the job and found Cornell very supportive.[13]

However one judges Johns Hopkins's treatment of Lattimore, the American academic world avoided him like the plague. As already noted, his speaking invitations all but disappeared—with one notable exception: John King Fairbank invited him to Harvard every year. This was not because of any exceptional commitment to academic freedom on Harvard's part; it was due solely to Fairbank's personal commitment. As Ellen Schrecker notes in *No Ivory Tower*, there was vigorous opposition to Lattimore at Harvard. The dean of students tried very hard to ban Lattimore on the grounds that his appearance would "bring added unfavorable publicity to the college."[14] Fairbank stood his ground; Lattimore appeared at Harvard each year.

Paul Lazarsfeld and Wagner Thielens, in a 1955 study of 2,451 college social science teachers, used attitudes toward a hypothetical Lattimore lecture on their campuses as a touchstone revealing the degree to which McCarthyism prevailed in academia. Eighty percent of their respondents would approve of Lattimore lecturing, but only 40 percent said they would protest vigorously if the president banned such a lecture. Schrecker is no doubt right: "The 1950's was the period when the nation's colleges and universities were becoming increasingly dependent upon and responsive toward the federal government. The academic community's collaboration with McCarthyism was part of that process. It was, in many respects, just another step in the integration of American higher education with the Cold War political system."[15]

If there was bitterness and consternation in the Justice Department over Judge Youngdahl's ruling, some FBI offices felt differently. At headquarters, Branigan asked Belmont to find out if the bureau could now forget about the "many leads outstanding on each of the counts dismissed. . . . These leads are widespread involving a number of offices as well as Bureau representatives in England, Germany, France, and Mexico." SAC Boardman in New York cabled headquarters almost gleefully, listing the "pending leads in NYO [that] will not be covered unless further request is received from Bureau or Baltimore."[16]

Relief for the bureau was short-lived. On May 6 three bureau representatives went to Rover's office for a conference. Rover announced that "he intended to appeal Youngdahl's decision and . . . desired that the Bureau continue its investigation on the four counts which were dismissed and 'keep moving as if nothing had happened.' " Headquarters passed the word to all field offices.[17]

Rover filed his notice of intent to appeal on May 14, 1953. As the *New York Times* noted,

> Mr. Rover said this action had been authorized by Herbert Brownell, Jr., the Attorney General. Today's steps opened up the possibility the Supreme Court might rule on the validity of the indictment before Mr. Lattimore ever was brought to trial on the charges contained in the true bill. A further possibility was that Mr. Lattimore might escape trial entirely if higher court rulings favored him.
>
> Mr. Rover said that if the Appeals Court sustained the rulings of Judge Youngdahl he would recommend to the Attorney General that the case be taken to the Supreme Court. It was considered likely a similar procedure would be followed by attorneys for Mr. Lattimore if Judge Youngdahl was overruled.[18]

The legal maneuvering, and the delays it occasioned, began to wear on Lattimore. After Rover filed his notice of appeal, Lattimore wrote a memo headed "Some questions for AF&P." Whether he gave this memo to Fortas is not clear; Bill Rogers does not remember it. The copy in Lattimore's papers expresses the agony of his situation.

> Are there any advantages to the case in further delays? What are they? Winning the case must of course be the first consideration. However if there are no advantages, or uncertain ones, there are disadvantages to us which are great enough so that we would like to raise the question as to whether any moves could be made to lessen delays. For instance— Appeal notice not yet filed—why? Shouldn't we ask why & when instead of meekly waiting?
>
> Since we must start now to prepare for the trial, could we not press for the bill of particulars on the remaining counts at an early date on the grounds that it is still necessary to our preparation?
>
> It seems to me there are two disadvantages in further delays, one of which directly affects the case. The other affects my career, reputation and productivity.
>
> 1. Since McCarthyism seems to be making more gains than losses, it will become more and more difficult for judges and juries to make

unprejudiced or courageous decisions. Should we not try to press the advantage of the Youngdahl decision as early as possible? The more time the government has the more forces they can marshal. Time is on their side because their resources are far greater than ours. Or are we still waiting for a miracle?

2. Until a decision is reached my life as a teacher, a writer, a lecturer, and in many instances as a friend, is at a standstill, and my seriously damaged reputation can not only not be repaired but will continue to deteriorate as the Flynns, Lawrences, Lewises etc. continue to blacken my name and the picture of me as a subversive character hardens in the public mind, and there is nothing I can do to change it. I have already lost three of what should be the best and most productive years of my life—Until I am acquitted I cannot begin to rebuild what has been destroyed. Examples: University treating as if guilty. Washington lawyers studying Flynn—Reports from all over of people reading Flynn. No answers available or possible until after court decision.[19]

The reference was to John T. Flynn's condensation of the SISS hearings, *The Lattimore Story*, discussed in chapter 25. Lattimore was right; the only counter to Flynn would be a verdict of not guilty by a jury of his peers.[20]

Ironically, as Lattimore despaired at the interminable delays in taking his case to a jury, legal circles in Washington were predicting that it was Rover who was in real trouble. The *New York Times* of May 17 said that government attorneys were unhappy that the indictment had been drawn so loosely and that unless a higher court reversed Youngdahl, Rover might be reluctant to go to trial "on what was left of an indictment apparently not too highly esteemed from a legal standpoint when it was whole."[21]

Rover and the prosecution team now intensified their efforts. They had "help" from the usual sources: Don Surine and the McCarran staff. Surine was plugging the Chinese Nationalists again, but Wacks and the bureau rejected this avenue as of "no pertinence." Then Surine volunteered the unhelpful report that Dorothy Borg of New York City appeared to be a friend of Lattimore's. She had come to Washington and sat in on every one of his hearings. Surine even knew the hotel where she stayed.[22]

Ben Mandel offered Hummer a new lead, which Hummer passed on to the bureau: Ruth Shipley of the Passport Office had information about Lattimore but had never been asked for it. Belmont commented that the FBI had checked out this information at the time of the Jarvinen affair, but perhaps they had not actually interviewed Shipley. They now did so;

she had nothing new.[23] Her batting average was not so high anyway; she had offered some of the wildest rumors during the Jarvinen fiasco.

On June 19, 1953, after unsuccessful last-minute appeals, the Rosenbergs were executed. None rejoiced over this more than McCarthy and Surine, who were out to get all the traitors, including Lattimore. Surine was working on a bill for McCarthy to introduce that would cover Lattimore's major crime, "policy treason." As Lou Nichols reported this new offense, "By this Surine means an instance where through manipulation of top-level policy which could deliver a whole country or group of nations as contrasted against an individual act of espionage or sabotage."[24]

Hundreds of leads were followed through during this period. Each new one seemed to the bureau more useless than the last. In desperation Rover resurrected Budenz. Budenz had never "furnished his opinion as to the probable role Lattimore played as a Communist propagandist, nor has he stated the Communist aims, policies and strategies pursued in the Far East during the period 1933 through 1949." Would the bureau please go back to Budenz and ask him to address this matter? So on June 24 FBI agents once again descended on Budenz in Crestwood, New York. The transcript is peculiarly stilted and formal. "Mr. Budenz: Inquiry is requested on my opinion of Owen Lattimore as a Soviet propagandist, concerning specifically his relations with top Soviet or Communist authorities in relation to such propaganda. . . . my opinion is that at all times from at least the year 1937, Owen Lattimore was under directives from Communist authorities as to what the line of the Communist International apparatus was, in regard to the Far East, and was commissioned to follow out those directives as a concealed Communist, with due regard to his position."[25]

There follows, outlined as if in a lecture, a twenty-two-page digest of what Budenz had told SISS two years earlier, supported this time with references to Communist publications showing that Stalin was very clever to have kept out of war with Japan for so long, that the Soviet line on Chiang changed several times, that the Communists were against retention of the emperor in Japan, that Mao was totally subservient to Stalin, and so forth. Budenz did have a new and different timetable for the change in Party line on Chiang, and he asserted now that Lattimore had spent four months in Yenan in 1937. Otherwise it was vintage Budenz, warmed over.

Rover needed help. Hummer, Davitt, Anastos, and George J. Donegan were experienced attorneys assigned full-time to the Lattimore case, but apparently the Youngdahl setback induced Justice to seek another prestigious appointment. Rover suggested John W. Jackson, a former U.S. attorney. Rover got Robert Morris, Senator Harry F. Byrd, and Fulton Lewis, Jr., to support Jackson. Rover knew where the power lay; Morris's task was to get McCarran's approval.[26] He did, and Jackson was made assistant U.S. attorney and appeared on government briefs from July 1953 on.

The pressures on Rover and his team are revealed by the lengths they went to in attempting to secure testimony against Lattimore. On July 30 Rover sent Hummer to Belmont requesting that the bureau contact a potential witness who was not being "fully cooperative." The man had been born abroad and was a naturalized citizen. Rover wanted the FBI to threaten to report him to the Immigration and Naturalization Service, recommending cancellation of his citizenship unless he cooperated on Lattimore. Belmont told Hummer the bureau would not agree to any pressure of this kind; it would backfire. Hoover agreed.[27]

The government did not file its brief appealing the Youngdahl decision until August 24, 1953. The story was the second lead in the *New York Times* the next day. Rover asked that Youngdahl be reversed on all four of the counts dismissed and attacked Youngdahl's reasoning on each of them.[28]

The vital first count, Rover held, could not be thrown out on First Amendment grounds. SISS had not inquired into Lattimore's beliefs; rather, Lattimore had volunteered his beliefs, and the First Amendment "does not protect the speech which willfully, falsely, and fraudulently expresses such a belief." Further, the indictment could not be dismissed before trial for vagueness: "in a perjury prosecution, prior to trial, vagueness or indefiniteness as to the meaning of words cannot be an issue. Determination of their meaning to the defendant awaits the trial. . . . The state of a man's mind is as much a fact as the state of his digestion." Questions of materiality, likewise, "must await determination at the trial and are not now before the Court." Youngdahl's discussion of the background of Lattimore's testimony to SISS could "have no bearing upon the legal sufficiency of the indictment."

The only significant press comment on Rover's brief was restatement of the consensus in legal circles that the case would go to the Supreme Court.

Government prosecutors were pleased with the brief. Hummer told FBI Supervisor J. F. Wacks that it "had been furnished a number of prominent attorneys in the District and elsewhere for review and that each of these attorneys had indicated that it contained very good arguments and was a well organized and documented treatise. Hummer stated that the general opinion of these attorneys was that it was 'a cinch' that the lower court would be reversed."[29]

Four days after this optimistic report Wacks got another request from the prosecution, this time from Donegan. The Justice Department "understood" that General Willoughby had a great deal of information in his Tokyo files. Had the bureau checked them? Wacks had his programmed response down pat. "I advised Donegan that we have neither the time or the money to conduct a search of our files to ascertain the answer to his query and I suggested to him that he cause a search to be made of the reports we have furnished the Department in instant case in order to determine whether General Willoughby's files were reviewed by us." Hoover's inevitable comment: "Right. We are not going to do their plowing." Throughout the remaining twenty-four months Lattimore was under indictment, prosecution requests to the FBI for documents and other services met rejection and ever-more-acerbic comments from Hoover. "Let him get it himself. We are not messenger boys, certainly not for him" was typical.[30]

Prosecution response to FBI recalcitrance was to channel requests through higher-ranking Justice Department officials, hoping that Hoover would be more receptive to them. This ploy did not work. William Foley, one of Olney's subordinates in the Criminal Division, handled one such request. A "third party" (probably an SISS staffer or Surine) had told the department that a Captain Ernest J. Lissner of the army had served in the Far East Command Counter-Intelligence Corps and had written a report that "was most derogatory concerning Lattimore." When Rover tried to get the Lissner report from Army, they denied having it. Rover thought Army had originally "buried" the report, as Lattimore was then "in the good graces of the White House." Army would not now release it since they had buried it when originally written. Foley wondered if perhaps the FBI could pry it loose.[31]

Foley brought his request to Inspector Carl Hennrich, who was not sympathetic, lecturing Foley about jurisdictional matters and correct procedures. If the Rover team wanted FBI investigation in this matter, they should put it in writing. Foley, sufficiently chastised, agreed. Hennrich reported this encounter to Belmont, with this recommendation: "When a request is made by the Department in connection with the Lissner report, we will carefully consider the request in the light of available information and, in the absence of indication of some shenanigans, I think we should make the investigation." When this memo came to Hoover's attention, he responded, "Watch it carefully. I am not as trusting as you fellows are." The request did come through in writing. The bureau followed the Lissner trail, and it led to yet another fiasco. Lissner had been fired by MacArthur for blackmailing various persons and for other irregularities. He had been reassigned as an assistant PX officer at Fort Meade, then shifted around several times. The bureau finally traced Lissner to an artillery unit in Germany. He told them he had never investigated Lattimore and had no information about him.[32]

On October 1, 1953, AFP filed its brief with the court of appeals, answering Rover's brief of August 24. This response was also headline news.[33] The defense brief was explosive, describing the Lattimore prosecution as "unique in the history of perjury. It brings into this court a meaningless and trivial residue of a once-sensational espionage charge culled from the transcript of the longest Congressional interrogation of one man ever conducted." Ironically, the best summary of the defense brief is the one prepared in the bureau by Wacks. There is room here only for Wacks's discussion of the Sixth Amendment aspects of count one.

> The lower court was correct in holding that Count I violates the Sixth Amendment, which insures an accused the right to be informed of the nature and the cause of the accusation against him.
> The brief sets out that Lattimore testified, "I am not and never have been a Communist, a Soviet agent, a sympathizer or any other kind of promoter of Communism or Communist interests . . ." The Government did not pick from this statement those parts which would be capable of proof and from which Lattimore could anticipate what the Government would attempt to prove. Rather, the indictment charges Lattimore with perjury based on the words "sympathizer" and "Communist interests," which have different meanings at different times and defy analysis in addition to being vague and all embracing. This count offers the Government a target to shoot at, covering any writing, act, opinion or association of Lattimore during the past twenty years and any letter, conversation or episode of whatever period may be introduced in evidence for the jury's evaluation in the light of today's understandings. To prepare any sort of defense, Lattimore must examine all the policies which he has advocated, must interview all his associates and must present his entire life in review. Such a case would be interminable and he would not know where to begin or end. This charge does not deal with facts at all, but with personal evaluations, surmises, conjectures, opinions and speculations, the nature of which Lattimore could not know before he goes to trial.[34]

Wacks presented similarly incisive summaries of the First Amendment issue, the question of materiality, and the minor counts. He did not comment on the cogency of defense arguments.

Rover and the prosecution took no comfort from the defense brief. Presumably they still expected the court of appeals to overturn Youngdahl, as they continued to pursue evidence that would be needed at trial for the first count. They were taking seriously the charges coming from Tai Li via Commander Miles (see chapter 16), but realized that Miles's history of mental problems would make him a shaky witness, as would the fact that he had only hearsay to offer. And with the government's massive investment in the Lattimore case, now amounting to more than twenty thousand pages of FBI reports alone and twenty-two hundred interviews, they could not afford to fail.[35] The force of their anxiety compelled them to canvas the world for a magisterial witness. They came up with: Generalissimo Chiang Kai-shek!

On October 29, 1953, Jackson and Donegan called on Hennrich, who reported to Belmont:

> These gentlemen said they considered it desirable to make overtures to determine whether Chiang Kai-shek would be available for use as a witness in the Lattimore case, either through personal testimony or through a deposition. Jackson and Donegan stated that they wanted to discuss these matters with me prior to sending an official request to the Bureau to conduct investigation in this matter, since they thought the Bureau might have specific suggestions in the matter. They also suggested that they had been considering the question as to whether a Bureau agent could go to China and conduct further inquiries, inasmuch as they had confidence the Bureau would be able to develop more information than CIA or G-2 or State Department investigators would be able to develop.[36]

Hoover disposed of the last suggestion summarily: "NO."

Hennrich's memo reported in detail the lecture he then gave Jackson and Donegan. The prosecution team had to straighten itself out and put requests for investigations in writing before Justice started its own investigation, rather than running to the bureau for help after they had muddied the waters. "I pointed out that if they had been conducting investigations, we will find out during our investigation, and they will then be in the position of not acting in good faith if they fail to tell us now." As to Chiang Kai-shek, they should take it up with the State Department.[37] There is no record that Rover followed through. The idea of soliciting testimony from a head of state nine thousand miles away was so hare-brained that Olney or Brownell undoubtedly killed it.

President Dwight Eisenhower, largely unaware of the turbulence in his Justice Department and completely ignorant of the Lattimore prosecution, nonetheless sensed that the internal security field was contaminated by overreliance on professional former Communists to ferret out subversives. On November 4, 1953, Ike wrote Attorney General Brownell about his concerns: "We must search out some positive way to put ourselves on the side of individual right and liberty as well as on the side of fighting Communism to the death. We might decide that this is a matter on which I or someone else should make a speech. We might decide that we needed to bring in two or three outstanding individuals of the caliber of Learned Hand to help us devise a policy or 'formula.' "[38]

One paragraph of Eisenhower's memo inadvertently scored a direct hit on the Lattimore prosecution and on the prime former Communist witness, Budenz: "The Communists are a class set apart by themselves. Indeed, I think they are such liars and cheats that even when they apparently recant and later testify against someone else for his Communist convictions, my first reaction is to believe that the accused person must be a patriot or he wouldn't have incurred the enmity of such people. So even when these 'reformed' Communists have proved useful in helping us track down some of their old associates, I certainly look for corroborating evidence before I feel too easy in my mind about it."[39]

Brownell got the message. He may not have agreed with Eisenhower's rationale, but he discovered that the government was maintaining a list of security informants and paying them regularly. In February 1954 he quietly put a stop to this operation. Herbert Philbrick, Mary Markward, Elizabeth Bentley, Louis Budenz, and seven others were dropped from the list of security informants.[40] Brownell, in his 1971 Columbia University oral history, says it happened this way:

> *Brownell:* I found developing out of the war years there had been built up a list of, say, half a dozen or so informants in the area of subversive activity who are actually on the payroll of the Justice Department, and were paid almost on a salary basis under a system which gave them a regular income, and they testified in one case after another. As soon as I discovered this, I stopped that system, and we either dispensed with their services entirely, or saw to it that in any future cases they would only be paid

what a regular witness would be paid for their attendance at court, in this way avoiding any danger of having a stable of witnesses who were more or less beholden
to the government and might have their testimony tainted
by the fact that their income came from this source. . . .

Interviewer: Did you actually find documentation that their evidence
was tainted, or was there fear that it might be?

Brownell: We dropped several prosecutions for fear that it might
have been. [41]

The spectacular Matusow recantation may have influenced Brownell.
Even the FBI had been taken in by Matusow, and Olney, in his oral history, tells how Justice discovered the FBI sanitizing its files: "Tommy
Tompkins . . . went up to the files to get the original FBI reports in which
Matusow's story was given. There it appeared that Matusow was described as an informant of 'known reliability.' He also found an FBI agent
there taking the file out, in the process of removing the first page and
substituting another page, in which Harvey Matusow was described as an
informant of 'unknown reliability.' "[42]

The list of possible witnesses against Lattimore was further depleted.
On March 5, 1954, the bureau learned that Elizabeth Boody Schumpeter,
the Japanophile who had been one of Lattimore's most persistent accusers,
had died the previous year. [43]

Unaware of the rumblings in the White House and the demotion of so
many ex-Communist witnesses, but beginning to worry about what would
happen in the court of appeals, Rover filed another brief with the court on
November 12, 1953, answering the defense brief of October 1. The defense contentions were "nonsense." The sole issue was "Did the accused
willfully falsify his oath by testifying to the truth of a matter which he
did not believe to be true?" Hummer reported that the date set for oral
argument on the appeal, November 17, had been indefinitely postponed
and that instead of the usual bank of three judges the entire court would
sit on the Lattimore case. [44]

By now suspicion of Lattimore had metastasized throughout the body
politic. On November 13, 1953, Robert C. Jewel, school board member in
Shaftsbury, Vermont, announced that *Our Neighbors in the Pacific* had
been removed from the school library shelves because it had been written
by "the Owen Lattimore gang." He did not identify the authors. [45]

Nineteen fifty-three ended with a veritable blizzard of investigation
requests to the bureau from Warren Olney. The prosecution was running

scared. FBI responses to most of these requests do not survive, but on December 4 Hennrich commented on one potential witness in Europe who wanted to be paid. Jackson asked if the bureau knew anything about this person. Hennrich noted that the man "does not profess to have information but merely to be able to get information. I pointed out to Jackson that Europe is full of individuals who are looking for American dollars in exchange for so-called intelligence services. I told Jackson that if he cared to submit a memorandum relative to this matter, the Bureau would look it over."[46]

On December 31 the court of appeals set oral argument in the Lattimore case for January 25, 1954.

The massive government resources thrown into prosecuting Lattimore were not all devoted to establishing the legal sufficiency of the vital count one or to gathering evidence to prove that count in a trial. There were still five minor counts that Rover needed to prove. The Justice Department and the FBI had active investigations under way in all of them. The effort and time devoted to these trivial matters is mind-boggling.

Take the search for Asiaticus. Count three charged that Lattimore falsely denied that he knew Asiaticus was a Communist. This claim was based on Lattimore's testimony to SISS in executive session July 13, 1951, and in public session February 29, 1952.

> *Morris:* And yet, Mr. Lattimore, you were able to recommend him [Asiaticus] as a qualified performer for the Institute of Pacific Relations.
>
> *Lattimore:* I didn't recommend him. He wrote in some material for me which I thought was a good article on the subject and I published it. One of the articles was on railway loans in China at the turn of the century, the late 1890's and the early 1900's. It concerned some of the British Railway loans of that period. I sent the article, as I always did in such cases, to the Royal Institute of International Affairs in London, and they disagreed with some of his interpretations but not with his statements of facts.
>
> *Morris:* You knew at the time he was at least a Marxist, didn't you?
>
> *Lattimore:* I didn't know whether he was a Marxist or not. I thought he was a left-winger. . . .
>
> *Morris:* And it is your testimony that you did not know he was a Communist?

> *Lattimore:*   I didn't know he was a Communist. I would have said,
>   speaking as of the late 1930's, that I would have thought
>   he was possibly a Socialist, but not a Communist.[47]

After this executive session testimony had been reviewed in the public hearing, Morris had some more questions. Did Lattimore want to stick with his statement that he did not know Asiaticus was a Communist? He did.[48]

Some twenty-five hundred pages of the FBI file record the four-year search for Asiaticus. The investigation went literally to the ends of the earth. It soon took on a life of its own. By the time it was over, the investigators were no longer even expecting to find evidence that Lattimore knew Asiaticus to be a Communist; they were just doggedly following a trail to which they had been assigned. At the end of this trail they could at best talk to someone who, fifteen or more years earlier, had actually met Asiaticus. In the end the bureau accumulated enough information to write a biography of Asiaticus up to 1944, when he disappeared. After that rumor took over, and he was variously reported to be dead or to be living in disguise in the United States, or in Montevideo, or in Europe.

One false lead threw the bureau off the scent for a while. A muddled informant in San Francisco claimed that Asiaticus was really Lattimore, who used that pen name "to write his most aggressive articles." When this suggestion was disproved, the bureau discovered that the real Asiaticus was born Moses Wolf Grzyb (pronounced "ship") on June 13, 1897, in Krakow, Poland. He led a fascinating life. He used at least two aliases in addition to Asiaticus: M. G. Shippe (the name under which Lattimore corresponded with him) and Hans Mueller or Moeller. His early years as a student in Krakow left no traces, but his employment with various German periodicals in the 1920s did. Every known survivor of those periodicals was tracked down. Asiaticus had several tours in China as Comintern representative, journalist, bar owner, and Du Pont foreman; survivors of those enterprises were located. Du Pont records were found in Wilmington, Delaware; others had to be located on three other continents. Grzyb's sister and brother, after many false starts and wild goose chases from Israel to Germany, were interviewed; they had last heard from him in 1939. His second wife, Trudy Rosenberg, was traced from Shanghai to New York to Israel to Italy to Germany, but when U.S. army agents found her in March 1953, she would tell them nothing about her husband. His first wife's brother was located in South Africa. Informants in

Taipei, Hong Kong, Melbourne, Sydney, Seattle, Baltimore, St. Louis, Boston, San Francisco, New York, Tokyo, Manila, Geneva, Paris, Heidelberg, Bonn, Tel Aviv, Berlin, Johannesburg, Montevideo, and no doubt a dozen other places claimed to know something about him, and all of it is reported in the bureau's voluminous files. The report of the U.S. consul in Montevideo is still classified for "national security" reasons.[49]

One informant told the Baltimore FBI office that Rudolph Slansky, vice premier of Czechoslovakia until he was "terminated with extreme prejudice" by that Stalinist government in November 1952, was actually Asiaticus. Pictures of Slansky were therefore shown to Wittfogel and two other persons who had seen Asiaticus. Wrong suspect. Woodrow W. Kelly, resident regional security officer in the U.S. embassy at Tel Aviv, spent December 1953 through April 1954 chasing around Europe and the Middle East to locate Asiaticus's relatives. At the end of it Kelly was an accomplished (if unwilling) genealogist and a fine storyteller.[50]

An amazing amount of information was thus gathered, but the FBI could reach no conclusions about Asiaticus's current whereabouts, dead or alive. Three informants claimed he was arrested in Shanghai in 1944 and never seen again.

Asiaticus was in fact dead, and an accurate report was in FBI files. It came from John S. Service, reporting under date of October 4, 1944, from Yenan, and it was among the papers found in the *Amerasia* offices in 1945. Service recorded a statement by Chu Teh to journalist Maurice Votaw that Asiaticus had been killed by the Japanese while he was traveling with the Communist New Fourth Army in 1941. His demise was confirmed by Janice and Stephen MacKinnon in 1980 when they interviewed Trudy Rosenberg, by then back in China.[51]

None of the far-flung Asiaticus informants (except Wittfogel) claimed to believe that Lattimore knew Asiaticus at all, much less as a Communist. Indeed, the informants abroad had never heard of Lattimore. The search for Asiaticus was a boondoggle to defy the imagination.

The search for evidence from Chinese Nationalist police files was equally quixotic. This was the source Surine had cultivated through informant T-7, the source touted and then canceled by Navy Commander Miles, the source the FBI tapped via Far East Command's Lieutenant Malim. FBI knew the Taipei files were bankrupt; Rover's prosecution team persisted in its hallucinations.

Several times during 1953 Rover suggested that a bureau agent go to Taiwan. Each time the bureau said no, emphasizing that all government agencies operating in Taiwan had already made what scrappy information they could get available to the bureau. The prosecution was persistent. On September 18, 1953, Hummer telephoned Wacks to report that Chiang Kai-shek's son (presumably Chiang Ching-kuo) was coming to the United States; there would be cocktail parties at which the attorney general could ask Chiang's son "to induce his father to furnish the 'real' information concerning Lattimore in his files." To prepare for this, would Wacks please review FBI records to see if Chiang had ever been interviewed? Wacks agreed to review the files. Hoover's response to this report: "This should not have been done. They have copies of our reports & can plow through them themselves. We are doing entirely too much 'wet-nursing' of Hummer et al."[52]

By January 1954 the prosecution had given up its proposal to get Chiang as a witness, but it was still pushing to send a bureau agent to Taipei. On January 7 Branigan was on the receiving end. The precise request is classified, but Branigan reported that he had assured Rover the bureau would let the prosecution know if anyone found something new about Lattimore in Taipei. Branigan also let out his frustration and his skepticism about what they were getting from Taipei: "In the past, it has been noted that the Chinese Nationalist Government officials have not been wholly cooperative with respect to instant case and the only pertinent information from this source has consisted of undocumented, hearsay data contained in memoranda which, from their contents, are undoubtedly of recent vintage. These documents, all of which are similar in certain respects, contain biographical data on Lattimore and unsubstantiated allegations which have been brought against Lattimore, including those of Senator McCarthy and Louis Budenz and others. These documents fail to reflect independent investigation by the Chinese."[53]

But Branigan's doubts were not passed on to Rover. On February 11 Jackson and Donegan called on Hennrich: same agenda. As of 1981 the FBI was still withholding what transpired in this conference; only Hoover's comment at the end of Hennrich's report was released: "I agree with positions taken in this memo. We are not going to send anyone out of the country; we are not going to do any research work & we are not going to directly contact any foreign diplomatic representatives."[54]

Whatever Hennrich told Jackson and Donegan, the Justice Department did not accept it. Two days later Olney wrote Hoover, again pushing for the bureau to interview a Nationalist diplomat. Hoover again turned it down: "It seems to me since the Dept. has initiated this angle it should carry it out—not the FBI."[55] Mild, but the tension was building.

Branigan got much of this pressure. He complained in a three-page letter to Belmont on March 23, 1954. Rover wanted the bureau to "furnish summaries of information" that might stimulate the Chinese Nationalists to provide more. This request, Branigan thought, was ridiculous. "The Criminal Division's attorneys are now preparing for trial. They know better than we what the weaknesses in the case from a prosecution standpoint are."[56]

Rover did know the weaknesses of his case, but he continued to believe that the Chinese could rescue him if pressed sufficiently. This belief led him to a curious maneuver. FBI documents about this operation are heavily censored, but sometime in March Rover communicated to John W. Ford, State Department regional security supervisor, Far East, requesting that Ford obtain from the Chinese Nationalist government a formal statement that all information it had about Lattimore had been given to the United States government. On the face of it this request was ridiculous, but Ford was a diplomat. The uncensored part of his reply says only that "past experience has shown the Nationalist Government to be reluctant to give information, especially where such data concerned American citizens. It was felt that an actual formal statement from the Nationalist Government to the effect that the United States Government had been furnished all information in its files would be extremely difficult, if not impossible, to obtain."[57] Presumably no such request was made.

But the pressure continued, and Taipei released one more document. "Informations on the Activities of Owen Lattimore and His Associates in Rendering Assistance to the Chinese Communist Party in Its Attempt to Overthrow the Nationalist Government" was turned over to the U.S. embassy May 17, 1954. Its primary subjects were Lattimore, Service, Vincent, and Davies. This forty-page document purported to contain three surveillance reports on the activities of these individuals. It was obviously written after the Tydings and McCarran hearings, but it contained more factual inaccuracies than previous documents from Taipei. Hoover received "Informations" June 21, 1954, a month after the embassy in Taipei got it. He passed a copy to Olney July 6, noting that it was similar to earlier documents from Taipei.[58]

This was not the end of prosecution attempts to squeeze more out of the Nationalists. In August 1954, when an unnamed high Nationalist official visited Washington on financial business, Davitt and Donegan quietly interviewed him. The bureau did not even know such an interview took place until December 2, when Assistant Attorney General William F. Tompkins (who replaced Olney) wrote the FBI to report on this interview. Tompkins wanted the bureau to follow up suggestions from the

Nationalist official, including an interview with Hollington Tong, by then Nationalist ambassador in Tokyo.[59]

Belmont inherited this problem. Most of his response is still denied, but his first recommendation got by the FBI censors: "It is recommended that we accede to the request of AAG Tompkins despite the fact that it took four months to advise us _____ interview and to request investigation. . . . if we now tell the Department to cover these leads itself and the case is lost, the Department would undoubtedly try to place the blame on us."[60]

When this story got to Hoover, he exploded. Two paragraphs of his letter of December 15 to the attorney general are denied, but one can get the general idea from what is released.

> I am calling this request to your attention because there are fundamental principles involved. Certainly if the Federal Bureau of Investigation is to be responsible for investigations, we must insist that our representatives conduct interviews where there appear to be available facts which would reflect upon investigations within our jurisdiction. Just as certainly it is unfair for the Department to hold facts for four months requiring investigative attention and then request investigation shortly before trial is scheduled to begin.
>
> I must protest vigorously the inconsiderate manner in which this matter has at this late date been referred to us for handling.[61]

There is no record of what the bureau learned from Hollington Tong or from any of the other fourteen interviews requested.

The bureau was forced into other "fishing expeditions" by a jittery prosecution team. One of them required hundreds of hours of agent time to search the chaotic Army Intelligence records at Fort Holabird in Baltimore for any mention of Lattimore in files covering thirty-four persons who had been in Asia and might have known him. Nothing came of this search.[62]

On January 25, 1954, the United States Court of Appeals for the District of Columbia Circuit sat for three hours to hear oral arguments in the Lattimore case. All nine judges were present. Rover said that he was "ask[ing] for a full court hearing because of what he called the crippling effect of Judge Youngdahl's ruling, if allowed to stand, on the right of Congress to conduct investigations."[63]

Most of the argument centered on the first count. Nothing new was presented. The arguments were all in the printed briefs. The judges seemed to assume that count one was nebulous, and they asked lawyers for both sides to discuss whether a bill of particulars would cure this defect. Rover said it wasn't nebulous at all; O'Mahoney said it was "basically vague and indefinite" and could not be cured.[64] AFP and the Lattimore lawyers were cautiously optimistic; nobody expected an early decision.

From Eleanor Lattimore's letter to the Barretts three days after the hearing, we know that the Lattimores did not share AFP's optimism. It was still unreal to her, "having to sit and listen to Owen being discussed and described by a serious representative of his government as if he were a criminal and a traitor." And when the case was "announced as United States of America versus Owen Lattimore it sounds like such an uneven contest to start with, especially when they describe Owen as 'Criminal No. 1879-52.' " As she saw it, the stress of the hearing gave her a bad cold, and "Owen woke up with a bad sacro-iliac, one of the worst he's ever had." Their doctor was convinced these illnesses were both largely psychosomatic. But this hearing was over, and she wrote, "We can now settle down to forgetting that the USA is against Owen Lattimore and doing some nice things like painting the house and digging the garden and chopping firewood."[65]

A week after the court of appeals hearing, one of the landmark events of the McCarthy era took place at the Department of Defense. John G. Adams, army counsellor, assigned by Secretary of the Army Robert Stevens as liaison to Senator McCarthy, had to decide whether to honor McCarthy's demand that the famous left-wing dentist, Irving Peress, be kept in the service. Peress had been hounded by McCarthy and wanted to be discharged—right away. Secretary Stevens was out of the country. Adams decided that the only reason to hold Peress was to appease McCarthy, since Peress was eligible for immediate discharge. Sick of appeasing McCarthy, Adams let the Peress discharge go through. McCarthy and Cohn declared war on the army, and Eisenhower was finally forced in his limp-handed way to back up the army. The televised Army-McCarthy hearings showed McCarthy to the electorate in all his nastiness, and by the end of 1954 the "Wisconsin Whimperer" (Lattimore's phrase) had been censured and shunned by the Senate.[66] Lattimore had the last laugh.

In spring 1954 the Lattimores were able to get away from Baltimore and its fanatics. They took several weeks to go north, first to visit the Stefanssons. Eleanor Lattimore described this visit in glowing terms. Then came Lattimore's annual Harvard lecture. There was fear of trouble by the Harvard authorities, largely because of threats by the local American Legion, so the area was swarming with police. But there was no trouble, and about a thousand people (Eleanor's estimate) packed the hall. Fairbank as usual entertained the Lattimores, and they dined with Zechariah Chafee, Ralph Barton Perry, Bernard De Voto, and other Cambridge friends. The next stop was New York, staying with Joe and Betty Barnes, dining with Santha Rama Rau, Dorothy Borg, and A. J. Liebling. *U.S. versus Lattimore* receded, for a while, into the background.[67]

Months dragged by, and no word came from the court of appeals. There were occasional words from McCarran. Speaking to the New Hampshire Catholic War Veterans in Manchester May 1, 1954, McCarran said the Communist party was more dangerous than ever. It had decentralized and gone underground. "This decentralization has already tripled the number of Communist Party clubs," he said. And the Party had "selected the secret leaders for its underground apparatus. It has established and is operating a far reaching and vigorous 'loyalty' program of its own."[68] The *New York Times* account does not say whether he mentioned Lattimore as one of the leaders of the new Communist apparatus.

On May 11 Hummer finally had word on how the court of appeals would rule. It was a rumor, he admitted to Wacks, but the vote would be 7–2 in favor of the prosecution. This time Hummer was wrong. On July 8, 1954, the appeals court issued its opinion. By a vote of 8–1 the court upheld Youngdahl in striking the vital first count and the trivial seventh count. The court overruled Youngdahl on counts three and four, but on a 5–4 vote. A vigorous minority opinion on counts three and four made Youngdahl look good.[69] It had taken six months, but the forty-four-page decision was worth it to the Lattimore camp.

The court based rejection of count one primarily on the vagueness argument: "The word 'sympathizer' is not of sufficiently certain meaning to sustain a charge of perjury. . . . There is no definition of the term 'sympathizer' or any concrete specification of its content either in the indictment or in the statute." Judge E. Barrett Prettyman, who wrote the opinion on count one, cited the dictionary; there were at least five distinguishable meanings. And the vagueness of the count "cannot be cured by a bill of particulars."[70]

Count seven, about the Yenan trip, was dismissed on a technicality. Robert Morris, in questioning Lattimore during the SISS hearings, had been inept. Morris asked in one place about prearrangements with "Communist authorities" and in another about "the Communist Party." The court held that these were two different things, and Lattimore had acknowledged writing the Communist authorities in Yenan.[71]

The majority opinion on the first count did not accept the First Amendment arguments of Lattimore's lawyers; that count was invalidated on the basis of vagueness. On the two counts reversing Youngdahl, Judges Henry W. Edgerton, Bennett Champ Clark, David L. Bazelon, and Wilbur K. Miller filed a powerful dissent. "Few terms are vaguer than 'Communist.' It may mean a member of the Communist Party, or a sympathizer and promoter of Communism and Communist interests, or a believer in dialectical materialism, or a radical, or an opponent of inherited wealth, or many other things." They felt that this vagueness alone should invalidate counts three and four.[72]

But the dissenters' most interesting analysis dealt with materiality.[73] Both counts (that Lattimore lied when he said he did not know that Chi Cha'o-ting and Asiaticus were Communists) were irrelevant to the mission of the committee before which Lattimore testified.

> Counts III and IV relate to the period between 1934 and 1941. But the Committee was authorized, at the end of 1950, to investigate current matters. . . . The Resolution expresses no interest in persons who *were*, or *may have been*, Communist-dominated years ago, when Hitler, not Russia, was threatening the world and many people were Communist sympathizers who are now anti-Communists. The Committee is to study what goes on in the 1950's, not what went on in the 1930's. It is to be a watchman, not a historian. If the Resolution left this point in doubt, legislative history would remove the doubt. . . . If these counts go to trial, and if the government offers to prove that Lattimore did publish "subversive" articles and also that their authors were Communists, it will remain immaterial whether or not Lattimore knew they were Communists. (Italics in original)[74]

There follows a lengthy indictment of SISS for overstepping its bounds. The dissenters *did* accept the First Amendment argument. They could not "avoid the conclusion that a congressional inquiry into what an editor knew, between 1934 and 1941, about the views of the authors whose work he published, would abridge the freedom of the press guaranteed by the First Amendment. . . . The court overlooks the fact that what is not pertinent cannot be material and the *Rumely* rule that pertinence cannot be decided without regard to constitutional limits on congressional power."[75] Here was a notable rebuke to McCarran, SISS, the Department of Justice, and the whole McCarthy saturnalia. This time it was a minority opinion, but in the end Edgerton and his fellow dissenters triumphed.

The press appreciated what had happened: the *Times* headline the next day read "Lattimore Upheld on Battle to Kill Key Count in Case." Rover knew he had been slapped down; he "acknowledged that he considered the first count the core of the case. Mr. Rover said he 'could go to trial' with what was left of the indictment, but made it clear that he would have been much happier if the first count had been reinstated."[76]

Lattimore said the decision was "clearly a major victory," and O'Mahoney claimed that the 8–1 vote of the court on the major count "has destroyed any substantial case" against Lattimore. A *New York Times* editorial on July 11 agreed.[77]

Rover was now at a crossroads. After a long and successful career, he had taken on a landmark prosecution that he expected to solidify his reputation. Seventeen months into that prosecution, things were beginning to fall apart. The whole anti-Communist crusade was losing its luster. McCarthy had been made a fool of by Joseph Welch and on July 20, as a result of the Army-McCarthy hearings, had to fire Roy Cohn and Don Surine. And the court of appeals—how could they have found for the heretic Lattimore?

Hummer relayed the deliberations of the prosecution team to the bureau. Rover's first plan was to take the case to the Supreme Court. Chief Judge Harold Stephens of the court of appeals, the lone dissenter in the 8–1 decision to dismiss count one, advised Rover to appeal to the Supreme Court.[78] But FBI coolness to the prosecution, and doubts as to whether Solicitor General Simon Sobeloff would agree to appeal the case, caused Rover to change his mind.

FBI reluctance to push the prosecution was apparent when Rover sent Jackson to the bureau to talk informally to an unidentified supervisor. Jackson raised several topics, then got to the bottom line: "Jackson then asked if a Bureau agent would be permitted to serve in court to identify the public source material used in preparation of the Bureau memorandum sent to the Department" and also if someone "would read, review, and analyze the Department's final written brief in the Lattimore case." The supervisor Jackson talked to said he could not handle that matter; it would have to go upstairs. Upstairs, in the person of Director Hoover, was as usual blunt. His terminal comment: "Absolutely no."[79]

Rover wrote Sobeloff July 16, 1954. Rover then believed that an appeal to the Supreme Court would take so long that the prosecution would lose momentum, and the best course would be to seek a new indictment "framed to meet the objections of the Court to the language in count one." This new indictment would then be consolidated with the still-standing minor counts of the first indictment. There would be two general counts in the new indictment, with the terms clearly defined, eliminating the vagueness problem.[80] Soberoff approved this recommendation.

Victims of the inquisition often felt they were facing an all-powerful, highly coordinated behemoth that could bludgeon its way to triumph over truth and justice. This was not always the situation. In the Hiss and Rosenberg cases the FBI, the Justice Department, the courts, and sometimes the White House worked together effectively. In the Lattimore case the FBI and Justice had serious fights, which, along with doubts in the bureau about Lattimore's alleged guilt, contributed to the failure of the prosecution.

After deciding to seek a second indictment, Rover made another tactical error: he wanted to reinterview twenty-one key witnesses. He sent Jackson to see Branigan at 6:45 P.M. on July 22, requesting that the bureau (1) furnish the current addresses of the witnesses and (2) "contact these witnesses tonight and request that replies be received by tomorrow, July 23." Branigan hit the roof. The bureau would not be hustled in this fashion. Justice could get the addresses itself. Jackson then retreated and told Branigan that "he did not mean to impress a deadline for action but desired only that the Bureau give the matter its usual prompt attention."[81] Hoover's comment: "We should not be stampeded in this."

Incredibly, after this display of arrogance the prosecution came back July 23 to ask that a bureau agent accompany the departmental attorney on each interview and that the various bureau offices outside Washington provide transportation for traveling department attorneys. Now Branigan dropped his formal language. These requests were "completely out of line."[82] Hoover agreed: "We are not going to start acting as chauffeurs, valets, witnesses, nor aides-de-camp for Dept attorneys." But this wasn't the end. Department attorneys Donegan and Davitt, on a western interview tour, tried to get the Los Angeles FBI office to drive them to San Diego. Hoover was apoplectic.[83]

Donegan and Davitt made their trip to San Diego on their own. The potential witness they went to see was Clay Osborne, who had begun his vendetta against Lattimore when he worked for OWI in 1943. Osborne was by this time in a state mental institution; he had periods of rationality followed by total incoherence. Donegan reported that he had "no doubt whatsoever that Clay Osborne would not make a satisfactory witness."[84]

By August 11, 1954, the prosecution team had prepared a fifty-two-page memorandum for Rover, giving the pros and cons of seeking a new indictment. Rover studied this memorandum and on August 19 made his announcement: he would seek from the grand jury then sitting in the District of Columbia an indictment based on matters not covered in the original indictment, using new evidence and new witnesses. The only clue he gave the press was that the new material dealt with Lattimore's "promotion of Communist interests." Lattimore did not comment publicly, but AFP, joined by O'Mahoney, issued a statement. "The United States Attorney has announced that he will not appeal the 'key' count of the Lattimore indictment which has been condemned by two courts on grounds which are fundamental to our liberties. Instead he will seek a new indictment containing the same charge in slightly different words. If Mr. Rover believes that the issue should be litigated, it seems to us a pity and an unjust hardship to the defendant that he has decided to adopt this strategy rather than to submit the fundamental question to the Supreme Court of the United States."[85]

The defense team was puzzled and downhearted. What new evidence, what new witnesses, could Rover possibly have that would lead him to seek another indictment on the vague grounds of "promoting Communist interests?" They were on a treadmill. After a successful two-year struggle to get one vague count thrown out, they were now confronted with the same thing all over again.

But it was not really the same thing over again; it was worse. The Lattimores and their lawyers had been constantly under stress for fifty-four months. The funds raised by George Boas had been exhausted. The government with its infinite resources had added new prosecutors, activated the immense power of the Hearst, Scripps Howard, and McCormick press, floated rumors about surprise witnesses, and carefully concealed the bankruptcy of its hunt for credible evidence. Lattimore wrote Fortas August 21, 1954, two days after Rover's announcement; the letter does not survive, but Fortas's answer tells us how things stood.

Fortas's response is dated August 25. So sensitive was the matter that he said he wanted "to write a few things to you which would be too difficult to say personally." Fortas acknowledged that the lawyers had concealed from Lattimore, who had been in their office at the time of Rover's announcement, their great distress. This was part of a lawyer's habitual "spare the client" reaction to bad news. But Lattimore's letter now made Fortas's anguish no longer concealable: "Your letter indicates that you have now reached what may be the point of unbearable stress." So Fortas had to level with Lattimore.

One thing he revealed was that he and Thurman Arnold were in disagreement: "Thurman, being of an optimistic turn of mind and being full of good red blood, strongly asserts that the case against you cannot pre-vail. I think that the outcome is entirely unpredictable and that it depends to a substantial extent upon the state of the world and of the nation at the time the case goes to the jury." Then to the crux of Lattimore's letter: "As to the immediate problem with which you are wrestling—whether to go before the grand jury or to hold a press conference after the indict-ment—I believe you are aware of the problems involved. Ultimately, the decision will have to be yours after you have had another exposure to the legal view. Please regard this as a personal communication from me to you. Thurman is out of town and has not seen this letter."[86]

Thus descended on Lattimore and his wife one more dark night of the soul, a rending decision whether to go by the traditional legal procedures or to venture into the volatile realm of public counterattack. Should they attempt to convince the keepers of public opinion that no matter how many hundreds of charges had been thrown at Lattimore, they were all frauds? By the time I came to question him, Lattimore no longer recalled the soul-searching that accompanied this decision, and no documents pre-serve it. In any case, the legal route won out. They would go by the book.

By September 19 Lattimore had recovered his composure sufficiently to write his sister-in-law with remarkable sanguinity. They had had a wonderful New England holiday, his gardening was therapeutic, his grandson Michael was so beautiful it was dangerous to take him out on the street, and there was a new granddaughter, Maria, who would prob-ably be a trapeze artist as well as an intellectual. The grand jury had subpoenaed fifty new letters from the IPR files, and their line of attack was evident: "The IPR will be pictured afresh as a nest of pro-Russian intrigue, and I as chief cuckoo in the nest. Even things like favoring US recognition in 1933 will be interpreted as 'pro-Russian,' to get me indicted as having been a 'promoter' of Communist causes, but leaving out, this time, the word 'sympathizer.' Thurman Arnold gets so mad when trying to discuss it that he can't talk, only huff and puff. . . . Ever'n ever so much love; and, paraphrasing McCarran: Don't think! Write!"[87]

What Lattimore and his lawyers did not know was that Rover was mis-stating his intentions just enough to throw the defense off the track. What he intended to seek was a two-count indictment, the first count being that Lattimore lied when he said he had never been a follower of the Com-munist line; when this falsehood was established by citing Lattimore's voluminous writings, Rover would use the same evidence to get a second count showing that Lattimore had thereby promoted Communist interests. There would be two major counts now, instead of one, and "follower of the Communist line" was sufficiently precise to avoid dismissal on Sixth Amendment grounds.[88]

Rover had a secret weapon. It was an impressive 515-page "analysis" of Lattimore's writings done by "outside experts" which showed that "in approximately 97% of the cases, Lattimore agreed with the Communist line."[89] To a grand jury, this analysis must have had the weight of Moses' tablets when he came down from Mount Sinai. Of course, the jurors couldn't read it all. Even if they had read it, in the absence of knowing the pathology of the compilers, the selectivity of the passages cited, the omissions of vast chunks of contradictory material, and the paranoid fantasies on which it was based, they would not have known how misleading it was.

Analyses of Lattimore's writings to show that he followed the Communist line had begun with Kohlberg's attack on the IPR. Freda Utley presented a similar analysis to the Tydings committee and in her 1951 book *The China Story*. Richard L. Walker filled a special section of the *New Leader* (March 31, 1952) with an anti-Lattimore article that included analysis of Lattimore's *Pacific Affairs* editing. The FBI had its Central Research Desk make a comparison of Lattimore's writings with the Party line. The Department of State did the same thing in 1951. McCarran's staff was constantly working up such comparisons; a June 1952 document headed "Parallel with Communist Line" was produced by Mandel, Morris, and "Burnham" (probably James Burnham). In addition to these known analysts, six unidentified individuals volunteered their studies of Lattimore's writings to McCarthy, McCarran, or the FBI.[90]

Hummer had no impressive comparison of Lattimore's writings with the Communist line in December 1952, but soon thereafter the prosecution set about getting one. On January 30, 1953, Rover wrote Hoover, noting that an article by Harold Lasswell showing how the new technique of "content analysis" could "prove a person's writings may follow a given propaganda line" had appeared in a back issue of *Public Opinion Quarterly*. Would the bureau get him a copy?[91] The bureau complied.

Then Rover visited Belmont February 24. Would the bureau agent who had analyzed Lattimore's writings in 1950 be available to testify at trial? Belmont did not think so. Whoever testified should have been a Communist so he could have personal knowledge of the Party line. No bureau agent could do this; no agent would be allowed to testify in any case. Hoover agreed.[92] Rover set about getting his own experts.

But he needed a library of Lattimore's writings for the experts to work with. On April 10 he dumped in the bureau's lap a request for two copies of everything Lattimore had ever written or spoken: books, magazine articles, public statements, book reviews, newspaper articles, OWI directives. At first the bureau attempted to comply with this request, but as hitherto unknown Lattimore articles began to surface, the bureau grew tired of tracking them down. Justice Department attorneys were told to go to the Library of Congress. By June the bureau had provided 322 articles and 5 books; Rover got the rest of the books from the Library of Congress. Rover's major problem now was finding the right persons to analyze them. All candidates for this task were screened by the bureau.[93]

By July 2 the apparatus was all in place. Rover had found an institutional base for the project: American University's Bureau of Social Science Research, Robert T. Bower, Director. Staff members working on the Lattimore project were Harold Mendelson, Ivor Wayne, and Stanley K. Bigman. Listed as consultants were William J. Morgan of the president's Psychological Strategy Board, Charles A. H. Thomson of the Brookings Institution, and W. Phillips Davison and Alexander George of Rand Corporation. Or so attorney Donegan told Belmont.[94]

In 1985 none of the American University people could be located. Fortunately, Alexander George, Phillips Davison, and Charles Thomson, the "consultants" on the project, responded to my inquiries. Alexander George's response was typical: "I am happy to have an opportunity to clarify the record as regards the [FBI] statement that I was a consultant to the Department of Justice in the Lattimore case. I and several other specialists in content analysis were asked to attend a meeting to discuss whether this technique could be used to prepare evidence against Lattimore. Ralph K. White, also present at the meeting, and I both emphatically stated that in our judgment the technique of content analysis was not capable of providing valid evidence for this kind of purpose. I was not asked to participate in such a project."[95]

Rover was not put off by the adverse judgment of the consultants. Bower said they could do it, so a contract was drawn up with American University for a "sample analysis" at a cost of eight thousand dollars. Hummer and Donegan related to Belmont how this analysis was working. Belmont thought:

> The method of analysis appears to be quite complicated; however, briefly, it is to be entirely objective and based on the treatment afforded subject matter by Lattimore as to whether it follows the Communist Party line or is more favorable to Russian interests than the interests of the United States. This is to be accomplished by utilizing the yardstick of some 400 key words and phrases; for example, Stalin, China, reactionary, impe-

rialist, opportunist, etc. For example, take the word "Stalin"; a list would be made up of the number of times this word appeared in Lattimore's writings and would be broken down as to whether Stalin was mentioned favorably or unfavorably. By this factual analysis, on a percentage basis, it is expected that these researchers can testify that Lattimore's writings were pro-Communist and that he favored or promoted Communist or Russian interests.[96]

The American University team set about its task. Apparently the university library was not adequate for their research; they were constantly plying Rover with requests for needed materials, which Olney passed on to the FBI: background data on the Overseas News Agency, a copy of the theses of the Sixth World Congress of the Communist party, *China's New Democracy* by Mao Tse-tung, the *China White Paper*, George Sokolsky's *Tinder Box of Asia*, and so on.[97]

Sometime in October 1953 the American University team finished a sixty-page report, which "concluded that the content analysis techniques used by them at this time cannot prove the proposition that Lattimore was a promoter and sympathizer of Communist interests." But they thought it was entirely possible that Lattimore's views could be compared with the Communist party line by some other means. Rover was back to square one. In November he started all over. This time he had a new list of expert prospects, all to be screened by the bureau: Herbert Feis, W. Yandell Elliott, Stefan Possony, Cyrus H. Peake, and Nelson T. Johnson. H. G. Creel and Wilmoor Kendall were later added to the list, but none of these people was selected. Perhaps they weren't expensive enough; Olney told Hummer "that no economy should be used on this search or any other aspect of instant case."[98]

Sometime in January 1954 Rover got his new team together. It was announced to the bureau February 4: Joseph Ballantine, David Dallin, Nicholas Poppe, and Timothy Taracouzio (henceforth designated by the initials of their last names, BDPT).[99] This group replicated the ideology of McCarran and his SISS. Three of them were known enemies of Lattimore. Rover chose well for the purpose of getting an analysis to overwhelm a grand jury; but were this team to be subject to skillful cross-examination in a public trial, their biases would hurt Rover's cause.

Joseph Ballantine had been chief of the Far Eastern division of the State Department in 1945—one of the Japanophiles Lattimore told Truman should be replaced. Ballantine thought Lattimore had been "very anxious to get us into a war with Japan" in 1941. After the war he objected to Lattimore's position on the emperor. At the October 1949 roundtable conference on China, Ballantine sided with Stassen and the group opposed to dealing with Peking. In his oral history for Columbia University, Ballantine said that *"Solution in Asia* goes 100 percent along the line of the Communist solution in Asia."[100]

David Dallin was a Russian national who had fled the Soviet Union in 1922. He came to New York in 1940 and made a name as a student of Soviet foreign policy. Naturally he read Lattimore, who was insufficiently anti-Communist for his tastes. In Dallin's 1948 book, *Soviet Russia and the Far East,* he claimed that Lattimore was following the Soviet line in advocating a coalition government in China; chastised Lattimore for claiming that the Chinese Communists had democratic features; and in general said that *Solution in Asia* swallowed the Communist line. In a 1950 *New Leader* article he strengthened these views. Lattimore, in saying that the Soviet Union did not control China, "could not be serving the Kremlin more effectively were he on Stalin's payroll." A year later, also in the *New Leader,* Dallin took up Budenz's crusade: Wallace, Lattimore, and Vincent had worked to carry out a Kremlin objective when they recommended Wedemeyer (which, of course, Lattimore had nothing to do with). Wallace said Dallin's article "indicates a mind so diseased" that he would not answer it; Alsop said that "it seemed to me such trumped up and psychotic nonsense" that he canceled his *New Leader* subscription.[101]

Nicholas Poppe (see chapter 22) had lost none of his hostility to Lattimore when Rover asked him to take part in the BDPT analysis in 1954. Poppe remained convinced that Lattimore followed the Party line on Mongolia. Poppe does not mention his work on BDPT in his autobiography.[102]

Timothy Taracouzio was the only BDPT participant with no public record of hostility to Lattimore. He was also a Russian refugee, having come to the United States in 1923. He studied at the University of Southern California, took a Ph.D. at Harvard (1928), and was in charge of the Slavic department of Harvard's Law Library from 1928 to 1942. During World War II he served in the army; after the war he taught at the National War College for a year, then the Naval Intelligence School for a few months. There is a big gap in his *Who's Who* biography between 1947 and 1956.[103]

Taracouzio wrote three books, two of which do not help us understand why he was enlisted to impale Lattimore. His third book, *War and Peace in Soviet Diplomacy,* published by Macmillan in 1940, is enlightening. As Rupert Emerson notes in the *American Political Science Review,* Taracouzio "sets out with a basic hostility both to Marxist ideology and to

Russian practice," hence leaving no room for defense of Soviet policy anywhere. Taracouzio ignores the exclusion of Russia from the Munich conferences; Lattimore's view of Munich, that the Western powers treated the Soviets contemptibly, was anathema to Taracouzio. Taracouzio would also have despised Lattimore's 1950 geopolitics. Lattimore held that by tough negotiations the United States could reach a settlement with the Soviet Union in Asia; Taracouzio thought that the Kremlin would not deviate from its fundamental desire to conquer the world and that negotiations were useless. [104]

Quite a crew, BDPT. Asking them to evaluate Lattimore's work was like asking Luther, Calvin, Knox, and Wesley to evaluate papal encyclicals.

BDPT had research needs too. Requests to the bureau for research materials tripled. Jackson made some monumental demands, usually channeled through the new Assistant Attorney General for Internal Security, William F. Tompkins. On September 3 Tompkins wanted specific information about 237 Lattimore publications: "With respect to each book, periodical, or document, the name and address of the witness or witnesses who can testify to (1) the amount of circulation of the first edition and all subsequent editions, if any; (2) its printing and circulation in foreign languages; and (3) the names of all countries in which the writings were circulated and the amount of circulation therein." [105] Unfortunately, our lexicon of J. Edgar Hoover's expletives is the poorer due to absence of his reaction to this request.

On Monday, September 3, 1954, Rover, Jackson, Donegan, and Hummer went before the grand jury. They had the 515-page BDPT comparison of Lattimore's writings with the Party line; more than five hundred other exhibits including, so Hummer claimed, all of Lattimore's publications; and various witnesses. [106] We do not know about the witnesses, but the stacks of documents had to be overwhelming.

The BDPT analysis of Lattimore's writings was not released by the FBI or the Department of Justice. There is, however, a copy in Ballantine's papers at the Hoover Institution at Stanford. [107] This document is mimeographed; presumably it was the version displayed before the grand jury. Marginalia indicate that BDPT clearly had some internal disagreements. Poppe wrote the lengthy section on Mongolia; Dallin scribbled caustic comments all over this section. Ballantine wrote on Japan, Dallin on China; Taracouzio's contribution is not clear.

The BDPT analysis is organized by topics: Chiang Kai-shek, China,

Indonesia, Indochina, Japan, Korea, Lattimore and communism in general, Mongolia, Sinkiang, Soviet foreign policy, Soviet Union. There are 555 separate citations to Lattimore's writings, with some passages cited twice or three times. These passages come from

Overseas New Agency	195
Situation in Asia	100
Solution in Asia	71
Pacific Affairs	25
Amerasia	17
Other	170

Inner Asian Frontiers of China, Lattimore's most important and best-known work, is cited only five times. Out of perhaps four million words in Lattimore's collected works, BDPT analyzed some seventy-five thousand. How were they chosen? The selection was not on the basis of random numbers, or by taking every tenth paragraph, or any other rigorous principle. Careful reading of BDPT makes the conclusion inescapable that they selected passages that contradicted the right-wing wisdom of 1954: that Lattimore, as mastermind of the China hands, lost China; that Moscow brought Mao to power; that the People's Republic of China was subservient to the Kremlin; that the Korean invasion was Stalin's first step toward world conquest; that the United States should never recognize the PRC; and so on. It was easy to build up a pro-Communist score this way. For each citation to Lattimore's writings in BDPT, there is a classification: either agreement with or contradiction to the Communist position. About half of the pages have a column for the evaluator to indicate whether the passage cited agrees or disagrees with the official U.S. position. Usually the author finds a contradiction to the U.S. position, but even where he doesn't, if the U.S. position agrees with the Soviet position, he chalks up a score against Lattimore. On about half of the items related to Chiang Kai-shek, whom the Russians supported until 1946 and Lattimore until 1947, Lattimore could be classified as in agreement with both the Soviet position and the U.S. position. This gives him no credit. It was a no-win situation. If Lattimore said the world was round, BDPT would check Soviet doctrine. If the Soviets also said the world was round, BDPT would score one against Lattimore.

Most of the evaluations show Lattimore taking a heretical position—for instance, his belief that Soviet minority policies in the Sino-Soviet border areas were enlightened, so that the Soviets had a certain "power of attraction" for minorities on the Chinese side. Lattimore's position on this point is cited in ten or more places—hence ten scores against him. BDPT justify this approach by arguing that there had been minority unrest in the Ukraine; hence, Lattimore could not be correct about the Sino-Soviet border areas; hence, Lattimore was following the Communist line.

BDPT analysis of the five citations from *Inner Asian Frontiers* is especially interesting. In any scientific sample of his writings this book would have been cited far more than a mere five times. The first of the five citations does not appear on the page of *Frontiers* BDPT claim, nor does it appear anywhere else in Lattimore's book. In citation two, Lattimore says that most of the Inner Mongolian lamas were parasites, living off the profits of trade and agriculture that they controlled. This was true, but the Soviets believed it also. Score another agreement between Lattimore and the Communists. The third citation is lengthy and complicated; any analysis would necessitate a major historical inquiry. Since Lattimore says Soviet policy in Outer Mongolia (MPR) was nonexploitive and aided the Mongols against the Japanese encroachment, BDPT score it against Lattimore.

In citation four, Lattimore says the Khalka Mongols have "the most popular and representative government they have ever had, and a rising standard of living" under the MPR. There is much reason to believe this evaluation was correct, but Poppe didn't believe it. Score another point against Lattimore. In citation five, Lattimore describes a Soviet-Chinese negotiation of 1929. BDPT says his description is overly kind to the Soviet Union. Perhaps they were right. But these five instances (or four, if item one is a false citation), taken out of a treatise of 585 pages, *do not prove anything except that the compilers were out to get Lattimore.*

I cannot claim to have checked out every one of BDPT's 555 citations. Since *Solution in Asia* was the paradigm instance of Lattimorean fellow-traveling, according to Ballantine and Dallin as well as Eastman and Powell in their *Reader's Digest* article, I checked the seventy-one references to it carefully. In only three cases do BDPT find Lattimore in opposition to the Communist line. The other sixty-eight citations are in agreement with the Communists. In about ten cases the analyst throws in the additional comment "Propaganda."

However, there are certain anomalies in the BDPT analysis of *Solution*. Nineteen items repeat earlier citations under a new category; hence, only fifty-two different citations are actually used. The box score does not show this duplication. One item is classified as "Agreement with Communist position—propaganda" on page 180 of BDPT but on page 292 is classed as "Contradiction to Communist position." One of these has to be wrong.

Most of the analysis simply demonstrates that BDPT lived in a different historical environment from Lattimore. Did, as Lattimore claims, Chiang use the threat of the Chinese Communists to get aid from the United States? Of course. This is not Party-lining. Lattimore claimed Chiang was still in control of China in 1944 and that the Communists were not strong enough to nominate a candidate of their own for president. This is Party-lining? Lattimore said Marxist thought was "competitive" with capitalist thought in Asia. Was this not true? Lattimore pointed out the interaction of domestic and foreign policy—linkage, in current parlance—and so did Lenin. Does this warrant charging Lattimore with following the Party line? Nationalism, Lattimore said in 1944, is the most potent force in Indonesia; colonialism is dead. Stalin said this, too. Who is following whom? This tortured analysis of *Solution* emanated from bias and ideology. O'Mahoney, Fortas, Arnold, or Rogers would have made mincemeat of it.

The most compelling evidence of bias in BDPT's analysis of *Solution* is its total disregard of Lattimore's prescriptions for the economic and political health of Asia. *No single passage in which he argues for capitalistic free enterprise* is cited by these analysts. What BDPT cite is slanted; what they ignore is vital. Lattimore notes the desirability "of encouraging the development of independent local capital and industry in colonial territories." He praises Chiang, saying the "power of decisive action lies with the Chinese, and within China with the Kuomintang." He notes that Americans were welcomed back to the Philippines, proving that U.S. policies there had been enlightened. He says, "We need political stability and economic prosperity in China so that we can invest our capital there safely." He argues that "we should do our utmost to revive production in China, emphasizing the value of the profit motive, and therefore of private enterprise." And in the overall Asian scene, we need "a general policy of expanding investments and markets."[108]

But on August 18, 1954, Jackson could tell Branigan that "in approximately 97% of the cases, Lattimore agreed with the Communist line."[109]

The BDPT analysis is a scandal, and its use by the Eisenhower Department of Justice to wring a two-count indictment out of an uncomprehending District of Columbia grand jury was contemptible.

CHAPTER TWENTY-SEVEN

Second Indictment, Second
Dismissal

While the judicial system was laboring to settle the case of the *United States versus Lattimore*, attacks from the political arena continued. One of the more unusual ones, which remained clandestine, came via the chaplain of the Senate. The Reverend Frederick Brown Harris was a friend and supporter of J. Edgar Hoover. On July 13, 1954, Harris wrote Hoover urging that an anti-Lattimore activist who had called on Harris be allowed to "put into your hands some things you ought to have regarding the Lattimore case." This individual, according to Harris, "lives and moves and has his being in this matter of the communistic threat. . . . He has just completed a volume based on the testimony Lattimore has given at various hearings. . . . I can assure you that, after three-quarters of an hour interview with him, he is on fire with this subject and with his zeal to uncover the diabolical plottings of this system which is a conspiracy against all that is decent."[1] Hoover declined; Lou Nichols was commissioned to be baptized with zeal. There is no evidence that Nichols was converted.

Zeal flowed more openly July 28, 1954. In the grand ballroom of the Hotel Astor, Alfred Kohlberg's American Jewish League against Communism, Incorporated, gave a gala dinner for Roy Cohn, recently fired by the Senate Permanent Investigations Subcommittee.[2] Twenty-five hundred people crowded the ballroom; the sponsors said six thousand more had been turned away. Every right-wing organization in the country was represented; Frank Gibney, a senior editor of *Newsweek*, said of it, "Unquestionably, this was a most comprehensive assembly of 'McCarthyites.' Besides Roy, the Senator and a few of the more prominent boys on the McCarthy sub-committee staff, there was an assortment of zealots comparable in their intensity only to the personnel of meetings organized in past years by groups like the old Communist-sponsored League Against War and Fascism."[3]

Kohlberg made one of the many tributes to Cohn. Not trusting the press to distribute his encomium adequately, Kohlberg mailed copies of his remarks to his list of some thousand opinion makers: "Roy, stay away from the U.S. Senate. I say this entirely without prejudice. In fact, some of my best friends are Senators. But beware of them, Roy, they are just too mixed up."[4] The mixed-up senators were the anti-McCarthyites such as Ralph Flanders.

From the standpoint of Rover and the prosecution, the Senate *was* troublesome; Rover had real trouble getting an SISS member to appear in court. Rover wrote McCarran August 24, 1954, asking him to arrange for a member of SISS, preferably himself, to appear before the grand jury on September 13 to testify that SISS had a valid legislative purpose in questioning Lattimore.[5] McCarran declined. Two weeks later Rover was still hunting a Senate witness. We have this intelligence from Ed Hummer, reporting to Branigan:

> Hummer advised that for purposes of showing materiality, a senator who was on the McCarran Committee . . . will appear before the grand jury and again in the trial. He advised that former Senator O'Conor of Maryland has indicated his desire not to so appear since he is now a practicing attorney and the publicity might be adverse; that Senator McCarran does not want to appear because "he would lay himself open to attack by the Communists"; that United States Attorney Rover does not want Senator Eastland to appear because of his professed anti-Negro sentiment; that Senator Ferguson is willing but has advised Rover that he is in the midst of a political campaign from which he should not take time off; that former counsel for the McCarran Committee, Judge Robert Morris of New York City, is not wanted because Rover believes he would use such an appearance for self-aggrandizing; and that Senator Smith is not living. Hummer advised that the remaining two Senators, Jenner and Watkins, have been requested to appear and as yet no reply has been received.[6]

Lacking grand jury minutes, we do not know which senator appeared. Nor do we know very much that happened in the grand jury room. The only published account is in Fred Field's autobiography.

In 1953, a year after serving a jail sentence for refusing to tell a New York court about the affairs of the Civil Rights Congress Bail Fund, Field moved to Mexico. The climate in the United States was such that he could no longer be effective in the Communist-affiliated causes dear to him.

Rover was adamant that Field should appear before the grand jury, so a summons was served on him in Mexico City. Presumably, Field was called to identify letters from the IPR files; he cooperated in this request. But when Rover began to question him about his political beliefs and his relations with various people, he balked:

> Nine of the questions began in exactly the same way: "Have you ever been requested to act on behalf of the Soviet Union . . . ," and then the nine endings: "by Budenz?" "by Browder?" "by any member of the American Communist Party?" . . . "by any Soviet citizen?" "by any Chinese Communist?" "by Owen Lattimore?" To all those questions I invoked the Fifth Amendment. It is not too difficult to imagine what could have happened if I had answered them instead. For example, had I said no to the one about Budenz, they would have had Budenz on the stand in no time at all, and he would have said something like this: "Yes, I clearly remember the occasion when I passed on to Comrade Spencer [Field] the message from Moscow in which Comrade Stalin asked him to come over to have tea with him." As a result, I would have landed in jail for perjury. There was convincing testimony on the record to show that the Establishment would believe absolutely *anything* Budenz said. I would not have had a chance. (Field's italics)[7]

The grand jury learned nothing significant from Field except that one of Lattimore's friends was a Fifth Amendment Communist. This did not matter. The guts of Rover's case was the BDPT document, probably supported by one or more of its compilers.

September 26, 1954, the day before the grand jury was to adjourn, Walter Winchell broadcast a claim that Philip Jaffe had made "a sensational statement to the FBI." Donegan called the bureau early the next morning. If Jaffe had said anything about Lattimore, Rover wanted to hold the grand jury and bring Jaffe before it. Wacks checked the records. Jaffe had never been "wholly cooperative." In August he had appeared to waver, but nothing had come of it. Branigan, who reported the incident to Belmont, recommended "that Mr. Donegan be advised that all pertinent information received from Jaffe re Lattimore has been furnished to the Department; that if the Department wants to continue the grand jury on the basis of Winchell's comment, that is entirely up to them." Hoover concurred: "We are not responsible for what W W says, & Donegan should be so advised."[8]

Rover did not need a confession from Jaffe. The grand jury was convinced. On September 27, 1954, they unanimously voted a two-count indictment.[9]

While prosecution attorneys were polishing and printing the indictment, the most powerful force behind the Lattimore prosecution died. Patrick McCarran, age seventy-eight, suffered a heart attack after addressing a political rally in Hawthorne, Nevada, September 28.[10] He took his suspicions about the "one being" directing the Communist apparatus in the United States to the grave with him. The chances are that Lattimore was still a candidate. Jenner and Eastland, who succeeded McCarran as chairmen of SISS, did not give up his crusade.

The new indictment was issued October 7. It is one of the strangest documents ever to come from a grand jury. The two counts are simple: Lattimore lied about not being a follower of the Communist line and not promoting Communist interests. But the document runs to twelve pages. It presents a definition of "Communist line" so expansive as to include any statement ever made by a Soviet or left-wing writer. It lists twenty-five "topics" on which Lattimore is alleged to have followed the Communist line, and for each of these topics it gives a list of Lattimore's publications, with page numbers, presumably setting forth that line. Fourteen of these topics are declarative sentences, such as "Moscow Has Not Backed the Indo-Chinese Communists." The other topics have no predicate; they are simply phrases such as "The Marshall Plan." The Lattimore publications listed, as in the BDPT analysis, are overwhelmingly ONA dispatches, *Solution in Asia,* and *Situation in Asia.*[11]

And as with BDPT, Lattimore's extensive statements in favor of capitalistic free enterprise are nowhere to be found in the indictment. Lattimore had also clearly asserted the legitimacy of free-world efforts to counter Soviet influence, but the indictment does not mention them. How Rover expected to deal at trial with a cross-examiner who would demonstrate that the articles listed were overwhelmingly anti-Communist is a mystery.

The AFP brief of appellee, filed November 18, 1954, quotes definitions of "follower of the Communist line" from HUAC, the U.S. Civil Service Commission, and the Internal Security Act of 1950 that differ radically from that of the Lattimore indictment. Most such definitions are narrowly drawn and focus on shifts in Soviet positions. According to the defense brief, "The indictment is not limited to those who shift with Russia as it shifts its policy. It touches any writer whose opinion ever coincided with Russian policy at any time. Covering a period of fifteen years, as it does, and including events long antedating the cold war, it would force every British and American statesman to admit that he was a follower of the Communist line in the sense used in the indictment."[12]

In a statement Lattimore issued the same day the indictment was re-leased, he said, "Under this indictment, the entire Democratic and Republican administrations could be accused of perjury if they said they had never knowingly followed the communist line—so could Presidents Roosevelt, Truman and Eisenhower, all of whom have been accused of following the communist line. Inevitably this country cannot always take a position in exact opposition to the position taken by Russia."[13] The *New York Times* quoted Lattimore's statement approvingly.

Despite the unanimous grand jury vote on the new indictment, Rover was uneasy about it. Even before it was issued, he was planning ways to avoid having it overturned. Hummer is again the channel through which we can view prosecution plans; he talked to Branigan September 30.

> Hummer advised that United States Attorney Rover has contacted Chief Judge Laws to request that Youngdahl not be assigned the Lattimore case again. Laws reportedly told Rover that any such request must be in writing and that Youngdahl had already indicated his desire to remain assigned to this case. Hummer stated that Rover has prepared a petition of prejudice and bias against Youngdahl, based mainly on his statement concerning materiality, referred to above, and if Youngdahl once again is assigned to this case, he will present this petition to Youngdahl as the basis for a motion for Youngdahl to step down. Hummer stated that he expects "fireworks" with respect to this situation since he is convinced that Youngdahl wants to use the Lattimore case as a steppingstone to higher positions.[14]

Hummer may have been wrong about Youngdahl's ambitions, but he was right on the mark about Rover. On October 13 Rover filed his affidavit of bias, stating that Youngdahl had shown himself so biased in favor of Lattimore that he could not preside impartially over a trial. He should therefore remove himself, allowing the case to be assigned to another judge.[15]

The defense was stunned. Youngdahl and Lattimore had never met. Youngdahl had never shown any bias in favor of Lattimore anywhere; he had simply ruled on the legal sufficiency of an indictment. AFP reacted immediately. Their motion to strike affidavit of bias and prejudice was filed October 14.

> (1) The affidavit is a bald and undisguised attack on the decision of Judge Youngdahl dismissing the first count in the original indictment of Owen Lattimore. That decision was affirmed by an eight-to-one vote of the judges of the United States Court of Appeals.

(2) The affidavit is in plain defiance of all the decided cases which hold
     that a judge may not be disqualified because counsel objects to his
     opinions and rulings. . . .

The affidavit is clearly an attempt to manipulate the administration of justice. The Department of Justice wants to prevent Judge
Youngdahl from deciding this case. The reason it wants him out
of the case is because under his opinion in the previous indictment
the prosecution fears that its present indictment cannot stand. The
Government had an opportunity to appeal to the Supreme Court
of the United States, which it declined. It substitutes for that judicial review the oath of the United States Attorney that in his
opinion the written decision of Judge Youngdahl on its face is so
bad that it must have been the result not of judicial reasoning but
of unjudicial prejudice.

No such affidavit has been filed by the Government in any case
before this. It amounts to an assertion that Judge Youngdahl has
been in this case an untrustworthy judge who has allowed his
prejudices to run away with his reason. That assertion is made in
a *cause celebre*. All over the United States newspaper headlines
have reported that it is the opinion of the Department of Justice
that the judge who dismissed the first count against Lattimore was
not acting as an unbiased court.[16]

Thus, it was all laid out: subtly, but firmly, the Eisenhower administration was challenging the courts to deal harshly with the heretic Lattimore. The rule of law was now to feel the heat of the frustrated inquisitors. At the time, no one could know how much the courts would bow to
the anti-Communist hysteria. McCarthyism seemed to be on the wane,
but the China lobby was as vigorous as ever and more determined.
Youngdahl was vulnerable, and Attorney General Herbert Brownell swung
his prestige firmly behind Rover.

Thurman Arnold requested an appointment with Brownell. According
to the *New York Times* account, Arnold "asked Mr. Brownell at a conference this morning to disassociate the Justice Department from the challenge to Judge Youngdahl's fitness. The Attorney General refused and
told Mr. Arnold that he had 'the fullest confidence in Leo Rover.' "[17]

Rover maintained the initiative. At a news conference October 20 he
challenged the right of the Lattimore defense to object to his affidavit of
bias, claiming that it was a matter exclusively between him and Judge
Youngdahl. As the *Times* described it, Rover "asserted that the Lattimore
lawyers had 'no standing to interpose a motion' to dismiss his affidavit.
He described their motion as a 'frantic emotional attack' on his action."[18]

Two days later Youngdahl held court to hear arguments on the affidavit of bias.

It was a nasty scene in the district court the morning of October 22, 1954. There is an old saying in legal circles; when you have no case, abuse the opposition attorneys. Rover went that one better: he abused the judge. Of course, he had disdain aplenty for Lattimore's attorneys, but his harshest barbs were reserved for Youngdahl. The judge, Rover said, should never have commented on the possible immateriality of the counts in the first indictment. Materiality was a matter that could be decided only after hearing the government case at trial. "How can it be argued that Your Honor does not come into this case prejudging it, biased and prejudiced, whether you believe it or not, remembering, now, this is not any off-the-cuff statement. This is not something that the court might say in the heat of the trial. It is a cool, calm, deliberate opinion." Said the *Times*, "Torrents of emotional oratory swirled about Judge Youngdahl for two hours. Mr. Rover shouted that the jurist had been 'an advocate, not a judge' in earlier consideration of the Lattimore case. Judge Youngdahl had used language in an opinion, Mr. Rover asserted, that was 'a gratuitous insult to the Government of the United States.' "[19]

It was left to the genius of Thurman Arnold to counter this outburst of invective. His impassioned defense of the original Youngdahl ruling, and of the court of appeals that upheld the vital part of it, is a model for students of judicial pleading. Arnold's speech had more than the requisite citations of precedent for affidavits of bias. He articulated precisely the fanaticism that sparked the Lattimore prosecution. Rover was "the sincerest man I have ever known, but he has that type of mind that feels any opinion against him must be biased and prejudiced, because he is so sure that God is with him and that he is in the right. . . . Four out of the nine judges on the Court of Appeals said . . . on the face of the record, these counts cannot pass materiality. What does the United States Attorney propose to do? To get rid of you? Then he swears off those four judges, who went even further than you with respect to materiality. . . . I think that what Mr. Rover wants to do is to muzzle this court—not yourself, but other judges."[20]

Youngdahl listened to it all impassively and when it was over, took it under advisement.

Blind commitment to a cause comes to different people in different ways. McCarthy, for instance, began his anti-Communist career with no deep commitment whatever. Anticommunism was just another political tactic. Jack Anderson, who covered McCarthy for Drew Pearson, says,

"From day to day I could see the new cause tightening its grip on him, as though the compulsive upward thrusting that had so long driven him forward willy-nilly had at last found its true focus."[21] So McCarthy became a believer, internalized his own rhetoric, lost any sense of proportion.

Something similar happened to Ed Hummer. Beginning his contact with the Lattimore case as a thorough skeptic, prodded by Cohn's vendetta and Rover's fanaticism, Hummer came by 1954 to share the commitment of the prosecution team. It clouded his vision. After hearing the Rover-Arnold confrontation over the affidavit of bias, Hummer reported to Branigan that "Rover 'lowered the boom' on Youngdahl to such an extent that it is inconceivable to Hummer that any judge in Youngdahl's position would consider remaining on the case." Hummer, too, had lost his sense of proportion. The next day Youngdahl ordered the affidavit stricken from the record as scandalous.[22]

Rover *had* attempted to intimidate the courts. Hummer revealed this fact on October 27, when he told Branigan that the government would not appeal Youngdahl's action but would "first see how Youngdahl treats the defense motions." Hummer himself thought that "in view of the recent adverse publicity, Youngdahl now will 'bend over backwards.' " On October 28 AFP moved to dismiss the new indictment, claiming that it was worse than the original count one. The government's research into definitions of "follower of the Communist line" was "historically silly" and "could only have been conducted by consulting with witch doctors, for, whatever the process by which the Grand Jury was persuaded to bring this outrageous indictment, it could not have included any consideration of historical fact."[23] Momentum was now with the defense, but AFP took no chances. Their brief on appeal was 215 pages.

The storm in Judge Youngdahl's courtroom spread far beyond Washington. In England, "clamor raised by members of Parliament and large parts of the British press over the questioning of Britons in connection with Mr. Lattimore's trial" led Home Secretary Gwilym Lloyd George to announce that any future American requests for investigation in this or similar cases would be considered at a "high level" before granting them. The *New Statesman and Nation* called the Lattimore case a "battle for the soul of America."[24]

In Wyoming, Republicans opposing O'Mahoney's campaign to regain his seat in the Senate played up his part in the defense of Lattimore. One called the lawyer a "foreign agent" in full-page newspaper advertisements. O'Mahoney gave no ground. He not only refused to apologize for defending Lattimore but emphasized that his client was entitled to a pre-

sumption of innocence and to counsel of his own choosing. Ten days before the election O'Mahoney was thought to be ahead of his Republican
opponent, but his advisers urged him to downplay the Lattimore case.[25]

In the Senate, upholders of civil liberties began some of the actions that
eventually overthrew the McCarthy-McCarran forces. Senator Thomas
C. Hennings, Jr., Democrat of Missouri, presaging the full-scale hearings
he chaired on civil liberties in 1955 and 1956, called for an investigation
of Rover's affidavit of bias. Senator William Langer, chair of Judiciary, at
first went along with Hennings and requested Brownell, Rover, and
Youngdahl to appear at a hearing November 23. When the committee
met, none of the three invited witnesses appeared. Deputy Attorney General William P. Rogers appeared "to advise the Committee that the Department would produce no one for questioning . . . since the Department feels that this action [Rover's affidavit] was proper."[26] Langer
adjourned the hearing on the pretext that one of the senators was absent.
It never reconvened.

Midterm elections took place November 2, 1954. Democrats won back
control of both House and Senate. The campaign degenerated toward the
end into mudslinging and acrimony. Vice President Nixon, setting the
tone for the Republicans, charged that the Democrats were unfit to govern
because they were soft on communism. Democrats bridled at this charge,
and House Speaker-Designate Sam Rayburn told United Press that "Congress would demand that the Republicans 'put up or shut up' on their
claims of mass dismissals of Federal security risks" hired by previous
Democratic administrations.[27]

McCarthy was not a major force in the campaign. With a committee
recommendation to censure the Wisconsin senator waiting to be voted on
by the full Senate, Republican campaign managers invited him to sit out
the campaign. He didn't, quite; significantly, the Republican liberal who
sustained McCarthy's bitterest attacks, Clifford Case of New Jersey, won
reelection. In Wyoming, O'Mahoney also won, showing at least that support of the beleaguered Lattimore was not fatal. William S. White of the
Times felt that the elections were a rebuff to extremist candidates.[28]

John Foster Dulles didn't get the word. Three days after the election
Dulles accepted the recommendation of a special hearing panel charged
with evaluating John Paton Davies under Eisenhower's Executive Order
10450. The board did not find that Davies was in any way disloyal. It
found, contrary to every efficiency rating Davies had ever received, that
he lacked judgment, discretion, and reliability. His continued employment was therefore inconsistent with the national interest. Dulles fired

him. Hurley and McCarran won that battle. The last of the Chiang opponents was now out of government service. As Davies himself puts it,
Jonah was finally overboard.[29]

Several days later Dulles, who might have had a conscience, told Davies
he could use Dulles's name as a reference in seeking another job.

Rover now increased the number of senior attorneys working on the
Lattimore case from four to ten. He pressed the department to take
Youngdahl's rejection of the affidavit of bias to the court of appeals; Brownell
refused. According to Hummer, Rover was bitter about this decision.[30]

Youngdahl was seething. On November 18, in an unusual move, he
filed a memorandum with the district court asking the government to
disavow as "without substance" the affidavit of bias, which he described
as a "hit-and-run" attack that could affect any judge who heard the Lattimore case. Youngdahl noted "with regret the public announcement by
a Government spokesman that his ruling would not be appealed. The
judgment of the appellate court could have helped to dissipate the affidavit's thrust against the integrity and independence of the judiciary." The
Justice Department remained silent. AFP also asked Brownell publicly to
withdraw the affidavit: same result.[31]

Despite Brownell's refusal to disavow Rover, the Justice Department
had some uneasiness about how the Lattimore case was going. On November 24, 1954, they sent a new representative to the FBI to talk over a
proposed line of investigation. The new man, Tom Hall, admitted misgivings about the proposed investigation, which he considered a "fishing expedition." Hennrich, for the bureau, agreed. The specific proposal is still
classified. Whatever it was, the bureau, as usual, said put it in writing and
"we will carefully analyze it."[32]

Hummer brought new intelligence November 24. It was all wrong.
Hummer thought Youngdahl would step down if Rover removed himself
from the case, but Rover refused to do so. Rover also thought Youngdahl's fellow judges would pressure him to step down.[33] They did not do
so.

On December 2, after extended and bitter debate, the Senate condemned McCarthy, 67–22. This was occasion for rejoicing at Arnold, Fortas, and Porter. Senator Jenner, unwilling to let the debate end without
another attack on Lattimore, threatened Senator Flanders with a subpoena
to get him to testify about his relations with Lattimore.[34] This was gal-
lows humor. McCarran was dead, McCarthy was impotent, and the Lattimore persecution was winding down.

Youngdahl presided over oral arguments on the defense motion to dismiss the second indictment December 13. The substance was familiar, but Arnold and O'Mahoney had some new rhetorical flourishes. Arnold commented, "If the first indictment was too vague, the second is 100 times too vague." O'Mahoney noted that President Eisenhower now advocated peaceful coexistence with the Soviet Union; if Lattimore "had been the one who first wrote 'peaceful coexistence' he would have been indicted for it." The atmosphere in the court was quite different from that of the hearing on the bias affidavit: "Today, Judge Youngdahl smiled and exchanged pleasantries with Mr. Rover. When he had finished two hours of argument, Mr. Rover thanked the judge for his 'graciousness and consideration.' " No date was set for announcing a decision.[35]

Until December 1954 mainstream press coverage of the Lattimore case had been based almost exclusively on public hearings, speeches, and documents. On December 27 the *New Republic* published "New Light on the Lattimore Case," listing "Brian Gilbert" as the author. It was an amazingly accurate effort. "Brian Gilbert" was the pen name of Roger Kennedy, a Minnesota Republican then working for one of the major broadcasting networks. Because of his background and conservative appearance Kennedy had access to Rover, Hummer, and possibly other prosecution attorneys. He had also talked to Arnold, Lattimore, and Youngdahl (whom he knew). Kennedy had originally intended to use the Lattimore material for a network documentary, but the network decided the story was too controversial. Kennedy therefore wrote up his findings for *New Republic*.[36] His article excoriated McCarran, Cohn, and the Justice Department, whose conduct he termed scandalous. Lattimore, he wrote, had been framed.

SISS was outraged. Jay Sourwine called Michael Straight, *New Republic* editor. Sourwine's employers were "particularly interested in the assertion made in the course of the article that the committee had encouraged perjury." Would Straight put them in touch with "Brian Gilbert"?[37] Straight called Kennedy. The prospect of confronting SISS was worrisome, but Straight convinced Kennedy that a contempt of Congress indictment was more worrisome. Kennedy subsequently paid a private call on Sourwine and members of his committee.

As Straight tells the story, "They expected to see an unkempt radical; instead, they faced a well-groomed young Republican. Some intensive grilling followed, but the committee concluded that the net cast out by Sourwine had caught an unappealing fish."[38] Nothing came of this meeting, but it was not the end of SISS interest in Lattimore. The committee followed his career as long as Sourwine was with them. As for the Gilbert/Kennedy article, it remains a perceptive account of the whole fantasy.

Even as the influence of the McCarthy-McCarran Senate bloc was winding down, a group of intellectuals calling itself the American Committee for Cultural Freedom (ACCF) took up the cudgels against Lattimore. The Gilbert/Kennedy article in *New Republic* triggered the ire of Sol Stein and other reactionaries at ACCF; the executive committee of that organization drafted a reply to Kennedy. "Lattimore was indeed a willing instrument of the Soviet conspiracy against the free world," said ACCF; "This conspiracy triumphed in China, yet Lattimore, its 'articulate instrument,' is now defended in the pages of the *New Republic*."[39] ACCF's moderate members did not go along with this article; David Riesman, Richard Rovere, Arthur M. Schlesinger, Jr., and Herbert Muller all protested. ACCF, supported by CIA funds, moved steadily rightward, keeping Lattimore on their roster of subversives; he is still there, in the rogues' gallery of the neoconservatives.

The date for Lattimore's trial had been set for January 10, 1955; as that date approached and Youngdahl had not yet issued a decision on the motion to dismiss the second indictment, trial was postponed. On January 7 Rover finally filed a bill of particulars. It dealt only with the counts concerning Chi Ch'ao-ting, Oumansky, and the handling of Currie's mail. Nobody was enlightened. Unbelievably, on January 10 Rover again asked the FBI to prepare "charts and similar graphics" to display the BDPT findings. Hoover again did not "deem it desirable to have representatives of the Bureau prepare the visual data requested by Mr. Rover."[40]

On January 18 Rover's expectation of having intimidated Judge Youngdahl was dashed. Youngdahl threw out the second indictment in toto and with zest:

> Under Count I, perjury is charged to the statement by Lattimore that he was not a follower of the Communist line. The Government supplies a definition of this phrase in the indictment. The Government is prompt to concede that no such definition was presented to the defendant at the Committee hearing in 1952; that it was formulated after Lattimore testified; that it was prepared after independent research conducted by the United States Attorney's Office. The sources of such research, however, do not appear. The Government contends that it is a matter of common knowledge as to what is meant by "follower of the Communist line" and that people differ but little in their understanding of the term; (footnote: Common knowledge of whom? The man in the street? A newspaper man? A man of ordinary or superior intellect? A member

of the F.B.I.? The Department of Justice? The Internal Security Sub-committee? The State Department?) that it is not a minimal require-ment of following the Communist line to zig and zag with it, since it does not always zigzag; (footnote: The Government's position confuses the Court. In its "Supplemental Memorandum in Opposition to Mo-tion to Dismiss," p. 7, there is found the following: "It defies common sense to argue that the only test of recognizing a dog is a wagging tail and similarly that the only test of a follower of the Communist line is one who zigs or zags. True, a dog should have a tail and a follower should zig and zag, but as [we have] stated to the Court, it will be proven the defendant has zigged and zagged. As the bulk of a dog is not his tail, neither is the bulk of the line zigging and zagging; over-whelmingly its positions remain fixed from their inception." The Gov-ernment appears to be zigging and zagging as to its position and mean-ing of the indictment terms. . . .)

This count, even with its apparent definition, is an open invitation to the jury to substitute, by conjecture, their understanding of the phrase for that of the defendant. . . . To ask twelve jurors to agree and then decide that the definition of the Communist line found in the indict-ment is the definition that defendant had in mind and denied believing in, is to ask the jury to aspire to levels of insight to which the ordinary person is incapable, and upon which speculation no criminal indictment should hinge. . . .

The charges here serve only to inform the defendant that his sworn statements are to be tested against all his writings for chance parallel-ism with, or indirect support of, Communism regardless of any delib-erate intent on his part. They demonstrate that the Government seeks to establish that at some time, in some way, in some places, in all his vast writings, over a fifteen-year period, Lattimore agreed with some-thing it calls and personally defines as following the Communist line and promoting Communist interests. . . .

With so sweeping an indictment with its many vague charges, and with the existing atmosphere of assumed and expected loathing for Communism, it would be neither surprising nor unreasonable were the jury subconsciously impelled to substitute its own understanding for that of the defendant.

To require defendant to go to trial for perjury under charges so form-less and obscure as those before the Court would be unprecedented and would make a sham of the Sixth Amendment and the Federal Rule requiring specificity of charges.

The indictment will therefore be dismissed.[41]

Lattimore and his lawyers were delighted. Surely now the zealots would fold their tents and fade away. But AFP did not brag about their victory.

When a *Baltimore Evening Sun* reporter contacted Arnold, Arnold would only say, "The opinion speaks for itself."[42]

Rover was furious and immediately asked the Justice Department to appeal. Hummer thought that Assistant Attorney General Tompkins would support Rover, but Solicitor General Sobeloff might not.[43] Trial was put off again.

Defense morale was further boosted on February 2 when United Press carried another story about Matusow: he had been confessing and retracting his confessions for more than a year. Now he again said that everything he testified to about Lattimore's books carrying the Communist line was false. Within three months of this final recantation the FBI conducted a new reconsideration of its former Communist informants. No less than seventeen of the New York informants in the Lattimore case were downgraded from "reliable" to "credibility is not known."[44]

The government appealed Youngdahl's decision on February 4, 1955. Rover continued to act as if the case were still on course. BDPT were still analyzing, the FBI was still collecting documents, the State Department was still pursuing potential witnesses in Taiwan. There had been more than 3,000 interviews, and 214 of these had been pertinent enough for the bureau to forward the results to Rover.[45]

The defense, however, thought the case would never come to trial. Since Lattimore had been all but immobilized for five years, the invitations he was getting from scholars in Europe began to look irresistible. Frozen out of American academia (except for Fairbank's annual invitation to Harvard) and unable to lecture at Johns Hopkins, Lattimore, with the support of his lawyers, figured it was time to go abroad. His life had been in the hands of lawyers and politicians long enough. Why should he not accept invitations to address the British Association of Orientalists at Oxford in May and the International Congress of the Historical Sciences at Rome in September? There were also four other tentative invitations. On March 12 he applied for an extension of his passport.[46]

Ruth Shipley was still in charge of the Passport Office and was every bit as anti-Lattimore as before. But she had been overruled in 1951; perhaps it could happen again.

Passport dragged its feet. Arnold complained: "They won't say yes and they won't say no," he told reporters. No wonder: granting a passport to Owen Lattimore was a matter of sufficient moment to reach clear up to the Oval Office.

The brouhaha began when the State Department asked the FBI to send them relevant reports on their investigations of Lattimore to use in questioning him. Belmont, for one, did not want to accede to this request. These reports would reveal "the logical government witnesses" to be called for trial. Rover's office also opposed State's request; he would give them nothing on Lattimore. On April 15 Assistant Attorney General (AAG) Tompkins overruled Rover, and the bureau was instructed to furnish the reports to State. Shipley read them and on April 29 prepared a letter denying Lattimore a passport.[47]

The Shipley letter went to Scott McLeod for approval; he disagreed, recommending that a passport be issued. From McLeod the letter went to the office of Loy Henderson, then to general counsel Herman Phleger, and finally to Herbert Hoover, Jr., the undersecretary, with no decision. Arnold asked that Lattimore be granted a formal hearing. Rover opposed such a hearing; it would just give Arnold a chance for "blowing off steam" and would injure the government's legal case.[48] Rover lost. Frances Knight, a protegé of Senator Styles Bridges and as anti-Lattimore as Shipley, became chief of the Passport Office on May 1; Lattimore got his hearing with Knight. As he recalled in 1979, "Frances Knight asked me if I could show reason why I should get a passport. I said, 'If you give me a passport, you will face a stink on Capitol Hill. If you don't, you'll face a stink in Europe. Take your choice.'"

State was in an uproar, and a meeting was held in Sherman Adams's White House office May 11, with Adams, Herbert Hoover, Jr., Loy Henderson, Phleger, and Jerry Morgan in attendance. No decision was reached. The controversy went on at the undersecretary's level for another week.

On May 17, 12:15 P.M., Adams talked to Secretary of State Dulles. Adams was distraught. Brownell thought the passport should be issued, but according to Adams, "Certain U.S. Senators will make life miserable if we let him go over. . . . [You] are not in a position to issue a passport to a man who has a pending indictment." But Dulles was to make the decision.[49]

Brownell called Dulles early on the eighteenth. The attorney general thought the passport should be issued; after all, when Lattimore was first indicted, the judge had ruled that he could travel anywhere in the world so long as he was back for trial. Dulles told Brownell that Adams was against it, but he didn't know how strongly. Brownell told Dulles to call Adams again.[50]

Dulles relayed Brownell's advice to Adams and said he thought they would issue the passport. Adams expressed regret but did not try to change Dulles's mind. Adams asked if he should speak to Eisenhower about it. Dulles responded, "Has he been following it?" Adams said no. They agreed that Ike should be informed.[51] Dulles then put in a call to the president:

The Pres. returned the call, and the Sec. said we are having a problem re giving a passport to Lattimore. Adams thought I should speak to you about it. I have the feeling that it is better if you are not consulted about it as it is hot. I am in close touch with Brownell and what we do would be what we agree on. The Pres. asked if there is any law that affects it? The Sec. said he is under indictment. The Pres. said oh, he is? The Sec. said the Judge gave permission for him to go abroad. . . . If you are interested, I would be glad to discuss it with you. The Pres. said to take whatever action is necessary and let him know before he is questioned at a press conference.[52]

Whatever conclusions one may draw about a hands-off presidency, Eisenhower's total ignorance of the most celebrated prosecution then under way in his Department of Justice is astounding. Dulles decided, and Lattimore's passport was renewed May 20.[53] Presumably the president was notified.

While the highest officials of the United States were sweating over whether the man who lost China should get a passport, the Justice Department was reviewing its security index, officially titled "Program for Apprehension and Detention of Persons Considered Potentially Dangerous to the National Defense and Public Safety of the United States." AAG Tompkins sent a routine letter to the FBI March 28, 1955, recommending that Lattimore be kept on (the bureau held the index cards). Hoover asked the Lattimore case officers in headquarters and the Baltimore office what they thought. He then wrote a two-page letter to Tompkins reviewing the SISS findings and the bureau's many investigations. From this information Hoover concluded, "It does not appear that facts . . . depict Lattimore as a dangerous individual." The bureau wanted to take him off, and Tompkins yielded. Lattimore became officially "not dangerous" on June 17, 1955.[54]

Rover filed his appeal from the latest Youngdahl decision April 11. The second indictment, he said, was scrupulously drawn to make clear to Lattimore "the nature and causes of the accusation." On May 11 John Jackson resigned from the prosecution team; Hummer and Davitt were reassigned. Edward Troxell replaced Jackson.[55]

On May 20 the Lattimores left for Europe, in plenty of time for his opening lecture in Oxford. After the stress and nastiness of the previous five years England was a tremendous relief. The scholarly community there greeted him with open arms. He lectured to packed houses, and many European intellectuals sought his company. Lattimore's core beliefs, that the Chinese Communists won on their own and were not slaves of the Kremlin, were accepted truths in Europe, not venal heresies as they were in the United States. His four months in Europe were a time of great rejuvenation.

Oral arguments before the court of appeals took place June 1 in Lattimore's absence. The full court sat again, but there were only eight judges; Harold Stephens had died shortly before the hearing. One new judge had not participated in the 1954 decision. The *Washington Post* said it was a "bitter debate in the tense, crowded courtroom." William D. Rogers of AFP said the "argument was somewhat inconclusive." Certainly there was little new; both sides had developed their contentions fully in the briefs. AFP was confident, according to Rogers: "No one has any doubt about the eventual outcome. The only question in my mind is what the Government will do when the Court of Appeals decision comes down." No date for a decision was set.[56]

The death throes of the Lattimore prosecution were much like the beginnings. Poor, befuddled Clay Osborne wrote one of his last pathetic letters to the FBI on June 8. It was addressed to a Los Angeles agent who had been sympathetic to him. "I have either underestimated the total bulk of useful documentation, or else overestimated my own ability swiftly to correlate it. It appears, now, that about another week will be required to get everything organized for even minimum usefulness to our common purpose. I've dedicated so much time to this already that a little more seems justified to meet standards of duty."[57]

There followed descriptions of OWI documents Osborne had pilfered in 1943 and just dug out of his files. Presumably he was now out of the mental hospital and able to visit his storeroom. There were OWI staff orders, memoranda, analyses of "The significance of the Emperor of Japan," the article by Sun Fo, notes on a conference with Sir George Sansom, and so on. All of these documents, Osborne felt, should be photographed for use in the cause. He was very careful with his treasures: "All drawers are secured by long screws at any time I am absent—and during absences of a few hours or longer, I take with me in the rear of my car, all those documents being prepared for you [the FBI]. In my wallet I have placed a notation to notify you in any event of grave accident or death—that my locked briefcase is your property, and that you will pick it up. Same notation is on brief case." The government did, in the end, take some of Osborne's documents. The State Department determined that they were subject to security classification, and Osborne was ordered to return the originals.[58] The documents are still classified.

Of cranks and opportunists there was no end. A "mystery flight" informant was still being checked out in June. This conspiratorial talebearer told the bureau that Lattimore had commanded an Army Transport Command plane that carried military supplies to the Chinese Communists in 1944. This informant had talked to the pilot of the plane, who now lived in Milwaukee. The bureau tracked the pilot down. He had never met Lattimore, had not flown to China at the time alleged, had never delivered supplies to a Chinese Communist army.[59] Poor Rover. Nothing checked out.

BDPT were still at work, still asking for documents (in June 1955 they wanted copies of fifteen pages of the *Daily Worker* and *Pravda*). George Donegan passed the requests on to the bureau. Expedite, said Donegan.[60]

It was too late. On June 14 the court of appeals upheld Youngdahl on a vote of 4–4. It would have taken a majority vote to overrule. No opinion was issued, and the order of the court did not disclose how the judges voted. Rover told the *Washington Post* that as far as he knew, the government would go to trial with the remaining counts of the first indictment, but he would ask the Justice Department to take the appeals court decision to the Supreme Court.[61]

Celebration at AFP was muted. According to Bill Rogers, they were much surprised at the closeness of the vote.[62]

Well they might have been. The grounds for Youngdahl's decision, that such an indictment was vague and imprecise, became settled law. In 1956 an indictment of author Harvey O'Connor for contempt of Congress in refusing to tell Joe McCarthy whether he, O'Connor, had been "a member of the Communist conspiracy" was thrown out because the question was so "imprecise and ambiguous" that it was not a crime to refuse to answer it. The court of appeals panel in the O'Connor case consisted of two judges who had ruled on Lattimore plus Warren E. Burger. Their ruling was unanimous. O'Connor told an Illinois newspaper that he was "delighted that it is now possible for an American citizen to have contempt for Joe McCarthy without having to go to jail."[63]

Rover's assistants, Troxell and Donegan, were divided on whether there was any case at all in the absence of the two backdrop counts Youngdahl had thrown out; Troxell thought the minor counts were weak, but Donegan wanted to go with them. Sobeloff, Tompkins, and Rover were to meet June 27 to make a decision.[64]

Hummer's report to the bureau says that Rover had no part in the decision; Sobeloff and Brownell were responsible. They wasted no time. The headline to the page-one *New York Times* account of June 29, 1955, tells the story: "Lattimore Perjury Case Dropped by Government. Conviction Made Difficult by Courts' Killing Key Counts, Brownell Says."[65]

Brownell's one-page news release of June 28 gave a brief history of the case, carefully noting that the original indictment had come under the previous administration. It concluded: "Upon a consideration of all aspects of the case, it has been decided not to apply to the Supreme Court for review on certiorari on the two counts that were recently invalidated. In the absence of these counts there is no reasonable likelihood of a successful prosecution on the five counts remaining from the first indictment. Therefore, the United States Attorney for this District intends to take the necessary steps to bring about a dismissal of these counts, thus bringing this litigation to a conclusion."[66]

Now Leo Rover, spearhead of the Lattimore prosecution for two and a half years, faced the embarrassing prospect of going before Luther Youngdahl, whom he had excoriated as unfit, and asking that the case be dismissed. To Youngdahl's credit, he did not take advantage of his triumph. As Youngdahl told the story in December 1977:

> Chief Judge Laws—he was the one who gave me the case—had a place out near Goose Creek. Arthur Godfrey had a place out there, and there's a wonderful golf course. We played golf out there. One day during a golf game [Laws] said to me, "Luther, Rover has been to see me, and he said the Department of Justice wants to dismiss that entire"—this was after the second appeal, where they split 4–4, on this two-count indictment—"the Justice Department wants to dismiss that entire case, only they're afraid you'll come out with another barn-burning order." I said, "If they want to come in and dismiss it I'll be a good boy and grant the dismissal and adjourn court in a hurry." So Rover came in one morning, moved to dismiss, and I said, "Motion granted." And I got off the court, almost ran off the bench. That was the end of that.[67]

Actually, Youngdahl said more than that. The official notation reads, "Government's oral motion for leave to dismiss the remaining counts of this indictment is by Court granted; dismissal entered; Defendant discharged."[68]

It was time. There had never been a case against Lattimore. William C. Sullivan, at one time number three man in the FBI, says in his memoirs:

> The dangerous threat of Communism was, of course, one of Hoover's obsessions. During the Eisenhower years the FBI kept Joe McCarthy in business. Senator McCarthy stated publicly that there were Communists working for the State Department. We gave McCarthy all we had, but all we had were fragments, nothing could prove his accusations. For a while, though, the accusations were enough to keep McCarthy in the headlines. One of his major targets was a State Department employee

[*sic*] named Owen Lattimore who McCarthy thought was an important Soviet agent, and a lot of government money was spent on digging through FBI files for evidence to prove it. We investigated the hell out of Lattimore, read every letter and memo, everything he ever wrote, but we never found anything substantial to use against him. Mc-Carthy's accusations were ridiculous.[69]

Roy Cohn, of course, never saw it that way. In my interview with him in December 1979 he argued that only a subversive judge kept Lattimore from his due:

> *Cohn:* I never had the opportunity of legally defending that indictment in District Court. It was dismissed on a bunch of technicalities.
>
> *Newman:* Why did that prosecution fail?
>
> *Cohn:* That prosecution never failed because it never happened. When a judge throws out something on a technicality, I don't consider a prosecution failing.[70]

Warren Olney, looking back on the case from the perspective of the 1970s, thought the case could have been handled better. Even though it was weak, the government should have been more sophisticated. Olney was particularly unhappy about Rover's affidavit of bias: "To our consternation, Leo got so incensed at this adverse ruling that he made a very unwise blast at the judge in public. It got into the papers, and it was very embarrassing to us to have that happen. Of course, it made the judge furious, and his fellow judges also. It was disastrous for Leo himself. . . . He undoubtedly would have been a district court judge if he hadn't blown his stack and fired off at the judge when he shouldn't have."[71]

Roger Kennedy, again writing as "Brian Gilbert" in the *New Republic*, deserves the last word on the dismissal of the Lattimore case. He reviewed the poisonous climate of the times, the excesses of the congressional investigators, the dubious efforts of the government to use perjury as a vehicle to repress dissent, the brazen effort to intimidate the courts, and the need to preserve freedom of speech. His conclusion:

There is another, and more serious lesson: we cannot afford another Lattimore case. Certainly no other private litigant will be likely to find a law firm like Arnold, Fortas and Porter which will take such a case without fee. (Time charges for an "ordinary litigant" by such a firm would run close to $250,000.) But in a broader sense, the cost has been too high. The perjury case against Lattimore grew out of a political prosecution. It was forwarded by improper political pressure upon the Justice Department, upon the press (represented by the magazine *Pacific Affairs*) and, of course, upon the Judiciary. Luther Youngdahl, practicing constitutionalist and Christian, fierce defender of the rights of heretics, sat firm upon the bench and fought off a berserk attack upon the integrity of our judicial system. Now, finally, the attackers seem a little ashamed, as they wipe their eyes and feel the passing of the fever in whose grip they did so much that was ignoble. Luther Youngdahl has won his fight; and so have we, and liberty.[72]

When Brownell announced the end of the prosecution, Owen and Eleanor Lattimore were in Sweden, visiting one of their friends from the 1930s at a cottage in the country. They returned to their Stockholm hotel the evening of June 28, 1955. The telephone rang, and a "very Swedish voice" told them the news just in from Washington. They had not expected it so soon.

They telephoned several friends in Stockholm hoping to find someone to help them celebrate. No one was at home. As Lattimore wrote Joseph O'Mahoney, "We went to a hotel balcony overlooking an arm of the harbor and ordered champagne and smoked salmon and smoked reindeer, and drank a toast to all the many people without whom we'd never have survived."[73]

The rest of their European tour was one long celebration. European intellectuals had never understood the Lattimore prosecution. They had read Lattimore, many knew him personally, and they believed him to be a loyal American and capitalist to the core. They did not think him a liar. The Lattimores spent July and August in England, where he lectured to appreciative crowds at Oxford, London, and elsewhere. Then they attended the history congress in Rome and headed back to America.

PART THREE

Recovery and Triumph

CHAPTER TWENTY-EIGHT

Starting Over

When fall term opened at Johns Hopkins in September 1955, Lattimore was once more an active member of the faculty and teaching classes. But it was a close thing. One faction of the board of trustees had wanted to fire him from the time of the first McCarthy attack. Francis White, a State Department officer who once served in Peking, was adamant about Lattimore.[1] To White and fellow trustees John Nelson, Thomas Nichols, and Jacob France, probably the only adequate exoneration of Lattimore would have been a unanimous vote of "not guilty" after a jury trial; indeed, even that might not have sufficed. They were concerned not just about his heresy but about his disrespectful attitude toward the McCarran committee.

A majority of the board, with the apparent agreement of chairman Carlyle Barton, was less concerned about Lattimore's sins and more devoted to academic freedom. Lattimore had been given tenure by Isaiah Bowman. There was no longer a Page School for him to head, and trustee opposition was too great to give him an equivalent position elsewhere, so they made him a lecturer. The anti-Lattimore trustees went along with this treatment only because they believed, as Nelson said, that Lattimore was really unpopular with the faculty, which would finally "eliminate" him.[2]

Lattimore's situation at Johns Hopkins was therefore quite different from what it had been in the 1940s. There was no prestige appointment, no school for him to direct, no Mongol program, no department of Chinese studies. Geography, an area in which Lattimore was well qualified, was at first closed to him: George Carter was head of that department. Fortunately Sidney Painter, the very conservative chairman of the history department, was also a strong civil libertarian and appalled by the Senate attack on Lattimore; Lattimore could lecture in his department. And in 1958 Lattimore was again welcome in geography, as M. Gordon Wolman replaced Carter as head.

Lattimore was a popular lecturer, drawing such large crowds that Painter had to provide teaching assistants to help grade papers. This popularity was encouraging, but the absence of a graduate program under Lattimore's control, and the dispersal of his Mongols, canceled the satisfaction of an undergraduate following. Also, the university excluded him from several across-the-board salary increases.[3] Despite the strong support most of the faculty gave Lattimore, the bitter hostility of Carter, William F. Albright, Carl Swisher, and a few others made life unpleasant.

Even the few public lectures that now began to come his way brought problems. When the Hartford, Connecticut, chapter of the American Civil Liberties Union asked him to speak on December 16, 1955, they arranged use of the Phoenix Fire Insurance Company auditorium. Word got to Hartford veterans' groups and other unidentified organizations; some of them threatened to picket the lecture and protested to Phoenix. Phoenix got cold feet and on December 6 withdrew permission to use the hall. The ACLU looked for other places and received a willing response from the First Methodist Church, whose parish hall was available. Lattimore's talk came off as scheduled at the Methodist Church.[4]

The *New York Times* reported six hundred people in attendance, braving the hostility of five women standing outside the church distributing anti-Communist literature. The women declined to identify themselves to the *Times* reporter. Lattimore, in opening his speech, remarked that he was disappointed in not being able to speak at the Phoenix: he was a stockholder in the company.[5]

Lattimore's Hartford address was a repeat of one he had given the night before, sponsored by the Emergency Civil Liberties Committee in Manhattan, which had received less publicity. His title was "Freedoms and Foreign Policy."[6] His major focus was the effect of the inquisition on the accuracy of foreign reporting. He began by analyzing the Soviet fiasco in Finland in 1939. The Soviet military had vastly underestimated the will and the capacity of the Finns to resist. Why? Because Soviet agents reporting from Finland told their bosses what the bosses wanted to hear, namely, the Communist line. "The Finns were supposed to be groaning under Fascist tyranny, and the loyal party line was to assume that great numbers of them would swing over to the Communists, who were depicted as the true popular vanguard." Soviet intelligence was thus distorted; the Soviets endured some stunning defeats and had to quadruple their original force to crush the Finns.

The rigid ideology of the United States at midcentury, said Lattimore, similarly distorted what we heard about China. Only one line was tolerated: Chiang and his forces on Formosa were still China's true rulers, bound to regain the mainland once the Chinese learned the horrors of communism. Thus, American foreign service officers had to report what was "politically acceptable, not simply to the Republican party, but to the extreme right wing, the Formosa-first wing of that party." Those who did not were fired. John Paton Davies was the latest case; he lost his job for telling the truth. "As a result, we now have, I make bold to say, the weakest foreign service of any great country in dealing with problems of Asia, and especially China." Lattimore agreed with Walter Lippmann that Knowland, Dulles, and Henry Cabot Lodge were ruining the foreign service with their insistence that everyone tell the same false story about China.

There was scant reference to Lattimore's own experience in this speech, but at the end he acknowledged the cost to him of his long immobilization. "If the study of international relations is to be productive, it has to be a continuous process of self-education, and over the past five years my self-education has been subjected to a certain amount of interruption. . . . Any opinions I may now express are not as well informed as they were before 1950. I am having to start all over again."

Lattimore had already started one new line of inquiry during his leave from Johns Hopkins: figuring out how the stock market worked. His wife told him, when he became restless at the absence of his normal activities, "You need something to do. Look at our investments and see if you can do something with them."[7] By 1945 Lattimore had saved a tidy sum, most of it in war bonds. He was forced to cash in many of these bonds between 1950 and 1952 to meet the expenses of his bouts with Tydings and SISS (the FBI faithfully recorded every bond he redeemed). The defense fund started by Boas in 1953 provided enough money to meet out-of-pocket expenses during the indictment period, and Lattimore still held some low-yield government bonds.

Lattimore approached the stock market just as he had approached the frontier area of Central Asia, studying it systematically and consulting people who had been there, then taking the plunge himself. Of the investment newsletters he consulted, one stood out as the best: the *Value Line*, published by Arnold Bernhard. In October 1955 Lattimore wrote

Bernhard to express his satisfaction with *Value Line*, which provided "a most realistic underpinning to my interest in international affairs; I had largely been without this realistic kind of contact since, many years ago, I worked for one of the great trading firms in China."[8] Bernhard responded cordially, inviting Lattimore to lunch and to visit with *Value Line*'s statisticians and analysts.

In January 1956 Lattimore was in New York and lunched with Bernhard. The two hit it off immediately and began a professional and personal association that lasted three decades. For Lattimore, writing to Bernhard replaced the Overseas News Agency (now defunct) as an outlet for his thoughts about world affairs. Bernhard valued Lattimore's communications enough to put him on a substantial retainer as a consultant.[9] Occasionally *Value Line* carried an article over Lattimore's byline; more often Bernhard simply incorporated Lattimore's ideas without attribution.

Value Line's advice proved lucrative for Lattimore: Xerox, Syntex, Phoenix Insurance, General Motors, IBM, and Santa Fe Industries all performed well. For the rest of his life he read *Value Line* eagerly; it was the periodical he took up first when it came in the mail.

Bernhard also got his money's worth, if only in pithy observations about the world's statesmen, such as John Foster Dulles. In a long letter of March 1, 1956, Lattimore responded to a *Value Line* story about the dangers of U.S. flirtation with Arab princes; Lattimore agreed, unwilling to believe that "patronized Sheikhs are pliant and reliable instruments of policy." As to Dulles:

> Lack of ordinary professional competence in high places is horribly illustrated by the story of Dulles' press interview in yesterday's Baltimore Sun. It seems that on the subject of Saudi Arabia Dulles airily and offhandedly "attributed to the Arabs a centuries-old hatred of Jews and explained that it derived from a Moslem belief that Mohammed had been assassinated by Jews. But when an aide more conversant with Islamic scripture, which says Mohammed died in a wife's arms and of natural causes, whispered something admonitory to Dulles, the latter tempered his explanation to the extent of asking leave to amend the hearing record if he found he had erred."
>
> Where does a Secretary of State pick up such Protocols of Zion poison? What company is he keeping? And what is indicated by a disposition to use such stuff in serious "enlightenment" of public opinion on matters of state in which the difference between war and peace is involved?[10]

After a trip to Finland, Lattimore wrote Bernhard an extensive commentary on that feisty nation. He admired the Finns tremendously and thought private investment in Finland would be worthwhile. One anecdote from his letter had unusual poignancy: "As for the Finnish attitude toward Russians, it can be illustrated by the wry reaction of a Finn when I asked him what Finns thought of the Russian policy of downgrading Stalin. He thought it was perhaps going a little bit too far. As far as the Finns were concerned, they had found that Stalin was a man with whom it was possible to negotiate, even in very tough circumstances; and when he made an agreement with the Finns, he kept it. 'Also,' he said, 'we cannot forget that Stalin killed far more Communists than we Finns ever did.' " [11]

As in his ONA articles, Lattimore wrote about a wide range of subjects and ventured risky predictions, many of which panned out. In a letter of December 29, 1956, he predicted that the main danger to Chiang Kai-shek was neither an invasion of Taiwan by Communist forces nor a revolt of the indigenous Taiwanese but rather a "colonel's putsch" by underemployed senior officials who wanted to return to their mainland homes and were impressed by the good jobs given by Mao to former anti-Communist warlords. This revolt did not happen. In the same letter, however, he foresaw Japan edging out the United States in international commerce. [12]

On June 25, 1957, Lattimore wrote Bernhard that competition in giving development aid was good because "countries that keep us on our toes by making us compete against German, Japanese, French, Italian, British investors are likely to be more stable than countries in which the US economic interest is lopsidedly dominant. . . . and competition is the essential hormone of both economic and political freedom." [13]

Throughout the 1956–59 period Lattimore provided Bernhard with provocative running commentary on the state of the world. He had plenty of time for it. The lecture circuit remained largely closed to him, though some brave organizations such as the Community Church of Boston, the Baltimore chapter of Americans for Democratic Action, and Temple Emanuel in Newton, Massachusetts, invited him.

Most summers during the rest of his tenure at Johns Hopkins he and Eleanor went to Europe, continuing to enjoy the prestige and welcome they had in 1955. In 1956 Lattimore received another invitation from India to teach the next year at the University of New Delhi. This offer was even more attractive than lecturing in Europe, since Indian scholars were in contact with the Mongolian People's Republic and had acquired what was described to Lattimore as "a very fine collection of source materials" not available in the West. Furthermore, Mongolian diplomats in New Delhi were eager for contact with Western scholars. Lattimore evaluated this opportunity in a letter to the Barretts.

> Eleanor and I could learn in New Delhi more about what is actually going on in Central Asia (and in China too) than by any other means short of actually going to those countries. These opportunities, however, might have certain liabilities attached to them. Our own intelligence services must obviously keep tabs on any contacts that Americans in India have with those dreadful Mongols and Chinese, and so on our return to America we might once more find ourselves listed, not as people who have been able to learn something about Central Asia and China but as people who have actually talked politely with Communists without spitting in their faces. So the gamble involved is: In a couple of years will the general situation between America and the Communist countries be more hostile than ever, or will there be any degree of relaxation? [14]

Lattimore decided that he would take his chances with possible "contamination" in India and applied to Johns Hopkins for a leave of absence.

The Lattimores were invited to the annual Arnold, Fortas, and Porter office party in December 1956. This was a gala occasion, since Thurman Arnold's arguments in the Lattimore case, accepted by Youngdahl and narrowly affirmed by the District of Columbia Court of Appeals, had now been unanimously affirmed in the O'Connor case. Lattimore reported to the Barretts, "Thurman Arnold was feeling very good—levitating several inches above the ground, in fact—and proclaiming that in a long career I was the only innocent man he had ever defended, and never would he defend an innocent man again. With a guilty man, you know just what you are defending, and how to go about it, and besides, you earn a good living. Whereas with an innocent man you never quite know what you are defending, it's a hell of a lot of work, and besides it costs you money." [15]

Euphoria at AFP was not duplicated at Johns Hopkins. Milton Eisenhower, now president of Hopkins, turned down Lattimore's leave request in an insulting letter: "Your career at Johns Hopkins is dependent on your demonstrating your desire and intention to devote yourself henceforth to scholarly work in this university in harmony with Hopkins' tradition. . . . Your primary concern for the advancement of scholarship at Johns Hopkins is yet to be persuasively demonstrated, and the work in India would, as I understand it, be primarily in the field of administration, organization, and policy, rather than in personal research, scholarship, and teaching."[16]

Lattimore was outraged. He had several long, frustrating conferences with Eisenhower, who retracted some of his more fatuous statements but did not yield on the leave of absence. The whole episode was traumatic; Lattimore was depressed for months. Eleanor summed up their reaction in a letter to the Barretts March 17, 1957: "Of course we are tempted to say 'to hell with you' and go off mad, but that wouldn't have hurt anybody but ourselves, since we don't really have a better place to go—yet. When we find a better one, or even one that can be made to appear better, we're all set to hop off to it, and no little pension will hold us."[17]

Milton Eisenhower had an effective veto over Lattimore getting a full year's leave, but European academic schedules were different from American schedules and enabled Lattimore to lecture at the Sorbonne during the spring terms of 1958 and 1959 without permission from Johns Hopkins. He had enough time while at the Sorbonne to finish preparing his collected papers, *Studies in Frontier History*, published by Oxford University Press in 1962.

Despite Lattimore's belief that the Maoists were giving China a new sense of dignity and improving the lot of the peasants, he knew that revolutions devour their children and that the course of the People's Republic would not be one of uninterrupted progress and enlightenment. He voiced his reservations in *Pacific Affairs* of December 1958. "China's old Confucianism was, whenever it had the power to be, dogmatic and authoritarian; for the true Confucian, if the book said one thing and the facts another, it was always the book that was right. Confucian rule has been shattered by Marxist rule, but if, at the same time, the dogmatic tendencies in Marxism fuse with the authoritarian heritage of Confucianism, the worst excesses of Byzantium, Moscow, and the Empress Dowager could be exceeded."[18] It was a startlingly prophetic analysis.

One piece of unfinished business concerned Lattimore during the late 1950s. The Institute of Pacific Relations was still under fire. From its founding in 1927 the IPR had enjoyed tax-exempt status as an educational institution. In 1954 McCarran wrote T. Coleman Andrews, Eisenhower's commissioner of internal revenue, asking Andrews to withdraw IPR's tax-exempt status. Andrews was as willing as McCarran was to view IPR as subversive; in 1955 he revoked the tax exemption and in 1956 assessed IPR $568.62 for the previous year, plus penalties and interest. IPR paid this sum and filed a claim for a refund. Internal Revenue did not respond. In July 1957 IPR filed suit. The sum was trivial, but the principle was important. Commissioner Andrews had cited the SISS report as basis for revoking IPR's exemption.[19]

Charles L. Kades of New York represented the IPR, and Arnold, Fortas, and Porter cooperated in preparing for trial. William Holland was to be the chief IPR witness; because of Lattimore's notoriety, he was not to be called unless needed for rebuttal. Bill Rogers wrote Lattimore October 22, 1959, telling him of Kades's strategy and saying that AFP was "standing by and raring to go."[20]

The case came to trial in Federal District Court for the Southern District of New York, Judge David Edelstein presiding, on March 31, 1960. Although the tax year at issue was 1955, the government's case was based exclusively on the findings of McCarran's SISS in 1952. Kades easily showed that the SISS hearings were biased and malicious and the report untruthful. Edelstein was scathing in his denunciation of the government's case:

> There is not in this case the shadow of a scintilla of evidence to meet the plaintiff's case. . . . Moreover, it is in this case that the plaintiff has for the first time had its "day in court" on those charges. . . . The plaintiff utilized its "day in court" to make its record in the way in which it thought it ought to be made, as any plaintiff in any lawsuit is allowed to do. The legislative report [SISS Report] was based upon hearings in which the plaintiff was not free to present its own case in its own way. In choosing to rely exclusively on the latter, the Government has not only not truly joined issue, but it appears to invite the court's adverse decision.
>
> The plaintiff is entitled to judgment against the defendant.[21]

Lattimore's testimony was not needed. Judge Edelstein's decision reads as if the SISS hearings were so poisonous that the IPR need not have presented any witnesses at all.

For all of Edelstein's eloquence, winning the tax case did not rehabilitate the IPR. The American IPR folded, and the International Council of the IPR moved to Vancouver in December 1960. Having a judicial finding that McCarran had loaded the dice against the IPR was no more than a moral victory. James O. Eastland was now chairman of Senate Judiciary, Jay Sourwine was one of his lieutenants, and the Committee of One Million against the Admission of Communist China to the United Nations was in full operation. Not until the miraculous conversion of Richard Nixon in 1972 did the China lobby lose its power.

Eastland and the FBI maintained their interest in Lattimore all through the 1960s and 1970s. The CIA joined them. Perhaps CIA interest was sparked, or maintained, by James Jesus Angleton, the controversial head of CIA counterintelligence. Angleton for years denied that the apparent split between the Soviet Union and China was anything more than an act of deception. Lattimore's doctrines would have caused a high degree of suspicion on Angleton's part. In any case, had it not been for the CIA's intercept program, we would know less about Lattimore's relations with foreign scholars and his trips abroad. In 1986, nine years after Lattimore's Freedom of Information request, the CIA finally released some of his letters abroad.

Periodically, the credulous Sourwine would refer some wild rumor about Lattimore to the FBI; predictably, the FBI would shoot it down. Every public lecture that Lattimore gave and every story about him anywhere in the country wound up in FBI and CIA files and in the private collection of J. B. Matthews.

By 1959, in the last years of the Eisenhower presidency, Lattimore assumed that the new willingness of the U.S. government to talk to the Russians offered a chance for him to again visit the Soviet Union. He was in contact with Soviet Asian scholars whom he met at various academic congresses in Western Europe. He wrote one of them, Professor S. L. Tikhvinskii of Moscow, in September 1959. He understood that there was to be a gathering of orientalists in Leningrad the next summer. Could he get an invitation? He would be happy to give a paper on Marco Polo.[22]

Hostilities were easing on the Soviet side also. The "learned lackey of imperialism" was no longer persona non grata. Lattimore was invited to the Leningrad Congress and got his visa at the Soviet embassy in Washington April 11, 1960. It was something he had long wanted; Russian scholarship on Mongolia was still worth absorbing. Lattimore and his wife left for a long tour of Europe June 3, with three weeks in Russia.

The opportunity to talk to his Russian counterparts was all he expected of it. But a related opportunity was even more valuable: he made friends among scholars from the Mongolian People's Republic participating at Leningrad. They knew who he was. They had read his books and felt that his descriptions of life in Inner Mongolia in the 1930s rang true. One of them told him, "Your Mongols are *real* Mongols."[23] He met Natsagdorj, a member of the Mongolian Academy of Sciences, one of whose books Lattimore had translated into English; Bira, a prominent Tibetanist; and a young historian named Dalai. The Mongols invited him to visit.

If there was a scholarly summum bonum for Lattimore, it was the opportunity to study and travel in the MPR. He knew a lot about it from reading everything available in non-Mongol languages, from the few Mongol publications available in the West, and from endless conversation with the Dilowa, John Hangin, Urgunge Onon, and other Mongol expatriates. But the kind of on-the-spot experience he had had of Inner Mongolia was lacking. The three days he had spent in Ulan Bator with Wallace in 1944 had merely piqued his curiosity. Since that trip was "official" and Wallace was in the charge of Russians, Lattimore was not free to explore on his own. Now, at last, he would have a chance to see for himself.

Lattimore got back to Baltimore in September 1960 to find the presidential election under way. Nixon versus Kennedy: obviously he could not support Nixon, who had done so much to fan anti-Peking hysteria and who still maintaned an allegiance to the Nationalists on Formosa. Kennedy seemed more reasonable about Asian policy, believing that the Nationalists should evacuate Quemoy and Matsu islands. But it was a mere fifteen years since Kennedy, campaigning in Massachusetts, had charged Lattimore and John King Fairbank with losing China to the Communists. And Kennedy's belligerent rhetoric about the nonexistent "missile gap" was disturbing. Lattimore did not have high hopes for a Kennedy presidency.

In March 1961, however, when Lattimore asked the State Department if his passport could be validated for travel to Mongolia, they readily agreed.[24] And there were rumors afloat that the United States was considering exchanging diplomatic missions with the MPR. Lattimore could hardly believe this news. It was precisely the suggestion for which he had been castigated by William Bullitt and the China lobby. But on April 21 the *New York Times* carried a page-one story with the apparent blessing of the government: "Ties with Mongolia Are Planned by U.S." The reasons given for the action were nonsensical: "to determine whether Outer Mongolia is in fact an independent state." But Lattimore was impressed. The Kennedy administration might be more progressive than he had anticipated.

The Lattimores left for Europe in early June 1961, visiting Czechoslovakia for two weeks then taking the train through Russia to Mongolia. He knew the trip was a gamble. However friendly the Mongol intellectuals he had met in Leningrad, he was well aware that the political bosses back home might not be enchanted with a visitor fluent in the language prying into all kinds of affairs. As he puts it in *Nomads and Commissars*, "The auspices were good, but in Communist-ruled countries the opportunities allowed to foreign scholars can be cut off abruptly."[25]

The Lattimores arrived in Ulan Bator July 9 in the middle of celebrations marking the fortieth anniversary of Mongolia's Declaration of Independence (from China). As he wrote his father, there were "parades, vast drills of athletic organizations, and the traditional Mongol horse-racing, archery, and wrestling. These traditional sports, as we used to see them in Inner Mongolia, had become rather broken-down. Here, they are now restored with all the details of costume and heraldry. The people are passionately interested. After one horse race, the herald presenting the third horse and chanting its praises in alliterative verse got more applause than the herald presenting the winning horse, because his poetry was better!"[26]

The major celebration was on July 11. A colorful crowd of fifty thousand paraded for two hours before a reviewing stand, with MPR President Sambuu, Soviet Party Secretary Suslov, and Polish leader Gomulka taking the salutes. It seemed as if the whole of Mongolia's 950,000 people had turned out for the festivities. Lattimore wrote his father:

> The old costumes abound, and the tiers of seats at the great stadium are a mosaic of colors. Mongol girls and women dress better, and in better taste, with a faultless eye for color and line, than the women of any other country of the Soviet bloc that we have seen. Checking with a French and an Italian and a British correspondent, I find them a little in despair because, they say, if they report simply their straightforward observations, everyone will say they have been "taken in by communist propaganda." As a matter of fact, it is impossible to work up an honest opinion that Mongolia is being run by anybody but the Mongols—and they are enjoying themselves hugely doing it.[27]

After the ceremonies Lattimore was introduced to the treasures of the National Library and conferred with scholars "full of the zest and exhilaration of discovery. Dialects, folklore, shaman chants—all are being tape recorded."[28] The head of the one big surviving Lama Buddhist monastery turned out to be a former disciple of the Dilowa and gave Lattimore extraordinary attention. Lattimore was inundated with historical materials. He found no oppressive Marxist doctrine dampening scholarly conversations in Mongolia, as it so often did with the Soviets.

From July 24 to August 4 the Lattimores were taken on a tour of the country, visiting five collective farms. As he wrote in a letter to Justice William O. Douglas, they were in "the original heartland of the history of the Huns, the Turks, and later the Mongols themselves. . . . Marvellous country, marvellous people. We also saw a lot of the new, collectivized pastoral economy. I was impressed by the intelligent way it builds on old traditions of cooperation (I put my yaks with your yaks, you put your sheep with my sheep, we'll both put our horses with that other fellow's horses) and so is more readily understood and accepted. The present degree of prosperity is too general, and we have travelled too widely, for there to be any question of specially-dressed-up show-places for foreigners."[29]

It was in this heartland of the Huns and Mongols that Lattimore was introduced to the "richest paleological find" that the great Russian archaeologist, Okladnikov, had ever seen. Artifacts half a million years old were found at the site, and Okladnikov told Lattimore how he had known to dig there. The Orkhon River made a bend, leaving a terrace suitable for a fishing camp. Near this terrace a small stream entered the Orkhon, and fluttering white rags were tied to bushes on the shores of the stream. "Right there under those bushes," Okladnikov said, "there is a mineral spring. Until quite recently, the local Mongols regarded it as magical and used its water to cure sickness. Probably it has been revered continually since the time of paleolithic man, because we know from other sites that men in the Old Stone Age were as aware as we are of the difference between mineral springs and ordinary springs. So when we found a mineral spring and a natural fishing camp within 50 yards of each other, we knew we had only to dig."[30] The chance to tour archaeological sites with Okladnikov was worth as much to Lattimore as anything on the trip.

Lattimore's forty-two days in Mongolia sped by mercilessly. Toward the end, he was asked to address the Academy of Sciences. It was a fitting climax. He was complimentary to his hosts, telling them to be proud of their nomad past as well as their startling leap into modernity. Justice Douglas, for whom Lattimore arranged a visit to Mongolia in September 1961, says, "A member of the Academy of Sciences in that country told me that Lattimore addressed them for an hour in Ulan Bator, speaking Mongolian. He paid Lattimore the highest compliment possible: 'If I had closed my eyes and listened, I would have sworn the speaker was Mongolian.' "[31]

On August 19 the Lattimores flew to Irkutsk, Moscow, and Copenhagen, where Owen was to give a series of lectures. The Monglian customs officials did not even open their baggage.[32]

The American initiative to open diplomatic relations with the MPR stirred up the China lobby while Lattimore was gone. Marvin Liebman, secretary of the Committee of One Million, raised hell. Recognition of Mongolia, he told the *New York Times* and a dozen or so prominent members of the China bloc in Congress, was just the opening wedge in an attempt to push through recognition of the People's Republic of China. On June 29, 1961, the State Department announced that negotiations with Mongolia were progressing; Chester Bowles, undersecretary of State, and Roger Hilsman, director of State's Bureau of Intelligence and Research, were pushing this initiative.[33]

The effort was premature. Had there been no other obstacles, word of Lattimore's presence in Ulan Bator that summer would have killed it. The *Washington Post* story of July 12 called the attention of official Washington to the fact that Lattimore and his wife were attending the Mongolian fortieth anniversary celebrations, and that news set off a new round of China lobby outrage. On July 13 the National Republican Congressional Committee "accused the Kennedy Administration of 30 actions that the committee said were withdrawals from the policies of the Eisenhower Administration in dealings with the Communists." Among them was the fact that the State Department had "granted a visa to Owen Lattimore for a 'study trip' to Outer Mongolia, although Lattimore has been named by a Senate subcommittee as a 'conscious, articulate instrument of the Communist party.' " Senator Everett Dirksen and Representative Charles Halleck, Republican leaders, denounced the reported proposal to recognize Mongolia.[34]

Unique among the ultraconservative fulminations was the July 16 ABC radio broadcast of George Sokolsky, the text of which was printed in the *Brooklyn Tablet*. Sokolsky was alarmed at Lattimore's trip: "How he got there, I don't know. What kind of passport he's using, I don't know. We have no regulations with Mongolia; our passport doesn't hold there, but he's gone there." Sokolsky reviewed the "great power of Ghengis [*sic*] Khan, which in the 13th Century conquered China and conquered much of Europe, east of Germany. It held Russia for a prolonged period. It held India and the Mongol Empire in India. It is Mongolia which is being revived as a power in this attempt to force upon the world the United Nations. This is a peril which is really greater than one imagines because, to us, the name Mongolia hardly means anything anymore and yet, out of that desert land has come this great power which at one time dominated much of the world and which can do it again if armed and given the direction and guidance that could lead to that. This, then, is our peril at the time."[35]

It is hard to excuse such crass ignorance. Sokolsky should have known that Mongolia was a sparsely populated country of fewer than one million and that it was totally surrounded by Russia and China, who would hardly give the Mongols the arms, direction, and guidance to conquer the Eurasian continent. Sokolsky did not name his candidate for a modern Genghis Khan.

David Nelson Rowe, at Yale, was also alarmed at Lattimore's travels. On August 9, 1961, he cabled Senator Eastland: "STRONGLY RECOMMEND INVESTIGATION OF PART PLAYED BY OWEN LATTIMORE IN OUTER MONGOLIA RECENTLY AND POSSIBLE COOPERATION WITH LATTIMORE BY DEPT OF STATE INABLING HIS PRESENCE THERE AND CURRENT SUGGESTION UNITED STATES ENTER INTO DIPLOMATIC RELATIONS WITH SOVIET PUPPET OF OUTER MONGOLIA." Eastland politely declined, telling Rowe that unless "information could be obtained that would furnish a sound basis for such a hearing" it would be a mere fishing expedition.[36]

The entire right-wing press jumped on the issue. Pressure was too great for Bowles to continue. On August 11 President Kennedy ordered plans for the exchange of diplomats with the MPR dropped.[37]

Senator Thomas Dodd of Connecticut didn't believe it was all over. On August 22 he told the Senate that it was no accident that Lattimore was in Mongolia "at the very moment when there was a big drive on" to recognize that country. Dodd threatened to call Lattimore before SISS "to establish all of the facts about his visit."[38] The threat was never carried out.

Justice William O. Douglas came back from two weeks in Mongolia in late September, calling for recognition of the MPR since it was independent of both China and Russia.[39] He was too late: the issue was dead.

The United Nations presented a different situation. A package deal, in which admission of Mongolia and Mauritania (wanted by the French African bloc) were linked, passed the Security Council October 25, 1961. The Mongolian People's Republic became a member of the community of nations.

Lattimore returned to Johns Hopkins October 1 with a treasure trove of historical materials, notes from manuscripts, records of interviews, and photographs. He now had the raw materials to flesh out an account of Outer Monglia to match his 1934 *Mongols of Manchuria*. He set about producing a contemporary description of the MPR with enough background to explain how things came to be the way he found them in the summer of 1961.

Nomads and Commissars, published by Oxford University Press in June 1962, was the result. It is still a valuable exposition of the development of Outer Mongolia in the modern period, beginning with the Mongol revolution against Manchu rule in 1911. This revolution established an autonomous state lasting about ten years. During this period czarist Russia began to take an interest in Mongolia. It was a barren time; Mongol leadership was weak, and the dominance of the Buddhist monasteries was suffocating. Lattimore refers to this period as the "years of frustration."

Modern Mongolia began to take shape with the Partisan Rebellion of Sukebator in 1921; this was the revolution celebrated by the MPR when Lattimore first came in the summer of 1961. There was much controversy about the extent to which Marxist practices were imposed on the Mongols by the Bolsheviks and about responsibility for the confiscation of private property and the purges of 1929–32, known as the Left Deviation. Though sympathetic to the Mongols, Lattimore concludes that left-wing Mongols rather than Soviet agents were responsible for the terror. It was, in fact, under Comintern guidance that the policy of forced collectivization was reversed.[40] Western assumptions about Soviet tyranny in Mongolia, Lattimore asserts, are mistaken. The Soviet Union could easily have annexed Mongolia but did not, and Soviet protection of Mongolia from Japanese encroachment in the 1930s saved the Mongols from the brutalization Japan inflicted on Manchuria.

It was of great significance to Lattimore that Mongolia had no capitalist past yet moved rapidly from feudalism to the modernity of 1961 with Soviet aid. He saw it as a model for other developing countries. The progress of Mongolia as he observed it did not decrease the enthusiasm for free enterprise capitalism in developing countries, which he had touted in *Solution* and *Situation*; he recognized that Mongolia was a special case. Other developing countries had at least a modest bourgeois capitalist class on which to build.

Nomads and Commissars remained Lattimore's primary volume on the subject of Outer Mongolia. In 1987, when he wrote "Mongolia as a Leading State" for the *Journal of the Mongolia Society*, he conformed closely to the conclusions he had reached in 1962.

After the stimulus of the trip to Ulan Bator in 1961, life at Johns Hopkins seemed tame. The Lattimores again went to Europe in 1962, visiting England, France, and Switzerland during June. They were barely settled back in Baltimore when a wholly unexpected invitation came.

Leeds University decided in 1962 to establish a department of Chinese studies, concentrating on contemporary China with language, literature, history, geography, economics, and sociology all represented. There would be classes for undergraduates, but also a strong research and graduate program. No such department existed in Great Britain; there were few anywhere. In August 1962 Leeds got in touch with Lattimore. Would he be interested in heading this department? He was, and in September the Lattimores again went to England to explore Leeds's plans. The Leeds vice-chancellor and his search committee decided Lattimore was the right man.

For Lattimore, the decision was easy to make. He was sixty-two, eligible for retirement at Johns Hopkins. His opportunities in the United States were still restricted by the fallout from the McCarthy-McCarran period. United States universities were rigidly compartmentalized, and Lattimore tended to disregard jurisdictional boundaries. U.S. foreign policies, still cretinous in regard to China, apoplectic about Cuba, and already beginning the long perverse involvement in Vietnam, caused him great anguish; yet he had no effective forum in which to oppose them. His close friend, Vilhjalmur Stefansson, had died of a stroke August 26, 1962.[41] Most of all, the Hopkins situation was stultifying: no graduate students, no research seminar on a topic dear to him, and a campus still bitterly divided over his presence. The announcement of his appointment to Leeds was made November 12.[42] He flew to Leeds again in January 1963 to make housing and other arrangements.

The opportunity to build a department from the ground up was itself attractive, but there was a bonus. As Lattimore bragged to Academician B. I. Pankratov at Leningrad, he would be able to add Mongol studies and to take Urgunge Onon with him.[43] Britain was far more open to unconventional views. The British had no McCarran-Walter Act. He could bring visiting scholars from the MPR to Leeds.

The main handicap Lattimore faced in developing Chinese and Mongol studies at Leeds was the absence of a good library collection. This problem was taken up by Mortimer Graves, a long-time Lattimore supporter recently retired from the post of administrative secretary of the American Council of Learned Societies. Graves wrote several hundred Asian scholars and bibliophiles, explaining the need for books at Leeds and asking them to cull their libraries for relevant items they no longer needed. Graves then arranged with the International Exchange Service of the Smithsonian Institution to assemble and ship the books to Leeds.[44]

Cutting a twenty-five-year tie with Johns Hopkins was easy. At a farewell party given by the history department, Lattimore said that the department had been good to him, but the university had not.[45] Chester Wickwire, Hopkins chaplain, says that Lattimore told him "getting out of here is like getting out of prison." His farewell lecture was packed. As David Harvey put it, "Everyone expected him to talk about Mc-

Carthyism. He talked about society and culture in Mongolia. I suspect that is where his heart was all along."[46]

As Lattimore was packing to leave Hopkins, a group of history junior faculty and graduate students stopped by his office to wish him well. Waldo Heinrichs, later a prominent diplomatic historian at Temple University, was among them. They noticed a half-dozen boxes in a corner with what appeared to be correspondence tossed inside. Heinrichs asked Lattimore what he intended to do with the boxes. He replied, "Throw them out." The visitors protested; could they take the boxes over to the library? Lattimore did not mind.[47] Sixteen years later this discarded correspondence was in the Hamburger Archives at Johns Hopkins, providing one of the few contemporary records of Lattimore's activities as director of the Walter Hines Page School and of his scholarly enterprises during the years 1946 to 1952.

CHAPTER TWENTY-NINE

Ascendancy at Leeds

The Lattimores arrived in Leeds early June 1963, with the first challenge house hunting. Owen had done a lot of this in January but hadn't settled on anything. Now Eleanor took over, with an assist from Dorothy Borg, who spent a week with them. By mid-June they had settled on a place in Linton, near Wetherby, some distance from Leeds but with room for Owen's books, his father, and guests. The house was officially called "Old Rose Cottage." Eleanor thought this name "icky" and wanted to change it; Owen thought it corny enough to be funny and insisted they keep it.[1]

Starting a new department involved Owen in unending conferences and paperwork. Bureaucratic chores were not his favorite occupations, but the excitement of building a program to his own specifications compensated for the drudgery. In addition, there was none of the opprobrium his heretical views had brought him in the United States. He was welcomed into the social and intellectual life of Yorkshire, with much broader contacts than either Johns Hopkins or the reactionary Baltimore suburbs had provided. On June 25 Eleanor wrote Evelyn Stefansson that "Owen hasn't been so happy in years."[2]

Only one bit of bad news distracted from the euphoria of those first days at Leeds: the Dilowa had fallen ill with cancer. When the Page School folded, the Dilowa made his primary residence with the exile Mongol community in New Jersey, but he traveled frequently to universities where his linguistic skills were in demand. One of the places he visited often was New Haven; Lattimore's son David was a graduate student at Yale. Wesley Needham, curator of the Tibetan collection at Yale, hosted the Dilowa frequently for work on Yale's extensive collection of Buddhist texts. It was during an August 1963 visit to New Haven that the Dilowa fell ill and was hospitalized.

The Dilowa did not want news of his illness to reach Lattimore, but the *New York Times* published the story of his hospitalization, and David sent a copy to his father.[3] At Grace New Haven Community Hospital, high-voltage radiation treatment seemed to stabilize the Dilowa's condition, and David wrote that he seemed to be in no immediate danger. The Dilowa was eighty; Lattimore knew complete recovery was impossible.

At Leeds the British tradition of public inaugural lectures for prestige appointments was strong. Lattimore's was scheduled for October 21, 1963. Lattimore was determined to distill for a general audience the most important influences in making China what she then was. Titled "From China, Looking Outward," the lecture presents the core of what he intended to develop as his magnum opus, a rendition of the theme "China in World History" showing both the impact of "barbarian" invasion on China and China's impact on Western cultures.

The lecture hall at Leeds that night was packed, and the address was carried on BBC television. Reaction in Britain was uniformly laudatory. Strangely, those in America who might have been expected to monitor Lattimore's latest heresies seemed to miss it. Several of his judgments could have been distorted to imply that he welcomed the triumph of communism in China, but none of his detractors commented on the lecture. The core of his analysis endures as a sound rendition of China's route to communism:

Only from China, looking outward, can it be clearly seen that a Communist revolution would have been impossible without the century of Western and Japanese domination that began in 1840–2 when in the name of law, order and security for business (opium was not mentioned in the Treaty of Nanking) the Treaty Port system was created, and subsequently elaborated into a system of indirect controls and sanctions. It was this system of herding, coercing, coaxing, and at the same time frustrating the Chinese, so different from direct colonial rule, that fostered the growth in China of new economic interests, new social classes, new antagonisms, new alliances, and, because of a sovereignty that was impaired but not, as under colonial rule, destroyed, an increasingly impatient search by the Chinese for methods, however radical, by which to fuse all the discordant forces at work into a mighty national effort to break out of the net. . . .

It was not an upheaval from within, but Japanese invasion, that ruptured the net. Upheavals which had been premature, like the Taiping

Rebellion, or too primitive to know what direction to take, like the Boxer Rising, could now be followed by a much more intricate process of detonation and fusion, at great speed: open class conflict, accompanied by new class alliances, with the explosion confined, and its energy concentrated, by the pressure of a foreign invasion. When the enclosing Japanese pressure collapsed, the energy released within China went into a second stage of expansion in which . . . Chiang Kai-shek's regime was consumed. It was destroyed not only because it was corrupt, but because so much of its corruption was rooted in its function of being the end-product, the last and most hated phenomenon, of relying on foreign support in order to keep the upper hand in China.[4]

Two weeks after his inaugural lecture Lattimore was contacted by the British foreign office. The adventure to which this call led brought glee to his voice when he described it twenty years later:

Very soon after I got to England, the Mongols and the British recognized each other, and the Mongols appointed their first Ambassador to Britain. One morning, I'd just got to the office at the University, and the phone rang. The voice said, "My name is—whatever [Dugald Malcolm]—at the foreign office. In a few days, the new Mongolian ambassador will present his letters to the queen. Would you consent to be the interpreter?" I said, "Well, that would be a great honor, but I'm not qualified. In the first instance, I'm not even a British subject." And the voice said, "Oh yes, we know all that, but you're the man we want." So I did that function. The man who was in attendance on the queen during the ceremony [Sir Harold Caccia], the queen, and I and the Mongol Ambassador were the only people in the room. The queen's attendant was a man I had met first in Peking when he was secretary at the embassy. . . . That whole ceremony shows how skillfully the British handle that kind of thing. The Mongol had, of course, his own English-speaking aide with him. But the British thought that for British prestige, they must have the interpreter on the British side, not on the visitor's side. To prepare for it—again very British—they sent the ambassador up to Leeds, to see me. They put him in that famous resort hotel, and sent me over there to dine with him so we could get acquainted. We had a good talk. He was a crafty ambassador, too. He said, "I suppose there will be some small talk, and they will ask me how I like England. What should I talk about?" I said, "There's one sure thing. All the royal family are crazy about horses. So say something about horses." When we got there, the queen sure enough asked him if he'd had a good time so far in England. He said "Yes, I went to Yorkshire, and since we Mongols are crazy about horses, we know there are two great breeds in the world, the Arab horse, and the English thoroughbred. So while I was in Yorkshire I went to several stables and saw your English thoroughbreds." "Oh," said the queen very interested. "And you have horseracing in Mongolia?" "Yes, at the big festival every summer we have the great national horse race. Only our horseracing is a little bit different from yours. You see, for us the race is a test of the horse, and not of the jockey. So we don't put a strong rider on the horse. We put a young rider on it. The race is about twenty-five kilometers and it has to be a horse that is willing to run that on his own, without being driven by his jockey. Our jockeys are retired for age when they are twelve years old." And that's the first and only time I have seen British royalty do a double-take.

The ceremony at Buckingham Palace took place November 14. Ten days later Lattimore got another call from London. This time it was the BBC: John F. Kennedy had been assassinated in Dallas. Would Lattimore explain to British listeners what this terible act of violence meant?

Lattimore hesitated to accept this invitation also. He had had his own exposure to the dark places of the American mind, but he did not feel prepared to deal with a presidential assassination and declined. Later BBC invitations called for commentary that would draw more directly on his own background, and he became less reticent about appearing. By the time he retired from Leeds in 1970, he was a frequent BBC commentator.

Lattimore heard in early November 1963 that a memorial service was to be held in London for Chi Ch'ao-ting, the Chinese economist whose articles he had published in *Pacific Affairs*. Chi had died in Peking August 9. Joseph Needham, fellow of the Royal Society and president of Gonville and Caius College, Cambridge, organized the service and asked Lattimore to speak about Chi's career. Joan Robinson, Cambridge economist, and John Keswick, prominent British businessman, were also to speak. Lattimore accepted but was unable to attend because his father fell ill. He sent remarks to Needham to read for him.

The service was held December 5. In his eulogy Lattimore did not have to explain why he had not known Chi was a Communist; he was free to describe the man he had known in Chungking in 1941. Chi was then confidential private secretary to H. H. K'ung, Chiang's minister of finance. As Lattimore and the sponsors of the memorial service had known him, Chi was a statesman and scholar no matter whether he was serving the Kuomintang or the Communists. Lattimore's was a moving tribute, one of those beautifully crafted encomia that deserve a place in the enduring literature of human achievement. Lattimore could never have given it in the United States. To speak of a Communist leader who was "hu-

mane to the marrow of his bones" would have again brought down the
wrath of the Peking haters.[5]

During his last years at Johns Hopkins and his first year at Leeds Lattimore kept up his correspondence with Arnold Bernhard of *Value Line.*
The letters these two exchanged offer a fascinating commentary on world
events during the last half of the Eisenhower administration and the two
years of Kennedy. On December 15, 1963, when Lattimore had six months'
experience living in England, he described his reactions for Bernhard. Lattimore found himself "a little to my surprise, more intrigued by economic
than by political questions."

> As soon as I got here I started reading all I could find that is readily
> available to the ordinary investor, and I was—and still am—aghast. In
> Britain, the classical country of the industrial revolution and of the
> forms of saving and investment that accompanied and followed the in-
> dustrial revolution, it is exceedingly difficult, if you are native born and
> not a foreigner bringing with you your own sources of information, to
> get hold of basic data and plan your investments. Not only is there no
> hard-headed advisory service remotely comparable to the Value Line;
> there is no equivalent of the Wall Street Journal or—very significant—
> of Merrill Lynch. On the native heath of modern capitalism, there just
> isn't any "people's capitalism." In America, I thought that a rather
> corny slogan. Here—because of its absence—I see what it means.[6]

Two days before Christmas 1963, Lattimore's father was operated on
for colon cancer in the Leeds hospital. The operation only postponed the
inevitable. David Lattimore died March 3, 1964, at the age of ninety.

Periodically, reporters from American papers would appear in Leeds to
survey the new career of the onetime flagship heretic. Clyde Farnsworth
of the *New York Times* was one of the earliest, visiting in February 1964.
He found Lattimore ecstatic about the program's success in teaching spoken Chinese: "By the end of the first term, we had students taking simple
dictation in Chinese characters." Farnsworth mentioned the "brain drain"
of many British scholars leaving for the United States because of higher
pay. Lattimore was a "brain drain" in reverse. Why had he come there?
"Some people are interested in going where the money is, others where
the brains are. That's why I am in Britain. In my field there is more
original thinking here than in the United States."[7]

Lattimore put it more colorfully in a letter to Bernhard: "As soon as
possible, you and Janet *must* come over. Eleanor and I are happier than
we've been in years. So many interesting things going on, so many inter-

esting people. It's as if, in a weird way, Baltimore were the sleepy English village where nothing ever happened, and Leeds the driving, creative American city, with people thinking and doing all the time."[8]

In May an Associated Press story probed Lattimore's reactions to the McCarthy years. " 'I was angry at the time,' Prof. Lattimore said in an interview, 'as anyone would be had they been falsely accused. But it is no use sitting around nursing rancor.' " Lattimore had kind words for Charles de Gaulle, who had just recognized the People's Republic of China. This was a much-needed breakthrough. China was a great power, and her quarrel with the Soviet Union was a danger to the rest of the world; while recognition "will not make the Chinese all sweet and reasonable, at least then we would have some way of dealing with them."[9]

Lattimore was encouraged, in March 1964, to think that even he might have a way of dealing with the Chinese. Edgar Snow had met Chou En-lai in Africa and wrote Lattimore that Chou had expressed interest in the Department of Chinese Studies at Leeds.[10] Lattimore decided to write Chou. Even though his own connection with the Mongols might make him persona non grata in Peking (Mongol-Chinese relations at the time were bitter), he desperately wanted other members of his staff to have access to China. The PRC chargé d'affaires in London was not responsive to inquiries from Leeds. Chou, at the time, was no better.

During August 1964 Lattimore went back to Mongolia. Eleanor was not able to go, so Lattimore's son David accompanied him. He described his trip in a letter to Mortimer Graves: "We did about 2,500 miles in a jeep-like vehicle, then came back to Ulan Bator and I saw a lot of my scholar friends. They did just about everything except make me a member of the University and the Academy, and we came back loaded with loot. In addition, we are getting eight students to come here [Leeds] this month for an intensive six-months' English course. A real scoop, first ever west of the Iron Curtain."[11] David remembers that more than anything else on their trip, his father enjoyed talking with Okladnikov, whom the elder Lattimore regarded as the most impressive scholar-adventurer he ever knew.

The Lattimore house in the fall of 1964 was like a hotel. The rector of the Mongolian National University was just one of hundreds of guests who made the Lattimore residence a visitor's center. Americans, Mongols, British, French, Swedes—every conceivable nationality sent somebody to visit Lattimore. Reading Eleanor Lattimore's letters, one wonders how her husband ever had time for scholarly activity. The long Christmas vacation was a blessing. Lattimore took seven days of it for a trip to Rome and Paris but spent the rest in his study.

In March 1965, at the end of the Leeds winter term, the Lattimores went to the United States, visiting David and family, Joe and Betty Barnes, Evelyn Stefansson and her new husband John Nef, Bill and Suki Rogers, and friends in California. While they were attending the Association for Asian Studies conference in San Francisco in early April, word came from David that the Dilowa, then in a New York hospital, was rapidly losing strength. Lattimore flew immediately to New York: "I found him very weak, but not in pain. I sat by his bed, holding his hand. He could only say a few words at a time, but wanted to be assured that all was well with me and my wife. At last I left, to go up to New Haven to see my son, saying that I would be back the next day: but he died in the night."[12] The date was April 7, 1965; the Dilowa was eighty-one.

Of all the fascinating Mongols Lattimore knew, the Dilowa was the closest to him and the greatest influence on his life. They differed on many things, especially religion. As Lattimore explained it, the Dilowa "told me in a tolerant, friendly way that I had no vocation for religion and it was no use trying to explain Buddhism to me."[13] But Lattimore did not disparage the old man's religion, and when he finally published the Dilowa's autobiography in 1982, his introduction gave a most sympathetic account of his friend's religious beliefs.

Sentiment among Lattimore's friends in the United States about the Vietnam War was rising. Particularly while he was in California, leaders of the antiwar movement urged him to speak out about American policy. He agreed and chose the medium of a long letter published in the *New York Times* April 9, 1965. The CIA recorded a remarkably accurate summary of his arguments.[14] The summary did not, however, display the flavor of his impassioned prose. His last three paragraphs do that well:

> Is the next Pearl Harbor to be an American bombing of China? Is that the meaning of the smooth, cold, authoritative, hypnotically evasive voices of McGeorge Bundy, Dean Rusk, Robert McNamara, and the imperfectly civilianized Gen. Maxwell Taylor?
>
> One difference between Japan then and America now is that we are more free to protest. We must use that freedom. Between here and the Pacific Coast I have heard and read enough to know that many have been ahead of me in raising their voices and many of them are more influential than I.
>
> But unless we all unite in a great outcry of horror, repudiating this

obsessed policy of doom, we shall not waken from the nightmare in time.[15]

Predictably, Lattimore's blast called forth equally fervent defenses of American policy. The *Times* carried one on April 20. Bruno Shaw, a former AP correspondent in China, interpreted our Vietnam adventure quite differently. We were, said Shaw, trying to "help save the free nations of South Asia and the Western Pacific from onslaught and domination by Red China's puppet armies," which, if allowed to conquer Vietnam, would set off World War III and dim the outlook for freedom all over the world. The paradigm had now shifted: Ho Chi Minh was the puppet of China, just as Mao had been the puppet of the Soviet Union. Perhaps the most obscurantist response to Lattimore's letter was that of his old enemy Robert Morris. *His* paradigm had not shifted at all. Red China and Red Russia were still "firm allies in war against us and have always said so." Lattimore, said Morris, was once again trying to guide us to disaster. Lattimore compounded his offense as soon as he got back to England. He joined in the formation of the Society for Anglo-Chinese Understanding, described by UPI as a "breakaway from the Britain-China Friendship Association, which always has been tied to the Moscow-aligned British Communist Party."[16]

Lattimore did not participate in any of the British protests against U.S. policy in Vietnam. In June 1965 he told Norman Moss of the North American Newspaper Alliance, "I think it is more proper to confine my protests to my own country." On the larger world scene he was quite willing to comment, giving Moss an extensive analysis of the Sino-Soviet split. This split "is the kind that great powers have regardless of ideology. But don't count on it lasting forever. In international affairs, neither friends nor enemies are forever." As to relations between China and Vietnam, his sight was 20/20: if the Chinese tried to move into Vietnam, "they'd have insurrection on their hands. And they wouldn't be able to handle it any more than we can."[17]

The summer of 1965 was one of Lattimore's best. In May he gave the Chichele Lectures at Oxford; on June 4 he received, finally, a university degree, Glasgow's D. Litt.; and in July he hosted at Leeds 170 participants in the International Congress of Chinese Studies. To keep up to speed he and Eleanor toured the continent again in August with granddaughter Maria (age eleven), taking in a history congress in Vienna along with Alpine scenery and Parisian dining.[18]

Fall term at Leeds in 1965 brought heavy work and dank weather. The

Lattimores were determined to make up for the frustrations and tragedies of the previous Christmas and arranged to spend Christmas this time in sunny Israel. Letters to their friends were glowing; Eleanor took painting lessons, Owen lectured and consulted with Israeli scholars. The kibbutzim, he felt, were solidly established; Oriental and Occidental Jews, some Marxist and some not, got along because rugged pioneer conditions dampened "theoretical differences of ideology." But the economy of Israel was overwhelmingly capitalist, and if the socialized kibbutzim were "to start growing rapidly, the capitalist interest, backed by America, would very rapidly call them to order."[19]

In March 1966 Lattimore was back in the United States for an Asian studies meeting in New York, several lectures, and parties in Washington given by John and Evelyn Nef. Two of Lattimore's lectures can be documented: at Harvard March 26 and at Brown on the twenty-eighth. He was on American soil, free again to criticize American policy—Asian policy. Our policy in Europe had been a great success, but in Asia an increasingly disastrous failure. We had not learned to cut our losses and get out of a hopeless mess. He likened the situation to an American investor telling his broker one week that a stock the broker recommended at $100 was too high, then asking the broker to buy the stock a week later at $125.[20]

The FBI followed Lattimore's lecture tour fitfully. They knew he lectured at Brown but were apparently unaware of the Harvard speech.

Lattimore had not written Arnold Bernhard for almost a year, blaming the hiatus on his obsession with the "Vietnam tragedy." He called on Bernhard when he was in New York April 5, 1966, and Bernhard encouraged him to write a signed article on the war for *Value Line*. This article appeared in the June edition, saying all the negative things about America's counterproductive approach to stopping communism that Lattimore had been telling audiences for several years. *Value Line* got some static because of the Lattimore article; William F. Buckley, Jr., and other columnists who still had an investment in the inquisition attacked the piece strongly. Bernhard did not regret carrying it. On June 23 he sent Lattimore a check for $1,000 and said that while *Value Line* had received a few cancelations because of the Lattimore article, he was glad and proud to have been able to print it.[21]

While Lattimore was in Washington during April 1966, he used a private channel to further his objective of ending the Vietnam War. He believed that the power of the president to obtain public support for a change of policy was great enough that "it ought to be possible to adopt either a 'hard' or a 'soft' policy, or to switch from one to the other, and have the decision or the switch hailed as a stroke of genius." Thus President Johnson could successfully reverse course in Vietnam. Lattimore discussed this matter with Walter Lippmann and James Reston; both agreed. Reston, to support the idea, noted "that at the time of the Cuban Missile crisis Kennedy had the option of acting in several ways other than the way he finally adopted, and could have counted on a strong public support whichever way he acted."[22]

Thus encouraged, Lattimore sought the best channel to LBJ. No public proposal stood a chance of adoption by the president; Johnson was gunshy of having an idea "sold" to him or "planted" on him by someone else. The best channel was Lattimore's old friend and now Supreme Court Justice Abe Fortas, a presidential confidant. Lattimore went to Fortas with his idea. "My suggestion was that LBJ should make a startling, unexpected switch in policy. He should get away from the sterile insistence that all the trouble in South Vietnam was invented by Hanoi, and the Vietcong are mere puppets and instruments of Hanoi. In dropping this line he would get away from the endless blind alley argument about whether Hanoi should be allowed to bring some Vietcong representatives along with them to a negotiation. Instead, he should say boldly, we intend to negotiate with the people against whom we are fighting, the Vietcong. If the Vietcong want to bring along with them some delegates from Hanoi, that is up to them. This move, I believe, would act as a catalyst on the whole situation."[23]

The meeting with Fortas was quite different from any of his other discussions of Vietnam. "With Abe, there was obviously no question of a 'conversation.' He . . . would never even talk to an old friend in a way that might indicate how far he is privy to LBJ's thinking. So all I could do was to talk to Abe as persuasively as I could, and this I did."[24] Shortly after Lattimore saw Fortas, Senator J. William Fulbright published *The Arrogance of Power*, which proposed ideas similar to Lattimore's. Johnson's choler at Senator "Halfbright" knew no bounds. The war continued.

Lattimore wanted to take David to Mongolia again the summer of 1966, but David was working hard on his dissertation and decided he shouldn't go. Eleanor preferred another visit to the United States, so Lattimore went to Mongolia with Urgunge Onon. He had a glorious month, recording songs and legends and visiting for the first time Gurban Nor, the alleged birthplace of Genghis Khan. He had all of July in the MPR, then met Eleanor in Copenhagen for a week before returning to Leeds.[25]

Lattimore was now sixty-six, and retirement was creeping up. Leeds gave him a special dispensation to stay on active duty until he was seventy, but he and Eleanor began to plan their life after he had to give up his post at Leeds. Eleanor wanted to return to the United States, where friends and family were clustered in the Boston-to-Washington corridor. Owen was more inclined to stay in England, where the intellectual rewards were greater and the continent a mere train ride away. Apparently the deciding factor was a warning from Bill Rogers that were either of the Lattimores to die in England, the inheritance taxes would be colossal. American rates were much more modest. Rogers urged the Lattimores to buy land near them in Virginia.[26]

Grappling with the retirement problem caused Lattimore to reflect on his attitudes toward the United States and Britain. In a letter to Bill Rogers October 10, 1966, he wrote, "I will be perfectly frank in saying that I am depressed at the prospect of having to return to live in America. England has its drawbacks, and the British support for American imperialism, almost unquestioning, is a scandal, but nevertheless university life is very much more stimulating than in America. I suppose that in England my views could be classed as more radical Tory than Left. Certainly I have no sympathy for the bogus socialism of people like Harold Wilson and George Brown, but I do find many points of sympathy for the views of a conservative like Enoch Powell."[27]

During the Lattimores' years at Leeds, entertaining was so heavy that they moved to a larger house near the university. Lattimore wrote in 1975, "We lived successively in two houses, each made beautiful by Eleanor's genius for knowing both what to do to a house and how to live in it."[28] Part of their entertaining was of potential donors to the Chinese and Mongol programs. Lattimore spent much time with Stanley Burton, an internationally minded businessman in Leeds who contributed both ideas and funds to advance the study of Asia. On March 18, 1968, the British Royal Society of Arts held one of its periodic celebrations; Lattimore was featured, delivering a lecture titled "China Today: Some Social Aspects." Then he flew to the United States for a lecture tour and came back into CIA cognizance; that organization clipped a report in the *Boston Herald Traveler* of his lecture at the Community Church of Boston headlined "Lattimore Says U.S. Fails on Intelligence."[29]

The cost of this constant activity—and of constant traveling—was reduced scholarship. Books that he was committed to review piled up on his desk. Letters from scholar-friends around the world, asking for advice or information, were answered months after arrival, if at all. The major work he intended on Chinese history was untouched. He wanted to edit and publish the Dilowa's memoirs and started Eleanor working on it, but it made little progress.

A constant stream of scholars from all over the globe came to the grimy Midlands industrial town because Lattimore was there. One of these visitors was S. L. Tikhvinskii, Asian expert and member of the Soviet Academy of Sciences, whom Lattimore had known for a long time. Lattimore's colleagues at Leeds were a bit uneasy at this visit: Tikhvinskii was believed to be a KGB general.[30] Lattimore didn't care. He wasn't doing anything classified, and he claimed to have learned more from Tikhvinskii than Tikhvinskii had learned from him. (When Soviet and American historians held their first joint conference on post–World War II relations in Moscow June 16–18, 1987, Tikhvinskii headed the Soviet historians; George F. Kennan headed the American delegation.)[31]

Lattimore heard rumors during the mid-1960s that he had been proposed as a full member of the Mongolian Academy of Sciences but that Party authorities had vetoed the proposal. In 1967, though, it finally happened. He was notified that he had been voted in as the only foreign member. Investiture was to take place the summer of 1969.

Lattimore thought, in the first months of 1968, that it might now be time to revisit China. Accordingly he wrote Madame Sun, thinking her more likely to be able to answer his letters than Mao or Chou. He was right; she did answer, on February 13. But the answer was hardly comforting. She was pleased to hear of his Chinese curriculum at Leeds, welcomed his interest in events in China, and thought the "great changes" of the "Great Proletarian Cultural Revolution" should be studied by Westerners—*but* "Relations between China and the United States being what they are due to the hostile attitude and actions of the United States government, there is little hope for an invitation."[32] She sent best wishes to him and his family.

Unable to visit China, the Lattimores decided to attend the European Congress of Chinese Studies to be held in Prague. Many of their Czech friends had visited them in Leeds and had promised reciprocal hospitality during the congress. Two days before the Lattimores were to leave, the Russians invaded Czechoslovakia, and the congress was canceled. This was a catastrophe of major dimensions to the entire European intellectual community. Lattimore worried over the Czech invasion for months. His final evaluation was expressed in a letter to Arnold Bernhard December 9, 1968:

> Was the Soviet action "red imperialism?" No. It was a colossal blunder, a misreading of the situation, an unneeded security measure. Czechoslovakia was *not* trying to play the West, especially West Germany,

against Russia. The Russians were guilty of thick-skinned, "big brother" insensitivity to a small nation's justifiable confidence in its own intelligence and competence to manage its own affairs. The Russians are prone to the great power attitude. "We are in the big time. We deal with the U.S., atomic problems, and all that. You little fellows are only bush-league players. Your politics, and your understanding of world problems, are parochial." That is the Russian Big Power insensitivity.[33]

There followed a five-page analysis going beyond the immediate Czech crisis to long-term prospects for the Soviet Union. Lattimore foresaw, in the distance, perestroika.

The final years of his Leeds professorship were the best years of Lattimore's life. Even though the administrative and teaching burden was oppressive, the rewards made it worthwhile. His department had more than fifty undergraduate majors, several graduate students on their own, two Leverhulme Trust Sino-Soviet fellows, and "the recent British ambassador to Mongolia who is with us as a research fellow on a year of sabbatical leave from the Foreign Office."[34] There were even students from the U.S. Department of State specializing in Mongol studies. Lattimore had seven faculty members directly under him and three "lecturers planted as infiltrators in other departments." When he wrote Joe Barnes in November 1966, he was negotiating for three more faculty appointments and spending several hours a week with three students from Mongolia. He and Eleanor were their "godparents" while they were at Leeds.

The program of Mongol studies was the capstone of Lattimore's academic achievements. Having Urgunge Onon with him made it academically possible; Lattimore's stature in the global intellectual community made it financially possible. No university funds were available for Mongol studies; Lattimore financed them by tapping private donors, a rarity in Britain. His was the only program in the English-speaking world actively serving visiting Mongols and dealing with contemporary Mongol culture and politics.

Christmas 1968 the Lattimores again spent in the United States, primarily arranging architects and builders for the retirement home they were to build on the land in Southdown estates near Great Falls, Virginia, adjoining the new home of Bill and Suki Rogers. In addition to visiting in the East, they went to California to see the Robert LeMoyne Barretts. Barrett was now ninety-seven, living in a mountain retreat near Los Angeles. He was hard of hearing and almost blind but still "fantastically healthy," according to Eleanor, and still supportive of Lattimore's travels and heresies.[35] On March 5, 1969, two months after they visited him, Barrett died. Since Barrett admired Lattimore's fortitude in opposing the senatorial inquisition, a substantial part of Barrett's estate was left to Owen Lattimore and went to further Mongol studies. Joe McCarthy and Pat McCarran never knew how they had thus strengthened academic study of the MPR.

The summer of 1969 was special for Lattimore. He was to retire from Leeds after the next school year and return to the United States. Before making this move, he and Eleanor had a major tour to make.

They began with a week of frustration in Paris, where Lattimore had to deal with Soviet consular officials for a visit to Moscow and a transit visa to Ulan Bator. Lattimore's respect for most of the Soviet scholars he knew was high, but the bureaucracy drew his unmitigated contempt. His language describing the 1969 hassle was scathing. Soviet consuls were, among other things, "constipated."[36]

Then to a happy week in Italy, attending the European Congress of Chinese Studies and visiting old friends. On to Moscow: Intourist fouled up again, and no one met them at the airport. But Lattimore had that valuable possession, a Moscow telephone number (for the Soviet Academy of Sciences). The Academy came to their rescue and put them up in the VIP scholars' hotel. As Lattimore described events in a letter to his son on October 12, 1969, there began a week of

long talks with individuals and small discussion groups on China, Mongolia, the history of Central Asian nomadism—all very professional, and real discussion possible. This is the fifth time I have been in Moscow since 1960, and never have I found people so relaxed and open. Not a single sign of the war-with-China scares that we have had all summer in the Western press. . . . On China, the Cultural Revolution, Mao himself the Russians are *very*, very tough, but they have shifted gears. Instead of vulgar abuse, a serious attempt to analyze Chinese history and society. . . .

We saw a lot of dear old Zlatkin, the chap who did that ponderous critique of my life and works in 1960. I become fonder and fonder of him as the years go by. He is undoubtedly the most flat-footed, unimaginative, do-it-by-the-book-and-by-the-rules Marxist I have ever encountered; but at the same time he is decent, honest, likeable. He is now engaged on an enormous steam-roller exercise in flattening out Arnold Toynbee's theory of nomadic history. He asked me to read this and criticise it (which I did). I also told him that I would see to it that Toynbee gets a translation of the critique when published, and said that Toynbee would not take offense at strong but honest criticism. (As a matter of fact he will chuckle at Zlatkin's ponderousness.) Zlatkin knows my critique of Toynbee, published some years ago, but when he found that we are very good friends of the Toynbees he wanted to know all kinds of personal details. Finally he asked me solemnly to assure Toynbee that his criticism is in no way a personal attack, and not meant to be offensive; that he hopes Toynbee will live many more years and write many more books. (Arnold will be delighted.)[37]

The Lattimores arrived in Ulan Bator in mid-September 1969 to what he described as a homecoming. The MPR was liberally sprinkled with former students from Leeds who competed with each other in providing both Owen and Eleanor hospitality to repay what the students had experienced in England. On hand to welcome him were not only former students but also friends like Dalai, the young historian whom Lattimore had met in Moscow years before and had as a companion during his travels in Mongolia in 1961. Dalai had just served a tour in the MPR embassy in Peking, where hostility between the two countries was, if anything, worse than that between China and Russia. Dalai was glad to be back in Ulan Bator; the isolation of Mongols in Peking he described as "deadening."

Lattimore found that he was now extended an unofficial honor in some ways more significant than membership in the Academy of Sciences; he was "La Bagsh." This title, which came from Manchu days, simply meant "teacher." Only three Mongol professors were addressed this way before the summer of 1969, and Lattimore became the fourth by consensus of the academic community. Even the president of the Academy was not so addressed.

Lattimore wrote David a long description of his investiture at the Academy. The president of the Academy, Shirendyb, began with a welcoming speech. Then two academicians presented him with a traditional scarf (Lattimore described it as magnificent) and a colorful gown. Eleanor was also honored with a "gorgeous Manchu-style sleeveless jacket." There followed a reading of Lattimore's biography by academician Lobsanvandan, and Lattimore then spoke.

Urgunge Onon had warned Lattimore to prepare his speech in English and get someone to help translate it into Mongol, but the press of socializing had been so great there hadn't been time for this preparation. Lattimore "just thought about it the night before and memorised the general outline. The only thing I carefully composed and memorised was a closing invocation to world peace, which I did in the traditional alliterative rhapsodic style—a five-line stanza. As I had opened with some very common-language, vernacular passages (they like changes of pace and the mixing

of style), this was a great success." Lattimore, who had never earned a
college degree, took academic ceremonies lightly, except for his induction
into the Mongolian Academy. Compared with the top scientific bodies in
major-power states it may have been insignificant, but to him the Mongolian Academy epitomized all the glamour and glory of the ancient Central Asian kingdoms. He wore his Mongol gown from then on when he
took part in academic ceremonies throughout the Western world.

Shortly after the investiture ceremony the Lattimores were invited to
an official audience with Tsedenbal, first secretary of the Mongolian Communist party and premier of the government. Tsedenbal remembered
Lattimore from the trip with Wallace in 1944 and produced a photograph
of the two of them with Marshal Choibalsan. Surprisingly, Tsedenbal
seemed indifferent to this opportunity to "prime" Lattimore with the
Mongol version of the raging battles within the Communist bloc. Lattimore wrote David, "In fact, I was the one who tried a political demarche.
Tsedenbal asked about our years in China, and my starting to learn Mongol there. I told him, and then said that some of the things happening in
China recently must remind Mongols of their own period of 'leftist excesses,' about 1928–32. 'Yes, but the Chinese have been much more extreme,' he said, and went on to other things."

Owen and Eleanor were taken on a tour of the countryside, but extreme
weather conditions (early snow squalls and heavy rain) kept them from
enjoying it as much as usual. Mongol hospitality was greater than ever,
however; Lattimore was now introduced with a whole new set of superlatives in villages they visited. He recalled David's explanation of why he
got on so well with the Mongols: he was "culturally interesting, but no
longer politically dangerous." At one village sending-off party someone
asked him how many children he had: "I replied in the old set phrases,
one single, solitary son, but from him six grandchildren, four mere girls
and two girdled youths. An intellectual man spoke up: Nowadays, you
know, we just say four females, two males. Yes, I said, but you can see
that I am in my declining years, and for me the old way of speaking is
better; I am, after all, just a feudal remnant, a relic of the bad old times.
They nearly fell apart laughing."[38]

In October 1969 the Lattimores returned to Leeds for their last year. It
flew by unmercifully. The endless rounds of entertaining, the streams of
visitors from abroad, the preparations for turning the department over to
his successor, all kept Lattimore from digesting and writing up the huge
amount of Mongolian material he had gathered. But these necessities did

not keep him from dictating long letters to Arnold Bernhard and to the recipient of his most reflective writing: Joe Barnes. He was, he wrote Barnes October 20, increasingly glad he was not a Marxist. He thought there had been a lot of devotion to blind ideology when the Russians panicked over Prague Spring and invaded that backsliding country. As for himself: "England, I love you. How sad that our principal reason for our Christmas visit this year [to the United States] will be not to observe the quaint manners and customs of the natives, but to get on with building our place of exile among the bien-pensants of Virginia."[39]

Lattimore had now become fond of John Nef, Evelyn Stefansson's new husband, and had some philosophical reflections for him too in November. Lattimore was working on a lecture titled "Peking Seen from Moscow and Ulan Bator." As he wrote Nef, he got along well with both Russians and Chinese, but they were hard to argue with; there was a lot of "big nation" arrogance, similar to that of Americans. But the Mongols were different: "Perhaps the reason I get on best of all with the Mongols is that they are a powerless people. If they were a big nation, throwing its weight about in the world, I would probably have reservations about them."[40]

Eleanor, for all her grace as a hostess, was weary by the end of their time at Leeds. The last year had been particularly trying, largely because of an important Mongol visitor and his wife, neither of whom spoke English. Eleanor bore the brunt of accommodating their needs, and her letters to Evelyn Nef in early 1970 showed her quite ready to give up the job of department chairman's wife and get on with her dream house in Southdown. The Lattimores were saddened by Joe Barnes's death from cancer on February 28; Owen had vowed to spend long hours with Joe when they returned to the United States, catching up on the mood of the country and tapping in to Barnes's fabulous journalistic pipeline. Owen was more hesitant to leave Leeds than Eleanor was, but even he welcomed the leisure that retirement would bring, enabling him to get back to writing. And the Library of Congress would be available.

On Saturday, March 21, 1970, he and Eleanor boarded a plane for Washington to inspect progress on the Southdown house, after which they would return to Leeds to close out the house and make their last farewells.

CHAPTER THIRTY

After Leeds

As the plane carrying the Lattimores landed at John F. Kennedy Airport on March 21, 1970, Eleanor suffered a massive, fatal pulmonary embolism. Owen described it as "a crowning mercy. She never knew what happened. No pain, no fear, no premonition. But that was the end of what one of her friends called 'a honeymoon of forty-four years.'"[1] Eleanor was seventy-five, five years older than her husband.

Eleanor had not exactly been in the background during her husband's years of prominence; she was more a partner than an assistant. In those thousands of routine tasks on which any enterprise depends, she was the stalwart: arranging, organizing, encouraging, substituting if need be. She shared the limelight and dominated the shadows. Owen was adrift without her.

Without exception, Owen's friends were also Eleanor's friends, and the ties between the Lattimores and the many people they knew and loved were nurtured primarily by Eleanor. She was by all accounts an extraordinary personality, with a warmth that offset her husband's sometimes abrasive manner. Evelyn Stefansson Nef organized and published a beautiful memorial booklet for Eleanor, with Brian Hook's London *Times* obituary and tributes by Étienne Balazs, George Boas, Pearl Buck, Bill Rogers, and others.

Lattimore was taken in by Bill and Suki Rogers at their Southdown home in Great Falls, Virginia, in the first days of his bereavement. The Lattimore house at Southdown, planned by Eleanor, was not yet ready for occupancy. Owen could not have moved in so soon in any case; it was really her house. After short stays with the Rogers and a visit with his son David he returned to Leeds for the closing days of the school year.

Lattimore had traded barbs with the fiercest of Senate inquisitors and faced down malevolent Asian camel drivers in the middle of the Gobi, but the loss of his wife was almost more than he could bear. A letter to Evelyn Nef from Leeds May 15, 1970, displays the depth of his anguish and the slowness of his recovery.

> Your letter was very sweet and much needed, coming at a time when I was badly demoralized—as you foresaw. Things are not so bad now. I've been away from home a couple of times and back again. I don't know what primitive psychology it is that makes each coming back diminish the hauntedness a bit. But I still break down—I did in Cambridge a couple of days ago—when I meet for the first time people of whom Eleanor was especially fond.
>
> I think I told you of my idea of a possible long stay in Mongolia, but wondered if the Mongols would agree. I needn't have worried. By the time I got back to England there was a message waiting for me—come to Mongolia, we'll make you Dean of all our Far Eastern studies. You can do as much or as little work as you like, but we'll look after you for always. Of course I couldn't do quite that—it would be a kind of running away—but I was so touched that I cried and cried.[2]

On June 24 students and faculty of the Leeds Center for Chinese and Mongolian Studies gave Lattimore a farewell dinner, with the Mongolian Ambassador to the Court of St. James in attendance. It was a subdued occasion. Every person present had been Eleanor's guest.

Equally painful was the prospect of returning to Asia without Eleanor. Lattimore was due to go back the summer of 1970 to attend a congress of Mongolists in Ulan Bator and to visit, for the first time as a scholar, the libraries and archaeological sites in the Soviet areas bordering on China and Mongolia. He had visited some of these with Wallace but had had no opportunity to do research. The Soviet initiative for this invitation came from Okladnikov. All the scholarly riches of Central Asia were opening up for Lattimore, and he would be exploring them alone. On March 27, 1970, he wrote a sad note to Okladnikov, telling of Eleanor's death and recalling times when they had all been together at scholarly meetings: "it warmed my heart to see how, when you met [Eleanor], each appreciated the other so quickly and so rightly. . . . So that is the end of a marriage of 44 years that was perfect from beginning to end—thanks to her. What more can I say? I turn to you, and the comradeship of those who . . ." Here the CIA photocopy machine malfunctioned, and the conclusion of the letter to Okladnikov is not readable.[3]

Edgar Snow, living in Switzerland, was unaware of Eleanor's death when he addressed a letter to both Owen and Eleanor May 20. Snow had heard of Joe Barnes's death and wrote, "I know what a loss it has been to you both." But most of Snow's letter was comment springing from Lattimore's introduction to the 1970 reprinting of Jack Belden's *China Shakes the World.*[4] Lattimore had written this brief introduction in January 1970 at Leeds; he admired Belden's book and put it in context by comparing it with two other classic descriptions of the rise of the Chinese Communists: Snow's *Red Star over China* and William Hinton's *Fanshen.*

In his introduction to Belden's book, Lattimore comments, "I remember talking to a Communist about Snow, years ago, at a time when adherents of Chiang Kai-shek were denouncing him [Snow] as nothing but a mouthpiece for Communist propaganda. The Communist shook his head. No, he said, they respected Snow as a completely honest man. His reporting of facts could be relied on. But his *interpretations* did not entitle him to rank as a 'spokesman,' because he did not really understand Marxism."[5] Lattimore then notes that Belden's book was even more important in 1970 than it had been in 1949 when it was first published: "Page after page is a reminder that the stupid, obvious, unnecessary mistakes made by the American political and military establishments in China have been made over again, and are still being made, in Vietnam." The United States had in the late 1940s, and still had, a "bewitched belief that the incantation of words like 'freedom' and 'democracy' (accompanied by the spending of lots of money) could somehow conjure up an Ohio-like or New England–like regime capable of reversing a revolution already in being." America was still a "society blinded by imperialistic preconceptions."[6]

Snow, in his letter to Lattimore, agreed.

I noticed that you quote some Chinese as saying that Snow is an honest man but doesn't understand Marxism. That I could never have been a Chinese Communist "spokesman" ought not to have done me any harm in the councils of our great ones at home—but few of them ever heard that. (Besides, it was OL speaking.) In fact I have (though not very recently) spent a vast amount of time reading Marx and Engels and, even more, their various disciples, from orthodox to revisionist. After living in Russia several years (and away from realities in Washington) my early tendency to subscribe to the "exceptionalism" notion about the U.S. was strongly reinforced. It was not even entirely shattered by McCarthyism; I thought the inner structure was still sound and that the good in the American democratic process was still viable and would prevail to overcome a banal fulfillment of the role of imperialism. It was not until Kennedy fell in step with the Pentagon and CIA and deceived himself and us in Vietnam that I saw the "exceptionalism" truly was and had to have been a mirage, a subjective thing with me— which was understandable because I, like you, had been taken in by the Establishment, tolerated for a while as an "exception" myself, a kind of house nigger. Yes, Virginia, there is an American imperialism—the most vicious and dangerous kind yet seen, and all the more so because people, thinking themselves free, could not imagine carrying anything but freedom elsewhere.[7]

Lattimore noted on Snow's letter "Answered 19 June 70." His answer does not survive. It would have been interesting. He did not agree with Snow that American imperialism was the "most vicious kind": he thought the Fascists worse.

Closing up the Leeds house was more than Lattimore could handle alone. He prevailed on Charlotte Riznik, with whom he and Eleanor had been friends ever since Riznik had been his office manager at OWI in San Francisco, to help him dismantle and ship his possessions. Riznik arrived at Leeds in early June, and by June 14 Lattimore could report to the Nefs that Charlotte had taken over and things were beginning to work: "I have been crippled by hesitation, inability to make decisions. She sorts things out up to a certain point, then comes to me and says 'I want a decision.' Good for my morale, because it gives me the illusion of being the boss, while gently disguising the fact that I am being managed, which of course is what I still can't do without."[8] He was so pleased with Riznik's help that he offered her a job as "manager secretary," but she would promise no more than helping him get settled in Virginia.

Charlotte Riznik must indeed have been good for his morale. When he wrote Academician Y. V. Peive, chief scientific secretary of the Soviet Academy of Sciences, on June 26, 1970, suggesting dates for his trip to Soviet Central Asia, he was brimming with confidence about his future scholarly endeavors. He outlined on two single-spaced pages the historical-ethnographic studies he intended to accomplish for the next ten years— emphasizing that while he hoped his knowledge would be of use to Russian and Mongolian colleagues, "I have much more to learn . . . than I can teach." Peive must have been impressed. The travel schedule came off exactly as Lattimore suggested. And when he wrote the Nefs July 1, he was manic; that coming winter, he would be "finishing up 'China in History' and planning long-term research on Mongolia." He was looking forward to the winter of 1970–71 in the Southdown house; "I've suffered a shattering defeat, but the retreat is ending and an advance into new terrain is in sight. Thank God for friends."[9]

On July 16 he and Riznik flew to the United States, she to California to work in a political campaign until Lattimore was back from his summer in Asia, he to Washington, where he stayed with the Rogers, inspected progress on his almost-completed house, and made arrangements for unpacking his furniture when it arrived from Leeds. After a few days in New York with Gerard and Eleanor Piel and a visit to David in Providence, he was off to the Soviet Union. He arrived in Moscow August 17, 1970.

During his 1970 Asian trip Lattimore took pains to report more fully than he ever had to friends in the United States. These reports, or diary-letters, went to Bill Rogers at Arnold and Porter (Fortas had dropped out of the firm when he went to the Supreme Court), who photocopied them for a half-dozen relatives and friends. On this trip he had no companion, which no doubt impelled him to more comprehensive letter writing.

He wrote Rogers from Ulan Bator on August 22, reporting events on the plane from Moscow.

> Yesterday I was badly shaken. I met some Mongols. All strangers, but as soon as they got my name they said, with a mixture of grave courtesy and personal tenderness, how sorry they were about Eleanor. . . . The Mongols always gave my work a kind of professional respect, but were very impatient of my political misguidedness, wrongheadedness, even stupidity. I think for years they really did think I was some kind of imperialist ideologue. Then, in 1960, we met their delegation to the Orientalist Congress, were invited to Mongolia for six weeks in 1961, and did a long trip into the Aru Khangai. In 1964 I came to Mongolia with David, and they saw what kind of son she and I had brought up. In the Leeds years, all the Mongols who came to England met her. Finally there was last year, and you've seen the account of that. The truth is that the Mongols decided that if I'd been happily married for so many years to a woman like Eleanor, I just couldn't be a wrong 'un. I might be politically askew (but not maliciously) and in any showdown involving human decency I could be trusted to come down on the right side.[10]

However much he missed Eleanor, and possibly because of it, Lattimore plunged wholeheartedly into his duties for the congress. There were papers to be translated into the official languages (Mongol, Russian, English, French), his own remarks to polish, a book on English for Mongol schools to be edited, courtesy calls on various Academy figures he knew. On August 24, when he was leaving his hotel, several American tourists accosted him. He reported to Rogers sarcastically that such incidents had happened before and that the tourists asked him to talk to their group "and explain to them what country they've been in." Most tourists, he found, had read nothing about Mongolia before coming and at most had heard of Genghis Khan and the Gobi Desert. Then they fell in love with the country and were "pathetically delighted to have bits of things explained." Big-game hunters from Texas were especially prone to captivation by their Mongol guides: the hunters were "marvellously confused between their truly Texan detestation of communism" and the fact that their guides "more than qualified by Texas he-man standards."[11]

Lattimore and Urgunge Onon spent August 26, 1970, with Shirendyb, president of the Mongolian Academy of Sciences. They drove out to Shirendyb's country place in the valley "where the Wallace safari was quartered in 1944." Lattimore was fascinated by the Shirendyb entourage, especially by a former Buddhist monk, well read in the Tibetan scriptures, who had been a chauffeur to Shirendyb and was now retired on pension. The ex-monk loved to cook, and Shirendyb kept him around for that purpose. After an elaborate lunch the party played dominoes; Lattimore wrote, "The ex-monk kibitzed over my shoulder, so I came out on the winning side. Note: must remember to tell my clerical friends about the pleasures of being a pensioned ex-monk in an atheist country."[12]

Shirendyb asked Lattimore about the history of a telescope given the Mongols by Peggy Braymer of the Questar Corporation at Lattimore's suggestion. Lattimore had wanted to "do something really different" for the Mongols to repay their hospitality. He saw an ad in *Scientific American* for a Questar telescope and asked Gerard Piel if it were a first-class job and if he might get a discount for a gift to the Mongols. Piel said it was indeed a terrific and expensive instrument, but no discounts were available. However, Piel knew the Braymers, and at his suggestion they gave a Questar to the Mongols. It was a tremendous hit and was used by the Mongols to establish accurately their far-flung borders by stellar observation and measurement. Peggy Braymer's letter of gift noted that Lattimore had worked for "better understanding" between the United States and the MPR. Lattimore wrote Rogers that this letter meant a great deal to the Mongols: "For them, 'peace and friendship' is not the malarky of international humbug. It's what they're hooked on. It means survival. . . . Driving home [from Shirendyb's] Urgunge said, 'There's one woman [Braymer] who's going to have no difficulty if she ever wants to visit Mongolia. And my bet is, she's going to get a hunk of dinosaur bone.' "

Dinosaur bone was the supreme present for someone hung with medals and vacuous honors. [13]

The night of September 14, 1970, brought a welcome surprise to Lattimore. As he described it in a letter to Rogers:

> After dinner I had gone to my room when, as I was reading, not being quite ready for bed, someone came in and asked me to come up to the top floor—and there was a surprise supper party, to honour my seventieth year. At least 30 people. It was overwhelming. Speeches and toasts in Mongol, Russian, German, French, Japanese. . . . Practically everybody referred to the McCarthy business, including the top Russian (I was sitting between him and Shirendyb, who was presiding), who said that in the Soviet Union, despite differences of politics, I am honoured for my defence of the human values and dignity of scholarship. After that, do I put two exclamation points, or three? But isn't it the irony of ironies that McCarthy should have opened the way for me to a whole new, international life of intellectual interest and activity! . . . When we were dispersing, old Damdinsuren said: "We have a lot of learned foreign friends here tonight, but among them all it is you who are a Mongol." [14]

The rest of September, Lattimore worked at translating and editing the papers of the Congress of Mongolists and inspecting the new industrial city of Darkhan. He found Darkhan far more impressive than Dalstroi, and of course no one was hiding slave labor camps. After a round of farewell parties he was escorted on October 1 to Irkutsk and the beginning of his tour of Siberian archives and libraries.

It seems hardly possible that this tour could have been more profitable professionally than his deep immersion in Mongolia, yet his glowing descriptions of manuscripts and libraries almost warrant that conclusion. One conclusion is clearly warranted: had the historical and archaeological treasures of Central Asia been available to him in his early career, rather than in his seventieth year, his scholarly output would have been immensely increased. Age and the demoralization of losing Eleanor denied him opportunity to reflect on, analyze, and incorporate in his published work the riches that came to him in the 1970s.

His stay in Irkutsk was brief, two days for the library and museum. Ulan-Ude was next; it was the center of Buryat studies, and Lattimore stayed there a full week. The Buryats were at first stiff and formal, but he reported on October 9:

Things are livening up. It works the same way, over and over again. The locals are apt to begin by thinking that you've been wished off on them by some distant higher-up. They're polite and considerate, but they stand off a bit. Then, as they find you are not joy-riding but working really hard, and trying to learn, they warm up. Today there was an invitation—from the children themselves, not the teachers—to come to the intensive-English school and talk to the 10th and 9th year classes about American schools and education generally. . . . I was simple, but I tried to be honest. I talked about the differences between private and public schools, and between tax-supported schools in "good" residential districts where parents demand good teaching, and in slum districts and above all black districts. I explained why, in a country dominated by a bourgeois establishment, technological training is sound and scientific research and teaching are excellent, but in history, sociology, politics, economics you can get away with all kinds of slop, and in literature and poetry "individualism" justifies anything. . . . I'm telling you all this because of the payoff. It came back to me, over the grapevine, that one of the teachers had said, "We used to have two classics in Buryatia, but now we have three—Marx, Lenin, Lattimore." . . . Later in the afternoon I was pulled out of the library, and there was a deputation of kids with some nice little gifts. [15]

From Ulan-Ude, Lattimore went to Novosibirsk. This visit brought back vivid memories:

This is the city where Eleanor left the Trans-Siberian in 1927 to take the then uncompleted Turk-Sib to Semipalatinsk, and on by sled to her Turkestan Reunion with me in Chuguchak. . . . I thought sadly, as I have thought so many times since her death, that I never did justice (and she never claimed credit for herself) to Eleanor's ingenuity and persistence, and above all incredible courage in making that journey. It was February, the cruellest month of winter, she didn't know more than a couple of words of Russian, and she had to struggle to get herself and more baggage than she could personally carry through a Siberia still wrecked by the revolution and civil war. [16]

Novosibirsk was the home of Okladnikov, the master historian-archaeologist who had arranged Lattimore's trip. The scholarly riches there were greater than at any other stop. Lattimore found that librarians, archivists, even minor bureaucrats were willing, when they learned of his interests, to offer him out-of-print books to take back with him. For this largesse, he explained to Rogers, he would have to spend a small fortune buying books to send his Russian hosts after he got home—but it was worth it.

Lattimore wrote some thirty pages on his stay in Novosibirsk; his main theme was amazement. "This town is incredible. There are 5 million books in the library. And the Siberian Section, Academy of Sciences . . . they get all they want, for the most recondite researches" (ellipsis in original). Again Lattimore was struck with Soviet tolerance here of "Old Believers," most of them living in remote valleys and earning their living by sable hunting. They also "kept up the ancient tradition of illuminating MSS in the Byzantine and Old Slavonic styles, and the atheistic government, instead of persecuting them, subsidizes them."[17]

Okladnikov arranged a side trip for Lattimore to archives in Biisk and Kyzyl. These were places he had known about only by name; he found them more than worth his time. On Biisk he remarked:

> The people are terribly nice, and I am going to like them. . . . They are so full of interest—and it isn't drawing-room, curiosity interest. They were all professionals, and they wouldn't give up until they were able to "place" me professionally. Why had I come? What interest of mine could they help me with? . . . Why so short a visit? Could I learn enough? So I said, "You know your own Okladnikov. Other archeologists go over an area and say, No Paleolithic here. Then Okladnikov comes to the same area, walks straight to a point, says 'Dig here'—and there's a big Paleolithic find." They all laughed—everybody knows the Okladnikov stories.

Lattimore then explained his interest in nomadic peoples, Central Asian history, migrations, the relations of minorities to empires, geography, and so forth, to his audience:

> As professionals, they were quite satisfied, but as individuals, they were more curious than ever. Where had I travelled? In what years? Under what conditions? The questions got more and more personal—right down to Chiang Kai-shek and Mao Tze-tung and Senator McCarthy and all. By the end, it was an unbelievable transvaluation of values . . . by the end of the evening these nice people had hypnotised themselves into thinking of me as a "romantic bourgeois." This is possible because in the Soviet Union today—and I say that instead of "Russia" because so many millions of peoples other than Russians make the Soviet Union what it is—only ancient characters like me can remember what the world was like before 1917.[18]

The Biisk archaeologists took Lattimore on a long drive. The Altai Mountains into which they drove were much like the Heavenly Mountains of Lattimore's early travels. They showed him a Paleolithic site sim-

ilar to that of Peking Man, though they had found no comparable skull or
bones. The final three days of his stay in Biisk were hectic and went
unrecorded. He never got around to writing about them.

His next stop was Kyzyl in the Tuvinian republic. Lattimore, who at
age seventy had seen most of the world and tasted of the richness of its
cultures, here in the land of the Reindeer People found his Shangri-la.

> Tuva has been the best yet. Of all the Soviet countries I have been in,
> it is the one that can be quite simply described as ravishing. It is bigger
> than Switzerland, Holland, Belgium, Denmark combined, and they have
> a map to prove it. They are the Centre of Asia, and they have a mon-
> ument, and obelisk, to prove that, too. They are enclosed by snow-
> capped mountains, but the internal valleys of the streams that are the
> headwaters of the lordly Yenesei are comparatively windless, and the
> winter is of a cheerful coldness. . . . They speak an ancient Turkish—
> very pure, few loan words. And the people are as ravishing as their
> country. They have a Gallic gaiety and lightness, combined with pre-
> cision—and rather Gascon at that. Perhaps in the Soviet Union some
> of the small tribes of the Caucasus can match them for dash and ele-
> gance. They are mostly of middle height, and I never saw a fat one,
> man or woman. . . . I fell for them, hard (Mongols, look out—I may
> never come home), and thank goodness they took me to their hearts.
> The Director of the Pedagogical Institute and the Director of the Insti-
> tute of History, Language, and Literature (he speaks good Mongol, though
> a bit literary) the two highest academic posts in the country, came each
> morning for breakfast and were with me until after dinner. . . .
>
> We drove out southward toward the Tannu-tuva, the range dividing
> Tuva from Mongolia. Came to a place called Tuvakobalt, where there
> is a big cobalt mining and refining enterprise. Top engineer-manager a
> Russian (Ukrainian), but most of the technical posts were held by Tu-
> vinians. This is the way the Russians work, with every minority na-
> tionality, they do not try to preserve "living museums" (Navahoes),
> but to develop "cadres" of mathematicians, physicists, chemists, engi-
> neers. At the same time, they encourage (not merely preserve) the local
> language and cultural traditions. Thus you get the local electronics-
> automation expert whose hobby is the poetic legends of his own people.[19]

The remainder of his stay in Kyzyl is described in similarly glowing
language. He didn't understand a thing about the cobalt works but knew
he had to act impressed. When they asked him the usual Soviet questions,
"Any criticisms? Any questions?" he responded, "What do you do about
industrial waste?" They described an elaborate process of burying it in
deep pits in a deposit of impermeable clay. When he left the cobalt works,

"They gave me a nicely-mounted set of test tubes of their product, in successive stages. I said, 'You'd better be careful. The American Customs might take this off me and turn it over to the CIA, and then I might be in for some questioning.' They all know 'CIA,' and they laughed, but I noticed that the test tubes never turned up in my luggage."[20]

He spent only four days in Tuva, but it made the most lasting impression of his whole trip. The only article about the trip that he wrote for publication afterwards was an encomium of Tuva sent to the London *Times* on November 23, 1970.

Lattimore went back to Novosibirsk October 25 for a last few days with Okladnikov. He described these days as frenzied, with much time spent sorting books to take with him from books to be mailed and making lists of books to be bought in the West and sent to his Siberian hosts. Farewell parties occupied the rest of his time, with the "real farewell party" the afternoon of October 29: "Warm speeches. Everybody embraced everybody—big Russian bear-hugs. Okladnikov has really done all this for me out of the overflowing kindness of his Siberian heart. An unforgettable man."[21]

On October 30 Lattimore was back in Moscow for a brief stop en route to Prague, Leeds, and home. There were the usual bureaucratic foul-ups. Given the friendliness of the academicians, it was hard for him to believe that Okladnikov and the Tuvians were part of the same country as the Moscow functionaries.

On November 20, 1970, Lattimore took possession of the house in Great Falls, Virginia, that he and Eleanor had expected to call home for the rest of their lives. This was probably more painful than anything he had ever experienced. His travels since her death in March postponed confronting the full domestic consequences of her absence. The warmth of his reception in Mongolia and Siberia had been therapeutic, but now he had to start up a household de novo, every decision reminding him of how much he had depended on her. Charlotte Riznik was there and as helpful as she had been in Leeds. Setting up a household, however, was more difficult than dismantling one. Riznik took over housekeeping; Lattimore was now absolutely dependent on her.

Books, manuscripts, correspondence, and other scholarly pursuits were another matter. He had a massive accumulation of scholarly materials, some from Leeds, more from his recent trip, with an avalanche of books yet to come: these were an insuperable challenge. Eleanor's control of the flow of paper, based on a lifetime of sharing Lattimore's professional activities, could not be duplicated by anyone new. Now the paper was out of control, flooding the room Lattimore used for a study and several other rooms besides, boxed and unboxed, stacked, spread on tables, scattered almost without pattern. The unending requests to critique manuscripts, write articles, furnish recommendations, advise about academic programs—this avalanche of mail, which Eleanor had controlled and Owen had then turned over to secretaries, now got quite beyond him. In his despair he began drinking heavily. Despite the problems he did complete three articles that winter: one for a book edited by Toynbee, another for a book edited by Denis Sinor of Indiana University, and the "Mongols" entry for *Encyclopaedia Brittanica*. Gerry Piel's request for an article for *Scientific American* on ancient caravans had to be put off.[22] And no work got done on "China in History" or the major Mongolian project.

Some relief came on January 25, 1971, when Fujiko Isono came to Great Falls. Fujiko had been a student of Lattimore at Leeds. She and her husband, Seiichi Isono, had been dissenters from Japan's aggressive policies in the 1930s and spent the war years studying in the Mongol areas of North China. Fujiko had been inspired to endure the hardships this entailed by reading Eleanor's *Turkestan Reunion*. When she read that the Lattimores were in England, she wrote and then visited them. During 1968–69 the Isonos both studied at Leeds.

Now she came to Great Falls to be of assistance to her former professor, bringing an offer from Japan's Asian Affairs Research Council and the Mainichi Newspapers (who would provide financing) to come to Tokyo the summer of 1971 to lecture. Lattimore accepted. Fujiko's knowledge of Lattimore's professional interests helped him deal with the mountain of paperwork, but Fujiko and Charlotte Riznik did not take to each other, and tension in the household did not improve Lattimore's morale.

In February 1971 Lattimore heard from Edgar Snow, just returned from China to his home in Switzerland. Snow again had interesting news. "Responsible persons" in Peking were asking whether Lattimore would accept an invitation to visit China. Snow told them he was sure Lattimore would want to come. But this was a period of poisonous relations between the Chinese and the Soviet Union; would Lattimore's ties with Ulan Bator and various Russian scholars make a visit to China awkward? The Chinese assured Snow that Lattimore's Soviet connections would be no obstacle. These things worked slowly, and Lattimore did not expect an invitation in time for a 1971 trip.[23]

Lattimore stayed in Great Falls until May 1971, leaning heavily on Bill and Suki Rogers for friendship and moral support. He made little progress on his backlog of paperwork but did manage to arrange visits to Mongolia and to friends in Bulgaria, East Berlin, and Denmark after his coming appearance in Japan. By May, when he left for Leeds en route to Tokyo, he was beginning to wonder if he could survive in a house where every feature bore Eleanor's imprint and every day's passage highlighted the need for her talents.

Lattimore had by now put behind him the trauma of the inquisition. His career since leaving Johns Hopkins had been so all-absorbing that there was no occasion to dwell on the ugly past. He was therefore startled when he went through the mail awaiting him at Leeds and found this letter:

8 Chemin des Roches
Fribourg, Switzerland
30 April 1971

Professor Owen Lattimore
University of Leeds
England

Sir:

This is written by a Russian witness against you during the Senate investigations in 1952 (Igor Bogolepov).

I have written a manuscript dealing with memoirs about American and Western in general politics of the cold war against my country, the Soviet Union. In these memoirs I explain the background of my testimony. I believe I have finally to tell the truth: I have very little time left to live and must hurry as much as I can. All my previous efforts to find a publisher either in America or England or elsewhere were in vain; the material is very hot in other aspects, too.

Would you be interested in assisting me to tell the truth? But you must take into consideration that my writings are very critical of the US government and American way of life in general. I had been and still am a patriot of my Soviet country; as Machiavelli told, one can serve his country con gloria e con ignomia. You may understand that I cannot say more until I learn about your attitude.

The manuscript is in Russian.

Very truly yours

I. Nyman[24]

Bogolepov! The surprise witness so valued by SISS that he got more space in the committee's final report than any other did. The double defector from the Russians to the Nazis to the Americans. The witness who said Soviet propagandists flooded IPR publications with their writings. The witness who quoted Litvinov as saying Lattimore was the most appropriate agent for "mobilizing public sentiment" in the West.

Lattimore was astounded. Could Nyman/Bogolepov actually be defecting again, back to the Russians? Why would he contact Lattimore? Why assume Lattimore could find him a publisher if his own efforts had failed? Was this a setup engineered by the CIA, or James O. Eastland, or Robert Morris, or someone else attempting to implicate Lattimore in some treasonous activity? Or was Nyman simply a very disturbed, possibly pathological character?

There was no time to stew about it. Lattimore was due to leave for Japan. Only one safe course came to mind: send the letter to Bill Rogers, who would know how to deal with it. Rogers did; he wrote Nyman June 4, 1971, saying that Lattimore was in Asia, but Nyman could send the manuscript to Arnold and Porter, where Rogers would hold it for Lattimore's return.[25] The manuscript did not come, but this was not the end of Nyman.

Lattimore arrived in Tokyo June 4, 1971. He was whisked through customs; the customs man had read some of his writings and wished him a happy visit.

> Explanation of this recondite literacy of a Customs inspector, surely unmatched anywhere else in the world: At the end of the war "The Making of Modern China," which Eleanor and I had written during the war, was quickly translated into Japanese. It is a very one-syllable-word, primer-like book, as indicated by the fact that it was also reprinted in a huge paperback edition for the use of U.S. troops. Anyhow, lots of Japanese have told me that it gave them their first glimpse of a China different from the official Japanese views of the 1930's. As the MacArthur occupation evolved into the Cold War years, another generation of Japanese came to fall back on it as a non–Cold War American depiction of China.[26]

He later learned that *The Making of Modern China* was in its thirty-second Japanese printing.

Lattimore had not been in Japan since 1945. To his delight he discovered that Saburo Matsukata, one of the prewar Japanese IPR stalwarts, was still alive and anxious to see him. They visited for several hours. And at a luncheon of "big brass" from Mainichi and the Japanese Research Council, he was amazed to hear some of those present claim that they had read his book and agreed with much of it even in the 1930s. "I seem to have had, at the time, an influence that I never knew about, on Japanese who, while working within the Japanese military-industrial-academic-imperialistic complex, were sceptical about its aims, its conduct, and its eventual outcome. Of course it was an ineffectual influence. What it all amounted to was that it helped a few people to say 'I told you so' when the party was over and the broken glass and crockery were being swept up."[27]

Lattimore discovered a strong interest among Japanese scholars and businessmen in Mongolia, some of this interest apparently coming from his writings. "I sensed that with every one of them it began with a romantic interest which then developed into political partisanship, though all of them had been in either the political or military service of Japanese imperialism. It is strange that the Japanese have a particular and not dissimilar sentimentality about the Mongols, who under Khubilai [Khan] tried and failed to conquer them, and the Americans, who did conquer them. Whatever (as the Irish say), it seems it was the Japanese I subverted with my nefarious doctrines, not the Americans. Tut-tut."[28]

On June 7, 1971, Lattimore gave his major lecture, sponsored by the Research Council and Mainichi. He used a contemporary theme: the United States, in the person of Richard Nixon, was finally dealing with the People's Republic of China. The shift in policy was greater than met the eye; in previous years Nixon had made much of American determination to negotiate only from a position of strength. And what was Nixon doing now? Not only dealing with the People's Republic of China, but dealing with it precisely because America's position in Vietnam was weak. "Today, whatever the way the Americans might take to cover up their defeat, one thing is no longer possible—the escalation of the war. Public opinion in America would not stand for it."[29] The *Mainichi Daily News* gave Lattimore's speech page-one treatment.

Lattimore's letters to Bill Rogers detail dozens of fascinating discoveries about Japanese intellectual and political currents. Not all of those he met were liberals disenchanted with Japan's previous expansionist policies; some still defended them as superior to the imperialist policies of Western governments. The bureaucrats of the foreign office were "smooth and condescending," content to be "wallowing in Washington's wake." They were as gullible as their American counterparts, ready to swallow the Hong Kong monitoring of Chinese press and radio, which was being done by refugees wanting to "get the hell out of Hongkong" and willing to select and translate the mainland press to please the prejudices of their American employers.[30]

Mainichi staged an eight-day tour of the islands for Lattimore; it was a tourist's delight. He rode the bullet trains to Kyoto, Osaka, and Nagoya, saw the temples and monuments Fujiko recommended, and traded opinions about the world with civic leaders all over Japan. Mainichi seemed to think they got their money's worth; they asked him to report for them from China in 1972 if he made it there.

Fujiko was also delighted with Lattimore's visit. She and her husband, Seiichi Isono, conferred about her future career and decided that she should join Lattimore in Leeds or Virginia on a semipermanent basis to work with him on several specific projects and to assume his mantle when, as he put it, total senility set in. She was then fifty-three, with at least a decade of vigorous scholarship before her. Their first joint task: translating and annotating the memoirs of the Dilowa, which they would start the spring of 1972 when she finished a course she was giving at Tokyo University.[31]

Lattimore enjoyed his VIP treatment in Japan and appreciated the Japanese intelligentsia with whom he mingled. But in his letters home he expressed less empathy for the affluent Japanese than he had earlier shown for the Mongols and Tuvinians. The ethos of the Central Asian caravan never really left him. He sailed from Yokohama June 16, 1971, for the Soviet Union and Mongolia.

Nakhodka, the Soviet port city for ships from Japan, plunged him again into the bloody-mindedness of Soviet officialdom. The two-page description of his encounter with Soviet customs at Nakhodka is hilarious. He was breaking all the rules: he had a tape recorder; he forgot to declare a broken camera in his luggage; he had a copy of a bitterly anti-Soviet article in Russian that he was carrying to Ulan Bator at the request of a Mongol scholar; and on examining his clothing, the custom officers found a pair of new trousers with stiffening in the waistband. Very suspicious. They were about to slit the waistband open, but Lattimore protested: "I was lucky my Russian was good enough to explain everything." Customs confiscated the anti-Soviet article but let him pass with the rest of his impedimenta in time to make his train to Khabarovsk.[32]

He was traveling with Urgunge Onon and family. Since the group constituted a "party" by Intourist standards, they got a first-class guide in Khabarovsk. To no avail. There was no significant intellectual life, no friendly scholarly community, no first-rate museum here; Lattimore described it as "a pleasant provincial city, but that's about all." The rest of his journey through Siberia to Mongolia was touristy, comfortable, but somewhat strained. Lattimore and the Onons had no Mongolian visas, not even a written invitation. Intourist was afraid they'd be stuck with these five careless travelers indefinitely. At the border stop the Intourist people "gaped when we telephoned, and the Mongolian consul, instead of telling us to come to the consulate, insisted on coming round to the hotel himself, with the visas all made out."[33]

Despite extensive preparations going on to celebrate the MPR's fiftieth anniversary, Lattimore and his party were met at the Ulan Bator station by a delegation of his friends. One can sense the emotion as Lattimore greeted Dalai, who reported that a beautiful picture of Eleanor now hung in a "place of honour" with his family portraits; as he met again "the pretty waitress who cried last year when she learned of Eleanor's death" (she almost cried again); and as he ran into old friends in the street, including the lama who had known the Dilowa.[34] It was old home week.

By now Lattimore had developed his diary-letters into an art form. The one of July 1, 1971, as usual to Bill Rogers, was exemplary, describing in fascinating detail his four-day stay in the Ulan Bator hospital.

Lattimore had a mild blood-pressure problem. When he called on Shirendyb, president of the Academy, for a "long, very pleasant and very profitable conversation" soon after his arrival in Ulan Bator, the subject of Lattimore's health came up. He mentioned the blood pressure. Shirendyb, not only concerned as a friend but also anxious to procure maximum editing and translating services while Lattimore was in Mongolia, suggested that he check into the hospital for rest and observation. "I thought, why not? What a marvellous opportunity to get an idea of Mongolian medicine and hospitals!"

Registration was simple and quick. He was in a semiprivate (two-bed) room with bath and washbasin, but the toilet was down the hall. Sanitation was superb. The heart specialist who examined him was "a hell of a nice guy." Before long Lattimore had learned most of the doctor's life history. Nurses were efficient and colorful. Nobody pulled rank in the hospital, neither doctors nor administrators nor the higher grades of nurses. The elderly cleaning lady noticed Lattimore's pouch of pipe tobacco and confessed that she too smoked a pipe; he offered her a fill if she brought her pipe the next day. Later that night she came back with a cigarette paper and asked if she could have enough tobacco to roll a cigarette. As she smoked, they "talked about what a pity it is that you can't get the old trade tobacco from China anymore." Lattimore had entered with a systolic blood-pressure reading of 175; by the time he left, it was 140. He was pronounced sound.[35]

Lattimore always called on the British ambassador when in Mongolia.

In 1971 John Colvin was the new envoy. Lattimore's judgment: "He is the kind of High Tory I can like and respect." Colvin had previously served in North Vietnam and observed that when he was there, the Russians were always baffled because the Vietnamese wouldn't do things the Russian way. This description, wrote Lattimore to Bill Rogers, "touches on one of the great similarities between Russians and Americans. Both are so convinced of their own righteousness that they can only see the fact, never the 'why,' when disagreed with. This is bad for the conduct of foreign policy, for both nations, but the Russians have been winning, on balance, since there are more peoples wanting to pull down their rotten governments than there are who want to stand by while we prop them up."[36]

Lattimore's stature with the Mongols, always high since he first visited there, reached a new level in 1971, partly because of the devotion and praise of Urgunge Onon: "He goes around propagandizing me like a PRO." Lattimore was flattered, but in his letter of July 8 he revealed that the pedestal on which he was placed had its disadvantages. He was depressed, despite the adulation. "I have been thinking that this winter it will be 40 years since I started to learn Mongol (45 years since the long journey through [Inner] Mongolia to Sinkiang, at a time when I spoke only Chinese). And what have I got to show for it? A damn sight less than ought to have been possible. I don't speak anything like perfect Mongol, in spite of what people say, and my knowledge of history, tribes, traditions, manners, customs, is all bits and patches, never properly coordinated into a rounded whole. The chief thing is that I was able to begin in Mongolia in the very years when the old order was falling apart, and new forces, emotions, instinctive strivings beginning to emerge. To put this all in order, I've got to train Fujiko as my successor. Urgunge too."[37]

Depression, however, could not last in the excitement and ceremony of the fiftieth anniversary celebration. Shirendyb gave a glorious picnic in a valley several miles from Ulan Bator. Lattimore said of the setting, "The scene was lovely beyond any words of mine." At the picnic, and at later parties in the city, he heard ancient tribal songs of haunting beauty. The formal celebrations on July 12 were boring, "listening for hours to speeches in different languages saying the same thing," but a parade of veterans of the 1921 revolution fascinated him. "My God, what warriors they look, even in old age (few are under 70)! A fierce crowd they must have been in their fighting years. . . . Except for the rifles, the cavalry of Chingis Khan."[38]

There was no Chinese delegation in the reviewing stand and more Russians than Lattimore had ever seen in Mongolia before. Kosygin had the position of greatest eminence and at the big official reception in the evening had "tough" things to say pointed at the Chinese.

A hiatus in Mongol festivities drew some typical Lattimorean sarcasm: "14 July. Bastille Day reception at the French Embassy. Someone less likely to have stormed the Bastille than the French Ambassador I defy anybody to imagine. But then, can any of you recall having met an American Ambassador, to any country, who looked as if he could have served at Valley Forge? Well, one exception: Averell Harriman."[39]

Several days later Lattimore had lunch "with a chap who was in the Party Institute of History, and in that capacity had written a devastating criticism of my Nomads and Commissars. [This] year, by an intermediary, he asked if I would let him come to see me. I said, of course. When he turned up, he said: That review I wrote. Of course, we have to keep the orthodoxy orthodox. But personally, I think you're a very good guy, with a lot of bright ideas. I said, Naturally, we have to keep the record straight. I'm not a Marxist, and never likely to become one. No hard feelings. Since then, we have been very good friends."[40]

Lattimore heard with wonderment the news that Nixon was going to Peking. His first comment on this phenomenon was in a letter of July 22, 1971. He had dined at the French embassy, with three other ambassadors and wives also present.

> As the only non-diplomat, I thought I would be the naughty boy, so I raised the topic of Nixon going on bombing and burning and gassing the hell out of the Indo-Chinese, and Mao saying, "Never mind that, but do drop in for breakfast some day." Got no rise out of this (though all the diplomats here are passionate fishermen), but it did become clear that Nixon-Mao would be talking, in the opinion of everybody but me, principally about Taiwan. I was utterly surprised. I may be 100 degrees disoriented, from having been out of America for a while, but I pontificated to the obviously disbelieving diplomats as follows:
>
> In America, Taiwan is a dead issue. People are bored—not fed up and outraged, as over Indochina. Just bored. There is no "military-industrial complex" committed to Taiwan anymore. . . . under the new deal (not New Deal!) with Japan, the cynical ditching of Taiwan is immaterial. Japan-Okinawa is a much more solid base, because the object now— and there is no material difference between the Rostow and Kissinger versions of amateur Machiavellianism—is no longer the roll-back of China, but setting China and Russia against each other, and for that Japan is better (so these poor dopes think). . . . No, in my opinion the emotional issue in America will no longer be Taiwan, but Indochina.[41]

Lattimore cherished his role as a heretic, which extended even to his contacts with Soviet historians. One of them, Gol'man, had published an analysis of American writing on Mongolia. Lattimore thought Gol'man had been fair except on one dimension. Gol'man made much of the attempts of one "Duke" Larson, an adventurer who had tried to persuade American firms to invest in Mongolia during the pre-Soviet years, with, of course, due dividends for Larson himself. Gol'man called Larson "odious" and treated him as a paradigm capitalist exploiter.

> When Gol'man comes in again I'm going to give it to him hot and strong. I'm going to say, "You accuse me of defending Larson. I wasn't defending him. I was trying to accuse you Russian Marxists, in a mild, polite way. You didn't get the point, so now just sit still while I attack you in a rough, Bolshevik way. You Russian Marxists are falling down on the job. You make a political accusation: The American imperalist-capitalists wanted to dominate the Mongolian market—and you produce one figure, old Franz Larson, who was ridiculous, rather than sinister. That's not good enough. There *were* American interests—and British, and other. A description of their operations and affiliations, plus a clear Marxist economic analysis, would be a valuable contribution to economic history and would interest a lot of people, me included. But you never deliver. Now why don't you get busy?"
>
> Gol'man came in. I was in my bath, reading his book, and as an author he had to acknowledge that that was a compliment. I climbed out, wrapped a towel around myself, and went at it, hammer and tongs, with my criticisms. We had a fine time, and are better friends than ever. I told him about "capitalist-imperialist" business in Mongolia in the 1920's, drawing on personal experience, reminiscences, and remembered hearsay—the gossip of the trade in my time. He was fascinated. He knows about these things only from Marxist theory, and had never met anybody who had actually been engaged in such nefarious doings.[42]

Lattimore's seventy-first birthday, on July 29, seemed to affect him more than his last. He described it as "weird and solitary," even though he had lunch with two of his best Mongol friends and took great interest in the family of Bira, a noted Tibetanist whose wife was originally a physician but became a scholar of Turkish after her children were born. Lattimore was always fascinated by the career choices, and changes, of people in a Communist system. Bira's son, a child prodigy painter, also captivated him. The rest of his birthday was hardly solitary; half a dozen friends called on him to offer many happy returns.

Nonetheless, he did not sleep that night. "It's a sorry business, turning

71, mourning the past and not quite daring to believe that the future can be as bright as its present promise. The Buddhists are right on one thing: it's a terrible fate to be a human being." Yet his fate was not terrible. He was as interested as ever in the peoples and cultures of Central Asia and was contemplating accepting Mongol offers to spend a year in some scenic valley, watching the full cycle of the herding year, recording the life experiences, the songs and legends, the reactions to communism of these formerly nomadic tribes. He confided to Bill Rogers, "It is so tempting. . . . [But it] would never end. My real problem is that I already have so much that may never get on paper, but I have this hunger for more and more knowledge."[43]

He concluded that tempting as a long stay in Mongolia was, he had to first put in at least a year of "book and typewriter work." He would help Urgunge do his *Mongolian Heroes of the Twentieth Century;* do a new edition of his own *Nomads and Commissars;* complete several promised articles; work with Fujiko on the Dilowa memoirs; "go through untold quantities of my unfinished work, and see what I complete, what I turn over to Fujiko, and what we work on together. She's going to have plenty to do when I'm gone. . . . And there's always that *China in History.* And, oh God, my memoirs. Gives me writer's cramp to think of it all."[44]

He got his mind off of it all July 31 when he and Dalai left Ulan Bator for his annual "field trip," this time two full weeks in Hövsgöl Province at the headwaters of the Selenge River. Here Lattimore was back again with herdsmen and hunters, Mongols (and Kazakhs and Reindeer People and other still-distinct tribes) whom he had learned to love and trust forty-five years earlier on the desert road to Turkestan.

Dalai was a master tour arranger. Lattimore observed that when Dalai introduced him to ordinary Mongols, his line was "This old chap is 71. Solid old bastard, isn't he?" But when Dalai went to the authorities in charge of housing, transportation, and the like, his line was "I've got a very frail old chap here. Very distinguished, of course, but very frail. Anything you can do to help me out? Wouldn't like to have anything happen to him while he's in my charge and in your territory."[45] So they got the best of everything. The hotel in Hövsgöl was better than the one in Ulan Bator, as was the food. Lattimore had a ball.

Thirty-nine pages of his diary-letter of July 31, 1971, describe the weeks in Hövsgöl. Seventy-one years to the contrary, living with these friendly, happy, curious people restored his morale, blotted out the pain of Eleanor's death, and eased the worry of coping with his massive scholarly projects when he returned to the West. At each settlement he and Dalai visited, after they learned the lore of the villagers, heard the ancient songs, visited the schools, herds, and cottage industries, they responded to questions: Dalai reciting his experiences as a Mongol diplomat in China, Lattimore describing how he happened to be there and what he was up to. It was a different apologia from the one he presented to Soviet scholars. At their first village,

> about 80 people gathered in a triple ring on the greensward, and I stood in the middle and began: I have travelled a strange road through life to be among you here today, and went right on. There were no intellectuals there except the teacher, so I used very simple language. I told them about that first long Gobi journey when I didn't know any Mongol, about how I first started to learn Mongol and became interested in the politics of Inner Mongolia. I didn't disguise the fact that my friends of those days were regarded as shady and presumptively dangerous characters in Outer Mongolia, but that didn't matter. Their attitude would be: That's the way things were in those times, and that's where he was. And anyhow, he was interested in us Mongols. . . . I went on to tell about being in Ulan Bator in 1944 with Wallace—that always fascinates them, and then about my repeated visits here since 1961, with Eleanor, with David, and by myself, and wound up with due (and genuine) admiration of the progress I have seen in these 10 years. The young people were listening intently, a lot of the older people were wiping their eyes. The sentimentality of the Mongols is winningly simple. When they can tell that you really like them, everything they have is yours.[46]

It would be hard to overstate the therapeutic effect of Lattimore's 1971 stay in Mongolia. When he left for Hungary August 19, his health was good and his spirits high. The rest of 1971 was all downhill.

After the Orientalists' Congress in Hungary, Lattimore spent a week each in Bulgaria and East Berlin and two weeks in Copenhagen; on September 28 he was back in Leeds, teaching the fall term despite his retirement. Among the letters waiting for him was a package from Evelyn Nef with copies of the memorial brochure for Eleanor. It pleased him immensely but brought on renewed anguish.

In early November he flew to the United States, hoping that another try at establishing residence in Virginia would work. It was a vain hope. Despite the help of the Rogers and Evelyn Nef, he could not bring himself to stay in the house that Eleanor planned. Nor could he manage the household routine. His drinking increased, and he wandered between Virginia, New York, and Providence, visiting the Piels, David, and other friends.

By 1971, twenty years had passed since McCarran and his Senate Internal Security Subcommittee set out to pillory Lattimore. A few institutions (besides Harvard) were now overcoming their skittishness about asking the great heretic to lecture. Johns Hopkins was not one of them, but another Baltimore institution, Goucher College, brought him in for a lecture December 9.

At Goucher he was still derogating the conventional wisdom. All the talk of China "coming out of its isolation," he said, was nonsense. "China has diplomatic relations with all kinds of countries. In my opinion they have not been nearly as isolated as Washington." He also dismissed widespread speculation about a full-scale war between the Soviet Union and China. Of course there was great hostility, but the common bond of dedication to Marxist theory made war unlikely. "I think we should understand this, instead of simply sensationalizing frontier clashes." [47]

Lattimore's visit to Goucher produced a long story in the *Baltimore Sun*.[48] Interestingly, the headline was not about his views on world affairs but about his plans to visit China once again. *New York Times* columnist James Reston had been in Peking in August; Chou En-lai told Reston then that Lattimore would be welcome in the People's Republic. Lattimore told the *Sun* reporter that he would probably seek a visa for summer 1972.

Lattimore made his last appearance at the Council on Foreign Relations January 11, 1972. Gerard Piel was there: "His message was to assure his hearers that they were as wrong now about the possibility of successfully playing the China card against the U.S.S.R. as they had been when they fused both powers in a monolithic communist conspiratorial dictatorship. The border questions that divided them and their competition for the territory and loyalty of the frontier peoples, he said, were far outweighed by their shared antipathy to the hegemony of Western capitalism and their fear of the U.S.A." Piel says Lattimore's message was as unwelcome as ever.[49]

By the end of January 1972 Lattimore had come to doubt the viability of establishing his main residence in the United States. With considerable relief he returned to Leeds in early February to spend six weeks on duties he still had as professor emeritus. His report to Bill Rogers on February 22 did not deal with the Leeds routine, however. It was all about his delicate negotiations with the Chinese. Two secretaries of the Chinese chargé d'affaires in London visited Leeds, nominally as guests of the local Society for Anglo-Chinese Understanding. They were presumably interested in the science and Chinese studies departments. Lattimore soon discovered they were more interested in finding out what he would expect were he now to visit the PRC.

He had several objectives: seeing Manchuria, Inner Mongolia, Sinkiang, and Tibet and visiting old friends. And since he was "an old man, no longer able to totter about alone," he needed Fujiko along as a research associate—secretary. The Chinese thought that would be fine. Could Lattimore bring Fujiko along to the consulate in London soon? Yes, she would be in England February 14. He would bring her down to London the twenty-first.

> So we went down. At King's Cross, no need for a taxi. At the ticket barrier, a secretary was waiting for us. Outside, an Embassy—excuse me, a Chargé d'Affaires—car. We're in, I said in Fujiko's ear; we're in. A superb lunch, at exactly the right spaced-out interval between "home cooking" and "fancy feast." Conversation easy, affable. You'd never think the humourless Cultural Revolution had ever occurred. They knew Nixon wanted Pandas, but what on earth were the musk oxen? I explained. If you can do *that* in Chinese, you needn't worry about future conversational traps. Yes, but why, they wanted to know. Well, you wouldn't expect the President of a capitalistic nation not to try a bit of dealing on the side, would you? I asked. This was well received.
>
> Mind you, all this time—it's been going on for nearly two years now—I've never had a written or other direct invitation from China. (And I've never asked for a visa.) Everything has been relayed indirectly, through Ed Snow, a Reston news story, etc. At this lunch, the Chargé said openly, for the first time, that both the Chairman (Mao) and the Premier (Chou En-lai) had expressed a personal interest in my coming.[50]

So the China trip was set. As anticipated, the Mainichi newspapers and Japan Television wanted Lattimore to report for them; Fujiko was to make these arrangements when, at the end of March, she returned to Japan and Lattimore to the United States.

Before Lattimore returned to the United States, an incident occurred that brought out his lingering sensitivity about the inquisition. Henry Steele Commager wrote a letter to the *New York Times*, carried by that paper March 6, 1972, under the heading "To Right a Wrong." Commager noted that the Truman and Eisenhower administrations had "destroyed the careers of two distinguished scholars and public servants, Dr. Robert Oppenheimer and Prof. Owen Lattimore." Presidents Kennedy and Johnson had made apologies and restitution to Oppenheimer. Wasn't it time for Nixon, who had finally seen the merit of the formerly heretical policies advocated by Lattimore, to do the same for him?

Lattimore's answer was carried March 23: "Owen Lattimore Asks: 'To Right What Wrong?' " Lattimore acknowledged Commager's friendly in-

tent and his long service to the cause of academic freedom. But Commager
had accepted too quickly the myth that Lattimore had been done in by the
inquisition.

> It is misleading to say that I "never recovered from the effects of official
> harassment and eventually removed to England, where (I) could carry
> on (my) China studies without interference." During the years in which
> I was under indictment my university in America did not suspend me,
> but put me on leave with full pay. It is true that in America, the articles
> and paid lectures on which I had always relied for supplementary in-
> come became few and far between.
>
> On the other hand, my career internationally was definitely en-
> hanced. I lectured for two half-years at the Sorbonne. I gave a course
> of lectures at the University of Copenhagen and lectured widely in En-
> gland, Scotland, and Wales. My wife and I were invited to Mongolia,
> and this led to a revival of the Mongolian part of my career. The out-
> rageous Department of Justice indictment became an international
> passport.
>
> Finally, the invitation to come to the University of Leeds was any-
> thing but an offer of asylum to "carry on China studies without inter-
> ference." It gave me seven years—the happiest and most productive of
> my academic career—in which to found a completely new Department
> of Chinese Studies, putting into operation my own ideas and unencum-
> bered by the traditions and uncompleted programs that might have been
> problems if I had simply taken over a long-established department.[51]

Lattimore then described the successes of his Leeds program, ending with
a jab at Nixon. "My record from the McCarthy era to the present day
does not need to be prettied up. President Nixon's record of the same
period could do with, and is getting, a lavish application of the cosmetic
art." There was truth in this.

Four days after his letter was carried in the *Times*, Lattimore was back
in New York for the Twenty-fourth Annual Meeting of the Association
for Asian Studies. When the CIA finally condescended to disgorge a minor part of its holdings on Lattimore, it produced a heavily censored report by its China Political and Military Branch on this convention. In the
one page released of an eight-page report, the CIA agent said kind things
about Lattimore, approved his election as first president of the newly formed
Mongolia Society, and even praised a Soviet-produced movie shown at
the convention touting the achievements of the MPR since the revolution.[52]

On April 27, 1972, the most prominent witness against Lattimore, Louis

Budenz, quietly departed this earth. His last years were marred by ill health and the increasingly shrill warnings he issued of the imminent triumph of the Soviet Union over the now-impotent United States. Budenz's last book, *The Bolshevik Invasion of the West,* is embarrassingly fanatical. It was published by the notorious Bookmailer and largely ignored. Margaret Budenz complained, "It never earned a cent of royalties."[53] The Associated Press obituary noted that Budenz's major contributions to the American inquisition had been his accusations against Lattimore and Gerhart Eisler. The story concluded, "In most instances, his accusations were denied and never actually proven in court."[54]

On June 14, 1972, twenty years and three months after SISS released him from its grasp, Lattimore again appeared before a committee of Congress. This time the auspices were friendly: he was appearing before Senators Proxmire, Fulbright, and Javits and Representative Boggs of the Joint Economic Committee. The JEC was holding hearings on economic developments in mainland China. Calling Lattimore as a witness was anomalous; he did not pretend to be an economist, he had not been in China for twenty-seven years, and he could be expected to come up with some abrasive remarks. But there he was, and the senators, even the Republican Javits, treated him with deference.

Proxmire apologized for the "indignities you suffered in the early 1950's" and implied that Lattimore had been "hounded" out of the country. Lattimore responded with the same lecture he had given Commager: he was not hounded out of the country: he went to a better job. Proxmire accepted the correction.

There was little talk of economics. Inevitably the conversation turned to geopolitics. What were the Chinese up to? The Russians? Was China a threat to the United States? Lattimore unburdened himself of his firm opposition to the Vietnam War but made it clear that he was still not promoting communism. "Any country has a sovereign right to do everything it can to limit or restrict the spread of Communism. That is not the real question. The real question is if you adopt methods intended to stop the spread of Communism and find those measures are creating Communists faster than you can kill them, then the sensible thing is to change the policy."[55]

The committee seemed to accept that statement. They asked reasonable questions and got the full exposition of Lattimore's foreign policy views. These views were largely incompatible with the conventional wisdom, but *this* Congress was not on a heresy hunt.

Lattimore moved restlessly from place to place during the spring and summer of 1972. He could not stay in the United States. The Southdown house, without a compatible housekeeper, was impossible. Perhaps Fujiko could have made it work, but she was unwilling to reside steadily in the United States. Lattimore was still drinking heavily. David wanted him to enter a prominent Boston center for treatment of alcoholism and took him to see it, but he reacted negatively and did not check in. He decided he could go on the wagon by himself.[56]

The trip to China was lining up nicely. Fujiko arranged an assignment from Japan Television to film Lattimore's return to China; this project was in addition to reporting for the Mainichi Newspapers. Chinese visas were in order. By the end of July Lattimore had given up on the house in Virginia and decided to rent it out. He would move to Paris. Fujiko could get an apartment near him and would not be tied down as she would have been in Virginia. Lattimore's French was still fluent. The intellectual life in Paris was superior to that of Washington. Paris was also closer to England and Scandinavia. By late August Lattimore was in Paris and had contracted to purchase an apartment there. That done, he and Fujiko were off to China.

On August 29, 1972, twenty-seven years after he was last in China on the Pauley mission, Lattimore returned to Peking. This time it was with VIP status. The New China News Agency reported a dinner given in his honor by the vice president of the Institute of Foreign Affairs.[57] Since neither he nor Fujiko was capable of operating the camera provided by Japan Television, Lattimore asked the Chinese to allow his grandson Michael to accompany them as cameraman. This request was granted; Lattimore sent for Michael to come in a hurry, and he arrived just in time for their trip to Sinkiang.

Despite the ceremony and the nostalgia, Lattimore's reports from China are remarkably low-keyed. In Peking he saw the latest in archeological holdings and was taken on routine tours of factories, schools, and communes. He wrote Bill Rogers, "I don't mind; it helps me to get the feel and mood of people." He met Rewi Alley and George Hatem, both prominent Westerners who had stayed in China after the Communists took over in 1949, and through Hatem he got to see contemporary Chinese medicine close up. This subject he found fascinating. Doctors visiting Peking were, according to Lattimore, "the most unabashedly admiring visitors, and there are a lot of them." Chinese health was indeed vastly improved. One contrast with the old days elicited a bit of excitement from

Lattimore: "the healthy, active, clean children—not one of the majority we used to see with distended bellies, runny noses, inflamed eyes, scabby heads."[58]

The China of 1972 was still not free of the Cultural Revolution. Chou En-lai was ascendant, with Mao's backing, and had managed the Nixon visit of February 1972.[59] But China's quarrel with Russia was at fever heat, and not even Chou's friendship with Lattimore could entirely cancel out the taint of Lattimore's collaboration with Soviet scholars nor the fact that he had been "adopted" by the Mongolian People's Republic.

Furthermore, Lattimore kept asking embarrassing questions, as his grandson Michael remembers: "During the 1972 trip he often inquired, especially during the weeks in Peking, after individuals, mainly Chinese and mainly intellectuals only to be told 'Oh they're doing work in the countryside.' Thus, although I was completely unaware of it myself at the time, he was acutely aware of the ongoing Cultural Revolution, even though the Chinese tried hard to give the impression that the 'revolution' was essentially over. It's to his credit that he was not only not taken in but also not in the least bit hesitant to annoy our hosts with his inquisitiveness."[60] And despite Lattimore's only slightly rusty Chinese, two full-time interpreters were assigned to his party, in addition to the usual politically unsophisticated tour guides.

One consequence of Lattimore's independent ways was that Mao refused to see him. (Chou was very friendly, as will be noted later, but the Great Helmsman remained aloof.) A second consequence was that Lattimore's itinerary was more restricted than he had expected. Michael believes that the restricted itinerary developed out of Lattimore's refusal to

> be had or used. This is genuine. I'm sure we paid for this as we were not only denied Tibet, but also Kashgar, where Owen had been before, and where Joris Ivens was allowed to go while we were only treated to Urumchi and Turfan. Ivens was engaged in making his epic on the emergence of "socialist man" in China. I met him and had several conversations with him and his sound person . . . I was very impressed with them both. However on further reflection I have to hand it to my Grandfather for standing by his principles, especially since he'll never get the credit for doing so he really deserves. After all we could have come out of China with a vastly more salable product in terms of film, photos, and articles had he played the game and had we been able to go to those places.[61]

But they did get to Sinkiang; Reuters noted Lattimore's departure from Peking on September 10, and the *Washington Post* picked up the story. In Urumchi, Kalja, Aksu, and Turfan they were seeing country that Owen and Eleanor had traveled through forty-five years earlier. It was almost unrecognizable. Stone River, a hundred miles west of Urumchi, had been just a marsh when Owen and Eleanor had been there. Now it was restored to its pre-1920s state, with "God knows how many thousand people; a rich agriculture, large herds of animals—and the factories are humming," as Lattimore wrote Bill Rogers. Urumchi, too, had been built up enormously, with Han laborers and management brought in to staff the factories. After two weeks in Sinkiang and Inner Mongolia, Lattimore observed, "Some things make me feel like a dinosaur returning to his ancient mud-bath and finding it's been taken over by a porcelain works." The major exception was Turfan. There the Uighurs were still dominant, the underground irrigation channels functioning as they had for generations, the vines and lattices shading the streets. Lattimore, Michael, and Fujiko feasted under the grape arbors in the nearby valley just as Lattimore and Eleanor had done on their honeymoon. Michael, a budding musician, was captivated by Uighur folk songs.[62]

On October 5 they were back in Peking. Now there was "a pilgrimage to a shrine: the hospital where David was born; the labour room where he was delivered, after 27 hours of agony for Eleanor."[63] To Lattimore's amazement, Dr. Katie Lim, the obstetrician who had attended Eleanor, was still at the hospital. She had survived Japanese occupation, war, Nationalist recovery, and Communist takeover. Now, at seventy years, she was a respected member of the People's Consultative Council and about to visit the United States with a medical group organized by Dr. E. Gray Dimond of the University of Missouri at Kansas City. Dr. Lim was delighted to meet Michael and to have word of the American child (David) she had delivered so many years earlier.

Also during this stay in Peking, Lattimore was taken to visit a "Committee of Housewives" who ran several cottage industries. This group supervised a lock factory, a knitted-wear workshop, and similar operations.

Of course, everybody was prepared for us, but still—instant rapport. Like an old lady from Shantung, 70, who had been a famine refugee in Manchuria. Story of hardship, still-born child, etc. When she heard Eleanor and I had been in Manchuria in those days, and knew something of the conditions, no stopping her. Fujiko and I have been getting a little, let's say satiated, with all the paeans about the Chairman, but when old women like this express their liberation, their happiness after toil and hardship, their secure old age in a clean two-room apartment with clean bedding and "look, a closet all my own," in terms of what the Chairman did for them, we just about break down and cry. It's so different from the incantations of the intellectuals.[64]

But the high point of their Peking stay was dinner with Chou. This event was not announced in advance. Late one afternoon Lattimore, who was writing in his hotel room, was suddenly told to get ready to dine with the premier. The atmosphere was friendly, and Chou greeted Lattimore and his party effusively; nonetheless, secretaries were present to take down every word. Chou spoke only through an interpreter, who had been a classmate of David Lattimore at Harvard. Of course Chou understood every word of English, but his official position had to be formal, and Lattimore did not break protocol except late in the evening, when he slipped occasionally into Chinese.

One of Chou's first comments was to the effect that "your grandson is very feminine looking [Michael had long hair] and if I didn't know otherwise I might think he was a woman." Michael recalls, "I don't think Owen knew quite how to reply to this, and he knew what had been said well before I did, but I jumped right in and gave my prepared answer, since I had been reading up on Chou, which was that long hair for us American youth was a political statement just as it had been a political statement for Chou at one time to cut off his long pig tail. Chou really appreciated this, whether for its cheekiness or because it showed him I knew a little bit more about him than he thought. Anyway he laughed, and after that we got along famously."[65]

The serious conversation was dominated by Chou's long list of grievances against the Russians. Chou listed all the agreements with Russia, going back to the czars, that the Chinese had lived up to but the Russians had not. Lattimore did not want to hear this diatribe but he listened sympathetically. There were lighter moments in the conversation. The diners were liberally supplied with mao-t'ai, and Michael asked Chou about the report that on the Long March the Communists had burned down all the distilleries. " 'Yes,' Chou replied, 'it is true that I ordered the distilleries closed down' (he wouldn't admit to actually burning them) 'but first we confiscated all the liquor.' He then went on to recount that the Red Army had been required to cross a river, so he had himself ensconced up on a cliff where he could watch the crossing, a process which took about eight hours. While this was going on, according to Chou he was enjoying some of the confiscated product, 'but we weren't drinking it out of those puny little glasses like you're doing because all we had there were big tin cups.' This is a tall tale if I've ever heard one."[66]

Pictures were taken at the dinner with Chou and appeared with an account of the event on the front pages of Peking newspapers.

After two weeks in Peking, Lattimore and his party toured Manchuria, Nanking, and Shanghai. Lattimore wrote little about these travels. All the Chinese officials with whom he talked expounded vigorously their grievances against the Soviet Union. In Dairen, Lattimore was taken down in the deep air-raid shelters; had there been no other convincing evidence that Chinese fear of the Russians was profound, these shelters would have established it. By the end of October, Lattimore was ready to leave China. He canceled visits to Hangchow and other places; he and Fujiko entrained for Mongolia October 27. Michael went to Tokyo with his film.

Lattimore's unease in China shows clearly in a letter to Bill Rogers: "When we were at last across the frontier and trundling along toward Ulan Bator, Fujiko and I looked at each other and it was a 'now we're home' look. I just don't know how to say it, but there's always that shade of difference between Chinese and Mongols. Everywhere in China people were wonderful to us, and it was genuine, not put on. But always, somehow, however faint, that touch of condescension—'how tolerant we are, we Chinese, to treat you as people, and not rub it in that you're barbarians.' The Russians have their own form of that, too. But with the Mongols, you're not being 'admitted'—you're there."[67]

Two weeks in Ulan Bator were predictably glorious. There was "a marvellous dinner with Shirendyb," much book buying and seeing old friends, and a new collection of folk songs taped by a former professor who had been exiled by the Party but was now rehabilitated. Lattimore's letters as usual described the state of the agricultural economy and how the Mongols were preparing to compensate for a bad hay crop that year by utilizing old herdsman lore—whereas the Chinese were "relying on the Thought of Chairman Mao."[68]

Lattimore wanted to introduce Fujiko to Okladnikov after their Mongolian stay. Unfortunately, Okladnikov was in Moscow and going after that to Hungary; his itinerary meant an unplanned trip to Moscow for Lattimore and Fujiko. Lattimore's report on their Moscow stay was ambivalent. The good news was that he could have a give-and-take, seminar-type discussion in Russia. Such discussion had not been possible in China. Counterbalancing this, Muscovite food and manners were atrocious. Seeing Okladnikov was worthwhile, but they were glad to leave for Tokyo. "Food and manners much better on the Aeroflot flight to Japan. International competition. Something to be said for it."[69]

In Tokyo on November 19, Lattimore began work on his stories for Mainichi. Mainichi decided to publish his commentaries in a special New Year's supplement and asked him to write a half-page introduction to "hook people's interest" and "show them I'd been around for a while."

> So I began: "Freshly severed human heads were nailed to the telephone poles of Peking." That ought to hook them, I thought. Then, to show I've been around for a while, I went on: "That is one of my childhood memories, from Peking in the winter of 1911–12."
>
> I proudly brought it in. Fujiko ascended to the ceiling in a puff of steam. You can't do that! Not in Japan, in a New Year's Special Issue! People would think it a bad omen, and simply throw the whole paper away! So . . . whole thing to do again. (Ellipsis in original.)[70]

There was much entertainment by Mainichi and Japan Television, interminable and unsatisfactory editing of Michael's film, renewed discussions with Fujiko's intellectual friends. On December 11, 1972, Lattimore boarded a plane for Washington, to pack his belongings once again.

CHAPTER THIRTY-ONE

Paris

Christmas 1972 was melancholy. John Carter Vincent had died just before Lattimore left Japan, and giving up the house in Virginia was traumatic. It was to have been his final residence. Everything he had taken to Leeds in 1963 and accumulated since then was now in Southdown; it all had to be reclassified: some furniture and books to Paris, other furniture and books into storage, some furniture to be left in the house. He sorted and packed during most of December, spent Christmas with David and family, then finished the packing.

In February 1973 Lattimore moved in to his flat on the rue Danton in Levallois Perret, a Paris suburb. The flat was sparsely furnished and had no telephone. Mornings he worked on scholarly materials until Fujiko came, then they discussed the day's agenda, had lunch, and wrote until dark. Afternoons he devoted largely to the "incredible number" of necessary letters. Evenings he spent reading in bed.[1]

His furniture and books arrived from the United States in early April. All was then "pandemonium." It took weeks to get bookcases installed and filled and housewares unpacked. Getting his materials organized in such small space was agonizing.[2]

During his first month in Paris Lattimore received another letter from Nyman/Bogolepov in Switzerland. This letter does not survive, nor does Lattimore's answer, which he said was noncommittal about Nyman's publishing ambition. Noncommittal Lattimore may have been, but Nyman took his answer as encouragement and wrote Lattimore again on April 10, 1973. This letter is still in Lattimore's files. (I have not tampered with Nyman's tortured English.)

Dear Professor:

It was a surprise of my life, I would say, to get your letter—and
especially such a friendly one. I know that I had contributed to your
ordeal by trial although this was far from being my intention or
motive. Please believe me that I deeply regret this. Now when we
both are not too far from leaving this world when cold war situation
forces people to say and to act often in contradiction to their inner-
most feelings and intentions, I hope we may consider our relations
in a more detached and philosophical mood and to try to repair
what can be repaired. . . .

In my vain efforts to find a Western publisher for my critical
evaluation of the Western policies toward my country—both before
and after revolution, I met with several occasions when some dark
hand intervened in order to prevent the publications of my memoirs
in which, besides general critical attitude toward the Western politics and institutions, first of all of the CIA, I expose the crime committed in the West toward Soviet Russian exiles which otherwise
than a genocide I cannot qualify. Only recently, one British publisher retracted from a written contract and met with a silence all
my requests to give reasons. This may explain why I became so
suspiceous toward vague offers. In my reply to your lawyer [Ny-
man had contacted Arnold and Porter, but the firm has no surviving
record], while accepting with a grateful amazement your willingness to read my memoirs, I noted that I wish I could have a more
formal promise to assist me with the publication—if the text would
meet your endorsement.

I presume that whatever your own views, you would approach
my critical attitude just as a human document that reflects the
impressions of a modern Russian intellectual who—whatever the
attitude of Soviet bureaucrats remains a loyal Soviet citizen.

The main question is however whether you might associate
yourself somehow with my testimony about my "testimony" before the US Senate in which I had to say about you what the circumstances beyond my will forced me to say. You certainly noted
that I refused to say what was demanded from me, namely that you
were a Soviet agent—and I paid dearly for this refusal!

Briefly, I did this because there was no other way for me to
intervene against the policies of the preventive war that was then in
full preparation and of which the attitude toward the Maoist China
had been a main component. In those times I was really scared and
had no other choice in my plans to oppose the menace of a new
war. As a former member of the CP and a high Soviet official I was
barred from coming to the States as a DP [displaced person] immigrant. There was but one way to go to your country and to try to
divert the furies of the war-mongering from the external adventure
toward the home "traitors" from the liberal Establishment, to support the views of the Tafts and the Maccartys that enemy is not

outside but inside the USA; this was the more logical as the liberals of those days from the supporters of the Truman administration (Marschall and Acheson, Clark and Forrestal) were for an attack upon Soviet Russia, whereas Taft represented the views of isolationists with his idea of the Fortress America. Thus, it remained to me to follow the maxim of Machiavelli that one can serve his country con gloria e con ignomia. It was not easy for me to do. And also I was not a free man but a humble, defenceless DP already in the claws of the CIA, as all other Soviet prisoners of the West whom were hypocrticlally called as those who "choosed freedom." . . .

This forced my participation in the attack upon you, this attack, as I was told openly by my exploiters in Washington, being directed merely through Lattimore against Truman, Acheson, Marshall. Indeed, their motives were quite different from mines; they wanted to come to power to continue the preparation of the preventive war. But I believed that Taft as president would stick merely to his conception of the Fortress and thus make me their bed fellow.

I believe you might understand now better my reasons. What trouble me however is the fact that the Nixon administration returned to the conception of the alliance with Mao and against the USSR. This may look as a vindication of your views, and makes my explanations more difficult for I do not want to associate you with the sinister plans of the US warmongers who try again the carrot while keeping the big stick behind their backs. In the whole, it is the single point on which we have to reach some understanding. The rest of the manuscript dealing with my struggle against the enslavement of the CIA and revelations of the criminal attitudes in the West against the Soviet exiles, as well as my views of American policies, press, Congress e,t.c. certainly, if not fully shared, might well be accepted by you as my personal impressions.

Sincerely, yours I. Nyman[3]

Incredible. Here was the confused but unconstrained confession of the witness who, judging by the SISS report, was regarded by McCarran as giving the most incriminating testimony against Lattimore. Nyman says nothing about having testified before the grand jury; we do not know whether he was called.

As Lattimore later recalled, he was by then convinced that Nyman was sincere and genuinely contrite, not fronting for anybody. But he was clearly a tortured soul. Lattimore did not respond to the letter immediately: "Sometime later I was going to Switzerland anyway, so I wrote him and said I was coming, would he make an appointment. The letter came back from the Swiss post office 'Addressee left for Sweden leaving no forwarding address,' which would very likely mean that he had gone to Sweden on his—that he had got the Soviets to reaccept him." Perhaps. But we will never know.[4]

Lattimore went to Ulan Bator in early May 1973 for a congress on the role of nomadism in Central Asia. At the same time Britain's Granada Television wanted to do a documentary on Mongolia and needed Lattimore as a consultant to smooth the way with Mongol authorities. He made a quick trip to London to consult with Granada before he left for Ulan Bator on May 4.

Arriving in Ulan Bator, Lattimore had three hours of rest before going to

> a reception by Shirendyb, the President of the Academy . . . as the only foreign member of the Academy, I always get a place of honour at his left hand. The reception was copiously irrigated. I had thought I was going to be able to ride past on the wagon, because Shirendyb, an old drinking companion, has been on the wagon. No luck. A man in Germany sent him a new German concoction that has "cleaned out his old blood vessels and opened new ones," so that he no longer has high blood pressure. So he has jumped off the wagon. I have descended only cautiously, one foot at a time, and playing the old Russian tricks of pretending to drink "bottoms up" when you only take a sip.[5]

The congress was delightful, with seventy participants from all over the world. Lattimore's paper, "Some Problems of Periodisation in Nomadic History," was well received. Two weeks of meetings, concerts, interviews, and visits to the countryside went by like a flash. On May 19, after a three-day stopover in Moscow, he was back in Paris.

His flat in Levallois Perret was now functional, and he again set to work on the mountain of letters and scholarly projects that had accumulated. But he could not settle down; that summer he went to England several times. He had things to do at Leeds and wanted to visit Rosemary Carruthers, the widow of British explorer Douglas Carruthers, who had helped Lattimore in 1929 when he came to England after his first book was written. Rosemary invited Lattimore to visit in Norfolk and look through her late husband's travel diaries and photographs. He and Rosemary got along well, and she invited him to return anytime he wanted to relax in the Norfolk countryside.

In November 1973 he flew to the United States. One of his missions was to establish a foundation to promote Mongol studies. With the Barrett bequest and money that had been left to Eleanor by a wealthy aunt, he now felt that he could establish a fund for scholarly purposes. Arnold and Porter were still his attorneys, and over Thanksgiving he arranged the details with them.

Back to Paris in December for a month, then again to England. He now contemplated spending some time in Leeds and bought a small house there within walking distance of the university. He told Bill Rogers that it would be perfect should he or Fujiko want to spend a whole term there.[6]

By January 1974 Granada Television was ready to send one of its producers, Brian Moser, and Lattimore to Mongolia to begin talks with Montsame, the Mongolian news agency that would control arrangements for the documentary. Lattimore and Moser flew to Ulan Bator January 23.

Lattimore found that in his new capacity, as adviser to a commercial organization in Mongolia on business, the rules had changed. When he was in Mongolia as a scholar, the Academy provided a car; Granada had to rent one. "Brian and I, to show that we are not capitalists who are *that* rich, walk to whatever we can reach on foot." Negotiations with Montsame went slowly. The Mongols wanted Granada to pay a flat fee for the privilege of filming; Moser said they had never paid such a fee and couldn't now. Montsame replied that Japan Television had paid such a fee. Moser wouldn't budge. Several times it seemed as if negotiations had broken down completely, but each side left a loophole somewhere, and talks would resume.[7]

Lattimore vowed never to undertake another business engagement in Mongolia. Few of his academic friends came around to see him. He observed, "In these socialist countries your manner of earning a living—I suppose one could try to be witty and say your 'mode of production'— puts you in an identifiable compartment. From this there are channels up and down, to higher and lower compartments in the same hierarchy, but much less definite cross-channels."[8] On this trip Lattimore was in the television compartment of the Mongolian bureaucracy, and many of his academic friends were wary of intruding.

Granada wanted to film the daily life of at least two families in a rural village, preferably in the Altai Mountains. Moser was to do a reconnaissance of several villages and work out in detail what they would film. When the scenario was agreeable to the village authorities, to Montsame, and to Granada, a camera crew would come out from London. It took several weeks for Montsame to agree to the details of Moser's reconnaissance trip; finally on February 6, 1974, Moser, Lattimore, and two Montsame men flew to the Altai and took a truck to a village collective called Biger.

The chairman of the collective was not happy with Granada's proposal. Filming the daily routine of his families would be an invasion of their privacy. He was willing to allow Granada to film what Moser called "a string of picture post cards," for which a week would be enough. Moser thought his project would take three to four weeks. Lattimore, as the only person involved who knew Mongol folkways as well as British practices, mediated as best he could. After five days satisfactory arrangements were tentatively reached, and the Granada party flew back to Ulan Bator.[9] Lattimore left in mid-February 1974 for Paris, Moser for London.

While Lattimore was in Mongolia, the Gang of Four in Peking, headed by Chiang Ch'ing, Mao's wife, stepped up their attack on Lin Piao and Confucius. This conflict had started in 1973; now, as Joseph Lelyveld of the *New York Times* put it, they were addressing their "sharpest polemics" to foreigners visiting China since "ping-pong diplomacy" began. In a pamphlet denouncing Confucius, "The scholar Owen Lattimore is castigated as 'an American reactionary historian' and 'an international spy' on the basis of a bland allusion to the Sage in one of his books. Professor Lattimore was one of the first Americans invited to return to China in the summer of 1971 by Premier Chou En-lai when relations between the two countries started to warm."[10]

Was Chou vulnerable as a "revisionist"? A dispatch from John Burns noted, "After several years of pragmatism and calm, China is returning to the more militant attitudes characteristic of the Cultural Revolution— and everyone from the elevator operator who is wearing his Mao badge again to the soldier outside the diplomatic compound who no longer returns a friendly smile is falling into step."[11]

Lattimore was disturbed. His standing in China was now less important to him than his ties with the Mongolian People's Republic, but he still wanted to maintain access to China. Gradually word filtered out to him after discreet inquiries: the Gang of Four would not prevail, and no one in China really thought he was an "international spy." So far as he was able to tell, the incident blew over with no lasting effects.

After short visits to Paris and Leeds, Lattimore arrived in Boston April 1, 1974, for the annual meeting of the Association for Asian Studies and a related session of the Mongolia Society. The CIA monitored this session, noting that Lattimore was failing in health, apparently unable to stand for more than a few minutes without support. The CIA also thought his popularity with Asian scholars had declined.[12]

For the rest of April 1974 and all of May, Lattimore was in constant motion. To England, to inspect his Leeds house and arrange for someone to take care of the furniture he was shipping from Virginia. To Paris, where he was preparing to move to a new flat with a telephone. All the while, he was waiting for a call from Granada announcing departure for Ulan Bator with the film crew.[13]

From Paris, Lattimore made his first major probe for funds to extend the work of the Lattimore Institute of Mongolian Studies. This was a long letter on April 15 to Cyrus S. Eaton. Eaton had invited Lattimore to one of the Pugwash conferences, at which prominent Soviet bloc and Western scholars and businessmen discussed ways to moderate the cold war. Lattimore had then just started at Leeds and could not attend. Now Mongol studies were firmly established in the West; wouldn't Eaton like to underwrite them? Especially at Leeds, whose program the Mongols most admire? Eaton was not interested.[14]

Not until June 6 did the call come from Granada; the MPR was ready for filming. This trip to Mongolia was disillusioning. Lattimore was now exposed to Montsame bureaucrats who had been trained in the propaganda tradition of the Soviet Union. Only the best new buildings and machinery could be filmed; people in factories, farms, and stores must have their best clothes on; no spontaneous targets of opportunity could be filmed. Lattimore described one irritating incident in a diary-letter of July 7:

> We were allowed to photograph the inside of a bookstore. When we got there, the shop was jammed with specially recruited people in their best, brightest, neatest clothes. There were so many you couldn't swing a camera, and some had to be asked to leave. When the film crew left, the "extras" left too. I stayed behind to buy books. The manager and personnel were terribly pleased about this. They even took me to their store-rooms at the back to make sure I didn't miss anything I might want. I got some interesting stuff, including an Art Buchwald collection translated into Mongol. (I'll send it to him.) By the time I got back into the front of the shop, it had filled again, this time with genuine customers. As in any bookstore in Mongolia, most of them were in their working clothes, some a bit shabby. Now the truth about Mongolia is that it is nearly 100% literate, people have a hunger for books, and there is a steady supply of books to satisfy the hunger. Which picture would do the most for Mongolia, abroad: the true picture of the people who really buy books, or the faked picture of dressed-up people pretending to buy books?[15]

Lattimore got a nice fee as consultant to the project, and more was to come during a winter filming session, but he swore he would never do it again.[16]

Filming was over by the first of July, and Lattimore resumed his scholarly role. Now he saw many of his old friends, dined at the embassies, attended National Day celebrations, made plans for the future with Academy people and the rector of the university. After talking to a Chinese diplomat at one of the parties, he was moved to rare sarcasm about the personality cult of the Great Helmsman: "It sometimes seems to me that Maoists believe that to make cows produce milk, and hens lay eggs, all you have to do is read the Little Red Book."[17]

After Mongolia, the rest of 1974 was constant movement: Denmark, London, Norfolk, Cambridge, Leeds, Paris, Languedoc, New York, Baltimore, Washington. By a considerable margin, Lattimore spent less time in Paris that year than elsewhere. The scholarly production of his partnership with Fujiko was hardly under way.[18]

In early January 1975 Lattimore was in London conferring with Granada; he then spent a relaxing weekend with Rosemary Carruthers in Norfolk. Even there work went with him. As he told David, he wrote a long review of *The Horse in Fifty Thousand Years of Civilisation* for the *Times Literary Supplement*, noting that the book was interesting, but weak on the importance of cavalry in Asia.[19]

After his visit with Rosemary, Lattimore and Brian Moser left for Mongolia, arriving January 22. Now he had to deal with Montsame again, and his adjectives this time were more colorful than those of the previous summer. He put some prime invective in a letter to David. By February 5 Montsame had cleared the winter shooting script and the Granada party was off to the Altai. At Biger, where the head man of the collective had previously been obstreperous, things were now friendly. Granada got the desired shots of schools, winter farm operations, family celebrations of the lunar new year, and a spectacular valley opening into the high mountains. The Granada expedition wound up with more cordiality than Lattimore had expected, and everybody got back to England by the end of February.[20]

Lattimore made the rounds of London, Norfolk, and Leeds, staying in his new Leeds house until mid-April. There he claimed to catch up on the "urgent" mail, but he still felt snowed under by all his obligations. He was lecturing some at Leeds and went to London several times to see rushes of the Granada film. He was himself in much of the footage:

a chastening experience for me to see and hear. God never designed me to be a television star.

So Granada's got under its wing, tra-la,
A most unattractive old thing, tra-la,
With a caricature of a face.

So for television, let Kenneth Clark have it.[21]

Lecturing was still his favorite activity. Fairbank had him at Harvard that spring. He worked into his presentation at the Harvard Faculty Club on May 28, 1975, many of the themes he had developed during his last five years of travel in Siberia and Mongolia but had not yet been able to turn into books. His title was "Asia from the Landward Side." The major thrust was that Western scholars had dealt with China almost exclusively by considering the interaction of Chinese and foreigners along the China coast. He sought to emphasize the significance to China of contact with people spreading eastward from the civilizations of the Middle East, bringing with them languages, trading practices, and agricultural systems that had strongly influenced China. Even Chinese historians tended to overlook the importance of cultural influences from the West; he found an "obsessive assumption" that all Central Asian cultures were heavily influenced by China, but not the other way around. He referred to the rich holdings of the library at Ulan-Ude, in the Buryat Soviet Socialist Republic, written by political exiles sent to Siberia by the czars but allowed to continue their intellectual life. Buryatia had irrigated agriculture very early, using methods derived from Turkic rather than Chinese models. Siberia was not a cultural desert, Central Asian peoples were not primitives, and Mongols were not marauding savages.[22]

Inevitably, in the question period Lattimore was grilled about Mongolia:

Herbert Levin asked Mr. Lattimore for his comments on contemporary thinking in Mongolia about relations with other countries. Mr. Lattimore made three points. First, the Mongols attribute their survival as a nation to their alliance with the Soviet Union. They greatly resent the allegation that they are a Soviet satellite. When Mr. Lattimore used that word to refer to Mongolia in the 1930's, he intended no pejorative meaning. Later the term became pejorative, making the Mongols upset. Even today, the idea is popular that Mongolia is squeezed between two giants. Since the Mongols are on one side, however, they do not feel squeezed.

Secondly, the Mongols are proud of their national independence. They take part in the United Nations and UNESCO, and bitterly resent the State Department attitude that the Soviet Union controls Mongolia.

Recently the Mongols published a book on "Mao and the Maoists." It criticizes the Chinese minority policies, but is restrained in comparison with the Chinese language used to describe the Mongols as "the new serfs of the new Tsars."

Finally, the Mongols understand China better than China understands Mongolia. The weak understand the strong.[23]

The rest of the summer of 1975 Lattimore spent visiting in the United States. Brown University awarded him an Ll.D. on June second, and in August he went to California, lecturing at Berkeley, where he had lunch with old friends Jack Service and Philip Lilienthal. He also attended the International Congress of the Historical Sciences in San Francisco. This was an important milestone: for the first time a delegation of Mongol scholars attended a conference in the United States. Feeling so deeply indebted for the hospitality shown him in Ulan Bator, Lattimore tried hard to see that the Mongols had an easy time of it. Bira and Natsagdorj, friends of his, and a younger historian, Isjants, made up the Mongol delegation. After the congress Lattimore accompanied the Mongols on a visit to Indiana University, Bloomington, the foremost center of Mongol studies in the United States. John Hangin, one of the two Mongols Lattimore had brought to Baltimore in 1948, was a professor at Indiana. Then the party went on to New York, where Lattimore put the Mongols in touch with various foundations he hoped would support cultural exchanges when the United States finally recognized the MPR.[24]

In late 1975 Lattimore seemed to control his urge to travel. He spent several months in Leeds, mostly working with Urgunge Onon on translations. The first three months of 1976 he stayed put in Paris, working with Fujiko on the Dilowa's memoirs and tape-recording recollections of his earlier life in China and the United States. He actually passed up an opportunity to work for American Express, helping them "get started doing business in Mongolia."[25]

Fujiko was working on the history of a Japanese adventurer–intelligence agent named Kodama, who had profited from contacts with high-ranking Mongols. As Lattimore heard about this kind of commerce, he reflected, "It makes me look back on my own life, crestfallen. I could have worked that racket. The timing would have been right, too. By the McCarthy era I would have been in the CIA and shielded as a target; by the time the investigations of the CIA came along, I would have been retired and living on a much fatter pension than I draw now."[26] What Lattimore did not add to this bit of persiflage, but should have, was "And I would have been miserable."

Even when Lattimore managed to stay in one place long enough to settle into a work routine, fame stood in the way of scholarly accomplishment. He wrote Gerard Piel February 20, 1976: "In the afternoon post, a letter from a learned man in England who wants to know about trypanosomiasis in camels. By the way he writes, he's a nice chap, so I'll have to answer, but how many hours of work will it mean? . . . I could do a full 8-hour day, just on letters, because too often answering a letter doesn't deal with the matter—it starts a correspondence. I can't even dictate on tape and send out for typing: too much slow spelling out of foreign words. Trypanosomiasis is bad enough, but when you get to the Mongol vocabulary of the disease . . ." (ellipses in original).[27]

Even when relatively stationary, Lattimore would put off working on his major projects because he was so incurably interested in everybody he met and spent much time drawing out their life histories. Asian caravan men, Chinese merchants and peasants, diplomats of all countries, fellow passengers on planes and trains, the concierge of his Paris apartment building, surgeons, nurses, and charwomen in a hospital—Lattimore "interviewed" them all. In the years after Eleanor's death, when he wrote his diary-letters to Bill Rogers or his son David, he filled more space with biographical vignettes than with all other subjects.

He attributed his acquaintance with so many languages to this curiosity about people: "My mother once—in my hearing—explained to a visitor: 'My husband and my son Richmond are both scholars. Owen isn't a scholar, but he travels a lot and wherever he goes he picks up a bit of the language, because he just can't bear not talking to people.'"[28] In some ways this talk contributed to his understanding of the contemporary world and its citizens; it also meant he was not concentrating on his major projects. Had Eleanor lived longer, there would have been fewer miniature biographies and more scholarly projects.

One of the major items on Lattimore's agenda was a translation into English of a Mongol herdsman's manual by Sambuu, one of the founders of the Mongolian People's Republic who befriended Choibalsan and rose to a high rank in the MPR hierarchy. Sambuu's book developed out of lectures on herdsmanship. It was colloquial yet scientific; Lattimore said he wanted to preserve its color and practicality. He told Gerard Piel, "As a Mongol said to me, when you read Sambuu, you can smell the scent of a cowdung fire. I want to keep that."[29] The publishing house affiliated with Piel's *Scientific American* was interested in the Sambuu translation. Lattimore worked at it for ten years, checking his translation with Mongol scholars, seeking the most authoritative version of each chapter from among several editions of Sambuu, but ultimately bogging down in the attempt to get Linnaean names for the many flora mentioned in the book.

After congressional passage of the 1975 amendments to the Freedom of Information Act, Lattimore began to consider requesting his government files. Arnold and Porter advised him against this project: "Too expensive and you won't get the juicy stuff."[30] Lattimore decided in April 1976 not to try.

Lattimore still spent time at Leeds, tutoring promising students in Mongol and consulting with the Department of Chinese Studies, for which he still felt some responsibility. And he began to spend vacation periods with Rosemary Carruthers in Norfolk, where he found cutting and splitting firewood beneficial for an ailing back. In 1976 he spent mid-April to mid-May in England. The rest of the year he was peripatetic: a month in Mongolia, a holiday in the south of France, a conference in Switzerland, another month in England, conferences in Bonn and Copenhagen.

January 14, 1977, was a big day. He wrote exultantly to Gerard Piel, enclosing the last chapters of the Sambuu translation: "Lift up your eyes unto the Lord with proper amazement."[31] He and Fujiko had also completed the Dilowa's memoirs and mailed them to Harrassowitz, the publisher, in Wiesbaden. Transliteration of Mongol was now governed by new rules, and when this book finally came out in 1982, "Dilowa Hutukhtu" had become "Diluv Khutagt."

Michigan State University lured Lattimore back to the United States in February 1977 to give the concluding talk at a conference on Soviet frontiers in Asia. He spent six weeks in America and discovered that he was once again salable to academic audiences: Colgate, Michigan, Illinois, Chicago, Pittsburgh. One outcome of these visits was a change in his attitude toward applying for his government files. No one remembers exactly how this decision came about, but on June 22, 1977, Bill Rogers wrote the FBI and the CIA requesting Lattimore's files under the Freedom of Information Act and the Privacy Act. The CIA was the first to reply, on June 30: "We are processing your request and will provide you with the results under the Privacy Act as soon as possible."[32] As soon as possible turned out to be exactly nine years later, July 21, 1986. The CIA never acknowledged Lattimore's claim under the Freedom of Information Act; they did recognize Privacy Act rights, but the restrictive provisions of that act enabled them to ignore the vast bulk of their Lattimore holdings. The FBI was much faster, and documents from the bureau began appearing within a year. Lattimore asked me to screen them for him, using what I needed for articles about events in which he was involved and sending copies of salient items to him in Paris.

Lattimore did not get to Mongolia in 1977; it was the first year he had missed in a decade. He shuttled for the rest of the year between Paris, Leeds, Norfolk, and London, with side trips to Copenhagen, Oxford, and Switzerland. He wrote the Piels on April 11, "It's been hard to settle down. Travelling around and talking to people was easy; getting out books, references and typewriter is WORK." [33] He bemoaned the lack of a secretary but never got around to hiring one, which would have cut into his travel funds. However, he did get several chapters of an autobiography written. Lattimore spent the Christmas season of 1977 in Switzerland and visited Lois Snow (Edgar Snow had died in 1972), who had delightful tales about her recent visit to China.

By April 22, 1978, Lattimore was back in Mongolia. He wrote David that his main purpose in being there was to check his translation of Sambuu, which of course he did; but visiting old friends occupied more of his time. In his twenty-eight page diary-letter beginning April 25 and running through May 6, most of his minibiographies are of sons and daughters of Mongol scholars he had known for years. Career choices always fascinated Lattimore. He was especially pleased that Dalai was having a book translated into Russian, for which Dalai would get the Russian equivalent of Ph.D. [34]

From John Gibbens, the first Leeds student Lattimore had picked to study in Ulan Bator, Lattimore learned that the MPR was now troubled with juvenile delinquency. Gibbens said he "thinks it begins with preteen agers, coming home from school before either parent is home from work. Idle and bored, they get into gangs, vandalize, fight, steal." This was one of the dangers of rapid urbanization that Lattimore had not before considered. The Mongols were working hard to counter it; Gibbens was hoping to learn from them, since he felt that the Mongol methods were effective. [35]

Much of Lattimore's 1978 letter was about the ethnohistory of the Mongols, a subject he pursued now with even more enthusiasm than he had shown for "China in History." He was absolutely convinced that the Mongol conquests were not just a product of "bloody-mindedness" but a reaction to oppression by conquerors from older centers of civilization. He and Dalai discussed this hypothesis endlessly.

Lattimore had a long interview with the *Izvestia* correspondent for Mongolia and North Korea; as usual, he learned as much about the correspondent as the correspondent did about him. During this interview Lattimore came up with a new formulation to explain Chiang Kai-shek's fall: "he had one foot in the past and one in the present (the war-time present) and tripped over himself because he couldn't get either foot into the future." The *Izvestia* man had interesting stories about the alienation of children of Siberian minorities, such as the Eskimos and Yakuts, who were put into boarding schools where they learned Russian and forgot their parents' tongue.

On May 1 Lattimore watched the May Day parade. There were no military units. It was the first such celebration Lattimore had seen where there were few all-Russian units; Russians were "mingled in with the Mongols." He left Ulan Bator on May 4, carrying with him to Paris yet another cache of scholarly materials and another storehouse of poignant memories.

In Paris he found the first gleanings from his FBI file, the papers showing that the bureau had begun full-scale surveillance of him after Barmine's accusations in 1949. This discovery stimulated another effort on his autobiography, but he could not settle down to it for any length of time. And he had to finish a paper, "Marxism and Nationalism in Mongolia," for a December conference. He wrote Bill Rogers on August 21, 1978, "As you know, it was the McCarthy/McCarran accusations that principally aroused my interest in Marxism, but I have followed up the interest in only a desultory way, always with the feeling that it's too late in life to master all *that*. However, just a couple of days ago, having run out of elevated discourse in print like Time, Newsweek, New Statesman, Economist, I got off a shelf, for bedside reading, a volume of Marx-Engels correspondence that I must have acquired in the 1950s but had never read." Here Lattimore found a critique of Ricardo's theory of rent that fit very closely his own 1940 analysis of agricultural productivity in China. "Does that make me a marxiste gentilhomme?" he asked Rogers.

Several months in France and he was restless—so back to England. He spent most of his time with Rosemary Carruthers in Norfolk. By October 1978 he and Rosemary had decided to marry.[36] Her house in Norfolk was small, so they looked for a larger place. He would sell the house in Leeds, but moving to England from France would be expensive. Rutgers University invited him to teach there winter term 1979 at a good salary. He accepted the offer, hoping that Rosemary would come with him. She was reluctant. He stayed with her through the Christmas holidays then went to New York to stay with the Piels. He commuted from there to Rutgers.

The undergraduates he faced at Rutgers and the University of Pittsburgh during Rutgers' spring break were a quite different breed from the Asian specialists he had taught at Leeds. Lattimore took them in stride. At seventy-nine he realized the dangers of living in the past and took special pains to relate the turmoil of ancient Central Asia to the contemporary Middle East, Cambodia, Chile, and other trouble spots. One of the liabilities he saw coming from the McCarthy period was fear of anyone who could be termed controversial; this fear caused the hiring of only "safe" and hence second-rate public servants. These second-raters were now in control at the State Department and elsewhere in the bureaucracy. No wonder they did not understand what was really going on in Iran, Southeast Asia, and so on.[37] Undergraduates of 1979 could understand this criticism.

Shortly before Lattimore finished his tour in the United States, the American Society of Newspaper Editors, meeting in New York, invited him to attend a discussion of Asia. When it came his turn to speak, according to the *UPI Reporter*, "the meeting room became deathly still." He explained how he and others who knew the Chinese Communists were not tools of the Kremlin were vilified and persecuted in the 1950s. When someone asked him why no one would listen at the time, he replied, "Because it did not fit the conventional wisdom." The *UPI Reporter* noted that there was "the barest trace of bitterness in his words."[38]

In June 1979, when he returned to England, Rosemary was having second thoughts about marriage. She was happy to have Lattimore's company, and he spent much of his time in Norfolk; but to leave her cozy house for a man with wanderlust seemed too much. Lattimore decided to settle in Cambridge, where he had easy access to Norfolk and could spend frequent weekends there. July saw him apartment hunting and selling his house in Leeds.

In August he returned to Mongolia again. He described it as a "successful trip," but no diary-letter survives.

The move to Cambridge in November was harder than the moves to Paris and Leeds had been: he had to fit more impedimenta, including an "Augean cloaca" of FBI papers, into less space. He was now, he said, "as tightly wedged in among books as if I were bound between book covers myself." As for the ambience, Cambridge was more stimulating intellectually than was Paris.[39]

CHAPTER THIRTY-TWO

Cambridge and Pawtucket

Lattimore's years with Cambridge as his base (1979–85) were the happiest of any after Eleanor's death. He already had friends there. One of the closest was Caroline Humphrey, formerly his student at Leeds. She had become head of the Mongolian and Inner Asia Studies Unit established at Cambridge in 1986 when Leeds was unable to sustain its Mongol program. Others he knew well included Joseph Needham, authority on Chinese science, ex-president of Gonville and Caius College, and Fellow of the Royal Society; Joan Robinson, frequent visitor to China and a prominent economist who specialized in the Third World; David's wife's sister, married to a don at Selwyn College; Edmund Leach, provost of King's College, who had started his career in China as Lattimore did, with an export-import firm; Sir Moses Finley, master of Darwin College, a great economic historian of classical times who had been hounded out of the United States by the splenetic Karl Wittfogel; and E. H. Carr, prominent historian at Trinity College.

Lattimore was made a member of High Table at King's College and dined there several times a term; the conversation was brilliant and the food superb. He was also made an honorary member of University Centre, "an endowed, club-like organization for visiting professors and the like. Rather good for me: no fees, better than average food." And he was "fast making new friends: many of them, which is cheering at my age, very young and promising." London was within commuting distance. He went there frequently for meetings of the Royal Geographical Society and the Royal Central Asian Society.[1]

He soon fell into a routine. Up at seven, when his "internal clock" always woke him. After breakfast he worked on his autobiography: "In theory (and I must say, generally in practice), nothing else is done until several pages of that have been tapped out."[2] After lunch, chores, shopping, and exercise—at least half an hour of walking or cycling. Afternoon was also for "secondary productive work"—book reviews, articles, anything that would get into print. But there were troubles:

> Theoretically, again, evening is for correspondence, and theoretically the structure is right. I have two typewriters: one in my study for the "primary" and one on a table in my bedroom for the "secondary" work. But the performance isn't up to the theory. In the first place, my filing is at least a year behind. . . . In the second place, there's the occasional visitor, or going out to dinner. Thirdly, I've developed an addictive vice: I read too many papers and weeklies (lucky I don't have television). That's because I'm fascinated by the American election, Iran, Afghanistan, China, Kampuchea, and what-all. Finally, by evening I am often just plain tired. (After all, I've just had my 80th birthday.)[3]

Almost as important as the sociability and structured routine of Cambridge was the "refuge with Rosemary" in Norfolk. She had a guest room with a typewriter, and he could take work with him if he felt like it. Rosemary was a fine cook, and his descriptions of special meals like Christmas dinner are glowing. The thing he mentioned most in his letters to friends, however, was his Norfolk exercise: splitting wood. When he started visiting Norfolk, Rosemary had a huge pile of sawed logs too wide for the fireplace. At first Lattimore worked on them with an axe. In April 1980 Gerry Piel sent him a splitting maul from L. L. Bean. It revolutionized his favorite sport. Most of his letters during 1980 and 1981 describe the glee with which he reduced Rosemary's woodpile to fireplace size. He bragged, "I've split two mountains of firewood."[4]

Toward the end of 1980 there were rumblings on the grapevine from China:

> The Chinese are making noises—very discreet noises—about inviting me again next year. They are doing it just the way they did in 1972; not a thing in writing, but messages passed by word of mouth along a relay chain. It would be interesting, but I don't *have* to go. As things stand, it looks as though they want me more than I need them. I've heard that under the new dispensation in China (that blessed word, pragmatism) even invited guests have to pay their own hotel and travel expenses inside China. So I've passed the message back that (a) I can't afford that much, and they'll have to pay my expenses inside the country; and (b) I'm getting too old to go racketing about all on my own, so I must have David with me. He's legitimate. He's a solid expert on

medieval Chinese poetry, which is now once more a respectable pursuit. . . . Like last time, I have to make it clear (but not vulgarly clear) to the Chinese that they are not capturing me from my Soviet and Mongol friends—any more than those friends have captured me from the Chinese.[5]

Nineteen eighty-one marked the sixtieth anniversary of the Mongolian revolution, and as the first foreign member of the Academy of Sciences Lattimore was to help the Mongols celebrate. He arranged his trip that year to provide a fortnight each in China, Mongolia, and the Soviet Union, leaving in late June. David was unable to accompany him, so Lattimore asked Maria, his twenty-seven-year-old granddaughter, to come along. She was a musician and published poet. Lattimore observed later, "It's interesting that in all three revolutionary countries qualities like that got her an instant, enthusiastic welcome. Also, in all three societies, the Soviet as well as the Chinese and Mongol, the idea of the faithful granddaughter accompanying and looking after the decrepit grandfather was cordially approved."[6]

Lattimore and Maria arrived in Peking on June 22, 1981, after a nineteen-hour flight from London. He found the atmosphere much more relaxed than in 1972 in one way: people felt more free to talk. But the talk was often anti-Soviet diatribe. Maria recalls that all of their guides in China "were feeding us the line that the U.S. should supply them with nuclear weapons to counter the Soviet threat."[7] Lattimore and Maria argued against this position, but the Chinese were unyielding. Maria says, "No matter how many counter-arguments we offered, they simply reiterated their initial position: 'The U.S. must help China defend against Soviet hegemony.'" Lattimore and Maria speculated inconclusively as to Chinese motives for this stultifying rigidity.

Lattimore was quite clear that the Chinese expected him to report to his friends in the West that things had improved since the Cultural Revolution. Of course they had, and Lattimore was pleased at this. But it was a bittersweet pleasure. One of his old Peking friends, whom he had asked to see in 1972 but was told the man was "on vacation," was available in 1981. The man had been sent off to the country and tortured, yet Lattimore had not suspected this treatment in 1972. He was now disturbed by his earlier blindness to the horrors of the Cultural Revolution, and he told Maria it was a personal failure analogous to the "good Germans not knowing about the concentration camps." Here he was probably too hard on himself: Michael remembered that his grandfather had been distinctly aware of the repression in 1972.

Lattimore's Chinese itinerary had been arranged to accommodate David's interest in Tu Fu, the great eighth-century poet who had lived in Chengtu. This stop was still on his schedule. John Stewart Service had been born in Chengtu, and Lattimore sent him a postcard from there. He and Maria also visited Sian, one of the most fascinating areas for archaeologists in all China. At the Ch'in dynasty site near Sian, where a massive vault containing life-size terra-cotta armies had been excavated, Lattimore was delighted to discover that the six thousand buried warrior figures were of many races, not just Han Chinese. Even the horses and weapons of the buried armies showed great individual detail and tribal distinctions. At Sian's T'ang dynasty tombs he and Maria "happened" to meet one of China's chief archaeologists, also a victim of the Cultural Revolution, once again practicing his profession.

Back in Peking, Lattimore was interviewed by Bradley Martin of the *Baltimore Sun*. The lead of Martin's story captured the Lattimore ethos precisely: "He walks with a stoop now, and the wrinkles earned during a career that ranged from scholarly field work with nomads on China's borders to jousting with the red-baiting Senator Joseph McCarthy are etched deeply as he squints through a cloud of smoke from Chinese Double Happiness brand cigarettes. But as he nears his 81st birthday, Owen Lattimore . . . retains the quick and effective way with words and the critical eye for American foreign policy that persuaded McCarthy wire-pullers that the professor was a dangerous man."[8]

Lattimore told Martin that Chinese intellectuals were indeed more relaxed than they had been in 1972 and reported a conversation with an official of the Chinese Nationalities Institute. This official acknowledged that the Cultural Revolution had purged thousands of competent men and installed "second-raters" whose main virtue was that they were conformists, just as happened in the United States during the McCarthy purges. Still heretical, Lattimore went on to observe that Mao Tse-tung once said the Chinese converted to communism because they "had the best teachers in the world—Japanese imperialists and Chiang Kai-shek. 'What worries me,' Mr. Lattimore said, 'is: aren't we, in El Salvador and elsewhere, becoming the best teachers of Communism? I've always said the government of a capitalist country not only has the right, it has the *duty*, to stop the spread of Communism. . . . but for God's sake let's try to stop resorting to methods that will recruit more new Communists.' "[9]

The Chinese spared no effort to make Lattimore's visit enjoyable, but at the end of two weeks he was ready for Mongolia. On July 4 he and Maria entrained for Ulan Bator. At the Sino-Mongolian border, where the train carriages had to be refitted with Russian-gauge wheels, the passengers disembarked and went to the railyard restaurant for dinner. Maria describes it as "the Chinese equivalent of a truck stop; the food was superb." Here Lattimore was in his glory. At his table were a Frenchman, a Malay, and several other nationalities, none of whose Chinese was in working order. Lattimore translated the menu into five languages and ordered for all of them.

Lattimore was one of the highest-ranking guests as the MPR celebrated its sixtieth anniversary. Tsedenbal, the premier, received him and Maria for a full hour. The polemics were now reversed: Tsedenbal was worried about an infiltration of Chinese spies, mostly men who married Mongol women and moved to the MPR to gather defense secrets and carry out sabotage. Maria gave Tsedenbal a poem she had composed celebrating the anniversary. The poem, Lattimore said, delighted him. It included a reference to the Mongol cosmonaut who had recently gone on a Soviet space flight; this Russian-Mongol venture was a symbol for the celebration.

Lattimore's formal part in the proceedings was a speech (in Mongol) at the Academy. Maria says he practiced on her during the train ride and then spoke without notes. His theme was the significance of China's Great Wall. He did not see it as merely a barrier to keep out barbarians. Construction of the wall would have required either large numbers of resident workers or incredibly long supply lines. The Chinese aim must have been at least partly to extend the area inhabited by ethnic Chinese. This was a theme the Mongols appreciated.

There were the usual reunions with friends and former students, picnics in the countryside, attendance at the festival games, visits to the library and bookstores. Possibly the high point of the trip for Lattimore occurred the day he made his call on the British embassy. He and Maria walked to and from their hotel. His back was hurting on the return trip, and he stopped to rest on one of the benches lining Ulan Bator streets. At this bench an elderly Mongol, dressed in traditional robe and boots with turned-up toes, noticed Lattimore's coral and silver ring of Mongol design. The old man whispered almost inaudibly, "Where did you get the ring?" He was not sure whether he should pry into the affairs of this foreigner, was not sure the foreigner spoke Mongol, and did not fully expect an answer. Lattimore heard and responded, starting a long conversation. The Mongol knew that this was someone special; Lattimore knew that he was "one of them."

Two weeks in Ulan Bator were again too short; on July 18, 1981, Lattimore and Maria were on the Trans-Siberian railway en route to Novosibirsk. His old friend Okladnikov was seriously ill, hospitalized with advanced diabetes. During the three days Lattimore was in Novosibirsk, Okladnikov persuaded his doctors to allow him out of the hospital so he could entertain Lattimore for a last nostalgic visit. Okladnikov took Lattimore to the museum to see the latest of the stone markers from Central Asian archaeological digs and gave a magnificent banquet for him. The respect of the Novosibirsk academic community for Lattimore was shown at a meeting with the rector of the university; Maria says they served "vodka, expresso, and chocolates all at one time, the first two in exquisite containers which were never allowed to be empty." Okladnikov died within the year.

In Moscow the Lattimores were guests of the Soviet Academy of Sciences. He was tired. A daylong journey to a monastery museum wore him out. His eighty-first birthday party on July 29, which the Academy gave at what Maria describes as a "very fashionable restaurant," revived his spirits, but anticipation of the work awaiting him in Cambridge soon bore down on him. He had planned to continue his journey by train, visiting several European cities where friends were expecting him, but decided to fly back instead. He and Maria caught a plane for England July 31.

Fujiko came over from Paris for a week soon after his return to Cambridge to work on the proofs of their book about the Dilowa. This work postponed his dealing with the "unbelievable mountain of correspondence" that had accumulated in his absence.[10] Maria stayed in England until the end of November, visiting friends and helping Lattimore with shopping and housekeeping. When he caught up on his correspondence and started on his memoirs, he got a writing block at the point where he first met Eleanor in Peking. Maria was visiting and got him to talk to her about it; the next day he was able to put it on paper. When she left, he spent several weekends and the Christmas season with Rosemary in Norfolk.

He learned in February 1982 that Shirendyb had been deposed as president of the Mongolian Academy of Sciences. Only the Chinese commented publicly on this event; the Chinese embassy in London sent Lattimore their "official news agency report on Shirendyb, which suggests that he was attacked for 'not being pro-Russian enough,' which doesn't convince me. I have known him for more than 20 years, and he always struck me as the most romantically, as well as politically, pro-Russian (not just pro-Soviet) among my Mongol friends."[11] Eventually he learned that Shirendyb fell because the MPR thought he lived too well, and enabled his relatives to live too well, on the perquisites of his position.

Lattimore was still working fitfully on his autobiography, but his major interest now seemed to be a "big" article for *Scientific American* on ancient long-distance caravans. He previewed it this way:

> Everybody knows there was a Silk Road from China to the Mediterranean. (There wasn't; there was a network of alternative routes.) But who knows what was the day's march (in sand, over steppe, in hilly country); the weight carried by each camel; seasonal variations and so on. I do, and so do a number, a dwindling number, of old Mongol and Chinese caravan men (and their techniques were different in important ways). For all this, you don't get the real thing by reading the great travellers, the Aurel Steins or whoever; they hired their caravans, they didn't work their own animals as I did; or, when I travelled in company with Chinese trading caravans, sit around the camp fire and hobnob with the men.[12]

Despite his travel weariness the previous summer, when the fire bell rang, he was off again. The last week of August 1982 it was to the Fourth International Congress of Mongolists in Ulan Bator. He was "head" of the three-person English-speaking delegation; he appeared on Mongol television, translated documents, solicited the life histories of delegates he had not previously met, and visited friends. Surprisingly, in the one surviving letter written from Ulan Bator, he does not comment on Shirendyb's fall or his successor.[13]

In the fall of 1982 he was back in the United States to lecture and see David, the Piels, the Nefs, and the Rogers. Mark Spencer of the *Kansas City Times,* who caught up with Lattimore at the University of Kansas, noted that he was constantly smoking unfiltered Pall Malls. He told Spencer somewhat ruefully that he had been "knocking around loose" since he retired from Leeds. But he did not mind being out of the headlines now.[14]

This lecture trip was the last major excursion. Old age was overcoming wanderlust. In a letter to the Piels April 5, 1983, he described his aching back, caused by his "spine shrinking down on thinned-out discs."[15] Walking brought acute discomfort; cycling and swinging his splitting maul at Rosemary's seemed to loosen him up. And he had a serious infection of the inner ear, which took many months to heal.

By the time the ear was healed, he had reduced Rosemary's woodpile "to a few gnarled chunks," and his favorite exercise was no longer available. It became a chore even to go to London. And he was again drinking heavily. Everything was slowing down, even the requests for information and advice that had previously descended in torrents. The mail was probably decreasing, he said, "because of my slowness in correspondence."[16]

There was one bright spot in 1984; he went to Leeds for an honorary degree, his third, on May 11.

David began to get letters from his father's friends in 1985, saying that it was no longer safe to leave him alone in Cambridge and that no live-in housekeeper or practical nurse would suffice. He needed the frequent attention and authority of a member of the family. David flew to England in July 1985 and agreed; the old man could no longer make it on his own. David called in the movers and packed up his father to come live near him in Pawtucket. It was a wrenching move. According to Lattimore, "I had to give in, though it was agony to leave Cambridge, where I'd been blissful."[17]

Two things had to be done in Pawtucket: find a house and get a complete physical examination. David's place was too small to add his father and his impedimenta. Within a month Lattimore found a beautiful eighteenth-century house three blocks from David, but modernization took almost a year. The medical exams went faster. He was basically sound, but teeth and eyes needed attention. The doctors forbade alcohol and caffeine and put him on a strict diet. Many of his teeth had to come out, and the dentures he got were agonizing: "The new teeth are an occupying army, and they never let me forget who's occupied and who's doing the occupying."[18] When he moved into his house, he had a full-time practical nurse, and in 1987 his grandson Evan and fiancée moved in upstairs.

Despite age and poor eyesight Lattimore continued to work away at his remaining projects. Fujiko was still his collaborator on a part of his memoirs, to be handled separately from the full-length autobiography: this was the story of his service with Chiang. She came every year from Paris or Tokyo, where she had moved in 1986, to visit him. They mailed the manuscript back and forth between visits. John DeFrancis, still living in Hawaii, also got it through the mail for editing.

The Association of American Geographers, very conservative and long uneasy about Lattimore, finally awarded him its "highest honors" at its convention in May 1986. The citation reviewed his career approvingly, concluding, "In his 86th year we, the Association of American Geographers, humbly add our formal recognition to the wide range of accolades he has received both in his homeland and abroad. He has reminded us again that formal academic credentials do not necessarily equate with scholarly achievement and excellence.''[19] In the summer of 1986 Lattimore learned that the State Museum in Ulan Bator had named a newly discovered dinosaur after him: *Goyocethale lattimorei*. The Mongolian embassy in London wished him a happy eighty-sixth birthday by telephone July 29.

Nothing could keep Lattimore from addressing the Mongolia Society's annual convention in New York November 8, 1986. His title, ''Mongolia as a Leading State,'' reflected his long-held admiration and affection for the Mongols. Mongolia, he said, was a leader in industrial and social development, melding the new with the old in a fashion that was an example to others.[20] The address was subsequently published in the society's bulletin.

Now that Lattimore was back in the United States, I was able to visit him regularly. He had much to say about the various publications I had written based primarily on his FBI file. One of the things he argued about was my contention that the FBI, despite its hostility toward him, had behaved better than had the senatorial inquisitors and the politicized Justice Department and had shown a basic professionalism in evaluating the so-called evidence that he was a Communist. For him the FBI was and would remain a scurrilous part of the midcentury witch-hunt, and incompetent to boot. He constantly admonished me to acknowledge his errors and not to ''overjustify'' him.[21]

Nineteen eighty-seven brought good news. The United States government, after sixty-six years, had extended diplomatic recognition to the Mongolian People's Republic. Invigorated by this belated sanity in American behavior, Lattimore made plans to attend the International Congress of Mongolists in Ulan Bator in September. David and granddaughter Clare, a nurse, would go with him. His health was holding steady, perhaps even improving, and he wanted to give a paper on ''a Manchu folk-history legend that I garnered in Kirin in 1929.''[22]

On June 2, 1987, Lattimore wrote the Piels bubbling over with plans for publishing.[23] This was one of his last letters. On July 17 he suffered a stroke, with substantial loss of his ability to speak. The Mongol trip was canceled. Now it was necessary to bring in a full-time practical nurse. Lattimore's ability to walk, eat, read, and understand others was unimpaired. He could start a sentence orally, but his aphasia prevented its completion.

One can imagine the agony for a man who had always been quick with a response. Now the "opium" (David's word) of reading endless newspapers and magazines and his interest in world affairs sustained his spirit. He was cut off from the world, but the world was not cut off from him.

The world missed much in the contributions Lattimore could have made had he not lost his indispensable wife and partner in 1970. "China in History" was never finished, nor were the major article on long-haul caravans, the autobiography, or the Sambuu translation. Only the fragment of a memoir, centering on his service with Chiang, was finished through the efforts of Fujiko Isono. Gerard Piel particularly regretted that Lattimore "never put together a comprehensive picture of his field." But as late as February 1987, commenting on my account of his service with Chiang, he was still sharp and articulate. He commented on the enormous enigma of Western relations with the Soviet Union:

> Chiang did tell me, early on [1941] that after the war China's Communists would have to be dealt with militarily. No use trying to negotiate. I discounted this, knowing that powerful warlords like Chang Ch'un in Szechuan, Yen Hsi-shan in Shensi, the Ma family Muslims in Kansu would manoeuvre to prevent total power from falling into Chiang's hands. He told me also that he could trust Stalin and work with him. I discounted this, too, thinking that Stalin would walk in if there were a vacuum—yet Stalin never gave Mao a pistol or a cartridge during the war and after the war he delayed the Soviet withdrawal from Manchuria—at Chiang's request, because Chiang was afraid that Mao would get there ahead of him. It was only after Chiang's collapse, with the Communists already triumphant in the field, that Stalin moved into the "vacuum." Mao never forgot or forgave this. It is a very tricky, delicate problem of analysis to determine when the Soviets make decisions because they claim to be the senior communists of the world, and when they act as the rulers of a Great Power. They have a number of times acted in *restraint* of what they regard as "revolutionary excess" in neighboring countries. I have never been able to get a clear discussion of this with a Soviet (or any other) Marxist, because their briefcases are always stuffed with old slogans, cliches, and long-ago doctrinal rulings—and so, all too often, are ours. (Lattimore's italics)[24]

One way to gauge a scholar's worth is to examine with hindsight the wisdom of that scholar's judgments. Lattimore's track record is remarkable. Of course, there was some bad advice from his pen. He said in 1940 that Japan was no danger to the United States. He was wrong about Stalin's purge trials. He thought too highly of Chiang's ability as a politician and statesman. He thought the Czechs would be able to maintain their independence of the Soviet Union, as Finland had. James Cotton faults Lattimore's interpretation of the role of Buddhism in Mongolia.[25] But in far more judgment calls, his heresies now look very good.

When the Japanese launched their major offensive against North China in 1937, Lattimore was all but alone in saying that Japan would not win, that the Chinese would stem the Japanese advance and hold their heartland. Going against the common opinion of journalists, he saw clearly that the Chinese Communist support of coalition with Chiang was only a tactical maneuver and that Mao was a dedicated Marxist. His prescriptions for the Chinese Nationalist government to recover the areas lost to Japan in such fashion as to win peasant allegiance and roll back Communist gains can now be seen as enlightened. His constant early warnings that colonialism was doomed in Asia were right on the mark, however offensive they were to conservatives and the European powers. He knew, and said, that the United States could not prop up the Nationalist government after it had lost the mandate of heaven, that foreign intervention would be the kiss of death, and that we should cut our losses and come to terms with Peking.

He was right about Marshall Plan aid being wasted in futile colonial wars in Southeast Asia; about Ho Chi Minh being strong in 1949, and about United States backing of Bao Dai being a mistake; and about the inapplicability of the domino theory in that area. He knew the ill-fated *China White Paper* would be counterproductive. He knew Chinese control of Tibet would be destructive and unpopular, and he tried to rescue the Tibetan monastery manuscripts. He foresaw the rigidity and excesses of the Chinese Communists and predicted a repression in China such as the Great Proletarian Cultural Revolution. He anticipated long in advance Japan edging out the United States in international commerce. He constantly warned of serious consequences of great power arrogance and hegemonism, both from the United States and from Russia. Russian arrogance, he held, would eventually alienate Soviet minorities. He knew, and said, that the Vietnamese were no more puppets of the Chinese than the Chinese were of the Russians.

As to the Senate Internal Security Subcommittee of 1950–54, he was right to hold it in contempt. As to the most visible inquisitor, McCarthy, Lattimore's judgment was ultimately upheld by that most conservative senator, Arthur V. Watkins of Utah, who said that McCarthy took the nation to "depths as dark and fetid as ever stirred on this continent."[26]

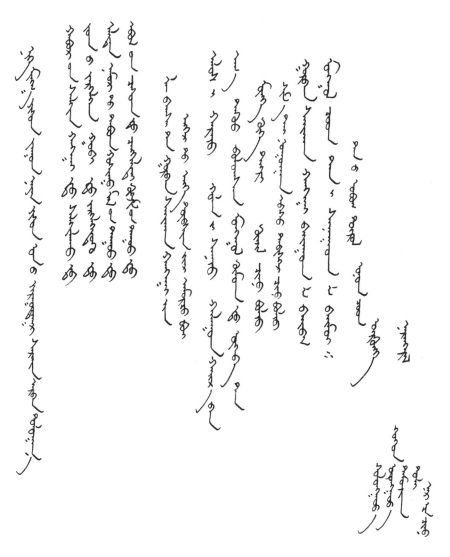

Mongol text of poem read by Urgunge Onon at Lattimore's memorial service, 1989.

Even the State Department finally came around to recognizing the MPR in 1987; Lattimore had pushed recognition with Bullitt in 1936.

It is a record to admire.

We also owe to Lattimore clear proof that it is possible for a single individual to prevail against a powerful committee of the U.S. Senate, a committee that was accumulating perhaps the greatest mass of lies and perjuries ever assembled in the halls of Congress. We cannot know how much Lattimore's refusal to knuckle under, confess imagined sins, or run away stiffened the spines of others under attack; we do know that his courage was applauded throughout the world.

Owen Lattimore died of pneumonia May 31, 1989, in Providence, twenty-nine days short of his eighty-ninth birthday. At a memorial service on the Brown University campus three of his oldest friends, Evelyn Stefansson Nef, Urgunge Onon, and Gerard Piel, came to pay their respects. Were Lattimore to select a eulogy to grace his memory, it would undoubtedly be the poem written by Urgunge Onon and read by him at the memorial service.

> When the spring wind blows in Khangqai,
> When the summer mirage appears in the Gobi,
> When the five kinds of livestock make sounds in the golden autumn,
> When the joyful music sounds on the winter snow
> La bagshi, rest peacefully on the sunlit side of Gurban Saikhan Khangqai.
>
> Thinking and gazing from afar,
> You have given your love to the Mongols
> Who have all become your brothers.
> The blue sky is now your quilt,
> The green grass your blanket;
> As long as Gurban Saikhan Khangqai stands,
> The Mongols will remember you.

NOTES

Abbreviations

FBI/OL   FBI Headquarters File 100-24628, Owen Lattimore, Espio-
          nage—R (Russia). Documents in FBI files are identified by
          serial numbers and are roughly chronological. Where no se-
          rial number is given, the document is identified by date, ori-
          gin, or other datum.

FDRL   Franklin D. Roosevelt Library, Hyde Park, N.Y.

FR   *Foreign Relations of the United States.*

HSTL   Harry S Truman Library, Independence, Mo.

LP   Lattimore Papers. After publication of this book, the Latti-
          more Papers will be placed in the Library of Congress.

O'Mahoney MS Autobiographical sketch written by Lattimore in March 1953
          for Joseph C. O'Mahoney, one of his lawyers. Located in Box
          175, O'Mahoney Papers, William Robertson Coe Library,
          University of Wyoming, Laramie.

NA   National Archives, Washington, D.C.

RG   Record Group.

SISS/IPR U.S. Senate, Committee on the Judiciary, Subcommittee on
          Internal Security, *Institute of Pacific Relations, Hearings and
          Report;* Senator Patrick McCarran, chair: July 24, 1951,
          through June 20, 1952; 82d Congress, 1st and 2d sess. Pub-
          lished in fourteen parts.

Tydings   U.S. Senate, Subcommittee of the Committee on Foreign Re-
          lations, *State Department Employee Loyalty Investigation,
          Hearings and Report;* Senator Millard Tydings, chair; March
          8 to June 28, 1950; 81st Congress, 2d sess. Published in five
          parts.

1. A Fascination with Central Asia

1. FBI/OL, 3204.
2. This and other unattributed quotations derive from the author's conversations with Lattimore.
3. Lattimore, *Desert Road to Turkestan,* 232.
4. O'Mahoney MS, 23.
5. Lattimore, *Studies in Frontier History,* 14.

6. Lattimore, *Desert Road to Turkestan* 107, 40, 253.
7. Ibid., 149.
8. Ibid., 83.
9. Ibid., 86.
10. Ibid., 245.
11. Lattimore, *High Tartary*, 85.
12. O'Mahoney MS, 5.
13. Lattimore and Isono, *Diluv Khutagt*, 2.
14. Ibid., 3.
15. Lattimore, *High Tartary*, 227.
16. The phrase "Slavic Manchukuo" implies that the Soviet Union had control over North China similar to that of Japan when it established the puppet state of Manchukuo.
17. Lattimore, *High Tartary*, 264. To the Mongols, the greatest threat was Chinese overpopulation and the expansion of Chinese farmers onto their grazing lands. The Russian population presented no such threat. For a full exposition of Lattimore's analysis of the extent to which Russian expansion under both czars and Communists incorporated Asian minorities rather than subjecting them, see *Studies in Frontier History*, 165–79.
18. The name of the Chinese capital, "Peking," was changed to "Peiping" in 1928, when the capital was moved south; in 1949 the Communist government restored "Peking," the name used throughout this book for convenience' sake.
19. O'Mahoney MS, 7–8.
20. Lattimore and Isono, *Diluv Khutagt*, 10.
21. Ibid., 10–11.
22. Lattimore, *Studies in Frontier History*, 438.
23. Cotton, "Owen Lattimore and China," 255.
24. O'Mahoney MS, 11.

2.   The IPR Years

1. On the establishment and objectives of IPR, see Thomas, *Institute of Pacific Relations*, chap. 1. Information about Fred Field and Joseph Barnes comes from Thomas and from Betty Barnes to author, January 14, 1989.
2. Lattimore to Joseph Barnes, October 14, 1934.
3. Lattimore, "My Audience with Chingghis Khan."
4. O'Mahoney MS, 13.
5. Lattimore was well-informed about Japanese plans for China. Just before he left for the United States in 1937, he managed to get a series of interviews with knowledgeable Japanese both in Peking and in Tokyo during a stopover there. Those he talked to were Matsukata, Shimanouchi, Kuga, Sakatana, Mori, Sogo, Kishi, Saionji, Ushiba, and members of the Tokyo branch of the IPR. Several of those with whom he talked were close to Prince Konoye. Lattimore made extensive notes of these conversations, which survive in his personal files.
6. O'Mahoney MS, 6.
7. Thomas, *Institute of Pacific Relations*, 12.
8. FBI/OL, 4183.
9. SISS/IPR, 5122.
10. Thomas, *Institute of Pacific Relations*, 13.
11. O'Mahoney MS, 18.
12. FBI/OL, 2722.

13. SISS/IPR, 3319.
14. FBI/OL, 2722.
15. Ibid.
16. A good summary of Borodin's career is in Spence, *China Helpers*, chap. 7.
17. FBI/OL, 2722.
18. Ibid.
19. W. L. Holland and Kate Mitchell, eds., *Problems of the Pacific, 1936* (Chicago: University of Chicago Press, 1936), is an extensive record of the conference.
20. Ibid., 91.
21. Ibid., 92.
22. For a brief account of the Sian Incident, see Clubb, *Twentieth Century China*, 202–9.
23. SISS/IPR, 3289.
24. Lattimore, foreword to Bisson, *Yenan in June 1937*, 8.
25. Ibid., 16.
26. For the 1950s controversy over this trip, see, inter alia, FBI/OL, 5341.
27. O'Mahoney MS, 30.
28. Lattimore, foreword to Bisson, *Yenan in June 1937*, 9.
29. Lattimore, "Unpublished Report from Yenan." Also found as attachment to Frank P. Lockhart to Secretary of State, August 2, 1937, 893.00/14179, RG 59, NA.
30. Lattimore's batting average as a prophet was also enhanced by an article he wrote at the same time for the *Saturday Evening Post*, in which he predicted that the Chinese would rally effectively and ultimately frustrate Japanese advances. The conventional wisdom of the time was that the Japanese would cut through Chinese forces "like a knife through butter" when they attacked seriously. Lattimore's article had actually been set in print by the *Saturday Evening Post* before the Marco Polo Bridge incident; when the editors got word that Japan had launched a full-scale offensive, they pulled out the Lattimore article, thinking they were saving his reputation.
31. O'Mahoney MS, 9.
32. Ibid., 35.
33. Lattimore, "On the Wickedness." For a perceptive analysis of the development of Lattimore's beliefs about the North China frontiers, see Cotton, "Owen Lattimore and China."
34. W. W. Wheeler II, letter to the editor, *Pacific Affairs* 11 (March 1938): 101–4.
35. *Pacific Affairs* 11 (March 1938): 106.
36. See discussion of this incident in SISS/IPR, 3433–46.
37. SISS/IPR, 1225.

3. At Johns Hopkins

1. Evelyn Stefansson Nef, introduction to Owen and Eleanor Lattimore, *Silks, Spices, and Empire*, x.
2. O'Mahoney MS, 36–37.
3. Van Kleeck, "The Moscow Trials," *Pacific Affairs* 11 (June 1938): 233–37. *Pacific Affairs* coverage of the purge trials, and IPR attitudes toward them, are discussed in SISS/IPR, 5149–68.
4. Chamberlain, "The Moscow Trials," *Pacific Affairs* 11 (September 1938): 367–70.

5. *Pacific Affairs* 11 (September 1938): 370–72.

6. The full story of Stalin's China operatives did not come out until 1971 with the publication of Vera Vishnyakova-Akimova's *Two Years in Revolutionary China, 1925–1927*. The chief agent of this enterprise was the legendary Borodin, but there were dozens of others, all of whom fled China in 1927 when Chiang Kai-shek turned on the Communists. Stalin "lost" China in 1927. Vishnyakova-Akimova's tale is mainly a necrology. She identifies 148 Russians who took part in Stalin's great effort to capture the Chinese revolution. By the time she wrote, 43 of them were known dead or in prison camps, another thirty probably dead. See Salisbury, "Amerasia Papers," for a good comparison between Stalin's and America's efforts to influence China.

7. The writer who castigated Lattimore most fiercely was Sidney Hook, in "Lattimore on the Moscow Trials." For more recent and contrasting views, see Conquest, *Great Terror*, and Getty, *Origins of the Great Purges*.

8. Lattimore, "Can the Soviet Union Be Isolated?" *Pacific Affairs* 11 (December 1938): 492–93.

9. SISS/IPR, 3226.

10. Churchill, *Second World War*, 393–94.

11. *Pacific Affairs* 12 (Sept. 1939): 245–62.

12. *Problems of the Pacific, 1939* (New York: IPR and Oxford University Press, 1940), v.

13. Ibid., 24–25.

4. "China Will Win"

1. Lattimore, "American Responsibilities."

2. Ibid., 161–62.

3. Ibid., 174, 165.

4. Ibid., 162, 164, 168. Ironically, this article was quoted selectively in 1950 to show that Lattimore was pro-Communist. Ironically again, it figured in the FBI search for evidence that Lattimore had been paid off by the Soviets. When the bureau began to investigate Lattimore's finances in an attempt to show that his net worth was more than could be accounted for by legitimate sources of income, they checked out every cent he had received for his articles. They discovered after some difficulty that *VQR* had paid Lattimore their standard rate of five dollars per page; he earned seventy dollars for this article. FBI/OL, 2023.

5. FBI/OL, no serial number, 3. The document was transmitted from Dennis A. Flinn of the Department of State to J. Edgar Hoover under a cover letter of April 27, 1955.

6. Ibid., 14.

7. FBI/OL, 6.

8. Tydings, 739, 740.

9. "Comment and Correspondence," *Pacific Affairs* 13 (June 1940): 196–97.

10. "As China Goes, So Goes Asia," *Amerasia* 4 (August 1940): 256.

11. Ibid., 255, 257.

12. Memorandum for Discussion, Territorial Group, CFR October 5, 1940, CFR Archives.

13. Schulzinger, *Wise Men*, 66.

14. "The Soviet View of the Far East," *Pacific Affairs* 13 (December 1940): 446–52.

15. FBI/OL, 647.

16. Memorandum, "Possible Effects of an Agreement between Russia and Japan," Territorial Group, CFR, April 3, 1941, CFR Archives.

17. Lattimore, "Stalemate in China," 621–22, 624.

18. Lattimore, "America Has No Time to Lose," 161–62.

19. Memorandum, "The Chinese Communists, the Comintern, and the Russo-Japanese Neutrality Agreement," Territorial Group, CFR, May 6, 1941, CFR Archives.

20. Wohl, "American 'Geopolitical Masterhand.'"

21. FBI/OL, 1.

22. FBI/OL, 3.

23. "After Four Years," *Pacific Affairs* 14 (June 1941): 143.

24. Kristol, "Ordeal by Mendacity," 316.

5. Adviser to Chiang

1. Johnson to Secretary of State, October 24, 1941, *FR* 4:429.

2. Schaller, *U.S. Crusade*, 43–44. For another account of McHugh's politics, see Tuchman, *Stilwell*, 338–40.

3. See the account in Schaller, *U.S. Crusade*, 46–54.

4. Ibid., 47.

5. Currie to President Roosevelt, March 15, 1941, *FR* 4:81–95; and FBI/OL, 1936.

6. Schaller, *U.S. Crusade*, 50.

7. FBI/OL, 1936; see also Currie to Messersmith, April 1, 1941, Currie Papers, Box 1, Hoover Institution.

8. Currie did not remember who first recommended Lattimore; Lattimore heard the story from Gaus, whom he met at a Washington dinner party in the late 1940s.

9. Currie, Memorandum for the President, April 29, 1941, FDRL.

10. Bowman to Currie, May 2, 1941, FDRL; Yarnell to Currie, May 2, 1941, FDRL.

11. Currie, Memorandum for the President, May 6, 1941, *FR* 5:644; Roosevelt, Memorandum for the Secretary of State, May 19, 1941, FDRL.

12. Hull, Memorandum for the President, May 21, 1941, *FR* 5:648.

13. Secretary of State to Ambassador in China, May 29, 1941, *FR* 5:651; Ambassador in China to Secretary of State, June 2, 1941, *FR* 5:657; Currie, Memorandum for the President, June 5, 1941, FDRL; FBI/OL, 5864.

14. Currie, Memorandum for the President, June 20, 1941, FDRL.

15. *New York Times*, June 29, 1941; FBI/OL, 4117.

16. FBI/OL, 1201.

17. McHugh to Curry, July 22, 1941, McHugh Papers, Cornell University Libraries.

18. SISS/IPR, 5253.

19. "Washington Seeks Chinese-Red Peace," *New York Times*, July 22, 1941.

20. McHugh to Currie, July 22, 1941, McHugh Papers.

21. Richard Watts, Jr., "China Stirred by Assignment of Lattimore," *Baltimore Sun*, August 24, 1941.

22. FBI/OL, 5864.

23. Ibid.

24. Cable to Lauchlin Currie from Owen Lattimore, August 2, 1941, *FR* 4:362; Lauchlin Currie to Acting Secretary of State, August 3, 1941, *FR* 4:361.

25. McHugh to Currie, August 3, 1941, McHugh Papers.

26. For an extensive discussion of the perversion of Tai Li's files during the inquisition, see Newman, "Clandestine."

27. SISS/IPR, 5254.

28. McHugh to Currie, August 25, 1941, McHugh Papers.

29. Lattimore, *Studies in Frontier History*, 20.

30. Lloyd E. Eastman, "Who Lost China?" 660.

31. Currie, Memorandum for the President, summarized in Roosevelt, Memorandum for the Secretary of State, August 30, 1941, FDRL.

32. Currie to Lattimore, September 18, 1941, LP.

33. Lattimore to Madame Chiang Kai-shek, October 13, 1941, LP.

34. Memorandum of conversation with Lung Yun, October 30, 1941, LP.

35. Lattimore to Currie, November 2, 1941, FR 5:747; "Defenders Ready, Lattimore Says," *New York Times*, November 4, 1941.

36. Wohl, "American 'Geopolitical Masterhand.'"

37. Omita (Lattimore's code name) to Currie, October 11, 1941, FDRL. The date on the FDRL copy of the cable is probably wrong. Lattimore's correspondence with Madame Chiang shows a November 11 date.

38. Memorandum of conversation with Bishop Paul Yu-pin, October 13, 1941, LP.

39. Memorandum of conversation with Tsang (Chang) Han-fu, November 11, 1941, LP.

40. Memorandum of conversation with Chou En-lai, November 24, 1941, LP.

41. Mayling Soong Chiang to Lattimore, September 12, 1941, LP.

42. Conversation with Gimo (Chiang Kai-shek), November 16, 1941, LP; Omita to Currie, November 14, 1941, FDRL.

43. Lattimore to Madame Chiang Kai-shek, November 13, 1941, LP.

44. Dinner with Generalissimo, November 14, 1941, LP.

45. Conversation with Gimo (Chiang Kai-shek), November 16, 1941, LP.

46. Currie, Memorandum for the President, November 21, 1941, FDRL.

47. Madame Chiang to Currie, November 29, 1941, Currie Papers.

48. This discussion leans heavily on Feis, *Road to Pearl Harbor*, chaps. 37–42.

49. Final draft of proposed "Modus Vivendi" with Japan, FR 4 (1941): 661–64.

50. Lattimore to Currie, November 25, 1941, FR 4: 652.

51. Winant to Secretary of State, November 26, 1941, FR 4: 665.

52. Secretary of State to Roosevelt, November 26, 1941, FR 4: 665–66.

53. Tansill, *Back Door to War*, 648–49; Greaves, "Secretary Knox and Pearl Harbor," 1271.

54. Toland, *Infamy*, 267.

55. McCarthy to Hickenlooper, June 28, 1950, Hickenlooper Papers, Foreign Relations, "Amerasia-McCarthy," Box 2, Herbert Hoover Presidential Library.

6. War

1. Memorandum, Recent Conversations with Generalissimo, November 30, 1941, LP.

2. Ibid.

3. Omita (Lattimore) to Currie, November 27, 1941, FDRL.

4. Memorandum, Recent Conversations with Generalissimo, November 30, 1941, LP.

5. Mayling Soong Chiang to Lattimore, December 3, 1941, LP.

6. Memorandum, Generalissimo: Northeast China, December 4, 1941, LP.

7. Memorandum, Generalissimo: Counteracting Propaganda of Chinese Communists in U.S., December 4, 1941.

8. Memorandum, Generalissimo: Fundamental Question of the Pacific Area, December 4, 1941, LP.

9. Memorandum, Generalissimo: Economics, December 4, 1941, LP.

10. Memorandum, Generalissimo: Military, December 5, 1941, LP.

11. Memorandum, Generalissimo: December 5, 1941, LP.

12. McHugh to Currie, December 3, 1941, McHugh Papers.

13. Lattimore to Currie, December 9, 1941, *FR* 4: 738–39.

14. Omita to Currie, December 11, 1941, FDRL.

15. Untitled three-page memorandum with note at end, "Submitted through Madame, December 14, 1941. No Chinese translation," LP.

16. Omita to Currie, December 21, 1941, FDRL; see also the discussion of this loan in Tuchman, *Stilwell*, 251–52.

17. Aide Memoire, Submitted through Madame, December 21, 1941, LP.

18. Ibid.

19. Omita to Currie, December 28, 1941, FDRL.

20. Omita to Currie, January 1, 1941 (error: should read 1942), FDRL; Omita to Currie, January 4, 1942, FDRL.

21. Omita to Currie, January 7, 1942, FDRL.

22. Chiang Kai-shek to President Roosevelt, January 12, 1942, FDRL.

23. FBI/OL, 5864.

24. Hamilton Owens, "Back from China, Lattimore High in Praise of Chiang's War Leadership," *Baltimore Sun*, February 9, 1942.

25. "Roosevelt Signs Chinese Loan Bill," *New York Times*, February 14, 1942.

26. FBI/OL, 5864.

27. Lattimore to Madame Chiang, February 16, 1942, LP.

28. Creighton Hill to Currie, February 25, 1942, LP.

29. Lattimore to Chiang Kai-shek, March 4, 1942, LP.

30. Memorandum, "Studies of American Interests in the War and the Peace," Territorial Group, CFR, March 18, 1942, CFR Archives.

31. Lattimore to Hollington Tong, March 15, 1942, LP.

32. FBI/OL, 1752.

33. Canadian Club Meeting No. 1 (Season of 1942–43), Chateau Laurier, Ottawa, May 7, 1942, LP.

34. Currie to Roosevelt, May 15, 1942, *FR*, China, 46.

35. FBI/OL, 5864.

36. Lattimore, "How to Win the War," 15.

37. Ibid., 111.

38. Tuchman, *Stilwell*.

39. Schaller, *U.S. Crusade*, 111.

40. Ibid., 111–13.

41. Ibid, 113–14.

42. FBI/OL, 3693. The McCarthyite charge that Lattimore "had an office in the Department of State" was entirely false. Currie's was an Executive Department office, located in the Old State Department Building, but it had no connection with State at that time.

43. "Conference with Dr. Owen Lattimore," June 10, 1942, Preston Goodfel-

low Papers, Box 3, Hoover Institution. In 1978 even so careful a scholar as Christopher Thorne misinterpreted this document to suggest that Lattimore thought that the Chinese Communists were not genuine ideologues. This was not what he thought at all; he knew well that Chu Teh's "Democratic regime" was a temporary tactical expedient. See Thorne, *Allies of a Kind,* 183.

44. Lattimore, *Asia in a New World Order,* 150, 161. A decade later this even-handed discussion triggered a bitter attack on Lattimore by isolationist-turned-McCarthyite John T. Flynn. In *While You Slept* and *The Lattimore Story,* Flynn outrageously distorts Lattimore's position, grossly misrepresenting *Asia in a New World Order* to paint Lattimore as a Kremlin agent.

45. "Tribute Is Accorded Chinese Army Deeds; Adviser to Chiang Urges U.S. to Send More Planes Quickly," *New York Times,* July 27, 1942.

46. Mayling Soong Chiang to Lattimore, August 5, 1942, LP.

47. O'Mahoney MS, 42.

48. Draft telegram for Generalissimo, no date, LP.

49. Roosevelt to Generalissimo, September 16, 1942, FDRL.

50. Clipping from unidentified newspaper, LP.

51. "New Front in China Seen," *New York Times,* October 24, 1942.

52. O'Mahoney MS 44. The five thousand dollar gift figured prominently in McCarran's SISS hearings. McCarran could not accept it as a genuine indication of Chiang's satisfaction with Lattimore's services; it had to be seen as routine.

53. H. H. K'ung to Lattimore, November 15, 1942, LP.

54. Seagrave, *Soong Dynasty,* 380–81; Schleit, *Shelton's Barefoot Airlines,* 21–24. There were adventures on this trip. Jeanette Kung had no money and borrowed nineteen hundred dollars from Lattimore to buy watches in Brazil. She repaid it when she got access to her father's U.S. accounts. FBI/OL, 3005.

55. "Lattimore Stresses We Must Win in China," *New York Times,* December 8, 1942.

56. *War and Peace in the Pacific* (New York: Institute of Pacific Relations, 1943), vi. McCarran's SISS made much of the fact that William W. Lockwood, IPR secretary, had solicited from Alger Hiss suggestions as to who should be invited to Mont Tremblant. Hiss obliged, suggesting Dean Acheson, Adolf Berle, Adlai Stevenson, and Harvey Bundy, among others. None of them attended; they were nonetheless damned by this recommendation. Those who did attend were also damned. Among the twenty-six American delegates were Philip Jessup, Frank Coe, Lauchlin Currie, Len De Caux, Fred Field, and Owen Lattimore.

57. Memorandum, "Studies of American Interests in the War and the Peace," Territorial Group, CFR, December 15, 1942, CFR Archives.

58. Draft of letter from Lattimore to Generalissimo Chiang Kai-shek, no date, *FR* 1942, China 185–187.

59. Currie to Lattimore, December 28, 1942, LP.

60. Lattimore to Currie, January 1, 1943, LP.

7. OWI, San Francisco

1. Tape recording from Riznik, January 30, 1988.
2. FBI/OL, 6614.
3. *American Mercury* 46 (April 1939): 510.
4. FBI/OL, 6235.
5. FBI/OL, 6614.

6. FBI/OL, 6235, 6054.

7. FBI/OL, 6614; see the statements by Lattimore on Osborne, SISS/IPR, 3598.

8. FBI/OL, 6097, 6707.

9. FBI/OL, 908.

10. Tydings, 434.

11. Tong, *Dateline: China*, 213.

12. FBI/OL, 2943.

13. FBI/OL, 405, 1678.

14. FBI/OL, 3728.

15. FBI/OL, 2089.

16. Ibid. In this and subsequent FBI documents, copy censored by the FBI is indicated by a long dash.

17. Lattimore, "Yunnan, Pivot of Southeast Asia," 492; Memorandum, Mongolia and the Peace Settlement, Territorial Series, CFR, June 8, 1943, CFR Archives.

18. FBI/OL, 2732, 2948, 2984. In 1950, after McCarthy had fingered Lattimore as the "top Soviet spy," Upton Close, a right-wing radio commentator with experience in China started a campaign to prosecute Lattimore for scripts he allegedly wrote for "The Pacific Story" series. Close wrote Senators Tydings, Hickenlooper, and Lodge on May 3, 1950, urging them to subpoena scripts and call witnesses on this matter; Hickenlooper Papers. Close also contacted the FBI, who discovered that he was wrong about who wrote "Pacific Story" scripts.

19. Lattimore, *America and Asia*, 45.

20. "American Falsifiers on the Policy of the USA in Relation to the Chinese Revolution of 1925–1927," *Voprosy Istorii* (Moscow), April 1949; translation by FBI; FBI/OL, 1327.

21. Lattimore to Madame Chiang, March 30, 1943, LP.

22. Lattimore to Madame Chiang, April 20, 1943, LP.

23. One of the writers most concerned about the state of Kuomintang morale was T. A. Bisson, whose article "China's Part in a Coalition War" went much too far in labeling the Chinese Communists "democratic." Lattimore knew, and said, that they were genuine ideological Communists, however moderate their political program at any one time.

24. Lattimore to Currie, July 20, 1943, LP.

25. Studies of American Interests in the War and the Peace, Territorial Series, CFR, December 14, 1943, CFR Archives.

26. Colegrove's account: SISS/IPR, 912. Lattimore's account: SISS/IPR, 3577.

27. For Edwin O. Reischauer's response to Colegrove, see SISS/IPR, 4931. For Eugene Staley's response, see SISS/IPR, 5313–16. For Colegrove's operations as a "mind-guard" at Northwestern University, see Thompson, "Miller Center Discussions," 25–26; Cook, *Nightmare Decade*, 365, has a brief comment on Colegrove's support of McCarthy.

28. O'Mahoney MS, 45.

8. Mission with Wallace

1. Sending "missionaries" or personal investigators was akin to Roosevelt's habit of having multiple intelligence sources; he could select from among a number of conflicting reports.

2. Hull, *Memoirs*, 1585–86; Wallace, *Soviet Asia Mission*, 17; Tuchman, *Stilwell*, 464.

3. Harriman, *Special Envoy to Churchill and Stalin*, 331.

4. Wallace, *Soviet Asia Mission*, 17–18.

5. Madame Chiang to Lattimore, April 28, 1944, LP.

6. Secretary of State to Ambassador in China (Gauss), May 23, 1944, *FR, China*, 228.

7. Lattimore, "New Road to Asia."

8. O'Mahoney MS, 46.

9. Wallace, *Soviet Asia Mission*, 33–34.

10. Yuri A. Rastvorov, "Red Fraud and Intrigue in Far East," 180. Rastvorov's claim that all stockades along the Wallace route had been torn down does not square with John Hazard's memory. As Wallace's translator, Hazard was in the lead car in the convoy and hence not handicapped by the dust swirling around the following cars. During the McCarthy years Lattimore asked Hazard if there had been any prison stockades visible near Magadan. Hazard replied, " 'Oh yes, there were plenty of those, and when I asked the Russians what they were, they replied perfectly frankly that they were the stockades of prison camps.' The point is that he never told me on the trip. He was an extremely discreet man." Lattimore to author, January 11, 1982. What Hazard saw so clearly Wallace should also have seen, but not Lattimore.

11. Harriman, *Special Envoy*, 331.

12. Wallace, *Soviet Asia Mission*, 128–29.

13. J. R. Hildebrand to Lattimore, August 30, 1944, National Geographic Society Archives. The most reprehensible attack on Lattimore's *National Geographic* article came years after it was published, in Paul Hollander's misleading *Political Pilgrims* (1981). Hollander set out to show how certain intellectuals, alienated from Western society and seeking utopias, visited the Soviet Union, China, and other Communist nations as pilgrims visiting a shrine. Lattimore's trip with Wallace in 1944 met none of the criteria Hollander established for his pilgrims. It was at the wrong time: Hollander's pilgrims traveled to Russia in the 1930s. It was to Siberia, the wrong place: what "political pilgrim" went there? Lattimore went for the wrong reasons: he was not estranged from the United States but was a well-adjusted, practicing, enthusiastic capitalist. He went under the wrong auspices: he was not on a utopia-seeking tour but on an official mission sent by the president of the United States. Hollander betrays his total ignorance of Lattimore's beliefs as displayed in his extensive writings; Hollander gives evidence of having read only Lattimore's *National Geographic* article and a letter to the editor of the *New Statesman* in 1968. There are eight references in Hollander to Lattimore; the best that can be said of this work is that Hollander knew nothing about Lattimore's trip. Robert Conquest, who also frequently attacked Lattimore's account, at least knew what Lattimore was doing in Kolyma.

14. This and all subsequent quotations from Lattimore's diary are from the copy in the Lattimore Papers, Library of Congress.

15. Department of State, *United States Relations with China*, 551–54.

16. Ibid., 554.

17. Seagrave, *Soong Dynasty*, 293.

18. May, *China Scapegoat*, 83.

19. On the Kunming events, see May, *China Scapegoat*, 105–7; Merrell to Secretary of State, June 28, 1944, *FR, China*, 235–37; SISS/IPR, 1403–89, 1809–16.

20. See the Alsop account in "Strange Case."

21. See Tuchman, *Stilwell*, 89.

9. "Who Lost China?" Begins

1. Graebner, *New Isolationism*, 27.
2. Lattimore, *Solution in Asia*, 12, 82–85, 99–100, 104–7, 122.
3. Ibid., 121, 120.
4. Ibid., 140, 139, 152–53, 173.
5. Ibid., 158.
6. Ibid., 191, 196, 197. When Lattimore was indicted in 1954 for following the Communist party line in his writings, the displaced and embittered foreign service officer Joseph W. Ballantine "analyzed" Lattimore's writings. *Solution*, said Ballantine, "goes 100 percent along the line of the Communist solution in Asia"; Ballantine Oral History, Columbia University Libraries, 216. The official Justice Department–sponsored analysis of Lattimore's writings in which Ballantine was involved, was equally mendacious; *Solution* was cited as Communist-lining in seventy-one places, but none of Lattimore's extensive argument for free enterprise, and for outflanking the Russians, was acknowledged. See chap. 26.
7. Lattimore, *Solution in Asia*, AMS edition, i–vi.
8. Keeley, *China Lobby Man*, 67.
9. Thomas, *Institute of Pacific Relations*, 41.
10. Keeley, *China Lobby Man*, 314.
11. Thomas, *Institute of Pacific Relations*, 41.
12. *Security in the Pacific* (New York: Institute of Pacific Relations, 1945).
13. SISS/IPR, 994.
14. SISS/IPR, 991–92.
15. Pacificus, "Dangerous Experts," *Nation* 160 (February 3, 1945): 128.
16. FBI/OL, 1683; SISS/IPR, 703–54.
17. I. F. Stone, "Pearl Harbor Diplomats," *Nation* 161 (July 14, 1945): 25–27. An accurate account of Grew's resignation is in Heinrichs, *American Ambassador*, 380.
18. FBI/OL, 5.
19. Lattimore, "International Chess Game," 732.
20. Ibid., 733.
21. Keeley, *China Lobby Man*, 87. Eastman also sought material from Freda Utley. A copy of the Eastman-Powell *Reader's Digest* article ("The Fate of the World") in Utley's papers at the Hoover Institution has "written by Freda Utley" on the cover page, and attached is what appears to be Utley's manuscript as submitted to Eastman. Some of the Utley manuscript does appear in the *Digest* article, but it also contains material not in her draft. When Utley published *The China Story* in 1951, she mentioned the Eastman-Powell article but did not hint at her part in it; *China Story*, 148.
22. O'Neill, *Last Romantic*, xvii.
23. Eastman and Powell, "The Fate of the World."
24. O'Neill, *Last Romantic*, 227.
25. SISS/IPR, 3353.
26. This account is taken from Latham, *Communist Controversy in Washington*, 203–16; Service, *Amerasia Papers*; Tydings, 431; *Congressional Record*, March 30, 1950, 81st Cong., 2d Sess., 4375–98.
27. Moos affidavit, April 5, 1950, LP; Tydings, 431. Innocent as Moos's participation in the Ruxton picnic was, his casual acquaintance with Lattimore, Service, and Roth may have cost him the presidency of the University of Maryland. An FBI memo of February 16, 1954, from Lee Pennington to D. M. Ladd, notes

that while Moos was being considered for the job, he was "tied up with Lattimore and the subversive group of professors at Johns Hopkins University"; FBI/OL, 5549. This handicap did not, however, prevent Moos from serving with distinction as one of President Eisenhower's speechwriters and later as president of the University of Minnesota.

28. FBI/OL, 1189, 544.
29. Author interview with Abel Wolman, February 13, 1984.
30. Weil, *Pretty Good Club*, 216.
31. SISS/IPR, 3087.
32. SISS/IPR, 3387.
33. SISS/IPR, 3388.
34. Ibid.
35. *New York Times*, August 6, 1945.
36. Ibid.; Ballantine Oral History, 218.
37. Byrnes, *All in One Lifetime*, 310.

10. Kohlberg and the Pauley Mission

1. Alfred Kohlberg sarcastically claimed that *he* was the China lobby, but common usage of the phrase included many others. Politicians, journalists, businessmen, retired generals and admirals, a handful of professors, and employees of the Nationalist government all worked for the same ends: continued recognition of and aid to Chiang Kai-shek and opposition to admission of the People's Republic of China to the United Nations. See Ascoli, "China Lobby"; Bachrack, *Committee of One Million*; and Koen, *China Lobby*.
2. Klehr and Radosh, "Anatomy of a Fix," 20.
3. Latham, *Communist Controversy in Washington*, 213.
4. Ibid., 214. Many commentators on *Amerasia* fail to realize how illegal entries by the OSS and the FBI vitiated the government case. A comprehensive description of the legal issues involved appears in Heald and Tyler, "Legal Principle."
5. The text of Sokolsky's broadcast was recorded by Chinese Nationalist officials; a transcript is in the Wellington Koo Papers, Columbia University. For an analysis of Sokolsky's character and ideological track record, see Cohen, *Chinese Connection*.
6. Kohlberg, "Owen Lattimore."
7. Lattimore, "Reply to Kohlberg," 15.
8. Shanahan, "False Solution," 22.
9. FBI/OL, 5768.
10. FBI/OL, 5518.
11. A chronology of the mission is in *Report on Japanese Reparations to the President of the United States*, Box 21, Records of the U.S. Mission on Reparations, RG 59, NA (hereafter cited as Pauley Mission Records).
12. Lattimore to Maxwell, November 6, 1945, Pauley Mission Records.
13. Ibid.
14. See the account of the Pauley mission in Schaller, *American Occupation of Japan*, 33–38.
15. *Presentation of Interim Program and Policy to FEC Committee Jan. 12, 1946*, Pauley Mission Records.

16. FBI/OL, 5768.
17. Ibid. We do not know whether Coons answered Lattimore. When the FBI interviewed Coons in 1950, he stated that "when he was first requested to serve on the mission he refused to do so because he learned that he would have to work under OWEN LATTIMORE." Coons had met Lattimore at the Hot Springs IPR conference and found him a "domineering character"; FBI/OL, 835. By 1950 he thought Lattimore pro-Communist.
18. FBI/OL, 835.
19. Lattimore to Pauley, November 28, 1945. Pauley Mission Records.
20. FBI/OL, 5768. This memorandum should also be in the Pauley Mission Records, but I did not find it when I searched those records.
21. FBI/OL serial numbers 227, 236, 246, 253, 295, 322, 402, 412, 432, 462, 744, 829, 835, 886, 912, 944, 963, 978, 1098, 1132, 1292, 1592, 1631, 1925, 2625, 2740, 2985, and 6074 report interviews about Lattimore with members of the Pauley mission.
22. See note 11 above.
23. Schaller, *American Occupation of Japan*, chap. 2, gives a good description of the attempt of the occupation to destroy the cartels.
24. Tydings, 558–68.
25. FBI/OL, 2619.
26. See Willoughby to Bonner Fellers, November 23, 1949, de Toledano Papers, Box 5, Hoover Institution. Willoughby hoped to achieve fame as author of the first book on the Sorge spy ring; when this work brought him small reward, he went to Spain to work for Francisco Franco. On Willoughby's attempt to smear John K. Emmerson, see Emmerson's *Japanese Thread*, 312–13, 324–25. For an extended analysis of Willoughby's activities, see Bowen, *Innocence Is Not Enough*, esp. chap. 6.
27. FBI/OL, 7.
28. James R. Young to P. Stewart Macaulay, December 1, 1945, RG 03.001, Records of the Office of the Provost, Series 1, File 116, Page School of International Relations, 1945–54, Ferdinand Hamburger, Jr., Archives, Johns Hopkins University.
29. P. Stewart Macaulay to James R. Young, December 5, 1945, Hamburger Archives.
30. See Buhite, *Patrick J. Hurley*, chap. 11.

11. The Triumph of Ideology over Politics

1. Murray, *Red Scare*, is the definitive source for the early 1920s.
2. Wohl, "American 'Geopolitical Masterhand.' "
3. Levering, *American Opinion*, chap. 3. But see Sirgiovanni, "Undercurrent of Suspicion," for evidence that many Americans did not relax their hostility toward Russia during the war.
4. Irons, "Cold War Crusade," 76.
5. Ibid., 78–82.
6. Jefferson, "Rhetorical Restrictions," chaps. 3–4.
7. Irons, "Cold War Crusade," 79–80.
8. Ibid., 79.
9. "Two Thousand Reds Hold U.S. Jobs, Priest Asserts," *Washington Post*,

March 11, 1946; "Rep Rees to Ask Congressional Probe of Communists in U.S. Agencies Here," *Washington Post*, March 12, 1946.

10. Irons, "Cold War Crusade," 80.

11. Ibid.

12. Ibid., 81–82, 82–83.

13. O'Reilly, *Hoover and the Un-Americans*, chaps. 3–4.

14. Lattimore's ONA articles all appeared in the *York* (Pennsylvania) *Gazette and Daily*. No other paper carried them all. All citations to these ONA articles are to that paper; dates are those of publication. The Justice Department report is analyzed in chapter 26.

15. For a lurid account of the Gouzenko case and the Soviet espionage apparatus of which he was a part, see Pincher, *Too Secret, Too Long*.

16. Ray Richards, "Prof. Owen Lattimore's Job under Probe by House Sub-Committee," *Baltimore News-Post*, June 7, 1946.

17. FBI/OL, 173, 2418. The *Chicago Journal of Commerce* piece was traced back by the FBI to Today's World Publishing Company in St. Louis. Today's World had a brief existence from June 1946 to March 1947; it was founded by Virgil A. and Charles F. Kelly and supported by the Knights of Columbus. The FBI was not certain of this connection, however; Serial 2418 notes that the connection was only the "opinion" of Virgil Kelly.

18. Goodman, *The Committee*, 184.

19. Caute, *Great Fear*, 26.

20. Oshinsky, *Conspiracy So Immense*, 50–51.

21. Goodman, *The Committee*, 185.

22. Ibid., 186–87.

12. Cold War Declared

1. ONA dispatch in *York Gazette and Daily*, January 17, 1947. Subsequent ONA dispatches identified in text by date only.

2. Eastman, "Who Lost China?" 658–60. For the most complete discussion of why Mao triumphed, see Pepper, *Civil War In China*.

3. Salisbury, "Amerasia Papers."

4. Discussion Meeting Report, Far Eastern Affairs, March 5, 1947, CFR Archives.

5. Ibid.

6. Lattimore to Choibalsan, February 11, 1947, LP; Lattimore to Novikov, February 11, 1947, LP.

7. Undated mimeographed paper titled "Owen Lattimore," J. B. Matthews Papers, Liberty University Library.

8. FBI/OL, 173.

9. FBI/OL, 454.

10. Thomas, *Institute of Pacific Relations*, 41–44.

11. FBI/OL, 1324.

12. Ibid.

13. Ibid.

14. Ibid.

15. For the story of Vincent's struggle, and Clare's contemptible role in it, see May, *China Scapegoat*. An equally chilling report on Clare's bias and incompetence is in Kimball, *The File*.

13.　Europe Up, Asia Down

1.　Graebner, *New Isolationism,* 27.

2.　Bailey, *Diplomatic History,* 800.

3.　"Town Meeting," January 6, 1948. Transcripts of town meetings were published by the Town Hall, Inc., of Columbus, Ohio. This transcript was volume 13, number 37. This broadcast was also monitored by the Soviets, who castigated Lattimore over Radio Moscow as an opponent of communism; FBI/OL, 647.

4.　Blind transcript in CFR Archives, the first paragraph of which reads, "The discussion group on Japan held its third meeting at 6:00 p.m. on Tuesday, January 27, 1948, at the Harold Pratt House."

5.　Ibid.

6.　See discussion of the reversal of occupation policy in Schonberger, *Aftermath of War;* Bowen, *Innocence Is Not Enough,* 152–58; and Schaller, *American Occupation of Japan,* chap. 2.

7.　Keeley, *China Lobby Man,* 220.

8.　Ibid., 202.

9.　Ibid., 203.

10.　Goodman, *The Committee,* 226.

11.　See Acheson, *Present at the Creation,* chap. 34; Cochran, *Harry Truman,* chap. 15; Goldman, *Crucial Decade,* 83–90; and Rogin, *Intellectuals and McCarthy,* chap. 8.

14.　Barmine

1.　FBI/OL, 13.

2.　Barmine, "Russian View," 44.

3.　SISS/IPR, 183.

4.　Ibid., 221.

5.　Barmine, "New Communist Conspiracy," 28.

6.　FBI/OL, 503.

7.　FBI/OL, 1447, 420.

8.　Barmine, "New Defender for Yenan."

9.　FBI/OL, 503.

10.　FBI/OL, 420.

11.　Goodman, *The Committee,* chap. 8.

12.　FBI/OL, 503.

13.　SISS/IPR, 201.

14.　FBI/OL, 226.

15.　For a description of Berzin, see Deakin and Storry, *Case of Richard Sorge,* 61–63.

16.　Barmine, *Memoirs of a Soviet Diplomat,* and *One Who Survived,* chap. 40.

17.　SISS/IPR 211; FBI/OL, 3114.

18.　FBI/OL, 13, 19, 20.

19.　FBI/OL, 23.

20.　Ibid.

21.　FBI/OL, 34.

22.　FBI/OL, 45.

23. FBI/OL, 65.
24. FBI/OL, 61.
25. Ibid.
26. FBI/OL, 103.
27. This letter was not released by the FBI. We know its date from the CIA response cited in note 28.
28. Robert A. Schow to Director, FBI, August 10, 1949, CIA Lattimore files. As with the rest of the documents released after a nine-year delay, the CIA had censored this letter so heavily as to make it all but useless.
29. This letter does not survive, but Lattimore quoted it in an ONA article of February 22, 1947.
30. FBI/OL, 1082.
31. *Congressional Record*, February 21, 1949, 81st Cong., 1st Sess., A993. Theodore White told me in 1977 that on the campaign plane in 1960 Kennedy regretted having attacked Lattimore and Fairbank and wanted to make it up to them. White said he did not put this incident in his *Making of the President: 1960* because he did not want to stir up trouble for Lattimore and Fairbank, both friends of White. White did, however, recount this event in his *In Search of History*, 469–70.
32. Budenz, "Menace of Red China," 23.
33. Ibid., 48.
34. Ibid., 49.
35. Lattimore to Mrs. William Stanton, February 14, 1949, Lattimore Papers, Hamburger Archives.
36. Lattimore, *Situation in Asia*, 12, 202.
37. Ibid., 237.
38. Ibid., 233.
39. Ibid., 111.
40. "Owen Lattimore Is on Legion List," *Baltimore Sun*, May 6, 1949.
41. Lattimore to Lauterbach, May 26, 1949, Lattimore Papers, Hamburger Archives.
42. FBI/OL, 146.
43. FBI/OL, 48, 49.
44. Lattimore to Roche, July 12, 1949, Lattimore Papers, Hamburger Archives.
45. On the *White Paper*, see Newman, "Self-Inflicted Wound."
46. Mao, *Selected Works*, 4:425–59.
47. Kearney, "Disaster in China," 4.
48. FBI/OL, 149.
49. Ibid.
50. Varg, *Missionaries, Chinese, and Diplomats*, 249.
51. Quoted in Varg, *Missionaries, Chinese, and Diplomats*, 3.
52. See Swanberg, *Luce and His Empire*.
53. Stuart, *Fifty Years in China*, 242.
54. Dimond, "U.S. and China," 22–23.
55. Madsen, "The New China," 72.
56. Garrett, "Why They Stayed," 309.
57. FBI/OL, 1577.
58. SISS/IPR, 1551–1682 contains the complete transcript.
59. Ibid., 1583–95; and author interview with Philip Jessup, June 8, 1978.
60. FBI/OL, 2497; Bull to Lattimore, November 14, 1949, Lattimore Papers, Hamburger Archives.

61. FBI/OL, 146.
62. Lattimore to Evans, January 19, 1950, Rockefeller Foundation 1.1, Serial 2003, Box 354, Folder 4210, Rockefeller Archive Center.
63. FBI/OL, 133.

15. Top Soviet Spy

1. *Public Papers of the Presidents of the United States: Harry S. Truman, 1950* (Washington, D.C.: GPO, 1950), 11.
2. *Department of State Bulletin*, January 12, 1950, 111.
3. Lattimore expressed these views in an ONA article carried by the *York Gazette and Daily*, July 9, 1949.
4. Acheson, *Present at the Creation*, 469–70.
5. W. H. Lawrence, "G.O.P. Poses Issues for '50 as Liberty versus Socialism," *New York Times*, February 7, 1950.
6. Lattimore to Gardner, February 1, 1950, LP.
7. Lattimore to Evans, February 26, 1950, LP.
8. FBI/OL, 151.
9. Ibid.
10. Ibid.
11. FBI/OL, 164.
12. Author interview with Burkhardt, May 7, 1982.
13. FBI/OL, 228.
14. See the account in Reeves, *Joe McCarthy*, chaps. 8–9.
15. All sources mentioned in this paragraph are in the bibliography.
16. See Hofstadter, *Paranoid Style*, for a historical approach to conspiracy theory.
17. Goldman, *Crucial Decade*, 116.
18. Watkins, *Enough Rope*, ix.
19. Oshinsky, *Conspiracy So Immense*, 114.
20. Tydings. For narrative accounts of the Tydings hearings, see Reeves, *Joe McCarthy*, chaps. 12–13; Oshinsky, *Conspiracy So Immense*, chap. 8; Griffith, *Politics of Fear*, chap. 3.
21. Keeley, *China Lobby Man*, 98–99.
22. Oshinsky, *Conspiracy So Immense*, 121.
23. I heard this story from John F. Melby (interview, June 10, 1983), who in 1950 was a foreign service officer on the Philippine desk.
24. Anderson, *Confessions of a Muckraker*, 196–97.
25. FBI/OL, 192, 178.
26. FBI/OL, 178.
27. FBI/OL, 2462.
28. FBI/OL, 916.
29. Lattimore, *Ordeal by Slander*, 5.
30. Ibid., 8.
31. Ibid.
32. Ibid., 3.
33. Ibid., 4.
34. FBI/OL, 1699.
35. Ibid.
36. Ibid.

37. Anderson, *Confessions of a Muckraker*, 198.

38. Keeley, *China Lobby Man*, 3.

39. McCarthy to Utley, April 4, 1950, Utley Papers, Box 8, Hoover Institution; Reeves, *Joe McCarthy*, 267–68.

40. Anderson and May, *McCarthy*, 304. For a revealing account of Don Surine, see the extensive records of Tom Reeves's conversations with him in the Reeves Papers, Wisconsin State Historical Society.

41. Reeves, *Joe McCarthy*, 359, 366–69.

42. Ibid., 341–45, 363–64, 445.

43. Author interview with Burkhardt, May 7, 1982.

44. FBI/OL, 207.

45. FBI/OL, 226, 1221.

46. FBI/OL, 1447.

47. FBI/OL, 372, 1447.

48. Reeves, *Joe McCarthy*, 268.

49. FBI/OL, 243. The text of the McCarthy speech is also in *Congressional Record*, March 30, 1950, 81st Cong., 2d Sess., 4375–93.

50. Ibid., 4385; Oshinsky, *Conspiracy So Immense*, 145.

51. George McT. Kahin, then a graduate student at Johns Hopkins, went to McCarthy's office to check out the sources of McCarthy's charges against Lattimore. He told me, "I found it surprisingly easy to look for things that I wanted. I said, 'This has to be in the public domain, he's been talking about this.' " Kahin found that McCarthy had taken statements out of context, doctored them, even conjured some of them up. Author interview with Kahin, August 10, 1979.

52. FBI/OL, 3114.

53. See discussion of the *Amerasia* case in chapter 9.

54. On the Hobbs committee report, see *Congressional Record*, May 22, 1950, 81st Cong., 2d sess., 7428–68.

55. Hofstadter, *Paranoid Style*, 36.

56. *Congressional Record*, March 30, 1950, 81st Cong., 2d sess., 4380.

57. Stewart Alsop, *The Center*, 8.

58. *Time*, April 17, 1950, 22.

59. Edwards, "Lattimore Raked by Sen. McCarthy," *Chicago Daily Tribune*, March 31, 1950; Edwards, "Senator Will Give Evidence to FBI," *Washington Times-Herald*, March 31, 1950.

60. FBI/OL, 3114.

61. Ibid.

62. FBI/OL, 3711.

63. FBI/OL, 2778. See also Theoharis and Cox, *The Boss*, 285–87.

16.   Out of the Woodwork

1. Lattimore, *Ordeal by Slander*, 20–21.

2. FBI/OL, 200.

3. FBI/OL, 261.

4. FBI/OL, 219, 354.

5. FBI/OL, 1894. Tavenner was an informal agent for General Willoughby, who sent him various Sorge papers hoping that HUAC would take up the case and thus publicize Willoughby's forthcoming book on Sorge. See correspondence from Willoughby to Bonner Fellers, Ralph de Toledano Papers, Box 5, Hoover Institution.

6. FBI/OL, 1677.
7. FBI/OL, 2033.
8. FBI/OL, 1900.
9. FBI/OL, 2367.
10. Edwards, "M'Carthy Links Lattimore to Slain Red Spy," *Chicago Tribune*, August 2, 1950.
11. FBI/OL, 5116.
12. FBI/OL, 294.
13. Caldwell, *Secret War*; see also Davies, *Dragon by the Tail*, 287–89; and Miles, *A Different Kind of War*.
14. Miles to Nimitz, March 21, 1946, Miles Papers, Box 9, Hoover Institution; Schaller, *U.S. Crusade in China*, 248–49.
15. FBI/OL, 606.
16. Ibid.
17. Ibid.
18. FBI/OL, 1474.
19. FBI/OL, 1684.
20. FBI/OL, 1684, 1850.
21. FBI/OL, 2321.
22. FBI/OL, 2172.
23. FBI/OL, 2550.
24. FBI/OL, 2827.
25. FBI/OL, 2953.
26. FBI/OL, 3058, 3219.
27. FBI/OL, 944, 1318, 1806.
28. FBI/OL, 932.
29. Ibid.
30. FBI/OL, 942.
31. FBI/OL, 1279
32. FBI/OL, 1769.
33. FBI/OL, 962.
34. FBI/OL, 1306.
35. FBI/OL, 2389.
36. FBI/OL, 2692.
37. FBI/OL, 5536.
38. FBI/OL, 2625.
39. FBI/OL, 2355.
40. Ibid.
41. FBI/OL, 2728.
42. Ibid.
43. FBI/OL, 2987.
44. FBI/OL, 1686.
45. FBI/OL, 1691.
46. Ibid.
47. FBI/OL, 2461.
48. FBI/OL, 1272.
49. FBI/OL, 1686.
50. FBI/OL, 1688, 1687, 1362.
51. FBI/OL, 1690.
52. FBI/OL, 1355.
53. FBI/OL, 1575, 1437.
54. FBI/OL, 1691.

55. FBI/OL, 2054.
56. FBI/OL, 2461.
57. FBI/OL, 2330.
58. FBI/OL, 2830.
59. FBI/OL, 2330.
60. FBI/OL, 2705.
61. FBI/OL, 2600.
62. FBI/OL, 2662.
63. FBI/OL, 2759.
64. FBI/OL, 2803.
65. FBI/OL, 2830.
66. FBI/OL, 3875, 4035.
67. FBI/OL, 1932, 2381, 2382.
68. FBI/OL, 3285, 3286, 3290.
69. FBI/OL, 1831, 2014, 2233, 2265, 2358.

17.   A Fool or a Knave

1. Lattimore, *Ordeal by Slander*, 18.
2. Ibid., 19.
3. Ibid., 23.
4. Reeves, *Joe McCarthy*, 265.
5. Lattimore, *Ordeal by Slander*, 23.
6. "Lattimore's Statement," *Baltimore Sun*, April 2, 1950.
7. Ibid.
8. Lattimore, *Ordeal by Slander*, 27.
9. *New York Times*, April 4, 1950.
10. William S. White, "Lodge Asks Loyalty Inquiry Be Shifted to Private Board," *New York Times*, April 4, 1950.
11. FBI/OL, 345, 334.
12. FBI/OL, 1940.
13. Lattimore, *Ordeal by Slander*, 56–57.
14. In addition to the Tydings committee hearings, Lattimore's appearance was covered extensively in the *New York Times, Baltimore Sun, Washington Post,* and many other papers on April 7, 1950. See also Lattimore, *Ordeal by Slander*, 59–108.
15. Tydings, 417–18.
16. Ibid., 420.
17. Ibid., 425.
18. Ibid., 438–39.
19. Ibid., 439, 441.
20. Ibid., 484.
21. Oshinsky, *Conspiracy So Immense*, 148.
22. William S. White, "Lattimore Denies He Was Ever a Red; Hits 'China Lobby,' " *New York Times*, April 7, 1950.
23. FBI/OL, 518, 519.
24. FBI/OL, 1604.
25. FBI/OL, 3050, 6110.
26. FBI/OL, 2195, 2290.
27. FBI/OL, 447, 566.

28. FBI/OL, 2722.
29. FBI/OL, 1940.
30. FBI/OL, 2409.
31. FBI/OL, 686.
32. FBI/OL, 594.
33. FBI/OL, 552 (my assignment of serial number; the FBI did not mark it). This serial covers the whole Kohlberg interview story through his painful session with Belmont April 13, 1950.
34. "Kohlberg Says His File Has More on Lattimore," *New York Mirror,* April 13, 1950.
35. FBI/OL, 552.
36. Ibid.

18. Agony at the FBI: Louis Budenz

1. FBI Headquarters File 100-63, Louis Francis Budenz, Internal Security—C, Serial 122; hereafter cited as FBI/LB, plus the serial number.
2. Budenz, *This Is My Story,* preface, chaps. 10–11.
3. FBI/LB, 138.
4. FBI/LB, 149.
5. FBI/LB, 160.
6. FBI/LB, 211.
7. Ibid.
8. FBI/LB, 139.
9. FBI New York Office File 62-8988B, Serial 3. The New York office changed classifications on Budenz several times, and the different files were not kept clearly separate. Hereafter, New York files on Budenz will be cited as FBINY, Budenz, file number, and serial.
10. FBI/LB, 190.
11. In the period just before the Tydings hearings, and again in 1951 when Budenz was called before the McCarran committee, the changes in his recollections due to "refreshing his memory" were so numerous the FBI could hardly keep track of them. See FBI/OL, 728.
12. FBI/LB, 227.
13. FBI/OL, 2327, 1324.
14. The transcript of the Santo hearing is printed in Tydings, 1691–1725.
15. Anderson, *Confessions of a Muckraker,* 201.
16. FBI/LB, 257.
17. FBINY, Budenz, 62-8988B, Serial 11; Budenz, 66-6709B, Serial 203.
18. FBI/LB, 282.
19. FBI/LB, 288.
20. Budenz, "Menace of Red China," 23.
21. Margaret Budenz, *Streets,* 242.
22. FBI/OL, 515.
23. Ibid.
24. FBI/OL, 3114.
25. FBI/OL, 182.
26. FBI/OL, 226.
27. FBI/OL, 531.
28. FBI/OL, 515, 444.
29. FBI/OL, 463, 514.

30.   FBI/OL, 1821.
31.   FBI/OL, 532.
32.   FBI/OL, 501.
33.   Ibid.
34.   FBI/OL, 561.
35.   FBI/OL, 488.
36.   Ibid.
37.   Ibid.
38.   FBI/OL, 724.
39.   Ibid.
40.   Ibid.
41.   FBI/OL, 927.
42.   FBI/OL, 1151.
43.   FBI/OL, 1150.
44.   FBI/OL, 1823.
45.   FBI/OL, 1822.
46.   FBI/OL, 702.
47.   FBI/LB, 314.
48.   FBI/OL, 1332; Reeves, *Joe McCarthy*, 716.
49.   FBI/OL, 1032.
50.   Lattimore, *Ordeal by Slander*, 111–12.
51.   Field's testimony is in Tydings, 709–35; Dodd's testimony is in Tydings, 631–59; Thorpe's testimony is in Tydings, 5558–68. Charles Callas, who worked for SISS from February to June 1952, says Thorpe told him that contrary to statements made by Lattimore in *Ordeal by Slander*, Thorpe's expenses in Washington were paid by the Lattimore team; author interview with Callas, August 19, 1989. All the principals are now deceased, and it is impossible to find records settling the matter.
52.   William G. Weart, "Lattimore Bids U.S. Sever Formosa Tie," *New York Times*, April 16, 1950.
53.   Tydings, 488.
54.   Ibid., 489.
55.   Budenz's "four hundred" list included many persons whom he never accused publicly. The FBI has released only a fraction of those he named. Some of the more prominent: Kay Boyle, John Carter Vincent, Albert Einstein, Rockwell Kent, Senator Elbert D. Thomas, Henry Steele Commager, Clifford Durr, John K. Fairbank, Carey McWilliams, Linus Pauling, Thomas I. Emerson, Walter Gellhorn, Representative Adolph Sabath.
56.   Tydings, 489; FBI/OL, 214, 1621.
57.   FBI/OL, 344.
58.   Tydings, 496.
59.   Ibid., 534.
60.   Tydings, 491–95. The fifth of these charges Budenz retracted in FBI interviews of May 4 and June 2, 1950; FBI/OL, 2434.
61.   Bayley, *Joe McCarthy and the Press*, analyzes press failure to show McCarthy's mendacity.
62.   Krock, "Capital Is Disturbed by Budenz Testimony," *New York Times*, April 23, 1950.
63.   FBI/OL, 1065.
64.   FBI/OL, 1231.
65.   FBINY, Budenz, 62-8988, Serial 237; FBINY, Budenz, 66-6709, Serial 262.
66.   FBI/LB, 324.

19. Exit Tydings, Enter Kim Il-sung

1. Lattimore, *Ordeal by Slander*, 125; *New York Times*, April 22, 1950.
2. FBI/OL, 1051.
3. FBI/OL, 1785.
4. Tydings, 631–59.
5. Ibid., 660–67.
6. FBI/OL, 1463. The Kerley charge reached the *Times* in watered-down form; see "Bella Dodd Terms Budenz 'Dishonest,' " *New York Times*, April 26, 1950. In this story Huber had only been "assaulted."
7. FBI/OL, 1282, 1463.
8. Ibid.
9. Ibid.
10. Ibid.
11. FBI/OL, 1504.
12. FBI/OL, 1484, 1907.
13. "Budenz Cautions of Plot in Pacific," *New York Times*, April 24, 1950.
14. Tydings, 669–707.
15. Ibid., 709–35; Field, *From Right to Left*, 218. Field's description of the Tydings hearings, and the mendacious Budenz, is inaccurate in some details but is overall a shrewd account of the inquisition. See especially chapter 20.
16. Tydings, 768.
17. Ibid., 759. For an extensive discussion of Utley's political and ideological shifts, and of her belief that the Nazis in 1940 could be "humanized and democratized" and hence were preferable to the Communists, see Klotz, "Freda Utley," chaps. 7–8.
18. Author interview with Utley, December 3, 1977.
19. "Freda Utley Calls Lattimore No Red Spy, But a 'Judas Cow,' " *New York Times*, May 2, 1950.
20. Lattimore, *Ordeal by Slander*, 146.
21. Tydings, 802.
22. Shewmaker, *Americans and Chinese Communists*, 245.
23. Tydings, 807.
24. Ibid., 809.
25. Ibid., 809, 813.
26. *New York Times*, May 3, 1950.
27. Jansen, "Owen Lattimore and the China Policy," *Christian Science Monitor*, May 12, 1950.
28. *Congressional Record*, Senate, May 12, 1950, 81st Cong., 2d sess., 6969.
29. Ibid., 6970.
30. Ibid.
31. Ibid., 6971.
32. Ibid., 6972, 6971.
33. Ibid., 6973–74.
34. "Budenz Uses Catholic Church as a 'Shield,' Chavez Charges," *New York Times*, May 13, 1950; "Head of Fordham Champions Budenz," *New York Times*, May 14, 1950; "McCarthy Says Red Wrote Chavez Talk," *New York Compass*, May 26, 1950.
35. Mimeographed copy of speech in LP; "Seven G.O.P. Senators Decry 'Smear' Tactics of McCarthy," *New York Times*, June 2, 1950.

36. Stueck, *Road to Confrontation*, 217.

37. Buhite, *Soviet-American Relations*, 169. On the outbreak of the Korean War, see also Cumings, *Origins of the Korean War;* and Simmons, *Strained Alliance.*

38. Oshinsky, *Conspiracy So Immense*, 167.

39. *Congressional Record,* Senate, July 6, 1950, 81st Cong., 2d sess., 9715; "McCarthy Charges Files Destruction," *New York Times,* July 13, 1950.

40. *Chicago Daily Tribune,* July 10, 1950.

41. Mimeographed copy of speech, LP.

42. *Baltimore Evening Sun,* July 7, 1950.

43. Tydings *Report,* 167. For a critique of the Tydings *Report* and its reception, see Reeves, *Life and Times,* 304–14.

44. "Red Charges by McCarthy Ruled False," *New York Times,* June 18, 1950.

45. Lattimore, *Ordeal by Slander,* 216, 9.

46. Ibid., 222.

47. Friendly, "Lattimore Answers McCarthy," *Washington Post,* July 30, 1950. Koen's book was actually printed in 1960 by Macmillan and review copies sent out, but the book was then withdrawn. Lawyers for the Chinese Nationalist government threatened Macmillan with a lawsuit because of charges in Koen's preface of illegal smuggling of narcotics into the United States by Nationalist Chinese. The book was finally published by Harper and Row in 1974.

48. Stefansson to Lattimores, October 6, 1949, LP.

49. Evelyn Stefansson to Eleanor Lattimore, May 18, 1950, LP. For Stefansson's account of this event, see his *Discovery,* chap. 45.

50. Stefansson to Lattimores, June 12, 1950, LP.

51. Stefansson to Lattimores, June 17, 1950, LP.

52. Stefansson to Lattimores, July 25, 1950, LP; FBI/OL, 2523.

53. "M'Carthy Hits Sale of Lattimore House," *New York Times,* July 28, 1950.

54. "New McCarthy vs. Lattimore Dispute On," *Baltimore Sun,* July 28, 1950.

20.   China Attacks

1. Edwards, "M'Carthy Links Lattimore to Slain Red Spy," *Chicago Tribune,* August 3, 1950.

2. "AP Suppressed Charge on Reds, Says M'Carthy," *Chicago Tribune,* August 8, 1950.

3. "Resort Hotel Bans Lattimore Talk as Poll of Guests Shows Protest," *New York Times,* August 28, 1950.

4. Ibid.

5. "M'Carthy Attacks Cheered by V.F.W.," *New York Times,* August 31, 1950.

6. FBI/OL, 2887.

7. Ibid.

8. FBI/OL, 2873.

9. FBI/OL, 2887.

10. FBI/OL, 2854.

11. FBI/OL, 2895.

12. Cooney, *American Pope*, 285, 324.

13. FBI/LB, 353; Edwards, "Budenz Names 380 Top Reds for Probers," *Washington Times-Herald*, September 1, 1950.

14. FBI/OL, 377.

15. Lattimore to Colegrove, September 5, 1950, Lattimore Papers, Hamburger Archives.

16. Evelyn Stefansson to Eleanor Lattimore, August 21, 1950, LP; Stefansson to Lattimores, August 21, 1950, LP; Evelyn Stefansson to Eleanor Lattimore, September 11, 1950, LP.

17. Ibid.

18. Tanner and Griffith, "Legislative Politics and 'McCarthyism,' " 168–88.

19. "Wellesley Permits Lattimore to Speak," *New York Times*, September 26, 1950; Bert Wissman, "Wellesley Trustees May Ban Invitation to Prof. Lattimore," *Washington Times-Herald*, October 2, 1950.

20. FBI/OL, 2858.

21. Fried, "Electoral Politics and McCarthyism," 205.

22. For an excellent account of the Maryland campaign, see Reeves, *Joe McCarthy*, 331–46.

23. "Owen Lattimore Lauds Tydings Regarding Whitewash Charge," *Baltimore Sun*, November 15, 1950.

24. Lattimore to Eisenhart, October 31, 1950, LP; Lattimore to Pandit Kunzru, December 11, 1950, Lattimore Papers, Hamburger Archives.

25. "U.S. Accuses Red China of 'Open Aggression'; 'New War,' Says M'Arthur; Truman Sees Aides: 200,000 of Foe Advance up to Twenty-three Miles in Korea," *New York Times*, November 29, 1950; "Skiers in Northwest Unite as Defense 'Guerrillas,' " *New York Times*, December 19, 1950; "Priest Justifies Use of Bomb for Defense," *New York Times*, December 25, 1950. For the complete story of the defeat of the Eighth Army, see Marshall, *The River and the Gauntlet*.

26. On the concept of virile self-image, see Ralph White, *Nobody Wanted War*, chap. 7.

27. FBI/OL, 2925.

28. FBI/OL, 5070.

29. SISS/IPR, 3430.

30. FBI/OL, 2944.

31. FBI/OL, 3017.

32. FBI/OL, 4769.

33. FBI/OL, 3017.

21.   McCarran

1. Steinberg, "McCarran Lone Wolf," 90.

2. Pittman, "Senator Patrick A. McCarran," 47–50, 79. I am much indebted to Von Pittman for his account of McCarran's anticommunism.

3. Ibid., 85–88.

4. Notes of Conversation with Senator John Foster Dulles, August 18, 1949, Wellington Koo Papers, Box, 130, Columbia University Library; "$1,500,000,000 Help to Nanking Urged," *New York Times*, January 29, 1949.

5. Norman H. Biltz Oral History, Western Studies Center, University of Nevada, Reno, 177.

6. "The Senate," *ADA World*, September 1950, 4A.

7. *Congressional Record*, March 29, 1950, 82d Cong., 1st sess., A2762–63; Fried, "Electoral Politics," 198–99.

8. Notes of conversations with Don Surine, Reeves Papers, Wisconsin State Historical Society.

9. FBI/OL, 1886; J. Edgar Hoover to Sidney W. Souers, February 20, 1950, President's Secretary's File, Box, 168, HSTL.

10. Anderson and May, *McCarthy*, 344.

11. "Senators Predict Sensation in Files," *New York Times*, February 11, 1951.

12. "Full Inquiry Pledged on Pacific Institute," *New York Times*, February 12, 1951; FBI/OL, 1886.

13. Morris, "Counsel for the Minority," 80.

14. FBI/OL, 3078, 3176.

15. FBI/OL, 3170. For an expanded account of these and other documents released by the Chinese Nationalists, see Newman, "Clandestine."

16. FBI/OL, 3170.

17. FBI/OL, 5842.

18. FBI/OL, no serial number. This is a cable from APO 500 to G-2 in Washington, July 7, 1951.

19. FBI/OL, 3298.

20. FBI/OL, 5842, 3174, 3252.

21. FBI/OL, 3174.

22. "Ban on Lattimore Asked," *New York Times*, March 6, 1951; "Lattimore Speaks," *New York Times*, March 8, 1951.

23. *Congressional Record*, April 19, 1951, 82d Cong., 2d sess, 4129.

24. The Government Printing Office issue of these hearings, published in 1951, is censored. A declassified version later became available in microfilm from University Publications of America.

25. Senate, Foreign Relations and Armed Services Committee, *Military Situation in the Far East*, 25–29.

26. Ibid., 37.

27. FBI/OL, 3105.

28. Lipper, *Elf Jahre*.

29. Lipper, *Eleven Years*. Henry Regnery does not mention his addition to Lipper's book; see his *Memoirs of a Dissident Publisher*, 104–6. In the 1970s Lattimore lived in Paris, where he got to know Ruth Fischer, a former Communist of stature and an early anti-Stalinist. Lattimore told me about a conversation with Fischer: "One day we were talking about the different kinds of ex-Communists— the reasonable ones, the sectarian ones, the pathological ones, and I mentioned Lipper [meaning her attack on him in the American edition of her book]. 'That's strange,' said Ruth, 'I know Lipper and I'll find out for you. She's an honest woman.' In due course she told me—but did not show me the letter—that Lipper had written her that this derogatory passage had been inserted by the American publishers, without consulting her."

30. FBI/OL, 3227.

31. Tydings, 523.

32. SISS/IPR, 2795–2823, 2871–76.

33. "Communist Threat inside U.S.," *U.S. News and World Report*, November 16, 1951, 30

34. FBI Headquarters File 100-221869, Joseph Zack Kornfeder, Serial 26.

35. Ibid., Serial 12; FBI/OL, 3006.

36. SISS Executive Session Records, Hearing of June 8, 1951, RG 46, NA; FBI Headquarters File 100-221869, Kornfeder, Serial 12.

37. SISS/IPR, 886; Caute, *Great Fear*, 126; May, *China Scapegoat*, 345.

38. SISS Executive Session Records, July 3, 1951, 12–13, RG 46, NA.

39. "Field Summoned to Senate Inquiry," *New York Times*, July 11, 1951.

40. "Senators Examine Field for Two Hours," *New York Times*, July 13, 1951.

41. "Lattimore Quiz Based on New Material," *Baltimore Evening Sun*, July 13, 1951.

42. SISS Executive Session Records, July 13, 1951, RG 46, NA; SISS/IPR, 3261.

43. Lattimore to Edgar McInnis, July 30, 1951, Lattimore Papers, Subseries 2, Correspondence, 1946–51, Hamburger Archives.

44. Undated memo headed "Lattimore, Owen," in SISS Files, IPR Investigation, RG 46, NA; FBI/OL, 3204.

45. FBI/OL, 3187.

46. "G.O.P. Loses Fight for Open MacArthur Inquiry," *New York Times*, May 5, 1951.

47. "Richardson and Nimitz," *New York Times*, May 28, 1951.

48. SISS/IPR, 2–5.

49. Thomas, *Institute of Pacific Relations*, 81; SISS/IPR, 10.

50. SISS/IPR, 18.

51. Ibid., 40.

52. Ibid., 2991.

53. "Field Says He Was Invited to Seek Air Intelligence Post," *New York Times*, July 27, 1951.

54. "Senators to Hear Ex-Wife of Eisler," *New York Times*, July 28, 1951.

55. FBI/OL, 3114.

56. SISS/IPR, 222.

57. Ibid., 208–9; Krivitsky, *In Stalin's Secret Service*; FBI/OL, 3294.

58. FBI/OL, 3294.

59. "Lattimore and Barnes Linked to Soviet Spies but Deny It," *New York Times*, August 1, 1951.

60. SISS/IPR, *Report*, 25, 195.

61. Barmine, *One Who Survived* and *Memoirs*; "Ex-Russian Agent Heard by Senators," *Baltimore Sun*, August 1, 1951; *Who Was Who in the USSR* (Metuchen, N.J.: Scarecrow Press, 1972), 67.

62. Krivitsky, *In Stalin's Secret Service*, 37–38; Deakin and Storry, *Case of Richard Sorge*, 60; SISS/IPR, 3107.

63. See the analysis of the questioning of Barmine in "Draft Memorandum for Mr. Crossman," August 31, 1951, Philip Jessup Papers, Box 26, Library of Congress.

64. SISS/IPR, 211.

65. *Chicago Tribune*, August 1, 1951.

66. "Foundations Face Inquiry by House," *New York Times*, August 2, 1951.

67. SISS/IPR, 223–71.

68. FBI/OL, 4769.

69. Fairbank, *Chinabound*, 339.

70. SISS/IPR, 314, 316.

71. Ibid., 288, 289–90, 303, 327, 334; Ulmen, *Science of Society*, 189, 199, 203–4, 263–80, 283–99, 569–71.

72. FBI/OL, 3985; Packer, *Ex-Communist Witnesses*, 216.

73. SISS/IPR, 342–49.

74. Ibid., 353–401, 439.

75. Ibid., 437.

76. Barth, "McCarran's Monopoly," 25, 26.

77. SISS/IPR, 517.

78. Ibid., 515. During the South Bend interrogations with agent Pat Coyne, Budenz himself agreed that because he had never been to a Soviet school for Communist leaders he knew *less* than did other Politburo members; this admission was quite forgotten during the SISS hearings. See also chapter 18.

79. SISS/IPR, 521, 529.

80. Ibid., 552, 555, 556.

81. Ibid., 685–86.

82. "Sorge's Spy Ring Held Copied in U.S.," *New York Times,* August 23, 1951; FBI/LB, 431.

83. Ibid.

84. FBINY, Budenz, File 62-8988, Serial 402.

85. FBI/OL, 3203.

86. Ibid.

87. SISS/IPR, 704–5, 714.

88. Ibid., 718, 719; Edwards, "Calls Acheson a Tool in 1945 of Lattimore," *Chicago Tribune,* September 1, 1951. For more on Dooman, see chapter 9. The intensity of Dooman's vindictiveness toward those who disagreed with him about Japan does not come through in his SISS testimony. To gauge it fully, see Emmerson, *Japanese Thread,* 314–26, and Schonberger, *Aftermath of War.*

89. Joseph Alsop, "Is It Accurate?" *New York Herald Tribune,* September 12, 1951.

90. William S. White, "Democrats Blaze at Acheson Critics," *New York Times,* September 15, 1951; "Lehman Presses Security Inquiry," *New York Times,* September 25, 1951.

91. SISS/IPR, 864–95.

92. Ibid., 905, 912, 915, 922; FBI/OL, 955.

93. SISS/IPR, 948.

94. Ibid., 975–80, 959.

95. Ibid.,1009.

96. Ibid., 1011, 1019.

97. Ibid., 3614.

98. Author interview with Philip Jessup, June 8, 1978. Stassen's appearances are recorded in SISS/IPR, 1035–74, 1111–38, 1252–77.

99. White, "Parley of Experts Urged Recognition of Red China in '49," *New York Times,* October 12, 1951; SISS/IPR, 1252–77; "Lattimore and Douglas Cited on Asia," October 3, 1951. The CIA Lattimore file has an interesting Soviet comment on Lattimore made while Stassen was trying to make Lattimore out to be a Soviet agent. The Soviet Information Bureau broadcast a castigation of Lattimore as "one of the leading propagandists of American imperialism [who is] late in 'discovering' the new Asia." The Soviet attack was prompted by an article Lattimore wrote for the *Nation* commenting on the Korean War. This item did not find its way to McCarran.

100. SISS/IPR, 1077–1110.

101. Crosby, *God, Church and Flag,* 59.

102. SISS/IPR, 1195.

103. Ibid., 1234.

104. Alsop to Hibbs, October 10, 1951, Alsop Papers, Box 80, Library of Congress.
105. SISS/IPR, 1303–5.
106. Ibid., 1322.
107. Ibid., 1329–30.
108. Ibid., 1330.
109. Ibid., 1351.
110. Ibid., 1342.
111. Ibid., 1368.
112. Ibid., 1405.
113. Ibid., 1405–6.
114. Ibid., 1485–86.
115. Alsop to Smith, October 19, 1951, Alsop Papers; Alsop to Smith, October 23, 1951, Alsop Papers.
116. Alsop to Smith, November 1, 1951, Alsop Papers.
117. Alsop to author, July 28, 1981.
118. Robert B. Ekvall to Lattimore, July 24, 1951, LP; hereafter cited as Ekvall letter. For the story of the Tibetan takeover, see Weissman, "Last Tangle in Tibet."
119. Eleanor Lattimore to Barretts, December 10, 1951, Lattimore Papers. The Takster Lama's family name was Thubten Jigme Norbu. For his account of his trip to the United States, see Norbu, *Tibet Is My Country*, 239–46; and Grunfeld, *Making of Modern Tibet*, 106–7.
120. Lattimore to Ekvall, July 23, 1951, LP. Ekvall's somewhat different interpretation of events is in Ekvall letter.
121. Lattimore to Ekvall, July 23, 1951, LP.
122. Eleanor Lattimore to Barretts, December 10, 1951, LP.
123. Fortas to Dewey Anderson, December 28, 1950, LP.
124. Eleanor Lattimore to Barretts, December 10, 1951, LP.
125. Shipley to Nicholson, December 6, 1951, Lattimore Passport File, State Department.
126. FBI/OL, 5536, 3264.
127. Eleanor Lattimore to Barretts, December 10, 1951, LP.
128. See Newman, "Clandestine," 221–22; "M'Carthy Attacks Truman on an Aide," *New York Times*, January 16, 1952; White, "1952 Campaign Issues Begin to Take Shape," *New York Times*, December 23, 1951.
129. FBI/OL, 3305.

22.   Venom: Twelve Days with SISS

1. "A Senate Inquiry," *New York Times*, October 13, 1951.
2. "Death of Nimitz Board Frees M'Carran's Hand," *New York Times*, November 4, 1951.
3. See Thurman Arnold to Herbert M. Levy, in Gressley, *Voltaire and the Cowboy*, 410–11. Arnold objected to ACLU's "quibbling" about technicalities while ignoring fundamental "legal and constitutional issues."
4. "Observing Fair Procedure," *New York Times*, November 16, 1951.
5. "Lattimore Rebukes US Policy Makers," *New Haven Evening Register*, October 21, 1951.

6. SISS/IPR, 2900.

7. FBI/OL, 3248.

8. FBI/OL, 3242.

9. FBI/OL, 3242, 3248, 3259.

10. FBI/OL, 3297.

11. FBI/OL, 3283, 3297.

12. "Communist Threat inside U.S.," *U.S. News and World Report*, November 16, 1951, 27–28.

13. SISS/IPR, 2175.

14. May, *China Scapegoat*, 348.

15. SISS/IPR, 2021–22.

16. Ibid., 2281.

17. FBI/OL, no serial number. This is a memo from Branigan to Belmont, April 1, 1952.

18. Some of Poppe's background is given in SISS/IPR, 2691–2731. For much of what Poppe did not tell the Senate, see Simpson, *Blowback*, 118–23. See also Poppe, *Reminiscences*, 208–16.

19. Weiner, "Nazi Sympathizers."

20. Poppe to Robert Morris, October 24, 1952, Box 139, RG 46, NA.

21. SISS/IPR, 2724–26.

22. SISS/IPR, 2726.

23. Poppe, *Reminiscences*, 216.

24. Westerfield, *Foreign Policy and Party Politics*, 246; Rorty and Decter, *McCarthy and the Communists*, 14; Navasky, *Naming Names*, chap. 10.

25. SISS/IPR, 2947.

26. Ibid., 2926.

27. Ibid., 2933–35.

28. Ibid., 3022–33. During the Iran-Contra hearings in Washington in July 1987, the frequency, force, and length of objections by Lieutenant Colonel Oliver North's counsel to questions asked by congressmen contrasted sharply with the muzzle put on counsel before SISS thirty-five years earlier.

29. SISS/IPR, 2899.

30. Ibid., 3038, 3041.

31. Ibid., 3041–42.

32. Ibid., 3084.

33. Ibid., 3095–96.

34. Ibid., 3123–25.

35. Ibid., 3426. The McCarran demand that Lattimore answer without thinking appears on page 3527.

36. Ibid., 3426.

37. Arnold, *Fair Fights and Foul*, 216.

38. Olney Oral History, Bancroft Library, University of California, 358, 362.

39. SISS/IPR, 3262.

40. "Lattimore Lashes Out at Committee," *Washington Post*, February 27, 1952; "Lattimore the Witness," *New York Times*, March 2, 1952.

41. SISS/IPR, 2919, 2924.

42. Ibid., 2988.

43. Ibid., 3006.

44. Ibid., 3078.

45. Ibid., 3085.

46. Fairbank, *Chinabound*, 347; SISS/IPR, 3721, 3718; Fairbank, *Chinabound*, 345.

47. SISS/IPR, 3720.
48. See note 17.
49. SISS/IPR, 3199, 3125, 3130, 3126, 3290.
50. Ibid., 3674–76.
51. Ibid., 3677, 3679.
52. "Senators Accuse Lattimore of Untruths in Testimony," *New York Times*, March 22, 1952; *Baltimore Sun*, March 23, 1952; Owens, "The Committee versus the Professor," *Baltimore Sun*, March 24, 1952.
53. Lattimore to Vincent, May 7, 1952, LP.
54. Tuchman to Lattimore, February 27, 1952, LP.
55. Vincent to Lattimore, March 28, 1952, LP.
56. "No Action on Lattimore Planned," *New York Times*, March 29, 1952.

23. Matusow, Bogolepov, the CIA, and Other Liars

1. For Matusow's career, see Caute, *Great Fear*, 133–38, O'Reilly, *Hoover and the Un-Americans*, 236–40; and Albert Kahn, *Matusow Affair*.
2. Matusow, *False Witness*, 102–6.
3. SISS/IPR, 3823–47; Olney Oral History, 364.
4. SISS/IPR, 4523.
5. Ibid., 3634.
6. Ibid., 3973–76.
7. Ibid., 3993.
8. Ibid., 3997.
9. Ibid., 3984.
10. FBI/OL, 3494.
11. SISS/IPR, 4033–71, 4159–4288, 4358–91, 4455–78.
12. Ibid., 4478–88.
13. Ibid., 4487.
14. FBI/OL, 3171. For more about Nyman, see Simpson, *Blowback*, 241–43.
15. FBI/OL, 3519.
16. FBI/OL, 3171.
17. SISS/IPR, 3519.
18. SISS/IPR, 4517–18.
19. Ibid., 4518–19.
20. Ibid., 4496.
21. Ibid., 4511–12.
22. De Silva, *Sub Rosa*, 17.
23. "Cold War in Russia on Soviet Is Noted," *New York Times*, December 7, 1952; "Hiss' Red Tie Held Known to Dulles," *New York Times*, December 18, 1952.
24. FBI/OL, 3617, 3618.
25. FBI/OL, 3604. For a full account of the Jarvinen affair and its legal outcome, see Newman, "Red Scare in Seattle, 1952."
26. FBI/OL, 3608.
27. FBI/OL, 3606, 3585.
28. FBI/OL, 3601, 3666.
29. Ward, "U.S. Lays Lattimore Travel Ban to 'Official' Word He Planned Trip behind Iron Curtain," *Baltimore Sun*, June 21, 1952.
30. Ibid.

31. FBI/OL, 3617.
32. Sentner, "Lattimore Tip from Seattle," *Seattle Post-Intelligencer*, June 22, 1952.
33. FBI/OL, 3627.
34. Guthman, "False Tip on Lattimore Given by Employee of Travel Agency Here," *Seattle Daily Times*, June 26, 1952.
35. *New York Times*, June 27, 1952.
36. Sperber, *Murrow*, 387.
37. "Two U.S. Agents in Contempt of Court in Jarvinen Case," *Seattle Daily Times*, September 23, 1952.
38. FBI/OL, 3652.
39. SISS/IPR, 4763–4808.
40. Buckley, "Owen Lattimore and the 'Cold War,' " 54; Minutes, Senate Judiciary Committee, July 1, 1952, 82d Cong., RG 46, NA.
41. *Congressional Record*, July 2, 1952, 82d Cong., 2d sess., 8860, 8863.
42. SISS/IPR *Report*, 223–25.
43. "Senate Unit Calls Lattimore Agent of Red Conspiracy," *New York Times*, July 3, 1952; "Senate Report Calls Lattimore Soviet Conspiracy Instrument, Recommends Perjury Proceeding," *Baltimore Evening Sun*, July 2, 1952. See also the discussion of press coverage in Thomas, *Institute of Pacific Relations*, 97–99.
44. SISS/IPR *Report*, 21, 190–91.
45. SISS/IPR, 3891.
46. FBI/OL, 3552.
47. Truman to Attorney General, July 5, 1952, White House Central Files, Box 39, HSTL.
48. Westerfield, *Foreign Policy and Party Politics*, 250, 253.
49. Ibid., 246.
50. Harper, *Politics of Loyalty*, 217–19.
51. Kristol, "Ordeal by Mendacity."
52. Rorty and Decter, *McCarthy and the Communists*, 5 and throughout.
53. De Borchgrave and Moss, *The Spike*, 158, 208, 415.

24.   Roy Cohn as Torquemada

1. See chapter 17.
2. FBI/OL, 3017, 3203.
3. FBI/OL, 3538.
4. FBI/OL, 3578.
5. FBINY, Budenz, File 66-6709, Serial 101; FBI/LB, 458.
6. FBI/OL, 3580.
7. Cronin to author, April 17, 1981; FBI/OL, 4769.
8. FBI/OL, 4769.
9. Ibid.
10. FBI/OL, 3727.
11. The best biography of Cohn is von Hoffman, *Citizen Cohn*.
12. U.S. House of Representatives, Committee on the Judiciary, Special Subcommittee to Investigate the Department of Justice, 82d Cong., 2d sess., *Hearings on House Resolution 95*, part 2, 1782–1812.
13. SISS/IPR, 4627–4737; FBI/OL, 3531.

14. FBI/OL, 3560.
15. FBI/OL, 3562.
16. U.S. Senate, Committee on the Judiciary, *Hearings on the Nomination of James P. McGranery*, 25.
17. Reeves, *Joe McCarthy*, 425.
18. Matusow, *False Witness*, 107; von Hoffman, *Citizen Cohn*, 134.
19. Ross L. Malone to Myles J. Lane, September 10, 1952, James P. McGranery Papers, Box 70, Library of Congress.
20. Author interview with Cohn, December 28, 1979; FBI/OL, 3713.
21. Gilbert (Roger Kennedy), "New Light," 11.
22. Author interview with Cohn, December 28, 1979.
23. FBI/OL, 3725.
24. FBI/OL, 3726.
25. FBI/OL, 3730.
26. FBI/OL, 3742.
27. FBI/OL, 3729.
28. FBI/OL, 3749.
29. "M'Granery Pressed on Lattimore Case," *New York Times*, October 4, 1952.
30. FBI/OL, 3916.
31. FBI/OL, 3758.
32. FBI/OL, 3911.
33. Ibid.
34. Anastos to Foley, December 1, 1952, Lattimore File, Department of Justice.
35. "Lattimore Faces a Perjury Inquiry," *New York Times*, December 3, 1952.
36. "Clearing of Spies for U.N. Laid to State Department by Defiant U.S. Jury Here," *New York Times*, December 3, 1952.
37. FBI/OL, 3919.
38. Menon to Lattimore, May 15, 1952, Lattimore Papers, Hamburger Archives.
39. Lattimore to Beloff, May 19, 1952, Lattimore Papers, Hamburger Archives.
40. Lattimore, *Inner Asian Frontiers of China*, xxxvi.
41. Lattimore, "Inner Asia," 513–14.
42. FBI/OL, 3927.
43. "Lattimore Indicted on Perjury Counts: He Issues a Denial," *New York Times*, December 17, 1952. My petition to the U.S. District Court for the District of Columbia to unseal the 1952 Lattimore grand jury minutes was filed in June 1987 by attorney Patti A. Goldman of the Public Citizen Litigation Group. She had been successful in obtaining the grand jury minutes in the William W. Remington case from the U.S. District Court for the Southern District of New York for the use of historian Gary May. The D.C. court, however, denied my petition with no hearing and giving no reasons. The court of appeals for the D.C. circuit refused to hear an appeal. Since there are many conflicting district court opinions on release of grand jury minutes, Goldman petitioned the Supreme Court of the United States for a writ of certiorari. See Robert P. Newman v. United States of America, October Term, 1988, No. 88-548. Charles Fried, U.S. solicitor general, filed a brief in opposition, arguing that "this case, and cases like this one, are not exceptional cases, and they do not present a compelling claim for disclosure. . . . Even if dressed up as a significant project of historical scholarship, requests of the type made by petitioner could not easily be distinguished from journalistic in-

quiries . . . or requests based simply on individual or public curiosity." On January 9, 1989, the Court rejected my petition.

44. FBI/OL, 3996.
45. FBI/OL, 3998.
46. Kidd to McGranery, December 16, 1952, McGranery Papers.
47. Farley to Eleanor Lattimore, December 18, 1952, LP.
48. Toynbee to Lattimore, December 19, 1952, LP.
49. Wright to Hill, February 9, 1953, LP.
50. "U.S. Quashes Case M'Carthy Caused," *New York Times*, May 26, 1954; Shalett, "How to Be a Crime Buster," 502. See also Lamont, *Freedom Is as Freedom Does*, 156.

25. Youngdahl

1. Edwards, *Pat McCarran*, chap. 9; "Alien Law Bars 269 of Liberte's Crew," *New York Times*, December 24, 1952.
2. FBI/OL, no serial number (this is a memo from Nichols to Tolson, February 5, 1953, located behind serial 4143); FBI/OL, 3927.
3. FBI/OL, 3927.
4. U.S. Senate, Committee on the Judiciary, *Herbert Brownell, Jr., Attorney General–Designate*, January 19, 1953, 4.
5. "Issue Raised on Lattimore," *Baltimore Sun*, January 20, 1953.
6. Cronin to McCarran, January 21, 1953, Lattimore File, Department of Justice.
7. Payne to McCarran, January 28, 1953, Lattimore File, Department of Justice.
8. FBI/OL, 4127.
9. FBI/OL, 4143.
10. McCarran to Hummer, February 16, 1953, SISS Records, RG 46, Box 140, NA.
11. Hummer to McCarran, February 25, 1953, McCarran Papers, Eva Adams Files, University of Nevada, Reno.
12. "Issue Raised on Lattimore," *Baltimore Sun*, January 20, 1953.
13. Olney Oral History, 359–60.
14. FBI/OL, 4330.
15. FBI/OL, 4481.
16. Author interview with Fortas, March 18, 1981.
17. Lattimore, *Ordeal by Slander*, 111.
18. Gressley, *Voltaire and the Cowboy*, 86, 99.
19. Ibid., 86.
20. Author interview with Frank, May 15, 1986.
21. On Emerson and Countryman, see Schrecker, *No Ivory Tower*, 251–53.
22. Thomas I. Emerson Oral History, Columbia University, 2294.
23. Arnold, *Fair Fights*, 204.
24. Author interview with Fortas, March 18, 1981.
25. Author interview with Rogers, September 18, 1987.
26. FBI/OL, 4077, 4153, 4322.
27. FBI/OL, 4131.
28. "Lattimore Trial Date Set, May Be Changed," *Baltimore Evening Sun*, February 6, 1953.

29. "Far East Expert Claims Effort to Entrap Him," *Baltimore Sun*, February 17, 1953. All quotations from the defense brief are from the *Sun* story. For the full brief, see U.S. District Court for the District of Columbia, Criminal No. 1879–52, U.S. v. Owen Lattimore, Motion by Defendant to Dismiss the Indictment and Memorandum in Support of Motion, filed February 16, 1953.

30. Ibid.

31. Ibid.

32. FBI/OL, 4258, 4620.

33. FBI/OL, 4279, 916, 4418.

34. "M'Carran Opposes Bohlen as Envoy; Wiley Seeks 'Facts,' " *New York Times*, March 16, 1953.

35. "U.S. Calls Lying Only Lattimore Trial Issue," *Baltimore Evening Sun*, March 17, 1953.

36. FBI/OL, 4457.

37. "Dashiell Hammett Silent at Inquiry," *New York Times*, March 27, 1953. For an account of the Cohn-Schine trip to Europe, see Reeves, *Joe McCarthy*, 488–91.

38. See Esbjornson, *Luther W. Youngdahl*; "Luther Youngdahl," *Washington Post*, June 24, 1978; "Judge Luther Youngdahl," *Washington Post*, June 22, 1978.

39. "Lattimore's Trial Put Off till October," *Baltimore Sun*, April 1, 1953.

40. Eleanor Lattimore to Barretts, April 2, 1953, LP.

41. "OL's Notes on Hearings, March 31 and April 1, 1953," LP.

42. Ibid.

43. Ibid.

44. Ibid.

45. See note 39.

46. FDI/OL, 4536, 1632, 4781.

47. "McCarthy Critics Challenged by Twenty-eight," *New York Times*, April 6, 1953.

48. FBI/OL, 4713.

49. "Judge Throws Out Four Perjury Charges against Lattimore," *New York Times*, May 3, 1953. For the full text, see U.S. District Court for the District of Columbia, Criminal No. 1879-52, U.S. v. Owen Lattimore, Memorandum, May 2, 1953.

50. "Judge Also Sees 'Doubt' on Three Counts," *Baltimore Sun*, May 3, 1953; author interview with Rogers, September 18, 1987.

51. "Judge Throws Out," *New York Times*, May 3, 1953. Judge Youngdahl gave me the mail he received on his Lattimore rulings. Surprisingly, the congratulatory letters (350) outnumbered the hate letters (123). Only three members of Congress wrote, all approvingly; Senators Hubert Humphrey and J. William Fulbright and Congresswoman Coya Knutson. Many of the favorable letters were from other judges and lawyers. The hate mail was vicious, some of it addressed to "Comrade Youngdahl." Much of it was anonymous, very little of it from professionals. Mrs. Charles Clifton Moses of Bluffton, South Carolina, was consumed by the Lattimore case and Youngdahl's rulings. She wrote four letters to Youngdahl and at least two to Brownell (with copies to Youngdahl) expressing her horror at the "Washington–New York Egghead Axis" that was delivering America to the Communists. One of these letters included a seventeen-page, single-spaced analysis of the IPR and its minions on which she had spent three months of research.

26.   Rover, Asiaticus, and BDPT

1.   Harvey, "Owen Lattimore," 9; author interview with David Spring, October 26, 1982.
2.   "The Page School Is Being Closed," *New York Times*, April 17, 1953.
3.   FBI/OL, 4769.
4.   Author interview with Smith, June 25, 1984; with Harvey, October 24, 1982; with Shaffer, May 6, 1982.
5.   FBI/OL, 4274. *Lattimore the Scholar* was privately published in Baltimore; copies are located in Arnold and Porter files and LP.
6.   "Lattimore Defense Funds Sought," *Baltimore Evening Sun*, January 10, 1953; Esbjornson, *Luther W. Youngdahl*, 268.
7.   Author interview with Owens, May 6, 1982.
8.   FBI/OL, 5052.
9.   FBI Headquarters File 100-400471. Owen Lattimore Defense Fund, Serial 6.
10.   Ibid., Serials 18, 20.
11.   Author interview with DeFrancis, November 30, 1977.
12.   This is as Lattimore remembered it in 1981.
13.   Author interview with Kahin, August 10, 1979.
14.   Schrecker, *No Ivory Tower*, 89.
15.   Lazarsfeld and Thielens, *Academic Mind*, 93; Schrecker, *No Ivory Tower*, 340.
16.   FBI/OL, 4795, 4764.
17.   FBI/OL, 4796.
18.   "U.S. Files an Appeal in Lattimore's Case," *New York Times*, May 15, 1953.
19.   "Some Questions for AF&P," May 1953, LP.
20.   See the description of Flynn in Radosh, *Prophets on the Right*, chaps. 7–8.
21.   "Lattimore Case for the Supreme Court," *New York Times*, May 17, 1953.
22.   FBI/OL, 4872, 3599.
23.   FBI/OL, 5135.
24.   FBI/OL, 4031.
25.   FBI/OL, 5003, 5076.
26.   FBI/OL, 5115.
27.   FBI/OL, 5169. FBI clearance practices are capricious. Hundreds of documents are denied in toto to protect individuals named in them who may have done something illegal. Yet the incriminating document that shows Rover and Hummer attempting to blackmail a witness to get him to cooperate was released with only the name of the person blackmailed denied.
28.   "U.S. Says Quashings in Lattimore Case Violate Basic Law," *New York Times*, August 25, 1953. For the full text, see U.S. Court of Appeals for the District of Columbia Circuit, U.S. v. Owen Lattimore, No. 11849, Brief for Appellant, filed August 24, 1953.
29.   FBI/OL, 5263.
30.   FBI/OL, 5259, 5292.
31.   FBI/OL, 5304.

32. FBI/OL, 5304, 5370, 5504.
33. Major stories appeared in the *New York Times,* the *Washington Post,* and the *Baltimore Sun* on October 2, 1953. For the full record, see U.S. Court of Appeals for the District of Columbia Circuit, U.S. v. Owen Lattimore, No. 11849, Brief for Appellee, filed October 2, 1953.
34. FBI/OL, 5289.
35. FBI/OL, 5188.
36. FBI/OL, 5322.
37. Ibid.
38. Memorandum for the Attorney General, November 4, 1953, Ann Whitman Diary Series, Dwight D. Eisenhower Library, Abilene, Kansas.
39. Ibid.
40. FBINY, Budenz, 66-6709-B-119.
41. Herbert Brownell Oral History, Columbia University Library, New York, 297–98.
42. Olney Oral History, 364.
43. FBI/OL, 5600.
44. "U.S. Again Urges Lattimore Action," *Baltimore Sun,* November 13, 1953; FBI/OL, 5336.
45. "Second Book Banned in Town," *New York Times,* November 14, 1953.
46. FBI/OL, 5365.
47. SISS/IPR, 3131.
48. SISS/IPR, 3132.
49. FBI/OL, 1380, 5718.
50. FBI/OL, 5059, 5855.
51. FBI/OL, 2288; MacKinnon and MacKinnon, *Agnes Smedley,* 228; and Steve MacKinnon to author, September 1, 1988.
52. FBI/OL, 5263.
53. FBI/OL, 5455.
54. FBI/OL, 5546.
55. FBI/OL, 5547.
56. FBI/OL, 5752.
57. FBI/OL, 5842.
58. FBI/OL, 5921, 5946.
59. FBI/OL, 6347.
60. FBI/OL, 6348.
61. FBI/OL, 6347.
62. The FBI files have five major reports on the Holabird investigation: Serials 5455, 5460, 5505, 5519, 5551.
63. "Court Weighs Plea in Lattimore Case," *Baltimore Evening Sun,* January 26, 1954.
64. "U.S. Fights Ruling in Lattimore Case," *New York Times,* January 26, 1954.
65. Eleanor Lattimore to Barretts, January 29, 1954, LP.
66. See Adams, *Without Precedent.* This is the best and most accurate account of the Army-McCarthy fracas.
67. Eleanor Lattimore to Stefanssons, March 10, 1954, LP.
68. "M'Carran Warns on Reds," *New York Times,* May 2, 1954.
69. FBI/OL, 5874; "Lattimore Upheld on Battle to Kill Key Count in Case," *New York Times,* July 9, 1954.

70. U.S. Court of Appeals for the District of Columbia, No. 11849, U.S. v. Owen Lattimore, decided July 8, 1954, 2–4.

71. Ibid., 10–13.

72. Ibid., 14, 29–30.

73. Ibid., 31–33, 37.

74. Ibid., 40–43.

75. Ibid., 2–4.

76. *New York Times*, July 9, 1954.

77. "Dismissal of Key Lattimore Perjury Charge Upheld," *Baltimore Evening Sun*, July 8, 1954; "Court on Lattimore," *New York Times*, July 11, 1954.

78. FBI/OL, 5959.

79. FBI/OL, 5972.

80. FBI/OL, 5985.

81. FBI/OL, 5992.

82. FBI/OL, 5993.

83. FBI/OL, 6045.

84. FBI/OL, 6054.

85. FBI/OL, 6057; "Lattimore Facing a New Indictment," *New York Times*, August 20, 1954.

86. Fortas to Lattimore, August 25, 1954, LP.

87. Lattimore to Barbara Holgate, September 19, 1954, LP.

88. FBI/OL, 6065.

89. FBI/OL, 6069.

90. FBI/OL, 5536; Records of the SISS, Memo from Ben Mandel to Jay Sourwine, June 20, 1952, RG 46, Box 139, NA.

91. Charles B. Murray to Hoover, January 30, 1953, Lattimore File, Justice Department.

92. FBI/OL, 4271.

93. FBI/OL, 4680, 4974.

94. FBI/OL, 5040.

95. George to author, February 9, 1985.

96. FBI/OL, 5040.

97. FBI/OL, 5134, 5154.

98. FBI/OL, 5426, 5362, 5426.

99. FBI/OL, 5512.

100. Ballantine Oral History, 215, 216.

101. Dallin, *Soviet Russia*, 220, 229, 330; Dallin, "Writings of Owen Lattimore," 11; Dallin, "Henry Wallace and Chinese Communism," 14; Wallace to Daniel James, October 23, 1951, Alsop Papers; Alsop to Arthur G. McDowell, October 25, 1951, Alsop Papers.

102. Poppe, *Reminiscences*, 214.

103. See the listing in *Who Was Who in America*, vol. 3, 1951–60 (Chicago: Marquis, 1961), 841.

104. Emerson, review of *War and Peace*, by Taracouzio, 569; T. A. Taracouzio, *War and Peace*, 259, 273.

105. FBI/OL, 6089.

106. FBI/OL, 6163.

107. Joseph W. Ballantine Papers, Box 2, Hoover Institution, Stanford University. This document is not paginated.

108. Lattimore, *Solution in Asia*, 158–59, 170, 173, 191, 198, 205.

109. FBI/OL, 6069.

27. Second Indictment, Second Dismissal

1. FBI/OL, 5986.
2. "M'Carthy Accepts Cohn Resignation, Transfers Surine," *New York Times*, July 21, 1954. "Resignation" is a euphemism; the committee members forced Cohn out.
3. Gibney, "After the Ball."
4. Speech of Alfred Kohlberg at dinner honoring Roy M. Cohn, July 28, 1954, William Knowland Papers, Far East Files Carton 2, Bancroft Library, University of California, Berkeley.
5. Rover to McCarran, August 24, 1954, Eva Adams Papers.
6. FBI/OL, 6108.
7. Field, *From Right to Left*, 266.
8. FBI/OL, 6171.
9. FBI/OL, 6172.
10. "Senator McCarran Is Dead in Nevada," *New York Times*, September 29, 1954.
11. U.S. District Court for the District of Columbia, Grand Jury Impaneled July 2, 1954, U.S. v. Owen Lattimore, True Bill, returned October 7, 1954, 3–4.
12. U.S. Court of Appeals for the District of Columbia Circuit, No. 12,609, U.S. v. Owen Lattimore, Brief of Appellee, filed November 18, 1954, 8.
13. "Owen Lattimore Is Indicted Again in Perjury Case," *New York Times*, October 8, 1954. All major papers headlined the indictment.
14. FBI/OL, 6177.
15. "U.S. Attorney Asks Judge to Step Out of Lattimore Case," *New York Times*, October 14, 1954.
16. U.S. District Court for the District of Columbia, Criminal No. 1879–52, U.S. v. Owen Lattimore, Motion to Strike Affidavit of Bias and Prejudice, October 14, 1954.
17. "Brownell Backs Attack on Judge," *New York Times*, October 15, 1954.
18. "Lattimore Move Attacked by U.S.," *New York Times*, October 21, 1954.
19. U.S. District Court for the District of Columbia, Criminal Nos. 1016–54 and 1879–52, Motions, Official Transcript, October 22, 1954, 16; "Lattimore Judge Scored in Hearing," *New York Times*, October 23, 1954.
20. See case information cited in note 19.
21. Anderson, *Confessions of a Muckraker*, 194; see also Reeves, *Joe McCarthy*, chap. 10.
22. FBI/OL, 6200: "Judge Calls Bias Charge Scandalous," *Baltimore Sun*, October 24, 1954.
23. FBI/OL, 6209; U.S. Court of Appeals for the District of Columbia Circuit, No. 12,609, U.S. v. Owen Lattimore, Brief of Appellee, November 18, 1954, 7.
24. "British Interest in Case High," *New York Times*, October 29, 1954.
25. "O'Mahoney Holds Lead in Wyoming," *New York Times*, October 24, 1954.
26. "Inquiry Asked on Judge Attack," *New York Times*, October 30, 1954; "Lattimore Trial Inquiry Set," *New York Times*, November 21, 1954; FBI/OL, 6270.
27. "Rayburn Cites Inquiry Fields," *New York Times*, November 5, 1954.
28. White, "G.O.P. Future Involved in the M'Carthy Case," *New York Times*, November 7, 1954.
29. "Dulles Dismisses Davies as a Risk; Loyalty Not Issue," *New York Times*,

November 6, 1954; see also John W. Finney, "The Long Trial of John Paton Davies," *New York Times Magazine*, August 31, 1969. Author interview with Davies, April 26, 1981.

30.   FBI/OL, 6256, 6251. Hummer is probably wrong; Solicitor General Simon Sobeloff probably made this decision. See "Youngdahl Fight Is Dropped by U.S.," *New York Times*, November 18, 1954.

31.   "Youngdahl Bids U.S. Admit Error," *New York Times*, November 19, 1954; "Lattimore Counsel Ask Youngdahl Test," *New York Times*, November 20, 1954.

32.   FBI/OL, 6284.

33.   FBI/OL, 6278.

34.   "Final Vote Condemns M'Carthy," *New York Times*, December 3, 1954.

35.   "Lattimore Urges Quashing of Case," *New York Times*, December 14, 1954.

36.   FBI/OL, 6365, 6379.

37.   Straight, *After Long Silence*, 281.

38.   Ibid., 282.

39.   Stein, "Communication," 22.

40.   Harrington, "The Committee for Cultural Freedom," 119–20; see also McAuliffe, *Crisis on the Left*, 126–27; FBI/OL, 6406; "U.S. Files Evidence in Lattimore Case," *New York Times*, January 8, 1955; FBI/OL, 6457.

41.   U.S. District Court for the District of Columbia, Criminal No. 1016–54, U.S. v. Owen Lattimore, Memorandum Opinion, filed January 18, 1955; see also "Judge Youngdahl Drops Second Charge in Lattimore Case," *New York Times*, January 19, 1954.

42.   "New Lattimore Count Dismissed, Called Too Obscure," *Baltimore Evening Sun*, January 18, 1955.

43.   FBI/OL, 6462.

44.   FBI/OL, 6475; informant downgradings appear in serials 6595, 6598, 6603, 6611, 6616, 6620, 6621, 6631, 6632, 6635, 6642, 6643, 6644, 6648, 6649. One informant downgrading report has no serial number.

45.   "U.S. Plans Appeal in Lattimore Case," *New York Times*, February 5, 1955; FBI/OL, 6506, 6509.

46.   "Lattimore Talks Slated in Europe," *Baltimore Sun*, April 23, 1955.

47.   FBI/OL, 6556, 6567, 6571.

48.   FBI/OL, 6580, 6592.

49.   Telephone call from Governor Adams, May 17, 1955, Eisenhower Telephone Calls Series, Dwight D. Eisenhower Library.

50.   Memorandum of Telephone Conversation with the Attorney General, May 18, 1955, John Foster Dulles General Correspondence and Memoranda Series, Dwight D. Eisenhower Library.

51.   Memorandum of Telephone Conversation with Mr. Sherman Adams, May 18, 1955, John Foster Dulles General Correspondence and Memoranda Series, Dwight D. Eisenhower Library.

52.   Telephone Call to the President, May 18, 1955, John Foster Dulles Telephone Calls Series, Dwight D. Eisenhower Library.

53.   "Passport Ban Hit by Einstein Aide," *New York Times*, May 21, 1955.

54.   Tompkins to Hoover, March 28, 1955, Lattimore File, Department of Justice; FBI/OL, 6565; FBI/OL, 6646.

55.   "Lattimore Case Again Appealed," *New York Times*, April 12, 1955; FBI/OL, 6589.

56.   "Complex Points in Lattimore Case Argued before Full Appeals Bench,"

Washington Post, June 2, 1955; William D. Rogers to John P. Frank, June 9, 1955, Lattimore Files, Arnold and Porter.

57. FBI/OL, 6654.

58. FBI/OL, 6654, 6704.

59. FBI/OL, 6662.

60. FBI/OL, 6692.

61. "Court of Appeals Upholds Dismissal of Two Key Lattimore Perjury Charges," *Washington Post*, June 15, 1955; "Lattimore Wins New Court Test," *New York Times*, June 15, 1955.

62. Author interview with Rogers, September 18, 1987.

63. "Writer's Conviction Set Aside Because Red Query Was 'Vague,' " *New York Times*, December 21, 1956.

64. FBI/OL, 6671.

65. "Lattimore Perjury Case Dropped by Government," *New York Times*, June 29, 1955.

66. FBI/OL, 6673.

67. Author interview with Youngdahl, December 3, 1977.

68. FBI/OL, 6689.

69. Sullivan, *Bureau*, 45–46.

70. Author interview with Cohn, December 28, 1979.

71. Olney Oral History, 360–61.

72. Gilbert, "Judge Youngdahl Wins," 6.

73. Lattimore to O'Mahoney, July 13, 1955, O'Mahoney Papers, Box 184, Coe Library, University of Wyoming.

28. Starting Over

1. Francis White to John Nelson, September 19, 1955, Special Collections, White Papers, Eisenhower Library, Johns Hopkins University.

2. John Nelson to Francis White, September 14, 1955, White Papers.

3. Author interview with David Spring, October 26, 1982.

4. "Lattimore Talk Shifted," *New York Times*, December 7, 1955.

5. "Lattimore, in Hartford, Says He Has Stock in Company That Denied Him Auditorium," *New York Times*, December 17, 1955.

6. A text of this speech, including "revisions made as delivered at a dinner sponsored by the Citizens Committee to Preserve Academic Freedoms, Saturday, March 24, 1956, at Hollywood Athletic Club," is in the J. B. Matthews Papers. All quotations are from this text.

7. Author interview with David Lattimore, August 31, 1987.

8. Lattimore to Bernhard, October 26, 1955, LP.

9. Bernhard to Lattimore, April 6, 1956, LP.

10. Lattimore to Bernhard, March 1, 1956, LP.

11. Lattimore to Bernhard, August 29, 1956, LP.

12. Lattimore to Bernhard, December 29, 1956, LP.

13. Lattimore to Bernhard, June 25, 1957, LP. For a full analysis of Lattimore's beliefs about Point Four (development) aid, see Cotton, *Asian Frontier Nationalism*, 108–10.

14. Lattimore to Barretts, December 26, 1956, LP.

15. Ibid.

16. Milton Eisenhower to Lattimore, January 22, 1957, Eisenhower Papers, Special Collections, Eisenhower Library, Johns Hopkins University.

17.   Eleanor Lattimore to Barretts, March 17, 1957, LP.
18.   Lattimore, review of *To Lhasa and Beyond*, by Giusseppe Tucci, *Pacific Affairs* 31 (December 1958): 418.
19.   "McCarthy Target Finally Cleared," *Washington Post*, May 8, 1960.
20.   William D. Rogers to Lattimore, October 22, 1959, LP.
21.   Institute of Pacific Relations v. U.S., 5 AFTR 2d 1333.
22.   Lattimore to Tikhvinskii, September 15, 1959, Lattimore File, CIA.
23.   Lattimore, *Nomads and Commissars*, xviii. Despite the invitation and a warm reception when Lattimore got there, Mongol officials were still very divided in their opinions about him. According to Harrison Salisbury, who was in Ulan Bator in December 1961, Lattimore's picture "still hung in the State Revolutionary Museum, along with that of Roy Chapman Andrews, as an enemy of the Mongol people"; "Lattimore of the C.I.A.," *New York Times*, August 27, 1989.
24.   "Lattimore to Visit Outer Mongolia," *New York Times*, March 20, 1961.
25.   Lattimore, *Nomads and Commissars*, xix.
26.   Owen Lattimore to David Lattimore (father), July 2, 1961, Lattimore File, CIA.
27.   Ibid.
28.   Owen Lattimore to David Lattimore (son), July 17, 1961, Lattimore File, CIA.
29.   Lattimore to William O. Douglas, Aug. 4, 1961, Douglas Papers, Box 350, Library of Congress.
30.   Owen and Eleanor Lattimore, *Silks, Spices, and Empire*, 1.
31.   Douglas, *Go East, Young Man*, 382.
32.   Eleanor Lattimore to Mercedes Douglas, September 1, 1961, Douglas Papers.
33.   "Outer Mongolia's Status," *New York Times*, May 2, 1961; Bachrack, *Committee of One Million*, 202–3; see Hilsman's account, *To Move a Nation*, 305–7.
34.   "Mongolia Celebration United Old and New," *Washington Post*, July 12, 1961; "Finds Softening in Red Stand," *Washington Star*, July 13, 1961.
35.   "Sokolsky Scores Double Trickery," *Brooklyn Tablet*, July 29, 1961.
36.   Rowe to Eastland, August 9, 1961, Records of the SISS, Box 140, RG 46, NA; Eastland to Rowe, August 17, 1961, Records of the SISS.
37.   "U.S. Cancels Plan for Mongolia Tie," *New York Times*, August 12, 1961.
38.   "Dodd Urges Senate to Investigate Owen Lattimore's Visit to Mongolia," *Washington Post*, August 23, 1961; "Lattimore Trip Hit," *New York Times*, August 23, 1961.
39.   "Mongolia Tie Urged by Justice Douglas," *New York Times*, August 30, 1961.
40.   Lattimore, *Nomads and Commissars*, chaps. 6–7. For a critical view of this book, see Cotton, *Asian Frontier Nationalism*, chap. 7.
41.   See Lattimore's tribute to Stefansson, *Polar Notes*, November 1962, 47–48.
42.   "Lattimore to Teach at Leeds U.," *New York Times*, November 13, 1962.
43.   Lattimore to Pankratov, February 18, 1963, Lattimore File, CIA.
44.   Graves to Lattimore, February 23, 1963, LP.
45.   Author interview with David Spring, October 26, 1982.
46.   Author interview with Wickwire, May 6, 1982; Harvey, "Owen Lattimore," 10.
47.   Author interview with Heinrichs, August 3, 1978.

29.   Ascendancy at Leeds

1.   Eleanor Lattimore to Betty Barnes, August 13, 1963, Barnes private papers.

2.   Eleanor Lattimore to Evelyn Stefansson, June 25, 1963, Nef private papers.

3.   "Buddhist Leader Is Ill of Cancer in New Haven," *New York Times*, August 13, 1963.

4.   Lattimore, *From China Looking Outward*, 24–25.

5.   The text of his address is attached to Lattimore to Joseph Needham, December 1, 1963, LP.

6.   Lattimore to Bernhard, December 15, 1963, LP.

7.   Farnsworth, "Lattimore Holds Chair in Britain," *New York Times*, March 1, 1964.

8.   Lattimore to Bernhard, June 30, 1964, LP.

9.   "No Grudges, Lattimore Says," *Washington Star*, May 20, 1964.

10.   Lattimore to Graves, March 6, 1964, LP.

11.   Lattimore to Graves, October 7, 1964, LP.

12.   Lattimore and Isono, *Diluv Khutagt*, 15–16.

13.   Ibid., 15.

14.   Typed note headed "New York Times, April 9, 1965," Lattimore File, CIA.

15.   "Lattimore Warns of Disaster in Asia," *New York Times*, April 9, 1965.

16.   "Lattimore Disputed on U.S. Role in Asia," *New York Times*, April 20, 1965; Morris, "Lattimore Is Back," *Wanderer*, April 29, 1965; "Lattimore Joins Peking Amity Club," *Washington Post*, April 19, 1965.

17.   Moss, "Lattimore Happy in English University Post," *Washington Sunday Star*, June 13, 1965.

18.   Lattimore to Barnes, September 12, 1965, Barnes private papers.

19.   Lattimore to Barnes, December 25, 1965, Barnes private papers; Lattimore to Barnes, January 11, 1966, Barnes private papers.

20.   "Lattimore Calls U.S. Policy in Asia an Increasingly Disastrous Failure," *New York Times*, March 27, 1966.

21.   Lattimore, "Vietnam: An Investor's View," *Value Line*, June 1966; Bernhard to Lattimore, June 23, 1966, LP.

22.   Lattimore to Bernhard, January 26, 1967, LP.

23.   Ibid.

24.   Ibid. As we now know, Fortas was not as profoundly discreet at this stage of his life as Lattimore thought he was.

25.   Lattimore to David Lattimore, September 9, 1966, LP.

26.   Lattimore to Barnes, November 17, 1966, Barnes private papers.

27.   Lattimore to Rogers, October 10, 1966, LP. Enoch Powell was a British counterpart of Barry Goldwater.

28.   Lattimore, introduction to *Turkestan Reunion*, AMS edition, xiii.

29.   "Lattimore Says U.S. Fails on Intelligence," *Boston Herald Traveler*, April 1, 1968.

30.   Author interview with Brian Hook, September 3, 1986.

31.   American Historical Association, *Perspectives*, November 1987, 8.

32.   Madame Sun (Soong Ch'ing-ling) to Lattimore, February 13, 1968, LP.

33.   Lattimore to Bernhard, December 9, 1968, LP.

34.   Lattimore to Barnes, November 17, 1966, Barnes private papers.

35.   Eleanor Lattimore to Evelyn Stefansson Nef, January 9, 1969, Nef private
papers.
36.   Lattimore to David Lattimore, October 12, 1969, LP.
37.   Ibid.
38.   Ibid.
39.   Lattimore to Barnes, October 20, 1969, LP.
40.   Lattimore to John Nef, November 6, 1969, Nef private papers.

30.   After Leeds

1.   Lattimore, preface to *Turkestan Reunion*, AMS edition, xv.
2.   Lattimore to Nef, May 15, 1970, Nef private papers.
3.   Lattimore to Okladnikov, March 27, 1970, Lattimore File, CIA.
4.   Snow to Lattimores, May 20, 1970, LP; Lattimore, introduction to *China
Shakes the World*, by Belden, ix–xvi.
5.   Lattimore, introduction to *China Shakes the World*, by Belden, xi. For a
contrasting view of Snow's relationship to the PRC, see Fang Lizhi, "The Chinese
Amnesia," *New York Review of Books* 37 (September 27, 1990), 30–31.
6.   Lattimore, introduction to *China Shakes the World*, by Belden, xv, x, xvi.
7.   Snow to Lattimores, May 20, 1970, LP.
8.   Lattimore to Nefs, June 14, 1970, Nef private papers.
9.   Lattimore to Peive, June 26, 1970, Lattimore File, CIA; Lattimore to Nefs,
July 1, 1970, Nef private papers.
10.   Lattimore to Rogers, August 22, 1970, LP.
11.   Lattimore to Rogers, August 24, 1970, LP.
12.   Lattimore to Rogers, August 26, 1970, LP.
13.   Ibid.
14.   Lattimore to Rogers, September 14, 1970, LP.
15.   Lattimore to Rogers, October 9, 1970, LP.
16.   Lattimore to Rogers, October 11, 1970, LP.
17.   Lattimore to Nefs, October 13, 1970, Nef private papers.
18.   Lattimore to Rogers, October 21, 1970, LP.
19.   Lattimore to Rogers, October 25, 1970, LP.
20.   Ibid.
21.   Ibid.
22.   Lattimore to Piels, January 16, 1971, Piel private papers.
23.   Snow to Lattimore, February 15, 1971, LP.
24.   Nyman to Lattimore, April 30, 1971, LP.
25.   Rogers to Nyman, June 4, 1971, LP.
26.   Lattimore to Rogers, June 6, 1971, LP.
27.   Ibid.
28.   Ibid.
29.   "U.S. Concept of Confrontation Dangerous," *Mainichi Daily News* (Tokyo), June 8, 1971.
30.   Lattimore to Rogers, June 8, 1971, LP.
31.   Lattimore to Rogers, June 12, 1971, LP.
32.   Lattimore to Rogers, June 20, 1971, LP.
33.   Ibid.
34.   Lattimore to Rogers, June 25, 1971, LP.

35. Lattimore to Rogers, July 1, 1971, LP.
36. Lattimore to Rogers, July 8, 1971, LP.
37. Ibid.
38. Lattimore to Rogers, July 12, 1971, LP.
39. Ibid.
40. Ibid.
41. Lattimore to Rogers, July 22, 1971, LP.
42. Ibid.
43. Lattimore to Rogers, July 28, 1971, LP.
44. Lattimore to Rogers, July 31, 1971, LP.
45. Ibid.
46. Ibid.
47. "Lattimore to Seek China-trip Visa," *Baltimore Sun*, December 10, 1971.
48. Ibid.
49. Piel to author, August 22, 1988.
50. Lattimore to Rogers, February 22, 1972, LP.
51. "Owen Lattimore Asks: 'To Right What Wrong?' " *New York Times*, March 23, 1972.
52. Memorandum for Acting Chief, Production Group, from [name deleted] China Political and Military Branch, Trip Report, April 11, 1972, Lattimore File, CIA.
53. Budenz, *Bolshevik Invasion of the West*, incorporates most of the paranoid fantasies of the far Right. We were losing in Vietnam because Wall Street and the business community had joined the pacifists and Communist sympathizers. Television commercials were also doing us in. Germany was our only genuine ally. Jack Stachel and Alexander Bittelman, prominent leaders of the American Communist party, dictated what the United States did. There are eight references to Lattimore, including the "mere agrarian reformers" line and the charge that the Lattimore indictment was "squashed" by the kindly disposition of the courts to communism. The Margaret Budenz comment is from *Streets*, 434.
54. "Louis Budenz, Communist Who Aided Sen. McCarthy," *Washington Evening Star*, April 28, 1972.
55. House Joint Economic Committee, *Hearings on Economic Developments in Mainland China*, 54.
56. Author interview with David Lattimore, October 26, 1987.
57. Foreign Broadcast Information Service, "Owen Lattimore at Peking Dinner," August 30, 1972, Lattimore File, CIA.
58. Lattimore to Rogers, September 4, 1972, LP; Lattimore to Rogers, September 25, 1972, LP.
59. See Stanley Karnow, "U.S. Seen Aiming to Bolster Chou against His Enemies," *Washington Post*, March 16, 1972.
60. Michael Lattimore to author, August 3, 1988.
61. Ibid.
62. "Lattimore Leaves for North China," *Washington Post*, September 11, 1972; Lattimore to Rogers, September 12, 1972, LP; Lattimore to Rogers, September 25, 1972, LP.
63. Lattimore to Rogers, October 5, 1972, LP.
64. Ibid. See Lattimore, "Return to China's Northern Frontier," for another account of this trip.
65. Michael Lattimore to author, August 3, 1988.
66. Ibid.
67. Lattimore to Rogers, November 1972, LP.

68. Ibid.
69. Ibid.
70. Lattimore to Rogers, November 27, 1972, LP.

31. Paris

1. Lattimore to Rogers, March 24, 1973, LP.
2. Ibid.
3. Nyman (Bogolepov) to Lattimore, April 10, 1973, LP.
4. Robert Morris, in 1987 the only survivor of the SISS staff, told me that after several years in the United States, Nyman got homesick, lonesome, and depressed, and returned to the Soviet Union. Telephone conversation with Morris, August 26, 1987.
5. Lattimore to Rogers, May 6, 1973, LP.
6. Lattimore to Rogers, January 24, 1974, LP.
7. Ibid.
8. Lattimore to Rogers, February 4, 1974, LP.
9. Lattimore to Rogers, February 11, 1974, LP.
10. Lelyveld, "Peking Says the 'High Tide' of Its New Campaign Is Still to Come," *New York Times*, February 9, 1974.
11. Burns, "Peking Is Gripped by New Militancy," *New York Times*, February 10, 1974.
12. "The Mongolia Society Business Meeting Attended by Owen Lattimore," April 1, 1974, Lattimore File, CIA.
13. Lattimore to Rogers, May 7, 1974, LP.
14. Lattimore to Eaton, April 15, 1974, LP.
15. Lattimore to David Lattimore, July 7, 1974, LP.
16. Ibid.
17. Ibid.
18. Lattimore to David Lattimore, July 28, August 9, and September 14, 1974, LP.
19. Lattimore to David Lattimore, January 24, 1975, LP.
20. Ibid.
21. Lattimore to David Lattimore, March 29, 1975, LP.
22. Lattimore, "Asia from the Landward Side" (mimeographed), Harvard Faculty club, May 28, 1975, LP.
23. Ibid.
24. Lattimore to David Lattimore, July 29, 1975, LP.
25. Author interview with Fujiko Isono, August 27, 1988; Lattimore to David Lattimore, July 29, 1975, LP.
26. Lattimore to Piel, February 20, 1976, Piel private papers.
27. Ibid.
28. Lattimore to Piels, October 8, 1986, Piel private papers.
29. Lattimore to Piels, April 6, 1976, Piel private papers.
30. Lattimore to Piels, April 10, 1976, Piel private papers.
31. Lattimore to Piel, January 14, 1977, Piel private papers.
32. Gene F. Wilson to Lattimore, June 30, 1977, LP.
33. Lattimore to Piels, April 11, 1977, Piel private papers.
34. Lattimore to David Lattimore, April 25, 1978, LP.
35. This and other events of his 1978 stay in Mongolia are related in Lattimore's April 25–May 6 diary-letter to David Lattimore, LP.

36. Lattimore to author, October 5, 1978.
37. Lattimore presentation to Honors College seminar, University of Pittsburgh, March 20, 1979.
38. *UPI Reporter*, May 3, 1979.
39. Lattimore to author, November 30, 1979.

32.   Cambridge and Pawtucket

1. Lattimore to Piels, February 23, 1981, Piel private papers; Lattimore to author, February 23, 1980.
2. Lattimore to author, August 16, 1980.
3. Ibid.
4. Lattimore to Piels, April 8, 1980, Piel private papers; Lattimore to author, August 16, 1980.
5. Lattimore to Piels, December 25, 1980, Piel private papers.
6. Lattimore to author, October 12, 1981.
7. This and all subsequent references to the 1981 trip are from a telephone conversation with Maria Lattimore, January 10, 1988, and her letter to author, July 10, 1988.
8. Martin, "Lattimore, Disagreeing with U.S. Views, Revisits China at Eighty," *Baltimore Sun*, July 8, 1981.
9. Ibid.
10. Lattimore to author, October 12, 1981.
11. Lattimore to Piels, February 9, 1982, Piel private papers.
12. Lattimore to author, August 12, 1983.
13. Lattimore to Nefs, August 29, 1982, Nef private papers.
14. Spencer, "Scholar Says He Doesn't Mind Loss of Notoriety," *Kansas City Times*, October 23, 1982.
15. Lattimore to Piels, April 5, 1983, Piel private papers.
16. Lattimore to Piels, August 22, 1983, Piel private papers; Lattimore to author, August 12, 1983.
17. Author interview with David Lattimore, January 25, 1988; Lattimore to author, December 3, 1985.
18. Lattimore to author, April 4, 1986.
19. Association of American Geographers, *Newsletter*, 1986.
20. Lattimore, "Mongolia as a Leading State," 16–17.
21. Lattimore to author, August 2, 1986.
22. "U.S. and Mongolia in Ceremony Establishing Diplomatic Relations," *New York Times*, January 28, 1987; Lattimore to author, February 20, 1987.
23. Lattimore to Piels, June 2, 1987, Piel private papers.
24. Lattimore to author, February 6, 1987.
25. Cotton, *Asian Frontier Nationalism*, 148–49.
26. Watkins, *Enough Rope*, ix.

BIBLIOGRAPHY

Writings of Owen Lattimore

Books

America and Asia. Claremont, Calif.: Claremont Colleges, 1943.

Desert Road to Turkestan. Boston: Little, Brown, 1929.

High Tartary. Boston: Little, Brown, 1930.

Inner Asian Frontiers of China. New York: American Geographical Society, 1940. Reprint. Boston: Beacon Press, 1962.

Manchuria: Cradle of Conflict. New York: Macmillan, 1932.

Mongol Journeys. London: Jonathan Cape, 1941.

The Mongols of Manchuria. New York: John Day, 1934.

Nationalism and Revolution in Mongolia. New York: Oxford University Press, 1955.

Nomads and Commissars. New York: Oxford University Press, 1962.

Ordeal by Slander. Boston: Little, Brown, 1950. Reprint. Westport, Conn.: Greenwood Press, 1971.

Pivot of Asia. Boston: Little, Brown, 1950.

Situation in Asia. Boston: Little, Brown, 1949. Reprint. Westport, Conn.: Greenwood Press, 1969.

Solution in Asia. Boston: Little, Brown, 1945. Reprint. New York, AMS Press, 1975.

Studies in Frontier History. London: Oxford University Press, 1962.

Articles, Monographs, and Lectures

The following lists only those works quoted in this biography; it does not include articles written for Pacific Affairs *or the* Overseas News Agency. *For a complete bibliography of Lattimore's writings to 1972, see* Analecta Mongolica, *published by the Mongolia Society (Bloomington: Indiana University Press, 1972).*

"America and the Future of China." *Amerasia* 5 (September 1941): 296–97.

"America Has No Time to Lose." *Asia* 41 (April 1941): 159–62.

"American Responsibilities in the Far East." *Virginia Quarterly Review* 16 (Spring 1940): 161–74.

"Asia in a New World Order." *Foreign Policy Reports* 28 (September 1, 1942): 150–63.

From China, Looking Outward. Inaugural Lecture. Leeds: Leeds University Press, 1964.

"How to Win the War." *American Legion Magazine* 133 (June 1942): 14–15, 111–13.

"Inner Asia: Sino-Soviet Bridge." *Nation* 175 (December 6, 1952): 512–14.

"International Chess Game." *New Republic* 112 (May 28, 1945): 731–33.

"Mongolia as a Leading State." *Mongolian Studies* 10 (1986–87): 5–18.

"My Audience With Chingghis Khan." *Atlantic Monthly* 160 (July 1937): 1–10.

"New Road to Asia." *National Geographic Magazine* 86 (December 1944): 641–76.

"On the Wickedness of Being Nomads." *Asia* 35 (October 1935): 598–605.

"Reply to Mr. Kohlberg." *China Monthly* 6 (December 1945): 15–17.

"Return to China's Northern Frontier." *Geographical Journal* 139 (June 1973): 233–42.

"Stalemate in China." *Foreign Affairs* 19 (April 1941): 621–32.

"Unpublished Report from Yenan." In *Studies in the Social History of China and Southeast Asia,* ed. J. Chen and N. Tarling. London: Cambridge University Press, 1970.

"Yunnan, Pivot of Southeast Asia." *Foreign Affairs* 21 (April 1943): 476–93.

With Eleanor Lattimore

China: A Short History. New York: Norton, 1944.

Silks, Spices, and Empire. New York: Delacorte, 1968.

With Fujiko Isono

China Memoirs. Tokyo: Tokyo University Press, 1990.

The Diluv Khutagt. Wiesbaden: Otto Harrassowitz, 1982.

Writings of Eleanor Lattimore

Turkestan Reunion. New York: John Day, 1934. Reprint. AMS Press, 1975.

Archives and Manuscript Collections

Arnold and Porter, Washington, D.C.
    Lattimore Files

Bancroft Library, University of California, Berkeley
    Warren Olney III Oral History
    William Knowland Papers

Central Intelligence Agency, Washington, D.C.
    Lattimore Files

Coe Library, University of Wyoming, Laramie
    Joseph C. O'Mahoney Papers
Columbia University Libraries, New York
    Joseph W. Ballantine Oral History
    Herbert Brownell Oral History
    Wellington Koo Papers
Cornell University Libraries, Ithaca, New York
    James McHugh Papers
Council on Foreign Relations Archives, New York
    Territorial Group Files
    Far Eastern Affairs Files
Dwight D. Eisenhower Library, Abilene, Kansas
    John Foster Dulles General Correspondence and Memoranda Series
    John Foster Dulles Telephone Calls Series
    Dwight D. Eisenhower Telephone Calls Series
    Ann Whitman Diary Series
Eisenhower Library, Johns Hopkins University, Baltimore
    Hamburger Archives, Lattimore Papers
    Special Collections, Francis White and P. Stewart Macaulay Papers
FBI Headquarters, Washington, D.C.
    Louis F. Budenz File
    Joseph Zack Kornfeder File
    Owen Lattimore Defense Fund File
    Owen Lattimore File
FBI Office, New York
    Louis F. Budenz Files
Franklin D. Roosevelt Library, Hyde Park, New York
    Lauchlin Currie Papers
Harry S. Truman Library, Independence, Missouri
    President's Secretaries File
    White House Central Files
    John F. Melby Papers
Herbert Hoover Presidential Library, West Branch, Iowa
    Bourke Hickenlooper Papers
Hoover Institution on War, Revolution and Peace, Stanford, California
    Joseph W. Ballantine Papers
    Lauchlin Currie Papers
    Ralph de Toledano Papers
    Preston Goodfellow Papers
    Milton E. Miles Papers
    Freda Utley Papers
Liberty University Library, Lynchburg, Virginia
    J. B. Matthews Papers
Library of Congress Manuscript Division, Washington, D.C.
    Joseph Alsop Papers
    William O. Douglas Papers
    Philip Jessup Papers

Owen Lattimore Papers
James P. McGranery Papers

National Archives, Washington, D.C.
RG 46, Records of the U.S. Congress
RG 59, Records of the Department of State

National Geographic Magazine Archives, Washington, D.C.
Owen Lattimore File

New England College Library, Henniker, New Hampshire
Styles Bridges Papers

Rockefeller Archive Center, North Tarrytown, New York
Detlev Bronk Collection
Rockefeller Foundation Archive

University of Nevada Western Studies Center, Reno
Eva Adams Papers
Norman H. Biltz Oral History

U.S. Court of Appeals for the District of Columbia Circuit, Washington, D.C.
U.S. v. Owen Lattimore, No. 12,609

U.S. Department of Justice, Washington, D.C.
U.S. v. Owen Lattimore File

U.S. Department of State Passport Office, Washington, D.C.
Lattimore File

U.S. District Court, Washington, D.C.
U.S. v. Owen Lattimore, No. 1879–52.

U.S. Government Publications

Data on the SISS hearings and Report *on the IPR and the Tydings committee
hearings on State Department loyalty are given at the beginning of the Notes.*

Department of State. *United States Relations with China [China White Paper].*
Washington, D.C.: Government Printing Office, 1949. Reprint. Stanford, Calif.:
Stanford University Press, 1967.

House. Committee on the Judiciary, Special Subcommittee to Investigate the Department of Justice. *Hearings on House Resolution 95.* August 26–December 31, 1952. 82d Cong., 2d sess.

Joint Economic Committee. *Hearings on Economic Developments in Mainland
China.* June 14, 1972. 92d Cong., 2d sess.

Senate. Committee on the Judiciary. *Hearings on the Nomination of James P.
McGranery.* May 5, 1952. 82d Cong., 2d sess.

———. *Herbert Brownell, Jr., Attorney General–Designate.* Jan. 19, 1953. 83d
Cong., 1st sess.

Senate. Foreign Relations and Armed Services Committees. *Military Situation in
the Far East.* May 3–31, 1951. 82d Cong., 1st sess.

Interviews

Burkhardt, Daniel H. May 7, 1982.
Callas, Charles. August 19, 1989.

Cohn, Roy M. December 28, 1979.

Davies, John Paton. April 26, 1981.

DeFrancis, John. November 30, 1977.

Fortas, Abe. March 18, 1981.

Frank, John P. May 15, 1986.

Harvey, David. October 24, 1982.

Heinrichs, Waldo. August 3, 1978.

Hook, Brian. September 3, 1986.

Isono, Fujiko. August 27, 28, 1988.

Jessup, Philip. June 8, 1978.

Kahin, George McT. August 10, 1983.

Lattimore, David. August 31, 1987, and other dates.

Lattimore, Maria. January 10, 1988 (telephone).

Melby, John F. June 10, 1983.

Morris, Robert. August 26, 1987 (telephone).

Needham, Wesley. December 3, 1987 (telephone).

Nef, Evelyn Stefansson. December 29, 1987.

Owens, Gwinn. May 6, 1982.

Rogers, William D. and Suki Rogers. September 18, 1987, and other dates.

Shaffer, Wilson. May 6, 1982.

Smith, Neil. June 25, 1984.

Spring, David. October 26, 1982.

Utley, Freda. December 3, 1977.

White, Theodore H. June 22, 1977.

Wickwire, Chester. May 2, 1982.

Wolman, Abel. February 13, 1984.

Youngdahl, Luther. December 3, 1977.

Books and Articles

Acheson, Dean. *Present at the Creation*. New York: New American Library, Signet Books, 1969.

Adams, John G. *Without Precedent: The Story of the Death of McCarthyism*. New York: Norton, 1983.

Alsop, Joseph. "The Strange Case of Louis Budenz." *Atlantic Monthly* 189 (April 1952): 29–33.

Alsop, Stewart. *The Center: People and Power in Political Washington*. New York: Harper and Row, 1968.

Anderson, Jack, with James Bond. *Confessions of a Muckraker*. New York: Random House, 1979.

Anderson, Jack, and Ronald W. May. *McCarthy: The Man, the Senator, the Ism.* Boston: Beacon, 1952.

Arnold, Thurman. *Fair Fights and Foul.* New York: Harcourt, Brace and World, 1965.

Ascoli, Max, et al. "The China Lobby." In *Our Times: The Best from the Reporter,* ed. Max Ascoli. 3–49. New York: Farrar, Straus, and Cudahy, 1960.

Bachrack, Stanley D. *The Committee of One Million.* New York: Columbia University Press, 1976.

Bailey, Thomas A. *A Diplomatic History of the American People.* Ninth ed. Englewood Cliffs, N.J.: Prentice-Hall, 1970.

Barmine, Alexander (Alexandre). *Memoirs of a Soviet Diplomat.* Westport, Conn.: Hyperion, 1938.

————. "The New Communist Conspiracy." *Reader's Digest* 45 (October 1944): 27–33.

————. "New Defender for Yenan." *New Leader* 28 (April 7, 1945): 10, 14.

————. *One Who Survived.* New York: Putnam's, 1945.

————. "A Russian View of the Moscow Trials." *International Conciliation* 337 (February 1938): 43–52.

Barth, Alan. "McCarran's Monopoly." *Reporter* 5 (August 21, 1951): 25–50.

Bayley, Edwin R. *Joe McCarthy and the Press.* Madison: University of Wisconsin Press, 1981.

Belden, Jack. *China Shakes the World.* New York: Monthly Review Press, 1970.

Bell, Daniel, ed. *The Radical Right.* Garden City, N.Y.: Doubleday, Anchor Books, 1964.

Bisson, T. A. "China's Part in a Coalition War." *Far Eastern Survey* 12 (July 1943): 135–41.

————. *Yenan in June 1937: Talks with the Communist Leaders.* Berkeley: Center for Chinese Studies, University of California, 1973.

Boas, George, and Harvey Wheeler. *Lattimore the Scholar.* Baltimore: privately printed, 1953.

Bohlen, Charles E. *Witness to History, 1929–1969.* New York: Norton, 1973.

Bowen, Roger. *Innocence Is Not Enough: The Life and Death of Herbert Norman.* Vancouver and Toronto: Douglas and McIntyre, 1986.

Buckley, William F., Jr. "Owen Lattimore and the 'Cold War,' " *National Review* 41 (August 18, 1989): 54.

Buckley, William F., Jr., and L. Brent Bozell. *McCarthy and His Enemies.* Chicago: Henry Regnery, 1954.

Budenz, Louis F. *The Bolshevik Invasion of the West.* Linden, N.J.: Bookmailer, 1966.

————. "The Menace of Red China." *Colliers* 123 (March 19, 1949): 23, 48–50.

————. *This Is My Story.* New York: McGraw-Hill, 1947.

Budenz, Margaret. *Streets.* Huntington, Ind.: Our Sunday Visitor, 1979.

Buhite, Russell D. *Patrick J. Hurley and American Foreign Policy.* Ithaca: Cornell University Press, 1973.

―――. *Soviet-American Relations in Asia, 1945–1954.* Norman: University of Oklahoma Press, 1981.

Byrnes, James F. *All in One Lifetime.* New York: Harper and Brothers, 1958.

Caldwell, Oliver J. *A Secret War: Americans in China, 1944–1945.* Carbondale: Southern Illinois University Press, 1972.

Caute, David. *The Great Fear.* New York: Simon and Schuster, 1978.

Churchill, Winston S. *The Second World War: The Gathering Storm.* Boston: Houghton Mifflin, 1948.

Clubb, O. Edmund. *Twentieth Century China.* New York: Columbia University Press, 1964.

Cochran, Bert. *Harry Truman and the Crisis Presidency.* New York: Funk and Wagnalls, 1973.

Cohen, Warren F. *America's Response to China.* New York: Wiley, 1971.

―――. *The Chinese Connection.* New York: Columbia University Press, 1978.

Conquest, Robert. *The Great Terror.* New York: Macmillan, 1968.

Cook, Fred J. *The Nightmare Decade.* New York: Random House, 1971.

Cooney, John. *The American Pope: The Life and Times of Francis Cardinal Spellman.* New York: Dell, 1986.

Cotton, James. *Asian Frontier Nationalism: Owen Lattimore and the American Foreign Policy Debate.* Manchester, Eng.: Manchester University Press, 1989.

―――. "Owen Lattimore and China: The Development of a Frontier Perspective, 1928–1937." In *China and Europe in the Twentieth Century,* ed. Yu-ming Shaw. Taipei: National Chengchi University, 1986.

Countryman, Vern. *Un-American Activities in the State of Washington.* Ithaca: Cornell University Press, 1951.

Crosby, Donald F., S.J. *God, Church, and Flag: Senator Joseph R. McCarthy and the Catholic Church, 1950–57.* Chapel Hill: University of North Carolina Press, 1978.

―――. "The Politics of Religion." In *The Specter,* ed. Robert Griffith and Athan Theoharis. New York: Franklin Watts/New Viewpoints, 1974.

Cumings, Bruce. *The Origins of the Korean War.* Princeton: Princeton University Press, 1981.

Dallin, David J. "Henry Wallace and Chinese Communism." *New Leader* 34 (October 22, 1951): 14.

―――. *Soviet Russia and the Far East.* New Haven: Yale University Press, 1948.

―――. "Writings of Owen Lattimore Reflect Pro-Soviet Views." *New Leader* 33 (May 13, 1950): 11.

Davies, John Paton, Jr. *Dragon by the Tail.* New York: Norton, 1972.

Deakin, F. W., and G. R. Storry. *The Case of Richard Sorge.* New York: Harper and Row, 1966.

de Borchgrave, Arnaud, and Robert Moss. *The Spike.* New York: Avon, 1980.

de Silva, Peer. *Sub Rosa: The CIA and the Uses of Intelligence.* New York: New York Times, 1978.

Dimond, E. Gray. "U.S. and China: A Sympathetic Symbiosis." *Center Report*, April 1974, 22–23.

Douglas, William O. *Go East, Young Man.* New York: Random House, 1974.

Eastman, Lloyd E. "Who Lost China? Chiang Kai-shek Testifies." *China Quarterly* 88 (December 1981): 658–68.

Eastman, Max, and J. B. Powell. "The Fate of the World Is at Stake in China." *Reader's Digest* 46 (June 1945): 13–22.

Edwards, Jerome E. *Pat McCarran: Political Boss of Nevada.* Reno: University of Nevada Press, 1982.

Emerson, Rupert. Review of *War and Peace in Soviet Diplomacy*, by T. A. Taracouzio. *American Political Science Review* 35 (April 1941): 568–70.

Emerson, John K. *The Japanese Thread.* New York: Holt, Rinehart and Winston, 1978.

Esbjornson, Robert. *Luther W. Youngdahl: A Christian in Politics.* Minneapolis: T. S. Denison, 1955.

Fairbank, John King. *Chinabound.* New York: Harper and Row, 1982.

Feis, Herbert. *The Road to Pearl Harbor.* Princeton: Princeton University Press, 1950.

Field, Frederick Vanderbilt. *From Right to Left: An Autobiography.* Westport, Conn.: Lawrence Hill, 1983.

Flynn, John T. *The Lattimore Story.* New York: Devin-Adair, 1953.

———. *While You Slept.* New York: Devin-Adair, 1951.

Fried, Richard M. "Electoral Politics and McCarthyism: The 1950 Campaign." In *The Specter*, ed. Robert Griffith and Athan Theoharis. New York: Franklin Watts/New Viewpoints, 1974.

———. *Men against McCarthy.* New York: Columbia University Press, 1976.

———. *Nightmare in Red.* New York: Oxford University Press, 1990.

Garrett, Shirley Stone. "Why They Stayed." In *The Missionary Enterprise in China and America*, ed. John K. Fairbank. Cambridge: Harvard University Press, 1974.

Getty, J. Arch. *Origins of the Great Purges: The Soviet Communist Party Reconsidered, 1933–1938.* New York: Cambridge University Press, 1985.

Gibney, Frank. "After the Ball." *Commonweal* 60 (September 3, 1954): 531–35.

Gilbert, Brian [Roger Kennedy]. "Judge Youngdahl Wins His Fight." *New Republic* 133 (July 11, 1955): 5–6.

———. "New Light on the Lattimore Case." *New Republic* 131 (December 27, 1954): 7–12.

Goldman, Eric F. *The Crucial Decade—And After.* New York: Random House, Vintage Books, 1956.

Goodman, Walter. *The Committee.* Baltimore: Penguin, 1969.

Graebner, Norman A. *The New Isolationism.* New York: Ronald Press, 1956.

Greaves, Percy. "Secretary Knox and Pearl Harbor." *National Review* 19 (November 1966): 1266–72.

Gressley, Gene M. *Voltaire and the Cowboy: The Letters of Thurman Arnold.* Boulder: Colorado Associated Universities Press, 1977.

Griffith, Robert. *The Politics of Fear.* Lexington: University Press of Kentucky, 1970.

Grunfeld, A. Tom. *The Making of Modern Tibet.* Armonk, N.Y.: M. E. Sharpe, 1987.

Harper, Alan D. *The Politics of Loyalty.* Westport, Conn.: Greenwood Press, 1969.

Harriman, W. Averell, and Elie Abel. *Special Envoy to Churchill and Stalin.* New York: Random House, 1975.

Harrington, Michael. "The Committee for Cultural Freedom." *Dissent* 2 (Autumn 1955): 113–22.

Harvey, David. "Owen Lattimore: A Memoire." *Antipode* 15 (1983): 3–11.

Heald, Robert L., and Lyon L. Tyler, Jr. "The Legal Principle behind the *Amerasia* Case." *Georgetown Law Journal* 39 (January 1951): 181–215.

Heinrichs, Waldo H., Jr. *American Ambassador: Joseph C. Grew.* Boston: Little, Brown, 1966.

Hersey, John. *The Call.* New York: Knopf, 1985.

Hilsman, Roger. *To Move a Nation.* Garden City, N.Y.: Doubleday, 1967.

Hofstadter, Richard. *Anti-Intellectualism in American Life.* New York: Knopf, 1964.

———. *The Paranoid Style in American Politics and Other Essays.* New York: Random House, Vintage Books, 1967.

Hollander, Paul. *Political Pilgrims.* New York: Oxford University Press, 1981.

Hook, Sidney. "Lattimore on the Moscow Trials." *New Leader* 35 (November 10, 1952): 16–19.

Hull, Cordell. *Memoirs.* New York: Macmillan, 1948.

Irons, Peter H. "The Cold War Crusade of the American Chamber of Commerce." In *The Specter,* ed. Robert Griffith and Athan Theoharis. New York: Franklin Watts/New Viewpoints, 1974.

Jefferson, Bonnie S. "The Rhetorical Restrictions of a Devil Theory." Ph.D. diss., University of Pittsburgh, 1984.

Kahn, Alfred E. *The Matusow Affair.* Mount Kisco, N.Y.: Moyer Bell, 1987.

Kahn, E. J., Jr. *The China Hands.* New York: Viking, 1975.

Kearney, James F., S.J. "Disaster in China." *Columbia* 24 (September 1949): 4, 16–17.

Keeley, Joseph. *The China Lobby Man: The Story of Alfred Kohlberg.* New Rochelle, N.Y.: Arlington House, 1969.

Kimball, Penn. *The File.* New York: Avon, Discus Books, 1985.

Klehr, Harvey, and Ronald Radosh. "Anatomy of a Fix." *New Republic* 94 (April 21, 1986): 18–21.

Klotz, Daniel James. "Freda Utley: From Communist to Anti-Communist." Ph.D. diss., Yale University, 1987.

Koen, Ross Y. *The China Lobby in American Politics.* New York: Harper and Row, 1974.

Kohlberg, Alfred. "Owen Lattimore: Expert's Expert." *China Monthly* 6 (October 1945): 10–13, 26.

Kristol, Irving. "Ordeal by Mendacity." *Twentieth Century* 152 (October 1952): 315–23.

Krivitsky, Walter G. *In Stalin's Secret Service.* New York: Harper, 1939.

Kutler, Stanley I. *The American Inquisition: Justice and Injustice in the Cold War.* New York: Hill and Wang, 1982.

Lamont, Corliss. *Freedom Is as Freedom Does.* New York: Horizon, 1981.

Latham, Earl. *The Communist Controversy in Washington.* New York: Atheneum, 1969.

Lazarsfeld, Paul, and Wagner Thielens. *The Academic Mind.* Glencoe, Ill.: Free Press, 1958.

Levering, Ralph B. *American Opinion and the Russian Alliance, 1939–1945.* Chapel Hill: University of North Carolina Press, 1976.

Lipper, Elinor [Elinor Catala]. *Eleven Years in Soviet Prison Camps.* Chicago: Henry Regnery, 1951.

———. *Elf Jahre in sowjetischen Gefängnissen und Lagern.* Zurich: Oprecht, 1950.

Lipset, Seymour Martin, and Earl Raab. *The Politics of Unreason.* New York: Harper and Row, 1970.

McAuliffe, Mary Sperling. *Crisis on the Left.* Amherst: University of Massachusetts Press, 1978.

MacKinnon, Janice R., and Stephen R. MacKinnon. *Agnes Smedley.* Berkeley and Los Angeles: University of California Press, 1987.

Madsen, Richard. "The New China Confronts the Christian Theologian." *Holy Cross Quarterly* 7 (1975): 72–79.

Mao Tse-tung. *Selected Works.* Vol. 4. Peking: Foreign Languages Press, 1975.

Marshall, S. L. A. *The River and the Gauntlet.* New York: William Morrow, 1953.

Matusow, Harvey. *False Witness.* New York: Cameron and Kahn, 1955.

May, Gary. *China Scapegoat: The Diplomatic Ordeal of John Carter Vincent.* Washington, D.C.: New Republic Books, 1979.

Miles, Milton. *A Different Kind of War.* New York: Doubleday, 1967.

Morris, Robert. "Counsel for the Minority: A Report on the Tydings Investigation." *Freeman* 1 (October 30, 1950): 78–81.

Murray, Robert K. *Red Scare: A Study in National Hysteria, 1919–1920.* New York: McGraw-Hill, 1964.

Nahaylo, Bohdan, and Victor Swoboda. *Soviet Disunion.* New York: Free Press, 1989.

Navasky, Victor S. *Naming Names.* New York: Penguin, 1981.

Newman, Robert P. "Clandestine Chinese Nationalist Efforts to Punish Their American Detractors." *Diplomatic History* 7 (Summer 1983): 205–22.

————. "Lethal Rhetoric: The Selling of the China Myths." *Quarterly Journal of Speech* 61 (April 1975): 113–28.

————. "Red Scare in Seattle, 1952: The FBI, the CIA, and Owen Lattimore's 'Escape.' " *Historian* 48 (November 1985): 61–81.

————. "The Self-Inflicted Wound: The China White Paper of 1949." *Prologue—The Journal of the National Archives* 14 (Fall 1982): 141–56.

Norbu, Thubten Jigme. *Tibet Is My Country*. New York: Dutton, 1961.

O'Neill, William L. *The Last Romantic: A Life of Max Eastman*. New York: Oxford University Press, 1978.

O'Reilly, Kenneth. *Hoover and the Un-Americans: The FBI, HUAC, and the Red Menace*. Philadelphia: Temple University Press, 1983.

Oshinsky, David M. *A Conspiracy So Immense: The World of Joe McCarthy*. New York: Macmillan/Free Press, 1983.

Pacificus. "Dangerous Experts." *Nation* 160 (February 3, 1945): 128.

Packer, Herbert L. *Ex-Communist Witnesses*. Stanford: Stanford University Press, 1962.

Pepper, Suzanne. *Civil War in China*. Berkeley and Los Angeles: University of California Press, 1978.

Pincher, Chapman. *Too Secret, Too Long*. New York: St. Martin's Press, 1984.

Pittman, Von V., Jr. "Senator Patrick A. McCarran and the Politics of Containment." Ph.D. diss., University of Georgia, 1979.

Polsby, Nelson. "Towards an Explanation of McCarthyism." *Political Studies* 8 (October 1960): 250–71.

Poppe, Nicholas. *Reminiscences*. Bellingham: Western Washington University Press, 1983.

Rader, Melvin. *False Witness*. Seattle: University of Washington Press, 1969.

Radosh, Ronald. *Prophets on the Right*. New York: Simon and Schuster, 1975.

Rastvorov, Yuri A. "Red Fraud and Intrigue in Far East." *Life* 37 (December 6, 1954).

Reeves, Thomas C. *The Life and Times of Joe McCarthy*. New York: Stein and Day, 1982.

Regnery, Henry. *Memoirs of a Dissident Publisher*. New York: Harcourt, Brace, Jovanovich, 1979.

Rogin, Michael P. *The Intellectuals and McCarthy*. Cambridge: MIT Press, 1967.

Rorty, James, and Moshe Decter. *McCarthy and the Communists*. Boston: Beacon, 1954.

Salisbury, Harrison E. "The Amerasia Papers." *New York Times Book Review* (September 19, 1971).

Schaller, Michael. *The American Occupation of Japan*. New York: Oxford University Press, 1985.

————. *The U.S. Crusade in China, 1938–1945*. New York: Columbia University Press, 1979.

Schleit, Philip. *Shelton's Barefoot Airlines*. Annapolis, Md.: Fishergate, 1982.

Schonberger, Howard. *Aftermath of War*. Kent, Ohio: Kent State University Press, 1990.

Schrecker, Ellen W. *No Ivory Tower: McCarthyism and the Universities*. New York: Oxford University Press, 1986.

Schulzinger, Robert D. *The Wise Men of Foreign Affairs*. New York: Columbia University Press, 1984.

Seagrave, Sterling. *The Soong Dynasty*. New York: Harper and Row, 1985.

Service, John S. *The Amerasia Papers: Some Problems in the History of US–China Relations*. Berkeley: Center for Chinese Studies, University of California, 1971.

Shalett, Sidney. "How to Be a Crime Buster." *Saturday Evening Post* 227 (March 19, 1955): 501–6.

Shanahan, Carmac. "False Solution in Asia." *China Monthly* 6 (December 1945): 22–24.

Shewmaker, Kenneth E. *Americans and Chinese Communists, 1927–1945: A Persuading Encounter*. Ithaca: Cornell University Press, 1975.

Simmons, Robert. *The Strained Alliance: Peking, Pyongyang, Moscow, and the Politics of the Korean Civil War*. New York: Free Press, 1975.

Simpson, Christopher. *Blowback*. New York: Weidenfeld and Nicolson, 1988.

Sirgiovanni, George. "An Undercurrent of Suspicion." Ph.D. diss., Rutgers University, 1988.

Spence, Jonathan. *The China Helpers*. London: Bodley Head, 1969.

Sperber, A. M. *Murrow: His Life and Times*. New York: Freundlich, 1968.

Stefansson, Vilhjalmur. *Discovery*. New York: McGraw-Hill, 1964.

Stein, Sol. "A Communication." *New Republic* 132 (February 14, 1955): 20–22.

Steinberg, Alfred. "McCarran: Lone Wolf of the Senate." *Harper's Magazine* 201 (November 1950): 89–95.

Stone, I. F. "Pearl Harbor Diplomats." *Nation* 161 (July 14, 1945): 25–27.

Straight, Michael. *After Long Silence*. New York: Norton, 1983.

Stuart, John Leighton. *Fifty Years in China*. New York: Random House, 1954.

Stueck, William Whitney, Jr. *The Road to Confrontation: American Policy toward China and Korea, 1947–1950*. Chapel Hill: University of North Carolina Press, 1981.

Sullivan, William C. *The Bureau: My Thirty Years in Hoover's FBI*. New York: Norton, 1979.

Swanberg, W. A. *Luce and His Empire*. New York: Scribner's, 1972.

Tanner, William R., and Robert Griffith. "Legislative Politics and 'McCarthyism': The Internal Security Act of 1950." In *The Specter*, ed. Robert Griffith and Athan Theoharis. New York: Franklin Watts/New Viewpoints, 1974.

Tansill, Charles Callan. *Back Door to War*. Chicago: Henry Regnery, 1952.

Taracouzio, T. A. *War and Peace in Soviet Diplomacy*. New York: Macmillan, 1940.

Theoharis, Athan, and John Stuart Cox. *The Boss: J. Edgar Hoover and the Great American Inquisition*. Philadelphia: Temple University Press, 1988.

Thomas, John N. *The Institute of Pacific Relations.* Seattle: University of Washington Press, 1974.

Thompson, Kenneth. "Miller Center Discussion: McCarthyism and Consensus." In *McCarthyism and Consensus?* ed. William Bragg Ewald, Jr. Lanham, Md.: University Press of America, 1986.

Thorne, Christopher. *Allies of a Kind: The United States, Britain, and the War against Japan, 1941–1945* New York: Oxford University Press, 1978.

Toland, John. *Infamy: Pearl Harbor and Its Aftermath.* Garden City, N.Y.: Doubleday, 1982.

Tong, Hollington K. *Dateline: China.* New York: Rockport Press, 1950.

Tuchman, Barbara W. *Stilwell and the American Experience in China, 1911–45.* New York: Macmillan, 1971.

Ulmen, G. L. *The Science of Society: Toward an Understanding of the Life and Work of Karl August Wittfogel.* The Hague: Mouton, 1978.

Utley, Freda. *The China Story.* Chicago: Henry Regnery, 1951.

Varg, Paul A. *Missionaries, Chinese, and Diplomats.* New York: Octagon, 1977.

Vishnyakova-Akimova, Vera. *Two Years in Revolutionary China 1925–1927.* Cambridge: Harvard University Press, 1971.

von Hoffman, Nicholas. *Citizen Cohn.* New York: Doubleday, 1988.

Wallace, Henry A. *Soviet Asia Mission.* New York: Reynal and Hitchcock, 1946.

Warren, Frank A., III. *Liberals and Communism.* Bloomington: Indiana University Press, 1966.

Watkins, Arthur V. *Enough Rope.* Englewood Cliffs, N.J.: Prentice-Hall, 1969.

Weil, Martin. *A Pretty Good Club.* New York: Norton, 1978.

Weiner, Jon. "Bringing Nazi Sympathizers to the U.S." *Nation* 248 (March 6, 1989): 289, 306–9.

Weissman, Steve. "Last Tangle in Tibet." *Pacific Research and World Empire Telegram* 4 (July–August 1973): 1–18.

Westerfield, H. Bradford. *Foreign Policy and Party Politics: Pearl Harbor to Korea.* New York: Octagon, 1972.

White, Ralph K. *Nobody Wanted War.* Garden City, N.Y.: Doubleday, Anchor Books, 1970.

White, Theodore H. *In Search of History.* New York: Harper and Row, 1978.

Wohl, Paul. "An American 'Geopolitical Masterhand.'" *Asia* 41 (November 1941): 601.

INDEX

Compositor: Maple-Vail Book Mfg. Group
Printer: Maple-Vail Book Mfg. Group
Binder: Maple-Vail Book Mfg. Group
Text: 10/13 Aldus
Display: Aldus